Why Do You Need this New Edition?

1. A new box, **Eye on the Environment,** provides material that links culture with some aspect of the environment. Examples include Inuit place names and environmental knowledge, eagle protection among the Hopi Indians, and environmental destruction from oil drilling in Nigeria.

2. **New and Updated Maps** have been designed to provide complementary information for the textual material without distracting the reader with unnecessary details.

3. **New Photographs** have been carefully chosen to enliven the textual material and to be thought provoking. Photographs arranged in pairs or trios, with linked captions, offer a mini-photo essay for students to ponder.

4. **MyAnthroLab** is an interactive and instructive multimedia site designed to offer access to a wealth of resources geared to meet the individual teaching and learning needs of every instructor and student. Combining an ebook, video, audio, multimedia simulations, research support, and assessment, MyAnthroLab engages students and gives them the tools they need to enhance their performance in the course.

PEARSON

CULTURAL ANTHROPOLOGY IN A GLOBALIZING WORLD

SECOND EDITION

BARBARA MILLER

George Washington University

Prentice Hall

Boston Columbus Indianapolis New York San Francisco Upper Saddle River
Amsterdam Cape Town Dubai London Madrid Milan Munich Paris Montréal Toronto
Delhi Mexico City São Paulo Sydney Hong Kong Seoul Singapore Taipei Tokyo

VP, Editorial Director: Craig Campanella
Editor in Chief: Dickson Musslewhite
Publisher: Nancy Roberts
Editorial Assistant: Nart Varoqua
Editor in Chief, Editorial Development: Rochelle Diogenes
Development Editor: Ohlinger Publishing Services
Director of Marketing: Brandy Dawson
Senior Marketing Manager: Laura Lee Manley
Marketing Assistant: Pat Walsh
Managing Editor: Maureen Richardson
Project Manager: Marianne Peters-Riordan
Copy Editor: Gary Morris
Proofreader: Heather Mann
Senior Operations Supervisor: Nick Sklitsis
Operations Specialist: Cathleen Petersen
Senior Art Director: Nancy Wells
Art Director: Anne Bonanno Nieglos

Interior and Cover Designer: Anne DeMarinis
Manager, Visual Research: Beth Brenzel
Photo Researcher: Teri Stratford, Susanna Lesan
Manager, Rights and Permissions: Zina Arabia
Image Interior Permission Coordinator: Fran Toepfer
Manager, Cover Visual Research & Permissions: Karen Sanatar
Cover Art: Masai glass beaded jewelry: Big Stock Photo; Masai glass beads necklace: Michel Lizarzaburu/iStockphoto; Kenyan teenage Masai girls attend an alternative rite of passage at Kilgoris: Tony Karumba/Stringer/AFP/Getty Images
Media Director: Brian Hyland
Senior Media Editor: David Alick
Media Project Manager: Diane Lombardo
Full-Service Project Management: Jill Traut
Composition: MPS Limited
Printer/Binder and Cover Printer: Courier Companies, Inc.

This book was set in 10/13, Adobe Caslon.

Credits and acknowledgments borrowed from other sources and reproduced, with permission, in this textbook appear on the appropriate printed page within the text (or on pages 300–301).

Library of Congress Cataloging-in-Publication Data

Miller, Barbara D.
  Cultural anthropology in a globalizing world / Barbara Miller. — 2nd ed.
    p. cm.
  ISBN-13: 978-0-205-77698-6 (pbk.)
  ISBN-10: 0-205-77698-1 (pbk.)
  1. Ethnology. 2. Globalization—Social aspects. I. Title.
    GN316.M49 2010
    306—dc22   2009044753

10 9 8 7 6 5 4 3 2

Student Edition
ISBN 10: 0-205-77698-1
ISBN 13: 978-0-205-77698-6
Exam Edition
ISBN 10: 0-205-77704-X
ISBN 13: 978-0-205-77704-4
A la Carte
ISBN 10: 0-205-80951-0
ISBN 13: 978-0-20580951-6

Prentice Hall
is an imprint of

PEARSON

www.pearsonhighered.com

brief CONTENTS

PART I   INTRODUCTION TO CULTURAL ANTHROPOLOGY   3

1   ANTHROPOLOGY AND THE STUDY OF CULTURE   5
2   RESEARCHING CULTURE   29

PART II   CULTURAL FOUNDATIONS   49

3   ECONOMIC SYSTEMS   51
4   REPRODUCTION AND HUMAN DEVELOPMENT   77
5   DISEASE, ILLNESS, AND HEALING   101

PART III   SOCIAL ORGANIZATION   123

6   KINSHIP AND DOMESTIC LIFE   125
7   SOCIAL GROUPS AND SOCIAL STRATIFICATION   147
8   POLITICAL AND LEGAL SYSTEMS   167

PART IV   SYMBOLIC SYSTEMS   187

9   COMMUNICATION   189
10 RELIGION   211
11 EXPRESSIVE CULTURE   235

PART V   CONTEMPORARY CULTURAL CHANGE   255

12 PEOPLE ON THE MOVE   257
13 PEOPLE DEFINING DEVELOPMENT   277

CONTENTS

PREFACE xv

ABOUT THE AUTHOR xxi

PART I
INTRODUCTION TO CULTURAL ANTHROPOLOGY 3

1
ANTHROPOLOGY AND THE STUDY OF CULTURE 5

THE BIG QUESTIONS 5

INTRODUCING ANTHROPOLOGY 6

Biological or Physical Anthropology 7

Archaeology 7

Linguistic Anthropology 9

Cultural Anthropology 9

Applied Anthropology: Separate Field or Cross-Cutting Focus? 9

INTRODUCING CULTURAL ANTHROPOLOGY 9

◆ LESSONS APPLIED Orangutan Research Leads to Orangutan Advocacy 10

A Brief History of Cultural Anthropology 10

The Concept of Culture 13

◆ EVERYDAY ANTHROPOLOGY Latina Power in the Kitchen 16

Multiple Cultural Worlds 19

CULTURAMA San Peoples of Southern Africa 21

Distinctive Features of Cultural Anthropology 22

Three Theoretical Debates in Cultural Anthropology 23

CULTURAL ANTHROPOLOGY AND CAREERS 24

Majoring in Anthropology 25

Graduate Study in Anthropology 25

Living an Anthropological Life 25

THE BIG QUESTIONS REVISITED 26

Key Concepts 27   Suggested Readings 27

2
RESEARCHING CULTURE 29

THE BIG QUESTIONS 29

CHANGING RESEARCH METHODS IN CULTURAL ANTHROPOLOGY 30

From the Armchair to the Field 30

Participant Observation 30

DOING FIELDWORK IN CULTURAL ANTHROPOLOGY 31

Beginning the Fieldwork Process 31

◆ CRITICAL THINKING Shells and Skirts in the Trobriand Islands 32

CULTURAMA The Trobriand Islanders of Papua New Guinea 33

Working in the Field 34

Fieldwork Techniques 37

◆ EYE ON THE ENVIRONMENT Researching Inuit Place Names and Landscape Knowledge 41

Recording Culture 41

Data Analysis 43

URGENT ISSUES IN CULTURAL ANTHROPOLOGY RESEARCH 44

Ethics and Collaborative Research 44

Safety in the Field 45

THE BIG QUESTIONS REVISITED 46

Key Concepts 47   Suggested Readings 47

PART II
CULTURAL FOUNDATIONS 49

3
ECONOMIC SYSTEMS 51

THE BIG QUESTIONS 51

MODES OF LIVELIHOOD 52

Foraging 52

◆ EVERYDAY ANTHROPOLOGY The Importance of Dogs 54

Horticulture 56

Pastoralism 58

Agriculture 58

Industrialism and the Information Age 61

◆ CRITICAL THINKING Was the Invention of Agriculture a Terrible Mistake? 62

MODES OF CONSUMPTION AND EXCHANGE 62

Modes of Consumption 62

Modes of Exchange 66

◆ LESSONS APPLIED Assessing the Social Impact of Indian Casinos in California 69

GLOBALIZATION AND CHANGING ECONOMIES 71

Sugar, Salt, and Steel Tools in the Amazon 71

Global Networks and Ecstasy in the United States 71

CULTURAMA The Kwakwaka'wakw of Canada 72

Alternative Food Movements in Europe and North America 73

Continuities and Resistance: The Enduring Potlatch 73

THE BIG QUESTIONS REVISITED 74

Key Concepts 75   Suggested Readings 75

4

REPRODUCTION AND HUMAN DEVELOPMENT 77

THE BIG QUESTIONS 77

MODES OF REPRODUCTION 78

The Foraging Mode of Reproduction 78

The Agricultural Mode of Reproduction 78

The Industrial/Informatics Mode of Reproduction 79

CULTURAMA The Old Order Amish of the United States and Canada 80

CULTURE AND FERTILITY 81

Sexual Intercourse 81

Fertility Decision Making 83

Fertility Control 84

Infanticide 86

PERSONALITY AND THE LIFE CYCLE 86

Birth, Infancy, and Childhood 86

◆ LESSONS APPLIED Mediating Cultural Conflict about the Treatment of a Newborn Baby in a U.S. Hospital Nursery 87

Socialization during Childhood 88

Adolescence and Identity 90

◆ CRITICAL THINKING Cultural Relativism and Female Genital Cutting 92

Adulthood 94

THE BIG QUESTIONS REVISITED 98

Key Concepts 99   Suggested Readings 99

5

DISEASE, ILLNESS, AND HEALING 101

THE BIG QUESTIONS 101

ETHNOMEDICINE 102

Defining and Classifying Health Problems 102

Ethno-Etiologies 105

Healing Ways 106

◆ EYE ON THE ENVIRONMENT Local Botanical Knowledge and Child Health in the Bolivian Amazon 109

THREE THEORETICAL APPROACHES 110

The Ecological/Epidemiological Approach 110

The Interpretivist Approach 112

Critical Medical Anthropology 112

GLOBALIZATION AND CHANGE 114

New Infectious Diseases 115

Diseases of Development 115

Medical Pluralism 115

CULTURAMA The Sherpa of Nepal 116

Applied Medical Anthropology 118

◆ LESSONS APPLIED Promoting Vaccination Programs in Developing Countries 119

THE BIG QUESTIONS REVISITED 120

Key Concepts 121   Suggested Readings 121

PART III
SOCIAL ORGANIZATION 123

6

KINSHIP AND DOMESTIC LIFE 125

THE BIG QUESTIONS 125

HOW CULTURES CREATE KINSHIP 126

Studying Kinship: From Formal Analysis to Kinship in Action 127

Descent 128

◆ EVERYDAY ANTHROPOLOGY What's in a Name? 130

Sharing 130

CULTURAMA The Minangkabau of Indonesia 132

Marriage 133

HOUSEHOLDS AND DOMESTIC LIFE 137
The Household: Variations on a Theme 137
Intrahousehold Dynamics 138

CHANGING KINSHIP AND HOUSEHOLD DYNAMICS 139
Change in Descent 139
◆ LESSONS APPLIED Ethnography for Preventing Wife
Abuse in Rural Kentucky 140
Change in Marriage 141
Changing Households 142

THE BIG QUESTIONS REVISITED 144
Key Concepts 145   Suggested Readings 145

7

SOCIAL GROUPS AND SOCIAL STRATIFICATION 147

THE BIG QUESTIONS 147

SOCIAL GROUPS 148
Friendship 148
◆ EVERYDAY ANTHROPOLOGY Making Friends 150
Clubs and Fraternities 151
Countercultural Groups 152
Cooperatives 154
Self-Help Groups 154

SOCIAL STRATIFICATION 155
Achieved Status: Class 156
Ascribed Status: "Race," Ethnicity, Gender, and Caste 156
◆ EYE ON THE ENVIRONMENT Industrial Pollution and
Activism in an African American Community in
Georgia, the United States 159

CULTURAMA The Roma of Eastern Europe 160

CIVIL SOCIETY 162
Civil Society for the State: The Chinese Women's
Movement 162
Activist Groups: CO-MADRES 163
New Social Movements and Cyberpower 163

THE BIG QUESTIONS REVISITED 164
Key Concepts 165   Suggested Readings 165

8

POLITICAL AND LEGAL SYSTEMS 167

THE BIG QUESTIONS 167

POLITICS, POLITICAL ORGANIZATION,
AND LEADERSHIP 168

Bands 168
Tribes 169
Chiefdoms 170
States 171
◆ EYE ON THE ENVIRONMENT Water, Pollution, and
International Politics 173

SOCIAL ORDER AND SOCIAL CONFLICT 174
Norms and Laws 175
Systems of Social Control 175
◆ CRITICAL THINKING Yanomami: The "Fierce People"? 178
Social Conflict and Violence 178

CHANGE IN POLITICAL AND LEGAL SYSTEMS 181
Emerging Nations and Transnational Nations 181

CULTURAMA The Kurds of the Middle East 182
Democratization 183
The United Nations and International Peacekeeping 183

THE BIG QUESTIONS REVISITED 184
Key Concepts 185   Suggested Readings 185

PART IV
SYMBOLIC SYSTEMS 187

9

COMMUNICATION 189

THE BIG QUESTIONS 189

THE VARIETIES OF HUMAN COMMUNICATION 190
Language and Verbal Communication 190
Nonverbal Language and Embodied
Communication 192
◆ LESSONS APPLIED Anthropology and Public
Understanding of the Language and Culture of People
Who Are Deaf 193
Communicating with Media and Information
Technology 196

COMMUNICATION, DIVERSITY, AND INEQUALITY 197
Language and Culture: Two Theories 197
Critical Discourse Analysis: Gender and "Race" 198

LANGUAGE CHANGE 200
The Origins and History of Language 200
Historical Linguistics 201
Writing Systems 202
Colonialism, Nationalism, and Globalization 203

CULTURAMA The Saami of Sápmi, or Lapland 205
◆ CRITICAL THINKING Should Dying Languages Be
Revived? 206

Endangered Languages and Language Revitalization 206

THE BIG QUESTIONS REVISITED 208

Key Concepts 209   Suggested Readings 209

10
RELIGION 211

THE BIG QUESTIONS 211

RELIGION IN COMPARATIVE PERSPECTIVE 212

What Is Religion? 212

Varieties of Religious Beliefs 213

◆ **EYE ON THE ENVIRONMENT** Eagle Protection, National Parks, and the Preservation of Hopi Culture 214

Ritual Practices 217

Religious Specialists 219

WORLD RELIGIONS AND LOCAL VARIATIONS 219

Hinduism 221

Buddhism 222

Judaism 223

◆ **EVERYDAY ANTHROPOLOGY** Tattoos and Sacred Power 224

Christianity 225

Islam 227

CULTURAMA Hui Muslims of Xi'an, China 228

African Religions 229

DIRECTIONS OF RELIGIOUS CHANGE 230

Revitalization Movements 230

Contested Sacred Sites 231

Religious Freedom as a Human Right 231

THE BIG QUESTIONS REVISITED 232

Key Concepts 233   Suggested Readings 233

11
EXPRESSIVE CULTURE 235

THE BIG QUESTIONS 235

ART AND CULTURE 236

What Is Art? 236

◆ **CRITICAL THINKING** Probing the Categories of Art 237

Studying Art in Society 237

Performance Arts 239

Architecture and Decorative Arts 241

PLAY, LEISURE, AND CULTURE 243

Games and Sports as a Cultural Microcosm 244

Leisure Travel 245

CHANGE IN EXPRESSIVE CULTURE 246

CULTURAMA The Gullah of South Carolina 247

Colonialism and Syncretism 248

Tourism's Complex Effects 248

◆ **LESSONS APPLIED** A Strategy on Cultural Heritage for the World Bank 250

THE BIG QUESTIONS REVISITED 252

Key Concepts 253   Suggested Readings 253

PART V
CONTEMPORARY CULTURAL CHANGE 255

12
PEOPLE ON THE MOVE 257

THE BIG QUESTIONS 257

CATEGORIES OF MIGRATION 259

Categories Based on Spatial Boundaries 259

◆ **CRITICAL THINKING** Haitian Cane Cutters in the Dominican Republic: A Case of Structure or Human Agency? 260

Categories Based on Reason for Moving 260

CULTURAMA The Maya of Guatemala 264

THE NEW IMMIGRANTS TO THE UNITED STATES AND CANADA 265

The New Immigrants from Latin America and the Caribbean 266

The New Immigrants from Asia 268

The New Immigrants from the Former Soviet Union 270

◆ **LESSONS APPLIED** Studying African Pastoralists' Movements for Risk Assessment and Service Delivery 270

MIGRATION POLITICS, POLICIES, AND PROGRAMS IN A GLOBALIZING WORLD 271

Protecting Migrants' Health 271

Inclusion and Exclusion 271

Migration and Human Rights 273

THE BIG QUESTIONS REVISITED 274

Key Concepts 275   Suggested Readings 275

13
PEOPLE DEFINING DEVELOPMENT 277

THE BIG QUESTIONS 277

DEFINING DEVELOPMENT AND APPROACHES TO IT 278

Two Processes of Cultural Change 279

Theories and Models of Development 279

◆ **LESSONS APPLIED** The Saami, Snowmobiles, and the Need for Social Impact Analysis 280

Institutional Approaches to Development 282

CULTURAMA The Peyizan yo of Haiti 284

The Development Project 285

DEVELOPMENT, INDIGENOUS PEOPLE, AND WOMEN 288

Indigenous People and Development 288

Women and Development 292

◆ **EYE ON THE ENVIRONMENT** Oil, Environmental Degradation, and Human Rights in the Nigerian Delta 294

URGENT ISSUES IN DEVELOPMENT 295

Life Projects and Human Rights 296

Cultural Heritage and Development: Linking the Past and Present to the Future 296

Cultural Anthropology and the Future 297

THE BIG QUESTIONS REVISITED 298

Key Concepts 299   Suggested Readings 299

PHOTO CREDITS 300

GLOSSARY 302

REFERENCES 308

INDEX 325

boxed FEATURES

LESSONS applied

Orangutan Research Leads to Orangutan Advocacy 10

Assessing the Social Impact of Indian Casinos in California 69

Mediating Cultural Conflict about the Treatment of a Newborn Baby in a U.S. Hospital Nursery 87

Promoting Vaccination Programs in Developing Countries 119

Ethnography for Preventing Wife Abuse in Rural Kentucky 140

Anthropology and Public Understanding of the Language and Culture of People Who Are Deaf 193

A Strategy on Cultural Heritage for the World Bank 250

Studying African Pastoralists' Movements for Risk Assessment and Service Delivery 270

The Saami, Snowmobiles, and the Need for Social Impact Analysis 280

everyday ANTHROPOLOGY

Latina Power in the Kitchen 16

The Importance of Dogs 54

What's in a Name? 130

Making Friends 150

Tattoos and Sacred Power 224

CRITICAL thinking

Shells and Skirts in the Trobriand Islands 32

Was the Invention of Agriculture a Terrible Mistake? 62

Cultural Relativism and Female Genital Cutting 92

Yanomami: The "Fierce People"? 178

Should Dying Languages Be Revived? 206

Probing the Categories of Art 237

Haitian Cane Cutters in the Dominican Republic: A Case of Structure or Human Agency? 260

CULTURAMA

San Peoples of Southern Africa 21

The Trobriand Islanders of Papua New Guinea 33

The Kwakwaka'wakw of Canada 72

The Old Order Amish of the United States and Canada 80

The Sherpa of Nepal 116

The Minangkabau of Indonesia 132

The Roma of Eastern Europe 160

The Kurds of the Middle East 182

The Saami of Sápmi, or Lapland   205

Hui Muslims of Xi'an, China 228

The Gullah of South Carolina 247

The Maya of Guatemala 264

The Peyizan yo of Haiti 284

eye on the ENVIRONMENT

Researching Inuit Place Names and Landscape Knowledge 41

Local Botanical Knowledge and Child Health in the Bolivian Amazon 109

Industrial Pollution and Activism in an African American Community in Georgia, the United States 159

Water, Pollution, and International Politics 173

Eagle Protection, National Parks, and the Preservation of Hopi Culture 214

Oil, Environmental Degradation, and Human Rights in the Nigerian Delta 294

Maps

CHAPTER 1
MAP 1.1 Orangutan Regions in Malaysia and Indonesia 10
MAP 1.2 Weyéwa Region in Indonesia 14
MAP 1.3 Papua New Guinea 17
MAP 1.4 Ju/'hoansi Region in Namibia and Botswana 21

CHAPTER 2
MAP 2.1 Trobriand Islands of Papua New Guinea 33
MAP 2.2 Syria 35
MAP 2.3 Baffin Island in Northeast Canada 41
MAP 2.4 Spain 42

CHAPTER 3
MAP 3.1 Hare Region near Colville Lake in Northwest Canada 55
MAP 3.2 Precolonial Iroquois Region 57
MAP 3.3 Yanomami Region in Brazil and Venezuela 57
MAP 3.4 Location of the Kuru Epidemic in Papua New Guinea 65
MAP 3.5 Lese and Efe Region in the Democratic Republic of Congo 70
MAP 3.6 The Kwakwaka'wakw Region in Canada 72

CHAPTER 4
MAP 4.1 Old Order Amish Population of North America 80
MAP 4.2 Morocco 82
MAP 4.3 Mexico 84
MAP 4.4 Maasai Region of Kenya and Tanzania 91
MAP 4.5 Sierra Leone 93
MAP 4.6 Aka Region of the Central African Republic and the Democratic Republic of Congo 95

CHAPTER 5
MAP 5.1 The Philippines 103
MAP 5.2 The Republic of Bolivia 109
MAP 5.3 Precolonial Distribution of Indian Tribes in the 48 United States 112
MAP 5.4 Designated Reservations in the 48 United States 113
MAP 5.5 Nepal 116
MAP 5.6 Samoa and American Samoa 117

CHAPTER 6
MAP 6.1 Ireland 126
MAP 6.2 Hong Kong 131
MAP 6.3 Minangkabau Region in Indonesia 132
MAP 6.4 Ghana 133
MAP 6.5 Kentucky, United States 140

CHAPTER 7
MAP 7.1 Bangladesh 149
MAP 7.2 Caribbean Countries of South America 151
MAP 7.3 The Solomon Islands 153
MAP 7.4 Kuna Region in Panama 155
MAP 7.5 South Africa 158
MAP 7.6 Roma Population in Eastern Europe 160

CHAPTER 8
MAP 8.1 The Danube and Tisza Rivers in Eastern Europe 173
MAP 8.2 Central Asian States 180
MAP 8.3 Kurdish Region in the Middle East 182
MAP 8.4 Puerto Rico 183

CHAPTER 9
MAP 9.1 Pirahã Reservation in Brazil 191
MAP 9.2 Western Apache Reservation in Arizona 195
MAP 9.3 Hungary 197
MAP 9.4 Two Sites of Proto-Indo-European Origins 202
MAP 9.5 The Bantu Migrations in Africa 202
MAP 9.6 The Saami of Sápmi, or Lapland 205

CHAPTER 10
MAP 10.1 Klamath and Modoc Region in Oregon and California 214
MAP 10.2 Hopi Reservation in Arizona 215
MAP 10.3 England 217
MAP 10.4 Mainland Southeast Asia 225
MAP 10.5 Sacred Sites in the Old City of Jerusalem, Israel 226
MAP 10.6 The City of Xi'an in China 228

CHAPTER 11
MAP 11.1 Costa Rica 246
MAP 11.2 The Gullah Region of South Carolina 247
MAP 11.3 Turkey 249

CHAPTER 12
MAP 12.1 Tonga 262
MAP 12.2 Site of Three Gorges Dam in China 263
MAP 12.3 Guatemala 264
MAP 12.4 El Salvador 267
MAP 12.5 Sahel Region 272
MAP 12.6 Italy 273

CHAPTER 13
MAP 13.1 Walpole Island Reservation in Southern Ontario, Canada 278
MAP 13.2 Kerala, South India 282
MAP 13.3 Haiti 284
MAP 13.4 Senegal 287
MAP 13.5 Nunavut Province, Canada 290
MAP 13.6 Sudan 291
MAP 13.7 Nigeria and the Niger Delta 295

◆◆◆ PREFACE

"I had no idea all those cultures were out there," said one of my students after taking my introductory cultural anthropology course. Another commented, "I'm a business major, but I am going to keep the books from this course because they will help me in my career. I need to understand people."

Cultural anthropology opens up whole new worlds. Not just "out there," but here, there, and everywhere. The subject matter of cultural anthropology may seem distant, exotic, and "other"—jungle drumbeats and painted faces, for example. This book helps students to encounter those faraway cultures and also to realize that their culture has its own versions of jungle drumbeats and painted faces. "Making the strange familiar" is essential learning in a globalizing world where cultural diversity may equal cultural survival for all of us. "Making the familiar strange" is a priceless revelation because it reduces the divide between "us" and the "other." "We" become "other" through the insights of cultural anthropology.

To achieve this double goal, *Cultural Anthropology in a Globalizing World,* Second Edition, delivers rich and exciting information about the world's cultures and promotes critical thinking and reflective learning. Students will find many points at which they can interact with the material, view their own culture as a culture, and make connections between anthropology and their everyday life in, for example, hairstyles, food symbolism, sleep deprivation, doctor–patient dialogues, racism and sexism, and the meaning of gestures.

The study of the world's cultures involves learning new words and analytical categories, but the effort will pay off in terms of bringing the world's peoples and cultures closer to you. If this book achieves my aspirations, anyone who reads it will live a life that is more culturally aware, enriched, and tolerant.

HOW THIS BOOK IS ORGANIZED

The book's organization and pedagogical features are designed to help ensure student engagement and enhanced learning. The chapters are organized into five parts.

Part I, "Introduction to Cultural Anthropology," comprises two chapters that provide the foundation for the rest of the book. They describe what anthropology is and how cultural anthropologists do research. Part II, "Cultural Foundations," consists of three chapters that explain how people make a living, how they reproduce and raise children, and how different cultures deal with illness, suffering, and death. Part III, "Social Organization," provides three chapters about how people around the world organize themselves into groups

based on kinship and other forms of social ties, how they form political alliances, and how they deal with conflict and the need for order.

Part IV, "Symbolic Systems," presents three chapters that address communication and language, religion, and expressive culture.

Part V, "Contemporary Cultural Change," looks at two of the most important topics shaping cultural change in our times: migration and international development. These chapters explicitly put culture into motion and show how people both are affected by larger structures, such as globalization or violence, and exercise agency in attempting to create meaningful and secure lives.

SIGNIFICANT CHANGES IN THE SECOND EDITION

New Box, Eye on the Environment These boxes provide material that links culture with some aspect of the environment. Examples include Inuit place names and environmental knowledge, the protection of eagles among the Hopi, and environmental destruction from oil drilling in Nigeria. These boxes, along with many in-text references to how culture and the environment interact, enable students to make new connections and think critically.

New and Updated Maps The author has designed a number of new maps to complement the textual material without distracting the reader with unnecessary details.

New Photographs The new photographs are carefully chosen to enliven the textual material and to be thought provoking. Photographs arranged in pairs or trios, with linked captions, offer a mini–photo essay for students to ponder.

CONTINUED FEATURES

Several features continued from the first edition make this textbook distinctive and effective.

Anthropology Works Each of the book's five parts opens with a profile of an applied anthropologist, someone who uses his or her anthropology training in a professional career. Profiles include those of a business anthropologist, a medical anthropologist, a forensic anthropologist, a development anthropologist, and a federal relations anthropologist.

Culturama All chapters include a one-page profile of a cultural group, accompanied by a mini-panorama of two photographs and a map with captions. These brief summaries provide an enticing glimpse into the culture presented.

In-Text Glossary Definitions of the key concepts are provided on the page where the concept is first mentioned and defined. A paginated list of the key concepts appears at the end of each chapter. The glossary at the end of the book contains a complete list of key concepts together with their definitions.

Thinking Outside the Box The Thinking Outside the Box feature provides three or four thought-provoking questions in each chapter, displayed at the bottom of the page. These questions prompt readers to relate an issue to their own cultural experiences or provide an avenue for further research. They can promote class discussion and serve as a basis for a class project.

The Big Questions Three Big Questions are posed at the beginning of each chapter to alert readers to the chapter's overarching themes. They are carried through in the chapter outline as the three major headings. At the end of the chapter, The Big Questions Revisited provides a helpful review of the key points related to each Big Question.

BOXED FEATURES

Everyday Anthropology boxes present cultural examples that connect to everyone's lives and prompt reflective learning. **Critical Thinking** boxes introduce an issue and show how it has been studied or analyzed from different anthropological perspectives. These boxes provide tie-ins to the major theoretical debates in cultural anthropology presented in Chapter 1. Although students may appreciate the interesting material that cultural anthropology offers, they are still likely to ask, "Does this knowledge have any practical applications?" **Lessons Applied** boxes highlight how applied anthropologists work and the relevance of anthropology to addressing social problems.

COMMITMENT TO CULTURAL SURVIVAL

In confirming our commitment to the sustainability of the world's cultures, especially of endangered indigenous peoples, the author and the publisher donate a portion of the royalties from sales of new copies of this book to the organization called Cultural Survival (see its mission statement on the inside of the front cover). Cultural Survival helps support indigenous people worldwide in achieving and maintaining their preferred lifestyles and environments. Back issues of the journal *Cultural Survival Quarterly* are available on the Web at www.cs.org.

THE IMPORTANCE OF NAMES

Since the beginning of modern humanity, people have been naming each other, naming their groups and other groups, and naming features of the places they inhabit. People of earlier times often referred to themselves in terms that translate roughly into "The People." As far as they were concerned, they were The People: the only people on earth.

Things are more complicated now. European colonialism, starting in the fifteenth century, launched centuries of rapid contact between Europeans and thousands of indigenous groups around the world. The Europeans named and described these groups in their European languages. The names were not those which the people used for themselves, or if they were, the transliteration into a European language altered local names into something very different from the original.

The Spanish explorers' naming of all the indigenous peoples of North America as Indians is a famous example of a misnomer. Beyond being wrong by thinking they had reached India, the Spanish conquerors who renamed thousands of people and claimed their territory simultaneously erased much of the indigenous people's heritage and identity.

The challenge of using the preferred names for people and places of the world faces us today as people worldwide wrestle with the issue of what they want to be called. Until recently, indigenous peoples of the present-day United States mainland preferred to be called Native Americans, rejecting the pejorative term "Indian." Now, they are claiming and re-casting the term "Indian." In Alaska, the preferred term is "Alaska Native," and in Hawai'i it is "Native Hawai'ian." In Canada, preferred terms are "First Nations," "Native Peoples," and "Northern Peoples." From small-scale groups to entire countries, people are attempting to revive precolonial group names and place names. Bombay is now Mumbai, and Calcutta is Kolkata. Group names and place names are frequently contested. Is someone Hispanic or Latino? Is it the Persian Gulf or the Arabian Gulf? Is it Greenland or Kalaallit Nunaat? Does it matter? The answer is yes, resoundingly, yes.

This book strives to provide the most currently accepted names for people, places, objects, activities, and ideas. By the time it is printed, however, some names and their English spellings will have changed. It is an ongoing challenge to keep track of such changes, but doing so is part of our job as citizens of a transforming world.

THE COVER IMAGE

Throughout much of Africa, especially central and eastern Africa, young girls go through a coming-of-age ceremony that includes "female genital cutting." This Maasai girl of Kenya has just gone through an alternative ritual that is called "Circumcision through Words" and has been promoted by the government and non-governmental organizations since the 1990s. This alternative ceremony allows the girls to go through all the steps of a traditional initiation, including the usual period of seclusion in which elder women teach them about adult life, except the cutting.

The topic of female genital cutting, perhaps more than any other, challenges students and their teachers to use and assess longstanding and more recent concepts in the discipline such as cultural relativism, human rights, and bodily inscription.

IN THANKS

The breadth, depth, and quality of this edition are the result of many people's ideas, comments, corrections, and care. For the first edition of Cultural Anthropology, four anthropologists carefully reviewed multiple drafts of the book. I will always be grateful to them for their monumental contribution that helped make this book what it is today: Elliot Fratkin, Smith College; Maxine Margolis, University of Florida; Russell Reid, University of Louisville; and Robert Trotter II, University of Arizona.

The cultural anthropologists who have reviewed various editions of my *Cultural Anthropology* textbook and offered their critiques and detailed suggestions have shaped this book

from start to finish: Warren D. Anderson, Southeast Missouri State University; Jason Antrosio, Albion College; Diane Baxter, University of Oregon; Monica L. Bellas, Cerritos College; Barbara Bonnekessen, University of Missouri–Kansas City; Peter Brown, University of Wisconsin, Oshkosh; Howard Campbell, University of Texas, El Paso; (the late) Charles R. de Burlo, The University of Vermont; Elizabeth de la Portilla, University of Texas at San Antonio; William W. Donner, Kutztown University; Lisa Pope Fischer, Santa Monica College; Pamela J. Ford, Mount San Jacinto College; Mary Kay Gilliland, Pima Community College; Nancy Gonlin, Bellevue Community College; Jeanne Humble, Bluegrass Community & Technical College; Ann Kingsolver, University of South Carolina; Leslie Lischka, Linfield College; William M. Loker, California State University, Chico; Martin F. Manalansan IV, University of Illinois; Corey Pressman, Mt. Hood Community College; Ed Robbins, University of Wisconsin; Jacquelyn Robinson, Albany State University; Harry Sanabria, University of Pittsburgh; Kathleen M. Saunders, Western Washington University; G. Richard Scott, University of Nevada, Reno; Wesley Shumar, Drexel University; David Simmons, University of South Carolina; Kimberly Eison Simmons, University of South Carolina; Lori A. Stanley, Luther College; Jim Wilce, Northern Arizona University; Peter Wogan, Willamette University; and Katrina Worley, Sierra College.

Many anthropologists and others have provided encouragement, suggestions, feedback, references, and photographs: Lila Abu-Lughod, Abigail Adams, Vincanne Adams, Catherine Allen, Joseph Alter, Matthew Amster, Myrdene Anderson, Donald Attwood, Christopher Baker, Isabel Balseiro, Nancy Benco, Marc Bermann, Alexia Bloch, Elson Boles, Lynne Bolles, John Bowen, Don Brenneis, Alison Brooks, Judith K. Brown, D. Glynn Cochrane, Jeffery Cohen, Carole Counihan, Brian Craik, Liza Dalby, Loring Danforth, Patricia Delaney, Alexander Dent, Linus Digim'rina, Timothy Earle, Daniel Everett, Johannes Fabian, Ilana Feldman, Janina Fenigsen, Elliot Fratkin, Martin Fusi, Maris Boyd Gillette, Richard A. Gould, David Gow, Richard Grinker, Daniel Gross, (the late) Marvin Harris, Tobias Hecht, Cornelia Mayer Herzfeld, Michael Herzfeld, Barry Hewlett, Danny Hoffman, Michael Horowitz, (the late) Robert Humphrey, Lanita Jacobs-Huey, Vicki Jensen, Anstice Justin, Barry D. Kass, Patty Kelly, Laurel Kendall, David Kideckel, Diane E. King, Stuart Kirsch, Dorinne Kondo, Conrad Kottak, Jennifer Kramer, Donald B. Kraybill, Ruth Krulfeld, Joel Kuipers, Takie Lebra, David Lempert, Lamont Lindstrom, Susan Orpett Long, Luisa Maffi, Beatriz Manz, Debra Martin, Samuel Martínez, Catherine McCoid, Leroy McDermott, Kimber Haddox McKay, Jerry Milanich, Laura Miller, Madhushree Mukerjee, Kirin Narayan, Sarah Nelson, Gananath Obeyesekere, Ellen Oxfeld, Hanna Papanek, Michael G. Peletz, Deborah Pellow,

Gregory Possehl, David Price, Joanne Rappaport, Jennifer Robertson, Nicole Sault, Joel Savishinsky, David Z. Scheffel, Nancy Scheper-Hughes, Pankaj Sekhsaria, Bob Shepherd, Richard Shweder, Jennie Smith-Pariola, Chunghee Soh, Kate Spilde Contreras, Anthony Stocks, Patricia Tovar, Sita Venkateswar, Martha Ward, James (Woody) Watson, Rubie Watson, Van Yasek, and Kevin Yelvington.

For this edition, I am grateful to Nancy Roberts, my new publisher at Pearson/Prentice Hall, for her support and to Monica Ohlinger, my development editor who is the head of Ohlinger Publishing Services in Columbus, Ohio, for her contributions and care throughout the revision process.

I thank the Millers—my parents, siblings, aunts and uncles, and nieces and nephews—for their interest and support. My father's two comments about the book were that it has an awful lot of long words and how do I know so much about sex? "From reading, Dad," was my truthful reply. I am grateful to the Heatons—my former in-laws, including my ex-husband, (late) ex-parents-in-law, brothers- and sisters-in-law, and nieces and nephews—for their enduring friendship.

I thank, especially, my son, Jack Heaton. He was a superb traveling companion on our trip around the world with the Semester at Sea Program in 1996, when I wrote much of the first edition of *Cultural Anthropology*. He continues to be excellent company during our time together in DC. This book is dedicated to him.

Barbara Miller
anthropologyworks@gmail.com
Washington, DC

SUPPORT FOR INSTRUCTORS AND STUDENTS

This book is accompanied by an extensive learning package to enhance the experience of both instructors and students. The author is personally responsible for the material in the Instructor's Resource Manual, MyTest, and the PowerPoint™ slides.

Instructor's Resource Manual with Tests (0-205-77713-9): For each chapter in the text, this valuable resource provides a detailed outline, a list of objectives, discussion questions, and suggested readings and videos. In addition, test questions in multiple-choice, true–false, fill-in-the-blank, and short-answer formats are available for each chapter; the answers are page-referenced to the text. For easy access, this manual is available within the instructor section of MyAnthroLab for *Cultural Anthropology in a Globalizing World*, Second Edition, or at www.pearsonhighered.com/irc.

MyTest (0-205-77762-7): This computerized software allows instructors to create their own personalized exams, to edit any or all of the existing test questions, and to add new questions. Other special features of this program include the random generation of test questions, the creation of alternative versions of the same test, scrambling question sequences, and test previews before printing. For easy access, this software is available within the instructor section of MyAnthroLab for *Cultural Anthropology in a Globalizing World*, Second Edition, or at www.pearsonhighered.com/irc.

PowerPoint™ Presentation for Cultural Anthropology (0-205-77709-0) These PowerPoint slides combine text and graphics for each chapter to help instructors convey anthropological principles in a clear and engaging way. For easy access, they are available within the instructor section of MyAnthroLab for *Cultural Anthropology in a Globalizing World*, Second Edition, or at www.pearsonhighered.com/irc.

PEARSON myanthrolab MyAnthroLab is an interactive and instructive multimedia site designed to help students and instructors save time and improve results. It offers access to a wealth of resources geared to meet the individual teaching and learning needs of every instructor and student. Combining an ebook, video, audio, multimedia simulations, research support, and assessment, MyAnthroLab engages students and gives them the tools they need to enhance their performance in the course. Please see your Pearson sales representative or visit www.myanthrolab.com for more information.

Strategies in Teaching Anthropology, Sixth Edition (0-205-71123-5) Unique in focus and content, this book focuses on the "how" of teaching anthropology across all of the discipline's four fields and provides a wide array of associated learning outcomes and student activities. It is a valuable single-source compendium of strategies and teaching "tricks of the trade" from a group of seasoned teaching anthropologists, working in a variety of teaching settings, who share their pedagogical techniques, knowledge, and observations.

EthnoQuest® (0-13-185013-X) This interactive multimedia simulation includes a series of 10 ethnographic encounters with the culture of a fictional Mexican village set in a computer-based learning environment. It provides students with a realistic problem-solving experience and is designed to help students experience the fieldwork of a cultural anthropologist. Please see your Pearson sales representative for more information about **EthnoQuest®**.

about the AUTHOR

"*Cultural anthropology* is exciting because it **CONNECTS** with everything, from **FOOD** to **ART**. And it can help prevent or **SOLVE** world problems related to *social inequality* and injustice."

BARBARA D. MILLER

Barbara Miller is Professor of Anthropology and International Affairs and Director of the Culture in Global Affairs (CIGA) Research and Policy Program at The George Washington University. She received her Ph.D. in anthropology from Syracuse University in 1978. Before coming to GW in 1994, she taught at the University of Rochester, SUNY Cortland, Ithaca College, Cornell University, and the University of Pittsburgh. For 30 years, Barbara's research has focused on gender-based inequalities in India, especially the nutritional and medical neglect of daughters in northern regions of the country. In addition, she has conducted research on culture and rural development in Bangladesh, on low-income household dynamics in Jamaica, and on Hindu adolescents in Pittsburgh. Her current interests include continued research on gender inequalities in health in South Asia, the role of cultural anthropology in informing policy issues, and cultural heritage and public policy, especially as related to women, children, and other disenfranchised groups. She teaches courses on introductory cultural anthropology, medical anthropology, development anthropology, culture and population, health and development in South Asia, and migration and mental health.

She has published many journal articles and book chapters and several books: *The Endangered Sex: Neglect of Female Children in Rural North India*, Second Edition (Oxford University Press 1997), an edited volume, *Sex and Gender Hierarchies* (Cambridge University Press 1993), and a co-edited volume with Alf Hiltebeitel, *Hair: Its Power and Meaning in Asian Cultures* (SUNY Press 1998). In addition to *Cultural Anthropology in a Globalizing World*, Second Edition, she is the author of *Cultural Anthropology*, Fifth Edition (Pearson 2008) and the lead author of *Anthropology*, Second Edition (Pearson 2008).

Barbara launched a blog in 2009 (anthropologyworks. com) which includes her thoughts on important findings and debates in anthropology, a weekly feature covering anthropologists in the mainstream media, and guests posts. You can also follow her via Twitter @anthroworks.

CULTURAL
ANTHROPOLOGY
IN A GLOBALIZING
WORLD

1 ANTHROPOLOGY AND THE STUDY OF CULTURE

2 RESEARCHING CULTURE

PART I

INTRODUCTION TO CULTURAL ANTHROPOLOGY

ANTHROPOLOGY works

Susan Squires, a business anthropologist, is one of the brains behind the General Mills breakfast food Go-Gurt®. During its first year of production in 1991, Go-Gurt generated sales of $37 million. Squires, who earned a Ph.D. in cultural anthropology from Boston University, is one of the growing number of anthropologists who use their knowledge of anthropology in the business world.

Research into the development of Go-Gurt took Squires and an industrial designer into the homes of American families to observe their breakfast behavior and food choices. On their first day of research, they arrived at a residence at 6:30 a.m., laden with video cameras and other equipment, prepared to have breakfast with a family they had never met.

General Mills had learned from focus group studies that mothers want their families to eat whole-grain breakfast foods. Squires, in contrast, found a wide range of preferences and behavior related to individual hunger patterns and the need to leave home early for work or school.

She realized that the ideal breakfast food should be portable, healthy, fun, and come in a disposable container. The answer: yogurt packaged so that it does not require a spoon and can be frozen or refrigerated. One mother said that her daughter thinks she is eating a popsicle when she has Go-Gurt for breakfast.

The work of Susan Squires demonstrates how cultural anthropology can benefit the business world and the everyday lives of consumers. Two assets of cultural anthropology in the business world are, first, its attention to everyday life and, second, its attention to cultural variation, which exposes differences in preferences, values, and behavior.

A Maya dancer performs in Mexico City's Plaza de al Constitución, also called the Zócalo. Maya is a cluster term referring to 7 million indigenous people of southern Mexico and northern Central America.

ANTHROPOLOGY AND THE STUDY OF CULTURE

1

the BIG questions

◆ What is anthropology?

◆ What is cultural anthropology?

◆ How is cultural anthropology relevant to a career?

OUTLINE

Introducing Anthropology

Lessons Applied: Orangutan Research Leads to Orangutan Advocacy

Introducing Cultural Anthropology

Everyday Anthropology: Latina Power in the Kitchen

Culturama: San Peoples of Southern Africa

Cultural Anthropology and Careers

5

A member of the Dani people, of Irian Jaya, New Guinea, holding a stone adze, photographed in the 1990s.

Old bones, *Jurassic Park*, cannibalism, hidden treasure, *Indiana Jones and the Temple of Doom*. The popular impression of anthropology is based mainly on movies and television shows that depict anthropologists as adventurers and heroes. Many anthropologists do have adventures and discover treasures such as ancient pottery, medicinal plants, and jade carvings. But

most of their research is not glamorous. Some anthropologists spend years in difficult physical conditions, searching for the earliest fossils of our ancestors. Others live among people in Silicon Valley, California, and study firsthand how they work and organize family life in a setting permeated by modern technology. Some anthropologists conduct laboratory analyses of the contents of tooth enamel to reveal where an individual once lived. Others study designs on prehistoric pottery to learn what the symbols mean, or observe nonhuman primates such as chimpanzees or orangutans in the wild to learn how they live.

Anthropology is the study of humanity, including prehistoric origins and contemporary human diversity. Compared with other disciplines that study humanity (such as history, psychology, economics, political science, and sociology), anthropology is broader in scope. Anthropology covers a much greater span of time than these disciplines, and it encompasses a broader range of topics.

◆◆◆

Introducing Anthropology

In North America, anthropology is divided into four fields (see Figure 1.1) that focus on separate, but connected, subject matter related to humanity:

- **Biological anthropology** or *physical anthropology*— the study of humans as biological organisms, including evolution and contemporary variation.
- **Archaeology**—the study of past human cultures through their material remains.

---

anthropology   the study of humanity, including its prehistoric origins and contemporary human diversity.

biological anthropology   the study of humans as biological organisms, including evolution and contemporary variation.

archaeology   the study of past human cultures through their material remains.

linguistic anthropology   the study of human communication, including its origins, history, and contemporary variation and change.

cultural anthropology   the study of living peoples and their cultures, including variation and change.

culture   people's learned and shared behaviors and beliefs.

applied anthropology   the use of anthropological knowledge to prevent or solve problems or to shape and achieve policy goals.

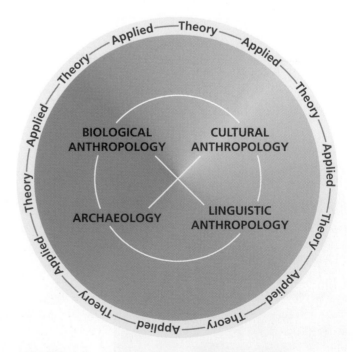

FIGURE 1.1   **The Four Fields of Anthropology**

Members of a team of anthropologists and students discuss their research project on Silicon Valley culture.

▶ *If you were given a grant to conduct anthropological research, where would you go and what would you study?*

• **Linguistic anthropology**—the study of human communication, including its origins, history, and contemporary variation and change.

• **Cultural anthropology**—the study of living peoples and their cultures, including variation and change. **Culture** refers to people's learned and shared behaviors and beliefs.

Some anthropologists argue that a fifth field, applied anthropology, should be added. **Applied anthropology** (or *practicing anthropology* or *practical anthropology*) is the use of anthropological knowledge to prevent or solve problems or to shape and achieve policy goals. The author of this book takes the position that the application of knowledge, just like theory, is an integral part of each of the four fields and should be integrated within each of them.

BIOLOGICAL OR PHYSICAL ANTHROPOLOGY

Biological anthropology encompasses three subfields. The first, *primatology*, is the study of the nonhuman members of the order of mammals called primates, which includes a wide range of animals from very small, nocturnal creatures to gorillas, the largest members. Primatologists study nonhuman primates in the wild and in captivity. They record and analyze how the animals spend their time, collect and share food, form social groups, rear offspring, develop leadership patterns, and experience and resolve conflicts. Primatologists are alarmed about the decline in numbers, and even the extinction, of nonhuman primates. Many apply their knowledge to nonhuman primate conservation.

The second subfield is *paleoanthropology*, the study of human evolution on the basis of the fossil record. One important activity is the search for fossils to increase the amount and quality of the evidence related to the way human evolution occurred.

The third subfield is the study of *contemporary human biological variation*. Anthropologists working in this area define, measure, and seek to explain differences in the biological makeup and behavior of contemporary humans. They study such biological factors as DNA within and across populations, body size and shape, human nutrition and disease, and human growth and development.

ARCHAEOLOGY

Archaeology means, literally, the "study of the old," but "the old" is limited to human culture. Therefore, the time depth of archaeology goes back only to the beginnings of *Homo sapiens*, between 300,000 and 160,000 years ago, when they first emerged in Africa. Archaeology encompasses two major areas: *prehistoric archaeology*, which concerns the human past before written records, and *historical archaeology*, which deals with the human past in societies that have written documents. Prehistoric archaeologists often identify themselves with broad geographic regions, studying, for example, Old World

THINKING OUTSIDE THE BOX

What are your impressions of anthropology? How did you acquire them? Make notes of these impressions and review them at the end of the course.

Maya people watch as forensic anthropologist Francisco de León conducts an exhumation of more than 50 bodies in a highland Guatemalan village in 1997.

▶ *Are courses in forensic anthropology offered at your school?*

archaeology (Africa, Europe, and Asia) or New World archaeology (North, Central, and South America).

Another set of specialties within archaeology is based on the context in which the archaeology takes place. For example, *underwater archaeology* is the study of submerged archaeological sites. Underwater archaeological sites may be from either prehistoric or historic times. Some prehistoric sites include early human settlements in parts of Europe, such as household sites discovered in Switzerland that were once near lakes but are now submerged.

The archaeology of the recent past is another important research direction. An example of what could be called the *archaeology of contemporary life* is the "Garbage Project" conducted by archaeologists at the University of Arizona at Tucson (Rathje and Murphy 1992). They have excavated part of the Fresh Kills landfill on Staten Island, near New York City. The mass of the Fresh Kills landfill is estimated at 100 million tons and its volume at 2.9 billion cubic feet. Thus, it is one of the largest human-made structures in North America. The excavation of pop-top can tabs, disposable diapers, cosmetics containers, and telephone books reveals much about recent consumption patterns and how they affect the environment. One surprising finding is that the kinds of garbage people often blame for filling up landfills, such as fast-food packaging and disposable diapers, cause less serious problems than paper. Newspaper, especially, is a major culprit because of its sheer quantity. This information can improve recycling efforts worldwide. The Fresh Kills landfill continues to grow rapidly due to everyday trash accumulation and other, less common sources of debris, such

Stephen Lubkemann, trained as a cultural anthropologist and an underwater archaeologist, documents the remains of the hull of DRTO-036, a vessel that wrecked in the Dry Tortugas in the mid-nineteenth century. The vessel lies within Dry Tortugas National Park in the Florida Keys.

▶ *You can access UNESCO's Convention on the Protection of Underwater Heritage on the Internet.*

as the remains from the World Trade Center in Manhattan following the 9/11 attack.

LINGUISTIC ANTHROPOLOGY

Linguistic anthropology is devoted to the study of communication, mainly (but not exclusively) among humans. Linguistic anthropology has three subfields: *historical linguistics*, the study of language change over time and how languages are related; *descriptive linguistics*, or structural linguistics, the study of how contemporary languages differ in terms of their formal structure; and *sociolinguistics*, the study of the relationships among social variation, social context, and linguistic variation, including nonverbal communication.

New directions in linguistic anthropology are connected to important current issues. First is a trend to study language in everyday use, or discourse, and how it relates to power structures at local, regional, and international levels (Duranti 1997a). In some contexts, powerful people speak more than less powerful people, whereas sometimes the more powerful people speak less. Power relations may also be expressed through intonation, word choice, and such nonverbal forms of communication as posture and dress. Second is increased attention to the role of information technology in communication, especially the Internet and cell phones. Third is attention to the increasingly rapid extinction of indigenous languages and what can be done about it. These topics are discussed in Chapter 9.

CULTURAL ANTHROPOLOGY

Cultural anthropology is the study of contemporary people and their cultures. The term *culture* refers to people's learned and shared behaviors and beliefs. Cultural anthropology considers variations and similarities across cultures, and how cultures change over time. Cultural anthropologists learn about culture by spending a long time, typically a year or more, living with the people they study (discussed in Chapter 2).

Prominent areas of specialization in cultural anthropology include economic anthropology, psychological anthropology, medical anthropology, political anthropology, and international development anthropology.

APPLIED ANTHROPOLOGY: SEPARATE FIELD OR CROSS-CUTTING FOCUS?

In the United States, applied anthropology emerged during and after World War II. Its first concern was with improving the lives of contemporary peoples and their needs, so it was more closely associated with cultural anthropology than with the other three fields.

Many anthropologists feel that applied anthropology should be considered a fifth field of anthropology, standing on its own. Many others think that the application of knowledge to solve problems, just like theory, should be part of each field (see Figure 1.1). The latter is the author's position, and therefore, many examples of applied anthropology appear throughout this book.

Applied anthropology is an important thread that weaves through all four fields of anthropology:

- Archaeologists are employed in *cultural resource management (CRM),* assessing the presence of possible archaeological remains before construction projects, such as roads and buildings, can proceed.

- Biological anthropologists are employed as *forensic anthropologists,* participating in criminal investigations through laboratory work identifying bodily remains. Others work in the area of primate conservation (see Lessons Applied box).

- Linguistic anthropologists consult with educational institutions about how to improve standardized tests for bilingual populations and conduct policy research for governments.

- Cultural anthropologists apply their knowledge to improve policies and programs in every domain of life, including education, health care, business, poverty reduction, and conflict prevention and resolution.

Applied roles of anthropologists are illustrated in the Anthropology Works profiles at the beginning of each part of this book and in the Lessons Applied boxes.

◆◆◆

Introducing Cultural Anthropology

Cultural anthropology is devoted to studying human cultures worldwide, both their similarities and differences. Cultural anthropology makes "the strange familiar and the familiar strange" (Spiro 1990). Therefore, it teaches us to look at ourselves from the "outside" as a somewhat "strange" culture. A good example of making the familiar strange is the case of the Nacirema, a culture first described in 1956:

> The Nacirema are a North American group living in the territory between the Canadian Cree, the Yaqui and the Tarahumara of Mexico, and the Carib and the Arawak of the Antilles. Little is known of their origin, though tradition states that they came from the east. According to Nacirema mythology, their nation was originated by a culture hero, Notgnihsaw, who is otherwise known for two great feats of strength—the throwing of a piece of wampum across the river Pa-To-Mac and the chopping down of a cherry tree in which the Spirit of Truth resided. (Miner 1965 [1956]:415)

LESSONS applied

Orangutan Research Leads to Orangutan Advocacy

Primatologist Biruté Galdikas (pronounced Beer-OOH-tay GAL-dee-kas) first went to Indonesia to study orangutans in 1971 (Galdikas 1995). She soon became aware of the threat to the orangutans from local people who, as a way of making money, capture them for sale to zoos around the world. The poachers separate the young from their mothers, often killing the mothers in the process.

Orangutan juveniles are highly dependent on their mothers, maintaining close bodily contact with them for at least two years and nursing until they are around 8 years old. Because of this long period of orangutans' need for maternal contact, Galdikas set up her camp to serve as a way station for orphans. She became the maternal figure. Her first "infant" was an orphaned orangutan, Sugito, who clung to her as though she were its own mother for years.

The survival of orangutans on Borneo and Sumatra (their only habitats worldwide) is critically endangered by massive commercial logging and illegal logging, population resettlement programs, plantations, and other pressures on the rainforests where the orangutans live. A **rainforest** is an

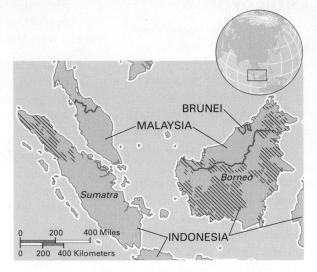

MAP 1.1 **Orangutan Regions in Malaysia and Indonesia.** Orangutans are the only great apes living outside Africa. Fossil evidence indicates that their habitats in the past extended throughout Southeast Asia and southern China. They are now limited to pockets of rainforest on the islands of Sumatra and Borneo.

environment, found at mid-latitudes, of tall, broad-leaf evergreen trees, with annual rainfall of 400 centimeters (or 60 inches) and no dry season.

Galdikas is focusing her efforts on orangutan preservation. She says, "I feel like I'm viewing an animal holocaust, and holocaust is not a word I use lightly . . . . The destruction of the tropical rainforest is accelerating daily" (Dreifus 2000:D3). Across all of the orangutan's ranges, it is estimated that during the twentieth century the orangutan population experienced a

huge decrease, from 315,000 in 1900 to 44,000 in 2000 (IUCN/SSC Conservation Breeding Specialist Group 2004). Aerial surveys (Ancrenaz et al. 2005) and DNA analysis of living orangutans (Goossens et al. 2006) confirm recent and dramatic declines that, if not halted, will lead to extinction of the animal in the next few decades.

Galdikas has studied orangutans longer than anyone else. She links her knowledge of and love for the orangutans with applied anthropology and advocacy on their behalf. Since the

---

The anthropologist goes on to describe the Nacirema's intense focus on the human body. He provides a detailed account of a daily ritual performed within the home in a specially constructed shrine area:

> The focal point of the shrine is a box or chest which is built into the wall. In this chest are kept the many charms and magical potions without which no native believes he could live. These preparations are secured from a variety of specialized practitioners. The most powerful of these are the medicine men, whose assistance must be rewarded with substantial gifts. . . . Beneath the charm box is a small font. Each day every member of the family, in succession, enters

the shrine room, bows his head before the charm-box, mingles different sorts of holy water in the font, and proceeds with a brief rite of ablution. (1965:415–416)

If you do not recognize this tribe, try spelling its name backwards. (*Note:* Please forgive Miner for his use of the masculine pronoun in describing Nacirema society in general; his writings are several decades old.)

A BRIEF HISTORY OF CULTURAL ANTHROPOLOGY

The beginning of cultural anthropology goes back to writers such as Herodotus (fifth century BCE; note: BCE stands for "Before the Common Era," a secular transformation of BC, or "Before Christ"), Marco Polo (thirteenth to fourteenth centuries), and Ibn Khaldun (fourteenth century), who traveled extensively and wrote reports about cultures they

---

rainforest an environment found at mid-latitudes, of tall, broad-leaf evergreen trees, with annual rainfall of 400 centimeters (or 60 inches) and no dry season.

(LEFT) Lowland rainforest in Borneo in the morning mist. (RIGHT) Biruté Galdikas has been studying orangutans in Borneo, Indonesia, for over three decades and is an active supporter of conservation of their habitat.
▶ *Learn about her work and the status of wild orangutans by searching on the Web.*

beginning of her fieldwork in Borneo, she has maintained and expanded the Camp Leakey field site and research center (named after her mentor, Lewis Leakey, who inspired her research on orangutans). In 1986, she cofounded the Orangutan Foundation International (OFI), which now has several chapters worldwide. She has published scholarly articles and given public talks around the world on her research. Educating the public about the imminent danger to the orangutans is an important part of her activism. Galdikas and other orangutan experts are lobbying international institutions such as the World Bank to promote forest conservation as part of their loan agreements.

Camp Leakey employs many local people in diverse roles, including antipoaching guards. The OFI sponsors study tours to Borneo for international students and opportunities for them to contribute to conservation efforts.

The success of Galdikas's activism depends on her deep knowledge of orangutans. Over the decades, she has filled thousands of notebooks with her observations of orangutan behavior, along with such details about their habitat as the fruiting times of different species of trees. A donor recently gave software and funding for staff to analyze the raw data (Hawn 2002). The findings will indicate how much territory is needed to support a viable orangutan population and will ultimately facilitate conservation policy and planning.

◆ **FOOD FOR THOUGHT**

• Some people claim that science should not be linked with advocacy because it will create biases in research. Others say that scientists have an obligation to use their knowledge for good causes. Where do you stand in this debate and why?

encountered. More recent conceptual roots are found in writers of the French Enlightenment, such as the philosopher Charles Montesquieu, who wrote in the first half of the eighteenth century. His book *The Spirit of the Laws*, published in 1748 [1949], discussed the temperament, appearance, and government of various people around the world. He explained cultural differences as due to the different climates in which people lived.

In the second half of the nineteenth century, the discovery of the principles of biological evolution by Charles Darwin and others offered for the first time a scientific explanation for human origins. Biological evolution says that early forms evolve into later forms through the process of natural selection, whereby the most biologically fit organisms survive to reproduce while those that are less fit die out. Darwin's model is thus one of continuous progress toward increasing fitness through struggle among competing organisms. The concept of evolution was important in the thinking of early cultural anthropologists.

The most important founding figures of cultural anthropology in the late eighteenth and early nineteenth centuries were Sir Edward Tylor and Sir James Frazer in England and Lewis Henry Morgan in the United States (see Figure 1.2). Inspired by the concept of biological evolution, they developed a model of cultural evolution whereby all cultures evolve from lower to higher forms over time. This view placed non-Western peoples at a "primitive" stage and Euro-American culture as "civilization" and assumed that non-Western cultures would either catch up to the level of Western civilization or die out.

Polish-born Bronislaw Malinowski is a major figure in modern cultural anthropology (see photo p. 32). In the first half of the twentieth century, he established a theoretical

FIGURE 1.2 Key Contributors to Cultural Anthropology

Late Nineteenth Century

Sir Edward Tylor	Armchair anthropology, first definition of culture
Sir James Frazer	Armchair anthropology, comparative study of religion
Lewis Henry Morgan	Insider's view, cultural evolution, comparative method

Early Twentieth Century

Bronislaw Malinowski	Functionalism, holism, participant observation
Franz Boas	Cultural relativism, historical particularism, advocacy
Margaret Mead	Personality and culture, cultural constructionism, public anthropology
Ruth Benedict	Personality and culture, national character studies
Zora Neale Hurston	Black culture, women's roles, ethnographic novels

Mid- and Late Twentieth Century and Early Twenty-First Century

Claude Lévi-Strauss	Symbolic analysis, French structuralism
Beatrice Medicine	Native American anthropology
Eleanor Leacock	Anthropology of colonialism and indigenous peoples
Marvin Harris	Cultural materialism, comparison, theory building
Mary Douglas	Symbolic anthropology
Michelle Rosaldo	Feminist anthropology
Clifford Geertz	Interpretive anthropology, thick description of local culture
Laura Nader	Legal anthropology, "studying up"
George Marcus	Critique of culture, critique of cultural anthropology
Gilbert Herdt	Gay anthropology
Nancy Scheper-Hughes	Critical medical anthropology
Leith Mullings	Anti-racist anthropology
Sally Engle Merry	Globalization and human rights

functionalism   the theory that a culture is similar to a biological organism, in which parts work to support the operation and maintenance of the whole.

holism   the perspective in anthropology that cultures are complex systems that cannot be fully understood without paying attention to their different components, including economics, social organization, and ideology.

cultural relativism   the perspective that each culture must be understood in terms of the values and ideas of that culture and should not be judged by the standards of another culture.

cultural materialism   a theory that takes material features of life, such as the environment, natural resources, and mode of livelihood, as the bases for explaining social organization and ideology.

interpretive anthropology   the view that cultures can be understood by studying what people think about, their ideas, and the meanings that are important to them.

structurism   a theoretical position concerning human behavior and ideas that says large forces such as the economy, social and political organization, and the media shape what people do and think.

agency   the ability of humans to make choices and exercise free will even within dominating structures.

approach called **functionalism**: the view that a culture is similar to a biological organism, in which the parts work to support the operation and maintenance of the whole. Religion and family organization, for example, contribute to the functioning of the whole culture. Functionalism is linked to the concept of **holism**, the view that one must study all aspects of a culture in order to understand it.

Franz Boas is considered the founder of North American cultural anthropology. Born in Germany and educated in physics and geography, he came to the United States in 1887 (Patterson 2001:46ff). He brought with him a skepticism toward Western science gained from a year's study with the Inuit, the indigenous people of Baffin Island (see Map 2.4). He learned from the Inuit that people in different cultures may have different perceptions of even basic physical substances, such as "water." Boas came to recognize the individuality and validity of different cultures. He introduced the now widely known concept of **cultural relativism,** or the view that each culture must be understood in terms of the values and ideas of that culture and not be judged by the standards of another. According to Boas, no culture is more advanced than any other. His position thus contrasted markedly with that of the nineteenth-century cultural evolutionists.

Margaret Mead is Boas's most famous student. She contributed to knowledge of South Pacific cultures, gender roles, and the impact of child-rearing practices on personality. Her scholarly works, as well as her columns in popular magazines, had wide influence on U.S. child-care patterns in the 1950s. Mead was thus an early *public anthropologist* who took seriously the importance of bringing cultural anthropology knowledge to the general public in order to create positive social change.

Following World War II, cultural anthropology in the United States expanded substantially in terms of the number of trained anthropologists and departments of anthropology in colleges and universities. Along with this growth came increased theoretical diversity. Several anthropologists developed theories of culture based on environmental factors. They suggested that similar environments (for example, deserts or tropical rainforests or mountains) would predictably lead to the emergence of similar cultures.

At the same time, French anthropologist Claude Lévi-Strauss was developing a quite different theoretical perspective, known as *French structuralism*. He maintained that the best way to understand a culture is to collect its myths and stories and analyze the underlying themes in them. French structuralism inspired the development of *symbolic anthropology*, or the study of culture as a system of meanings, which was especially prominent in the United States in the latter part of the twentieth century.

In the 1960s, Marxist theory emerged in anthropology, stating the importance of people's access to the means of production. It inspired the emergence of a new theoretical school in the United States called **cultural materialism**. Cultural materialism is an approach to studying culture by emphasizing the material aspects of life, especially the natural environment and how people make a living. Also arising in the 1960s was the theoretical position referred to as **interpretive anthropology**, or *interpretivism*. This perspective developed from both U.S. symbolic anthropology and French structural anthropology. It says that understanding culture should focus on what people think about, their ideas, and the symbols and meanings that are important to them. These two positions are discussed in more detail later in this section.

Since the 1990s, two other theoretical directions have gained prominence. Both are influenced by *postmodernism*, an intellectual pursuit that asks whether modernity is truly progress and questions such aspects of modernism as the scientific method, urbanization, technological change, and mass communication. The first theory is termed **structurism** (I coined this term), the view that powerful structures such as economics, politics, and media shape cultures, influencing how people behave and think, even when they don't realize it. The second theory emphasizes human **agency**, or free will, and the power of individuals to create and change culture by acting against structures. These two positions are revisited at the end of this section.

Cultural anthropology continues to be rethought and refashioned. Over the past few decades, several new theoretical perspectives have transformed and enriched the field. *Feminist anthropology* is a perspective that emphasizes the need to study female roles and gender-based inequality. In the 1970s, early feminist anthropologists realized that anthropology had overlooked women. To address this gap, feminist anthropologists undertook research that explicitly focused on women and girls, that is, half of the world's people. A related area is *gay and lesbian anthropology*, or *queer anthropology*, a perspective that emphasizes the need to study gay people's cultures and discrimination based on sexual identity and preferences. This book presents findings from both these areas.

In North American anthropology, African American, Latino, and Native American anthropologists are increasing in number and visibility. Yet anthropology in North America and Europe remains one of the "whitest" professions (Shanklin 2000). Some steps for moving the discipline toward *antiracist anthropology* include the following (Mullings 2005):

- Examine and recognize anthropology's history of, and implications for, racism.
- Work to increase the diversity of professors, researchers, staff, and students in the discipline.
- Teach about racism in anthropology classes and textbooks.

Worldwide, non-Western anthropologists are increasingly questioning the dominance of Euro-American anthropology and offering new perspectives (Kuwayama 2004). Their work provides useful critiques of anthropology as a largely Western-defined discipline and promises to lead it in new directions in the future.

THE CONCEPT OF CULTURE

Although cultural anthropologists are united in the study of *culture*, the question of how to define it has been debated for decades. This section discusses definitions of culture today, characteristics of culture, and bases for cultural identity.

DEFINITIONS OF CULTURE   Culture is the core concept in cultural anthropology, so it might seem likely that cultural anthropologists would agree about what it is. In the 1950s, an effort to collect definitions of culture produced 164 different

THINKING OUTSIDE THE BOX

This brief history of cultural anthropology describes early contributions by anthropologists, most of whom were white, European or Euro-American, and male. Compare this pattern with the history of some other discipline you have studied. What are some of the similarities and differences?

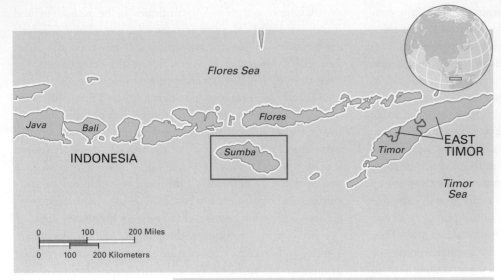

MAP 1.2 Weyéwa Region in Indonesia.
Sumba, one of Indonesia's many islands, is 75 miles long. The Weyéwa people number about 85,000 and live in small settlements on grassy plateaus on the western part of the island. They grow rice, maize, and millet, and they raise water buffaloes and pigs.

ones (Kroeber and Kluckhohn 1952). Since then, no one has tried to count the number of definitions of culture used by anthropologists.

British anthropologist Sir Edward Tylor proposed the first definition in 1871. He stated, "Culture, or civilization . . . is that complex whole which includes knowledge, belief, art, law, morals, custom, and any other capabilities and habits acquired by man as a member of society" (Kroeber and Kluckhohn 1952:81). The phrase "that complex whole" has been the most durable feature of his definition.

In contemporary cultural anthropology, the cultural materialists and the interpretive anthropologists support two different definitions of culture. Cultural materialist Marvin Harris says, "A culture is the total socially acquired life-way or life-style of a group of people. It consists of the patterned repetitive ways of thinking, feeling, and acting that are characteristic of the members of a particular society or segment of society" (1975:144). In contrast, Clifford Geertz, speaking for the interpretivists, believes that culture consists of symbols, motivations, moods, and thoughts. This definition focuses on people's perceptions, thoughts, and ideas and does not include behavior as a part of culture. The

microculture a distinct pattern of learned and shared behavior and thinking found within larger cultures.

definition of culture used in this book is that culture is learned and shared behavior and beliefs, and thus is broader than Geertz's definition.

Culture exists among all human beings. It is something that all humans have. Some anthropologists refer to this universal concept of culture as *Culture* with a capital *C*. Culture also exists in a more specific way. The term **microculture**, or local culture, refers to distinct patterns of learned and shared behavior and ideas found in local regions and among particular groups. Microcultures are based on ethnicity, gender, age, and more.

CHARACTERISTICS OF CULTURE Understanding of the complex concept of culture can be gained by looking at its characteristics.

CULTURE IS NOT THE SAME AS NATURE The relationship between nature and culture is of great interest to cultural anthropologists in their quest to understand people's behavior and thinking. This book emphasizes the importance of culture.

A good way to see how culture diverges from, and shapes, nature is to consider basic natural demands of life within different cultural contexts. Universal human functions that everyone must perform to stay alive are eating, drinking, sleeping, and eliminating. Given the primary importance of these four functions in supporting a human being's life, it seems logical that people would fulfill them in similar ways everywhere. But that is not the case.

EATING Culture shapes what people eat, how they eat, when they eat, and the meanings of food and eating. Culture also defines foods that are acceptable and unacceptable. In China, most people think that cheese is disgusting, but in France, most people love cheese. Throughout China, pork is a widely favored meat. The religions of Judaism and Islam, in contrast, forbid the consumption of pork. In many cultures where gathering wild plant foods, hunting, and fishing are important, people value the freshness of food. They would consider a package of frozen food on a grocery store shelf as way past its time.

Perceptions of taste vary dramatically. Western researchers have defined four supposedly universal taste categories: sweet, sour, bitter, and salty. Cross-cultural research disproves these categories as universals. For example, the Weyéwa (wuh-YAY-wuh) people of the highlands of Sumba, Indonesia (see Map 1.2), define seven categories of flavor: sour, sweet, salty, bitter, tart, bland, and pungent (Kuipers 1991).

How to eat is also an important aspect of food behavior. Rules about proper ways to eat are one of the first things a person needs to learn when living in another culture. Dining rules in India require using only the right hand. The left hand is considered polluted because it is used for personal cleansing after elimination. A person's clean right hand is the preferred eating utensil. Silverware that has been touched by others, even though it has been washed, is considered unclean. In some cultures, it is important to eat only from one's own plate, whereas in others, eating from a shared central platter is considered proper.

Another area of cultural variation involves who is responsible for cooking and serving food. In many cultures, domestic cooking is women's responsibility, but cooking for public feasts is more often something that men do. Power issues may arise about who cooks what for whom (see Everyday Anthropology).

DRINKING Cross-cultural variations related to drinking are also complex. Every culture defines the appropriate substances to drink, when to drink and with whom, and the meanings of the beverages and drinking occasions. French culture allows for the consumption of relatively large amounts of table wine with family meals, including lunch. In the United States, water is generally served and consumed during family meals. In India, water is served and consumed at the end of the meal. Around the world, different categories of people drink different beverages. In cultures where alcoholic beverages are consumed, men tend to consume more than women.

Culture often defines the meaning of particular drinks and the style of drinking and serving them. Social drinking—whether the beverage is coffee, beer, or vodka—creates and reinforces bonds. Beer-drinking rituals in U.S. college fraternities are a good example. In an ethnographic film entitled *Salamanders*, filmed at a large university in the northeastern United States, the fraternity brothers run to various "stations" in the fraternity house, downing a beer at each (Hornbein and Hornbein 1992). At one point, a brother chugs a beer, turns with a stagger toward the next station, falls flat on his face, and passes out. The movie documents another drinking ritual in which both young men and women at fraternity parties swallow live salamanders, sometimes two or three at a time, with large gulps of beer. (This practice is now forbidden by law.)

SLEEPING Common sense might say that sleep is the one natural function that is not shaped by culture because people tend to do it at least once every 24 hours, everyone shuts their eyes to do it, everyone lies down to do it, and most people sleep at night. Going without sleep for an extended period can lead to insanity and even death.

Sleep, however, is at least as much culturally shaped as it is biologically determined. Cultural influences on sleep include the questions of who sleeps with whom, how much

Ethiopian women dining at an Ethiopian restaurant. The main meal consists of several meat and vegetable dishes, cooked with special spices and laid out on injera bread, a soft, flat bread that is torn into small pieces and used to wrap bite-sized bits of meat and vegetables. The entire meal can be eaten without utensils.

▶ *How does this dining scene resemble or differ from a recent meal that you have had in a restaurant?*

THINKING
OUTSIDE
THE BOX

Think about your everyday drinking patterns (no matter what the liquid), and then think about your drinking patterns on special occasions, including weekends, holidays, or special events such as weddings. What beverages do you consume, and with whom, and what are the meanings and wider social implications involved?

everyday ANTHROPOLOGY

Latina Power in the Kitchen

Within a family, cooking food for other members can be a sign of love and devotion. It may carry a message that love and devotion are expected in return. Among Tejano (tay-HAH-no) migrant farm workers in the United States, preparing tamales is a symbol of a woman's commitment to her family and thus of the "good wife" (Williams 1984). The Tejanos are people of Mexican descent who live in Texas. Some of them move to Illinois in the summer, where they are employed as migrant workers.

For Tejanos, tamales are a central cultural identity marker. Tamales contain a rich inner mash of pig's head meat wrapped in corn husks. Making tamales is extremely time consuming, and it is women's work. Typically, several women work together over a few days to do the necessary tasks: buying the pigs' heads, stripping the meat, preparing the stuffing, wrapping the stuffing with the corn husks, and baking or boiling the tamale.

Tamales symbolize and emphasize women's nurturance of their husbands. One elderly woman, at home in Texas for Christmas, made 200 tamales with her daughters-in-law, nieces, and god-daughter. They distributed the tamales to friends, relatives, and local taverns. The effort and expense involved were enormous. But for the women, it was worth it. Through their tamale making, they celebrate the holiday, build ties with people whom they may need to call on for support, and maintain communication with tavern owners so that they will watch over male kin who drink at their bars.

Tejano women also use tamale making as a statement of domestic protest. A woman who is dissatisfied with her husband's behavior will refuse

Tamales consist of fried meat and peppers in a cornmeal dough that is encased in cornhusks.

▶ *What is a similarly important food item in your cultural world?*

to make tamales, a serious statement on her part. The link between being a good wife and making tamales is strong, so a husband can take his wife's unwillingness to make tamales as grounds for divorce. One young Tejano sued his wife for divorce in Illinois on the grounds that she refused to cook tamales for him, in addition to

dancing with other men at fiestas. The judge refused to grant a divorce.

◆ FOOD FOR THOUGHT

- Provide an example from your microcultural experience about food being used as a way of expressing social solidarity or social protest.

sleep a person should have, and why some people have insomnia or what are called sleep disorders. Across cultures, marked variation exists in rules about where infants and children should sleep: with the mother, with both parents, or by themselves in a separate room? Among indigenous peoples of the Amazon region of South America, mothers and babies share the same hammock for many months and breastfeeding occurs whenever the baby is hungry.

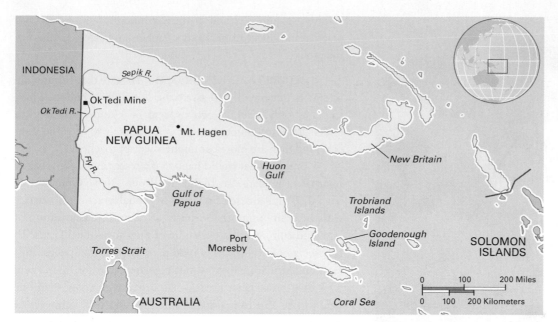

MAP 1.3 Papua New Guinea.
The Independent State of Papua New Guinea (PNG) gained its autonomy from Australia in 1975. Mostly mountainous with coastal lowlands, PNG is richly endowed with gold, copper, silver, natural gas, timber, oil, and fisheries. Its population is around 5,700,000. Port Moresby, the capital, has a high rate of HIV/AIDS infection among the working-age population.

Culture shapes the amount of time a person sleeps. In rural India, women sleep fewer hours than men because they have to get up early to start the fire for the morning meal. In fast-track, corporate North America, "type A" males sleep relatively few hours and are proud of that fact—to sleep too much is to be a wimp. A disorder in Japan called *excessive daytime sleepiness* (*EDS*) is common in Tokyo and other large cities (Doi and Minowa 2003). Excessive sleepiness is correlated with more accidents on the job, more absenteeism, decreased productivity, deteriorated personal and professional relationships, and increased rates of illness and death. Women are almost twice as likely as men to experience EDS, and married women are especially vulnerable.

ELIMINATING Given its basic importance in cross-cultural experience, it is ironic that elimination receives little attention (in print) from anthropologists. Anyone who has traveled internationally knows that there is much to learn about elimination in an unfamiliar context.

The first question is where to eliminate. Differences emerge in the degree to which elimination is a private act or can be done in more or less public areas. In many European cities, public options include street urinals for males but not for females. In most villages in India, houses do not have interior bathrooms. Instead, early in the morning, groups of women and girls leave the house and head for a certain field, where they squat and chat. Men go to a different area. Everyone carries, in his left hand, a small brass pot full of water with which he splashes himself clean. Think about the ecological advantages: This system adds fertilizer to the fields and leaves no paper litter. Westerners may consider the village practice unclean and unpleasant, but village-dwelling people in India would think that the Western system is unsanitary because using toilet paper does not clean one as well as water does, and

they would find the practice of sitting on a toilet less comfortable than squatting.

In many cultures, the products of elimination (urine and feces) are considered polluting and disgusting. Among some groups in Papua New Guinea (see Map 1.3), people take great care to bury or otherwise hide their fecal matter for fear that someone will find it and use it for magic against them. A negative assessment of the products of elimination is not universal, however. Among some Native American cultures of the Pacific Northwest region of Canada and the United States, urine, especially women's urine, was believed to have medicinal and cleansing properties and was considered the "water of life" (Furst 1989). In some death rituals, it was sprinkled over the corpse in the hope that it might rejuvenate the deceased. People stored urine in special wooden boxes for ritual use, including for a baby's first bath. (The urine was mixed with water.)

CULTURE IS BASED ON SYMBOLS Our entire lives—from eating breakfast to greeting our friends, making money, creating art, and practicing religion—are based on and organized through symbols. A **symbol** is an object, word, or action with a culturally defined meaning that stands for something else with which it has no necessary or natural relationship. Symbols are arbitrary (bearing no necessary relationship to that which is symbolized), unpredictable, and diverse. Because symbols are arbitrary, it is impossible to predict how a particular culture will symbolize something. Although one might assume that people who are hungry would have an expression for hunger involving the stomach no one could predict that in Hindi, the language of northern India, a

---

symbol an object, word, or action with culturally defined meaning that stands for something else; most symbols are arbitrary.

In India, a white sari (women's garment) symbolizes widowhood.

▶ *What might these women think about the Western custom of a bride wearing white?*

colloquial expression for being hungry is saying that "rats are jumping in my stomach." The linguistic history of Barbara—the name of the author of this book—reveals that originally, in the Greek, it referred to people who were outsiders, "barbarians," and, by extension, uncivilized and savage. On top of that, the Greek term referred to such people as "bearded." The symbolic content of the American name Barbara does not immediately convey a sense of beardedness in its current context because symbolic meaning can change. It is through symbols, arbitrary and amazingly rich in their attributions, that culture is shared, stored, and transmitted over time.

CULTURE IS LEARNED   Because culture is based on symbols that are arbitrary, culture must be learned anew in each context. Cultural learning begins from the moment of birth, if not before. (Some people think that an unborn baby takes in and stores information through sounds heard from the outside world.) A large but unknown amount of people's cultural learning is unconscious, occurring as a normal part of life through observation. Learning in schools, in contrast, is a formal way to acquire culture. Most cultures throughout history have not passed on learning through formal schooling. Instead,

---

globalization   increased and intensified international ties related to the spread of Western, especially U.S., capitalism that affects all world cultures.

localization   the transformation of global culture by local cultures into something new.

class   a way of categorizing people on the basis of their economic positions in society, usually measured in terms of income or wealth.

children acquire cultural patterns through observation and practice and advice from family members and elder members of the group.

CULTURES ARE INTEGRATED   To state that cultures are internally integrated is to assert the principle of holism. Thus, studying only one or two aspects of culture provides an understanding so limited that it is more likely to be misleading or wrong than are more comprehensive approaches.

Consider what would happen if a researcher were to study intertribal warfare in highland Papua New Guinea (see Map 1.3) and focused only on the actual practice of warfare without examining other aspects of culture. A key feature of highland culture is the exchange of pigs at political feasts. To become a political leader, a man must acquire many pigs. Pigs eat yams, which men grow, but pigs are cared for by women. This division of labor means that a man with more than one wife will be able to maintain more pigs and rise politically by giving more feasts. Such feasting enhances an aspiring leader's status and makes his guests indebted to him. With more followers attracted through feasting, a leader can gather forces and wage war on neighboring villages. Success in war brings gains in territory. So far, this example pays attention mainly to economics, politics, and marriage systems. But other aspects of culture are involved, too. Supernatural powers affect the success of warfare. Painting spears and shields with particular designs is believed to increase their power. At feasts and marriages, body decoration (including paint, shell ornaments, and elaborate feather headdresses) is an important expression of identity and status. Looking at warfare without attention to its wider cultural context yields an extremely narrow view.

Cultural integration is relevant to applied anthropologists interested in proposing ways to promote positive change. Years of experience show that introducing programs for change in one aspect of culture without considering their effects in other domains is often detrimental to the welfare and survival of a culture. For example, Western missionaries and colonialists in parts of Southeast Asia banned the practice of head-hunting. This practice was connected to many other aspects of the people's culture, including politics, religion, and psychology. A man's sense of identity depended on the taking of a head. While preventing head-hunting might seem like a good thing, its cessation had disastrous consequences for the cultures in which it was practiced because of its central importance.

CULTURES INTERACT AND CHANGE   Cultures interact with each other and change each other through contact such as trade networks, international development projects, telecommunications, education, migration, and tourism. **Globalization**, the process of intense global interconnectedness and movement of goods, information, and people, is a major force of contemporary cultural change. It has gained momentum through recent technological change, especially the boom in information and communication technologies.

Clash of civilizations	Conflict model
McDonaldization	Takeover and homogenization model
Hybridization	Blending model
Localization	Local cultural remaking and transformation of global culture

FIGURE 1.3 Four Models of Cultural Interaction

Globalization does not spread evenly, and its interactions with, and effects on, local cultures vary substantially from positive change to cultural destruction and extinction. Four models of cultural interaction capture some of the variation (see Figure 1.3).

The *clash of civilizations* argument says that the spread of Euro-American capitalism and lifeways throughout the world has created disenchantment, alienation, and resentment among other cultural systems. This model divides the world into the "West and the rest."

The *McDonaldization* model says that, under the powerful influence of U.S.-dominated corporate culture, the world is becoming culturally homogeneous. "Fast-food culture," with its principles of mass production, speed, standardization, and impersonal service, is taken to be at the center of this new global culture.

Hybridization, also called *syncretism* and *creolization,* occurs when aspects of two or more cultures combine to form something new—a blend. In Japan, for instance, a grandmother might bow in gratitude to an automated banking machine. In the Amazon region and in the Arctic, indigenous people use satellite imagery to map and protect the boundaries of their ancestral lands.

A fourth pattern is **localization**, the transformation of global culture by local microcultures into something new. Consider the example of McDonald's restaurants. In many Asian settings, people resist the pattern of eating quickly and insist on leisurely family gatherings (Watson 1997). The McDonald's managers accommodate this preference and alter the pace of service to allow for a slower turnover of tables. In Riyadh, Saudi Arabia, McDonald's provides separate areas for families and for heterosexual couples. Many other examples of cultural localization exist, throwing into question the notion that a form of Western "mono-culture" is taking over the entire world and erasing cultural diversity.

MULTIPLE CULTURAL WORLDS

Within large cultures, a variety of microcultures exist, as discussed in this section (see Figure 1.4). A particular individual in such a complex situation is likely to be a member of several microcultures. Microcultures may overlap or may be

A view into the yard of a house in a low-income neighborhood of Kingston, Jamaica. People in these neighborhoods prefer the term "low-income" to "poor."

related to each other hierarchically in terms of power, status, and rights.

In discussing microcultures, the contrast between *difference* and *hierarchy* is important. People and groups can be considered different from each other in terms of a particular characteristic, but they may or may not be unequal on the basis of it. For example, people with blue or brown eyes might be recognized as different, but this difference does not entail unequal treatment or status. In other instances, such differences do become the basis for inequality.

CLASS Class is a category based on people's economic position in society, usually measured in terms of income or wealth and exhibited in terms of lifestyle. Class societies may be divided into upper, middle, and lower classes. Separate classes are, for example, the working class (people who trade their labor for wages) and the landowning class (people who own land on which they or others labor). Classes are related in a hierarchical system, with upper classes dominating lower classes. Class struggle, in the classic Marxist view, is inevitable, as those at the top seek to maintain their position while those at the bottom seek to improve theirs. People at the bottom may attempt to improve their class position by gaining access to resources and

Class	Gender and sexuality
"Race"	Age
Ethnicity and indigeneity	Institution

FIGURE 1.4 Some Bases of Microcultures

by adopting aspects of upper-class symbolic behavior, such as speech, dress, and leisure and recreation activities.

Class is a recent social development in human history, extending back in time for only about 10,000 years. It does not exist today in remote local cultures where everyone has equal wealth and sharing food and other resources among the group is expected.

"RACE," ETHNICITY, AND INDIGENOUS PEOPLES

"Race" refers to groups of people with supposedly homogeneous biological traits. The term "race" is extremely complicated as it is used in diverse ways in different parts of the world and among different groups of people. Therefore, it makes sense to put the word in quotation marks in order to indicate that it has no single meaning. In South Africa, as in the United States, "race" is defined mainly on the basis of skin color. In pre–twentieth-century China, body hair was the key biological basis for racial classification (Dikötter 1998). The "barbarian" races had more body hair than the "civilized" Chinese people.

Chinese writers referred to bearded, male missionaries from Europe as "hairy barbarians." Into the twentieth century, some Chinese anthropologists divided humans into evolutionary stages on the basis of amounts of body hair.

Anthropological and other scientific research demonstrates that biological features alone do not explain or account for a person's behavior or lifestyle. Rather than being a biological category, racial classifications are cultural constructions. They are often associated with discrimination against, and cruelty toward, those "races" considered less worthy by those in power.

Ethnicity refers to a sense of identity among a group based on a sense of a common heritage, language, religion, or other aspect of culture. Examples include African Americans and Italian Americans in the United States, the Croats of Eastern Europe, the Han of China, and the Hutu and Tutsi of Rwanda. This sense of identity may be expressed through political movements to gain or protect group rights and recognition or more quietly stated in how one lives one's daily life. Compared with the term "race," "ethnicity" appears to be a more neutral, less stigmatizing term. But it, too, has been, and still is, a basis for discrimination, segregation, and oppression. The "ethnic cleansing" campaigns conducted in the early 1990s by the Serbs against Muslims in the former Yugoslavia are an extreme case of ethnic discrimination. In China, Han ethnic domination over minority ethnic groups has been a reality for centuries. Han political repression of the Tibetan people prompted thousands of Tibetans to flee their homeland. Living in exile, they struggle to keep their ethnic heritage alive.

Indigenous peoples, according to guidelines laid down by the United Nations, are defined as groups that have a long-standing connection with their home territories, a connection predating colonial or other societies that prevail in that territory (Sanders 1999). They are typically a numerical minority and often have lost the rights to their original territory. The United Nations distinguishes between indigenous peoples and *minority ethnic groups* such as the Roma, the Tamils of Sri Lanka, and African Americans. The San peoples of Southern Africa, as well as their several subgroups, are an important example of indigenous peoples whose way of life was dramatically affected first by colonialism and now by globalization (see Culturama).

GENDER Gender refers to culturally constructed and learned behaviors and ideas attributed to males, females, or sometimes a blended, or "third," gender. Gender differs from *sex*, which is based on biological markers, such as genitals and hormones, to define categories of male and female. Cultural anthropology shows that a person's biological makeup does not necessarily correspond to gender. Biology directly determines only a few roles and tasks, such as giving birth and nursing infants.

Cross-culturally, gender differences vary from societies in which male and female roles and worlds are similar or overlapping to those in which gender roles are sharply differentiated. In much of rural Thailand, men and women are about the same size, their clothing is similar, and their agricultural tasks are complementary and often interchangeable (Potter 1977). In contrast, among many groups in highland Papua New Guinea, extreme gender segregation exists in most aspects of life, including the kinds of food men and women eat (Meigs 1984). The men's house physically and symbolically separates the worlds of men and women. Men engage in rituals that purge them of female substances: nose or penis bleeding, vomiting, tongue scraping, sweating, and eye washing. Men possess sacred flutes, which they parade through the village from time to time. If women dare to look at the flutes, men have the right, by tradition, to kill them.

AGE The human life cycle, from birth to old age, takes people through cultural stages for which appropriate behavior and thinking must be learned anew. In many African herding societies, elaborate age categories for males define their roles and status as they move from being boys with few responsibilities and little status, to young men who are warriors and

---

"race" a classification of people into groups on the basis of supposedly homogeneous and largely superficial biological traits such as skin color or hair characteristics.

ethnicity a shared sense of identity among a group based on a heritage, language, or culture.

indigenous peoples groups of people who have a long-standing connection with their home territories that predates colonial or outside societies prevailing in that territories.

gender culturally constructed and learned behaviors and ideas attributed to males, females, or blended genders.

CULTURAMA

San Peoples of Southern Africa

San is a cluster name for many groups of people in southern Africa who speak related languages that have glottal click sounds. Around 2,000 years ago, the San were the only people living in southern Africa, but today they are restricted to scattered locations throughout the region. European colonialists referred to San people as "Bushmen," a derogatory term at the time but one that San people now prefer over what some locals call them. Some San also refer to themselves with the English term "First People."

For many centuries, the San supported themselves through collecting food such as roots and birds' eggs and by hunting eland, giraffe, and other animals. Now, pressure from African governments, farmers, ranchers, game reserves, diamond companies, and international tourism has greatly reduced the San's access to their ancestral land

and their ability to survive. Some have been arrested for hunting on what they consider their land.

The Ju/'hoansi ("True People") are a subgroup of San numbering between 10,000 and 15,000 people who live in a region crossing the borders of Namibia and Botswana. As described by Richard Lee in the early 1960s, they were highly mobile food collectors and quite healthy (1979). Today, most have been forced from their homeland and live as poor, urban squatters or in government-built resettlement camps. Many work as farm laborers or in the international tourist industry, serving as guides and producing and selling crafts. Others are unemployed. The specific living conditions of the San people depends on government policy toward indigenous people in the particular country where they live.

Transnational advocacy organizations, including the Working Group of Indigenous Minorities in Southern Africa (WIMSA) and First People of the Kalahari (FPK), are making progress in protecting the rights of San peoples. Recently, WIMSA waged an international legal case with a large pharmaceutical company and succeeded in ensuring that the San receive a portion of the profits from the commercial development of hoodia (*Hoodia gordonia*). Hoodia is extracted from a cactus indigenous to the Kalahari region. An effective appetite suppressant, it is now widely available in North America and on the Internet as diet pills.

Thanks to Alison Brooks, George Washington University, for reviewing this material.

  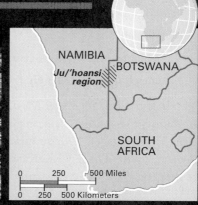

(LEFT) Richard Lee (wearing a shirt) asks Ju/'hoansi men about food plants of the Kalahari desert. This photograph was taken in 1968. Lee and many other researchers affiliated with the Harvard Kalahari research project learned to speak the Ju/'hoansi language.
(CENTER) San people eat part of the hoodia cactus when on long treks in the desert because it suppresses hunger and thirst. Now they cultivate it for commercial production in a diet pill sold in rich countries.

MAP 1.4 Ju/'hoansi Region in Namibia and Botswana. Before country boundaries were drawn, the Ju/'hoansi ranged freely across their traditional territory (shaded area), depending on the seasonal availability of food and water. Now they must show a passport when crossing from one country to another.

live apart from the rest of the group, to adult men who are allowed to marry, have children, and become respected elders. "The Hill," or the collective members of the United States Senate and the House of Representatives, is a highly age-graded microculture (Weatherford 1981). The Hill is a *gerontocracy* (a group ruled by senior members) in which the older politicians dominate younger politicians in terms of amount of time they speak and how much attention their words receive. It may take a junior member between 10 and 20 years to become as effective and powerful as a senior member.

INSTITUTIONS *Institutions*, or enduring group settings formed for a particular purpose, have their own characteristic microcultures. Institutions include hospitals, schools and universities, and prisons. Anyone who has entered such an institution has experienced a feeling of strangeness. Until you gain familiarity with the often unwritten cultural rules, you may do things that offend or puzzle people, that fail to get you what you want, and that make you feel marginalized and insecure.

Anthropologists who study educational institutions have shown that schools often replicate and reinforce stereotypes, power relations, and inequalities of the wider society. A study of middle schools in the southwestern Rocky Mountain region of the United States found a situation in which teachers marginalized Mexican immigrant girls (Meador 2005). In this school, Mexican immigrant students are labeled as ESL (English as a second language) students because they are not fluent in English and take special courses designed to improve their English. In addition, the teachers' mental model of a "good student" is a student who is

- motivated to do well in school and gets good grades.
- an athlete.
- popular and has good students as friends.
- comes from a stable family.

It is difficult for many Mexican immigrant children to conform to this image. Mexican girls, or Mexicanas, are especially disadvantaged because most are not interested in, or good at, sports. The few Mexicanas who are motivated to try to get good grades are consistently overlooked by the teachers,

who instead call on students who are confident, bright, and popular, and who sit in front of the classroom and raise their hands eagerly.

DISTINCTIVE FEATURES OF CULTURAL ANTHROPOLOGY

Cultural anthropology has two distinct research goals and two distinct guiding concepts. Researchers and teachers in other disciplines have begun to adopt these goals and concepts in recent decades, so they are now found beyond cultural anthropology. Such cross-disciplinary contributions are something of which cultural anthropology can be proud.

CULTURAL RELATIVISM Most people grow up thinking that their culture is *the* way of life and that other ways of life are strange and inferior. Cultural anthropologists label this attitude **ethnocentrism**: judging other cultures by the standards of one's own culture rather than by the standards of other cultures. Ethnocentrism has fueled centuries of efforts to change "other" people in the world, sometimes through religious missionary work, sometimes in the form of colonial domination.

The opposite of ethnocentrism is cultural relativism, the idea that each culture must be understood in terms of its own values and beliefs and not by the standards of another culture. Cultural relativism assumes that no culture is better than any other.

One way that some anthropologists have interpreted cultural relativism is *absolute cultural relativism*, which says that whatever goes on in a particular culture must not be questioned or changed because it would be ethnocentric to question any behavior or idea anywhere (see Figure 1.5). The position of absolute cultural relativism, however, can lead in dangerous directions. Consider the example of the Holocaust during World War II, in which millions of Jews, Roma, and other minorities in much of Eastern and Western Europe were killed as part of the German Nazis' Aryan supremacy campaign. The absolute cultural relativist position becomes boxed in, logically, to saying that because the Holocaust was undertaken according to the values of the culture, outsiders have no business questioning it. Can anyone feel comfortable with such a position?

Absolute Cultural Relativism	Whatever goes on within a particular culture cannot be questioned or changed by outsiders, as that would be ethnocentric.
Critical Cultural Relativism	Anyone can pose questions about what goes on in various cultures, including their own culture, in terms of how particular practices or beliefs may harm certain members; follows Lévi-Strauss' comment that no society is perfect and that, therefore, all societies may be able to learn from others and improve.

FIGURE 1.5 Cultural Relativism: Two Views

Native American dancers perform at the annual Gateway Pow Wow in Brooklyn, New York.

▶ *Think of possible examples in your microculture of attempts to revitalize aspects of the culture.*

Critical cultural relativism offers an alternative view that poses questions about cultural practices and ideas in terms of who accepts them and why, and who they might be harming or helping. In terms of the Nazi Holocaust, a critical cultural relativist would ask, "Whose culture supported the values that killed millions of people on the grounds of racial purity?" Not the cultures of the Jews, Roma, and other victims. It was the culture of Aryan supremacists, who were just one group among many. In other words, the situation was far more complex than a simple absolute cultural relativist statement suggests. Rather, it was a case of *cultural imperialism,* in which one dominant group claimed supremacy over minority cultures and took actions in its own interests and at the expense of the subjugated cultures. Critical cultural relativism avoids the trap of adopting a homogenized view. It recognizes internal cultural differences: winners and losers, and oppressors and victims. It pays attention to the interests of various power groups. It can illuminate the causes and consequences of recent and contemporary conflicts, such as those in Rwanda, Iraq, and Afghanistan.

Many cultural anthropologists seek to *critique* (which means "to probe underlying power interests," not just "to offer negative comments," as in the general usage of the term "criticism") the behavior and values of groups from the standpoint of a set of generally agreed-on human rights and values. Two issues emerge in this endeavor. First, it is difficult, if not impossible, to generate a universal list of what all cultures would agree to as good and right. Second, as Claude Lévi-Strauss said, "No society is perfect" (1968:385).

VALUING AND SUSTAINING DIVERSITY Anthropologists value and are committed to maintaining cultural diversity throughout the world, as part of humanity's rich heritage. Many cultural anthropologists share their expertise and knowledge to support the survival of indigenous peoples and other small-scale groups worldwide.

In the United States, an organization called Cultural Survival helps indigenous peoples and ethnic minorities deal as equals in their interactions with outsiders. Cultural Survival's guiding principle is outlined in the preface of this book. Cultural Survival sponsors programs to help indigenous peoples and ethnic minorities protect and manage their natural environment, claim land rights, and protect their cultural heritage.

THREE THEORETICAL DEBATES IN CULTURAL ANTHROPOLOGY

Transitioning to theory, this section describes three debates in cultural anthropology that go to the heart of its basic questions about how people behave and think cross-culturally and why people behave and think the way they do. Introduced briefly here, they reappear throughout the book.

BIOLOGICAL DETERMINISM VERSUS CULTURAL CONSTRUCTIONISM Biological determinism seeks to explain why people do and think what they do by considering biological factors such as people's genes and hormones. Thus, biological determinists search for the gene or hormone that contributes to behavior such as homicide, alcoholism, or adolescent stress. They also examine cultural practices in terms

---

ethnocentrism judging another culture by the standards of one's own culture rather than by the standards of that particular culture.

biological determinism a theory that explains human behavior and ideas as shaped mainly by biological features such as genes and hormones.

of how they contribute to the "reproductive success of the species," or how they contribute to the gene pool of subsequent generations by boosting the number of surviving offspring produced in a particular population. In this view, behaviors and ideas that have reproductive advantages are more likely than others to be passed on to future generations. Biological determinists, for example, have provided an explanation for why human males apparently have "better" spatial skills than females. They say that these differences are the result of evolutionary selection because males with "better" spatial skills would have an advantage in securing both food and mates. Males with "better" spatial skills impregnate more females and have more offspring with "better" spatial skills.

Cultural constructionism, in contrast, maintains that human behavior and ideas are best explained as products of culturally shaped learning. In terms of the example of "better" male spatial skills, cultural constructionists would provide evidence that such skills are passed on culturally through learning, not genes. They would say that parents and teachers socialize boys and girls differently in spatial skills and are more likely to promote learning of certain kinds of spatial skills among boys. Though recognizing the role of biological factors such as genes and hormones, anthropologists who favor cultural construction and learning as an explanation for behaviors such as homicide and alcoholism point to childhood experiences and family roles as being perhaps even more important than genes or hormones. Most cultural anthropologists are cultural constructionists, but some connect biology and culture in their work.

INTERPRETIVE ANTHROPOLOGY VERSUS CULTURAL MATERIALISM
Interpretive anthropology, or interpretivism, focuses on understanding culture by studying what people think about, their explanations of their lives, and the symbols that are important to them. For example, in understanding the eating habits of Hindus, interpretivists ask why Hindus do not eat beef. Hindus point to their religious beliefs, according to which cows are sacred and it is a sin to kill and eat them. Interpretivists accept this explanation as sufficient.

Cultural materialism attempts to learn about culture by first examining the material aspects of life: the natural environment and how people make a living within particular environments. Cultural materialists believe that these basic facts of life shape culture, even though people may not realize it. They use a three-level model to explain culture. The bottom level is *infrastructure*, a term that refers to basic material factors such as natural resources, the economy, and population. According to this model, infrastructure tends to shape the other two domains of culture: *structure* (social organization, kinship, and political organization) and *superstructure* (ideas,

values, and beliefs). This book's chapters are organized roughly in terms of these three categories, but with the recognition that the layers are not neat and tidy but rather have interconnections.

A cultural materialist explanation for the taboo on killing cows and eating beef involves the fact that cattle in India play a more important role alive than dead or carved into steaks (Harris 1974). The many cattle wandering the streets of Indian cities and villages look useless to Westerners. A closer analysis, however, shows that the seemingly useless population of bovines serves many useful functions. Ambling along, they eat paper trash and other edible refuse. Their excrement is "brown gold," useful as fertilizer or, when mixed with straw and formed into dried patties, as cooking fuel. Most important, farmers use cattle to plow fields. Cultural materialists take into account Hindu beliefs about the sacred meaning of cattle, but they see its relationship to the material value of cattle, as symbolic protection keeping these extremely useful animals out of the meat factory.

Some cultural anthropologists are strong interpretivists, whereas some are strong cultural materialists. Many combine the best of both views.

INDIVIDUAL AGENCY VERSUS STRUCTURISM
This debate concerns the question of how much individual will, or agency, affects the way people behave and think, compared with the power of forces, or *structures*, that are beyond individual control. Western philosophical thought gives much emphasis to the role of agency, the ability of individuals to make choices and exercise free will. In contrast, structurism emphasizes that free choice is an illusion because choices are structured by larger forces such as the economy, social and political organization, and ideological systems.

A prime example is the study of poverty. Those who emphasize agency focus their research on how individuals attempt to act as agents, even in situations of extreme poverty, in order to change their situation as best they can. Structurists, by contrast, would emphasize that the poor are trapped by large and powerful forces. They would describe how the political economy and other forces provide little room for agency for those at the bottom. An increasing number of cultural anthropologists seek to blend a structural perspective with attention to agency.

◆◆◆

Cultural Anthropology and Careers

Some of you reading this book may take only one anthropology course to satisfy a requirement. Others may become interested in the subject matter and take a few more. Some will decide to major or minor in anthropology. Just one course

---

cultural constructionism a theory that explains human behavior and ideas as shaped mainly by learning.

in anthropology may change your way of thinking about the world and your place in it. More than that, anthropology coursework may enhance your ability to get a job.

MAJORING IN ANTHROPOLOGY

An anthropology B.A. is a liberal arts degree. It is not, however, a professional degree, such as a business degree or a degree in physical therapy. It provides a solid education relevant to many career directions that are likely to require further study, such as law, criminal justice, medicine and health services, social services, education, humanitarian assistance, international development programs, and business. Students interested in pursuing a B.A. major in anthropology should know that anthropology is at least as useful as other liberal arts majors for either graduate study or a professional career.

Anthropology has several clear advantages over other liberal arts majors, and employers and graduate schools are increasingly recognizing these features. Cultural anthropology provides knowledge about the world's people and diversity. It offers insights about a variety of specialized research methods. Cross-cultural awareness and communication skills are valuable assets sought by business, government, health-care providers, and nongovernmental organizations.

The recurrent question is this: Will it be possible to get a good job related to anthropology with a B.A. in anthropology? The answer is yes, but it takes planning and hard work. Do the following: Gain expertise in at least one foreign language, study abroad, do service learning during your undergraduate years, and conduct an independent research project and write up the results as a professional report or conference paper. Package these skills on your résumé so that they appear relevant to employers. Do not give up. Good jobs are out there, and coursework and skills in anthropology are increasingly valued.

Anthropology is also an excellent minor. It complements almost any other area of study by adding a cross-cultural perspective. For example, if you are majoring in music, courses about world music will enrich your primary interest. The same applies to subjects such as interior design, psychology, criminal justice, international affairs, economics, political science, and more.

GRADUATE STUDY IN ANTHROPOLOGY

Some of you may go on to pursue a master's degree (M.A.) or doctoral degree (Ph.D.) in anthropology. If you do, here is some advice: Be passionate about your interest, but also be aware that a full-time job as a professor or as a professional anthropologist is not easy to get.

To expand your possibilities of getting a good job, it is wise to consider combining a professional skill or degree with your degree program in anthropology, such as a law degree, an M.A. degree in project management, a master of public health (M.P.H.), a certificate in disaster relief, or participation in a training program in conflict prevention and resolution.

LIVING AN ANTHROPOLOGICAL LIFE

Studying cultural anthropology makes for smart people and people with breadth and flexibility. In North America, college graduates are likely to change careers (not just jobs, but careers) several times in their lives. Because you never know where you are going to end up working, or in what endeavor, it pays to be broadly informed about the world.

Cultural anthropology prompts you to ask original and important questions about the world's people and their relationships with one another, and it helps provide some useful answers.

Beyond career value, cultural anthropology will enrich your daily life by increasing your exposure to the world's cultures. When you pick up a newspaper, you will find several articles that connect with what you have learned in your anthropology classes. You will be able to view your own everyday life as culturally constructed in interesting and meaningful ways. You will be a different person, and you will live a richer life.

1

the BIG questions REVISITED

◆ What is anthropology?

Anthropology is an academic discipline, like history or economics. It comprises four interrelated fields in its attempt to explore all facets of humanity from its origins through the present. Biological or physical anthropology is the study of humans as biological organisms, including their evolution and contemporary variation. Archaeology is the study of past human cultures through their material remains. Linguistic anthropology is the study of human communication, including its origins, history, and contemporary variation and change. Cultural anthropology is the study of living peoples and their cultures, including variation and change. Culture is people's learned and shared behaviors and beliefs.

Each field makes both theoretical and applied contributions. The perspective of this book is that applied anthropology, just like theoretical anthropology, should be an integrated and important part of all four fields, rather than a separate, fifth field. Examples of applied anthropology in the four fields include forensic anthropology, nonhuman primate conservation, assisting in literacy programs for refugees, and advising businesses about people's preferences.

◆ What is cultural anthropology?

Cultural anthropology is the field within general anthropology that focuses on the study of contemporary humans and their cultures. It has several distinctive features that set it apart from the other fields of general anthropology and from other academic disciplines. The concept of cultural relativism, attributed to Franz Boas, is a guiding principle that other disciplines have widely adopted. Cultural anthropology values and works to sustain cultural diversity.

Culture is the key concept of cultural anthropology, and many definitions for it have been proposed throughout the history of anthropology. Many anthropologists define culture as learned and shared behavior and ideas, whereas others equate culture with ideas alone and exclude behavior as a part of culture. It is easier to understand culture by considering its characteristics: Culture is related to nature but is not the same as nature; it is based on symbols and it is learned; cultures are integrated within themselves; and cultures interact with other cultures and change. Four models of cultural interaction involve varying degrees of conflict, blending, and resistance. People participate in cultures of different levels, including local microcultures shaped by such factors as class, "race"/ethnicity/indigeneity, gender, age, and institutions.

Cultural anthropology has a rich history of theoretical approaches and changing topical focuses. Three important theoretical debates are biological determinism versus cultural constructionism, interpretive anthropology versus cultural materialism, and individual agency versus structurism. Each, in its own way, attempts to understand and explain why people behave and think the way they do and to account for differences and similarities across cultures.

◆ How is cultural anthropology relevant to a career?

Coursework in cultural anthropology expands one's awareness of the diversity of the world's cultures and the importance of cross-cultural understanding. Employers in many fields—such as public health, humanitarian aid, law enforcement, business, and education—increasingly value a degree in cultural anthropology. In today's diverse and connected world, being culturally informed and culturally sensitive is essential.

Graduate degrees in cultural anthropology, either at the M.A. or Ph.D. level, are even more likely to lead to professional positions that directly use your anthropological education and skills. Combining graduate coursework in anthropology with a professional degree, such as a master's degree in public health or public administration, or a law degree, is a successful route to a meaningful career outside academia. Cultural anthropology, beyond its career relevance, will enrich your everyday life with its insights.

KEY CONCEPTS

agency, p. 13
anthropology, p. 6
applied anthropology, p. 7
archaeology, p. 6
biological
    anthropology, p. 6
biological
    determinism, p. 23

class, p. 19
cultural anthropology, p. 7
cultural
    constructionism, p. 24
cultural materialism, p. 13
cultural relativism, p. 12
culture, p. 7
ethnicity, p. 20

ethnocentrism, p. 22
functionalism, p. 12
gender, p. 20
globalization, p. 18
holism, p. 12
indigenous people, p. 20
interpretive
    anthropology, p. 13

linguistic
    anthropology, p. 7
localization, p. 19
microculture, p. 14
"race," p. 20
rainforest, p. 10
structurism, p. 13
symbol, p. 17

SUGGESTED READINGS

Thomas J. Barfield, ed. *The Dictionary of Anthropology*. Malden, MA: Blackwell Publishing, 1997. This reference work contains hundreds of brief essays on concepts in anthropology, such as evolution, myth, functionalism, and applied anthropology, and on important anthropologists.

Stanley R. Barrett. *Anthropology: A Student's Guide to Theory and Method*. Toronto: University of Toronto Press, 2000. This book organizes the theoretical history of cultural anthropology into three phases and summarizes trends in each. The author discusses how to do research in cultural anthropology.

Mario Blaser, Harvey A. Feit, and Glenn McRae, eds. *In the Way of Development: Indigenous Peoples, Life Projects and Globalization*. New York: Zed Books, in association with the International Development Research Centre, 2004. Twenty chapters contributed by indigenous leaders, social activists, and cultural anthropologists address indigenous peoples' responses to capitalism and indigenous ideas about future change that is positive for them and for the environment.

Ira E. Harrison and Faye V. Harrison, eds. *African-American Pioneers in Anthropology*. Chicago: University of Illinois Press, 1999. This collection of intellectual biographies highlights the contributions of 13 African American anthropologists to the development of cultural anthropology in the United States.

Takami Kuwayama, ed. *Native Anthropology: The Japanese Challenge to Western Academic Hegemony*. Melbourne, Australia: Trans Pacific Press, 2004. The chapters in this book discuss various topics in Japanese anthropology, including "native anthropology," the marginalization of Asian anthropologists, folklore studies, and how U.S. anthropology textbooks present Japan.

James H. McDonald, ed. *The Applied Anthropology Reader*. Boston: Allyn and Bacon, 2002. This collection of over 50 brief essays explores topics in applied cultural anthropology, including ethics, methods, urban settings, health, international development, the environment, education, and business.

R. Bruce Morrison and C. Roderick Wilson, eds. *Native Peoples: The Canadian Experience*, 3rd ed. Toronto, Ontario: Oxford University Press, 2004. This sourcebook on Northern Peoples contains 26 chapters with sections divided by region. Chapters about various cultural groups provide historical context and updates on the current situation.

Thomas C. Patterson. *A Social History of Anthropology in the United States*. New York: Berg, 2001. This history of anthropology in the United States emphasizes the social and political context of the discipline and how that context has shaped theories and methods.

Richard J. Perry. *Five Key Concepts in Anthropological Thinking*. Upper Saddle River, NJ: Prentice-Hall, 2003. The five key concepts are evolution, culture, structure, function, and relativism. The author raises thought-provoking questions about anthropology as being Eurocentric and about the appropriation of the culture concept beyond anthropology.

Pat Shipman. *The Evolution of Racism: Human Differences and the Use and Abuse of Science*. Cambridge, MA: Harvard University Press, 1994. This book offers a history of the "race" concept in Western thought from Darwin to contemporary DNA studies. The author addresses thorny issues such as racism in the United States and Nazi Germany's use of Darwinism.

Cultural anthropologist Robert Bailey and biological anthropologist Nadine Peacock, members of a Harvard University fieldwork team, conversing with some Ituri people who live in the rainforests of the eastern part of the Democratic Republic of Congo.

RESEARCHING CULTURE

2

OUTLINE

Changing Research Methods in Cultural Anthropology

Doing Fieldwork in Cultural Anthropology

Critical Thinking: Shells and Skirts in the Trobriand Islands

Culturama: The Trobriand Islanders of Papua New Guinea

Eye on the Environment: Researching Inuit Place Names and Landscape Knowledge

Urgent Issues in Cultural Anthropology Research

the **BIG** questions

◆ How do cultural anthropologists conduct research about culture?

◆ What does fieldwork involve?

◆ What are some urgent issues in cultural anthropology research today?

This chapter is about how cultural anthropologists do research to learn about people's shared and learned behavior and beliefs and how their research methods have changed over time. The first section discusses how methods in cultural anthropology have evolved since the late nineteenth century. The second section covers the steps involved in a research project. The chapter concludes by addressing two urgent topics in cultural anthropology research.

◆◆◆

Changing Research Methods in Cultural Anthropology

Methods in cultural anthropology today are different in several ways from those used during the nineteenth century. Most cultural anthropologists now gather data by doing **fieldwork**, going to the *field*, which is wherever people and cultures are, to learn about culture through direct observation. They also use a variety of specialized research techniques.

FROM THE ARMCHAIR TO THE FIELD

The term *armchair anthropology* refers to how early cultural anthropologists conducted research by sitting and reading about other cultures. They read reports written by travelers, missionaries, and explorers but never visited those places or had any kind of direct experience with the people.

In the late nineteenth and early twentieth centuries, anthropologists hired by European colonial governments moved a step closer to learning directly about the people of other cultures. They traveled to colonized countries in Africa and Asia, where they lived near, but not with, the people they were studying. This approach is called *verandah anthropology* because, typically, the anthropologist would send out for "natives" to come to his verandah for interviewing. Verandah anthropologists, like armchair anthropologists, were men.

A bit earlier, in the United States during the mid-nineteenth century, Lewis Henry Morgan had taken steps toward learning about people through direct observation. A lawyer, Morgan lived in Rochester, New York, near the Iroquois territory. He became well acquainted with many of

Ethnographic research in the early twentieth century often involved photography. The girl shown here wears the skull of her deceased sister. Indigenous people of the Andaman Islands revere the bones of their dead relatives and would not want them to be taken away, studied, or displayed in a museum.

the Iroquois (Tooker 1992). These experiences provided Morgan with important insights into their everyday lives. His writings changed the prevailing Euro-American perception of the Iroquois, and other Native American tribes, as "dangerous savages." Morgan showed that Iroquois behavior and beliefs make sense if an outsider spends time learning about them through direct experience.

PARTICIPANT OBSERVATION

A major turning point in how cultural anthropologists do research occurred in the early twentieth century, during World War I, laying the foundation for the current cornerstone method in cultural anthropology: fieldwork combined with participant observation. **Participant observation** is a research method for learning about culture that involves living in a culture for an extended period while gathering data.

The "father" of participant observation is Bronislaw Malinowski. He adopted what was, at the time, an innovative approach to learning about culture while he was in the Trobriand Islands in the South Pacific during World War I (see Culturama, p. 33). For two years, he lived in a tent alongside the local people, participating in their activities and living, as much as possible, as one of them. Through this process adopted by Malinowski, the key elements of participant observation were established:

- Living with the people
- Participating in their everyday life
- Learning the language

By living with the people and participating in their daily round of life, Malinowski learned about their culture in context,

---

fieldwork   research in the field, which is any place where people and culture are found.

participant observation   basic fieldwork method in cultural anthropology that involves living in a culture for a long time while gathering data.

multisited research   fieldwork conducted in more than one location in order to understand the behaviors and ideas of dispersed members of a culture or the relationships among different levels, such as state policy and local culture.

rather than through secondhand reports. By learning the local language, he could talk with the people without the use of interpreters and thus gain a much more accurate understanding of their culture.

In this early phase of fieldwork and participant observation, a primary goal was to record as much as possible of a people's language, songs, rituals, and social life because many cultures were disappearing. Most early cultural anthropologists did fieldwork in small, relatively isolated cultures. They thought they could study everything about such cultures; those were the days of holism (defined in Chapter 1). Typically, the anthropologist (a White man) would go off with his notebooks to collect data on a standardized list of topics, including economics, family life, politics, religion, language, art and crafts, and more.

Today, few if any such seemingly isolated cultures remain. Cultural anthropologists have devised new research methods so that they can study larger-scale cultures, global–local connections, and cultural change. One methodological innovation of the late twentieth century helps to address these new issues: **multisited research**, which is fieldwork conducted on a topic in more than one location (Marcus 1995). Although especially helpful in studying migrant populations in both their place of origin and their new location, multisited research is useful for studying many topics.

Lanita Jacobs-Huey conducted multisited fieldwork in order to learn about the language and culture of hair styles among African American women (2002). She chose a range of sites throughout the United States and in London, England, in order to explore the many facets of the far-from-simple topic of hair: beauty salons, regional and international hair expos and training seminars, Bible study meetings of a nonprofit group of Christian cosmetologists, stand-up comedy clubs, a computer-mediated discussion about the politics of Black hair, and a cosmetology school in Charleston, South Carolina.

◆◆◆

Doing Fieldwork in Cultural Anthropology

Fieldwork in cultural anthropology can be exciting, frustrating, scary, boring, and sometimes dangerous. One thing is true: It transforms the lives of everyone involved. This section explores the stages of a fieldwork research project, starting with the initial planning and ending with the analysis and presentation of the findings.

BEGINNING THE FIELDWORK PROCESS

Before going to the field, the prospective researcher must select a research topic and prepare for the fieldwork itself. These steps are critical to the success of the project.

PROJECT SELECTION Finding a topic for a research project is a basic first step. The topic should be important and feasible. Cultural anthropologists often find a topic to research by carrying out a *literature review,* or reading what others have already written about the subject to learn whether a gap in previous research exists. For example, cultural anthropologists realized during the 1970s that anthropological research had bypassed women and girls, and this is how feminist anthropology began (Miller 1993).

Notable events sometimes inspire a research topic. The HIV/AIDS epidemic and its rapid spread continue to prompt research. The recent rise in the numbers of international migrants and refugees is another pressing area for study. The fall of state socialism in Russia and Eastern Europe shifted

Lanita Jacobs-Huey's field sites include hair-styling competitions throughout the United States and in London, England. Here, a judge evaluates the work of a student stylist at the Afro Hair & Beauty Show in London.

THINKING
OUTSIDE
THE BOX

As you read this chapter, consider the similarities and differences between research in cultural anthropology and research in other disciplines, such as biology, psychology, political science, economics, and history.

CRITICAL thinking

Shells and Skirts in the Trobriand Islands

A lasting contribution of Bronislaw Malinowski's ethnography, *Argonauts of the Western Pacific* (1961 [1922]), is its detailed examination of the kula, a trading network linking many islands in the region, in which men have long-standing partnerships for the exchange of everyday goods, such as food, as well as highly valued necklaces and armlets.

More than half a century later, Annette Weiner (1976) traveled to the Trobriand Islands to study wood carving. She settled in a village less than a mile from where Malinowski had done his research. She immediately began making startling observations: "On my first day in the village, I saw women performing a mortuary [death] ceremony in which they distributed thousands of bundles of strips of dried banana leaves and hundreds of beautifully decorated fibrous skirts" (1976:xvii).

Nowhere in Malinowski's voluminous writings did he mention the women's activities. Weiner was intrigued and decided to change her research project to investigate women's goods, exchange patterns, and prestige. Men, as Malinowski showed, exchange shells, yams, and pigs. Women, as Weiner learned, exchange bundles of banana leaves and intricately made skirts. Power and

Bronislaw Malinowski during his fieldwork in the Trobriand Islands, 1915–1918.
▶ *What are some of the differences between what Malinowski's field research revealed about men's lives in the Trobriand Islands compared with what a "verandah anthropologist" might have learned?*

prestige derive from both exchange networks.

Reading Malinowski alone informs us about the world of men's status systems and describes them in isolation from half of the islands' population: women. Weiner's book *Women of Value, Men of Renown* (1976) provides an account of women's trading and prestige activities as well as how they are linked to those of men. Building on the work of her

predecessor, Weiner shows how a full understanding of one domain requires knowledge of the other.

◆ **CRITICAL THINKING QUESTIONS**

- Is it possible that Malinowski overlooked women's exchange patterns?
- Do the findings of Annette Weiner simply provide another one-sided view?
- What might a cultural anthropologist discover in the Trobriand Islands now?

---

attention to that region. Conflicts in Afghanistan, Iraq, Sudan, and other places spur cultural anthropologists to ask what causes such conflicts and how post-conflict reconstruction can be most effectively accomplished (Lubkemann 2005).

Some cultural anthropologists choose to study the cultural context of a particular item or commodity, such as sugar (Mintz 1985), cars (D. Miller 2001), beef (Caplan 2000), money (R. Foster 2002), shea butter (Chalfin 2004), wedding dresses (Foster and Johnson 2003), coca (Allen 2002), or cocaine

(Taussig 2004). The item provides a focus for understanding the social relations surrounding its production, use, and trade, and what it means in terms of people's changing identities.

Another idea for a research project is a *restudy*, fieldwork conducted in a previously researched community. Many decades of previous research provide baseline information on which later studies can build. It makes sense to examine changes that have occurred or to look at the culture from a new angle. For her doctoral dissertation research, Annette Weiner (1976) decided to go to the Trobriand Islands, following in the footsteps of Malinowski, to learn what people's lives were like over 50 years after his fieldwork. What she found there prompted her to change her original research plans (see Critical Thinking and Culturama).

---

kula a trading network, linking many of the Trobriand Islands, in which men have long-standing partnerships for the exchange of everyday goods, such as food, as well as highly valued necklaces and armlets.

CULTURAMA

The Trobriand Islanders of Papua New Guinea

The Trobriand Islands are named after eighteenth-century French explorer Denis de Trobriand. They include 22 flat coral atolls east of the island of New Guinea. The indigenous Trobriand population lives on four main islands. Kiriwina is by far the most populated, with about 28,000 people (digim'Rina, personal communication 2006). The Papua New Guinea (PNG) district office and an airstrip are located on Kiriwina at Losuia.

The islands were first colonized by Great Britain and then ceded to Australia in 1904 (Weiner 1988). The British attempted to stop local warfare and to change many other aspects of Trobriand culture. Christian missionaries introduced the game of cricket as a substitute for warfare (see Chapter 11 for further discussion). In 1943, Allied troops landed as part of their Pacific operations. In 1975, the islands

became part of the state of Papua New Guinea.

Island-to-island cultural differences exist. Even within one island, people may speak different dialects, although everyone speaks a version of the language called Kilivila (Weiner 1988). The Trobrianders grow much of their own food, including root crops such as yams, sweet potatoes, and taro; beans and squash; and bananas, breadfruit, coconuts, and betel nuts. Pigs are the main animal raised for food and as prestige items. In the latter part of the twentieth century, Trobrianders were increasingly dependent on money sent to them by relatives working elsewhere in PNG. Current development projects are encouraging people to plant more fruit trees, such as mango (digim'Rina 2005).

Kinship emphasizes the female line, meaning that mothers and daughters form the core of coresidential groups.

Fathers, though not coresidential, are nonetheless important family members and spend as much time caring for children as women do (Weiner 1988). Fathers of political status give their babies and children, both boys and girls, highly valued shell earrings and necklaces to wear. Mothers give daughters prized red skirts. Trobriand children attend Western-style schools on the islands, and many go to mainland PNG and beyond for further studies.

Today, elders worry that young people do nothing but dream about "money" and fail to care for the heritage of their ancestors. Another concern is that commercial overfishing is endangering the coral reefs.

Thanks to Linus S. digim'Rina, University of Papua New Guinea, and Robert Foster, University of Rochester, for reviewing this material.

(LEFT) Trobriand men's coveted trade goods include this shell necklace and armlet. (CENTER) A Trobriand girl wears a valued skirt at a dance in honor of the ancestors on Kiriwina Island. She and other female participants coat their skin with coconut oil and herbs and wear decorative flowers.

MAP 2.1 Trobriand Islands of Papua New Guinea. Also known as the Kiriwina Islands, these islands are an archipelago of coral atolls lying off the eastern coast of the island of New Guinea.

TROBRIAND ISLANDS

Kaileuna • Losuia • Lagoon • Kiriwina • Kitava • Vakuta

0   20   40 Miles
0   20   40 Kilometers

PREPARING FOR THE FIELD   After defining the research topic, it is important to secure funding to carry out the research. Academic anthropologists can apply for grants from a variety of sources, governmental and nongovernmental. Several sources of funding are also available for advanced graduate students. Undergraduate students have a more difficult time finding grants to support fieldwork, but many succeed.

Related to the funding question is whether it is appropriate for an anthropologist to conduct research while employed in the research setting. Employment provides financial support for the research, but it raises some problems. A basic dilemma, discussed later in the chapter, is the ethical principle that anthropologists cannot do "undercover" research. If you are working in a factory, for example, while studying what goes on in the factory, you must get people's permission for your study, something that is not always easy. More positively, a work role can help gain people's trust and respect. A British graduate student worked as a bartender in a tourist town in Ireland (Kaul 2004). This position placed him at the center of the village, and people respected him as a hard-working person, thus greatly adding to his ability to learn about the local culture, at least as revealed from a bartender's perspective.

If the project involves international travel, the host government may require a visa and an application for permission to conduct research. These formalities may take a long time and may even be impossible to obtain. The government of India, for example, restricts research by foreigners, especially research related to "sensitive" topics such as tribal people, border areas, and family planning. China's restrictions against foreign anthropologists doing fieldwork have been eased since the 1980s, but it is still not easy to get permission to do fieldwork and participant observation.

Many countries require that researchers follow official guidelines for the *protection of human subjects*. In the United States, universities and other institutions that support or conduct research with living people must establish *institutional review boards* (*IRBs*) to monitor research to make sure that it conforms to ethical principles. IRB guidelines follow a medical model related to the need to protect people who participate as "subjects" in medical research. Normally, IRBs require informed consent, in writing, from the research participants. **Informed consent** is an aspect of research ethics requiring that the researcher inform the research participants of the intent, scope, and possible effects of the study and seek their agreement to be in the study. Obtaining written consent from research participants is reasonable and feasible in many anthropological research projects. Written consent, however, is often not reasonable or feasible, especially in oral-based cultures where most people are not literate. Fortunately, IRBs are gaining more experience with the contexts in which most cultural anthropologists do research. Some universities' IRBs will waive the requirement for written informed consent, allowing oral informed consent instead. IRB guidelines do change, so check your institution's website for the latest policy.

Depending on the project's location, preparation for the field may involve buying specialized equipment, such as a tent, warm clothing, waterproof clothing, and sturdy boots. Health preparations may require immunization against contagious diseases such as yellow fever. For research in a remote area, a well-stocked medical kit and basic first-aid training are essential. Research equipment and supplies are another important aspect of preparation. Cameras, video recorders, tape recorders, and laptop computers are now basic field equipment.

If a researcher is unfamiliar with the local language, intensive language training before going to the field is critical. Even with language training in advance, cultural anthropologists often find that they cannot communicate in the local version of the standardized language they studied in a classroom. Therefore, many fieldworkers rely on help from a local interpreter throughout their study or, at least, in its early stages.

WORKING IN THE FIELD

A basic first step in establishing a fieldwork project is to decide on the particular location or locations for the research. The second is to find a place to live.

SITE SELECTION   A research *site* is the place where the research takes place, and sometimes a project involves more than one site. The researcher often has a basic idea of the area where the fieldwork will occur, for example, a shantytown in Rio de Janeiro, a village in Scotland or a factory in Malaysia. But it is often impossible to know in advance exactly where the project will be located. Selecting a research site depends on many factors. It may be necessary to find a large village if the project involves class differences in work patterns, or a clinic if the study concerns health-care behavior. It may be difficult to find a village, neighborhood, or institution in which the people welcome the researcher and the project. Often, housing shortages mean that even the most welcoming community cannot provide space for an anthropologist.

GAINING RAPPORT   **Rapport** is a trusting relationship between the researcher and the study population. In the early stages of research, the primary goal is to establish rapport with key leaders or decision makers in the community who may serve as *gatekeepers* (people who formally or informally control access to the group or community). Gaining rapport involves trust on the part of the study population, and that trust depends on how the researcher presents herself or himself. In many cultures, people have difficulty understanding why a

---

informed consent   an aspect of fieldwork ethics requiring that the researcher inform the research participants of the intent, scope, and possible effects of the proposed study and seek their consent to be in the study.

rapport   a trusting relationship between the researcher and the study population.

person would come to study them because they do not know about universities and research and cultural anthropology. They may provide their own explanations based on previous experience with outsiders whose goals differed from those of cultural anthropologists, such as tax collectors, family planning promoters, and law-enforcement officials.

Stories about *false role assignments* can be humorous. During his 1970s fieldwork in northwest Pakistan, Richard Kurin reports that, in the first stage of his research, the villagers thought he was an international spy from America, Russia, India, or China (1980). Over time, he convinced them that he was not a spy. So what was he? The villagers came up with several roles for Kurin. First, they speculated that he was a teacher of English because he was tutoring one of the village boys. Second, they guessed that he must be a doctor because he gave people aspirin. Third, they thought he might be a lawyer who could help them in local disputes because he could read court orders. Last, they decided that he was a descendant of a local clan because of the similarity of his last name and that of an ancestral king. For Richard Kurin, the last of these—being a true "Karan"—was best of all.

Being labeled a spy continues to be a problem for anthropologists. Christa Salamandra, a Western-trained doctoral student in anthropology, went to Damascus, Syria (see Map 2.2), to do research for her dissertation in anthropology

(2004). Although Damascus has an ancient history, it is increasingly cosmopolitan. Damascenes, however, have little exposure to anthropology. Syria has no university with a department of anthropology, and there are no Syrian anthropologists. Salamandra's research interests in popular culture (movies, cafés, and fashion) perplexed the local people, who decided she must be a foreign spy. One person said to her, "Your question is CIA, not academic" (2004:5). Nevertheless, she managed to carry out her study and write a book about popular culture in Damascus.

GIFT GIVING AND EXCHANGE   Giving gifts to people involved in the research can help the project proceed, but gifts should be culturally and ethically appropriate. Learning the local rules of exchange is important (see Figure 2.1).

Matthews Hamabata, a Japanese American who did fieldwork in Japan, learned about the complexities of gift giving among Japanese business families (1990). He developed a close relationship with one family, the Itoos, and helped their daughter apply for admission to universities in the United States. When the applications were completed, Mrs. Itoo invited him to an expensive restaurant to celebrate. After the dinner, she handed him a small, carefully wrapped package, expressing her embarrassment at the inadequacy of her gift in relation to all that he had done for her daughter. When he returned home, he opened the gift. It was a box of chocolates. Upon opening the box, he discovered 50,000 yen (about US$250). Hamabata felt insulted: "Who do the Itoos think they are? They can't buy me or my services!" (1990:21–22). He asked some Japanese friends what he should do. They told him that the gift signaled the Itoos' wish to have a long-standing relationship and that returning the money to the Itoos would be an insult. They advised him to give a return gift later on, in order to maintain the relationship. His gift should leave him ahead by about 25,000 yen, given his status as an anthropologist in relation to the Itoos'

MAP 2.2   Syria.
The Syrian Arabic Republic historically included the present-day territories of Lebanon, Israel, the Palestinian Territories, and parts of Jordan, but not the Jazira region in Syria's northeast. The population of Syria is 19 million people. The capital city, Damascus, with a population of 3 million people, is one of the oldest continually occupied cities in the world.

- What an appropriate or an inappropriate gift is
- How to deliver a gift
- How to behave as a gift giver
- How to behave when receiving a gift
- If and how to give a follow-up gift

FIGURE 2.1   Culture and Gift-Giving in the Field

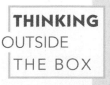

THINKING OUTSIDE THE BOX

Recall a situation in which either you did not know what would be an appropriate gift to give someone (in terms of quality, cost, or some other factor) or you were faced with some other puzzling situation related to gift exchange. What were the cultural meanings underlying the situation?

Tobias Hecht plays a game with some of the street children in his study in Rio de Janeiro, Brazil.

status as a rich business family. This strategy worked, and the relationship between Hamabata and the Itoos remained intact.

MICROCULTURES AND FIELDWORK   Class, race, gender, and age all affect how the local people will perceive and welcome an anthropologist. Some examples illustrate how microcultures influence rapport and affect the research in other ways.

CLASS   In most fieldwork situations, the anthropologist is more wealthy and powerful than the people studied. This difference is obvious to the people. They know that the anthropologist must have spent hundreds or thousands of dollars to travel to the research site. They see the anthropologist's expensive equipment (camera, tape recorder, video recorder, even a vehicle) and valuable material goods (stainless steel knives, cigarettes, flashlights, canned food, and medicines).

Many years ago, Laura Nader urged that anthropologists should also *study up* by doing research among powerful people such as members of the business elite, political leaders, and government officials (1972). As one example of this approach, research on the high-fashion industry of Japan placed the anthropologist in touch with members of the Japanese elite—influential people capable of taking her to court if they felt she wrote something defamatory about them (Kondo 1997). Studying up has prompted greater attention to accountability to the people being studied, whether or not they are able to read what the anthropologist has written about them or are wealthy enough to hire a lawyer if they do not like how they and their culture have been presented.

culture shock   persistent feelings of uneasiness, loneliness, and anxiety that often occur when a person has shifted from one culture to a different one.

deductive approach (to research)   a research method that involves posing a research question or hypothesis, gathering data related to the question, and then assessing the findings in relation to the original hypothesis.

"RACE"/ETHNICITY   For most of its history, cultural anthropology has been dominated by Euro-American White researchers who study "other" cultures that are mainly non-White and non-Euro-American. The effects of "Whiteness" on role assignments range from the anthropologist being considered a god or ancestral spirit to being reviled as a representative of a colonialist past or neocolonialist present. While doing research in a village in Jamaica called Haversham, Tony Whitehead learned how "race" and status interact (1986). Whitehead is an African American from a low-income family. Being of a similar "race" and class as the rural Jamaicans with whom he was doing research, he assumed that he would quickly build rapport because of a shared heritage. The people of Haversham, however, have a complex status system that relegated Whitehead to a position that he did not predict, as he explains:

> I was shocked when the people of Haversham began talking to me and referring to me as a "big," "brown," "pretty-talking" man. "Big" was not a reference to my weight but to my higher social status as they perceived it, and "brown" referred not only to my skin color but also to my higher social status. . . . More embarrassing than bothersome were the references to how "pretty" I talked, a comment on my Standard English speech pattern. . . . Frequently mothers told me that their children were going to school so that they could learn to talk as pretty as I did. (1986:214–215)

This experience prompted Whitehead to ponder the complexities of "race" and status cross-culturally.

GENDER   If a female researcher is young and unmarried, she is likely to face more difficulties than a young unmarried man or an older woman, married or single, because people in most cultures consider a young unmarried female on her own as extremely unusual. Rules of gender segregation may dictate that a young unmarried woman should not move about freely without a male escort, attend certain events, or be in certain places. A woman researcher who studied a community of gay men in the United States says:

> I was able to do fieldwork in those parts of the setting dedicated to sociability and leisure—bars, parties, family gatherings. I was not, however, able to observe in those parts of the setting dedicated to sexuality—even quasi-public settings such as homosexual bath houses. . . . Thus my portrait of the gay community is only a partial one, bounded by the social roles assigned to females within the male homosexual world. (Warren 1988:18)

Gender segregation may also prevent male researchers from gaining access to a full range of activities. Liza Dalby, a White American, lived with the geishas of Kyoto, Japan, and trained to be a geisha (1998). This research would have been impossible for a man to do.

AGE Typically, anthropologists are adults, and this fact tends to make it easier for them to gain rapport with people their age than with children or the aged. Although some children and adolescents welcome the participation of a friendly adult in their daily lives and respond to questions openly, others are more reserved.

American anthropologist Liza Dalby in formal geisha dress during her fieldwork on geisha culture in Kyoto, Japan.

▶ *Besides learning to dress correctly, what other cultural skills did Liza Dalby probably have to learn?*

CULTURE SHOCK **Culture shock** is the feeling of uneasiness, loneliness, and anxiety that occurs when a person shifts from one culture to a different one. The more different the two cultures are, the more severe the shock is likely to be. Culture shock happens to many cultural anthropologists, no matter how much they have tried to prepare themselves for fieldwork. It also happens to students who study abroad, Peace Corps volunteers, and others who spend a long time living in another culture.

Culture shock can range from problems with food to language barriers and loneliness. Food differences were a major problem in adjustment for a Chinese anthropologist who came to the United States (Huang 1993). American food never gave him a "full" feeling. An American anthropologist who went to Pohnpei, an island in the Federated States of Micronesia (see Map 5.6), found that her lack of skills in the local language caused her the most serious adjustment problems (Ward 1989). She says, "Even dogs understood more than I did. . . . [I will never] forget the agony of stepping on a woman's toes. Instead of asking for forgiveness, I blurted out, 'His canoe is blue'" (1989:14).

A frequent psychological aspect of culture shock is the feeling of reduced competence as a cultural actor. At home, the anthropologist is highly competent, carrying out everyday tasks, such as shopping, talking with people, and mailing a package, without thinking. In a new culture, the simplest tasks are difficult and one's sense of self-efficacy is undermined.

Reverse culture shock may occur after coming home. An American anthropologist describes his feelings on returning to San Francisco after a year of fieldwork in a village in India:

> We could not understand why people were so distant and hard to reach, or why they talked and moved so quickly. We were a little frightened at the sight of so many white faces and we could not understand why no one stared at us, brushed against us, or admired our baby. (Beals 1980:119)

FIELDWORK TECHNIQUES

The goal of fieldwork is to collect information, or *data*, about the research topic. In cultural anthropology, variations exist about what kinds of data to emphasize and the best ways to collect data.

DEDUCTIVE AND INDUCTIVE RESEARCH A **deductive approach** is a form of research that starts from a research question or *hypothesis*, and then involves collecting relevant data through observation, interviews, and other methods. An

THINKING OUTSIDE THE BOX

Think of an occasion in which you experienced culture shock, even if as the result of just a brief cross-cultural encounter. How did you feel? How did you cope? What did you learn from the experience?

FIGURE 2.2 Two Research Approaches in Cultural Anthropology

Research Approach	Process	Data
Deductive (Etic)	Hypothesis followed by data collection	Quantitative data for hypothesis testing
Inductive (Emic)	No hypothesis, data collection follows from participants' lead	Qualitative data for descriptive insights

inductive approach is a form of research that proceeds without a hypothesis and involves gathering data through unstructured, informal observation, conversation, and other methods. Deductive methods are more likely to collect **quantitative data**, or numeric information, such as the amount of land in relation to the population or the numbers of people with particular health problems. The inductive approach in cultural anthropology emphasizes **qualitative data**, or nonnumeric information, such as recordings of myths and conversations and filming of events. Most anthropologists, however, combine deductive and inductive approaches and quantitative and qualitative data.

Cultural anthropologists have labels for data collected in each approach. **Etic** (pronounced like the last two syllables of "phonetic," or eh-tik) refers to data collected according to the researcher's questions and categories, with the goal of being able to test a hypothesis (see Figure 2.2). In contrast, **emic** (pronounced like the last two syllables of "phonemic," or ee-mik) refers to data collected that reflect what insiders say and understand about their culture, and insiders' categories of thinking. Cultural materialists (review Chapter 1) are more likely to collect etic data, whereas interpretivists are more likely to collect emic data. Again, however, most cultural anthropologists collect both types of data.

PARTICIPANT OBSERVATION The phrase *participant observation* includes two processes: participating, or being part of the people's lives, and, at the same time, carefully observing. These two activities may sound simple, but they are actually quite complex.

Being a participant means that the researcher adopts the lifestyle of the people being studied, living in the same kind of housing, eating similar food, wearing similar clothing, learning the language, and participating in the daily round of activities and in special events. The rationale is that participation over a long period improves the quality of the data. The more time the researcher spends living among the people, the more likely it is that the people will live their "normal" lives. In this way, the researcher is able to overcome the *Hawthorne effect*, a research bias that occurs when participants change their behavior to conform to the perceived expectations of the researcher. The Hawthorne effect was discovered in the 1930s in a study of an industrial plant in the United States. During the study, research participants altered their behavior in ways they thought would please the researcher.

TALKING WITH PEOPLE Common sense tells you that participating and observing are important, but what about talking to people and asking questions such as "What is going on here?" "What does that mean?" and "Why are you doing that?" The process of talking to people and asking them questions is such an important component of participant observation that the method should actually be called *participant observation and talking*. Cultural anthropologists use a variety of data-collection techniques that rely on talking with people, from informal, casual, and unplanned conversations to more formal methods.

An **interview** is a technique for gathering verbal data through questions or guided conversation. It is more purposeful than a casual conversation. An interview may involve only two people, the interviewer and the interviewee, or several people in what are called *group interviews* or *focus groups*. Cultural anthropologists use different interview styles and formats, depending on the kinds of information they seek, the amount of time they have, and their language skills. The least structured type of interview is an *open-ended interview*, in which the respondent (interviewee) takes the lead in setting the direction of the conversation, determining the topics to be covered, and choosing how much time to devote to a particular topic. The interviewer does not interrupt or provide prompting

---

inductive approach (to research) a research approach that avoids hypothesis formation in advance of the research and instead takes its lead from the culture being studied.

quantitative data numeric information.

qualitative data non-numeric information.

etic an analytical framework used by outside analysts in studying culture.

emic insiders' perceptions and categories, and their explanations for why they do what they do.

interview a research technique that involves gathering verbal data through questions or guided conversation between at least two people.

questionnaire a formal research instrument containing a pre-set series of questions that the anthropologist asks in a face-to-face setting, by mail, or by e-mail.

questions. In this way, the researcher discovers what themes are important to the person.

A **questionnaire** is a formal research instrument containing a preset series of questions that the anthropologist asks in a face-to-face setting or by mail or e-mail. Cultural anthropologists who use questionnaires favor a face-to-face setting. Like interviews, questionnaires vary in the degree to which the questions are *structured* (close ended) or *unstructured* (open ended). Structured questions limit the range of possible responses—for example, by asking research participants to rate their positions on a particular issue as "very positive," "positive," "negative," "very negative," or "no opinion." Unstructured interviews generate more emic responses.

When designing a questionnaire, the researcher should have enough familiarity with the study population to be able to develop questions that make cultural sense. Researchers who take a ready-made questionnaire to the field with them should ask another researcher who knows the culture to review the questionnaire in advance to see whether it makes sense. Further revisions may be required in the field to make the questionnaire fit local conditions. A *pilot study* using the questionnaire among a small number of people in the research area can expose areas that need further revision.

COMBINING OBSERVATION AND TALKING A combination of observation of what people actually do with verbal data about what people *say* they do and think is essential for a well-rounded view of a culture (Sanjek 2000). People may say that they do something or believe something, but their behavior may differ from what they say. For example, people may say that sons and daughters inherit equal shares of family property when the parents die. Research into what really happens may reveal that daughters do not, in fact, inherit equal shares. Similarly, an anthropologist might learn from people and their laws that discrimination on the basis of skin color is illegal. Research on people's behavior might reveal clear examples of discrimination. It is important for an anthropologist to learn about both what people say and what happens. Both are "true" aspects of culture.

SPECIALIZED METHODS Cultural anthropologists also use several kinds of specific research methods. The choice depends on the anthropologist's research goals.

LIFE HISTORY A *life history* is a qualitative, in-depth description of an individual's life as narrated to the researcher. Anthropologists differ in their views about the value of the life history as a method in cultural anthropology. Early in the twentieth century, Franz Boas rejected this method as unscientific because research participants might lie or exaggerate (Peacock and Holland 1993). Others disagree, saying that a life history reveals rich information on individuals and how they think, no matter how "distorted" their reports are. For example, some anthropologists have questioned the accuracy of parts

Marjorie Shostak (RIGHT) interviewing Nisa during fieldwork among the Ju/'hoansi in 1975.
▶ *What would you tell an anthropologist about your life?*

of *Nisa: The Life and Times of a !Kung Woman* (Shostak 1981), probably the most widely read life history in anthropology. It is a book-length story of a Ju/'hoansi woman of the Kalahari desert of southern Africa (review Culturama, Chapter 1, p. 21). Presented in Nisa's voice, the book offers rich details about her childhood and several marriages. The value of the narrative is not so much whether it is "true" or not; rather, the value is that we learn from Nisa what she wants to tell us, her view of her experiences. That counts as "data" in cultural anthropology, for it is "truly" what she reported to Marjorie Shostak.

In the early days of life history research, anthropologists tried to choose an individual who was somehow typical, average, or representative. It is not possible, however, to find one person who is representative of an entire culture in the scientific sense. Instead, anthropologists now seek individuals who occupy particularly interesting social niches. For example, Gananath Obeyesekere (oh-bay-yuh-sek-eruh) analyzed the life histories of four Sri Lankan people, three women and one man (1981). Each became a Hindu religious devotee and ascetic, distinguished by their thickly matted hair, which is permanently matted into long, twisted coils that look like snakes. If they try to comb out the tangles, they cannot succeed because, according to the devotees, a deity is present in their matted hair. Obeyesekere suggests that all four people had suffered deep psychological afflictions during their lives, including sexual anxieties. Their matted hair symbolizes their suffering and provides them with a special status as holy, thus placing them beyond the rules of married life including conjugal sexual relations.

THINKING OUTSIDE THE BOX

Given the emphasis on observation in fieldwork, is it possible for a blind person to become a cultural anthropologist?

This Sri Lankan woman, whose life story Gananath Obeyesekere analyzed, is a priestess to a deity. She stands in the shrine room of her house, holding her matted, snaky hair.

▶ *How do hair styles in your culture express a person's religion, marital status, or sexuality?*

TIME ALLOCATION STUDY   A *time allocation study* is a quantitative method that collects data on how people spend their time each day on particular activities. This method relies on standard time units as the basic matrix and then labeling or coding the activities that occur within certain time segments (Gross 1984). Activity codes must be adapted to fit local contexts. For example, activity codes for various kinds of work would not be useful in a time allocation study in a retirement home. Data can be collected through observation that may be continuous, at fixed intervals (for instance, every 48 hours), or on a random basis. Continuous observation is extremely time-consuming and means that the number of people observed is limited. Spot observations help increase the number of observations but may inadvertently miss important activities. Another option for data collection is to ask people to keep daily time logs or diaries.

TEXTS   Many cultural anthropologists collect *textual material*, a category that includes written or oral stories, myths, plays, sayings, speeches, jokes, and transcriptions of people's everyday conversations. In the early twentieth century, Franz Boas collected thousands of pages of texts from American Indians of the Northwest Coast of Canada, including myths, songs, speeches, and accounts of how to perform rituals. These collections provide valuable records of cultures that have changed since the time of his fieldwork. Surviving tribal members have consulted them in order to recover forgotten aspects of their culture.

ARCHIVAL AND HISTORICAL SOURCES   Many cultural anthropologists who work in cultures with a written history gain important insights into the present from records of the past preserved in archives maintained in institutions such as libraries, churches, and museums. Ann Stoler pioneered the use of archival resources in understanding the present in her study of Dutch colonialism in Java (1985) (see Map 1.2, p. 14). Her archival research exposed details about colonial policies, the culture of the colonizers, and relationships with indigenous Javanese people.

National archives in London, Paris, and Amsterdam, to name just a few places, contain records of colonial contact and relations. Regional and local archives contain information about land ownership, agricultural production, religious practices, and political activities. Parish churches throughout Europe keep detailed family histories extending back hundreds of years.

MULTIPLE RESEARCH METHODS AND TEAM PROJECTS   Most cultural anthropologists use a mix of several different methods for their research because just one would not provide all the varieties of data necessary to understand a given topic. For example, consider what interviews with people in 100 households would provide in breadth of coverage, and then add what you could learn from life histories collected from a subset of five men and five women to provide depth, as well as what long-term participant observation with these people would contribute.

Anthropologists, with their in-depth insights about real people and real people's lives, are increasingly taking part in multidisciplinary research projects, especially projects with an applied focus. Such teamwork strengthens the research by

A multidisciplinary team comprising anthropologists, engineers, and agricultural experts from the United States and Sudan meet to discuss a resettlement project.

---

toponymy   the naming of places.

indigenous knowledge   local understanding of the environment, climate, plants, and animals.

Researching Inuit Place Names and Landscape Knowledge

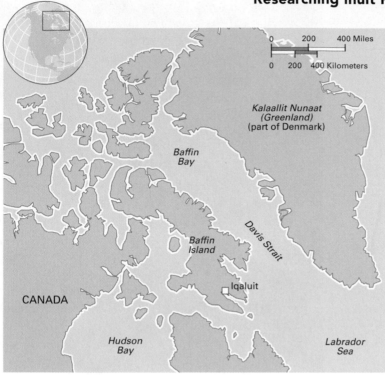

MAP 2.3 Baffin Island in Northeast Canada.
Baffin Island is the largest island in the Canadian Arctic and has a population of around 11,000. The Inuit name for the island is Qikiqtaaluk. It is part of the territory of Nunavut of which Iqaluit, a town of about 3,000 people, is the capital.

The South Baffin Island Place Name Project is dedicated to collecting and recording Inuit place names and landscape knowledge as a means to preserving climatically important information (Henshaw 2006). *Inuit* is a cluster name for many indigenous peoples who live in the Arctic region of Canada, Alaska, and Greenland. Before contact with Europeans, Inuit life was one of constant mobility. Now, most Inuit are settled in villages and towns. As a result, their detailed knowledge of migration routes, locations along these routes, and how to adapt to changing conditions when on the move are being lost.

Anthropologists and other researchers seek to work with Inuit people to document their traditional knowledge of places and routes. One project looks at **toponymy (to-PAH-nuh-mee)**, or the naming of places. Inuit toponymy is one aspect of a rich set of **indigenous knowledge,** or local understanding of the environment, climate, plants, and animals.

The South Baffin Island Place Names Project used several methods for collecting data. The first step was community-wide workshops, with 10 to 15 people gathered together in a community hall. The researchers laid out large maps, and the Inuit added place names to the map and explained their importance.

The second step was conducting one-on-one interviews with Inuit elders. These elders have lived in particular areas and can provide specialized knowledge about them in terms of their use (for shelter, for fishing and hunting, and for storage), routes to and from the site, and likely weather conditions.

The third step was participant observation. The anthropologists, with Inuit collaborators, went to many of the sites. They gained first-hand experience about travel conditions to and from the sites and conditions at the sites themselves. They made video recordings and took photographs.

The fourth step was analytical and archival. The researchers created a computer database, linking the ethnographic data to maps.

This research project has many uses. It will provide a data baseline, starting with elders' memories and narratives of important living sites and migration routes. It will show, over time, environmental changes that have occurred and how people are adapting to them. It will create an archive of indigenous knowledge that can be used by future generations of Inuit in protecting their cultural heritage and ways of making a living.

◆ **FOOD FOR THOUGHT**

• Choose an ordinary day in your week, create a map of where you go, and take notes about how key locations are named (such as your dorm room, dining hall, classrooms, and other locations). What names do you use for key sites, and what do the place names mean to you? How would you change your daily route depending on differences in the weather or season?

adding more perspectives and methods. For example, a team project uses mixed methods such as data from group interviews, one-on-one interviews, participant observation, and mapping to provide detailed information on Inuit place names and environmental knowledge (see Eye on the Environment).

RECORDING CULTURE

How does an anthropologist keep track of all the information collected in the field and record it for future analysis? As with everything else about fieldwork, things have changed since the

MAP 2.4   Spain.
The Kingdom of Spain is the largest of the three countries occupying the Iberian Peninsula. The geography is dominated by high plateaus and mountain ranges. Spain's population exceeds 40 million. Spain's administrative structure is complex, including autonomous communities, such as Andalucia and Catalonia, and provinces. The central government is granting more autonomy to some of the localities, including the Basque area.

The "autonomous community" of Asturias is located in the far north of Spain. It has extensive coastal beaches but the inland is mainly mountainous. The traditional economy was based in fishing and agriculture. Coal mining and steel production were important in the mid-twentieth century but have declined.

early times when a notebook and typewriter were the major recording tools. Taking detailed notes, nonetheless, is still a cultural anthropologist's trademark method of recording data.

FIELD NOTES   *Field notes* consist of daily logs, personal journals, descriptions of events, and notes about those notes. Ideally, researchers should write up their field notes each day. Otherwise, a backlog accumulates of daily "scratch notes," or rough jottings made on a small pad or note cards (Sanjek 1990). Trying to capture, in the fullest way possible, the events of even a single day is a monumental task and can result in dozens of pages of handwritten or typed field notes. Laptop computers now enable anthropologists to enter many of their daily observations directly into the computer.

TAPE RECORDINGS, PHOTOGRAPHS, AND VIDEOS
Tape recorders are a major aid to fieldwork. Their use may raise problems, however, such as research participants' suspicions about a machine that can capture their voices, and the ethical issue of protecting the identities of people whose voices are preserved on tape. María Cátedra reports on her use of tape recording during her research in the Asturias region of rural Spain (see Map 2.4):

> At first the existence of the "apparatus," as they called it, was part wonder and part suspect. Many had never seen one before and were fascinated to hear their own voice, but all were worried about what I would do with the tapes. . . . I tried to

solve the problem by explaining what I would do with the tapes: I would use them to record correctly what people told me, since my memory was not good enough and I could not take notes quickly enough. . . . One event helped people to accept my integrity in regard to the "apparatus." In the second *braña* [small settlement] I visited, people asked me to play back what the people of the first *braña* had told me, especially some songs sung by a group of men. At first I was going to do it, but then I instinctively refused because I did not have the first people's permission. . . . My stand was quickly known in the first *braña* and commented on with approval. (1992:21–22)

To be useful for analysis, tape recordings have to be transcribed (typed up), either partially or completely. Each hour of recorded talk takes between 5 and 8 hours to transcribe.

Like tape recordings, photographs or videos capture more detail than scratch notes. Any researcher who has watched people performing a ritual, taken scratch notes, and then tried to reconstruct the details of the ritual later on will know how much of the sequencing and related activity is lost to memory within just a few hours. Reviewing photographs or a video recording of the ritual provides a surprising amount of forgotten or missed material. The trade-off, however, is that if you are using a camera or video recorder, you cannot take notes at the same time.

DATA ANALYSIS

During the research process, an anthropologist collects a vast amount of data in many forms. How does he or she put the data into a meaningful form? In data analysis, as with data collection, two basic varieties of data exist: *qualitative* (prose-based description) and *quantitative* (numeric presentation).

ANALYZING QUALITATIVE DATA Qualitative data include descriptive field notes, narratives, myths and stories, songs and sagas, and more. Few guidelines exist for undertaking a qualitative analysis of qualitative data. One procedure is to search for themes or patterns. This approach involves exploring the data, or "playing" with the data, either "by hand" or with the use of a computer.

Many qualitative anthropologists use computers to help sort the data for *tropes* (key themes). Computer scanning offers the ability to search vast quantities of data more quickly and perhaps more accurately than with the human eye. The range of software available for such data management is expanding. The quality of the results, though, still depends on careful and complete inputting of the data, as well as an intelligent coding scheme that will tell the computer what it should be scanning for in the data.

The presentation of qualitative data relies on people's own words—their stories, explanations, and conversations. Lila Abu-Lughod followed this approach in conveying Egyptian Bedu (bed-oo) women's narratives in her book *Writing Women's Worlds* (1993). Abu-Lughod offers a light authorial framework that organizes the women's stories into thematic clusters such as marriage, production, and honor. Although she provides an introduction to the narratives, she offers no conclusion, thereby prompting readers to think for themselves about the meanings of the stories and what they say about Egyptian Bedu women's lives.

Some anthropologists question the value of such artistic, interpretive approaches because they lack scientific verifiability. Too much depends, they say, on the individual selection process of the anthropologist, and interpretation often depends on a small number of cases. Interpretive anthropologists respond that verifiability, in the scientific sense, is not their goal and, in fact, is not a worthwhile goal for cultural anthropology. Instead, they seek to provide a plausible interpretation or a fresh understanding of people's lives that offers detail and richness.

ANALYZING QUANTITATIVE DATA Analysis of quantitative, or numeric, data can proceed in several directions. Some of the more sophisticated methods require knowledge of statistics, and many require the use of a computer and a software package that can perform statistical computations. The author's research on low-income household budgets in Jamaica involved the use of computer analysis, first to divide the sample households into three income groups (lower, medium, and higher) and second to calculate percentages of expenditures in three categories of goods and groups of goods: food, housing, and transportation (see Figure 2.3). Because

Item	Urban				Rural			
	Group 1	Group 2	Group 3	Total	Group 1	Group 2	Group 3	Total
Number of Households	26	25	16	67	32	30	16	78
Food	60.5	51.6	50.1	54.7	74.1	62.3	55.7	65.8
Alcohol	0.2	0.4	1.5	0.6	0.5	1.1	1.0	0.8
Tobacco	0.8	0.9	0.9	0.9	1.1	1.7	1.2	1.4
Dry Goods	9.7	8.1	8.3	8.7	8.8	10.2	14.3	10.5
Housing	7.3	11.7	10.3	9.7	3.4	5.7	3.9	4.4
Fuel	5.4	6.0	5.0	5.6	3.7	3.9	4.1	3.9
Transportation	7.4	8.2	12.4	8.9	3.0	5.3	7.6	4.9
Health	0.3	0.6	0.7	0.5	1.5	1.4	1.7	1.5
Education	3.5	2.8	3.1	3.2	1.2	2.1	3.0	1.9
Entertainment	0.1	0.9	1.1	0.6	0.0	0.1	0.3	0.2
Other	5.2	8.3	6.9	6.8	2.1	6.0	6.9	4.6
Total*	100.4	99.5	100.3	100.2	99.4	99.8	99.7	99.9

*Totals may not add up to 100 due to rounding.

Source: From "Social Patterns of Food Expenditure Among Low-Income Jamaicans" by Barbara D. Miller in *Papers and Recommendations of the Workshop on Food and Nutrition Security in Jamaica in the 1980s and Beyond,* ed. by Kenneth A. Leslie and Lloyd B. Rankine, 1987.

FIGURE 2.3 Mean Weekly Expenditure Shares (Percentage) in 11 Categories by Urban and Rural Expenditure Groups, Jamaica, 1983–1984

the number of households was quite small (120), the analysis could have been done "by hand." But using the computer made the analysis proceed more quickly and more accurately.

REPRESENTING CULTURE Ethnography, a detailed description of a living culture based on personal observation and study, is the main way that cultural anthropologists present their findings about culture. The early ethnographers tended to treat a particular local group or village as a unit unto itself with clear boundaries. Since the 1980s, ethnographies have changed in several ways and now have the following characteristics:

- Ethnographies treat local cultures as connected with larger regional and global structures and forces.
- Ethnographies focus on one topic of interest and avoid a more holistic approach.
- Ethnographies describe Western, industrialized cultures as well as non-Western, non-industrialized cultures.

Urgent Issues in Cultural Anthropology Research

This section considers two urgent issues in cultural anthropology research: fieldwork ethics and safety during fieldwork.

ETHICS AND COLLABORATIVE RESEARCH

Anthropology was one of the first disciplines to devise and adopt a code of ethics. Two events in the 1950s and 1960s prompted cultural anthropologists to reconsider their role in research in relation to the sponsors of their research and to the people with whom they were studying. The first was *Project Camelot* of the 1950s; it was a plan of the U.S. government to influence political leadership in South America in order to strengthen U.S. interests (Horowitz 1967). The U.S. government employed several anthropologists to collect information on political leaders and events, without revealing their purpose.

The second major event was the Vietnam War (or the American War, as people in Vietnam refer to it). It brought to the forefront of anthropology questions about government interests in ethnographic information, the role of anthropologists during wartime, and the protection of the people with

whom anthropologists conduct research. Two bitterly opposed positions emerged within anthropology. On one side was the view that all Americans, as citizens, should support the U.S. military effort in Vietnam. People on this side said that any anthropologist who had information that could help subvert communism should provide it to the U.S. government. The other position stated that an anthropologist's responsibility is, first and always, to protect the people being studied, a responsibility that takes priority over politics. Anthropologists taking this position opposed the war and saw the people of South Vietnam as victims of Western imperialism. They uncovered cases in which some anthropologists submitted information about people's political affiliations to the U.S. government, with the result being military actions and death of the people exposed by the research.

This period was the most divisive in the history of U.S. anthropology. It led, in 1971, to the adoption by the American Anthropological Association (AAA) of a code of ethics. The AAA code of ethics states that an anthropologist's primary responsibility is to ensure the safety of the people participating in the research. A related principle is that cultural anthropology does not condone covert, or "undercover," research.

COLLABORATIVE RESEARCH A new direction in methods explicitly seeks to involve members of the study population in collaborative research—from data collection to analysis and presentation. **Collaborative research** is an approach to learning about culture that involves the anthropologist working with members of the study population as partners and teammates rather than as "subjects." This strategy, from the start, forces a reconsideration of how anthropologists refer to the people being studied, especially the long-standing term "informant." The term sounds hauntingly and negatively related to espionage or war and implies a passive role on handing over information to someone else. As noted earlier in this chapter, IRBs use the term "human subject," which cultural anthropologists reject for similar reasons. Cultural anthropologists favor the term *research participant*.

Luke Eric Lassiter is a pioneer in collaborative methods. In a recent project, Lassiter involved his undergraduate anthropology students in a collaboration with members of the African American community of Muncie, Indiana. This project resulted in a book with shared authorship among Lassiter, the students, and the community members (2004). The project collected information about African American life that is now housed in a library archive.

Cultural anthropologists are working to find better ways to share the benefits of research with the people and places they study. Research methods in cultural anthropology have come a long way from the armchair, to new strategies for nonhierarchical research. More progress lies ahead, however,

---

ethnography   a firsthand, detailed description of a living culture, based on personal observation.

collaborative research   an approach to learning about culture that involves anthropologists working with members of the study population as partners and participants rather than as "subjects."

The collaborative research team led by Luke Eric Lassiter includes Muncie community members (far left and far right) and students and faculty from Ball State University.

in democratizing anthropology and making everyone a "bare-foot anthropologist."

SAFETY IN THE FIELD

Fieldwork can involve serious physical and psychological risks to the researcher and to members of his or her family. The image of "the anthropologist as hero" has muffled, to a large degree, both the physical dangers and the psychological risks of fieldwork.

Dangers from the physical environment are often serious and can be fatal. In the 1980s, the slippery paths of the highland Philippines claimed the life of Michelle Zimbalist Rosaldo, a major figure in late twentieth-century cultural anthropology (review Figure 1.2, p. 12). Disease is a frequent problem. Many anthropologists have contracted infectious diseases that have chronic effects or that may be fatal.

Violence figures prominently in some, but not most, fieldwork experiences. During the five years that Philippe Bourgois lived in East Harlem, New York, he witnessed the following: a shooting outside his window, a bombing and machine-gunning of a numbers joint, a shoot-out and police car chase in front of the pizza parlor where he was eating, the aftermath of a fire-bombing of a heroin house, a dozen serious fights, and "almost daily exposure to broken-down human beings, some of them in fits of crack-induced paranoia, some suffering from delirium tremens, and others in unidentifiable pathological fits of screaming and shouting insults to all around them" (1995:32). He was rough-handled by the police several times because they did not believe that he was a professor doing research. He was once mugged for the sum of $8. Although his research placed him in danger, it also enabled him to gain an understanding, from the inside, of everyday violence in the lives of desperately poor and addicted people.

Likewise, some anthropological research involves danger from political violence or even war. A new specialty, *war zone anthropology,* or research conducted within zones of violent conflict, can provide important insights into topics such as the militarization of civilian lives, civilian protection, the cultural dynamics of military personnel, and postconflict reconstruction (Hoffman and Lubkemann 2005). This kind of research requires skills and judgment that anthropology classes or books on research methods do not typically address (Nordstrom 1997, Kovats-Bernat 2002). Previous experience in conflict zones as a worker in international aid organizations or the military is helpful.

What about fieldwork danger in supposedly normal situations? After more than 20 years of fieldwork in the Kalahari desert, southern Africa, Nancy Howell (1990) suddenly had to confront the issue of danger in the field when one of her teenage sons was killed and another injured in a truck accident in Botswana, southern Africa, while with their father, Richard Lee, who was doing fieldwork there at the time. In the months following the accident, she heard from many anthropologist friends who shared stories about other fieldwork accidents.

Howell contacted the American Anthropological Association (AAA) to see what advice it provides about fieldwork safety. The answer, she learned, was "not much." The AAA responded with financial support for her to undertake a detailed inquiry into fieldwork hazards in anthropology. Howell drew a sample of 311 anthropologists listed as employed in the AAA's *Guide to Departments.* She sent them a questionnaire asking for information on gender, age, work status, health status, and work habits in the field; she also asked for information on health problems and other hazards they had experienced. She received 236 completed questionnaires, a high response rate indicating strong interest in the study.

In her analysis, she found regional variation in risk and danger. The highest rates were in Africa, followed by India, the Asia/Pacific region, and Latin America. Howell offers recommendations about how anthropologists can prepare themselves more effectively for preventing and dealing with fieldwork risks. They include increasing risk awareness, training in basic medical care, and learning about fieldwork safety in anthropology classes.

Research methods in cultural anthropology have come a long way from the time of the armchair anthropologists. Topics have changed, as have techniques of data gathering and data analysis. New concerns about ethical research and responsibility and fieldworkers' safety continue to reshape research practices.

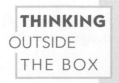

THINKING OUTSIDE THE BOX

Do you think that the AAA Code of Ethics places enough emphasis on protecting research participants from harm? To see the entire AAA Code of Ethics, go to http://www.aaanet.org.

2

the BIG questions REVISITED

◆ How do cultural anthropologists conduct research about culture?

Cultural anthropologists conduct research by doing fieldwork and using participant observation. In the nineteenth century, early cultural anthropologists did armchair anthropology, meaning that they learned about other cultures by reading reports written by explorers and other untrained observers. The next stage was verandah anthropology, in which an anthropologist went to the field but did not live with the people. Instead, the anthropologist would interview a few members of the study population where he (there were no women cultural anthropologists at this time) lived, typically on his verandah.

Fieldwork and participant observation became the cornerstones of cultural anthropology research only after Malinowski's innovations in the Trobriand Islands during World War I. His approach emphasized the value of living for an extended period in the field, participating in the daily activities of the people, and learning the local language. These features are the hallmarks of research in cultural anthropology today.

New techniques continue to develop in response to changing times. One of the most important is multisited research, in which the anthropologist studies a topic at more than one location.

◆ What does fieldwork involve?

Fieldwork in cultural anthropology involves several stages. The first is to choose a research topic. A good topic is timely, important, and feasible. Ideas for topics can come from a literature review, restudies, current events and pressing issues, and even sheer luck. Once in the field, the first steps include site selection, gaining rapport, and dealing with culture shock. Microcultures affect how anthropologists gain rapport and shape their access to particular cultural domains. Participating appropriately in the culture involves learning local forms of gift-giving and other types of exchange to express gratitude for people's hospitality, time, and trust.

Specific research techniques vary between being more deductive or more inductive and accordingly will emphasize gathering quantitative or qualitative data. Cultural materialists tend to focus on quantitative data, whereas interpretivists gather qualitative data. When in the field, anthropologists take daily notes, often by hand but now also using computers. Several other methods of documenting culture include photography, audio recording, and video recording.

Anthropologists' theoretical orientation, research goals, and the types of data collected affect their approach to data analysis and presentation. Quantitative data may involve statistical analysis and presentation in graphs or tables. The presentation of qualitative data is more likely to be descriptive.

◆ What are some urgent issues in cultural anthropology research today?

Questions of ethics have been paramount to anthropologists since the 1950s. In 1971, U.S. anthropologists adopted a set of ethical guidelines for research to address their concern about what role, if any, anthropologists should play in research that might harm the people being studied. The AAA code of ethics states that an anthropologist's primary responsibility is to maintain the safety of the people involved. Further, cultural anthropologists should never engage in covert research and should always explain their purpose to the people in the study and preserve the anonymity of the location and of individuals.

Collaborative research is a recent development that responds to ethical concerns by pursuing research that involves the participants as partners rather than as subjects.

Safety during fieldwork is another important issue. Danger to anthropologists can come from physical sources such as infectious diseases and from social sources such as political violence. A survey of anthropologists in the 1980s produced recommendations about increasing safety during fieldwork.

KEY CONCEPTS

collaborative research, p. 44

culture shock, p. 37

deductive approach
(to research), p. 37

emic, p. 38

ethnography, p. 44

etic, p. 38

fieldwork, p. 30

inductive approach
(to research), p. 38

indigenous
knowledge, p. 41

informed consent, p. 34

interview, p. 38

kula, p. 32

multisited research, p. 31

participant
observation, p. 30

qualitative data, p. 38

quantitative data, p. 38

questionnaire, p. 39

rapport, p. 34

toponymy, p. 41

SUGGESTED READINGS

Michael V. Angrosino. *Projects in Ethnographic Research*. Long Grove, IL: Waveland Press, 2005. This brief manual provides students with ideas about what conducting research in anthropology is like. It discusses the fundamental stages of three projects, with insights into how students can conduct their own research.

H. Russell Bernard. *Research Methods in Cultural Anthropology: Qualitative and Quantitative Approaches*, 3rd ed. Newbury Park, CA: Sage Publications, 2002. This is a sourcebook of anthropological research methods providing information about how to design a research project, methods of data collection, and data analysis and presentation.

Kathleen M. DeWalt and Billie R. DeWalt. *Participant Observation: A Guide for Fieldworkers*. New York: AltaMira Press, 2002. This book is a comprehensive guide to doing participant observation.

Alexander Ervin. *Applied Anthropology: Tools and Perspectives for Contemporary Practice*. Boston: Allyn and Bacon, 2005. Chapters discuss links between anthropology and policy, the history of applied anthropology, ethics, and specialized methods.

Carolyn Fluehr-Lobban. *Ethics and the Profession of Anthropology: A Dialogue for Ethically Conscious Practice*, 2nd ed. Philadelphia: University of Pennsylvania Press, 2003. The chapters in this volume address topics such as covert research, indigenous people's cultural rights, informed consent, and ethics in researching culture in cyberspace.

Peggy Golde, ed. *Women in the Field: Anthropological Experiences*. 2nd ed. Berkeley: University of California Press, 1986. Chapters in this classic collection discuss Margaret Mead's fieldwork in the Pacific, Laura Nader's fieldwork in Mexico and Lebanon, Ernestine Friedl's fieldwork in Greece, and Jean Briggs's fieldwork among the Inuit of the Canadian Arctic.

Joy Hendry. *An Anthropologist in Japan: Glimpses of Life in the Field*. London: Routledge, 1999. This book describes the author's original research design, how her focus changed, and how she reached unanticipated conclusions.

Choong Soon Kim. *One Anthropologist, Two Worlds: Three Decades of Reflexive Fieldwork in North America and Asia*. Knoxville: University of Tennessee Press, 2002. The author reflects on his fieldwork, conducted over 30 years, on Japanese industry in the American South and on Korean families displaced by the Korean war and partition.

Luke Eric Lassiter. *The Chicago Guide to Collaborative Ethnography*. Chicago: University of Chicago Press, 2005. This handbook for doing collaborative anthropology includes historical and theoretical perspectives on collaborative anthropology, exposing its roots in feminist, humanist, and critical anthropology.

Carolyn Nordstrom and Antonius C. G. M. Robben, eds. *Fieldwork under Fire: Contemporary Studies of Violence and Survival*. Berkeley: University of California Press, 1995. The chapters of this book discuss fieldwork experiences in Palestine, China, Sri Lanka, the United States, Croatia, Guatemala, and Ireland.

Tom Ric with Mette Louise Berg, eds. *Future Fields*, special issue of the online journal *Anthropology Matters*, Vol. 6, No. 2, 2004. This issue includes 11 articles that address a range of methodological issues cultural anthropologists face today, including emotional, financial, and ethical challenges as well as how to cope in situations of physical danger. The journal is accessible at no charge at http://www.anthropologymatters.com.

3   ECONOMIC SYSTEMS

4   REPRODUCTION AND HUMAN DEVELOPMENT

5   DISEASE, ILLNESS, AND HEALING

PART II

CULTURAL FOUNDATIONS

ANTHROPOLOGY works

Lara Tabac, medical anthropologist, works at the New York City Department of Health and Mental Hygiene (DOHMH), along with another cultural anthropologist and 6000 other employees. Her responsibilities with the department's Epidemiology Services require her to collect qualitative information from New Yorkers about their sexual practices and health.

Tabac describes her job as an "unusual joint venture of words and numbers." She explains that the department is traditionally highly quantitative; it uses statistics to determine health-action agendas. The numbers "tell how many, but they do not tell why. In order to be responsive to the health needs of New Yorkers, the DOHMH needs to know why. This is where I come in."

Anthropological training reinforced and shaped Tabac's natural tendency to observe and ask questions. She puts her skills and interests to work through direct interaction with people: "I do a lot of listening on a wide range of topics, and I need only a MetroCard to reach far-flung and eclectic neighborhoods peopled with individuals who share their health dilemmas and life struggles with me, as well as their suggestions for improving the services and programs that will ultimately affect them."

Tabac collects data about the sexual behavior of men who have sex with men. She wants to learn about when individuals in this group use condoms and why they do or do not do so. To gather qualitative information, Tabac has spent many hours conducting interviews. She says, "As a technique, interviewing is crucial for gaining a deep understanding of sensitive issues. . . . People tend to be more honest when they don't feel as though they are going to be judged by their peers." Tabac comments that every interview for this project has been valuable.

Tabac finds her position with the DOHMH challenging and socially relevant. She took the job because she wanted to help improve people's lives. She has not been disappointed.

*Dharavi is a low-income neighborhood of Mumbai (formerly
Bombay), India. It is perhaps the largest "slum" in Asia. Most
residents are poor and, if employed, work in low-paying and
insecure jobs. They also face an inadequate water supply,
lack of sanitation facilities, and constant threat of demolition
and displacement due to urban development. Dharavi has
been depicted in many Indian films, most recently the award
winning movie, Slumdog Millionaire.*

ECONOMIC SYSTEMS

3

the BIG questions

◆ What are the five major modes
of livelihood and their
characteristics?

◆ How are modes of livelihood
related to consumption
and exchange?

◆ How are livelihood, consumption,
and exchange changing in
contemporary times?

OUTLINE

Modes of Livelihood

Everyday Anthropology:
The Importance of Dogs

Critical Thinking: Was the
Invention of Agriculture a
Terrible Mistake?

**Modes of Consumption and
Exchange**

Lessons Applied: Assessing
the Social Impact of Indian
Casinos in California

**Globalization and Changing
Economies**

Culturama: The
Kwakwaka'wakw of Canada

Foraging	Horticulture	Pastoralism	Agriculture	Industrialism/Informatics
Reason for Production Production for use				**Reason for Production** Production for profit
Division of Labor Family-based Overlapping gender roles				**Division of Labor** Class-based High degree of occupational specialization
Property Relations Egalitarian and collective				**Property Relations** Stratified and private
Resource Use Extensive and temporary				**Resource Use** Intensive and expanding
Sustainability High degree				**Sustainability** Low degree

FIGURE 3.1 Modes of Livelihood

During the many thousands of years of human prehistory, people made their living by collecting food and other necessities from nature. All group members had equal access to life-sustaining resources. Most people throughout the world now live in economies much different from those of the past.

Economic anthropology is the subfield of cultural anthropology that cross-culturally focuses on economic systems. The term *economic system* comprises three areas: *livelihood,* or making goods or money; *consumption,* or using up goods or money; and *exchange,* or transferring goods or money between people or institutions.

This chapter first discusses the subject of production and introduces the concept of **mode of livelihood**: the dominant pattern in a culture of making a living in a culture. Ethnographic examples illustrate each of the five major modes of livelihood.

In addition, the section provides cross-cultural examples of the other two components of economic systems: **mode of consumption**, or the dominant pattern, in a culture, of using

up goods and services; and **mode of exchange**, or the dominant pattern, in a culture, of transferring goods, services, and other items between and among people and groups. The chapter's last section presents examples of contemporary change in livelihood, consumption, and exchange.

◆◆◆
Modes of Livelihood

Anthropologists define five major modes of livelihood. In this section, the modes of livelihood are discussed in order of their historical appearance in the human record (see Figure 3.1). This continuum does not imply that a particular mode of livelihood evolves into the one following it. For example, foragers do not necessarily transform into horticulturalists, and so on. Nor does the model imply a judgment about the sophistication or superiority of more recent modes of livelihood. For example, the oldest system involves complex and detailed knowledge about the environment that contemporary city dwellers would find difficult to learn quickly enough to ensure their survival.

While reading this section, bear in mind that most anthropologists are uneasy about typologies because they often do not reflect the complexity of life in any particular context. The purpose of the categories discussed is to help you organize the ethnographic information presented in this book.

FORAGING

Foraging is a mode of livelihood based on resources that are available in nature through gathering, fishing, hunting, or scavenging. The oldest way of making a living, foraging is a strategy that humans share with our nonhuman primate relatives. Although foraging has supported humanity since our beginnings, it is in danger of extinction. Only around

---

mode of livelihood   the dominant pattern, in a culture, of making a living.

mode of consumption   the dominant pattern, in a culture, of using things up or spending resources in order to satisfy demands.

mode of exchange   the dominant pattern, in a culture, of transferring goods, services, and other items between and among people and groups.

foraging   obtaining food available in nature through gathering, fishing, hunting, or scavenging.

extensive strategy   a form of livelihood involving the temporary use of large areas of land and a high degree of spatial mobility.

	Temperate-Region Foragers	Circumpolar-Region Foragers
Diet	Wide variety of nuts, tubers, fruits, small animals, and occasional large game	Large marine and terrestrial animals
Gender division of labor in food procurement	Men and women forage; men hunt large game	Men hunt and fish
Shelter	Casual construction, nonpermanent, little maintenance	Time-intensive construction and maintenance, some permanent

FIGURE 3.2 Temperate and Circumpolar Foraging Systems Compared

250,000 people worldwide provide for their livelihood predominantly from foraging now. Most contemporary foragers live in what are considered marginal areas, such as deserts, tropical rainforests, and the circumpolar region. These areas, however, often contain material resources, such as oil, diamonds, and gold, as well as other attractions including beautiful natural areas such as wetlands and rare animals such as mountain gorillas. The lifestyle of well-off outsiders places heavy demand on these natural resources and other attributes which leads to the conversion of foraging land to mines, plantations, or tourist destinations, in turn leading to the displacement of foragers from their homeland. Thus, the basis of the survival of many foragers is threatened by what is called the *resource curse.*

Depending on the environmental context, traditional foragers' food sources include nuts, berries and other fruits, and surface-growing vegetables such as melons, roots, honey, insects, and eggs. They trap and hunt a wide variety of birds, fish, and animals. Successful foraging requires sophisticated knowledge of the natural environment and the seasonal changes in it. Most critical is knowledge about the location of water sources and of various foods, how to follow animal tracks, how to judge the weather, and how to avoid predators. This unwritten knowledge is passed down over the generations (review Eye on the Environment, Chapter 2, p. 41).

Foragers rely on many kinds of tools for gathering, transporting, and processing wild foods. Tools include digging sticks for removing roots from the ground and for penetrating the holes dug by animals in order to get the animals out, bows and arrows, spears, nets, and knives. Baskets are important for carrying food. Foragers use stones to mash, grind, and pound the raw materials into edible food. Animal meat and fish can be dried in the sun or over fire. Fire is used for cooking either by boiling or by roasting. These activities involve few nonrenewable fuel sources beyond wood or other combustible substances for cooking. Foraging is an **extensive strategy**, a mode of livelihood involving the temporary use of large areas of land and a high degree of spatial mobility.

Cultural anthropologists distinguish two major varieties of foraging that are related to different environmental contexts: *temperate-climate foraging* and *circumpolar foraging* (see Figure 3.2). The Ju/'hoansi people of southern Africa are an

A Ju/'hoansi traditional shelter.

everyday ANTHROPOLOGY

The Importance of Dogs

Dogs were the first domesticated animal, with competing evidence of their domestication in Africa, China, and Eurasia. In spite of dogs' long-standing importance to humans around the world, few cultural anthropologists have focused attention on humans and their dogs. One of the rare ethnographies to do so provides insights about the economic, social, and psychological importance of dogs among a group of circumpolar foragers.

Fewer than 100 Hare Indians constitute the community of Colville Lake in Canada's Northwest Territories (Savishinsky 1974). They live by hunting, trapping, and fishing in one of the harshest environments in the world. Joel Savishinsky went to Colville Lake to study stress, tension, and anxiety among the Hare and how people cope with environmental stress. Environmental stress factors include extremely cold temperatures, long and severe winters, extended periods of isolation, hazardous travel conditions along with the constant need for mobility during the harshest periods of the year, and sometimes food scarcity. Social and psychological stress factors also exist, including contact with White fur traders and missionaries.

Savishinsky discovered the importance of dogs to the Hare people early in his research:

> Later in the year when I obtained my own dogteam, I enjoyed much greater freedom of movement, and was able to camp with many people whom I had previously not been able to keep up with. Altogether I travelled close to 600 miles by dogsled between mid-October and early June. This constant contact with dogs, and the necessity of learning how to drive, train and handle them, led to my recognition of the social and psychological, as well as the ecological, significance of these animals in the lives of the people. (1974:xx)

Among the 14 households in the Hare Indian community is a total of 224 dogs. Some households have as many as four teams, with an average of six dogs per team.

In addition to being economically useful, dogs play a significant role in people's emotional lives. They are a frequent topic of conversation:

> Members of the community constantly compare and comment on the care, condition, and growth of one another's animals, noting special qualities of size, strength, color, speed, and alertness. (1974:169)

Emotional displays are uncommon among Hare people, but they are significant between people and their dogs:

> The affectionate and concerned treatment of young animals is participated in by people of all ages, and the nature of the relationship bears a striking resemblance to the way in which people treat young children. Pups and infants are, in essence, the only recipients of unreserved positive affect in the band's social life. . . (1974:169–170)

---

example of temperate-climate foragers. As studied in the early 1960s before their lifestyle was dramatically changed by outside forces, they would move several times during a year, depending on the seasonal availability of water sources (review Culturama, Chapter 1, p. 21). Each cluster of families would regularly return to "their" territory, reconstructing or completely rebuilding their shelters with sticks for frames and leaf or thatch coverings. Shelters are sometimes attached to two or three small trees or bushes for support. In this traditional lifestyle, the amount of time involved in gathering and processing food and in constructing shelters is modest.

In contrast to foragers of temperate climates, those living in the circumpolar regions of North America, Europe, and Asia devote more time and energy to obtaining food and providing shelter. The specialized technology of circumpolar peoples includes spears, nets, and knives, as well as sleds and the use of domesticated animals to pull them. Dogs or other animals used to pull sleds are an important aspect of circumpolar peoples' technology and social identity (see Everyday Anthropology). Considerable amounts of labor are needed to construct and maintain igloos or log houses. Protective clothing, including coats, gloves, and boots, is another feature of circumpolar foraging that is time intensive in terms of construction and maintenance.

DIVISION OF LABOR Among foraging peoples, the *division of labor,* or occupational specialization (assigning particular tasks to particular individuals), is based on gender and age. Among temperate foraging cultures, a minimal gender-based division of labor exists. Temperate foragers get most of their everyday food by gathering roots, berries, larvae, small birds and animals, and fish, and both men and women collect these basic foods. Hunting large animals, however, tends to involve only men, who go off together in small groups on long-range expeditions. Large game provides a small and irregular part of the diets of temperate-climate foragers. In circumpolar groups, a significant part of people's diet comes

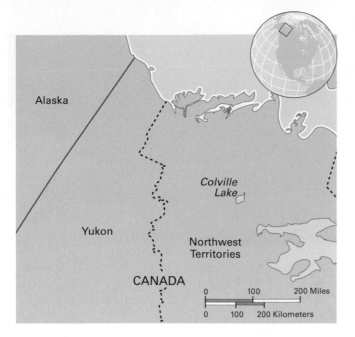

MAP 3.1 **Hare Region near Colville Lake in Northwest Canada.**
Early European colonialists named the local people Hare because of their reliance on snowshoe hares for food and clothing. The Hare people became involved in the wage-labor economy and were afflicted by alcoholism, tuberculosis, and other diseases. Efforts to reestablish claims to ancestral lands began in the 1960s.

Hare Indian children use their family's sled to haul drinking water to their village.

▶ *What tasks are children responsible for in a microculture that you know?*

◆ **FOOD FOR THOUGHT**

• Think of a culture (perhaps yours) in which dogs or some other domesticated animals are a focus of intense human interest. How do people and the animals in question interact? Are there age and gender differences in human relationships with domesticated animals?

---

from large animals such as seals, whales, and bears, as well as smaller quarry such as fish. Men do most of the hunting and fishing. Among circumpolar foragers, therefore, the division of labor is strongly gender divided.

Age is a basis for task allocation in all modes of livelihood, including foraging. Young boys and girls help collect food. Elderly people tend to stay at the camp area, where they are responsible for caring for young children.

PROPERTY RELATIONS The concept of *private property*, in the sense of owning something that can be sold to someone else, does not exist in foraging societies. Instead, the term **use rights** is more appropriate. It means that a person or group has socially recognized priority in access to particular resources, such as gathering areas, hunting and fishing areas, and water holes. This access is willingly shared with others by permission. Among the Ju/'hoansi, family groups control access to particular water holes and the territory surrounding them (Lee 1979:58–60). Visiting groups are welcome and will

be given food and water. In turn, the host group, at another time, will visit other camps and be offered hospitality there.

FORAGING AS A SUSTAINABLE SYSTEM When untouched by outside influences and with abundant land available, foraging systems are *sustainable*, which means that crucial resources are regenerated over time, in balance with the demand that the population makes on them. North Sentinel Island, one island in the Andaman Islands, provides a clear case because its inhabitants have long lived in a "closed" system. So far, the few hundred indigenous people live in almost complete isolation from the rest of the world, other than the occasional helicopter flying overhead and the occasional attempt by outsiders to land on their territory.

---

use rights a system of property relations in which a person or group has socially recognized priority in access to particular resources, such as gathering, hunting, and fishing areas and water holes.

One reason for the sustainability of foraging is that foragers' needs are modest. Anthropologists have typified the foraging lifestyle as the *original affluent society* because needs are satisfied with minimal labor efforts. The term *original affluent society* is a metaphoric reminder to people living in contemporary consumer cultures that foraging is not a miserable, inadequate way to make a living, contrary to most ethnocentric thinking.

Because foragers' needs for goods are limited, minimal labor efforts are required to satisfy them. Foragers typically work fewer hours a week than the average employed North American. In traditional (undisturbed) foraging societies, people spend as few as five hours a week collecting food and making and repairing tools. They have much time for storytelling, playing games, and resting. Foragers also traditionally enjoyed good health. During the early 1960s, the age structure and health status of the Ju/'hoansi compared well with the age structure and health status of people in the United States around 1900 (Lee 1979:47–48). The Ju/'hoansi had few infectious diseases and few degenerative diseases (health problems related to aging, such as arthritis).

HORTICULTURE

Horticulture is a mode of livelihood based on cultivating domesticated plants in gardens with the use of hand tools. Garden crops are often supplemented by foraging and by trading with pastoralists for animal products. Horticulture is still practiced by many thousands of people throughout the world. Prominent horticultural regions are found in sub-Saharan Africa, South Asia, Southeast Asia and the Pacific, Central America, South America, and the Caribbean islands. Major horticultural crops include yams, corn, beans, grains such as millet and sorghum, and several types of roots, all of which are rich in protein, minerals, and vitamins.

Horticulture involves the use of handheld tools, such as digging sticks, hoes, and carrying baskets. Rain is the sole source of moisture. Horticulture requires rotation of garden plots in order for them to regenerate. Thus, another term for horticulture is *shifting cultivation*. Average plot sizes are less than 1 acre, and 2.5 acres can support a family of five to eight for a year. Yields can support semipermanent villages of 200 to 250 people. Overall population density per square mile is low because horticulture, like foraging, is an extensive strategy. Horticulture is more labor intensive than foraging because of the energy required for plot preparation and food processing. Anthropologists distinguish five phases in the horticultural cycle (see Figure 3.3).

DIVISION OF LABOR Gender and age are the key factors structuring the division of labor in horticultural communities,

Cassava, also called manioc, is a root crop grown extensively in western Africa. This man displays a cassava plant in Niger. Cassava and millet, a grain, are the staple foods of many West Africans.

▶ *Do research to find some West African recipes that include cassava or millet.*

with men's and women's work roles often being clearly differentiated. Typically, men clear the garden area while both men and women plant and tend the staple food crops. This pattern exists in New Guinea, much of Southeast Asia, and parts of West and East Africa. Food processing involves women often working in small groups, whereas men more typically form small groups for hunting and fishing for supplementary food. Among many horticultural groups, women grow the staple food crops while men grow the "prestige foods" used in ritual feasts. In such contexts, men have higher public status than women.

Clearing: A section of the forest is cleared, partially or completely, by cutting down trees and brush and then setting the area on fire to burn off other growth. The fire creates a layer of ash that is rich fertilizer. The term *slash and burn cultivation* refers to this stage.

Planting: People use digging sticks to loosen the soil. They place seeds through the broadcasting method (scattering the seeds by hand) or place slips of plants by hand into the loose soil.

Weeding: Horticulture involves little weeding because the ash cover and shady growing conditions keep weed growth down.

Harvesting: This phase requires substantial labor to cut or dig crops and carry them to the residential area.

Fallowing: Depending on the soil and the crop grown, the land must be left unused for a specified number of years so that it regains its fertility.

FIGURE 3.3 Five Stages in Horticulture

---

horticulture a mode of livelihood based on growing domesticated crops in gardens, using simple hand tools.

Two unusual horticultural cases involve extremes in terms of gender roles and status. The first is the Iroquois of central New York State prior to contact with Whites (Brown 1975) (see Map 3.2). Iroquois women cultivated maize, the most important food crop, and they controlled its distribution. This control meant that they were able to decide whether the men would go to war, because a war effort depended on the supply of maize to support it. A contrasting example is that of the Yanomami of the Venezuelan Amazon (see Map 3.3) (Chagnon 1992). Yanomami men clear the fields and tend and harvest the crops. They also do much of the cooking for ritual feasts. Yanomami women, though, are not idle. They play an important role in providing the staple food that comes from manioc, a starchy root crop that requires substantial processing work: it has to be soaked for a long time to remove toxins and then scraped into a mealy consistency. Among the Yanomami, however, men are the dominant decision makers and have more social power than Yanomami women do.

Although anthropologists cannot explain the origins of the different divisions of labor in horticulture, they do know that the differences are related to men's and women's status (Sanday 1973). Analysis of many horticultural societies shows that women's contribution to food production is a necessary, but not sufficient, basis for women's high status. In other words, if women do not contribute to producing food, their status will be low. If they do contribute, their status may or may not be high. The critical factor appears to be control over the distribution of

MAP 3.3 Yanomami Region in Brazil and Venezuela. The Yanomami region is supposedly protected from outsiders. But miners, ranchers, loggers, and other commercial developers have encroached on the reserve, extracting natural resources and sexually exploiting women and children.

what is produced, especially public distribution beyond the family. Slavery is a clear example of how a major role in production does not bring high status because slaves have no control over the product and its distribution.

Children do more productive work in horticultural societies than in any other mode of livelihood (Whiting and Whiting 1975). *The Six Cultures Study* is a research project that examined children's behavior in horticultural, farming, and industrial settings. Children among a horticultural group, the Gusii (goo-see-eye) of western Kenya, performed the most tasks at the youngest ages. Gusii boys and girls care for siblings, collect fuel, and carry water. Among the Gusii and in other horticultural societies, children do so many tasks because adults, especially women, are busy working in the fields and markets. Children's work in the domestic domain fulfills what are adult roles in other economic systems.

PROPERTY RELATIONS Private property, as something that an individual can own and sell, is not characteristic of horticultural societies. Use rights are typically important, although they are more clearly defined and formalized than among foragers. By clearing and planting an area of land, a family puts a claim on it and its crops. The production of surplus goods allows the possibility of social inequality in access to goods and resources. Rules about sharing within the larger group decline in importance as some people gain higher status.

HORTICULTURE AS A SUSTAINABLE SYSTEM Fallowing is crucial in maintaining the viability of horticulture. Fallowing allows a plot to recover lost nutrients and improves soil quality by permitting the growth of weeds, whose root systems keep the soil loose. The benefits of a well-managed

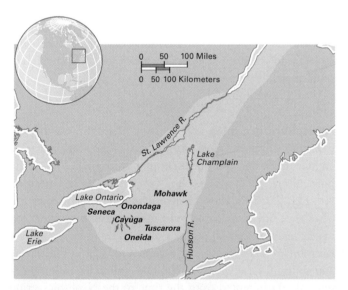

MAP 3.2 Precolonial Iroquois Region. At the time of the arrival of the European colonialists, the six nations of the Iroquois extended over a wide area. The Mohawk stood guard over the eastern door of the confederacy's symbolic longhouse, and the Seneca guarded the western door. The six nations worked out a peace treaty among them and established a democracy. A great orator named Hiawatha promoted the plan throughout the tribes, and a Mohawk woman was the first to approve it.

system of shifting cultivation are clear, as are the two major constraints involved: the time required for fallowing and the need for access to large amounts of land so that some land is in use while other land lies fallow. Using a given plot for too many seasons or reducing fallowing time quickly results in the depletion of soil nutrients, decreased crop production, and soil erosion.

PASTORALISM

Pastoralism is a mode of livelihood based on domesticated animal herds and the use of their products, such as meat and milk, for 50 percent or more of the diet. Pastoralism has long existed in the Middle East, Africa, Europe, and Central Asia, especially where rainfall is limited and unpredictable. In the Western Hemisphere, the only indigenous pastoralist system in existence before the arrival of the Spanish in the fifteenth century was in the Andean region of the New World; it was based on domesticated llamas (Barfield 2001). Sheep, goats, horses, and cattle became prominent after the Spanish conquest. Some Indian tribal groups in the southwestern United States still rely on herding animals.

Worldwide, the six major species of herd animals are sheep, goats, cattle, horses, donkeys, and camels. Three others have more restricted distribution: yaks at high altitudes in Asia, reindeer in northern sub-Arctic regions, and llamas in highland South America. Many pastoralists keep dogs for protection and for help with herding.

In terms of food, pastoralism provides primarily milk and milk products, with occasional slaughtering of animals for meat. Thus, pastoralists typically form trade links with foragers, horticulturalists, or farmers in order to obtain food and other goods that they cannot produce themselves. Prominent trade items are food grains and manufactured items, such as cooking pots, for which pastoralists offer milk, animals, hides, and other animal products.

Like foraging and horticulture, pastoralism is an extensive strategy. A common problem for all pastoralists is the continued need for fresh pasture and water for their animals. Herds must move, or else the grazing area will become depleted.

DIVISION OF LABOR Families and clusters of related families are the basic production unit. Gender and age are,

again, key factors in the allocation of work. In many pastoralist cultures, gender roles are clearly divided. Men are in charge of herding—moving the animals from place to place. Women are responsible for processing the herd's products, especially the milk. A cultural emphasis on masculinity characterizes many herding populations. For example, reindeer herding among the Saami of northern Scandanavia is closely connected to male identity to the extent that the definition of being a man is to be a reindeer herder (see Culturama, Chapter 9, p. 205). In contrast, women are the herders among the Navajo of the American Southwest. Navajo men's major work role is crafting silver jewelry.

PROPERTY RELATIONS The most important forms of property among pastoralists are, by far, animals, followed by housing (such as tents or yurts) and domestic goods (rugs and cooking ware). Depending on the group, ownership of animals is inherited, most commonly through males, less frequently through females, as among the Navajo. A concept of private property exists for animals, which the family head may trade for other goods. A family's housing materials are also its own. Use rights, however, regulate pasture land and migratory routes, and these rights tend to be informally regulated through an oral tradition.

PASTORALISM AS A SUSTAINABLE SYSTEM Pastoralists have developed sustainable cultures in extremely varied environments, from the relative lushness of Iran to the more depleted situation of Mongolia. Pastoralism is a highly successful and sustainable economic system that functions in coexistence with other economic systems. As with foraging and horticulture, however, when outside forces squeeze the space available for migration, overexploitation of the environment soon results.

AGRICULTURE

Agriculture is a mode of livelihood that involves growing crops on permanent plots with the use of plowing, irrigation, and fertilizer; it is also called *farming*. In contrast to foraging, horticulture, and pastoralism, agriculture is an **intensive strategy**. Intensification involves the use of techniques that allow the same plot of land to be used repeatedly without losing its fertility. Crucial inputs include substantial amounts of labor for weeding, the use of natural and chemical fertilizers, and control of the water supply. The earliest agricultural systems are documented from the time of the Neolithic period, beginning around 12,000 years ago in the Middle East. Agricultural systems now exist worldwide, on all continents except Antarctica.

Agriculture relies on the use of domesticated animals for plowing, transportation, and organic fertilizer in the form of manure or composted materials. It is highly dependent on artificial water sources, such as irrigation channels or terracing the land. Like the modes of livelihood already discussed,

---

pastoralism a mode of livelihood based on keeping domesticated animals and using their products, such as meat and milk, for most of the diet.

agriculture a mode of livelihood that involves growing crops with the use of plowing, irrigation, and fertilizer.

intensive strategy a form of livelihood that involves continuous use of the same land and resources.

family farming a form of agriculture in which farmers produce mainly to support themselves and also produce goods for sale in the market system.

FIGURE 3.4 Three Hypotheses to Explain Male Dominance in the Gender Division of Labor in Family Farming

agriculture involves complex knowledge about the environment, plants, and animals, including knowledge of soil types, precipitation patterns, plant varieties, and pest management. Long-standing agricultural traditions are now being increasingly displaced by methods introduced from the outside, so the world's stock of indigenous knowledge about agriculture is declining rapidly. In many cases, it has become completely lost, along with the cultures and languages associated with it.

Two types of agriculture are discussed next: family farming and industrial agriculture.

FAMILY FARMING **Family farming** (formerly termed *peasant agriculture*) is a form of agriculture in which production is geared to support the family and to produce goods for sale. Today, more than one billion people, or about one-sixth of the world's population, make their living from family farming. Found throughout the world, family farming is more common in developing countries than in more industrialized countries. Family farmers exhibit much cross-cultural variety. They may be full-time or part-time farmers, more or less closely linked to urban markets, and poor and indebted or wealthy and powerful. Major activities in family farming include plowing, planting seeds and cuttings, weeding, caring for irrigation systems and terracing, harvesting crops, and processing and storing crops.

DIVISION OF LABOR The family is the basic labor unit of production in agricultural societies, and gender and age are important in organizing work. Most family farming societies have a marked gender-based division of labor. Cross-cultural analysis of gender roles in 46 cultures reveals that men perform most of the labor in over three-fourths of the societies (Michaelson and Goldschmidt 1971). Anthropologists have proposed various theories to explain why productive work on so many family farms is male dominated (see Figure 3.4). The remaining one-fourth of the sample includes cultures in which men's and women's roles are balanced and cultures in which women play the dominant role.

In family farms in the United States and Canada, men typically have the main responsibility for daily farm operations; women's participation ranges from equal to minimal (Bartlett 1989). Women do run farms in the United States and Canada, but generally only when they are divorced or widowed. Women are usually responsible for managing the domestic domain. On average, women's daily work hours are 25 percent more than those of men.

Balanced work roles between men and women in family farming frequently involve a pattern in which men do the agricultural work and women do marketing. This gender-based division of labor is common among highland indigenous groups of Central and South America. For example, among the Zapotec Indians of Mexico's southern state of Oaxaca (wuh-HAK-uh), men grow maize, the staple crop, and cash crops such as bananas, mangoes, coconuts, and sesame (Chiñas 1992) (see Map 4.3, p. 84). Women sell produce in the town markets, and they make tortillas, which they sell from their houses. The family thus derives its income from the labor of both men and women working interdependently. Male status and female status are quite equal in such contexts.

Family farming in highland Ecuador. A man plows while women in the family follow, planting seed potatoes.

- Increased use of complex technology including machinery, chemicals, and genetic research on new plant and animal varieties.

  Social effects: This feature results in displacement of small landholders and field laborers. For example, replacing mules and horses with tractors for plowing in the U.S. South during the 1930s led to the eviction of small-scale share-croppers from the land because the landowners could cultivate larger units.

- Increased use of capital (wealth used in the production of more wealth) in the form of money or property.

  Social effects: The high ratio of capital to labor enables farmers to increase production but reduces flexibility. If a farmer invests in an expensive machine to harvest soybeans and then the price of soybeans drops, the farmer cannot simply switch from soybeans to a more profitable crop. Capitalization is most risky for smaller farms, which cannot absorb losses easily.

- Increased use of energy (primarily gasoline to run the machinery and nitrates for fertilizer) to grow crops. This input of energy often exceeds the calories of food energy yielded in the harvest. Calculations of how many calories of energy are used to produce a calorie of food in industrial agricultural systems reveal that some 2.5 calories of fossil fuel are invested to harvest 1 calorie of food—and more than 6 calories are invested when processing, packaging, and transport are taken into account.

  Social effects: This energy-heavy mode of production creates farmers' dependence on the global market of energy supplies.

Source: Adapted from "Industrial Agriculture" by Peggy F. Barlett in *Economic Anthropology*, ed. by Stuart Plattner. Copyright © 1989 by the Board of Trustees of the Leland Stanford Jr. University. Published by Stanford University Press.

FIGURE 3.5 Three Features of Industrial Agriculture and Their Social Effects

Female farming systems, in which women and girls play the major role in livelihood, are found mainly in southern India and Southeast Asia where *wet rice agriculture* is practiced. This method of growing rice is extremely labor intensive. It involves starting the seedlings in nurseries and transplanting them to flooded fields. Men are responsible for plowing the fields, using teams of water buffaloes. Women's labor is the backbone of this type of farming. Standing calf-deep in muddy water, they transplant rice seedlings, weed, and harvest the rice. Women can and often do own land in their own names, make decisions about planting and harvesting, and have substantial personal autonomy (Stivens et al. 1994). Why women have such a prominent position in wet rice agriculture as laborers as well as owners and managers is an intriguing question but impossible to answer. Its consequences, however, are clear in terms of women's relatively high status in relation to men.

Children's roles in agricultural societies range from prominent to minor, depending on the context (Whiting and Whiting 1975). The *Six Cultures Study*, mentioned earlier, found low rates of child labor in agricultural villages in North India and Mexico, compared with high rates among the horticultural Gusii in Kenya. In many agricultural contexts, however, children's labor participation is high. In villages in Java, Indonesia, (see Map 1.2, p. 14) and Nepal (see Map 5.5, p. 116), children spend more time caring for farm animals than adults do (Nag, White, and Peet 1978).

PROPERTY RELATIONS   Family farmers make substantial investments in land, such as clearing, terracing, and fencing, and these investments are linked to the development of firmly defined and protected property rights. Rights to land can be acquired and sold. Formalized, often written, guidelines exist about the inheritance of land and the transfer of rights to land through marriage. Social institutions such as law and police exist to protect private property rights.

In family farming systems where male labor and decision making predominate, women and girls are excluded from land rights. Conversely, in female farming systems, inheritance rules regulate the transmission of property rights more often through females.

INDUSTRIAL AGRICULTURE   **Industrial agriculture** produces crops through capital-intensive means, using machinery and inputs such as processed fertilizers instead of human and animal labor (Bartlett 1989). It is commonly practiced in the United States, Canada, Germany, Russia, and Japan and is increasingly being adopted in developing countries such as India, Brazil, Mexico, and China.

Industrial agriculture has brought with it the *corporate farm*, a huge agricultural enterprise that produces goods solely for sale and is owned and operated by a company that is entirely reliant on hired labor. Industrial agriculture has major social effects (see Figure 3.5).

---

industrial agriculture   a form of agriculture that is capital intensive, substituting machinery and purchased inputs for human and animal labor.

industrialism/informatics   a mode of livelihood in which goods are produced through mass employment in business and commercial operations and through the creation and movement of information via electronic media.

Migrant workers picking broccoli in Salinas, California.

Much of the labor demand in industrial agriculture is seasonal, creating an ebb and flow of workers, depending on the task and time of year. Large ranches hire seasonal cowboys for roundups and fence mending. Crop harvesting is another high-demand point. Some anthropologists study the lives of undocumented (illegal) migrant laborers. One researcher did participant observation with migrant laborers who work in the huge tomato, strawberry, and avocado fields owned by corporate farms in southern California (Chavez 1992). Many of the migrants are Maya from Oaxaca, Mexico (see Map 4.3, p. 84). They cross the border illegally in order to find work to support their families back home. In the San Diego area of southern California, they live temporarily in shantytowns or camps with minimal social services.

THE SUSTAINABILITY OF AGRICULTURE Agriculture requires more in the way of labor inputs, technology, and the use of nonrenewable natural resources than do the economic systems discussed earlier. The ever-increasing spread of corporate agriculture worldwide is now displacing other long-standing practices and resulting in the destruction of important habitats and cultural heritage sites in its search for land, water, and energy sources. Intensive agriculture is not a sustainable system. Furthermore, it is undermining the sustainability of foraging, horticulture, and pastoralism. For many years, anthropologists have pointed to the high costs of agriculture to the environment and to humanity (see Critical Thinking).

INDUSTRIALISM AND THE INFORMATION AGE

Industrialism/informatics is the mode of livelihood in which goods and services are produced through mass employment in business and commercial operations and through the creation, manipulation, management, and transfer of information via electronic media. In industrial capitalism, the form of capitalism found in most industrialized nations, most goods are produced not to meet basic needs but to satisfy consumer demands for nonessential goods. Employment in agriculture decreases while jobs in manufacturing and the service sector increase. In some industrialized countries, the number of manufacturing jobs is declining, with more people being employed in service occupations and in the growing area of information processing, such as computer programming, data processing, and communications.

An important distinction exists between the *formal sector* of the economy, which consists of salaried or wage-based work registered in official statistics, and the *informal sector*, which comprises work that is outside the formal sector, not officially registered, and sometimes illegal. If you have done babysitting and were paid cash that was not formally recorded by your employer (for tax-deduction purposes) or by you (for income tax purposes), then you have participated in the informal sector. Informal sector activities that are illegal are referred to as being part of the *underground economy*, a huge and uncounted part of global and local economies worldwide.

THINKING OUTSIDE THE BOX

On the basis of your personal experience and observations, how would you describe the gender division of labor in your culture, both in the domestic domain and in outside work?

CRITICAL thinking

Was the Invention of Agriculture a Terrible Mistake?

Most Euro-Americans have a *progressivist* view that agriculture is a major advance in cultural evolution because it brought with it so many things that Westerners admire, including cities, centers of learning and art, powerful state governments, and monumental architecture:

> Just count our advantages. We enjoy the most abundant and varied foods, the best tools, and material goods, some of the longest and healthiest lives, in history. . . . From the progressivist perspective on which I was brought up, to ask "Why did almost all our hunter–gatherer ancestors adopt agriculture?" is silly. Of course they adopted it because agriculture is an efficient way to get more food for less work. (Diamond 1994 [1987]:106)

Another claim about the advantage of agriculture is that it allows more leisure time, so art can flourish.

In contrast, many anthropologists, environmentalists, and other scholars raise serious questions about the advantages of agriculture. These *revisionists* take a critical approach and argue that agriculture may be "the worst mistake in the history of the human race," "a catastrophe from which we have never recovered" (Diamond 1994 [1987]:105–106). Some of the costs of agriculture, they maintain, are social inequality; disease; despotism; and destruction of the environment from soil exhaustion and chemical poisoning, water pollution, dams and river diversions, and air pollution from tractors, transportation, and processing plants.

With agriculture, life did improve for many people, but not for all. Elites emerged with distinct advantages, and the gap between the haves and the have-nots increased. Health improved for the elites, but not for the landless poor and laboring classes. With the vast surpluses of food created by agricultural production, elaborate state systems developed with new forms of power exercised over the common people.

◆ CRITICAL THINKING QUESTIONS

- What is your definition of "the good life"?
- What are the benefits and costs of achieving the good life among, say, the Ju/'hoansi compared with your vision of the good life in your microculture?
- Who gets to live the good life in each type of economy?

◆◆◆

Modes of Consumption and Exchange

Imagine that it is the late eighteenth century and you are a member of the Kwakwaka'wakw (KWA- kwuh- kayuh'- wah-kwah) of British Columbia in Canada's Pacific Northwest region (see Culturama at the end of this chapter, p. 72). You and your tribal group are invited to a **potlatch**, a feast in which the host lavishes the guests with abundant quantities of the best food and many gifts (Suttles 1991). The most honorable foods are fish oil, high-bush cranberries, and seal meat, and

they are served in ceremonial wooden bowls. Gifts include embroidered blankets, household articles such as carved wooden boxes and woven mats, canoes, and items of food. The more the chief gives, the higher his status rises and the more his guests are indebted to him. Later, when it is the guests' turn to hold a potlatch, they will give away as much as, or more than, their host did.

The Pacific Northwest region is rich in fish, game, berries, and nuts, among other foods. Nonetheless, given regional climatic variation, food supplies were often uneven, with some groups having surpluses each year while others would experience scarcity. The potlatch system helped to smooth out these variations: groups with a surplus would sponsor a potlatch, and those experiencing a leaner year were guests. In this way, potlatching established a *social safety net* across a wide area of the Northwest. This brief sketch of potlatching shows the linkages among the three economic processes of livelihood, consumption, and exchange (review Figure 3.1, p. 52). Potlatches are related to the food supply. They are also opportunities for consumption and exchange, the topics of this section.

MODES OF CONSUMPTION

Consumption has two meanings: First, it is a person's "intake" in terms of eating or other ways of using things; second, it is

---

potlatch a grand feast of Pacific Northwest cultures in which guests are invited to eat and to receive gifts from the hosts.

minimalism a mode of consumption that emphasizes simplicity, is characterized by few and finite consumer demands, and involves an adequate and sustainable means of achieving the demands.

consumerism a mode of consumption in which people's demands are many and infinite and the means of satisfying them are insufficient and become depleted in the effort to satisfy the demands.

Foraging	Horticulture	Pastoralism	Agriculture	Industrialism/Informatics
Mode of Consumption				**Mode of Consumption**
Minimalism				Consumerism
Finite needs				Infinite needs
Social Organization of Consumption				**Social Organization of Consumption**
Equality/sharing				Class-based inequality
Personalized products are consumed				Depersonalized products are consumed
Primary Budgetary Fund				**Primary Budgetary Fund**
Basic needs				Rent/taxes, luxuries
Mode of Exchange				**Mode of Exchange**
Balanced exchange				Market exchange
Social Organization of Exchange				**Social Organization of Exchange**
Small groups, face-to-face				Anonymous market transactions
Primary Category of Exchange				**Primary Category of Exchange**
The gift				The sale

FIGURE 3.6 Modes of Livelihood, Consumption, and Exchange

"output" in terms of spending or using resources to obtain those things. Thus, "intake" is eating a sandwich; "output" is spending money at the store to buy a sandwich. Both activities fit within the term "consumption."

People consume many things. Food, beverages, clothing, and shelter are the most basic consumption needs in most cultures. People also may acquire tools, weapons, means of transportation, computers, books and other items of communication, art and other luxury goods, and energy for heating and cooling their homes. In noncash economies, such as that of foragers, people "spend" time or labor in order to provide for their needs. In money-based economies, such as industrialized contexts today, most consumption depends on having cash or some virtual form of money.

In categorizing varieties of consumption, it makes sense to consider two contrasting modes, with mixed modes in the middle (see Figure 3.6). They are based on the relationship between *demand* (what people need or want) and *supply* (the resources available to satisfy demand):

- **Minimalism**: a mode of consumption characterized by few and finite consumer demands and an adequate and sustainable means to achieve them. Minimalism is most characteristic of free-ranging foragers but is also found to some degree among horticulturalists and pastoralists.
- **Consumerism**: a mode of consumption in which people's demands are many and infinite, and the means of satisfying them are never sufficient, thus driving

colonialism, globalization, and other forms of expansionism. Consumerism is the distinguishing feature of industrial/informatic cultures. Globalization is spreading consumerism throughout the world.

The social organization and meaning of consumption varies cross-culturally. As noted previously, foragers are generally egalitarian, whereas social inequality characterizes most agricultural and industrialism/informatics societies. In foraging peoples, sharing within the group is the norm and everyone has equal access to all resources. Among the Ju/'hoansi (review Culturama in Chapter 1, p. 21), "Even though only a fraction of the able-bodied foragers go out each day, the day's return of meat and gathered foods are divided in such a way that every member of the camp receives an equitable share" (Lee 1979:118).

The distribution of personal goods such as clothing, beads, musical instruments, or smoking pipes is also equal. *Leveling mechanisms* are unwritten, culturally embedded rules that prevent an individual from becoming wealthier or more powerful than anyone else. They are maintained through social pressure and gossip. An important leveling mechanism among the Ju/'hoansi requires that any large game animal killed be shared with the group and its killer must be modest, insisting that the meat is meager (Lee 1969). Ju/'hoansi hunters gain no social status or power through their provision of meat. The same applies to other foragers. Leveling mechanisms are important in horticultural and pastoralist societies,

Well-stocked and brightly lit candy shops are a prominent part of urban nightlife in Valencia, Spain. Sugarcane was introduced into Spain by the Arabs. Later, the Spanish established the first sugarcane plantations on Madeira and the Canary Islands, using enslaved laborers from Africa.

▶ *Log your food and drink consumption every day for a week, and assess the role that sugar plays in the results.*

too. For example, when someone's herd grows "too large," that person will be subject to social pressure to sponsor a large feast in which many of the herd animals are eaten.

The mode of consumption that contrasts with minimalism is consumerism, with the United States being the major consumerist country of the world. Since the 1970s, consumption levels in the United States have been the highest of any society in human history, and they show no sign of decline. Since China adopted features of capitalism, it has quickly become a consumerist giant. In the world's poorest countries, too, rising numbers of middle- and upper-class people are pursuing consumerism.

As consumerism spreads throughout the world, changes in the social relations involved in consumption also occur. In small-scale societies—such as those of foragers, horticulturalists, and pastoralists—consumption items are typically produced by the consumers themselves for their own use. If not, they are likely to be produced by people with whom the consumer has a personal, face-to-face relationship—in other words, *personalized consumption*. Everyone knows where products came from and who produced them. This pattern contrasts markedly with consumption in our contemporary globalized world, termed *depersonalized consumption*. Multinational corporations manage the production of most of the goods that people in industrialized countries consume. These products often are multisourced, with parts assembled in diverse parts of the world by hundreds of unknown workers. Depersonalized consumption, by distancing consumers from workers who actually produce goods, makes it more possible for workers to be exploited.

Even in the most industrialized/informatic contexts, though, depersonalized consumption has not completely replaced personalized consumption. Farmers' markets in urban centers in North America are an example of personalized consumption in which the consumer buys produce from the person who grew it and with whom the consumer may have a friendly conversation, perhaps while sampling one of the farmer's apples.

Homeless children rest by a storefront grate in Ho Chi Minh City, Vietnam.

▶ *Consider how the entitlement system affected children under pure socialism compared with the current transition to a more capitalist system.*

CONSUMPTION MICROCULTURES This section provides examples of three consumption microcultures: cultures based on class, gender, and "race." Microcultures often have distinct entitlement patterns that affect levels of lifestyle, identity, and welfare.

CLASS AND THE GAME OF DISTINCTION IN ISRAELI BIRTHDAY PARTIES

Class differences, defined in terms of levels of income, are reflected in distinctive consumption patterns. Although class differences in consumption may seem too obvious to be worth studying, they constitute an important and growing area in anthropology.

French anthropologist Pierre Bourdieu (1984) provides the concept of the *game of distinction,* in which people of the upper classes continually adjust their preferences to distance themselves from the lower classes, whereas members of the lower classes tend to adopt aspects of upper-class preferences in order to gain status. Cross-culturally, events such as weddings, funerals, and children's birthday parties are often occasions requiring large expenditures that send messages about the status (real or aspired) of the hosts. Children's birthday parties are a less studied topic but one with much potential, especially because such parties are becoming increasingly popular in cultures around the world.

In Israel, children's birthday parties have recently become expensive events among middle-class and upper-class urbanites (Goldstein-Gidoni 2003). Parents hire birthday party professionals to create special themes. "Around the World" themes are popular, especially those drawing on Japanese, Spanish, South American, and Middle Eastern motifs. A current craze for Japanese culture, such as gardens and food, means that the Japanese theme is one of the most popular. "Around the World" birthday party themes are ostensibly to help the children learn about other places and people. At the same time, they make a statement about how cosmopolitan, well off, and stylish the hosts are.

WOMEN'S DEADLY DIET IN PAPUA NEW GUINEA

Consumption patterns are often marked by gender and related to discrimination and inequality. Specific foods may be considered "men's food" or "women's food." An example of lethal gender inequalities in food consumption comes from highland Papua New Guinea (see Map 3.4).

The story begins with the emergence of a mysterious disease, with the local name of *kuru* (koo-roo), among the Fore (for-ay), a horticultural people of the highlands (Lindenbaum 1979). Between 1957 and 1977, about 2500 people died of kuru. The first signs of the disease are shivering tremors that are followed by a progressive loss of motor ability along with pain in the head and limbs. Kuru victims could walk unsteadily at first but would later be unable to get up. Death occurred about a year after the first symptoms appeared. Most victims were women.

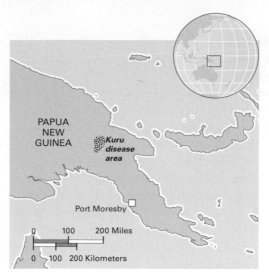

MAP 3.4 Location of the Kuru Epidemic in Papua New Guinea.

American medical researchers discovered that kuru was a neurological disease but they did not know how it was transmitted. Australian cultural anthropologist Shirley Lindenbaum pinpointed the cultural cause of kuru: cannibalism. Kuru victims had eaten the flesh of deceased people who had died of the disease.

Why were most of the kuru victims women? Lindenbaum learned that, among the Fore, it was considered acceptable to cook and eat the meat of a deceased person, although it was not a preferred food. The preferred source of animal protein is meat from pigs, and men receive preferential access to the best food. Fore women had begun to eat human flesh more often because of an increased scarcity of pigs. Population density in the region had risen, more land was being cultivated, and forest areas had decreased. Pigs live in forest areas, so, as their habitat became more restricted, their numbers declined. The Fore could not move to more pig-abundant areas because they were bounded on the east, west, and north by other groups. The south was a harsh and forbidding region. These factors, combined with the Fore's male-biased system of protein consumption, forced women to turn to the less-preferred protein source of human flesh. By eating the flesh, including brains, of kuru victims, they contracted the disease.

"RACE" AND CHILDREN'S SHOPPING IN NEW HAVEN

Throughout the world, in countries with "race"-based social categories, inequalities in consumption and quality of life exist, often in spite of antidiscrimination legislation. In the United States, racism affects many areas of life, from access to housing, neighborhood security and services, schooling, and health to whether a person is likely to be ignored or picked up by a taxi or be stopped by a police officer for speeding. Racial inequality between Black and White Americans has risen steadily since the 1970s in terms of income, wealth, and property ownership, especially home ownership (Shapiro 2004). Those at the top of the income distribution have increased their share of the wealth most.

The share of total income that goes to the top 1 percent of families is nearly the same size as the total income share of the bottom 40 percent.

How is this happening in a country dedicated to equality of opportunity? A large part of the answer lies in the simple fact that, in a capitalist system, inequality leads to more inequality through the transfer of wealth and property across generations. Those who have wealth and property are able to establish their children's wealth through college tuition payments, down payments on houses, and other financial gifts. The children of poor parents have to provide for their education and housing costs from their wages alone, a fact that makes it far less likely that they will be able to pursue higher education or buy a home.

As a graduate student in anthropology at Yale University, Elizabeth Chin decided to do her dissertation research on consumption patterns among schoolchildren in a poor, African American neighborhood in New Haven, Connecticut (2001). In terms of per capita income, Connecticut is the wealthiest state in the United States. It also harbors some of the most severe poverty and racial inequality in its major cities, exemplified in New Haven's clearly defined neighborhoods and in the fear and suspicion with which Whites and Blacks view each other. During her research in Newhallville, a Black neighborhood of New Haven, Chin found that 50 percent of the children age 5 and under were living in poverty.

Chin formed a relationship with one fifth-grade class of 22 students. She spent time in the classroom, visited the children and their families in their homes, and accompanied the children on shopping trips to the mall. The children are bombarded with media messages about consumption, but they have little money to spend. Some receive an allowance for doing household chores, some receive small amounts of pocket money on an ad hoc basis, and some earn money from

---

balanced exchange   a system of transfers in which the goal is either immediate or eventual equality in value.

unbalanced exchange   a system of transfers in which one party seeks to make a profit.

generalized reciprocity   a transaction that involves the least conscious interest in material gain or thought of what might be received in return and when the return might occur.

pure gift   something given with no expectation or thought of a return.

expected reciprocity   an exchange of approximately equally valued goods or services, usually between people roughly equal in social status.

redistribution   a form of exchange that involves one person collecting goods or money from many members of a group that, at a later time and at a public event, "returns" the pooled goods to everyone who contributed.

market exchange   the buying and selling of commodities under competitive conditions in which the forces of supply and demand determine value; a form of unbalanced exchange.

small-scale ventures such as a cucumber stand. They learn about the basics of household finances and the costs of daily life early on. Seeing their families strain every day to put meals on the table teaches them about the negative effects of overindulgence: "From divvying up the milk to figuring out where to sleep there is an emphasis on sharing and mutual obligation" (2001:5).

These practical lessons shape how the children spend their money when they go to the mall. Practicality and generosity guide their shopping choices. In order to learn about the children's decisions, Chin would give a child $20 and go with him or her to the mall. Most of the girls spent over half their money on gifts for family members, especially their mothers and grandmothers (2001:139). The girls knew their mothers' shoe sizes and clothing sizes. One boy, just before school was to start in the fall, spent $10 on a T-shirt to wear on the first day of school, $6 on a pair of shorts, and the rest on school supplies: pencils, pens, notebook paper, and a binder (2001:135). In her two years of research, Chin never heard a Newhallville child nag a caretaker about buying him or her something.

Birthday parties are rare events in Newhallville. Chin observed a birthday party that involved only an $18 ice-cream cake, but most birthday cakes are home-baked. Birthday gifts are few. One girl received three gifts on her tenth birthday: a jump rope and a bingo game from her mother, wrapped in brown paper made from a grocery bag, and an inexpensive plastic toy from her grandmother (2001:72).

MODES OF EXCHANGE

Exchange is the transfer of something that may or may not be material between at least two persons, groups, or institutions. Cultural anthropologists have done much research on gifts and other forms of exchange, such as Malinowski's early work on the kula in the South Pacific (review Culturama, Chapter 2, p. 33). In all economic systems, individuals and groups exchange goods and services with others. But variation exists in what is exchanged, how goods are exchanged, when exchange takes place, and the meaning of exchange.

Parallel to the two contrasting modes of consumption described earlier (minimalism and consumerism), two distinct modes of exchange can be delineated (see Figure 3.7):

- **Balanced exchange**: a system of transfers in which the goal is either immediate or eventual balance in value.
- **Unbalanced exchange**: a system of transfers in which one party attempts to make a profit.

BALANCED EXCHANGE The category of balanced exchange contains two subcategories based on the social relationship of the two parties involved in the exchange and the degree to which a "return" is expected. **Generalized reciprocity** is a transaction that involves the least conscious interest in material gain or thought of what might be received in return and when the return might occur. Such exchanges often involve

	Balanced Exchange			Unbalanced Exchange	
	Generalized Reciprocity	Expected Reciprocity	Redistribution	Market Exchange	Theft, Exploitation
Actors	Kin, friends	Trading partners	Leader and pooling group	Buyers/sellers	Nonkin, nonfriends, unknown
Return	Not calculated or expected	Expected at some time	Feast and give-away	Immediate payment	No return
Example	Buying coffee for a friend	Kula	Moka	Internet shopping	Shoplifting

FIGURE 3.7 Keeping Track of Exchange

goods and services of an everyday nature, such as a cup of coffee. Generalized reciprocity is the main form of exchange between people who know each other well and trust each other. Therefore, it is the main form of exchange in foraging societies. It is also found among close kin and friends cross-culturally.

A **pure gift** is something given with no expectation or thought of a return. The pure gift is an extreme form of generalized reciprocity. Examples of a pure gift include donating money for a food drive and making donations to famine relief, blood banks, and religious organizations. Some people say that a truly pure gift does not exist because one always gains something in giving, even if it is just the good feeling of generosity. Parental care of children is said to be a pure gift by some, but others do not agree. Those who say that parental care is a pure gift argue that most parents do not consciously calculate how much they have spent on their children with the intention of "getting it back" later on. Those who do not consider parental care a pure gift say that even if the "costs" are not consciously calculated, parents have unconscious expectations about what their children will "return" to them, whether the return is material (care in old age) or immaterial (making the parent feel proud).

Expected reciprocity is the exchange of approximately equally valued goods or services, usually between people of roughly equal social status. The exchange may occur simultaneously between both parties, or it may involve an understanding about the period within which the exchange will be completed. This aspect of timing contrasts with that of generalized reciprocity, in which there is no fixed time limit for the return. In expected reciprocity, if the second party fails to complete the exchange, the relationship will break down. Balanced reciprocity is less personal than generalized reciprocity and, according to Western definitions, more "economic."

The kula system, as found in the Trobriand Islands (review Culturama, Chapter 2, p. 33), is an example of expected reciprocity. Men exchange necklaces and armlets, giving them to their partners after keeping the items for a while. Partners include neighbors, as well as people on faraway islands who

are visited via long canoe voyages traversing rough waters. Trobriand men are distinguished by the particular armlets and necklaces that they exchange, and certain armlets and necklaces are more prestigious than others. One cannot keep one's trade items for long, because the kula code dictates that "to possess is great, but to possess is to give." Generosity is the essence of goodness, and stinginess is the most despised vice. Kula exchanges should involve items of equivalent value. If a man trades a very valuable necklace with his partner, he expects to receive in return a very valuable armlet as an equivalent gift. The equality of exchange ensures a strong bond between the trading partners and is a statement of trust. When a man arrives in an area that may be dangerous because of previous raids or warfare, he can count on having a friend to give him hospitality.

Redistribution is a form of exchange in which one person collects goods or money from many members of a group and provides a social return at a later time. At a public event, even several years later, the organizer "returns" the pooled goods to everyone who contributed by sponsoring a generous feast. Compared with the two-way pattern of exchange involved in reciprocity, redistribution involves some "centricity." It contains the possibility of inequality because what is returned may not always equal, in a material sense, what each individual contributed. The pooling group may continue to exist, however, because it benefits from the leadership skills of the person who mobilizes contributions. If a neighboring group threatens a raid, people turn to their redistributive leader for political leadership (discussed further in Chapter 8).

UNBALANCED EXCHANGE **Market exchange**, a form of unbalanced exchange, is the buying and selling of commodities

THINKING OUTSIDE THE BOX

Propose some examples of what might qualify as a "pure gift."

under competitive conditions in which the forces of supply and demand determine value and the seller seeks to make a profit. In market transactions, the seller and buyer may or may not have a personal relationship. They may or may not be social equals. Their exchange is not likely to generate social bonding. Many market transactions take place in a *marketplace,* a physical location in which buying and selling occur. The market system, which evolved from other, less formal contexts of **trade**, involves the formalized exchange of one thing for another according to set standards of value.

The market system is associated with regional specialization in producing particular goods and with trade between regions. Certain products are often identified with a town or region. In Oaxaca, Mexico (see Map 4.3, p. 84), some villages are known for their blankets, pottery, stone grinders, rope, and chili peppers (Plattner 1989). In Morocco, the city of Fez (see Map 4.2, p. 82) is famous for its blue-glazed pottery, whereas the Berber people of the Atlas Mountains are known for their fine wool blankets and rugs. Increasingly, producers of regionally distinct products, such as champagne, are legally copyrighting the regional name to protect it from use by producers of similar products from outside the region. Marketplaces range from informal, small stands that appear in the morning and disappear at night to huge multistoried shopping centers. One variety found in many parts of the world is a *periodic market,* a site for buying and selling that takes place on a regular basis (for example, monthly) in a particular location but without a permanent physical structure. Sellers appear with their goods and set up a table with perhaps an awning. In contrast, *permanent markets* are built structures situated in fixed locations. Marketplaces, however, are more than just places for buying and selling. They involve social interactions and even performances. Sellers solicit customers, shoppers meet and chat, government officials drop by, religious organizations may hold services, and traditional healers may treat toothaches.

Ted Bestor conducted research over many years in Tsukiji (tsee-kee-jee), the world's largest fish market, located in Tokyo (2004). Tsukiji connects large-scale corporations that supply most of the seafood with small-scale family-run firms that continue to dominate Tokyo's retail food trade. Bestor describes the layout of the huge market, with inner and outer sections as a basic division. The outer market attracts younger, more hip shoppers looking for unusual, trendy gourmet items and a more authentic-seeming shopping experience. It contains sushi bars, noodle stalls, knife shops, and chopstick dealers, as well as temples and graveyards. The inner market contains 11 fresh-produce market subdivisions. The seafood section by far overshadows the "veggie" markets in size and transaction level. It is subdivided into several main buildings where auctions occur, activities such as deliveries and dispatches

---

trade the formalized exchange of one thing for another according to set standards of value.

Workers at Tsukiji, the world's largest fish market in Tokyo, transport frozen tuna on hand carts for the upcoming auction.

▶ *For a research project, learn more about Ted Bestor's research on Tsukiji.*

take place, and rows of retail stalls serve 14,000 customers each morning. Stalls do not typically post prices, so buyers and sellers have to negotiate them. Experienced buyers and sellers use verbally coded conversations that yield a better price than what an inexperienced first-time buyer will get. The codes involve phrases such as "morning mist on a white beach" which, depending on the number of syllables in the phrase, conveys a price offer.

OTHER FORMS OF UNBALANCED EXCHANGE
Several forms of unbalanced exchange other than market transactions exist. In extreme instances, no social relationship is involved; in others, sustained unequal relationships are maintained over time between people. These forms include taking something with no expectation of giving any return. They can occur in any mode of livelihood but are most likely to be found in large-scale societies where more options (other than face-to-face) for balanced exchange exist.

GAMBLING *Gambling,* or gaming, is the attempt to make a profit by playing a game of chance in which a certain item of value is staked in hopes of acquiring the much larger return that one receives if one wins the game. If one loses, that which was staked is lost. Gambling is an ancient practice and is common cross-culturally. Ancient forms of gambling include dice throwing and card playing. Now one can gamble on the Internet. Many kinds of financial investments can be considered as forms of gambling, including investing in the stock market. Although gambling may seem an odd category within unbalanced exchange, its goals of making a profit seem to justify its placement there. The fact that gambling within "high" capitalism is on the rise justifies anthropological attention to it.

In 2006, the Center for California Native Nations (CCNN) at the University of California at Riverside released an evaluation of the effects of Indian gaming in California (Spilde Contreras 2006). (*Note:* According to current preferences of the people involved, the terms *Indian, American Indian,* and *Indian tribe* are used instead of *Native American.*)

Kate Spilde Contreras, applied cultural anthropologist, directed a multidisciplinary team of anthropologists, political scientists, economists, and historians. The team's research objective was to evaluate the social and economic effects of Indian gaming operations on tribal and local governments in California. The study relied mainly on public data, especially the 1990 and 2000 U.S. Censuses, to supply a "before" and "after" picture during the initial growth phase of Indian gaming in the state. To learn about more recent changes, the research team conducted surveys of tribal and local government officials and in-depth case studies of individual tribal governments.

The research revealed two important factors that shape the effects of Indian gaming in California: Gaming establishments are owned by tribal governments, and gaming establishments are located on existing tribal trust lands. Therefore, gaming revenues support community and government activities of the tribal communities, and employment generation is localized within the tribal communities.

Indian reservations in California are more economically heterogeneous than elsewhere in the United States.

Casino Sandia, located in the Sandia Pueblo in northern New Mexico, is one of many casinos in the state established in the hope of raising funds to improve the lives of Indian people.

Since the development of gaming, California also has greater economic inequality between gaming and nongaming reservations than is found in other states. By 2000, the fastest average income growth on California reservations occurred on gaming reservations. A policy response to this situation is a tribal-state gaming contract, the Revenue Sharing Trust Fund (RSTF), that provides for the sharing of gaming revenue with nongaming communities.

The research also considered the social effects of gaming beyond the reservation. Areas within 10 miles of gaming reservations experienced significant employment increases, greater income growth, and more educational expansion than those farther away.

Given the fact that reservations in California are located in the poorest regions, this effect is progressive; that is, it helps poorer communities more than it helps better-off communities.

Although the income and other effects of gaming in California are clearly substantial for Indians and their neighbors, Spilde Contreras points to the large gaps that still exist between conditions on Indian reservations and those for most Americans.

◆ **FOOD FOR THOUGHT**

- How does the recent development of Indian casinos connect with the theoretical perspectives of structure versus agency? (Review the discussion of these perspectives in Chapter 1.)

Indian tribal gambling establishments in the United States have mushroomed in recent years. Throughout the United States, Indian casinos are so financially successful that they are perceived as an economic threat to many state lotteries. The Pequot Indians of Connecticut, a small tribe of around 200 people, now operate the most lucrative gaming establishment in the world: Foxwoods Resort and Casino, established in 1992. Through gaming, many other Indian tribal groups have become successful capitalists. An important question is what impact casinos will have on Indian tribal people, and anthropologists are involved in trying to answer this question (see Lessons Applied).

THEFT *Theft* is the taking of something with no expectation or thought of returning anything to the original owner for it. It is the logical opposite of a pure gift. Anthropologists have neglected the study of theft, no doubt a reasonable response because theft is an illegal activity that is difficult to study and might involve danger.

A rare study of theft focused on food stealing by children in West Africa (Bledsoe 1983). During fieldwork among the Mende (men-day) people of Sierra Leone (see Map 4.5, p. 93), Caroline Bledsoe learned that children in town stole fruits such as mangoes, guavas, and oranges from neighborhood trees. At first Bledsoe dismissed cases of food stealing as rare exceptions, but then she realized that she "rarely walked through town without hearing shouts of anger from an adult and cries of pain from a child being whipped for stealing food" (1983:2). Deciding to look into children's food stealing more closely, she asked several children to keep diaries. Their writings were dominated by themes of *tiefing*, the local term for stealing. Fostered children, who are temporarily placed in the care of friends or relatives, do more food tiefing than children living with their birth families do. Such food stealing can be seen as children's attempts to compensate for their less-than-adequate food shares in their foster homes.

Although much theft worldwide is motivated by skewed entitlements and need, much is also driven by greed. Cultural anthropologists, for obvious reasons, have not done research on high-level theft involving expensive commodities such as drugs, gems, and art, nor have they examined corporate financial malpractice as a form of theft. Given the ethical requirement of informed consent, it is highly unlikely that any anthropologist would be given permission to study such criminal activity.

EXPLOITATION *Exploitation*, or getting something of greater value for less in return, is a form of extreme and persistent unbalanced exchange. Slavery is a form of exploitation in which people's labor power is appropriated without their consent and with no recompense for its value. Slavery is rare among foraging, horticultural, and pastoralist societies. Some degree of covert compulsion or dependence is likely to be present in order for relationships of unequal exchange to endure.

Relationships between the Efe (eff-ay), who are "pygmy" foragers, and the Lese (less-ay), who are farmers, in the Democratic Republic of Congo exemplify sustained unequal exchange (Grinker 1994) (see Map 3.5). The Lese live in small villages. The Efe are seminomadic and live in temporary camps near Lese villages. Men of each group maintain long-term, hereditary exchange partnerships with each other. The Lese give cultivated foods and iron to the Efe, and the Efe give meat, honey, and other forest goods to the Lese.

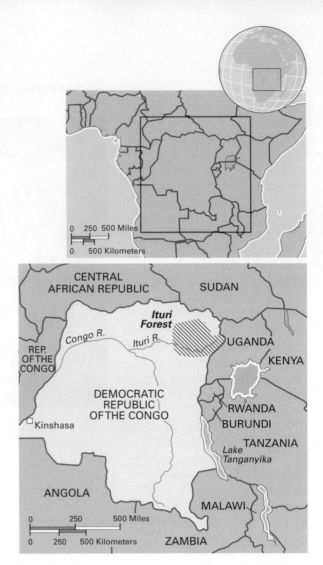

MAP 3.5 **Lese and Efe Region in the Democratic Republic of Congo.**
The Lese and Efe live in the Ituri Forest, a dense tropical rainforest in the northern part of the Congo River Basin. Cultural Survival, a nonprofit group promoting and defending the rights of indigenous peoples, supports the Ituri Forest Peoples Fund, which promotes the health and education of Efe foragers and Lese farmers. Go to the Internet to learn about the projects of the Ituri Forest Peoples Fund.

Each Efe partner is considered a member of the "house" of his Lese partner, although he lives separately. Their main link is the exchange of food items, a system conceptualized by the Lese not as trade but as the sharing of coproduced goods by partners living in a single unit. Evidence of inequality exists, however, in these relationships, with the Lese having the advantage. The Efe provide much-wanted meat to the Lese, but this role gives them no status. Rather, it is the giving of cultivated foods by the Lese to the Efe that conveys status. Another area of inequality is marital and sexual relationships. Lese men may marry Efe women, and their children are considered Lese. Efe men, however, cannot marry Lese women.

◆◆◆

Globalization and Changing Economies

Potent market forces controlled mainly by the most powerful industrialized countries (currently referred to as the *G-8 countries*), play a major role in shaping contemporary patterns of consumption and exchange worldwide. Local cultures, though, variously adopt and adapt global consumption messages, commodities, and their meanings. Sometimes they resist them outright.

SUGAR, SALT, AND STEEL TOOLS IN THE AMAZON

Katherine Milton, a biological anthropologist, has studied the nutritional effects of Western contact on the consumption patterns and health of indigenous foragers in the Brazilian Amazon. She comments:

> Despite the way their culture traditionally eschews possessions, forest-living people embrace manufactured goods with amazing enthusiasm. They seem to appreciate instantly the efficacy of a steel machete, ax, or cooking pot. It is love at first sight. . . . There are accounts of Indian groups or individuals who have turned their backs on manufactured goods, but such people are the exception. (1992:40)

The attraction to Western goods has its roots in the early decades of the twentieth century, when the Brazilian government sought to "pacify" Amazonian groups by placing cooking pots, machetes, axes, and steel knives along trails. This technique proved so successful that it is still used to "contact" remote groups. According to Milton:

> Once a group has been drawn into the pacification area, all its members are presented with various trade goods—standard gifts include metal cooking pots, salt, matches, machetes, knives, axes, cloth hammocks, T-shirts, and shorts. . . . Once the Indians have grown accustomed to these new items, the next step is to teach them that these gifts will not be repeated. The Indians are now told that they must work to earn money or must manufacture goods for trade so that they can purchase new items.
>
> Unable to contemplate returning to life without steel axes, the Indians begin to produce extra arrows or blowguns or hunt additional game or weave baskets beyond what they normally need so that this new surplus can be traded. Time that might, in the past, have been used for other tasks—subsistence activities, ceremonial events, or whatever—is now devoted to production of barter goods. (1992:40)

The adoption of Western foods has had detrimental effects on the nutrition and health of indigenous Amazonian peoples. Particularly harmful is the consumption of table salt and refined sugar. Previously, they consumed only small quantities of salt made by burning certain leaves and collecting the ash. Fructose from wild fruits was the only sweetener consumed. Sucrose, in refined sugar, tastes exceptionally sweet, and the Indians get hooked on it. Tooth decay, obesity, and diabetes are new and growing health risks. Milton comments, "The moment manufactured foods begin to intrude on the indigenous diet, health takes a downward turn" (1992:41).

GLOBAL NETWORKS AND ECSTASY IN THE UNITED STATES

In the late 1990s, a sharp increase in the use of ecstasy occurred in the United States (Agar and Reisinger 2003). Ecstasy, or MDMA (an abbreviation for its chemical name), is an illicit drug that produces a high without, apparently, leading to clinical dependence. Fieldwork and interviews in Baltimore, Maryland, revealed that ecstasy use "took off" in the late 1990s, and MDMA became the "up and coming" drug of choice among youth. As one research participant commented, "A lot of people I know like rolling, taking a pill of ecstasy and going to like a club or going to a school dance. I mean, alcohol is up and coming among like teenagers, like it's always been, but I think ecstasy's making a pretty powerful fight" (2003:2).

Official statistics confirmed this rise: In 1998, 10 percent of Baltimore County high school seniors reported that they had tried ecstasy; in 2001, the rate had increased to nearly 20 percent. Nationwide statistics on reported use the drug, arrests of distributors, and numbers of MDMA-related seizures reveal a similar pattern of increased use during the 1998–2001 period. What accounts for this change? Two anthropologists conducted research to assess their hypothesis that there was a major change in the systems that produced and delivered the drug, leading to its increased availability.

The standard story of the supply chain goes like this: Ecstasy is produced in the Netherlands and Belgium and is distributed to the United States by Israelis, with a fuzzy role for Russian organized crime along the way. Two anthropologists studied websites and media reports in 2000 and discovered a much more complicated story. They found a network of multiple and shifting production sites all over the world, including the largest illicit drug lab ever reported in Canadian history. Distribution channels are also highly diffuse. Although the simpler story may have been true in 1998, it was no longer true two years later. Perhaps as demand rose in the United States and elsewhere, this rise prompted the development of a wider network of production and distribution.

A bride wearing traditional wedding clothing in the city of Meknès, Morocco.

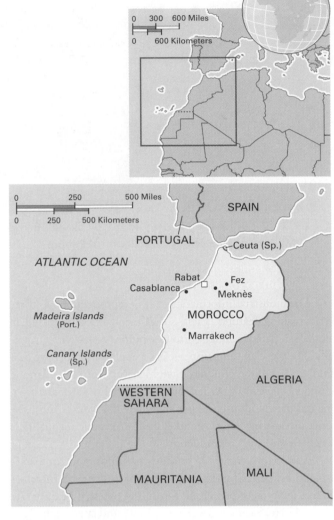

MAP 4.2 Morocco.
The Kingdom of Morocco is the westernmost country of the Arab world. A border dispute continues with the Western Sahara, which Morocco has administered since 1975. Morocco's population is 30 million. The terrain ranges from coastal lowlands to rugged interior mountains. Morocco's economy is based on mining phosphates, remittances, and tourism. It is one of the world's largest producers and exporters of cannabis and the world's largest per capita consumer of sugar. Most Moroccans are Sunni Muslims. The official language is classical Arabic, but Moroccan Arabic is widely spoken. Over 40 percent of the people speak a variety of Berber.

used option in some contexts. Biology, interacting with environment and culture, defines the time span within which a female is fertile: from **menarche** (pronounced men-ar-kee), the onset of menstruation, to **menopause**, the cessation of menstruation. Globally, the beginning of menarche varies from 12 to 14 years of age (Thomas et al. 2001). Generally, girls in richer countries reach menarche a few years earlier than girls in poorer countries do. For example, the estimated age at menarche in Japan is 12.5 years, but in Haiti it is 15.5 years. Worldwide, a trend is for the age at menarche to become earlier. The reasons for this change are not completely clear. Diet and activity patterns are likely factors involved. The underlying assumption is that today's diets and lifestyles are a sign of "progress" and thus an earlier age at menarche is an indicator of societal well-being.

Cultures, however, socialize children regarding the appropriate age to begin sexual intercourse, and cultural rules are more variable than the biological marker of menarche. Cultural guidelines vary by gender, class, race, and ethnicity. In many cultures, sexual activity should begin only with marriage. This rule often applies more strictly to females than to males. In Zawiya, a Muslim town of northern Morocco (see Map 4.2), a bride's virginity is highly valued, whereas that of the groom is ignored (Davis and Davis 1987). Most brides conform to the ideal. Some unmarried young women do engage in premarital sex, however. If they choose to have a traditional wedding, they must somehow meet the requirement of producing blood-stained wedding sheets after the first night. If the bride and the groom have been having premarital sexual relations, the groom may assist in the deception by nicking a finger with a knife and bloodying the sheets himself. Another option is to buy fake blood sold in drugstores.

menarche the onset of menstruation.

menopause the cessation of menstruation.

INTERCOURSE FREQUENCY AND FERTILITY Cross-culturally, the frequency of sexual intercourse varies widely. The relationship between frequency of sexual intercourse and fertility, though, is not simple. A common assumption is that people in cultures with high fertility rates have sexual intercourse frequently. Without modern birth control, such as condoms, birth control pills, and intrauterine devices (IUDs), intercourse frequency would seem, logically, to produce high rates of fertility.

A classic study of reported intercourse frequency among Euro-Americans in the United States and Hindus in India, however, throws this assumption into question (Nag 1972). The Indians had intercourse far less frequently (less than twice a week) than the Euro-Americans did (two to three times a week) in all age groups. Several features of Indian culture limit the frequency of sexual intercourse. First, the Hindu religion teaches the value of sexual abstinence, thus providing ideological support for limiting sexual intercourse. Hinduism also suggests that one should abstain from intercourse on many sacred days: the first night of the new moon, the first night of the full moon, the eighth day of each half of the month (the light half and the dark half), and sometimes on Fridays. As many as 100 days each year could be observed as days of abstinence. Another factor is Hindu men's belief in what anthropologists term the *lost semen complex*, which links men's health and strength to the retention of semen. An anthropologist learned about this complex during his fieldwork in North India:

> Everyone knew that semen was not easily formed; it takes forty days and forty drops of blood to make one drop of semen. . . . Semen of good quality is rich and viscous, like the cream of unadulterated milk. . . . Celibacy was the first requirement of true fitness, because every sexual orgasm meant the loss of a quantity of semen, laboriously formed. (Carstairs 1967:83–86, quoted in Nag 1972:235)

The fact remains, however, that fertility is higher in India than in many other parts of the world where such religiously based restrictions on sexual intercourse do not exist. Obviously, sheer frequency of intercourse is not the explanation because it takes only one act of sexual intercourse at the right time of the month to create a pregnancy. The point of this discussion is to show that *reverse reasoning* (assuming that high fertility means people have nothing better to do than have sex) is wrong. The cultural dynamics of sexuality in India function to restrain sexual activities and thus keep fertility lower than it otherwise would be.

FERTILITY DECISION MAKING

Within the context of the family unit, decision makers weigh factors influencing why and when to have a child. At the state level, governments plan their overall population goals on the basis of fertility goals that are sometimes pronatalist and sometimes *antinatalist* (opposed to many births). At the global level, powerful economic and political interests influence the reproductive policies of countries and, in turn, of families and individuals.

AT THE FAMILY LEVEL Within the family, parents and other family members consider, consciously or unconsciously, the value and costs of children (Nag 1983). Cross-cultural research indicates that four factors are most important in affecting the desire for children:

- Children's labor value
- Children's value as old-age support for parents
- Infant and child mortality rates
- Economic costs of children

The first three factors have a positive effect on fertility: When children's value is high in terms of labor or old-age support, fertility is likely to be higher; when infant and child mortality rates are high, fertility rates tend to be high in order to "replace" offspring who do die. In the case of child costs—including direct costs (for food, education, and clothing, for example) and indirect costs (employment opportunities that the mother gives up)—the relationship is negative. Higher costs reduce the desire for children. In industrial/informatic contexts, child costs are high and child labor value declines dramatically. Mandatory school attendance also pulls children out of the workforce and may involve direct costs for fees, uniforms, and supplies. States that provide old-age security and pension plans also reduce the need for children.

Husbands and wives may not always have the same preferences about the number of children they desire. In a highland village in the Oaxaca region of Mexico (see Map 4.3), men want more children than women do (Browner 1986). Of women with only one child, 80 percent were content with a family of that size. Most men (60 percent) who were satisfied with their present family size had four or more children. One woman said, "My husband sleeps peacefully through the night, but I have to get up when the children need something. I'm the one the baby urinates on; sometimes I have to get out of bed in the cold and change both our clothes" (1986:714).

Depending on the gender division of labor and on other social features, families may prefer sons, daughters, or a balance of each. Preference for sons is widespread, especially in South Asia (including India and Pakistan) and East Asia (China and Korea), but it is not universal. Throughout much of Southeast Asia, for

A family planning clinic in Egypt. Throughout much of the world, Western-style family planning advice is controversial because it may conflict with local beliefs and values.

▶ *In your cultural experience, what is the prevailing attitude about family planning?*

MAP 4.3 Mexico.
The United Mexican States is the most populous Spanish-speaking country in the world. It was subjected to Spanish rule for three centuries before gaining independence. Its population is 107 million, and the capital, Mexico City, has a population of 20 million people. Mexico has a mixed economy of industry, agriculture, and trade, and is the fourth-largest oil producer in the world. Ethnically, the population consists of Mestizos (60 percent), Indians (30 percent), and Whites (9 percent). Southern states have the highest proportion of Indians.

example, people prefer a balanced number of sons and daughters. A preference for daughters exists in some parts of Africa south of the Sahara and in some Caribbean populations.

AT THE STATE LEVEL State governments formulate policies that affect rates of population growth within their boundaries. These policies vary from being antinatalist to pronatalist, and they vary in terms of the methods of fertility management promoted. Factors that affect government policies include economic factors, such as projected jobs and employment levels, public services, and maintaining the tax base, as well as other factors, such as filling the ranks of the military, maintaining ethnic and regional proportions, and dealing with population aging.

AT THE GLOBAL LEVEL The most far-reaching layer that affects fertility decision making occurs at the international level, where global power structures such as pharmaceutical companies and religious leaders influence country- and individual-level decision making. In the 1950s, there was a wave of enthusiasm among Western nations for promoting family planning programs of many types in so-called developing countries. In the 1990s, the United States adopted a more restrictive policy toward family planning, withdrew support for such options as abortion, and began to promote abstinence as the foundation of population control.

FERTILITY CONTROL

People in all cultures since prehistory have had ways of influencing fertility, including ways to increase it, reduce it, and regulate its spacing. Some ways are direct, such as using herbs or medicines that induce abortion. Others are indirect, such as

long periods of breastfeeding, which reduce the chances of conception.

INDIGENOUS METHODS Hundreds of direct indigenous fertility control methods are available cross-culturally (Newman 1972, 1985).

Research in Afghanistan during the 1980s found over 500 fertility-regulating techniques in just one region (Hunte 1985). In Afghanistan, as in most nonindustrial cultures, it is women who possess this information. Specialists, such as midwives or herbalists, provide further expertise. Of the total number of methods in the Afghanistan study, 72 percent were for increasing fertility, 22 percent were contraceptives, and 6 percent were used to induce abortion. Most methods involve plant and animal substances. Herbs are made into tea and taken orally. Some substances are formed into pills, some steamed and inhaled as vapors, some vaginally inserted, and others rubbed on the woman's stomach.

INDUCED ABORTION A review of 400 societies found that induced abortion was practiced in virtually all of them (Devereaux 1976). Cross-culturally, attitudes toward induced abortion range from absolute acceptability to conditional approval (abortion is acceptable but only under specified conditions), tolerance (abortion is regarded with neither approval nor disapproval), and opposition and punishment for offenders. Methods of inducing abortion include hitting the abdomen, starving oneself, taking drugs, jumping from high places, jumping up and down, lifting heavy objects, and doing hard work. Some methods clearly are dangerous to the pregnant woman. In Afghanistan, a midwife inserts an object such as a wooden spoon or stick treated with copper sulfate

In Japan, people regularly visit and decorate *mizuko*, small statues in memory of their "returned" fetuses.

▶ *In your cultural world, what is the definition and status of a fetus? Does a fetus have rights? Should it?*

into the pregnant woman to cause vaginal bleeding and eventual abortion of the fetus (Hunte 1985).

The reasons women seek to induce abortion are usually related to economic and social factors (Devereaux 1976). Pastoralist women, for example, frequently carry heavy loads, sometimes for long distances. This lifestyle does not allow women to care for many small children at one time. Poverty is another frequent motivation. A woman who is faced with a pregnancy in the context of limited resources may find abortion preferable to bearing a child that cannot be fed. Culturally defined "legitimacy" of a pregnancy and social penalties for bearing an illegitimate child provide long-standing motivations for abortion, especially in Western societies.

Some governments regulate access to abortion, either promoting it or forbidding it. Since the late 1980s, China has pursued a rigorous campaign to limit population growth (Greenhalgh 2008). Its One-Child-per-Couple Policy, announced in 1978, restricted most families to having only one child. The policy involved strict surveillance of pregnancies, strong group disapproval directed toward women pregnant for the second time or more, and forced abortions and sterilizations. Inadvertently, this policy simultaneously led to an increase in female infanticide, as parents, prompted by a preference for sons, killed or abandoned infant daughters.

Religion and abortion are often related, but there is no simple relationship between what a particular religion teaches about abortion and what people actually do. Catholicism forbids abortion, but thousands of Catholic women have sought abortions throughout the world. Predominantly Catholic countries have laws making induced abortion illegal. This is the case in Brazil where, in spite of Catholic beliefs and the law, many women, especially poor women, resort to abortion. In one impoverished shantytown in the city of Recife in the northeast, one-third of the women said that they had aborted at least once (Gregg 2003:71–72). Illegal abortions are more likely to have detrimental effects on women's health than safe, legal abortion services. Several local studies conducted in the northeastern part of Brazil, the country's poorest region, report high percentages, up to one-fourth, of maternal deaths due to complications from illegal abortion (McCallum 2005:222).

Islamic teachings forbid abortion. Abortion of female fetuses is nonetheless practiced covertly in Pakistan and by Muslims in India. Hinduism teaches *ahimsa*, or nonviolence toward other living beings, including a fetus whose movements have been felt by the mother. Thousands of Hindus, however, seek abortions every year. In contrast, Buddhism provides no overt rulings against abortion. Japanese Buddhism teaches that all life is fluid and that an aborted fetus is simply "returned" to a watery world of unshaped life and may later come back (LaFleur 1992). This belief is compatible with people's frequent use of induced abortion as a form of birth control in Japan.

THE NEW REPRODUCTIVE TECHNOLOGIES Since the early 1980s, new forms of reproductive technology have been developed and have been made available in many places around the world.

In vitro fertilization (*IVF*) is an increasingly important part of the new reproductive technologies. This procedure, designed to bypass infertility, is highly sought after by many couples in Western countries, especially middle- and upper-class couples, among whom infertility is inexplicably high. It is also becoming more available in cities worldwide (Inhorn 2003). As IVF spreads globally, people interpret it within their own cultural frameworks. In much of the United States and the

THINKING
OUTSIDE
THE BOX

In your microculture, is there a preference about the desired number of sons and daughters? Is there a preference for their birth order?

United Kingdom, where IVF first became available, people consider its use to be an indication of "reproduction gone awry," of natural inadequacy, and failure (Jenkins and Inhorn 2003). A study of male infertility in two Middle Eastern cities—Cairo in Egypt and Beirut in Lebanon—reveals how closely linked masculine identity is with male fertility (Inhorn 2004). In these cities, infertile men face serious social stigma and feelings of deep inadequacy. In addition, third-party donation of sperm is not acceptable according to Islam.

INFANTICIDE

Infanticide, or the deliberate killing of offspring, is widely practiced cross-culturally, although it is rarely a frequent or common practice. Infanticide takes two major forms: direct infanticide and indirect infanticide (Harris 1977). *Direct infanticide* is the death of an infant or child resulting from actions such as beating, smothering, poisoning, and drowning. *Indirect infanticide*, a more subtle process, may involve prolonged practices such

In Bom Jesus, a shantytown in northeastern Brazil, a doctor at the local clinic told this mother that her son was dying of anemia and that she needed to feed him red meat. The mother said, "Now, where am I going to find the money to feed my hopeless son rich food like that?"

▶ *What is your perspective on Western bonding theory, and how did you come to have this view?*

as food deprivation, failure to take a sick infant to a clinic, and failure to provide warm clothing in winter.

The most frequent motive for direct infanticide reported cross-culturally is that the infant was "deformed" or very ill (Scrimshaw 1984:490–491). Other motives for infanticide include the infant's sex, an adulterous conception, an unwed mother, the birth of twins, and too many children in the family. A study of 148 cases of infanticide in contemporary Canada found that the mothers convicted of killing their offspring were relatively young and lacked financial and family resources to help them (Daly and Wilson 1984).

Among the poor of northeastern Brazil, indirect infanticide is also related to harsh conditions and poverty (Scheper-Hughes 1992). In a shantytown called Bom Jesus, in the state of Pernambuco, Brazil, life expectancy is low. Available data on infant and child mortality in Bom Jesus since the 1960s led anthropologist Nancy Scheper-Hughes to coin the painfully ironic phrase *the modernization of mortality*. The modernization of mortality in Brazil is class based, mirroring a deep division in entitlements between the rich and the poor. Economic growth in Brazil has brought rising standards of living for many. The *infant mortality rate* (deaths of children under the age of 1 year per 1,000 births) declined dramatically in recent decades. This decline, however, is unevenly distributed. High infant death rates are concentrated among the poorest classes of society. Poverty forces mothers to selectively (and unconsciously) neglect babies that seem sickly or weak, sending them to heaven as "angel babies" rather than struggling to keep them alive. People's religious beliefs, a form of Catholicism, provide psychological support for indirect infanticide by allowing mothers to believe that their dead babies are safe in heaven. (This ethnographic case is discussed further in the next section.)

◆◆◆

Personality and the Life Cycle

Personality is an individual's patterned and characteristic way of behaving, thinking, and feeling. Cultural anthropologists think that personality is formed largely through *enculturation* (sometimes called socialization), or the learning of culture through both informal and formal processes. They study how various cultures enculturate their members into having different personalities and identities. Cultural anthropologists also investigate how personalities vary according to cultural context, and some ask why such variations exist. Others study how changing cultural contexts affect personality, identity, and well-being over the life cycle.

BIRTH, INFANCY, AND CHILDHOOD

This section first considers the cultural context of birth itself. It then discusses cultural variations in infant care and how they may shape personality and identity. Last, it deals with the topic of gender identity formation in infancy.

Mediating Cultural Conflict about the Treatment of a Newborn Baby in a U.S. Hospital Nursery

Birth practices aim to ensure that the baby will develop properly, and they vary dramatically cross-culturally. This example considers an instance of cultural conflict about the treatment of a newborn. It takes place in a hospital that had recently been built in a suburban community in the central United States to provide services for its rapidly growing immigrant population (Deitrick 2002). Most of the nurses on staff were long-time residents of the community and had graduated from a local community college, where their training included no attention to cultural differences.

The conflict arose upon the birth of a baby to a Turkish immigrant family. The infant had not yet been brought to the mother's room, but family members had arrived to welcome the new baby. With them was a Muslim religious leader who came to administer the traditional honey blessing to the infant before his first feeding. Muslims believe that this ritual ensure that the baby will have a "sweet" life.

The nurse in charge denied the family access to the baby, saying that he first must have a medical examination and that unpasteurized honey could not be given to him. The baby's father was upset and claimed that the blessing must be administered because whatever the baby first tastes determines the quality of its life.

Fortunately, a nurse who also had training in cultural anthropology, Lynn Deitrick, entered into the discussions and was able to act as a **cultural broker**, a person—often, but not always, an anthropologist—who is familiar with the practices and beliefs of two different cultures and who can promote cross-cultural understanding to prevent or mediate conflicts. Deitrick listened to the views of the Turkish family and learned that only a tiny amount of honey would be placed on the baby's tongue for the blessing. She suggested a compromise to the medical staff whereby the baby would be taken for 10 minutes to the mother's room and the Muslim cleric could administer the blessing. The attending physician agreed, saying that she was not "on record" as approving the blessing but that she understood its importance. Deitrick took the baby to the family and returned 10 minutes later to find a smiling mother and father. The baby then underwent blood tests and other medically required procedures. He was discharged in good health—and assured of a sweet life—two days later.

◆ **FOOD FOR THOUGHT**

- In your cultural world, what are some practices at birth that are considered essential for ensuring the baby's welfare?

THE BIRTH CONTEXT The cultural context of birth affects an infant's psychological development. Brigitte Jordan (1983), a pioneer in the cross-cultural study of birth, conducted comparative research on birth practices in Mexico, Sweden, the Netherlands, and the United States. She studied the birth setting, including its location and who is present, the types of attendants and their roles, the birth event, and the postpartum period. Among Maya women in Mexico, the midwife is called in during the early stages of labor. One of her tasks is to give a massage to the mother-to-be. She also provides psychological support by telling stories, often about other women's birthing experiences. The husband is expected to be present during the labor so that he can see "how a woman suffers." The woman's mother should be present, too, along with other female kin, such as her mother-in-law, godmother, sisters, and friends. Thus, a Maya mother is surrounded by a large group of supportive people.

In the United States, hospital births are the norm. The newborn infant is generally taken to the nursery, where it is wrapped in cloth and placed in a plastic crate under bright lights, rather than being cared for by a family member. Some critics argue that the hospital-based system of highly regulated birth is extremely technocratic and too managed, alienating the mother—as well as other members of the family and the wider community—from the birthing process and the infant (Davis-Floyd 1992). This critique has prompted a consideration of how to improve the way birth is conducted in the United States.

The Western medical model of birth contrasts sharply with non-Western practices. Sometimes they come into direct conflict. In such situations, anthropological expertise can mediate the conflict by providing what medical specialists now refer to as *cultural sensitivity,* or cultural awareness and respect (see Lessons Applied).

BONDING Many contemporary Western psychological theorists say that parent–infant contact and bonding at the time of birth is crucial for setting in motion parental attachment to the infant. Western specialists say that if bonding is not established at the time of the infant's birth, it will not develop later. Explanations for juvenile delinquency or

---

infanticide   the killing of an infant or child.

personality   an individual's patterned and characteristic way of behaving, thinking, and feeling.

cultural broker   a person who is familiar with the practices and beliefs of two cultures and who can promote cross-cultural understanding to prevent or mediate conflicts.

other unfavorable child development problems often include references to a lack of proper infant bonding at birth.

Nancy Scheper-Hughes (1992) questions Western bonding theory. She argues that bonding does not necessarily have to occur at birth to be successful. Her observations in Brazil show that many low-income mothers do not exhibit bonding with their infants at birth. Bonding occurs later, if the child survives infancy, when it is several years old. She proposes that this pattern of later bonding is related to the high rate of infant mortality among poor people of northeast Brazil. If women were to develop strong bonds with their newborn infants, they would suffer untold amounts of grief. Western bonding is adaptive in low-mortality, low-fertility societies in which strong maternal attachment is reasonable because infants are likely to survive.

GENDER IN INFANCY Anthropologists distinguish between *sex* and *gender* (see Chapter 1). Sex is something that everyone is born with. In the view of Western science, it has three biological markers: genitals, hormones, and chromosomes. A male has a penis, more androgens than estrogens, and the XY chromosome. A female has a vagina, more estrogens than androgens, and the XX chromosome. Increasingly, scientists are finding that these two categories are not airtight. In all populations, up to 10 percent of people are born with indeterminate genitals, similar proportions of androgens and estrogens, and chromosomes with more complex distributions than simply XX and XY.

Gender, in contrast, is a cultural construction and is highly variable across cultures (B. Miller 1993). In the view of most cultural anthropologists, a high degree of human "plasticity" (or personality flexibility) allows for substantial variation in personality and behavior. More biologically inclined anthropologists, however, continue to insist that many sex-linked personality characteristics are inborn.

Proving the existence of innate (inborn) gender characteristics is made difficult by two factors. First, it is impossible to collect data on infants before they are subject to cultural treatment. Culture may begin to shape infants even in the womb, through exposure to sound and motion, but current scientific data on the cultural effects on the prenatal stage are slim. Once birth takes place, culture shapes infants in many ways, including how people handle and interact with them. There is thus no such thing as a "natural" infant.

Second, it is difficult, if not impossible, to study and interpret the behavior of infants to try to ascertain what is "natural" and what is "cultural" without introducing biases from the observers. Studies of infants have focused on assessing the potential innateness of three major Euro-American personality stereotypes (Frieze et al. 1978:73–78):

- That infant males are more aggressive than infant females
- That infant females are more social than infant males
- That infant males are more independent than infant females

What is the evidence? Studies conducted in the United States indicate that boy babies cry more than girl babies, and some people accept this difference as evidence of higher levels of inborn aggression in males. An alternative interpretation is that baby boys, on average, tend to weigh more than girls at birth. They therefore are more likely to have a difficult delivery from which it takes time to recover. So they cry more, but not because of aggressiveness. In terms of sociability, baby girls smile more often than boys, and some researchers claim that this difference confirms innate personality characteristics. But culture, not nature, may be the explanation because American caretakers smile more at baby girls than they smile at baby boys. Thus, the more frequent smiling of girls is likely to be a learned behavior. In terms of independence or dependence, studies thus far reveal no clear differences in how upset baby boys and girls are when separated from their caretakers. Taken as a whole, studies seeking to document innate differences between girls and boys are not convincing.

Cultural anthropologists who take a constructionist view make two further points. They note that, if gender differences are innate, it is odd that cultures go to so much trouble to enculturate offspring into a particular gender. Also, if gender differences are innate, then they should be the same throughout history and across all cultures, which they clearly are not. The following material explores cross-cultural cases of how culture constructs gender, beginning with childhood.

SOCIALIZATION DURING CHILDHOOD

The Six Cultures Study is a classic cross-cultural research project designed to provide comparative data on how children's activities and tasks shape their personalities (Whiting and Whiting 1975). Researchers used parallel methods at six sites (see Figure 4.4), observing children between the ages of 3 and 11 years. They recorded the children's behavior, such as caring for and being supportive of other children; hitting other children; and performing tasks such as child care, cooking, and errands. The data collected were analyzed in terms

Horticultural Groups
Gusii people, Kenya
Maya people, Oaxaca, Mexico
Tarong people, Philippines

Intensive Agriculture or Industrial Groups
Taira village, Okinawa, Japan
Rajput people, village in North India
Middle-class Euro-Americans, Orchard Town, New England, United States

Source: Whiting and Whiting (1975).

FIGURE 4.4 Groups in the Six Cultures Study

(LEFT) A Yanomami boy acquiring skills necessary for hunting and warfare through play. (RIGHT) An American boy playing a video game.

▶ *Consider examples of children's games that may provide learning and skills related to adult roles in your culture.*

of two major personality types: nurturant-responsible and dependent-dominant. A *nurturant-responsible personality* is characterized by caring and sharing acts toward other children. The *dependent-dominant personality* involves fewer acts of caregiving, more acts that assert dominance over other children, and more need for care by adults.

Of the six cultures, the Gusii children of southwestern Kenya had the highest frequency of a nurturant-responsible personality type. Gusii children were responsible for the widest range of tasks and at earlier ages than children in any other culture in the study, often performing tasks that an Orchard Town, United States, mother does. Although some children in all six cultures took care of other children, Gusii children (both boys and girls) spent the most time doing so. They began taking on this responsibility at a very young age, between 5 and 8 years old.

In contrast, Orchard Town children had the highest frequency of the dependent-dominant personality type. The differences correlate with the mode of livelihood. The people in Kenya, Mexico, and the Philippines all had more nurturant-responsible children, and their economies are reliant on horticulture. The study sites in Japan, India, and the United States were based on either intensive agriculture or industry. How do these different modes of livelihood influence child personality?

The key underlying factor is women's work roles. In the horticultural societies, women are an important part of the labor force and spend much time working outside the home. Their children take on many family-supportive tasks and thereby develop personalities that are nurturant-responsible. When women are mainly occupied in the home, as in the second group of cultures, children have fewer tasks and less responsibility. They develop personalities that are more dependent-dominant.

This study has many implications for Western child development experts. For one thing, what happens when the dependent-dominant personality develops to an extreme level—into a *narcissistic personality*? A narcissist is someone who constantly seeks self-attention and self-affirmation, with no concern for other people's needs. Consumerism supports the development of narcissism via its emphasis on identity formation through ownership of self-defining goods (clothing, electronics, cars) and access to self-defining services (vacations, therapists, fitness salons). The Six Cultures Study

THINKING OUTSIDE THE BOX

Try to recall your daily activities when you were 5 years old, 10 years old, and 15 years old. What tasks did you do? In terms of the Six Cultures Study categories, which type of personality do you have?

suggests that involving children more in household responsibilities might result in less self-focused personality formation and more nurturant-responsible people.

ADOLESCENCE AND IDENTITY

The transition from "childhood" to "adulthood" involves certain biological events, as well as cultural events, that shape the transition to adulthood.

IS ADOLESCENCE A UNIVERSAL LIFE-CYCLE STAGE?
Puberty is a time in the human life cycle that occurs universally and involves a set of biological markers. In males, the voice deepens and facial and body hair appear; in females, menarche and breast development occur; in both males and females, pubic and underarm hair appear and sexual maturation is achieved. **Adolescence**, in contrast, is a culturally defined period of maturation from around the time of puberty until the attainment of adulthood, usually marked by becoming a parent, getting married, or becoming economically self-sufficient.

Some scholars say that all cultures define a period of adolescence. A comparative study using data on 186 societies argues for the universal existence of a culturally defined phase of adolescence (Schlegel 1995, Schlegel and Barry 1991). The researchers point to supportive evidence in the fact that people in cultures as diverse as the Navajo and the Trobriand Islanders have special terms comparable to the American term "adolescent" to refer to a person between puberty and marriage. Following a biological determinist, Darwinian model, they interpret the supposedly universal phases of adolescence as being adaptive in an evolutionary sense. The logic is that adolescence provides training for parenthood and thus contributes to enhanced reproductive success and survival of parents' genes.

Other anthropologists view adolescence as culturally constructed, highly variable, and thus impossible to explain on only biological grounds. These researchers point out that people in many cultures recognize no period of adolescence. In some others, identification of an adolescent phase is recent. Moroccan anthropologist Fatima Mernissi (1987), for example, states that adolescence became a recognized life-cycle phase for females in Morocco only in the late twentieth century:

> The idea of an adolescent unmarried woman is a completely new idea in the Muslim world, where previously you had only a female child and a menstruating woman who had to be married off immediately so as to prevent dishonorable engagement in premarital sex. (1987:xxiv)

puberty a time in the human life cycle that occurs universally and involves a set of biological markers and sexual maturation.

adolescence a culturally defined period of maturation from the time of puberty until adulthood that occurs in some, but not all, cultures.

female genital cutting (FGC) a range of practices involving partial or total removal of the clitoris and labia.

Another line of evidence supporting a cultural constructionist view is that, in different cultures, the length and elaboration of adolescence varies for males and females. In many horticultural and pastoralist societies in which men are valued as warriors, a long period between boyhood and adulthood is devoted to training in warfare and developing solidarity among males of similar ages. This pattern occurs, for example, among the Maasai (sometimes spelled Masai). The Maasai are pastoralists, numbering over 500,000, who live in a large area crossing Kenya and Tanzania (see Map 4.4). The extended adolescent period for males has nothing to do with training for parenthood. Maasai females, by contrast, move directly from being girls to being wives with no adolescent period in between. They learn adult roles when they are children.

Among some highland groups in Papua New Guinea, long periods of male initiation that involve institutionalized homosexual relationships also do not fit within the Darwinian interpretation. Gilbert Herdt conducted research with the Sambia, highland horticulturalists, and learned about their secret male initiation practices (1987). The Sambia believe that, in order for a young boy to mature into a healthy adult, he must join a secret, all-male initiation group. A boy becomes a partner of a senior male who regularly transfers his semen to the youth orally. The Sambia believe that the youth is nourished by ingesting semen. After a certain length of time in the initiation group, the "grown" youth rejoins society as a man. At that time he will marry a woman and raise children.

In some cultures, females have long adolescent phases during which they live separated from the wider group and gain special knowledge and skills (Brown 1978). After this period of seclusion, they reemerge as full-fledged women and marry.

A cultural explanation exists for why gender affects whether a young person has an adolescent phase of life. Cultural materialism (Chapter 1) explains this variation by saying that a long and marked period of adolescence is preparation for any of several culturally valued adult roles: worker, warrior, or parent. Confirmation of this hypothesis comes from the finding that an extended adolescence for females in nonindustrial societies occurs in cultures where adult females are important as food producers (Brown 1978).

COMING OF AGE AND GENDER IDENTITY Margaret Mead made famous the phrase "coming of age" in her book *Coming of Age in Samoa* (1961 [1928]). The phrase can refer generally to the period of adolescence or specifically to a ceremony or set of ceremonies that marks the boundaries of adolescence. What are the psychological aspects of such special events for the children who go through them? Some ceremonies have a sacrificial element, with symbolic death and rebirth. Most coming-of-age ceremonies are gender specific, highlighting the importance of adult roles of men and women. These ceremonies often involve marking the body of the

A Maasai warrior's mother shaves her son's head during part of his initiation ceremony into adulthood. This ritual validates her status as a mother, as well as her son's adulthood.

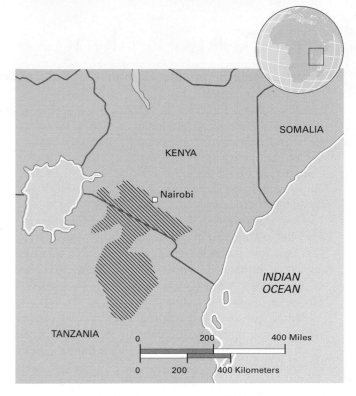

MAP 4.4 Maasai Region of Kenya and Tanzania.
An estimated 350,000 Maasai live in Kenya and 150,000 in Tanzania. The climate of both countries ranges from semiarid to arid.

initiate in some way. Such marking may include scarification, tattooing, and genital surgery.

In many societies, adolescent males undergo genital surgery that involves the removal of part of the skin around the tip of the penis; without this operation, the boy would not become a full-fledged male. Among many African pastoralist groups, such as the Maasai, adolescent males go through a circumcision ceremony that marks the end of adolescence and the beginning of manhood and full membership in the group. A young Maasai male, in a first-person account of his initiation into manhood, describes the "intolerable pain" he experienced following the circumcision, as well as his feeling of accomplishment two weeks later when his head was shaved and he became a warrior: "As long as I live, I will never forget the day my head was shaved and I emerged a man, a Maasai warrior. I felt a sense of control over my destiny so great that no words can accurately describe it" (Saitoti 1986:71).

Less common worldwide is **female genital cutting (FGC)**, or *female circumcision,* a term that refers to a range of practices involving partial or total removal of the clitoris and labia. In some contexts, FGC is practiced along with *infibulation,* the stitching together of the vaginal entry, leaving a small aperture for drainage of menstrual blood. These procedures are usually performed when a girl is between 7 and 15 years of age. In the Sahelian countries, extending from Africa's west to east coast (see Map 12.5, p. 272), many people practice some form of female genital cutting. The practice is also found in Egypt, in some groups of the Middle East (particularly among Bedu tribes), and among some Muslim groups in South and Southeast Asia. In terms of religion, FGC is often, but not always, associated with people who are Muslim. In Ethiopia, some Christian groups practice it. Genital cutting occurs in many groups in which female labor participation is high, but also in others where it is not.

Scholars have no good explanation for the regional and social distribution of female genital cutting. Anthropologists who study this practice ask the people involved for their views. Many young girls say they look forward to the ceremony so that they will be free from childhood tasks and can take on the more respected role of an adult woman. In other cases, anthropologists have reported hearing statements of resistance (Fratkin 1998:60). Fewer issues force the questioning of cultural relativism more clearly than female genital cutting (see Critical Thinking).

Initiation rites often involve themes of death and rebirth as the initiate loses his or her former identity and emerges with a new one. During the early 1990s, Abigail Adams conducted research on initiation rituals at what was then a men's military school, the Virginia Military Institute (VMI) (2002). Freshmen students, called "Rats," are each assigned to an upperclassman, called a "Dyke." The freshman year involves continuous humiliation and other forms of abuse for the Rats. Dykes treat their Rats like infants, telling them how to eat, bathe, and talk and yelling at them in baby talk. The culminating initiation ritual for the Rats takes place during March. The town's fire truck sprays the outskirts of the campus to create a large area of mud. The Rats have to crawl through the mud while sophomores and juniors attack them, shout at them, push them down, sit on them, and fill their eyes, ears, faces, and clothes with mud. The Rats can barely see as they grope their way along, and many lose their pants. The ordeal

CRITICAL thinking

Cultural Relativism and Female Genital Cutting

In cultures that practice female genital cutting (FGC), it is a necessary step toward full womanhood. Fathers say that an uncircumcised daughter is unmarriageable. Others say that removing the labia makes a woman beautiful by removing "male" parts. The prevailing Western view, increasingly being shared by many people who have long practiced female genital cutting, is that FGC is both a sign of low female status and an unnecessary cause of women's suffering.

Female genital cutting is linked with several health risks, including those related to the surgery itself (shock, infection) and future genito-urinary complications (Gruenbaum 2001). Infibulation scars the vaginal canal and may lead to problems during childbirth, sometimes causing the death of the infant and mother.

Having an infibulated bride's husband "open" her, using a stick or knife to loosen the aperture, is both painful and an opportunity for infection. After

giving birth, a woman is usually rein-fibulated, and the process begins again. Health experts say that repeated trauma to the woman's vaginal area increases the risk of contracting HIV/AIDS.

The Western view argues that the effects of both clitoridectomy and infibulation on a woman's sexual enjoyment are negative—for one thing, clitoral orgasm is no longer possible. Some experts say that FGC is related to the high level of infertility in many African countries, although a comparative study of fertility data from the Central African Republic, Côte d'Ivoire, and Tanzania found no clear relationship between FGC and infertility (Larsen and Yan 2000).

Outsiders often view these practices in oversimplified terms and in the most extreme forms. What are the views of insiders? Is there any evidence for female agency? Or is it all structure and should anthropologists support FGC liberation movements?

One voice that transcends insider–outsider divisions is that of Fuambai Ahmadu, who was born and raised in Washington, DC, and is descended from a prominent Kono lineage in Sierra Leone (2000).

In 1991, Ahmadu traveled to Sierra Leone with her mother and other family members for what she refers to as her "circumcision." Upon her return, she wrote about her initiation experience and what it meant to her. Although the physical pain was excruciating (in spite of the use of anesthetics), "the positive aspects have been much more profound" (2000:306). Through the initiation, she became part of a powerful female world. Her analysis addresses the effects of genital cutting on health and sexuality. Ahmadu argues that Westerners exaggerate these issues by focusing on infibulation rather than on the less extreme forms. She adds, however, that if global pressures against the practice continue, she will go along

continues over two banks of earth and a ditch, with continuous harassment from the sophomores and juniors. When the Rats finally reach the top of the second bank, the Dykes rush to greet them, tenderly wash the mud off them, and wrap them in blankets. The moment when the mud is washed away is the transition of the Rat into a cadet.

Adams interprets this ritual as a birthing event, with the newborn emerging blinded by and covered with fluids, then cleaned and blanketed. One senior said that being a Dyke "is like having my own child" (2002:39). Many aspects of this ritual, however, are ambiguous, not least of which is the term "Dyke" for male "mothers" (or "fathers"?). The Breaking Out initiation ritual is no longer practiced at VMI. In the mid-1990s, VMI, as the recipient of public funds, was under pressure to admit women in order to be compliant with the law. After a drawn-out legal battle that ended up in the Supreme Court, VMI admitted its first women students in 1997. Breaking Out has been replaced with a long weekend series of events involving physical and field challenges.

SEXUAL IDENTITY AND GENDER PLURALISM Scholars have long debated whether sexual preferences and gender

identity are biologically determined (ruled by genetic or hormonal factors) or culturally constructed and learned. Biological anthropologist Melvin Konner (1989) takes a middle position, saying that both factors play a part, but simultaneously

Breaking Out, a rite of passage at a military academy in Virginia when it was an all-men's school.

▶ *What rite of passage have you been through, and how would you analyze it anthropologically?*

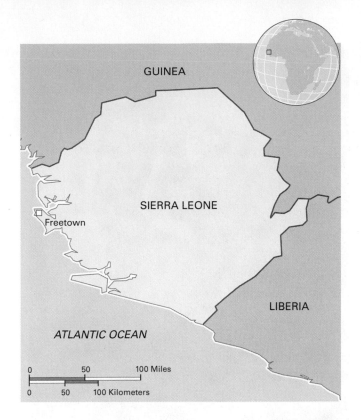

MAP 4.5 Sierra Leone.
The Republic of Sierra Leone was an important center of the transatlantic slave trade. Its capital, Freetown, was established in 1792 as a home for African slaves who fought with the British during the American Revolution. Sierra Leone's coast is covered with mangrove swamps, while the interior is plateau, forests, and mountains. The population is 6 million. Sierra Leone suffered a terrible civil war from 1991 to 2002, causing thousands of deaths and the displacement of 2 million people. It has the lowest per capita income in the world. English is the official language, but most people speak local, tribal languages.

with that movement and support "ritual without cutting" (2000:308).

◆ **CRITICAL THINKING QUESTIONS**

• Why do you think FGC is a prominent issue in human rights debates in the West, whereas male circumcision and other forms of initiation (such as fraternity and sorority hazing) are not?

• Where do you stand on FGC and why?

• What kinds of cultural remodeling of the female body are practiced in your culture?

warning that no one has a simple answer to the question of who is gay.

The cultural constructionist position emphasizes socialization and childhood experiences as more powerful than biology in shaping sexual orientation. These anthropologists find support for their position in the cross-cultural record and its cases in which people change their sexual orientation once, or sometimes more than once, during their lifetimes. The Sambia of Papua New Guinea are one example. In the Gulf state of Oman, the *xanith* (hah-neeth) is another example (Wikan 1977). A xanith is a man who, for a time, becomes more like a woman, wears female clothing, and has sex with other men. Later, the xanith returns to a standard male role, marries a woman, and has children. Thus, given the same biological material, some people assume different sexual identities over their lives.

No matter what one's theoretical perspective is, it is clear that homosexuals are discriminated against in many contexts in which heterosexuality is the norm. In the United States, homosexuals are disproportionately victims of hate crimes, housing discrimination, and problems in the workplace, including wage and benefits discrimination. They often suffer

from being stigmatized by their parents, peers, and the wider society. The psychological damage to their self-esteem by social stigma and discrimination is related to the fact that homosexual youth in the United States have substantially higher suicide rates than heterosexual youth.

Some cultures allow for a third gender, which is neither purely "male" nor purely "female," according to a particular culture's definition of those terms. As with the xanith of Oman, these gender categories offer ways for "males" to cross gender lines and assume more "female" behaviors, personality characteristics, and dress. Among some American Indians, a **berdache** (ber-DASH) is a male, in terms of genitals, who opts to wear female clothing, engages in sexual intercourse with a man or a woman, and does female tasks such as basket weaving and pottery making (Williams 1992). A person may become a berdache in a variety of ways. Sometimes parents, especially if they have several sons, choose one to become a berdache. Sometimes a boy who shows interest in typically

---

berdache a blurred gender category, usually referring to a person who is biologically male but who takes on a female gender role.

female activities or who likes to wear female clothing is allowed to become a berdache. Such a child is a focus of pride for the family, never a source of disappointment or stigma.

During decades of contact with Euro-American colonizers, including Christian missionaries, the outsiders viewed the berdache role with disapproval and ridicule (Roscoe 1991). American Indian cultures began to suppress their berdache tradition. Starting in the 1980s, as American Indians' cultural pride began to grow, the open presence of the berdache and the **amazon**, a woman who takes on male roles and behaviors, has returned. Contemporary American Indian cultures, compared with mainstream White culture, are more accepting of gender role fluidity and the contemporary concept of being gay.

In India, the counterpart of the berdache is a **hijra** (hij-ruh). Hijras dress and act like women but are neither truly male nor truly female (Nanda 1990). Many hijras were born with male genitals or with genitals that were not clearly male or female. Hijras have the traditional right to visit the home of a newborn, inspect its genitals, and claim it for their group if the genitals are neither clearly male nor clearly female. Hijras born with male genitals may opt to go through an initiation ceremony that involves cutting off their penis and testicles. Hijras roam large cities of India, earning a living by begging from store to store and threatening to lift their skirts if not given money. Because women do not sing or dance in public, hijras play an important role as performers in public events, especially as dancers or musicians. Mainstream Indians do not admire or respect hijras, and no family would be delighted to hear that their son has decided to become a hijra.

In mainland and island Southeast Asia, the situation is more open, with a wide range of gender options, or **gender pluralism**. Gender pluralism is the existence in a culture of multiple categories of femininity, masculinity, and blurred genders that are tolerated and legitimate (Peletz 2006:310). In Thailand, three gender categories have long existed: *phuuchai* (male), *phuuyung* (female), and *kathoey* (transvestite/transsexual/hermaphrodite) (Morris 1994). A kathoey is "originally" a male

The South Korean transgender musical group "Lady" includes four transsexuals.

who crosses into the body, personality, and dress defined as female. The sexual orientation of kathoeys is flexible, including either male or female partners. In contemporary Thailand, explicit discussion and recognition of homosexuality exists, usually couched in English terms, conveying a sense of its foreignness. The words for lesbian are *thom* (from the word "tomboy") and *thut* (an ironic usage from the U.S. movie *Tootsie*, about a heterosexual man playing the part of a woman).

ADULTHOOD

For most people, adulthood means entering into some form of marriage or long-term domestic relationship and having children. The following discussion considers the psychological aspects of parenthood and the "senior years."

BECOMING A PARENT In Euro-American culture, a woman becomes a mother when she gives birth. **Matrescence** is the cultural process of becoming a mother (Raphael 1975). Like adolescence, matrescence varies cross-culturally in terms of duration and meaning. In some cultures, a woman is transformed into a mother as soon as she thinks she is pregnant. In others, she becomes a mother and is granted full maternal status only when she delivers an infant of the "right" sex, as in much of northern India, where son preference is strong.

---

amazon   a person who is biologically female but takes on a male gender role.

hijra   in India, a blurred gender role in which a person, usually biologically male, takes on female dress and behavior.

gender pluralism   the existence within a culture of multiple categories of femininity, masculinity, and blurred genders that are tolerated and legitimate.

matrescence   motherhood, or the cultural process of becoming a mother.

patrescence   fatherhood, or the cultural process of becoming a father.

couvade   customs applying to the behavior of fathers during and shortly after the birth of their children.

An Aka father and his son. Aka fathers are affectionate caretakers of infants and small children. Compared with mothers, they are more likely to kiss and hug children.

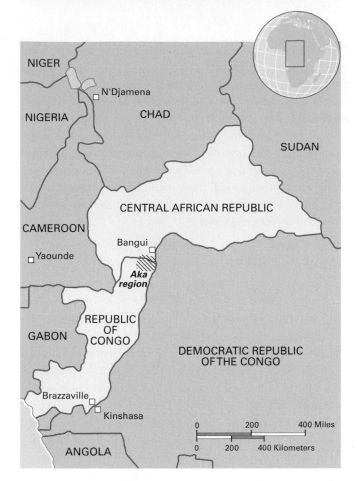

MAP 4.6 Aka Region of the Central African Republic and the Democratic Republic of Congo.
The 30,000 Aka are tropical forest foragers who know hundreds of plants and animals. They eat roots, leaves, nuts, fruits, mushrooms, honey, grubs, caterpillars, and meat from monkeys, rats, mongooses, and porcupines. They trade meat to farmers for manioc and other cultivated foods. They are socially egalitarian, and their religious beliefs are indigenous. Diaka, their main language, is tonal. The Aka territory is critically endangered by commercial loggers.

In many nonindustrial cultures, matrescence occurs in the context of supportive family members. Some cultures promote prenatal practices, abiding by particular food taboos, which can be regarded as part of matrescence. Such rules make the pregnant woman feel that she has a role in ensuring that the pregnancy turns out well. In the West, medical experts increasingly define the prenatal period as an important phase of matrescence, and they have issued many scientific and medical rules for potential parents, especially mothers (Browner and Press 1996). Pregnant women are urged to seek prenatal examinations, be under the regular supervision of a doctor who monitors the growth and development of the fetus, follow particular dietary and exercise guidelines, and undergo a range of tests such as ultrasound scanning. Some anthropologists think that such medical control of pregnancy leads to the greater likelihood of postpartum depression, as a result of the mother's lack of agency in the process of matrescence.

Patrescence, or the cultural process of becoming a father, is less marked cross-culturally than matrescence. One exception to this generalization is **couvade** (coo-VAHD), beliefs and customs applying to a father during his wife's pregnancy and delivery (Broude 1988). In some cases, the father takes to his bed before, during, or after the delivery, and he may experience pain and exhaustion. Couvade often involves rules for the expectant father: He may not hunt a certain animal, eat certain foods, or cut objects. Early theories of why couvade exists relied on Freudian interpretations that men were identifying with the female role in contexts where the father role was weak. Cross-cultural data indicate the opposite, because couvade occurs in societies where fathers have prominent roles in child care. In these contexts, couvade is a

phase of patrescence: The father's proper behavior helps ensure a safe delivery and a healthy baby. Another interpretation of couvade is that it offers support for the mother.

Once the baby is born, who takes care of it? The widespread pattern of women being the major caretakers of infants and children has led many people to think that something biologically innate about females makes them especially suited to caretaking roles. Most cultural anthropologists agree that child care is predominantly the responsibility of females worldwide—but not universally. They seek to provide a cultural construction explanation rather than a genetic or hormonal one. As evidence, they point to the cross-cultural variation in child-care roles. For example, throughout the South Pacific, child care is shared across families, and women breastfeed other women's babies. Paternal involvement varies cross-culturally as well. Among Aka foragers of the Central African Republic (see Map 4.6), paternal child care is prominent (Hewlett 1991).

Aka fathers are intimate, affectionate, and helpful, spending half their time each day holding or within close reach of their infants. Fathers are more likely to hug and kiss their infants than mothers are. The definition of good fatherhood among the Aka means being affectionate toward children and assisting the mother when her workload is heavy. Among the Aka, gender equality prevails and violence against women is unknown. This high level of paternal involvement is related to all these patterns and supports a constructionist view of parenting and gender roles rather than a biological determinist view.

MIDDLE AGE In many industrial/informatic societies, a major turning point for men is the fortieth birthday. According to a study of men turning 40 in the United States, the *40 syndrome* involves feelings of restlessness, rebelliousness, and unhappiness that often lead to family break-ups (Brandes 1985). A possible reason behind the emphasis on the age 40 as a turning point for males is that it is the current midpoint of a typical life span for a middle-class American man. In cultures with shorter life spans, a so-called midlife crisis would necessarily occur at some point other than the age of 40 years. The midlife crisis in America seems strongly embedded in contemporary culture and its fear and denial of death (Shore 1998).

Menopause, or the cessation of menstruation, is a significant aspect of middle age for women in many, but not all, cultures. A comparative study examined differences in the perception and experience of menopause among Maya women of Mexico and rural Greek women (Beyene 1989). Among the Maya women, menopause is not a time of stress or crisis. They consider menstruation an illness and look forward to its end. Menopause among these women is not associated with physical or emotional symptoms. None of the women reported hot flashes or cold sweats. No role changes were associated with menopause. In contrast, the rural Greek women recognized menopause, or *exapi* (eh-SHAP-ee), as a natural phenomenon that all women experience, which is a phase of hot flashes, especially at night, that may last about a year. The women did not think exapi was serious and did not regard it as worthy of medical attention. Postmenopausal women emphasized the relief and freedom they felt. Postmenopausal women can go into cafes by themselves, something they would never do otherwise, and they can participate more fully in church ceremonies. In Japan, likewise, menopause is minimally stressful and women rarely consider it something that warrants medical attention (Lock 1993).

THE SENIOR YEARS The senior life-cycle stage may be a development of contemporary human society, because, like most other mammals, our early ancestors rarely lived beyond their reproductive years. Cross-culturally, the category of the aged is variably recognized, defined, and valued. In many cultures, elders are highly revered as having great wisdom based on their life experiences. In others, aged people become burdens to their families and to society.

Cross-cultural comparisons reveal that the status of elderly people is higher and their welfare more secure in contexts where they continue to live with their families (Lee and Kezis 1979). This pattern is, however, more likely to be found in nonindustrial societies than in industrialized ones, where the elderly live with younger kin less frequently. Instead, they are increasingly experiencing a shift to living in age-segregated residences such as "retirement homes," where they have to create new social roles and ties and find new ways of gaining self-esteem and personal satisfaction. Research conducted in a retirement home in a small town in central New York state shows that having a pet promotes a person's sense of well-being (Savishinsky 1991).

THE FINAL PASSAGE: DEATH AND DYING It may be that no one in any culture welcomes death, unless he or she is in very poor health and suffering greatly. The contemporary United States, with its dependence on medical technology, appears to play a leading role in resistance to death, often at high financial and psychological costs. In many other cultures, a greater degree of acceptance prevails.

A study of attitudes toward death and dying among Alaskan Inuits revealed a pervasive feeling that people are active participants in their death rather than passive victims (Trelease 1975). The person near death calls friends and neighbors together, is given a Christian sacrament, and then, within a few hours, dies. The author comments, "I do not suggest that everyone waited for the priest to come and then died right away. But the majority who did not die suddenly did some degree of planning, had some kind of formal service or celebration of prayers and hymns and farewells" (1975:35).

Terminally ill people, especially in industrial/informatic societies with a high level of medical technology, are likely to be faced with choices about how and where they should die, at home or in a hospital, and whether they should prolong their lives with "unusual means" or opt for "physician-assisted suicide." Depending on the cultural context, the options are affected not only by the degree of medical technology and health-care services available but also by matters of kinship and gender role ideals (Long 2005). In urban Japan, terminally ill people have clear ideas of what is a "good death" and two major "scripts" for a "good death." A modern script of dying in a hospital is widely accepted, because it reduces burdens on family members. But a value on dying surrounded by one's family members still prevails;

Virginia Tech students, their relatives, faculty, and others hold a candlelight vigil on the campus in Blacksburg, Virginia, following the murders there in April 2007.

this practice reassures the dying person that he or she will be remembered.

In many cultures, the inability to perform a proper burial and funeral for a deceased person is a cause of serious social suffering. Among refugees from Mozambique living in neighboring Malawi, the greatest cause of stress was being forced to leave behind deceased family members without providing a proper burial for them (Englund 1998). Such improperly treated deaths mean that the unhappy spirit of the deceased will haunt the living. This belief is related to the high rate of mental-health problems among the refugees. A culturally informed recommendation for reducing their anxiety is to provide them with money to travel home and to perform a proper funeral for their deceased relatives. In that way, the living may carry on in greater peace.

Anthropologists know little about people's grief at the death of a loved one or a close community member. It might seem that sadness and grief, as well as a period of mourning, are only natural. But the outward expression of grief varies from extended, dramatic, public grieving that is overtly emotional to no visible sign of grief at all. The latter pattern is the norm in Bali, Indonesia (see Map 1.2, p. 14), where people's faces remain impassive at funerals and no vocal lamenting occurs (Rosenblatt et al. 1976). Do impassive faces and silence mean that the Balinese feel no sadness? Such different modes of expression of loss may be related to the healing process for the survivors by providing socially accepted rules of behavior—in other words, a script for loss. Either highly expressive public mourning or repressed grief may be equally effective, depending on the context.

4

the BIG questions REVISITED

◆ How are modes of reproduction related to modes of livelihood?

Cultural anthropologists define three modes of reproduction that are related to foraging, agriculture, and industrialism/informatics. They differ in terms of desired and actual fertility.

For thousands of years, foragers maintained a balanced level of population through direct and indirect means of fertility regulation. A classic study of the Ju/'hoansi shows how foragers' lifestyles, including a low-fat diet and women's physical activity, suppress fertility.

As sedentary lifestyles increased and food surpluses became more available and storable with agriculture, population growth increased. The highest rates of population growth in human prehistory and history are found among settled agriculturalists. Contemporary examples of high-fertility agriculturalists are the Amish and Mennonite people of North America.

◆ How does culture shape fertility in different contexts?

Cross-culturally, many techniques exist for increasing fertility, reducing it, and regulating its timing. From culture to culture, values differ about the right age for people to start having sexual relations and how often they do so. In terms of cultural practices that directly affect fertility, hundreds of different traditional methods exist, including the use of herbs and other natural substances for either preventing or promoting fertilization and for inducing abortion if an undesired pregnancy occurs.

In nonindustrialized societies, knowledge about fertility regulation, as well as its practice, is largely unspecialized and available to all women. In the industrial/informatics mode of reproduction, scientific and medical specialization increases, and most knowledge and expertise are in the hands of professionals rather than of women. Class-stratified access to fertility-regulating methods now exists both globally and within nations.

Population growth is also shaped through the practice of infanticide, which, though of ancient origin, still exists today. It is sometimes performed in response to limited family resources, perceptions of inadequate "fitness" of the child, or preferences regarding the gender of offspring.

◆ How does culture shape personality over the life cycle?

Cultural anthropologists emphasize the effects of infant care practices on personality formation, including gender identity. Other cross-cultural studies show that variations in the gender division of labor and children's work roles in the family correspond to varying personality patterns. Adolescence, a culturally defined time beginning around puberty and running until adulthood, varies cross-culturally from being nonexistent to involving detailed training and elaborate ceremonies.

In contrast to the sharp distinction between "male" and "female" in Euro-American culture, many cultures have traditions of third gender identities. Gender pluralism is found in many cultures, especially in some American Indian and Asian cultures.

Cross-culturally, adult roles usually involve parenthood. In nonindustrial societies, learning about motherhood is embedded in other aspects of life and knowledge about birthing and child care is shared among women. In industrialized/informatic cultures, science and medicine play a large part in defining the maternal role.

The senior years are generally shorter in nonindustrialized societies than in industrialized/informatic societies, in which life spans tend to be longer. Elderly men and women in nonindustrial cultures are treated with respect, are assumed to know the most, and retain a strong sense of their place in the culture. Increasingly in industrialized/informatic societies, elderly people live apart from their families and spend many years in age-segregated institutions such as retirement homes or alone.

KEY CONCEPTS

adolescence, p. 90
amazon, p. 94
berdache, p. 93
couvade, p. 95
cultural broker, p. 87

demographic transition, p. 79
female genital cutting
    (FGC), p. 91
fertility, p. 78
gender pluralism, p. 94

hijra, p. 94
infanticide, p. 86
matrescence, p. 94
menarche, p. 82
menopause, p. 82

mode of reproduction, p. 78
patrescence, p. 95
personality, p. 86
pronatalism, p. 78
puberty, p. 90

SUGGESTED READINGS

Kamran Asdar Ali. *Planning the Family in Egypt: New Bodies, New Selves.* Austin: University of Texas Press, 2002. The author, a Pakistani doctor and anthropologist, provides a critique of family planning policies and programs in Egypt that pressure women to act in the country's interest by limiting their fertility.

Robbie E. Davis-Floyd. *Birth as an American Rite of Passage*, 2nd ed. Berkeley: University of California Press, 2003. This book provides a cultural critique of the dominant U.S. model of birth as "technocratic" and patriarchal.

Jessica L. Gregg. *Virtually Virgins: Sexual Strategies and Cervical Cancer in Recife, Brazil.* Stanford, CA: Stanford University Press, 2003. Research with women residents of a poor urban area in northeast Brazil and with women cancer victims in a neighborhood maternity clinic shows how the women attempt to deal with racism, sexism, poverty, and violence.

Ellen Gruenbaum. *The Female Circumcision Controversy: An Anthropological Perspective.* Philadelphia: University of Pennsylvania Press, 2001. The author draws on her more than five years of fieldwork in Sudan and discusses how change is occurring through economic development, the role of Islamic activists, health educators, and educated African women.

Marcia C. Inhorn. *Infertility and Patriarchy: The Cultural Politics of Gender and Family Life in Egypt.* Philadelphia: University of Pennsylvania Press, 1996. Based on fieldwork in Alexandria, this book uses narratives from infertile Egyptian women to show how they and their families deal with cultural pressures to bear children.

Shahram Khosravi. *Young and Defiant in Tehran.* Philadelphia: University of Pennsylvania Press, 2008. This ethnographic study documents how youths in the Iranian capital contest official culture and parental domination.

Robert A. LeVine and Rebecca S. New, ed. *Anthropology and Child Development: A Cross-Cultural Reader.* Malden, MA: Blackwell Publishing, 2008. Twenty-four chapters discuss childhood around the world. The collection includes classic essays by Boas, Mead, and Malinowski, as well as recent studies. Some chapters present case studies and some are comparative. Topics range from child care in the Kalahari desert to children's play in Italy.

Michael Moffatt. *Coming of Age in New Jersey: College and American Culture.* New Brunswick, NJ: Rutgers University Press, 1991. Based on a year's participant observation in a college dormitory in a university in the eastern United States, this study discusses sexuality, race relations, and individualism.

Leith Mullings and Alaka Wali. *Stress and Resilience: The Social Context of Reproduction in Central Harlem.* New York: Kluwer Academic, 2001. Documenting the daily efforts of African Americans to contend with oppressive conditions, this ethnography focuses on the experiences of women during pregnancy.

Michael G. Peletz. *Gender Pluralism: Southeast Asia since Early Modern Times.* New York: Routledge, 2008. This book provides an understanding of the historical cultural traditions of cross-dressing and the current political climate toward transvestites and homosexuals in Southeast Asia.

Sarah Pinto. *Where There Is No Midwife: Birth and Loss in Rural India.* New York: Bergahn Books, 2008. Pinto examines women's experiences with childbirth and infant death in a poor region in rural northern India with high rates of infant mortality.

Nancy Scheper-Hughes. *Death without Weeping: The Violence of Everyday Life in Brazil.* Berkeley: University of California Press, 1993. This book is a landmark "ethnography of death," based on fieldwork in a shantytown in northeastern Brazil. The author argues that extreme social inequality in Brazil creates a stratified demography.

John W. Traphagan. *Taming Oblivion: Aging Bodies and the Fear of Senility in Japan.* Albany: State University of New York Press, 2000. The author conducted fieldwork in a small town north of Tokyo to investigate people's attitudes and practices related to old age, especially as aging people attempt to prevent the onset of the *boke* condition, or what Westerners call senility.

Andrea S. Wiley. *An Ecology of High-Altitude Infancy: A Biocultural Perspective.* New York: Cambridge University Press, 2004. Ladakh is a district in India's far north, high in the Himalayas. Wiley focuses on the links between biology and culture in birth, in infant health and survival, and in women's reproductive health.

Shaman Gray Squirrel of the Navajo of New Mexico prepares a sand painting as part of a four-day ritual to bring rain. Sand paintings are now also produced on paper or canvas for sale in the commercial art market. They have nothing to do with rain making.

DISEASE, ILLNESS, AND HEALING

5

the BIG questions

◆ What is ethnomedicine?

◆ What are three major theoretical approaches in medical anthropology?

◆ How are health, illness, and healing changing during globalization?

OUTLINE

Ethnomedicine

Eye on the Environment: Local Botanical Knowledge and Child Health in the Bolivian Amazon

Three Theoretical Approaches

Globalization and Change

Culturama: The Sherpa of Nepal

Lessons Applied: Promoting Vaccination Programs in Developing Countries

South African healer Magdaline Ramaota speaks to clients in Durban. In South Africa, few people have enough money to pay for HIV/AIDS drugs. The role of traditional healers in providing psychological and social support for victims is extremely important.

▶ *Do Internet research to learn about the current and projected rates of HIV/AIDS in African countries.*

Medical anthropology is one of the most rapidly growing areas of research in anthropology. This chapter first describes how people in different cultures think and behave regarding health, illness, and healing. The second section considers three theoretical approaches in medical anthropology. The chapter concludes by discussing how globalization is affecting health.

---

ethnomedicine the study of cross-cultural health systems.

Western biomedicine (WBM) a healing approach based on modern Western science that emphasizes technology for diagnosing and treating health problems related to the human body.

disease in the disease–illness dichotomy, a biological health problem that is objective and universal.

illness in the disease–illness dichotomy, culturally shaped perceptions and experiences of a health problem.

◆◆◆
Ethnomedicine

Since the early days of anthropology, the topic of **ethnomedicine**, or the study of cross-cultural health systems, has been a focus of research. A *health system* encompasses many areas: perceptions and classifications of health problems, prevention measures, diagnosis, healing (magical, religious, scientific, healing substances), and healers.

In the 1960s, when the term *ethnomedicine* first came into use, it referred only to non-Western health systems and was synonymous with the now abandoned term *primitive medicine*. The early use of the term was ethnocentric. Contemporary **Western biomedicine (WBM)**, a healing approach based on modern Western science that emphasizes technology in diagnosing and treating health problems related to the human body, is an ethnomedical system, too. Medical anthropologists now study WBM as a cultural system intimately bound to Western values. Thus, the current meaning of the term *ethnomedicine* encompasses health systems everywhere.

DEFINING AND CLASSIFYING HEALTH PROBLEMS

Emic diversity in labeling health problems presents a challenge for medical anthropologists and health-care specialists.

The Brazilian girl, aged 9 years, is HIV positive. Her mother contracted HIV from her husband and transmitted it to her child at birth.

Western labels, which biomedically trained experts accept as true, accurate, and universal, often do not correspond to the labels in other cultures. One set of concepts that medical anthropologists use to sort out the many cross-cultural labels and perceptions is the *disease–illness dichotomy*. In this model, **disease** refers to a biological health problem that is objective and universal, such as a bacterial or viral infection or a broken arm. **Illness** refers to culturally specific perceptions and experiences of a health problem. Medical anthropologists study both disease and illness, and they show how both must be understood within their cultural contexts.

A first step in ethnomedical research is to learn how people label, categorize, and classify health problems. Depending on the culture, the following may be bases for labeling and classifying health problems: cause, *vector* (the means of transmission, such as mosquitoes), affected body part, symptoms, or combinations of these.

Often, knowledgeable elders are the keepers of ethnomedical knowledge, and they pass it down through oral traditions. Among American Indians of the Washington–Oregon region, many popular stories refer to health (Thompson and Sloat 2004). The stories convey messages about how to prevent health problems, avoid bodily harm, relieve afflictions, and deal with old age. For example, here is the story of Boil, a story for young children:

> Boil was getting bigger.
>
> Her husband told her to bathe.
>
> She got into the water.
>
> She disappeared. (2004:5)

Other, longer stories about Boil add complexities about the location of the boil and how to deal with particular boils, revealing indigenous patterns of classification.

A classic study among the Subanun (soo-BAH-nun) people focused on their categories of health problems (Frake 1961). In the 1950s, the Subanun were horticulturalists living in the highlands of Mindanao, in the Philippines (see Map 5.1). An egalitarian people, all Subanun, even young children, had substantial knowledge about health problems. Of their 186 labels for health problems, some are a single term, such as "itch," which can be expanded on by using two words, such as "splotchy itch." Skin diseases are common afflictions among the Subanun and have several degrees of specificity (see Figure 5.1).

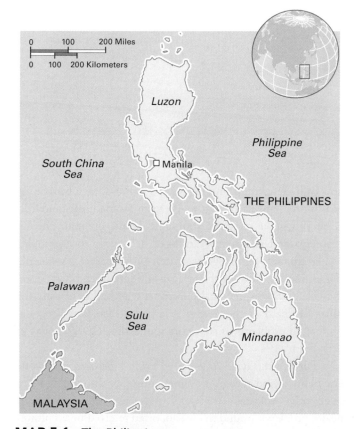

MAP 5.1 The Philippines.
The Republic of the Philippines comprises over 7000 islands, of which around 700 are populated. The population is 85 million, with two-thirds living on Luzon. The economy is based on agriculture, light industry, and a growing business-processing outsourcing (BPO) industry. Over 8 million Filipinos work overseas and remit more than $12 billion a year, a large part of the country's GDP. Although Filipino and English are the official languages, more than 170 languages are spoken. The Philippines has the world's third-largest Christian population, with Roman Catholicism predominant.

- Rash
- Eruption
- Inflammation
  — Eruption
  — Inflamed/Quasi-Bite
  — Ulcerated
- Sore
  — Distal Ulcer
    Shallow
    Deep
  — Proximal Ulcer
    Shallow
    Deep
  — Simple Sore
  — Spreading Sore
- Ringworm
  — Exposed
  — Hidden
  — Spreading Itch
- Wound

Source: Adapted from Frake 1961:118, Figure 1.

FIGURE 5.1 Subanun Categories of *Nuka*, Skin-Related Health Problems

Name of Syndrome	Distribution	Attributed Causes	Description and Symptoms
Anorexia nervosa	Middle- and upper-class Euro-American girls; globalizing	Unknown	Body wasting due to food avoidance; feeling of being too fat; in extreme cases, death
Hikikomori	Japan, males from adolescence through adulthood	Social pressure to succeed in school and pursue a position as a salaryman	Acute social withdrawal; refusal to attend school, or leave their room for months, sometimes years
Koro	China and Southeast Asia, men	Unknown	Belief that the penis has retracted into the body
Peito aberto (open chest)	Northeastern Brazil, especially women, perhaps elsewhere among Latino populations	Excessive worry about others	Enlarges the heart and "bursts" through it causing "openings in the heart"
Retired Husband Syndrome (RHS)	Japan, older women whose husbands are retired	Stress	Ulcers, slurred speech, rashes around the eyes, throat polyps
Sufriendo del agua (suffering from water)	Valley of Mexico, low-income people, especially women	Lack of access to secure and clean water	Anxiety
Susto	Spain, Portugal, Central and South America, Latino immigrants in the U.S. and Canada	Shock or fright	Lethargy, poor appetite, problems sleeping, anxiety

Sources: Chowdhury 1996; Ennis-McMillan 2001; Faiola 2005; Gremillion 1992; Kawanishi 2004; Rehbun 1994; Rubel, O'Nell, and Collado-Ardón 1984.

FIGURE 5.2 Selected Culture-Specific Syndromes

In Western biomedicine, panels of medical experts have to agree about how to label and classify health problems according to scientific criteria. Classifications and descriptions of thousands of afflictions are published in thick manuals that physicians consult before they give a diagnosis. In countries where medical care is privatized, the code selected may determine whether the patient's costs are covered by insurance or not. The *International Classification of Diseases (ICD)*, now in its tenth edition (1993), is a major source for coding health problems according to Western biomedical standards. Even though it contains abundant details on many health problems and is carefully arranged according to a complex coding system, its categories often prove to be inadequate. For example, following the attacks of September 11, 2001, on the United States, medical personnel who had to classify the cause of death of those who perished at the four sites and the health problems of survivors found the *ICD-10* codes of little help.

Further, the *ICD-10* is biased toward diseases that Western biomedicine recognizes and ignores health problems of many other cultures. Anthropologists have discovered many health problems around the world, often referred to as culture-specific syndromes. A **culture-specific syndrome** is a health problem with a set of symptoms associated with a particular culture (see Figure 5.2). Social factors such as stress, fear, or shock often are the underlying causes of culture-specific syndromes. Biophysical symptoms may be involved, and culture-specific syndromes can be fatal. **Somatization**, or embodiment, refers to the process through which the body absorbs social stress and manifests symptoms of suffering.

For example, **susto**, or "fright/shock disease," is found in Spain and Portugal and among Latino people wherever they

culture-specific syndrome a collection of signs and symptoms that is restricted to a particular culture or a limited number of cultures.

somatization the process through which the body absorbs social stress and manifests symptoms of suffering; also called embodiment.

susto fright/shock disease, a culture-specific illness found in Spain and Portugal and among Latino people wherever they live; symptoms include back pain, fatigue, weakness, and lack of appetite.

ethno-etiology a culturally specific causal explanation for health problems and suffering.

structural suffering human health problems caused by such economic and political situations as war, famine, terrorism, forced migration, and poverty.

live. People afflicted with susto attribute it to events such as losing a loved one or having a terrible accident (Rubel, O'Nell, and Collado-Ardón 1984). In Oaxaca, southern Mexico (see Map 4.3, p. 84), a woman said her susto was brought on by an accident in which pottery she had made was broken on its way to market, whereas a man said that his came on after he saw a dangerous snake. Susto symptoms include loss of appetite, lack of motivation, breathing problems, generalized pain, and nightmares. The researchers analyzed many cases of susto in three villages. They found that the people most likely to be afflicted were those who were socially marginal or experiencing a sense of role failure. For example, the woman with the broken pots had also suffered two spontaneous abortions and was worried that she would never have children. In Oaxaca, people with susto have higher mortality rates than other people. Thus, social marginality, or a deep sense of social failure, can place a person at a higher risk of dying. It is important to look at the deeper causes of susto.

Medical anthropologists first studied culture-specific syndromes in non-Western cultures. This focus created a bias in thinking that they exist only in "other" cultures. Now anthropologists recognize that Western cultures also have culture-specific syndromes. Anorexia nervosa and a related condition, bulimia, are culture-bound syndromes found mainly among White middle-class adolescent girls of the United States, although some cases have been documented among African American girls in the United States and among young males (Fabrega and Miller 1995). Since the 1990s, and perhaps as a result of Western globalization, cases have been documented in Hong Kong and in cities in Japan and India. Anorexia nervosa's cluster of symptoms includes self-perception of fatness, aversion to food, hyperactivity, and, as the condition progresses, continued wasting of the body and often death.

No one has found a clear biological cause for anorexia nervosa, although some researchers claim that it has a genetic basis. Cultural anthropologists say that much evidence suggests a strong role for cultural construction. One logical result of the role of culture is that medical and psychiatric treatments are notably unsuccessful in curing anorexia nervosa (Gremillion 1992). Extreme food deprivation can become addictive and entrapping, and the affliction becomes *embodied*, intertwined with the body's biological functions. Extended fasting makes the body unable to deal with ingested food. Thus, medical treatment may involve intravenous feeding to override the biological block. Sometimes nothing works, and the affliction is fatal.

Pinpointing the cultural causes of anorexia nervosa, however, is difficult. Some experts cite societal pressures on girls that lead to excessive concern with looks, especially body weight. Others feel that anorexia is related to girls' unconscious resistance to overcontrolling parents. For such girls, food intake may be one thing over which they have power.

ETHNO-ETIOLOGIES

People in all cultures, everywhere, attempt to make sense of health problems and try to understand their cause, or *etiology*. The term **ethno-etiology** refers to a cross-culturally specific causal explanation for health problems and suffering.

Among the urban poor of northeastern Brazil, people consider several causal possibilities when they are sick (Ngokwey 1988). In Feira de Santana, the second-largest city in the state of Bahia in the northeast (see Map 3.3, p. 57), ethno-etiologies can be natural, socioeconomic, psychological, or supernatural. Natural causes include exposure to the environment. For example, people say that humidity and rain cause rheumatism, excessive heat causes dehydration, and some types of winds cause migraines. Other natural explanations for illness take into account the effects of aging, heredity, personality, and gender. Contagion is another natural explanation, as are the effects of certain foods and eating habits. In the psychosocial domain, emotions such as anger and hostility cause certain health problems. In the supernatural domain, spirits and magic can cause health problems. The African–Brazilian religions of the Bahia region encompass many spirits who can inflict illness. They include spirits of the unhappy dead and devil-like spirits. Some spirits cause specific illnesses; others bring general misfortune. In addition, envious people with the evil eye cast spells on people and cause much illness. People also recognize the lack of economic resources, proper sanitation, and health services as structural causes of health problems. In the words of one person, "There are many illnesses because there are many poor" (1988:796).

The people of Feira de Santana also recognize several levels of causality. In the case of stomachache, they might blame a quarrel (*underlying cause*), which prompted the aggrieved party to seek the intervention of a sorcerer (*intermediate cause*), who cast a spell (*immediate cause*), which led to the resulting illness. The multilayered causal understanding opens the way for many possible avenues of treatment.

The multiple understandings of etiology in Bahia contrast with the scientific understandings of causality in Western biomedicine. The most striking difference is the tendency for biomedical etiologies to exclude structural issues and social inequality as causal factors of illness. Medical anthropologists use the term **structural suffering**, or social suffering, to refer to health problems caused by powerful forces such as poverty, war, famine, and forced migration. Such structural factors affect health in many ways, with effects ranging from anxiety and depression to death.

THINKING OUTSIDE THE BOX

Discuss some examples of culture-specific syndromes in your microculture or on your campus.

An example of a culture-specific syndrome that clearly implicates structural factors as causal is *sufriendo del agua*, or "suffering from water" (Ennis-McMillan 2001). Research in a poor community in the Valley of Mexico, located in the central part of the country (see Map 4.3, p. 84), reveals that sufriendo del agua is a common health problem, especially among women. The immediate cause is the lack of water for drinking, cooking, and washing. Women, who are responsible for cooking and doing the washing, cannot count on water coming from their taps on a regular basis. This insecurity makes the women feel anxious and constantly in a state of nervous tension. The lack of access to water also means that the people are at higher risk of cholera, skin and eye infections, and other biophysical problems. A deeper structural cause of sufriendo del agua is unequal development. The construction of piped water systems in the Valley of Mexico bypassed low-income communities in favor of servicing wealthier urban neighborhoods and supplying water for irrigation projects and the industrial sector. In Mexico, as a whole, nearly one-third of the population has inadequate access to clean drinking water and to a dependable supply of water for bathing, laundry, and cooking.

HEALING WAYS

The material that follows describes two approaches to healing, one in southern Africa and the other in Malaysia, Southeast Asia. It also discusses healers and healing substances.

COMMUNITY HEALING A general distinction can be drawn between private healing and **community healing**. The former addresses bodily ailments in social isolation, whereas the latter encompasses the social context as crucial to healing. Compared with Western biomedicine, many non-Western systems use community healing. An example of community healing comes from the Ju/'hoansi foragers of the Kalahari desert in southern Africa (review Culturama, Chapter 1, p. 21). Ju/'hoansi healing emphasizes the mobilization of community "energy" as a key element in the cure:

> The central event in this tradition is the all-night healing dance. Four times a month on the average, night signals the start of a healing dance. The women sit around the fire, singing and rhythmically clapping. The men, sometimes joined by the women, dance around the singers. As the dance intensifies, *num* or spiritual energy is activated by the healers, both men and women, but mostly among the dancing men.

As num is activated in them, they begin to *kia* or experience an enhancement of their consciousness. While experiencing kia, they heal all those at the dance. (Katz 1982:34)

The dance is a community event in which the entire camp participates. The people's belief in the healing power of num brings meaning and efficacy to the dance through *kia*.

Does community healing "work"? In both ethnic and Western terms, the answer is yes. It "works" on several levels. People's solidarity and group sessions may support mental and physical health, acting as a health protection system. When people fall ill, the drama and energy of the all-night dances may act to strengthen the afflicted in ways that Western science would have difficulty measuring. In a small, close-knit group, the dances support members who may be ill or grieving.

An important aspect of the Ju/'hoansi healing system is its openness. Everyone has access to it. The role of healer is also open. There is no special class of healers with special privileges. More than half of all adult men and about 10 percent of adult women are healers.

A Ju/'hoansi healer in a trance, in the Kalahari desert, southern Africa. Most Ju/'hoansi healers are men, but some are women.

▶ *In your microculture, what are the patterns of gender, ethnicity, and class among various kinds of healers?*

---

community healing   healing that emphasizes the social context as a key component and that is carried out within the public domain.

humoral healing   healing that emphasizes balance among natural elements within the body.

shaman/shamanka   a male and female healer, respectively.

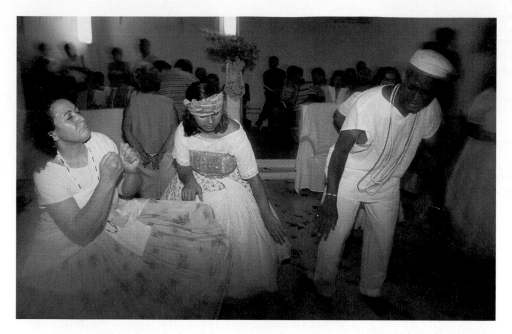

Umbanda is a popular religion in Brazil and, increasingly, worldwide. Its ceremonies are often devoted to healing through spiritual means. In this session, tourists at the back of the room watch as Umbanda followers perform a dance related to a particular deity.

▶ *What is your opinion on the role of spirituality in health and healing, and on what do you base your view?*

HUMORAL HEALING **Humoral healing** is based on a philosophy of balance among certain elements within the body and within the person's environment (McElroy and Townsend 1996). In this system, food and drugs have different effects on the body and are classified as either "heating" or "cooling"—the quotation marks indicate that these properties are not the same as thermal measurements. Diseases are the result of bodily imbalances—too much heat or coolness—that must be counteracted through dietary and behavioral changes or medicines that will restore balance.

Humoral healing systems have been practiced for thousands of years in the Middle East, the Mediterranean, and much of Asia. In the New World, indigenous humoral systems exist and sometimes blend with those which Spanish colonialists brought with them. Humoralism has shown substantial resilience in the face of Western biomedicine as a source of healing for many people. Local people also reframe Western biomedicine in classifying biomedical treatments as either heating or cooling.

In Malaysia (see Map 1.1, p. 10), several different humoral traditions coexist, reflecting the region's history of contact with outside cultures. Malaysia has been influenced by trade and contact between its indigenous culture and that of India, China, and the Arab-Islamic world for around 2000 years. Indian, Chinese, and Arabic health systems all define health as the balance of opposing elements within the body, although each has its own variations (Laderman 1988:272). Indigenous belief systems may have been compatible with these imported models because they also were based on concepts of heat and coolness.

Insights into these indigenous systems before outsiders arrived come from accounts about the Orang Asli, indigenous peoples of the interior who are relatively less affected by contact. A conceptual system of hot–cold opposition dominates

Orang Asli cosmological, medical, and social theories. The properties and meanings of heat and coolness differ from their counterparts in Islamic, Indian, and Chinese humoralism in several ways. In the Islamic, Indian, and Chinese systems, for example, death is the result of too much coolness. Among the Orang Asli, excessive heat is the primary cause of mortality. In their view, heat emanates from the sun and is associated with excrement, blood, misfortune, disease, and death. Humanity's hot blood makes people mortal, and their consumption of meat speeds the process. Heat causes menstruation, violent emotions, aggression, and drunkenness.

Coolness, in contrast, is vital for health among the Orang Asli. Staying in the forest protects against the harmful effects of the sun. Following this logic, the treatment of illness aims to reduce or remove heat. If someone were to fall ill in a clearing, the entire group would relocate to the coolness of the forest. The forest is also a source of cooling leaves and herbs. Healers are cool and retain their coolness by bathing in cold water and sleeping far from the fire. Extreme cold, however, can be harmful. Dangerous levels of coolness are associated with the time right after birth, because the mother is believed to have lost substantial heat. The new mother should not drink cold water or bathe in cold water. She increases her body heat by tying sashes around her waist that contain warmed leaves or ashes, and she lies near a fire.

HEALERS In an informal sense, everyone is a "healer," because self-treatment is always the first consideration in dealing with a perceived health problem. Yet, in all cultures, some people become recognized as having special abilities to diagnose and treat health problems. Cross-cultural evidence indicates some common criteria of healers (see Figure 5.3, p. 108).

In different cultures, specialists include midwives, bonesetters (those who reset broken bones), **shamans** or **shamankas**

- *Selection:* Certain individuals may show more ability for entry into healing roles. In Western medical schools, selection for entry rests on apparently objective standards, such as pre-entry exams and college grades. Among the indigenous Ainu of northern Japan, healers were men who had a special ability to go into a sort of seizure called *imu* (Ohnuki-Tierney 1980).

- *Training:* The period of training may involve years of observation and practice and may be arduous and even dangerous. In some non-Western traditions, a shaman must make dangerous journeys, through trance or use of drugs, to the spirit world. In Western biomedicine, medical school involves immense amounts of memorization, separation from family and normal social life, and sleep deprivation.

- *Certification:* Healers earn some form of ritual or legal certification, such as a shaman going through a formal initiation ritual that attests to his or her competence.

- *Professional image:* The healer role is demarcated from that of ordinary people through behavior, dress, and other markers, such as the white coat in the West and the Siberian shaman's tambourine for calling the spirits.

- *Expectation of payment:* Compensation in some form, whether in kind or in cash, is expected for formal healers. Payment level may vary, depending on the status of the healer and other factors. In northern India, strong preference for sons is reflected in payments to the midwife that are twice as high for the birth of a son as for a daughter. In the United States, medical professionals in different specializations receive markedly different salaries.

FIGURE 5.3   Criteria for Becoming a Healer

(male or female healers, respectively, who mediate between humans and the spirit world), herbalists, general practitioners, psychiatrists, nurses, acupuncturists, chiropractors, dentists, and hospice care providers. Some healing roles may have higher status and more power and may receive higher pay than others.

Midwifery is an example of a healing role that is endangered in many parts of the world because birth has become increasingly medicalized and brought into the institutional realm of the hospital rather than the home. In Costa Rica, a government campaign to promote hospital births with a biomedical doctor in attendance achieved a rate of 98 percent of all births taking place in hospitals by the end of the twentieth century (Jenkins 2003). This achievement means that midwives, especially in rural areas, can no longer support themselves, and they

phytotherapy   healing through the use of plants.

are abandoning their profession. The promotion of hospital births has destroyed the positive elements of community-based midwifery and its provision of social support and techniques such as massage for the mother-to-be.

HEALING SUBSTANCES   Around the world, thousands of different natural or manufactured substances are used as medicines for preventing or curing health problems. Anthropologists have spent more time studying the use of medicines in non-Western cultures than in the West, although a more fully cross-cultural approach is emerging that also examines the use and meaning of Western pharmaceuticals (Petryna, Lakoff, and Kleinman 2007).

Phytotherapy is healing through the use of plants. Cross-culturally, people know about and use many different plants for a wide range of health problems, including gastrointestinal disorders, skin problems, wounds and sores, pain relief, infertility, fatigue, altitude sickness, and more (see Eye on the Environment). Increasing awareness of the range of potentially useful plants worldwide provides a strong incentive for protecting the world's cultural diversity, because it is people, especially indigenous people, who know about botanical resources (Posey 1990).

Leaves of the coca plant have for centuries been a key part of the health system of the Andean region of South America (Allen 2002). Coca is important in rituals, in masking hunger pains, and in combating the cold. In terms of health, Andean people use coca to treat gastrointestinal problems, sprains, swellings, and colds. The leaf may be chewed or combined with herbs or roots and water to make a *maté (mah-tay)*, a medicinal beverage. Trained herbalists have

These boys are selling hyssop, a medicinal herb, in Syria. In Unani (Islamic) traditional medicine, hyssop is used to alleviate problems such as asthma.

▶ *Do research to learn more about hyssop and its medicinal uses.*

Local Botanical Knowledge and Child Health in the Bolivian Amazon

The Tsimané (see-mah-nay) are a foraging–horticultural society of Bolivia's northeastern Amazon region, numbering about 8000 (McDade et al. 2007). Although most Tsimané make a living from horticulture, complemented by some gathering and hunting, new opportunities for wage work are becoming increasingly available in logging camps or on cattle ranches, or by selling products from the rainforest. At the time of the study described here, in 2002–2003, the Tsimané were not much affected by outside forces and still relied heavily on local resources for their livelihood.

The study focused on mothers' botanical knowledge and the health of their children. The word *botany* refers to knowledge about plants. Household visits and interviews with mothers provided data on mothers' knowledge of plants. Children's health was assessed with three measures: concentrations of C-reactive protein (or CRP, a measure of both immunity and "infectious burden"), skinfold thickness (which measures body fat), and stature, or height (which indicates overall progress in growth and development).

The results of the study showed a strong relationship between mothers' knowledge of plants and the health of their children. Botanical knowledge promotes healthier children through nutritional inputs; that is, knowledgeable mothers tend to provide healthier plant foods to their children. It also improves children's health by providing herbal ways of treating their illnesses. The overall conclusion is that a mother's knowledge of local plant resources contributes directly to the benefit of her children. In contrast, levels of formal schooling of mothers and household wealth had little, if anything, to do with child health.

Given the positive effects of mothers' botanical knowledge and use of local plants to promote their children's health, it is critical that access to plant resources by indigenous people be protected and sustained and that local botanical knowledge be respected and preserved.

◆ **FOOD FOR THOUGHT**

- What do you know about the effects on your health of particular plants that you eat? When you eat herbs such as oregano or parsley, for example, do you think about their health effects?

MAP 5.2 The Republic of Bolivia.
Situated in the Andes Mountains, Bolivia is the poorest country in South America, although it is rich in natural resources, including the second-largest oil field in South America after one in Venezuela. The population of 10 million includes a majority of indigenous people of nearly 40 different groups. The largest are the Aymara (2 million) and the Quechua-speaking groups (1.5 million). Thirty percent of the population is mestizo and 15 percent is of European descent. Two-thirds of the people are low-income farmers. The official religion is Roman Catholicism, but Protestantism is growing. Religious syncretism is prominent. Most people speak Spanish as their first language, although Aymara and Quechua are also common. Bolivia's popular fiesta known as *El carnival de Oruro* is on UNESCO's Intangible Cultural Heritage list.

specialized knowledge about preparing matés. One maté, for example, is for treating asthma. The patient drinks the beverage, made of a ground root and coca leaves, three to four times a day until cured.

Minerals are also widely used for prevention and healing. For example, many people worldwide believe that bathing in

THINKING
OUTSIDE
THE BOX

What steps do you take to treat yourself when you have a cold or headache? If you take medicine, do you know what materials are in the medicine?

Ingredients for traditional medicines available in a shop in Singapore include deer and antelope horns, monkey gall bladders, amber, freshwater pearls, and ginseng.

▶ *Have you ever gone to a pharmacy in a non-Euro-American context? If so, what did you notice in terms of similarities to and differences from a Euro-American pharmacy?*

water that contains high levels of sulfur or other minerals promotes health and cures ailments such as arthritis and rheumatism. Thousands of people every year go to the Dead Sea, which lies beneath sea level between Israel and Jordan, for treating skin diseases. Bathing in the sulfur springs near the Dead Sea and plastering oneself with mud from the shore provide relief from skin ailments such as psoriasis. Throughout East Asia, including Japan, bathing in mineral waters is popular as a health-promotion practice.

In a more unusual practice, thousands of people worldwide visit "radon spas" every year, seeking the therapeutic effects of low doses of radon gas to alleviate the symptoms of arthritis and other afflictions. In the United States, many radon spas are located in mines in the mountains of Montana (Erickson

---

ecological/epidemiological approach an approach within medical anthropology that considers how aspects of the natural environment and social environment interact to cause illness.

historical trauma the intergenerational transfer of the detrimental effects of colonialism from parents to children.

2007). At one such spa, the Free Enterprise Mine, the recommended treatment is to go into the mine for one-hour sessions, two or three times daily, for up to a total of about 30 sessions. The mine contains benches and chairs, and clients read, play cards, chat, or take a nap. Some "regulars" come back every year and make plans to meet up with friends from previous visits.

Pharmaceutical medicines are becoming increasingly popular worldwide. Although these medicines have many benefits, some negative effects include over-prescription and frequent use without a prescription. The sale of patent medicines is often unregulated, and self-treating individuals can buy them in a local pharmacy. The popularity and overuse of capsules and injections has led to a growing health crisis related to the emergence of drug-resistant disease strains.

◆◆◆

Three Theoretical Approaches

The first major theoretical approach to understanding health systems emphasizes the importance of the environment in shaping health problems and how they spread. The second highlights symbols and meaning in people's expression of suffering and healing practices. The third points to the need to look at structural factors as the underlying causes of health problems and examines Western biomedicine as a cultural institution.

THE ECOLOGICAL/EPIDEMIOLOGICAL APPROACH

The **ecological/epidemiological approach** examines how aspects of the natural environment interact with culture to cause health problems and to influence their spread throughout the population. According to this approach, research should focus on gathering information about the environmental context

Women working in padi fields in southern China. Agricultural work done in standing water increases the risk of hookworm infection.

▶ *Is hookworm a threat where you live? What is the major infectious disease in your home region?*

and social patterns that affect health, such as food distribution within the family, sexual practices, hygiene, and degree of contact with outsiders. Research methods and data tend to be quantitative and etic, although a growing tendency is to include qualitative and emic data in order to provide a context for understanding the quantitative data (review Chapter 2).

The ecological/epidemiological approach seeks to yield findings relevant to public health programs. It can provide information about groups that are at risk of specific problems. For example, although hookworm is common throughout rural China, epidemiological researchers learned that rice cultivators have the highest rates. The reason is that hookworm spreads through *night soil* (human excrement used as a fertilizer) that is applied to the rice fields in which the cultivators work.

Another significant environmental factor that has important effects on health is urbanization. As archaeologists have documented about the past, settled populations living in dense clusters are more likely than mobile populations to experience a range of health problems, including infectious diseases and malnutrition (Cohen 1989). Such problems are apparent among many recently settled pastoralist groups in East and West Africa. One study compared the health status of two groups of Turkana men in northwest Kenya (see Map 4.4, p. 91): those who were mobile pastoralists and those who lived in a town (Barkey, Campbell, and Leslie 2001). The two groups differ strikingly in diet, physical activities, and health. Pastoralist Turkana eat mainly animal foods (milk, meat, and blood), spend much time in rigorous physical activity, and live in large family groups. Settled Turkana men eat mainly maize and beans. Their sedentary (settled) life means less physical activity and exercise. In terms of health, the settled men had more eye infections, chest infections, backache, and cough/colds. Pastoralist Turkana men were not, however, free of health problems. One-fourth of the pastoralist men had eye infections, but among the settled men, one-half had eye infections. In terms of nutrition, the settled Turkana were shorter and had greater body mass than the taller and slimmer pastoralists.

Cities present many stressors to human health as well as opportunities for improved health through greater access to health care. Typically, cities comprise diverse social categories, varying by class and ethnicity. These groups have different experiences of health risks. In the United States, the incidence of tuberculosis (TB) has increased in recent years, mainly in urban areas (DeFerdinando 1999). Tuberculosis is spread by infected humans, and its rate of spread is increased by crowding, poverty, poor housing, and lack of access to health care. In the United States, rates of tuberculosis are generally higher in southern than in northern states, with the exceptions of New York and Illinois, given their large urban populations. Beginning in the 1990s, outbreaks of *multidrug-resistant tuberculosis* (*MDRTB*), a new strain of TB that is resistant to conventional drugs, led to its being recognized by public health authorities as a major "new" infectious disease. Even more recently, the new threat

of *extra-multidrug-resistant tuberculosis* (*XMDRTB*) has emerged. New forms of the disease mutate more rapidly than scientists are able to develop drugs to combat them.

Anthropologists have applied the ecological/epidemiological approach to the study of the impaired health and survival of indigenous peoples resulting from colonial contact. They show that the effects of colonial contact are devastatingly detrimental, ranging from the quick and outright extermination of indigenous peoples, to resilient adjustment among other groups, to drastically changed conditions.

In the Western Hemisphere, European colonialism brought a dramatic decline in the indigenous populations, although disagreement exists about the numbers involved (Joralemon 1982). Research indicates that the precontact New World was largely free of the major European infectious diseases, such as smallpox, measles, and typhus, and perhaps also of syphilis, leprosy, and malaria. Therefore, the exposure of indigenous peoples to these infectious diseases likely had a massive impact, given those people's complete lack of resistance. One analyst compared colonial contact to a "biological war":

> Smallpox was the captain of the men of death in that war, typhus fever the first lieutenant, and measles the second lieutenant. More terrible than the conquistadores on horseback, more deadly than sword and gunpowder, they made the conquest by the whites a walkover as compared to what it would have been without their aid. (Ashburn 1947:98, quoted in Joralemon 1982:112)

This quotation emphasizes the importance of the three major diseases in New World colonial history: smallpox, measles, and malaria. A later arrival, cholera, also had severe effects because its transmission through contaminated water and food is enhanced in areas of poor sanitation.

Besides being ravaged by infectious diseases, indigenous populations were decimated by outright killing, enslavement and harsh labor practices, and the psychological damage produced by losing one's livelihood, social ties and support, and access to ancestral burial grounds (see Map 5.3 and Map 5.4).

Enduring effects of European colonialism among indigenous peoples worldwide include high rates of depression and suicide, low self-esteem, high rates of child and adolescent drug use, and high rates of alcoholism, obesity, and hypertension. **Historical trauma** refers to the intergenerational transfer of the emotional and psychological effects of colonialism from parents to children (Brave Heart 2004). It is closely associated with substance abuse as a way of attempting to cover the continued pain it induces. Troubled parents create a difficult family situation for children, who tend to replicate their parents' negative coping mechanisms. The concept of historical trauma helps to expand the scope of traditional epidemiological studies by drawing on factors from the past to explain the social and spatial distribution of contemporary health problems. Such an approach may prove more effective

MAP 5.3 Precolonial Distribution of Indian Tribes in the 48 United States.
Before the arrival of European colonialists, Indians were the sole occupants of the area.
The first English settlers were impressed by their height and robust physical health.

than a biomedical one in devising culturally appropriate ways to alleviate health problems.

THE INTERPRETIVIST APPROACH

Some medical anthropologists examine health systems as systems of meaning. They study how people in different cultures label, describe, and experience illness and how healing systems offer meaningful responses to individual and communal distress. Interpretivist anthropologists have examined aspects of healing, such as ritual trance, as symbolic performances. The French anthropologist Claude Lévi-Strauss established

---

placebo effect   a positive result from a healing method due to a symbolic or otherwise nonmaterial factor.

critical medical anthropology   an approach within medical anthropology involving the analysis of how economic and political structures shape people's health status, their access to health care, and the prevailing medical systems that exist in relation to them.

medicalization   the labeling of a particular issue or problem as medical and requiring medical treatment when, in fact, that issue or problem is economic or political.

this approach in a classic essay called "The Effectiveness of Symbols" (1967). He examined how a song sung by a shaman during childbirth among the Kuna Indians of Panama helps women through a difficult delivery. The main point is that healing systems provide meaning to people who are experiencing seemingly meaningless forms of suffering. The provision of meaning offers psychological support to the afflicted and may enhance healing through what Western science calls the **placebo effect,** or *meaning effect*, a positive result from a healing method due to a symbolic or otherwise nonmaterial factor (Moerman 2002). In the United States, depending on the health problem, between 10 and 90 percent of the efficacy of medical prescriptions lies in the placebo effect. Several explanatory factors may be involved in the meaning effect: the confidence of the specialist prescribing a treatment; the act of prescription itself; and concrete details about the prescription, such as the color and shape of a pill.

CRITICAL MEDICAL ANTHROPOLOGY

Critical medical anthropology focuses on analyzing how structural factors—such as the global political economy, global media, and social inequality—affect the prevailing

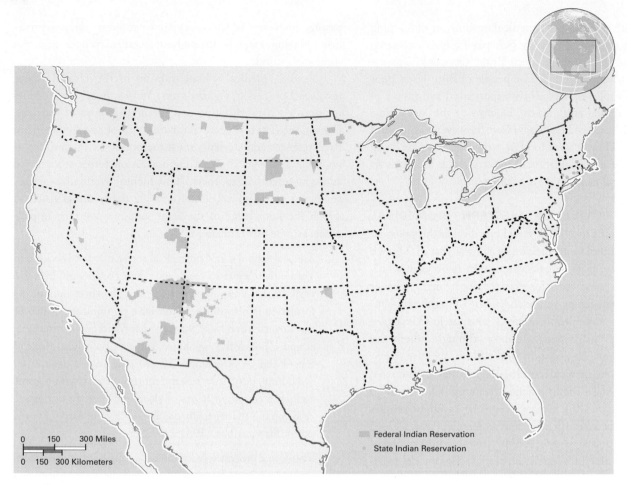

Federal Indian Reservation
State Indian Reservation

0 150 300 Miles
0 150 300 Kilometers

MAP 5.4 **Designated Reservations in the 48 United States.**
Indian reservations today make up a small percentage of the U.S. landmass. Reservations
are allocated to "recognized tribes." Several states recognize no tribes. Many Indians live
off of the reservations, often as poorly employed or unemployed urban residents.

health system, including types of afflictions, people's health status, and their access to health care. Critical medical anthropologists show how Western biomedicine itself often serves to bolster the institution of medicine to the detriment of helping the poor and powerless. They point to the process of **medicalization**, or labeling a particular issue or problem as medical and requiring medical treatment when, in fact, its cause is structural. In this way, people are prescribed pills and injections for poverty, pills and injections for forced displacement from one's home, and pills and injections for being unable to provide for one's family.

SOCIAL INEQUALITY AND POVERTY An important topic to launch this discussion is social inequality and poverty. No matter how you measure these factors, they always have something to say about health. Substantial evidence indicates that poverty is the primary cause of morbidity (sickness) and mortality (death) in both industrialized and developing countries (Farmer 2005). It may be manifested in different ways—for example, in child malnutrition in Chad or Nepal or

through street violence among the urban poor of wealthy countries.

At the broadest level comparing richer countries with poorer countries, distinctions exist between the most common health problems of rich, industrial countries and those of poor, less industrial countries. In the former, major causes of death are circulatory diseases, malignant cancers, HIV/AIDS, excess alcohol consumption, and the smoking of tobacco. In poor countries, tuberculosis, malaria, and HIV/AIDS are the three leading causes of death.

Within the developing world, rates of childhood malnutrition are inversely related to income. In other words, as income increases, so does calorie intake as a percentage of recommended daily allowances (Zaidi 1988). Thus, increasing the income of the poor is the most direct way to improve child nutrition and health. Yet, in contrast to this seemingly logical approach, most health and nutrition programs around the world focus on treating the health results of poverty rather than its causes.

Critical medical anthropologists describe the widespread practice of medicalization, or treating health problems caused by poverty with pills or other medical options, in developing countries. An example is Nancy Scheper-Hughes's research (1992) in Bom Jesus, northeastern Brazil (review Chapter 4 p. 86 and see Map 3.3, p. 57). The people of Bom Jesus, poor and often unemployed, frequently experienced symptoms of weakness, insomnia, and anxiety. Doctors at the local clinic gave them pills to take. The people were, however, hungry and malnourished. They needed food, not pills. In this case, as in many others, the medicalization of poverty serves the interests of pharmaceutical companies, not the poor.

CULTURAL CRITIQUE OF WESTERN BIOMEDICAL TRAINING Since the 1980s, critical medical anthropologists have studied Western biomedicine as a cultural system. Though recognizing many of its benefits, they point to ways in which WBM could be improved—for example, by reducing reliance on technology, broadening an understanding of health problems as they relate to structural conditions and not just biological conditions, and diversifying healing through alternative methods such as massage, acupuncture, and chiropracty.

Some critical medical anthropologists have conducted research on Western medical school training. One study of obstetric training in the United States involved interviews with 12 obstetricians, 10 male and 2 female (Davis-Floyd 1987). As students, they absorbed the technological model of birth as a core value of Western obstetrics. This model treats the body as a machine. The physician uses the assembly-line approach to birth in order to promote efficient production and quality control. One of the residents in the study explained, "We shave 'em, we prep 'em, we hook 'em up to the IV and administer sedation. We deliver the baby, it goes to the nursery and the mother goes to her room. There's no room for niceties around here. We just move 'em right on through. It's not hard to see it like an assembly line" (1987:292). The goal is the "production" of a healthy baby. The doctor is a technical expert in charge of achieving this goal, and the mother takes second place. One obstetrician said, "It is what we all were trained to always go after—the perfect baby. That's what we were trained to produce. The quality of the mother's experience— we rarely thought about that. Everything we did was to get that perfect baby" (1987:292).

This goal involves the use of sophisticated monitoring machines. One obstetrician said, "I'm totally dependent on fetal monitors, 'cause they're great! They free you to do a lot of other things. . . . I couldn't sit over there with a woman in labor with my hand on her belly, and be in here seeing 20 to 30 patients a day" (1987:291). The use of technology also conveys status to the physician. One commented, "Anybody in obstetrics who shows a human interest in patients is not respected. What is respected is interest in machines" (1987:291).

How do medical students learn to accept the technological model? Davis-Floyd's research points to three key processes. One way is through physical *hazing*, a harsh rite of passage involving, in this case, stress caused by sleep deprivation. Hazing extends throughout medical school and the residency period.

Second, medical school training in the United States involves a process of *cognitive retrogression*, in which students relinquish critical thinking and thoughtful ways of learning. During the first two years of medical school, most courses are basic sciences and students must memorize vast quantities of material. The sheer bulk of memorization forces students to adopt an uncritical approach. This mental overload socializes students into a uniform pattern, giving them tunnel vision in which the knowledge of medicine assumes supreme importance. As one obstetrician said,

> Medical school is not difficult in terms of what you have to learn—there's just so much of it. You go through, in a six-week course, a thousand-page book. The sheer bulk of information is phenomenal. You have pop quizzes in two or three courses every day the first year. We'd get up around 6, attend classes till 5, go home and eat, then head back to school and be in anatomy lab working with a cadaver, or something, until 1 or 2 in the morning, and then go home and get a couple of hours of sleep and then go out again. And you did that virtually day in and day out for four years, except for vacations. (1987:298–299)

Third, in a process termed *dehumanization*, medical school training works to erase humanitarian ideals through an emphasis on technology and objectification of the patient. One obstetrical student explained, "Most of us went into medical school with pretty humanitarian ideals. I know I did. But the whole process of medical education makes you inhuman . . . by the time you get to residency, you end up not caring about anything beyond the latest techniques you can master and how sophisticated the tests are that you can perform" (1987:299).

◆◆◆

Globalization and Change

With globalization, health problems move around the world and into remote locations and cultures more rapidly than ever before. The HIV/AIDS epidemic is one tragic example. Other new epidemics include severe acute respiratory syndrome (SARS) and H1N1 flu. At the same time, Western culture, including biomedicine, is on the move. Perhaps no other aspect of Western culture, except for the capitalist market system and the English language, has so permeated the rest of the world as Western biomedicine. But the cultural flow is not one-way: Many people in North America and Europe are turning to forms of non-Western and nonbiomedical healing, such as acupuncture and massage therapy. This section considers new and emerging health challenges, changes in healing, and examples of how applied medical anthropology has gained increasing relevance.

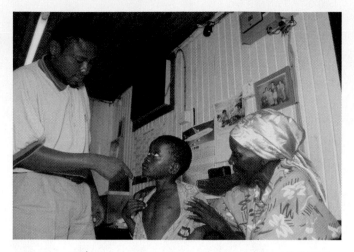

A woman takes her 8-year-old grandson, who has HIV/AIDS, to a clinic in Dar es Salaam, Tanzania. Throughout the world, increasing numbers of children are infected and, at the same time, are orphans because their parents have died of the disease.

NEW INFECTIOUS DISEASES

In the mid-twentieth century, scientific advances such as antibiotic drugs, vaccines against childhood diseases, and improved technology for sanitation dramatically reduced the threat from infectious disease. The 1980s, however, were the beginning of an era of shaken confidence, with the onset and rapid spread of the HIV/AIDS epidemic.

New contexts for exposure and contagion are created through increased international travel and migration, deforestation, and development projects, among others. Increased travel and migration have contributed to the spread of HIV/AIDS and SARS. Deforestation is related to higher rates of malaria, which is spread by mosquitoes; mosquitoes thrive in pools of water in open, sunlit areas, as opposed to forests. Development projects such as constructing dams and clearing forests often create unintended health problems for local people.

DISEASES OF DEVELOPMENT

A **disease of development** is a health problem caused or increased by economic development projects. For example, the construction of dams and irrigation systems throughout the tropical world has brought dramatically increased rates of *schistosomiasis* (shish-to-suh-my-a-sis), a disease caused by the presence of a parasitic worm in the blood system. Over 200 million people suffer from this debilitating disease, with prevalence rates the highest in sub-Saharan countries in Africa (Michaud, Gordon, and Reich 2005). The larvae hatch from eggs and mature in slow-moving water such as lakes and rivers. When mature, they can penetrate human (or other animal) skin with which they come into contact. Once inside the human body, the adult schistosomes breed in the veins around the human bladder and bowel. They send fertilized eggs into the environment through urine and feces. These eggs then contaminate water, in which they hatch into larvae.

Anthropologists' research has documented steep increases in the rates of schistosomiasis at large dam sites in developing countries (Scudder 1973). The increased risk is caused by the dams slowing the rate of water flow. Stagnant water systems offer an ideal environment for development of the larvae. Opponents of the construction of large dams have used this information in support of their position.

New diseases of development continue to appear. One of these is *Kyasanur forest disease*, or KFD (Nichter 1992). This viral disease was first identified in 1957 in southern India:

> Resembling influenza, at onset KFD is marked by sudden chills, fever, frontal headaches, stiffness of the neck, and body pain. Diarrhea and vomiting often follow on the third day. High fever is continuous for five to fifteen days, during which time a variety of additional symptoms may manifest themselves, including gastrointestinal bleeding, persistent cough with blood-tinged sputum, and bleeding gums. In more serious cases, the infection progresses to bronchial pneumonia, meningitis, paralysis, encephalitis, and hemorrhage. (1992:224)

In the early 1980s, an epidemic of KFD swept over 30 villages near the Kyasanur forest in Karnataka state, southern India. Mortality rates in hospitals ranged between 12 and 18 percent of those admitted. Investigation revealed that KFD especially affected agricultural workers and cattle tenders who were most exposed to newly cleared areas near the forest. In the cleared areas, international companies established plantations and initiated cattle raising. Ticks were the vector transmitting the disease from the cattle to the people. Ticks had long existed in the local ecosystem, but their numbers increased greatly in the cleared area. The ticks found many inviting hosts in the cattle and in the workers. Thus, human modification of the ecosystem through deforestation and the introduction of large-scale cattle raising caused the epidemic and shaped its social distribution.

MEDICAL PLURALISM

Contact between cultures may lead to a situation in which aspects of both cultures coexist: two (or more) different languages, religions, systems of law, or health systems, for example. The term **medical pluralism** refers to the presence

disease of development a health problem caused or increased by economic development activities that have detrimental effects on the environment and people's relationship with it.

medical pluralism the existence of more than one health system in a culture; also, a government policy to promote the integration of local healing systems into biomedical practice.

CULTURAMA

The Sherpa of Nepal

The word *Sherpa* means "person." About 35,000 Sherpa live in Nepal, mainly in the northeastern region (Fisher 1990). Another 10,000 reside in Bhutan and Sikkim, and another 5,000 live in cities of Europe and North America.

In Nepal, the Sherpa are most closely associated with the Khumbu region. Khumbu is a valley set high in the Himalayas, completely encircled by mountains and with a clear view of Mount Everest (Karan and Mather 1985). The Sherpa have a mixed economy involving animal herding, trade between Tibet and India, small businesses, and farming, with the main crop being potatoes. Since the 1920s and the coming of Western mountaineers, Sherpa men have become increasingly employed as guides and porters for trekkers and climbers. Many Sherpa men and women now run guest houses or work in guest houses as cooks, food servers, and cleaners.

The Sherpa are organized into 18 separate lineages, or *ru* ("bones"), with marriage taking place outside one's birth lineage. Recently, they have begun marrying into other ethnic groups, thus expanding the definition and meaning of what it is to be Sherpa. Because of increased intermarriage, the number of people who can be considered Sherpa to some degree is 130,000. Status distinctions include "big people," "middle people," and "small people," with the middle group being the largest by far (Ortner 1999:65). The main privilege of those in the top level is not to carry loads. Those in the poorest level are landless and work for others.

The Sherpa practice a localized version of Tibetan Buddhism that contains non-Buddhist elements having to do with nature spiritualism that connects all beings. The place name Khumbu, for example, refers to the guardian deity of the region.

Tourism has been, and still is, a major change factor for the Sherpa. In Khumbu, the number of international tourists per year exceeds the Sherpa population.

Global warming is also having significant effects. Glaciers are melting, lakes are rising, and massive flooding is frequent. Some of the swollen lakes are in danger of breaking their banks (United Nations Environment Programme 2002). Many community development projects are aimed at reforestation, planting fruit orchards, and protecting and expanding local knowledge of medicinal herbs.

Thanks to Vincanne Adams, University of California at San Francisco, for reviewing this material.

(LEFT) A Sherpa porter carries a load up a steep mountain path in the Himalayas. Porters earn relatively good wages, especially when they work for international tourists. (CENTER) Nepali children learn writing in a school supported by the Himalayan Trust, an organization founded by Sir Edmund Hillary in 1961, after he climbed Mount Everest and asked the local people he met how he could help them.

MAP 5.5   Nepal. The Kingdom of Nepal has a population of almost 30 million. Most of its territory is in the Himalayas, and Nepal has 8 of the world's 10 highest mountains.

of multiple health systems within a society. The coexistence of many forms of healing provides clients a range of choices and enhances the quality of health. In other cases, people are confronted by conflicting models of illness and healing, a situation that can result in misunderstandings between healers and clients and in unhappy outcomes.

SELECTIVE PLURALISM: THE CASE OF THE SHERPA

The Sherpa of Nepal (see Culturama) are an unusual example of a culture in which the preference for traditional healing systems remains strong and is combined with the selective use of Western biomedicine (Adams 1988). Healing therapists available in the Upper Khumbu (khoom-boo) region in northeastern Nepal fit into three categories:

- Orthodox Buddhist practitioners, including *lamas*, whom Khumbu people consult for prevention and cure through their blessings, and *amchis*, who practice Tibetan medicine, a humoral healing system.

- Unorthodox religious or shamanic practitioners, who perform divination ceremonies for diagnosis.

- Biomedical practitioners who work in a clinic that was first established to serve tourists. The clinic was established as a permanent medical facility in 1967, and many Sherpa selectively use it.

Thus, three varieties of health care exist in the region. Traditional healers are thriving, unthreatened by changes brought by the tourist trade, the influx of new wealth, and notions of modernity. The question of why Western biomedicine has not completely taken over other healing practices requires a complicated answer. One part of the answer is that high-mountain tourism does not deeply affect local production and social relations. Although it brings in new wealth, it does not require large-scale capital investment from outside as, for example, mega-hotel tourist developments have elsewhere. So far, the Sherpa maintain control of their productive resources, including trekking knowledge and skills.

CONFLICTING EXPLANATORY MODELS

In many other contexts, however, anthropologists have documented conflicts and misunderstandings between Western biomedicine and local health systems. Miscommunication often occurs between biomedical doctors and patients in matters seemingly as simple as a prescription that should be taken with every meal. The Western biomedically trained doctor assumes that this means three times a day. But some people do not eat three meals a day and thus unwittingly fail to follow the doctor's instructions.

One anthropological study of a case in which death resulted from cross-cultural differences shows how complex the issue of communication across medical cultures is. The "F family" are immigrants from American Samoa (see Map 5.6)

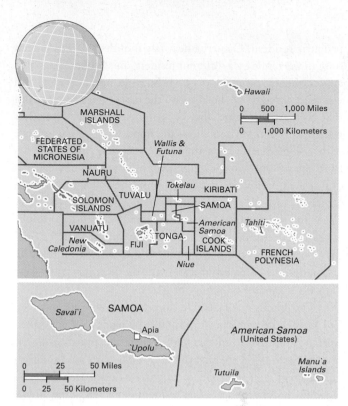

MAP 5.6 Samoa and American Samoa.
Samoa, or the independent state of Samoa, was known as German Samoa (1900–1919) and Western Samoa (1914–1997) until recognized by the United Nations as a sovereign country. Its population is around 177,000. American Samoa, or Amerika Samoa in Samoan English, is a territory of the United States with a population of about 57,000. During World War II, U.S. marines in American Samoa outnumbered the local population and had a strong cultural influence. Unemployment rates are now high and the U.S. military is the largest employer.

living in Honolulu, Hawai'i (Krantzler 1987). Neither parent speaks English. Their children are "moderately literate" in English but speak a mixture of English and Samoan at home. Mr. F was trained as a traditional Samoan healer. Mary, a daughter, was first stricken with diabetes at age 16. She was taken to the hospital by ambulance after collapsing, half-conscious, on the sidewalk near her home in a Honolulu housing project. After several months of irregular contact with medical staff, she was again brought to the hospital in an ambulance, unconscious, and she died there. Her father was charged with causing Mary's death through medical neglect.

In the biomedical view, her parents failed to give Mary adequate care, even though the hospital staff took pains to instruct her family about how to give insulin injections and Mary was shown how to test her urine for glucose and acetone and counseled about her diet. She was to be followed up with visits to the outpatient clinic, and, following the clinic's unofficial policy of linking patients with physicians from their own ethnic group, she was assigned to see the sole Samoan pediatric resident. Over the next few months, Mary was seen once in the clinic by a different resident, missed her next three appointments, came in once without an appointment, and was readmitted to the hospital on the basis of test results from that visit. At that time, she, her parents, and her older sister were once again advised about the importance of compliance with the medical advice they were receiving. Four months later, she returned to the clinic with blindness in one eye and diminished vision in the other. She was diagnosed with cataracts, and the Samoan physician again advised Mary about the seriousness of her illness and the need for compliance. The medical experts increasingly judged that "cultural differences" were the basic problem and that, in spite of all their attempts to communicate with the F family, they were basically incapable of caring for Mary.

The family's perspective, in contrast, was grounded in *fa'a Samoa*, the Samoan way. Their experiences in the hospital were not positive from the start. When Mr. F arrived at the hospital with Mary the first time, he spoke with several different hospital staff, through a daughter as translator. It was a teaching hospital, so various residents and attending physicians had examined Mary. Mr. F was concerned that there was no single physician caring for Mary, and he was concerned that her care was inconsistent. The family observed a child die while Mary was in the intensive care unit, reinforcing the perception of inadequate care and instilling fear over Mary's chance of surviving in this hospital.

Language differences between Mary's family and the hospital staff added to the problem:

> When they asked what was wrong with her, their perception was that "everyone said 'sugar.'" What this meant was not clear to the family; they were confused about whether she was getting too much sugar or too little. Mary's mother interpreted the explanations to mean she was not getting enough sugar, so she tried to give her more when she was returned home. Over time, confusion gave way to anger, and a basic lack of trust of the hospital and the physicians there developed. The family began to draw on their own resources for explaining and caring for Mary's illness, relying heavily on the father's skills as a healer. (1987:330)

From the Samoan perspective, the F family behaved logically and appropriately. The father, as household head and healer in his own right, felt he had authority. Dr. A, although Samoan, had been resocialized by the Western medical system and alienated from his Samoan background. He did not offer the personal touch that the F family expected. Samoans believe that children above the age of 12 are no longer children and can be expected to behave responsibly, so the family's assigning of Mary's 12-year-old sister to assist with her insulin injections and in recording results made sense to them. Also, the hospital in American Samoa does not require appointments. Cultural misunderstanding was the ultimate cause of Mary's death.

APPLIED MEDICAL ANTHROPOLOGY

Applied medical anthropology is the application of anthropological knowledge to further the goals of health-care providers. It may involve improving doctor–patient communication in multicultural settings, making recommendations about culturally appropriate health intervention programs, or providing insights about factors related to disease that medical practitioners do not usually take into account. Applied medical anthropologists draw on ethnomedical knowledge and on any of the three theoretical approaches or a combination of them.

REDUCING LEAD POISONING AMONG MEXICAN AMERICAN CHILDREN   An example of the positive impact of applied medical anthropology is in the work of Robert Trotter on lead poisoning among Mexican American children (1987). The three most common sources of lead poisoning of children in the United States are the following:

- Eating lead-based paint chips
- Living near a smelter where the dust has high lead content
- Eating or drinking from pottery made with an improperly treated lead glaze

The discovery of an unusual case of lead poisoning by health professionals in Los Angeles in the 1980s prompted investigations that produced understanding of a fourth cause: the use by many Mexican Americans of a traditional healing remedy, *azarcon,* which contains lead, to treat a culture-specific syndrome called *empacho.* Empacho is a combination of indigestion and constipation believed to be caused by food sticking to the abdominal wall.

The U.S. Public Health Service asked Trotter to investigate the availability and use of azarcon. He went to Mexico and surveyed the contents of herbal shops. He talked with *curanderos* (traditional healers). His findings convinced the U.S. government to place restrictions on azarcon and a related remedy called *greta.* Trotter also made recommendations about the need to provide a substitute remedy for the treatment of empacho that would not have harmful side effects. He offered ideas about how to advertise the substitute in a culturally effective way. Throughout his involvement, Trotter played several roles—researcher, consultant, and program developer—all of which brought anthropological knowledge to the solution of a public health problem.

---

applied medical anthropology   the application of anthropological knowledge to furthering the goals of health-care providers.

Vaccination programs in developing countries, especially as promoted by UNICEF, are introduced with much fanfare. But they are sometimes met with little enthusiasm by the target population. In India, many people are suspicious that vaccination programs are clandestine family planning programs (Nichter 1996). In other instances, fear of foreign vaccines prompts people to reject inoculations. Overall, acceptance rates of vaccination are lower than Western public health planners expected.

To understand why people reject inoculations, medical anthropologists conducted surveys in several countries. The results revealed that many parents have a partial or inaccurate understanding of what the vaccines protect against. Some people did not understand the importance of multiple vaccinations. Public health promoters incorporated findings from the survey in two ways:

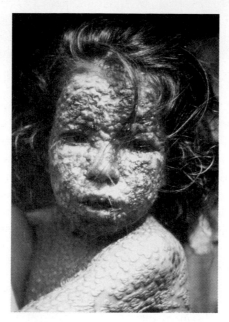

- Educational campaigns for the public that addressed its concerns

- Education for the public health specialists about the importance of understanding and paying attention to local cultural practices and beliefs

A young girl in Bangladesh, photographed in 1975, has the raised bumps of smallpox. In 1977, the World Health Organization announced that smallpox had been eradicated in Bangladesh.

▶ *Has smallpox been eradicated worldwide?*

◆ **FOOD FOR THOUGHT**

- If your job was to promote wider acceptance of vaccinations in your home country, what would you want to know before you began an education campaign?

PUBLIC HEALTH COMMUNICATION Much work in applied medical anthropology involves health communication (Nichter 1996). Anthropologists can help health educators in the development of more meaningful messages through these methods:

- Addressing local health beliefs and health concerns
- Taking seriously all local illness terms and conventions
- Adopting local styles of communication
- Identifying subgroups within the population that may be responsive to different types of messages and incentives
- Monitoring the response of communities to health messages over time and facilitating corrections in communication when needed
- Exposing and removing possible "blaming the victim" in health messages

These principles helped health-care officials understand local responses to public vaccination programs in several countries of Asia and Africa (see Lessons Applied).

WORKING TOGETHER: WESTERN BIOMEDICINE AND NONBIOMEDICAL SYSTEMS Since 1978, the World Health Organization has endorsed the incorporation of local healing practices into national health systems. This policy emerged in response to several factors. First is the increasing appreciation of the value of many non-Western healing traditions. Another is the shortage of trained biomedical personnel. Third is the growing awareness of the deficiencies of Western biomedicine in addressing a person's psychosocial context.

Debates continue about the efficacy of many traditional medical practices compared with biomedicine. For instance, opponents of the promotion of traditional medicine claim that it has no effect on such infectious diseases as cholera, malaria, tuberculosis, schistosomiasis, leprosy, and others. They insist that it makes no sense to allow for or encourage ritual practices against cholera, for example, when a child has not been inoculated against it. Supporters of traditional medicine as one component of a pluralistic health system point out that biomedicine neglects a person's mind, soul, and social setting. Traditional healing practices fill that gap.

the BIG questions REVISITED

◆ What is ethnomedicine?

Ethnomedicine is the study of the health systems of specific cultures. Health systems include categories and perceptions of illness and approaches to prevention and healing. Research in ethnomedicine shows how perceptions of the body differ cross-culturally and reveals both differences and similarities across health systems in perceptions of illness and symptoms. Culture-specific syndromes are found in all cultures, not just non-Western societies, and many are now becoming global.

Ethnomedical studies of healing, healing substances, and healers reveal a wide range of approaches. Community healing is more characteristic of small-scale nonindustrial societies. Community healing emphasizes group interaction and treating the individual within the social context. Humoral healing seeks to maintain balance in bodily fluids and substances through diet, activity, and behavior. In industrial/informatic societies, biomedicine emphasizes the body as a discrete unit, and treatment addresses the individual body or mind and frames out the wider social context. Biomedicine is increasingly reliant on technology and is increasingly specialized.

◆ What are three major theoretical approaches in medical anthropology?

Ecological/epidemiological medical anthropology emphasizes links between the environment and health. It reveals how certain categories of people are at risk of contracting particular diseases within various contexts in historical times and the present.

The interpretivist approach focuses on studying illness and healing as a set of symbols and meanings. Cross-culturally, definitions of health problems and healing systems for these problems are embedded in meanings.

Critical medical anthropologists focus on health problems and healing within a structurist framework. They ask what power relations are involved and who benefits from particular forms of healing. They analyze the role of inequality and poverty in health problems. Some critical medical anthropologists have critiqued Western biomedicine as being a system of social control.

◆ How are health, illness, and healing changing during globalization?

Health systems everywhere are facing accelerated change in the face of globalization, which includes the spread of Western capitalism as well as new diseases and new medical technologies. The "new infectious diseases" are a challenge to health-care systems in terms of prevention and treatment. Diseases of development are health problems caused by development projects that change physical and social environments, such as dams and mines.

The spread of Western biomedicine to many non-Western contexts is a major direction of change. As a consequence, medical pluralism exists in all countries. The availability of Western patent medicines has had substantial positive effects, but widespread overuse and self-medication can result in negative health consequences for individuals and the emergence of drug-resistant disease strains.

Applied medical anthropologists play several roles in improving health systems. They may inform medical care providers of more appropriate forms of treatment, guide local people about their increasingly complex medical choices, help prevent health problems by changing detrimental practices, or improve public health communication by making it more culturally informed and effective.

KEY CONCEPTS

applied medical
anthropology, p. 118

community healing, p. 106

critical medical
anthropology, p. 112

culture-specific
syndrome, p. 104

disease, p. 103

disease of
development, p. 115

ecological/epidemiological
approach, p. 110

ethno-etiology, p. 105

ethnomedicine, p. 102

historical trauma, p. 111

humoral healing, p. 107

illness, p. 103

medicalization, p. 113

medical pluralism, p. 115

phytotherapy, p. 108

placebo effect, p. 112

shaman/shamanka, p. 107

somatization, p. 104

structural suffering, p. 105

susto, p. 104

Western biomedicine
(WBM), p. 102

SUGGESTED READINGS

Eric J. Bailey. *Medical Anthropology and African American Health.* New York: Greenwood Publishing Group, 2000. This book explores the relationship between cultural anthropology and African American health-care issues. One chapter discusses how to do applied research in medical anthropology.

Ron Barrett. *Aghor Medicine: Pollution, Death, and Healing in Northern India.* Berkeley: University of California Press, 2008. This study of the Aghori, Hindu ascetics of India, shows how they have recently become involved in healing victims of stigmatized diseases.

Bernhard M. Bierlich. *The Problem of Money: African Agency and Western Biomedicine in Northern Ghana.* New York: Berghahn Books, 2008. Fieldwork among the Dagomba people provides the basis for this description of ambivalent attitudes toward Western biomedicine and other aspects of modernity.

Nancy N. Chen. *Breathing Spaces: Qigong, Psychiatry, and Healing in China.* New York: Columbia University Press, 2003. This ethnography explores *qigong* (chee-gung), a charismatic form of healing popular in China that involves meditative breathing exercises.

Paul Farmer. *Pathologies of Power: Health, Human Rights, and the New War on the Poor.* Berkeley: University of California Press, 2005. Farmer blends interpretive medical anthropology with critical medical anthropology in his study of how poverty kills through diseases such as tuberculosis and HIV/AIDS.

Bonnie Glass-Coffin. *The Gift of Life: Female Spirituality and Healing in Northern Peru.* Albuquerque: University of New Mexico Press, 1998. The author examines women traditional healers in northern Peru. She provides a descriptive account of their practices and an account of how two healers worked to cure her of a spiritual illness.

Richard Katz, Megan Biesele, and Verna St. Davis. *Healing Makes Our Hearts Happy: Spirituality and Cultural Transformation among the Kalahari Ju/'hoansi.* Rochester, VT: Inner Traditions, 1997. This book presents the story of how traditional healing dances help the Ju/'hoansi cope with recent and contemporary social upheaval. Their healing dances help them maintain a sense of community and are important for their cultural survival.

Carol Shepherd McClain, ed. *Women as Healers: A Cross-Cultural Perspective.* New Brunswick, NJ: Rutgers University Press, 1989. Case studies discuss women healers in Ecuador, Sri Lanka, Mexico, Jamaica, the United States, Serbia, Korea, Southern Africa, and Benin.

David McKnight. *From Hunting to Drinking: The Devastating Effects of Alcohol on an Australian Aboriginal Community.* New York: Routledge, 2002. McKnight documents the history of drinking in Australia, causes of excessive alcohol consumption, and vested interests of authorities in the sale of alcohol to Aboriginal people.

Ethan Nebelkopf and Mary Phillips, eds. *Healing and Mental Health for Native Americans: Speaking in Red.* New York. AltaMira Press, 2004. Chapters address mental health and substance abuse among Native North Americans and provide cases of healing that involve Native American culture.

Merrill Singer. *Something Dangerous: Emergent and Changing Illicit Drug Use and Community Health.* Long Grove, IL: Waveland Press, 2005. This ethnography combines theory with research and applied anthropology about drug use and public health responses in the United States.

Paul Stoller. *Stranger in the Village of the Sick: A Memoir of Cancer, Sorcery, and Healing.* Boston: Beacon Press, 2004. After being diagnosed with lymphoma, the author enters the "village of the sick" as he goes through diagnostic testing, chemotherapy, and eventual remission. He describes being a cancer patient in the United States and how he found strength through his earlier association with a West African healer.

Johan Wedel. *Santería Healing.* Gainesville: University of Florida Press, 2004. This book discusses Santería healing in Cuba. The author conducted interviews with priests and others knowledgeable about Santería and observed many Santería consultations.

6    **KINSHIP AND DOMESTIC LIFE**

7    **SOCIAL GROUPS AND SOCIAL STRATIFICATION**

8   **POLITICAL AND LEGAL SYSTEMS**

PART III

SOCIAL ORGANIZATION

ANTHROPOLOGY works

Fredy Peccerelli, a forensic anthropologist, risks his personal safety working for victims of political violence in Guatemala, his homeland. Peccerelli is founder and executive director of the Guatemalan Forensic Anthropology Foundation (FAFG). FAFG is dedicated to the recovery and identification of the remains of thousands of indigenous Maya whom Guatemalan military forces "disappeared" or outright killed during the brutal civil war that raged from the mid-1960s to the mid-1990s.

Peccerelli was born in Guatemala. His family immigrated to the United States when his father, a lawyer, was threatened by death squads. He grew up in New York City and attended Brooklyn College in the 1990s. But he felt a need to reconnect with his heritage and began to study anthropology as a vehicle that would allow him to serve his country.

The FAFG scientists excavate clandestine mass graves, exhume the bodies, and identify them through several means, such as matching dental and/or medical records. In studying skeletons, they try to determine the person's age, gender, ancestry, and lifestyle. DNA studies are few because of the expense. The scientists also collect information from relatives of the victims and from eyewitnesses of the massacres. Since 1992, the FAFG team has discovered and exhumed approximately 200 mass grave sites.

Peccerelli sees the foundation's purpose as applying scientific principles to basic human concerns. Bodies of identified victims are returned to their families to allow them some sense of closure about what happened to their loved ones. Families can honor their dead with appropriate burial ceremonies.

The scientists also give the Guatemalan government clear evidence on the basis of which to prosecute the perpetrators of these atrocities. Members of the long-standing military rulers still hold powerful positions within the government.

Peccerelli, his family, and his colleagues have been harassed and threatened. Bullets have been fired into Peccerelli's home, and it has been burglarized. Eleven FAFG scientists have received written death threats. Nevertheless, the United Nations and other human rights organizations have made it clear to the government that they support FAFG's investigations, and exhumations continue with heightened security measures.

The American Association for the Advancement of Science honored Peccerelli and his colleagues in 2004 for their work in promoting human rights at great personal risk. In 1999, *Time* magazine and CNN chose Peccerelli as one of 50 "Latin American Leaders for the New Millennium." During the same year, the Guatemalan Youth Commission named him an "icon" for the youth of the country.

ing how another culture's kinship system works is as
nging as learning another language. Robin Fox became
of this challenge during his research among the Tory
ers of Ireland (see Map 6.1) (1995 [1978]). Some Tory
kinship terms are similar to American English terms;
ample, the word *muintir* means "people" in its widest
as in English. It can also refer to people of a particular
category, as in "my people," and to close relatives. An-
similarity is in *gaolta*, the word for "relatives" or "those
blood." Its adjectival form refers to kindness, like the
sh word *kin*, which is related to "kindness." Tory Is-
rs have a phrase meaning "children and grandchildren,"
ike the English term "*descendants.*" One major difference
t the Tory Island word for "friend" is the same as the
for "kin." This usage reflects the cultural context of Tory
d with its small population, all related through kinship.
gically, a friend is also kin.

All cultures have ways of defining *kinship*, or a sense of
related to another person or persons. Cultures also pro-
guidelines about who are kin and the expected behavior
1. Starting in infancy, people learn about their particular
re's **kinship system**, the predominant form of kin rela-
hips in a culture and the kinds of behavior involved. Like
age, one's kinship system is so ingrained that it is taken
anted as something natural rather than cultural.

This chapter first considers cultural variations in three
res of kinship systems. It then focuses on a key unit of
estic life: the household. The last section provides ex-
es of contemporary change in kinship and household
nization.

◆◆◆

ow Cultures Create Kinship

I cultures, kinship is linked with modes of livelihood and
duction (see Figure 6.1). Nineteenth-century anthropolo-
found that kinship was the most important organizing
iple in nonindustrial, nonstate cultures. The kinship group
rms the functions of ensuring the continuity of the group
rranging marriages; maintaining social order by setting
l rules and punishing offenders; and providing for the
needs of members by regulating production, consump-
and distribution. In large-scale industrial/informatic
ties, kinship ties exist, but many other kinds of social ties
people together as well.

Nineteenth-century anthropologists also discovered that
itions of who counts as kin in the cultures they studied
red widely from those of Europe and the United States.
ern cultures emphasize as primary "blood" relations, or

---

hip system   the predominant form of kin relationships
culture and the kinds of behavior involved.

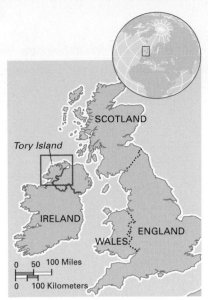

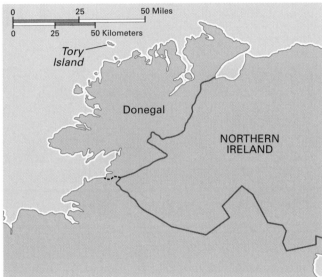

MAP 6.1   **Ireland.**

Ireland's population is about 4 million. The geography is low
central plains surrounded by a ring of mountains. Membership
in the European Union (EU) and the rising standard of living
earned Ireland the nickname of the Celtic Tiger. Its economic
opportunities are attracting immigrants from places as diverse
as Romania, China, and Nigeria. Most people are Roman
Catholics, followed by the Anglican Church of Ireland.

relations through birth from a biological mother and biological
father (Sault 1994). "Blood" is not a universal basis for kinship,
however. Even in some cultures with a "blood"-based understanding of kinship, variations exist in defining who is a
"blood" relative and who is not. For example, in some cultures,
male offspring are considered of one "blood," whereas female
offspring are not.

Among the Inuit of northern Alaska, behavior is a non-
blood basis for determining kinship (Bodenhorn 2000). In
this context, people who act like kin are kin. If a person stops
acting like kin, then he or she is no longer a kinsperson. So,
among the Inuit, someone might say that a certain person
"used to be" his or her cousin.

A Minangkabau bride in Sumatra, Indonesia, wears an elaborate gold headdress.

KINSHIP AN
DOMESTIC LI

6

the BIG questi

◆ How do cultures create kin

◆ What are cross-cu
patterns of househ
and domestic

◆ How are kinship
households chang

OUTLINE

How Cultures Create Kinship

Everyday Anthropology:
What's in a Name?

Culturama: The Minangkabau
of Indonesia

Households and Domestic Life

**Changing Kinship and
Household Dynamics**

Lessons Applied: Ethnography
for Preventing Wife Abuse
in Rural Kentucky

Foraging	Horticulture	Pastoralism	Agriculture	Industrialism/Informatics
Descent and Inheritance				**Descent and Inheritance**
Bilineal		Unilineal (matrilineal or patrilineal)		Bilineal
Marital Residence				**Marital Residence**
Neolocal or bilocal		Matrilocal or patrilocal		Neolocal
Household Type				**Household Type**
Nuclear		Extended		Nuclear or single-parent or single-person

FIGURE 6.1 Modes of Livelihood, Kinship, and Household Structure

STUDYING KINSHIP: FROM FORMAL ANALYSIS TO KINSHIP IN ACTION

Anthropologists in the first half of the twentieth century focused on finding out who, in a particular culture, is related to whom and in what way. Typically, the anthropologist would conduct an interview with a few people, asking questions such as "What do you call your brother's daughter?" "Can you (as a man) marry your father's brother's daughter?" and "What is the term you use to refer to your mother's sister?" The anthropologist would ask an individual to name all of his or her relatives, explain how they are related to the interviewee, and provide the terms by which he or she refers to them.

From this information, the anthropologist would construct a *kinship diagram,* a schematic way of presenting the kinship relationships of an individual, called *ego,* using a set of symbols to depict all the kin relations of ego (see Figure 6.2). A kinship diagram depicts ego's relatives, as remembered by ego. In cultures in which kinship plays a major role in social

relations, ego may be able to provide information on dozens of relatives. When I took a research methods course as an undergraduate, one assignment was to interview someone who was not an American and construct a kinship chart based on the information collected. I interviewed a student from an urban, middle-class business family in India. He recalled over 60 relatives on both his father's and mother's sides. My kinship diagram of his relatives required several sheets of paper taped together.

In contrast to a kinship diagram, a *genealogy* is a schematic way of presenting a family tree, constructed by beginning with the earliest ancestors that can be traced, then working down to the present. A genealogy, thus, does not begin with ego. When Robin Fox attempted to construct kinship diagrams beginning with ego, the Tory Islanders were uncomfortable with the approach. They preferred to proceed genealogically, so he followed their preference. Tracing a family's complete genealogy may involve archival research in the attempt to construct as

Characters		**Relationships**		**Kin Abbreviations**	
●	female	=	is married to	**Mo**	mother
△	male	≈	is cohabiting with	**Fa**	father
⊘	deceased female	≁	is divorced from	**Br**	brother
◬	deceased male	≉	is separated from	**Z**	sister
⬤	female "ego" of the diagram	⊙	adopted-in female	**H**	husband
▲	male "ego" of the diagram	◬	adopted-in male	**W**	wife
		|	is descended from	**Da**	daughter
		⊓	is the sibling of	**S**	son
				Co	cousin

FIGURE 6.2 Symbols Used in Kinship Diagrams

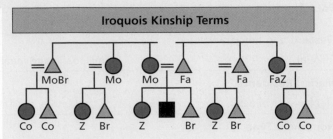

Eskimo Kinship Terms

Uncle | Aunt | Mo | Fa | Uncle | Aunt

Co Co | Co Co | Z Br | Co Co | Co Co

Eskimo kinship terminology, like that of most Euro-Americans, has unique terms for kin within the nuclear family that are not used for any other relatives: mother, father, sister, brother. This fact is related to the importance of the nuclear family. Another feature is that the same terms are used for relatives on both the mother's side and the father's side, a property that is related to bilineal descent.

Iroquois Kinship Terms

MoBr | Mo | Mo | Fa | Fa | FaZ

Co Co | Z Br | Z Br | Z Br | Co Co

Iroquois kinship terminology operates in unilineal systems. One result is that there are different terms for relatives on the mother's and father's sides and distinctions between cross and parallel cousins. Another feature is the "merging" of one's mother with one's mother's sister (both are referred to as "mother") and of one's father with one's father's brother (both are referred to as "father").

FIGURE 6.3 Two Kinship Naming Systems

complete a history as possible. In Europe and the United States, Christians have long followed a practice of recording their genealogy in the front of the family Bible. Many African Americans and other people are consulting DNA analysts to learn about their ancestry and cultural heritage.

Decades of anthropological research have produced a mass of information on *kinship terminology*, or the words people use to refer to kin. For example, in Euro-American kinship, a child of one's father's sister or brother or one's mother's sister or brother is referred to by the kinship term "cousin." Likewise, one's father's sister and one's mother's sister are both referred to as "aunt," and one's father's brother and one's mother's brother are both referred to as "uncle." "Grandmother" and "grandfather" refer to the ascending generation on either one's father's or one's mother's side. This merging pattern is not universal. In some cultures, different terms apply to kin on one's mother's and father's sides, so a mother's sister has a kinship term different from that referring to a

father's sister. Another type of kinship system emphasizes solidarity along lines of siblings of the same gender. For example, among the Navajo of the American southwest, one's mother and one's mother's sisters have the same term, which translates into English as "mother."

Early anthropologists classified the cross-cultural variety in kinship terminology into six basic types, named after groups first discovered to have those systems. Two of the six types, for purposes of illustration, are the Iroquois type and the Eskimo type (see Figure 6.3). Anthropologists place various cultures with similar kinship terminology, no matter where they lived, into one of the six categories. Thus, the Yanomami people of the Amazon are classified as having an Iroquois naming system. Contemporary anthropologists who study kinship have moved beyond these categories because they feel that the six kinship types do not shed light on actual kinship dynamics. This book, therefore, presents only the two examples and avoids going into detail on the six classic types.

Current interest in the study of kinship shows how it is related to other topics, such as globalization, ethnic identity, and even terrorism. Anthropologists have come a long way, from classifying kinship to showing how it matters. They focus on three key factors that, cross-culturally, construct kinship relations: descent, sharing, and marriage.

descent   the tracing of kinship relationships through parentage.

bilineal descent   tracing descent through both parents.

unilineal descent   tracing descent through only one parent.

patrilineal descent   a descent system that highlights the importance of men in tracing descent, determining marital residence with or near the groom's family, and providing for inheritance of property through the male line.

matrilineal descent   a descent system that highlights the importance of women by tracing descent through the female line, favoring marital residence with or near the bride's family, and providing for property to be inherited through the female line.

DESCENT

Descent is the tracing of kinship relationships through parentage. It is based on the fact that everybody is born from someone else. Descent creates a line of people from whom someone is descended, stretching through history. But not all cultures reckon descent in the same way. Some cultures have a bilineal descent system, in which a child is recognized as being related by descent to both parents. Others have a **unilineal descent** system, which recognizes descent through only one parent, either the father or the mother. The distribution of bilineal and unilineal systems is roughly correlated with different modes of livelihood (see Figure 6.1, p. 127). This correspondence makes sense because economic systems—production, consumption, and exchange—are closely tied to the way people are socially organized.

UNILINEAL DESCENT Unilineal descent is the basis of kinship in about 60 percent of the world's cultures, making it the most common form of descent. This system tends to be found in societies with a fixed resource base. Thus, unilineal descent is most common among pastoralists, horticulturalists, and farmers. Inheritance rules that regulate the transmission of property through only one line help maintain cohesiveness of the resource base.

Unilineal descent has two major forms. One is **patrilineal descent**, in which kinship is traced through the male line. The other is **matrilineal descent**, in which kinship is traced through the female line. In a patrilineal system, only male children are considered members of the kinship lineage. Female children "marry out" and become members of the husband's lineage. In matrilineal descent systems, only daughters are considered to carry on the family line and sons "marry out."

Patrilineal descent is found among about 45 percent of all cultures. It occurs throughout much of South Asia, East Asia, the Middle East, Papua New Guinea, northern Africa, and among some horticultural groups of sub-Saharan Africa. The world's most strongly patrilineal systems are found in East Asia, South Asia, and the Middle East (see Everyday Anthropology).

Matrilineal descent exists in about 15 percent of all cultures. It traces kinship through the female line exclusively, and the lineage consists of mothers and daughters and their daughters. Matrilineal descent is found among many Native North American groups; across a large band of central Africa; among many groups of Southeast Asia and the Pacific, and Australia; in parts of eastern and southern India; in a small pocket of northern Bangladesh; and in parts of the Mediterranean coast of Spain and Portugal. Matrilineal societies are found among foragers and in agricultural societies. Most matrilineal cultures, however, are horticulturalist economies in which women dominate the production and distribution of food and other goods. Often, but not always, matrilineal kinship is associated with recognized public leadership positions for women, as among the Iroquois and Hopi. The Minangkabau (muhnan-ka-bow, with the last syllable rhyming with "now") of Indonesia are the largest matrilineal group in the world (see Culturama).

BILINEAL DESCENT Bilineal descent traces kinship from both parents equally to the child. Bilineal descent is found in

(TOP) Some members of a Bedu household in Yemen. The Bedu are a small proportion of the Yemeni population. (BOTTOM) Boys playing in Hababa, Yemen. In this patrilineal culture, public space is segregated by gender.

▶ *If you were a cultural anthropologist working in Yemen, how would you proceed to learn about how Yemeni girls spend their time?*

about one-third of the world's cultures (Murdock 1965 [1949]:57). The highest frequency of bilineal descent is found at opposite ends of the modes-of-livelihood diagram (see Figure 6.1, p. 127). For example, Ju/'hoansi foragers have bilineal descent, as do most urban professionals in North America. Both foraging and industrialism/informatics cultures rely on a flexible gender division of labor in which both males and females contribute, more or less equally, to making a living. Bilineal descent makes sense for foraging and industrial/informatics groups because it allows for small family units and spatial mobility.

Marital residence tends to follow the prevailing direction of descent rules (see Figure 6.1, p. 127). *Patrilocality*, or marital residence with or near the husband's family, occurs in patrilineal societies, whereas *matrilocality*, or marital residence with or near the wife's family, occurs in matrilineal societies. *Neolocality*, or marital residence in a place different from

everyday ANTHROPOLOGY

What's in a Name?

Naming children is always significant. Parents may follow cultural rules that a first-born son receives the name of his father's father or a first-born daughter receives the name of her mother's mother. Some parents believe that a newborn should not be formally named for a year or two, and the child is instead referred to by a nickname. Others think that a name must convey some special hoped-for attribute for the child or that a name should be unique.

The village of Ha Tsuen is located in the northwest corner of a rural area of Hong Kong (Watson 1986). About 2500 people live in the village. All the males belong to the same patrilineage and all have the same surname of Teng. They are descended from a common male ancestor who settled in the region in the twelfth century. Daughters of Ha Tsuen marry into families outside the village, and marital residence is patrilocal.

Women do not own property, and they have no control over the household economy. Few married women are employed in wage labor. They depend on their husbands for financial support. Local politics is male dominated, as is all public decision making. A woman's status as a new bride is low, and the transition from daughter to bride can be difficult psychologically. Women's primary role is in reproduction, especially of sons. As a woman bears children, especially sons, her status in the household rises.

The local naming system reflects the power, importance, and autonomy of males. All children are first given a name, referred to as their *ming*, when they are a few days old. If the baby is a boy, the 30-day ceremony is as elaborate as the family can afford. It may include a banquet for many neighbors and the village elders and the presentation of red eggs to everyone in the community. For a girl, the 30-day ceremony may involve only a special meal for close family members. Paralleling this expenditure bias toward sons is the thinking that goes into selecting the *ming*. A boy's ming is distinctive and flattering. It may have a classical literary connection. A girl's ming often has negative connotations, such as "Last Child," "Too Many," or "Little Mistake." One common ming for a daughter is "Joined to a Brother," which implies the hope that she will be a lucky charm, bringing the birth of a son to her mother next. Sometimes, though, people give an uncomplimentary name to a boy, such as "Little Slave Girl." The reason behind this naming practice is protection—to trick the spirits into thinking the baby is only a worthless girl so that the spirits will do no harm.

Marriage is the next formal naming occasion. When a male marries, he is given or chooses for himself a *tzu*, or marriage name. Gaining a tzu is a key marker of male adulthood. The tzu is not used in everyday address, but appears mainly on formal documents. A man also has a *wai hao*, "outside name," which is his public nickname. As he enters middle age, he may take a *hao*, or courtesy name, which he chooses and which reflects his aspirations and self-perceptions.

---

either the bride's or groom's family, is common in Western industrialized society. Residence patterns have political, economic, and social implications. Patrilineal descent and patrilocal residence, for example, facilitate the formation of strongly bonded groups of men who can be mobilized for warfare.

SHARING

Many cultures emphasize kinship ties based on acts of sharing and support. These relationships may be either informal or ritually formalized. Godparenthood and blood brotherhood are examples of sharing-based kinship ties that are ritually formalized.

KINSHIP THROUGH FOOD SHARING Sharing-based kinship is common in mainland Southeast Asia, Australia, and Pacific island cultures (Carsten 1995). Among inhabitants of one of Malaysia's many small islands, sharing-based kinship starts in the womb when the mother's blood feeds the fetus. After birth, the mother's breast milk nourishes the infant. This tie is crucial. A child who is not breastfed will not "recognize" its mother. Breastfeeding is also the basis of the incest rule. People who have been fed from the same breast are kin and may not marry. After the baby is weaned, its most important food is cooked rice. Sharing cooked rice, like breast milk, becomes another way that kinship ties are created and maintained, especially between women and children. Men are often away on fishing trips, in coffee shops, or at the mosque and so are not likely to have rice-sharing kinship bonds with children.

ADOPTION AND FOSTERING Another form of sharing-based kinship is the transfer of a child or children from the birth parent(s) to the care of someone else. *Adoption* is a formal and permanent form of child transfer. Common motivations for adoption include infertility and the desire to obtain a particular kind of child (often a son). Motivations for the birth parent to transfer a child to someone else include a premarital pregnancy in a disapproving context, having "too many" children, and having "too many" of a particular gender.

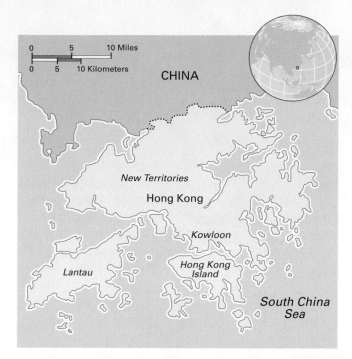

MAP 6.2 Hong Kong.

The formal name of Hong Kong is the Hong Kong Special Administrative Region of the People's Republic of China. A world center of finance and trade, it lacks natural resources and agricultural land, so it imports most of its food and raw materials. With 7 million residents, Hong Kong's population density is high. Most of the population is ethnic Chinese, and many practice ancestor worship. Ten percent of the population is Christian. Religious freedom is protected through Hong Kong's constitution.

In the case of a woman, her ming ceases to exist when she marries. She no longer has a name. Instead, her husband refers to her as *nei jen*, "inner person," because now her life is restricted to the domestic world of household, husband's family, and neighborhood. People may also refer to her by *teknonyms*, or names for someone based on their relationship to someone else, such as "Wife of So and So" or "Mother of So and So." In old age, she becomes *ah po*, "Old Woman."

Throughout their lives, men accumulate more and better names than women. They choose many of the names themselves. Over the courses of their lives, women have fewer names than men have. Women's names are standardized, not personalized, and women never get to choose any of their names.

◆ **FOOD FOR THOUGHT**

- Go to www.slate.com/id/2116505/ (Trading Up: Where Do Baby Names Come From? by Steven D. Levitt and Stephen J. Dubner), and read about the status game of child naming in the United States. How does your first name fit into this picture?

Among the Maasai pastoralists of East Africa, a woman with several children might give one to a friend, neighbor, or aged person who has no child to care for her or him.

Since the mid-1800s, adoption has been a legalized form of child transfer in the United States. Judith Modell, cultural anthropologist and adoptive parent, studied people's experiences of adoptees, birth parents, and adoptive parents in the United States (1994). She found that the legal process of adoption constructs the adoptive relationship to be as much like a biological one as possible. In *closed adoption,* the adopted child receives a new birth certificate and the birth parent ceases to have any relationship to the child. A recent trend is toward *open adoption,* in which adoptees and birth parents have information about each other's identity and are free to interact with one another. Of the 28 adoptees Modell interviewed, most were interested in searching for their birth parents. The search for birth parents involves an attempt to discover "who I really am." For others, such a search is backward looking instead of being a path toward identity formation. Thus, in the United States, adoption legalizes

sharing-based kinship but does not always replace a sense of descent-based kinship for everyone involved.

Fostering a child is sometimes similar to a formal adoption in terms of permanence and a sense of kinship. Or it may be temporary placement of a child with someone else for a specific purpose, with little or no sense of kinship. Child fostering is common throughout sub-Saharan Africa. Parents foster out children to enhance the child's chances for formal education or so that the child will learn a skill, such as marketing. Most foster children go from rural to urban areas and from poorer to better-off households. Fieldwork conducted in a neighborhood in Accra, Ghana (see Map 6.4), sheds light on the lives of foster children (Sanjek 1990). Child fostering in the neighborhood is common: About one-fourth of the children were foster children. Twice as many of the foster children were girls as boys. School attendance is biased toward boys. All of the boys were attending school, but only 4 of the 31 girls were. An important factor affecting the treatment of the child is whether the fostered child is related to his or her sponsor. Although 80 percent of the foster children as a

CULTURAMA

The Minangkabau of Indonesia

The Minangkabau are the world's largest matrilineal culture, numbering between 4 and 5 million (Sanday 2002). Most live in West Sumatra, Indonesia, and about 500,000 live in Malaysia. The Minangkabau are primarily farmers, producing substantial amounts of surplus rice. Many Minangkabau, both women and men, take up employment in Indonesian cities for a time and then return home.

In this strongly matrilineal kinship system, Minangkabau women hold power through their control of land passed down through the lineage, the products of that land, and agricultural employment on their land (Sanday 2002). Many have prominent positions in business, especially having to do with rice. Men are more likely to become scholars, merchants, and politi-cians. Inheritance of property, including farmland and the family house, passes from mothers to daughters.

Members of each submatrilineage, constituting several generations, live together in one house or several nearby houses. Often, men and older boys live in a separate structure, such as the village mosque. In the household, the senior woman controls the power, and she makes decisions in all economic and ceremonial matters. The senior male of the sublineage has the role of representing its interests to other groups, but he is only a representative, not a powerful person in his own right.

Water buffaloes are important in both the Minangkabau rice economy and symbolically. The roofline of a traditional house has upward curves that echo the shape of water buffalo horns. Minangkabau women's festive headdresses have the same shape. The Minangkabau are mostly Muslims, but they mix their Muslim faith with elements of earlier traditions and Hinduism. They have long-standing traditions of music, martial arts, weaving, wood carving, and making fine filigree jewelry of silver and gold.

Many of the traditional wooden houses and palaces in Western Sumatra are falling into a state of disrepair (Vellinga 2004). The matrilineal pattern of only women living in the house is changing, and today men and women are more likely to live together in nuclear households.

Thanks to Michael G. Peletz, Emory University, for reviewing this material.

MAP 6.3

(LEFT) A traditional wooden Minangkabau longhouse with its distinctive upward-pointing roof. The house interiors are divided into separate "bays" for submatrilineal groups. Many are no longer places of residence but are used as meeting halls or are falling into ruin.

(CENTER) The symbolic importance of water buffaloes, apparent in the shape of traditional rooftops, is reiterated in the shape of girls' and women's ceremonial headdresses. The headdress represents women's responsibilities for the growth and strength of Minangkabau culture.

MAP 6.3 **Minangkabau Region in Indonesia.** The shaded area shows the traditional heartland of Minangkabau culture in western Sumatra. Many Minangkabau people live elsewhere in Sumatra and in neighboring Malaysia.

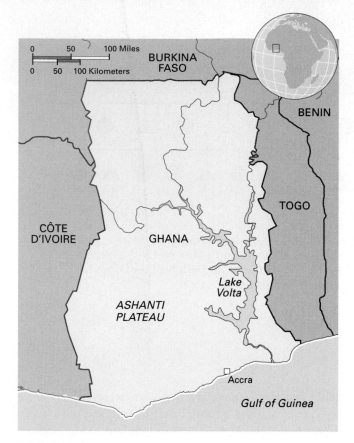

MAP 6.4 Ghana.
The Republic of Ghana has over 20 million people. Ghana has rich natural resources and exports gold, timber, and cocoa. Agriculture is the basis of the domestic economy. Several ethnic groups exist, with the Akan people constituting over 40 percent of the population. English is the official language, but another 80 or so languages are also spoken. Over 60 percent of the people are Christian, 20 percent follow traditional religions, and 16 percent are Muslim.

whole were kin of their sponsors, only 50 percent of the girls were kin. People who sponsor nonkin girls make a cash payment to the girl's parents. These girls cook, do housecleaning, and assist in market work by carrying goods or watching the trading area. Fostered boys, most of whom are kin of their sponsors, do not perform such tasks because they attend school.

RITUALLY ESTABLISHED KINSHIP Ritually defined ties between adults and children born to other people are common among Christians, especially Catholics, worldwide. Relationships between godparents and godchildren often involve strong emotional ties and financial flows from the former to the latter.

Among the Maya of Oaxaca, Mexico (see Map 4.3, p. 84), godparenthood is both a sign of the sponsor's status and the means to increased status for the sponsor (Sault 1985). A parent's request that a particular person sponsor his or her child is a public acknowledgment of the sponsor's standing. The godparent gains influence over the godchild and can call on the godchild for labor. Being a godparent of many children

means that the godparent can amass a large labor force when needed and gain further status. Most godparents in Oaxaca are husband–wife couples, but many are women alone, a pattern that reflects the high status of Maya women.

MARRIAGE

The third major basis for forming close interpersonal relationships is through marriage or other forms of "marriage-like" relationships, such as long-term cohabitation. The following material focuses on marriage.

TOWARD A DEFINITION Anthropologists recognize that some concept of *marriage* exists in all cultures, though it may take different forms and serve different functions. What constitutes a cross-culturally valid definition of marriage is, however, open to debate. A standard definition from 1951 is now discredited: "Marriage is a union between a man and a woman such that children born to the woman are the recognized legitimate offspring of both parents" (Barnard and Good 1984:89). This definition says that the partners must be of different genders, and it implies that a child born outside a marriage is not socially recognized as legitimate. Exceptions exist to both these features cross-culturally. Regarding the gender of partners, same-gender marriages are legal in Denmark, Norway, and Holland. Their legal status is a subject of ongoing debate in the United States and Canada.

Regarding the second, many cultures do not define the legitimacy of children on the basis of whether they were born within a marriage. Women in the Caribbean region, for example, typically do not marry until later in life. Before that, a woman has sequential male partners with whom she bears children. None of her children is considered more or less "legitimate" than any other.

Other definitions of marriage focus on rights over the spouse's sexuality. But not all forms of marriage involve sexual

Jillian Armenante (LEFT), actress, and her bride, Alice Dodd, call friends and family after their marriage ceremony in City Hall, San Francisco, in 2004.

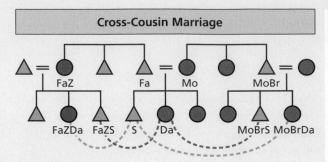

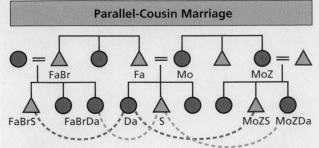

Cross-Cousin Marriage

Parallel-Cousin Marriage

Cross-cousin marriage: A daughter marries either her father's sister's son or her mother's brother's son. A son marries either his father's sister's daughter or his mother's brother's daughter.

Parallel-cousin marriage: A daughter marries either her father's brother's son or her mother's sister's son. A son marries either his father's brother's daughter or his mother's sister's daughter.

FIGURE 6.4 Two Types of Cousin Marriage

relations; for example, the practice of *woman–woman marriage* exists among the Nuer of southern Sudan (see Map 13.5, p. 290) and some other African groups (Evans-Pritchard 1951:108–109). In this type of marriage, a woman with economic means gives gifts to obtain a "wife," goes through the marriage rituals with her, and brings her into the residential compound just as a man would who married a woman. This wife contributes her productive labor to the household. The two women do not have a sexual relationship. Instead, the woman who marries into the household will have sexual relations with a man. Her children, though, will belong to the compound into which she married.

The many practices that come under the heading of marriage make it impossible to find a definition that will fit all cases. One might accept the following as a working definition of **marriage**: a more or less stable union, usually between two people, who may be, but are not necessarily, co-residential, sexually involved with each other, and procreative with each other.

SELECTING A SPOUSE All cultures have preferences about whom one should and should not marry or with whom one

should and should not have sexual intercourse. Sometimes these preferences are informal and implicit, and other times they are formal and explicit. They include both *rules of exclusion* (specifying whom one should not marry) and *rules of inclusion* (specifying who is a preferred marriage partner).

An **incest taboo**, or rule prohibiting marriage or sexual intercourse between certain kinship relations, is one of the most basic and universal rules of exclusion. The most basic and universal form of incest taboo is against marriage or sexual intercourse between fathers and their children and between mothers and their children. Although most cultures forbid brother–sister marriage, a few exceptions exist. The most well-known example of brother–sister marriage as an accepted practice comes from Egypt at the time of the Roman Empire (Barnard and Good 1984:92). Brother–sister marriage was the norm among royalty, and it was common among the general population, with between 15 and 20 percent of marriages between full brothers and sisters.

Further variations in close-relation marriage arise with regard to cousins. Incest taboos do not universally rule out marriage with cousins. In fact, some kinship systems promote cousin marriage, as discussed next.

Many preference rules exist cross-culturally concerning whom one should marry. Rules of **endogamy**, or marriage within a particular group, stipulate that the spouse must be from a defined social category. In kin endogamy, certain relatives are preferred, often cousins. Two major forms of cousin marriage exist. One is marriage between **parallel cousins**, either between children of one's father and one's father's brother or between children of one's mother and one's mother's sister—the term *parallel* indicates that the linking siblings are of the same gender (see Figure 6.4). Parallel-cousin marriage is favored by many Muslim groups in the Middle East and

---

marriage a union, usually between two people who are likely to be, but are not necessarily, coresident, sexually involved with each other, and procreative.

incest taboo a strongly held prohibition against marrying or having sex with particular kin.

endogamy marriage within a particular group or locality.

parallel cousin offspring of either one's father's brother or one's mother's sister.

cross-cousin offspring of either one's father's sister or one's mother's brother.

exogamy marriage outside a particular group or locality.

Hypergyny	The bride marries a groom of higher status.	The groom may be wealthier, more educated, older, taller.
Hypogyny	The bride marries a groom of lower status.	The bride may be wealthier, more educated, older, taller.
Isogamy	The bride and groom are status equals.	The bride and groom have similar wealth, education, age, height.

FIGURE 6.5 Status Considerations in Partner Selection (Heterosexual Pairing)

northern Africa. The second form of cousin marriage is that between **cross-cousins**, either between children of one's father and one's father's sister or between children of one's mother and one's mother's brother—the term *cross* indicates the different genders of the linking siblings. Hindus of southern India favor *cross-cousin marriage*. Although cousin marriage is preferred, it nonetheless is a minority of all marriages in the region. A survey of several thousand couples in the city of Chennai (formerly called Madras) in southern India showed that three-fourths of all marriages involved unrelated people, whereas one-fourth were between first cross-cousins or between uncle and niece, which is considered to be the same relationship as that of cross-cousins (Ramesh, Srikumari, and Sukumar 1989).

Endogamy may also be based on location. Village endogamy is preferred in the eastern Mediterranean among both Christians and Muslims. It is also the preferred pattern among Muslims throughout India and among Hindus of southern India. Hindus of northern India, in contrast, forbid village endogamy and consider it a form of incest. Instead, they practice village **exogamy**, or marriage outside a defined social group. For them, a spouse should live in a far-off village or town. In India, marriage distance is greater in the north than in the south, and northern brides are thus far less likely to be able to maintain regular contact with their birth family. Many songs and stories of northern Indian women convey sadness about being separated from their birth families.

Status considerations often shape spouse selection (see Figure 6.5). (The following discussion pertains to heterosexual marriage.) *Hypergyny*, or "marrying up," refers to a marriage in which the bride's status is lower than the groom's. Hypergyny is widely practiced in northern India, especially among upper-status groups. It is also prominent among many middle- and upper-class people in the United States. Because of hypergyny, women in top professions such as medicine and law—especially women medical students in North America—are having a difficult time finding appropriate partners, since there are few, if any, options for them to "marry up." The opposite pattern is *hypogyny*, or "marrying down," a marriage in which the bride has higher status than the groom. Hypogyny is rare cross-culturally. *Isogamy*, marriage between partners who are status equals, occurs in cultures where male and female roles and status are equal.

Physical features, such as ability, looks, and appearance, are factors that may be explicitly or implicitly involved in spouse selection. Facial beauty, skin color, hair texture and length, height, and weight are variously defined as important. Height hypergyny (in which the groom is taller than the bride) is more common in male-dominated contexts. Height-isogamous marriages are common in cultures where gender roles are relatively equal and where *sexual dimorphism* (differences in shape and size of the female body compared with the male body) is not marked, as in much of Southeast Asia.

The role of romantic love in spouse selection is debated by biological determinists and cultural constructionists. Biological determinists argue that feelings of romantic love are universal among humans because they play an adaptive role in uniting males and females in offspring care. Cultural constructionists, in contrast, argue that romantic love is an unusual factor influencing spouse selection (Barnard and Good 1984:94). The cultural constructionists point to variations in male and female economic roles to explain cross-cultural differences in the emphasis on romantic love. Romantic love is more likely to be an important factor in relationships in cultures where men contribute more to subsistence and where women are therefore economically dependent on men. Whatever the cause of romantic love, biological or cultural or both, it is an increasingly common basis for marriage in many cultures (Levine et al. 1995).

Within the United States, microcultural variations exist in the degree to which women value romantic love as a basis for marriage (Holland and Eisenhart 1990). One study interviewed young American women entering college from 1979 to 1981 and again in 1987 after they had graduated and begun their adult lives. The research sites were two southern colleges in the United States, one attended mainly by White Euro-Americans and the other by African Americans. A contrast between the groups of women emerged. The White women were much more influenced by notions of romantic love than the Black

THINKING OUTSIDE THE BOX

Do some research on www.match.com or www.chemistry.com to learn what cultural preferences people mention in their profiles.

FIGURE 6.6 Types of Marriage Exchange

	Type	Where Practiced
Dowry	Goods and money given by the bride's family to the married couple	European and Asian cultures; agriculturalists and industrialists
Groomprice	A form of dowry: goods and money given by the bride's family to the married couple and to the parents of the groom	South Asia, especially northern India
Brideprice (or bridewealth)	Goods and money given by the groom's family to the parents of the bride	Asian, African, and Central and South American cultures; horticulturalists and pastoralists
Brideservice	Labor given by the groom to the parents of the bride	Southeast Asian, Pacific, and Amazonian cultures; horticulturalists

women were. The White women were also less likely to have strong career goals and more likely to expect to be economically dependent on their spouse. The Black women expressed independence and strong career goals. The theme of romantic love supplies young White women with a model of the heroic male provider as the ideal, with her role being one of attracting him and providing the domestic context for their married life. The Black women were brought up to be more economically independent. This pattern is related both to African traditions in which women earn and manage their own earnings and to the racially discriminatory job market in the United States that places African American men at a severe disadvantage.

---

dowry   the transfer of cash and goods from the bride's family to the newly married couple and, sometimes, to the groom's family.

brideprice   the transfer of cash and goods from the groom's family to the bride's family and to the bride.

brideservice   a form of marriage exchange in which the groom works for his father-in-law for a certain length of time before returning home with the bride.

monogamy   marriage between two people.

polygamy   marriage involving multiple spouses.

polygyny   marriage of one husband with more than one wife.

polyandry   marriage of one wife with more than one husband.

family   a group of people who consider themselves related through a form of kinship, such as descent, marriage, or sharing.

household   either one person living alone or a group of people who may or may not be related by kinship and who share living space.

nuclear household   a domestic unit containing one adult couple (married or partners) with or without children.

extended household   a coresidential group that comprises more than one parent–child unit.

Arranged marriages are formed on the basis of parents' considerations of what constitutes a "good match" between the families of the bride and groom. Arranged marriages are common in many Middle Eastern, African, and Asian countries. Some theorists claim that arranged marriages are "traditional" and love marriages are "modern." They believe that arranged marriages will disappear with modernity. Japan presents a case of an industrial/informatics economy with a highly educated population in which arranged unions still constitute a substantial proportion of all marriages, about 25 to 30 percent (Applbaum 1995). The most important criteria for a spouse are the family's reputation and social standing; the absence of undesirable traits, such as a case of divorce or mental illness in the family; education; occupation; and income.

MARRIAGE GIFTS   Most marriages are accompanied by exchanges of goods or services between the families of the bride and groom (see Figure 6.6). The two major forms of marital exchanges cross-culturally are dowry and brideprice. **Dowry** is the transfer of goods, and sometimes money, from the bride's side to the new married couple for their use. The dowry includes household goods such as furniture, cooking utensils, and, sometimes, rights to a house. Dowry is the main form of marriage transfer in farming societies throughout Eurasia, from Western Europe through the northern Mediterranean and into China and India. In much of India, dowry is more accurately termed *groomprice*, because the goods and money pass not to the new couple but rather to the groom's family (Billig 1992). In China during the Mao era, the government considered dowry a sign of women's oppression and made it illegal. The practice of giving dowry in China has returned with increased personal wealth and consumerism, especially among the newly rich urban populations (Whyte 1993).

Brideprice, or *bridewealth*, is the transfer of goods or money from the groom's side to the bride's parents. It is common in horticultural and pastoralist cultures. **Brideservice**, a subtype of brideprice, is the transfer of labor from the groom

The Hausa are an important ethnic group of Ghana. This photograph shows a display of Hausa dowry goods in Accra, the capital city. The most valuable part of a Hausa bride's dowry is the *kayan dak'i* ("things of the room"), consisting of bowls, pots, ornamental glass, and cookware, which are conspicuously displayed in the bride's marital house so that the local women can get a sense of her worth. The bride's parents pay for these status items and for utilitarian items such as everyday cooking utensils.

to his parents-in-law for a designated period. It is practiced in some horticultural societies, especially in the Amazon.

Many marriages involve balanced gifts from both bride's and the groom's side. A longstanding pattern in the United States placed the major burden of the costs of the wedding and honeymoon on the bride's side, with the groom's side responsible for paying for the rehearsal dinner the night before the wedding. A trend toward shared costs by the bride and groom may indicate more equal relations in the marriage as well.

FORMS OF MARRIAGE Cultural anthropologists distinguish two forms of marriage on the basis of the number of partners involved. **Monogamy** is marriage between two people—a male or female if the pair is heterosexual, or two people of the same gender in the case of a homosexual pair. Heterosexual monogamy is the most common form of marriage cross-culturally, and in many countries it is the only legal form of marriage.

Polygamy is marriage involving multiple spouses, a pattern allowed in many cultures. Two forms of polygamous marriage exist. The more common of the two is **polygyny**, marriage of one man with more than one woman. **Polyandry**, or marriage between one woman and more than one man, is rare. The only place where polyandry is commonly found is in the Himalayan region that includes parts of Tibet, India, and Nepal. Nonpolyandrous people in the area look down on the people who practice polyandrous marriage as backward (Haddix McCay 2001).

◆◆◆

Households and Domestic Life

In casual conversation, North Americans might use the words *family* and *household* interchangeably to refer to people who live together. Social scientists, however, propose a distinction between the two terms. A **family** is a group of people who consider themselves related through kinship. In North American English, the term may include both "close" and "distant" relatives. All members of a family do not necessarily live together or have strong bonds with one another. But they are still "family."

A related term is the **household**, either a person living alone or one or more persons who occupy a shared living space and who may or may not be related by kinship. Most households consist of members who are related through kinship, but an increasing number do not. An example of a nonkin household is a group of friends who live in the same apartment. This section of the chapter looks at household forms and organization cross-culturally and at relationships between and among household members.

THE HOUSEHOLD: VARIATIONS ON A THEME

This section considers three forms of households and the concept of household headship.

Household organization is divided into types according to how many married adults are involved. The **nuclear household** (which many people call the nuclear family) is a domestic group that contains one adult couple (married or "partners"), with or without children. An **extended household** is a domestic group that contains more than one adult married couple. The couples may be related through the father–son line (making a *patrilineal extended household*), through the mother–daughter line (a *matrilineal extended*

THINKING
OUTSIDE
THE BOX

What is your opinion about the relative merits of love marriages versus arranged marriages, and on what do you base your opinion?

The woman on the lower right is part of a polyandrous marriage, which is still practiced among some Tibetan peoples. She is married to several brothers, two of whom stand behind her. The older man with the sash in the front row is her father-in-law.

household), or through sisters or brothers (a *collateral extended household*). Polygynous (multiple wives) and polyandrous (multiple husbands) households are *complex households,* domestic units in which one spouse lives with or near multiple partners and their children.

The precise cross-cultural distribution of these various types of households is not known, but some broad generalizations can be offered. First, nuclear households are found in all cultures but are the exclusive household type in only about one-fourth of the world's cultures (Murdock 1965 [1949]:2). Extended households are the most important form in about half of all cultures. The distribution of these two household forms corresponds roughly with the modes of livelihood (see Figure 6.1, p. 127). The nuclear form is most characteristic of economies at the two extremes of the continuum: foraging groups and industrialized/informatic societies. This pattern reflects the need for spatial mobility and flexibility in both modes of production. Extended households constitute a substantial proportion of households in horticultural, pastoralist, and farming economies.

INTRAHOUSEHOLD DYNAMICS

How do household members interact with each other? What are their emotional attachments, rights, and responsibilities? What are the power relationships between and among members of various categories, such as spouses, siblings, and those of different generations? Kinship systems define what the content of these relationships should be. In everyday life, people may conform more or less to the ideal.

SPOUSE–PARTNER RELATIONSHIPS This section discusses three areas of spousal relationships: marital satisfaction and sexual activity over the life course.

A landmark study of marriages in Tokyo in 1959 compared marital satisfaction of husbands and wives in love marriages and in arranged marriages (Blood 1967). In all marriages, marital satisfaction declined over time, but differences between the two types emerged. The decline was greatest for wives in arranged marriages and least for husbands in arranged marriages. In love-match marriages, both partners' satisfaction dropped dramatically (a bit earlier for wives and a bit later for husbands), but both husbands and wives reported nearly equal levels of satisfaction after they had been married nine years or more.

Sexual activity of couples can be both an indication and a cause of marital satisfaction. Analysis of reports of marital sex from a 1988 survey in the United States shows that frequency per month declines steadily with the duration of marriage, from an average of 12 times per month for people ages 19 to 24 years to less than once a month for people 75 years of age and older (Call, Sprecher, and Schwartz 1995). Older married people have sex less frequently. Less happy people have sex less frequently. Within each age category, sex is more frequent among three categories of people:

- Those who are cohabiting but not married
- Those who cohabited before marriage
- Those who are in their second or later marriage

SIBLING RELATIONSHIPS Sibling relationships are an understudied aspect of intrahousehold dynamics. One example comes from research in a working-class neighborhood of Beirut, Lebanon (Joseph 1994). The anthropologist became friendly with several families and was especially close to Hanna, the oldest son in one of them. Hanna was an attractive young man, considered a good marriage choice, with friends across religious and ethnic groups. Therefore, the author reports her shock when she once heard Hanna shouting at his 12-year-old sister Flaur and slapping her across the face. Further observation of the relationship between the two suggested that Hanna was playing a fatherly role to Flaur. He was especially irritated with her if she lingered on the street near their apartment building, gossiping with other girls: "He would forcibly escort her upstairs to their apartment, slap her, and demand that she behave with dignity" (1994:51). Adults in the household thought nothing was wrong. They said that Flaur enjoyed her brother's aggressive attention. Flaur herself commented, "It doesn't even hurt when Hanna hits me." She said that she hoped to have a husband like Hanna.

An interpretation of this kind of brother–sister relationship, common in Arab culture, is that it is part of a socialization process that maintains and perpetuates male domination in the household: "Hanna was teaching Flaur to accept male power in the name of love . . . loving his sister meant taking charge of her and that he could discipline her if his action was understood to be in her interest. Flaur was reinforced in learning that the love of a man could include that male's violent control and that to receive his love involved submission to control" (1994:52).

DOMESTIC VIOLENCE BETWEEN PARTNERS Violence between domestic partners, with males dominating as perpetrators and women as victims, is found in nearly all cultures, although in varying forms and frequencies (Brown 1999). Wife beating is more common and more severe in contexts where men control the wealth. It is less common and less severe where women's work groups and social networks exist (Levinson 1989). The presence of women's work groups is related to a greater importance of women in production and matrifocal residence. These factors provide women with the means to leave an abusive relationship. For example, among the Garifuna, an African–Indian people of Belize, Central America, incidents of spouse abuse occur, but they are infrequent and not extended (Kerns 1999). Women's solidarity in this matrifocal society limits male violence against women.

Increased domestic violence worldwide throws into question the notion of the house as a refuge or place of security. In the United States, evidence exists of high and increasing rates of intrahousehold abuse of children (including sexual abuse), violence between spouses or partners, and abuse of aged family members. Anthropological research helps policy makers and social workers better understand the factors affecting the safety of individuals within households so that they are able to design more effective programs to promote personal safety (see Lessons Applied).

The position of a widow or widower carries altered responsibilities and rights. Women's position as widows is often marked symbolically. In Mediterranean cultures, a widow must wear modest, simple, and black-colored clothing, sometimes for the rest of her life. Her sexuality is supposed to be virtually dead. At the same time, her new "asexual" status allows her greater spatial freedom than before. She can go to public coffeehouses and taverns, something not done by women whose husbands are living.

Extreme restrictions on widows are recorded for parts of South Asia where social pressures on a widow enforce self-denial and self-deprivation, especially among the propertied class. A widow should wear a plain white sari, shave her head, eat little food, and live an asexual life. Many widows in India are abandoned, especially if they have no son to support them. They are considered polluting and inauspicious. Widows elsewhere also experience symbolic and life-quality changes much more than do widowers. For example, in South Africa, a widower does not mark his body in any significant way, except to have his head shaved. He is required to wear a black button or armband for about six months. A widow, by contrast, is marked by shaving her head, smearing a mixture of herbs and ground charcoal on her body, wearing black clothes made from an inexpensive material, and covering her face with a black veil and her shoulders with a black shawl. She may wear her clothes inside out, wear one shoe, eat with her left hand, or eat from a lid instead of a plate (Ramphele 1996).

◆◆◆
Changing Kinship and Household Dynamics

This section provides examples of how marriage and household patterns are changing. Many of these changes have roots in colonialism, whereas others are the result of recent changes effected by globalization.

CHANGE IN DESCENT

Matrilineal descent is declining worldwide as a result of both European colonialism and contemporary Western globalization. European colonial rule in Africa and Asia contributed to the decline in matrilineal kinship by registering land and other property in the names of assumed male heads of household, even where females were the heads (Boserup 1970). This process eroded women's previous rights and powers. Western missionaries contributed further to transforming matrilineal cultures into patrilineal systems (Etienne and Leacock 1980). For example, European colonial influences led to the decline of matrilineal kinship among Native North Americans. Before European colonialism, North America

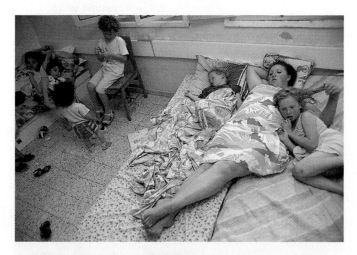

A shared bedroom in a battered-women's shelter, Tel Aviv, Israel. Many people wonder why abused women do not leave their abusers. Part of the answer lies in the unavailability and low quality of shelters throughout much of the world.

THINKING
OUTSIDE
THE BOX

In your microculture, what are the prevailing ideas about wedding expenses and who should pay for them?

LESSONS applied

Ethnography for Preventing Wife Abuse in Rural Kentucky

Domestic violence in the United States is reportedly highest in the state of Kentucky. An ethnographic study of domestic violence in Kentucky reveals several cultural factors related to the high rate of wife abuse (Websdale 1995). The study included interviews with 50 abused wives in eastern Kentucky and with battered women in shelters, police officers, shelter employees, and social workers.

Three categories of isolation exist in rural Kentucky that make domestic violence particularly difficult to prevent:

1. *Physical isolation:* The women reported a feeling of physical isolation in their lives. Abusers' tactics were more effective because of geographical isolation. The tactics include disabling motor vehicles so the wife cannot leave the residence; destroying motor vehicles; monitoring odometer readings on motor vehicles; locking the thermostat in winter; driving recklessly to intimidate the wife; and discharging firearms at, for example, a pet (1995:106–107).

It is difficult or impossible for an abused woman to leave a home located many miles from the nearest paved road, especially if the woman has children. In rural Kentucky, no public transportation serves even the paved road. Nearly one-third of households had no phones. Getting to a phone to report abuse results in delay, gives police the impression that the call is less serious, and increases a woman's sense of hopelessness. Sheriffs have acquired a very poor reputation among battered women in the region for not attending to domestic calls at all.

2. *Social isolation:* Aspects of the rural culture, including gender roles, promote a system of "passive policing." Men are seen as providers, and women are tied to domestic work and child rearing. When women do work outside the home, their wages are about 50 percent of men's wages. Marital residence is often in the vicinity of the husband's family. Thus, a woman is separated from the potential support of her natal family and is limited in seeking help in the immediate vicinity because the husband's family is likely to be nonsupportive of her. Local police officers view the family as a private unit, so they are not inclined to intervene in family problems. Because the home is the man's world and men are supposed to be dominant in the family, police are unwilling to arrest husbands accused of abuse. In some instances, the police take the batterer's side because they share the belief in a husband's right to control his wife.

3. *Institutional isolation:* Social services for battered women in Kentucky are scarce, especially in rural areas. The fact that abused women often know the people who run the services ironically inhibits the women from approaching them, given the value of family privacy. Other institutional constraints include low levels of schooling, lack of child-care centers to allow mothers the option to work outside the home, inadequate health services, and religious teaching of fundamentalist Christianity which supports values such as the idea that it is a woman's duty to stay in a marriage and "weather the storm."

These findings suggest some recommendations. First, rural women need more and better employment opportunities to reduce their economic dependency on abusive partners. To address this need, rural outreach programs should be strengthened. Expanded telephone subscriptions would decrease rural women's institutional isolation. Because of the complexity of the social situation in Kentucky, however, no single solution will be sufficient.

◆ FOOD FOR THOUGHT

- How do conditions in Kentucky differ from or resemble those in another cultural context where wife beating is frequent?

MAP 6.5 Kentucky, United States.
Located in the southeastern United States, in the wider Appalachian region, Kentucky has a population of over 4 million. It has more farmers per square mile than any other state. Per capita income is 43rd in the 50 states. Before being occupied by British settlers in the late eighteenth century, Kentucky was the hunting grounds of the Shawnees and Cherokees. The current population is about 91 percent White, 7 percent Black, 0.6 percent American Indian, and 0.9 percent Asian. Kentucky is known for thoroughbred horse breeding and racing, bourbon and whiskey distilling, and bluegrass music.

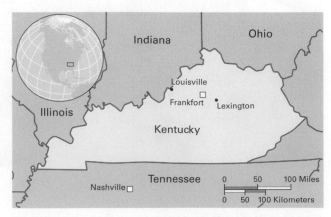

had one of the largest distributions of matrilineal descent worldwide. A comparative study of kinship among three reservation-based Navajo groups in Arizona shows that matrilineality is stronger where conditions most resemble the pre-reservation era (Levy, Henderson, and Andrews 1989).

Among the Minangkabau of Indonesia (review Culturama, this chapter), three factors explain the decline of matrilineal kinship (Blackwood 1995):

- Dutch colonialism promoted the image of male-headed nuclear families as an ideal.
- Islamic teachings idealize women as wives and men as household heads.
- The modernizing Indonesian state has a policy of naming males as household heads.

CHANGE IN MARRIAGE

Although the institution of marriage in general remains prominent, many of its details, including courtship, the marriage ceremony, and marital relationships, are changing. New forms of communication are profoundly affecting courtship. In a village in western Nepal (see Map 5.5, p. 116) people's stories of their marriages reveal that arranged marriages have decreased and elopement has increased since the 1990s.

Nearly everywhere, the age at first marriage is rising. The later age at marriage is related to increased emphasis on

A newly married husband and wife and their relatives in front of a church in Seoul, Republic of Korea.

▶ *How does this wedding group resemble or differ from a wedding you have attended?*

completing a certain number of years of education before marriage and to higher material aspirations, such as being able to own a house. Marriages between people of different nations and ethnicities are increasing, partly because of growing rates of international migration. Migrants take with them many of their marriage and family practices. They also adapt to rules and practices in their area of destination. Pluralistic practices evolve, such as conducting two marriage ceremonies—one conforming to the "original" culture and the other to the culture in the place of destination.

Marriage crises are situations in which people who want to marry cannot do so for one reason or another. They are more frequent now than in the past, at least as perceived and reported by young people in the so-called marriage market. Two examples illustrate variations in how a marriage crisis comes about and how it plays out for those caught up in it.

In a town of about 38,000 people in rural Niger, West Africa, the marriage crisis involves young men's inability to raise the necessary funds for the brideprice and for additional gifts to the bride's family (Masquelier 2005). Among these Muslim, Hausa-speaking people, called Mawri, marriage is the crucial ritual that changes a boy into a man. Typically, a prospective groom receives financial assistance from his kin and friends. In Niger, the economy has been declining for some time, and typical farm or other wages are worth less than they were in earlier times. Marriage costs for the groom have not declined, however—quite the opposite. Wealthy young men can afford to give a car to the bride's parents as a wedding gift. But most young Mawri men cannot afford such gifts and are caught in the marriage crisis. They remain sitting at home in their parents' house, something that, ordinarily, only females do. The many young, marriage-age women who remain single gain a reputation of being immoral, occupying a new and suspect social space between girl and wife.

The marriage crisis for African American women in Syracuse is related to policies promoted by the government of President George W. Bush (Lane et al. 2004). The Bush government earmarked millions of dollars to promote two-parent, heterosexual families. Furthermore, during the George W. Bush era, an increasing number of African American men were imprisoned. Besides suffering high rates of imprisonment, African American men die violent deaths at much higher rates than do men of other ethnic populations. In the population of Syracuse, a city in postindustrial decline, there are four African American women for every African American man, compared with an equal ratio among Whites. Given the strong preference for ethnic endogamous marriages, it is statistically impossible for many African American women to get married.

Weddings are important, culture-revealing events. Style changes in weddings worldwide abound. Factors to consider in examining changes in wedding styles are the ceremony, costs, appropriate clothing, and the possibility of a honeymoon.

The Western-style, so-named because the bride wears a white dress, is spreading around the world, though with fascinating local adaptations in terms of its features, including what the bride and groom wear, the design of the wedding cake and floral displays. Throughout much of East and Southeast Asia, advertisements and upscale stores display the Western-style white wedding gown, but not in India, where white clothing for women signifies widowhood and is inauspicious. A resurgence of local, folksy styles is occurring in some contexts. In Morocco, for example, an urban bride may wear a Western style white gown for one part of the wedding ceremony and an "exotic" Berber costume (long robes and ornate silver jewelry characteristic of the mountain pastoralists) at another stage of the ceremony. Such blending of Western and non-Western elements signals a family's complex identity in a globalizing world.

CHANGING HOUSEHOLDS

Globalization is creating rapid change in household structure and intrahousehold dynamics. One assumption is that the frequency of extended households will decline with industrialization and urbanization and the frequency of nuclear households will rise. Given what this chapter mentioned earlier about the relationship between nuclear households and industrialism/informatics, it is highly possible that the spread of this mode of production will cause an increase in the number of nuclear households, too.

This projection finds strong confirmation in the changes that have occurred in household structure among the Kelabit (kell-uh-bit) people of highland Borneo since the early 1990s (Amster 2000). One Kelabit settlement was founded in 1963 near the Indonesian border. At the time, everyone lived in one longhouse with over 20 family units. It was a "modern" longhouse, thanks to roofing provided by the British army and the innovation of private sleeping areas. Like more traditional longhouses, though, it was an essentially egalitarian living space within which individuals could freely move. Today, that longhouse is no more. Most of the young people have migrated to coastal towns and work in jobs related to the offshore oil industry. Most houses are now single-unit homes with an emphasis on privacy. The elders complain of a "bad silence" in the village. No one looks after visitors with the old style of hospitality. There is no longer one common longhouse for communal feasts and rituals.

(LEFT) A modern-style Kelabit longhouse built in the 1990s. It is the home of six families which formerly lived in a 20-family longhouse, seen in the background, that is being dismantled. (RIGHT) Since the 1990s, houses built for a nuclear unit have proliferated in the highlands. These houses stand on the site of a former multiunit longhouse.

International migration is another major cause of change in household formation and internal relationships (discussed further in Chapter 12). A dramatic decline in fertility can occur in one generation when members of a farming household in, for example, Taiwan or Egypt migrate to England, France, Canada, or the United States. Having many children makes economic sense in their homeland, but not in the new destination. Many such migrants decide to have only one or two children. They tend to live in small, isolated nuclear households. International migration creates new challenges for relationships between parents and children. The children often become strongly identified with the new culture and have little connection with their ancestral culture. This rupture creates anxiety for the parents and conflict between children and parents over issues such as dating, dress, and career goals.

In 1997, the people of Norway were confronted with the case of the kidnapping of an 18-year-old Norwegian citizen named "Nadia" (Wikan 2000). Her parents took her to Morocco and held her captive there. The full story is complicated, but the core issues revolve around conflict between Moroccan and Norwegian family values. Nadia's parents felt that she should be under their control and that they had the right to arrange her marriage in Morocco. Nadia had a Norwegian concept of personal autonomy. In the end, Nadia and her parents returned to Norway, where the courts ruled that, for the sake of the family, the parents would not be jailed for kidnapping their daughter. The case brought stigma to Nadia among the Muslim community of Norway, who viewed her as a traitor to her culture. She now lives at a secret address and avoids publicity. An anthropologist close to this case who served as an expert witness during the trial of the parents reports that, in spite of her seclusion, Nadia offers help to other young women.

At the beginning of the twenty-first century, three kinds of households are most common in the United States: households composed of couples living in their first marriage, single-parent households, and households formed through remarriage. A new, fourth category is the *multigenerational household*, in which an *adult child*, or *boomerang kid*, lives with his or her parents. About one in three unmarried adults between the ages of 25 and 55 share a home with their mother or father or both (*Psychology Today* 1995 [28]:16). In the United States, adult offspring spend over 2 hours a day doing household chores, with adult daughters contributing about 17 hours a week and adult sons 14.4 hours. Daughters spend most of their time doing laundry, cooking, cleaning, and washing dishes. Sons are more involved in yard work and car care. Parents in multigenerational households still do three-quarters of the housework.

Kinship and household formation are certainly not dull or static topics. Just trying to keep up with changing patterns in North America is a daunting task, to say nothing of tracking changes worldwide.

6

the BIG questions REVISITED

◆ How do cultures create kinship?

Key differences exist between unilineal and bilineal descent systems. Within unilineal systems, further important variations exist between patrilineal and matrilineal systems in terms of property inheritance, residence rules for married couples, and the relative status of males and females. Worldwide, unilineal systems are more common than bilineal systems. Within unilineal kinship systems, patrilineal kinship is more common than matrilineal kinship.

A second important basis for kinship is sharing. Sharing one's child with someone else through either informal or formal processes is probably a cultural universal. Sharing-based kinship is created through food transfers, including breastfeeding (in some cultures, children breastfed by the same woman are considered kin and cannot marry). Ritualized sharing creates kinship, as in the case of godparenthood.

The third basis for kinship is marriage, another universal factor, even though definitions of marriage may differ substantially. All cultures have rules of exclusion and preference rules for spouses. These rules affect factors such as kinship relationships of potential spouses, region, class, wealth, education, perceptions of "looks," and more.

◆ What are cross-cultural patterns of households and domestic life?

A household may consist of a single person living alone or may be a group comprising more than one person, each of whom may or may not be related by kinship; these individuals share a living space and, often, financial responsibilities for the household.

Nuclear households consist of a mother and father and their children, but they also can be just a husband and wife without children. Nuclear households are found in all cultures but are most common in foraging and industrial societies. Extended households include more than one nuclear household. They are most commonly found in cultures with a unilineal kinship system.

Household headship can be shared between two partners or can be borne by a single person, as in a woman-headed household. Studies of intrahousehold dynamics between parents and children and among siblings reveal complex power relationships as well as sharing and, sometimes, violence.

◆ How are kinship and households changing?

Recent forces of change, starting with European colonialism and now globalization, have had, and continue to have, marked effects on kinship formation and household patterns and dynamics. Matrilineal systems have been declining in distribution since European colonialist expansion began in the 1500s.

Many aspects of marriage are changing, including a trend toward later age at marriage in many developing countries. Although marriage continues to be an important basis for the formation of nuclear and extended households, other options (such as cohabitation) are increasing in importance in many contexts, including urban areas in developed countries.

Contemporary changes in kinship and in household formation raise several serious questions for the future, perhaps most importantly about the care of dependent members such as children, the aged, and disabled people. As fertility rates decline and average household size shrinks, kinship-based entitlements to basic needs and emotional support disappear.

KEY CONCEPTS

bilineal descent, p. 129

brideprice, p. 136

brideservice, p. 136

cross-cousin, p. 135

descent, p. 128

dowry, p. 136

endogamy, p. 134

exogamy, p. 135

extended household, p. 137

family, p. 137

household, p. 137

incest taboo, p. 134

kinship system, p. 126

marriage, p. 134

matrilineal descent, p. 129

monogamy, p. 137

nuclear household, p. 137

parallel cousin, p. 134

patrilineal descent, p. 129

polyandry, p. 137

polygamy, p. 137

polygyny, p. 137

unilineal descent, p. 129

SUGGESTED READINGS

Irwin Altman and Joseph Ginat, eds. *Polygamous Families in Contemporary Society*. New York: Cambridge University Press, 1996. This book provides a detailed account of polygyny as practiced in two fundamentalist Mormon communities of Utah, one rural and the other urban.

Dorothy Ayers Counts, Judith K. Brown, and Jacquelyn C. Campbell, eds. *To Have and to Hit: Cultural Perspectives on Wife Beating*. Champaign–Urbana: University of Illinois Press, 1999. Chapters include an introductory overview and cases from Australia, southern Africa, Papua New Guinea, India, Central America, the Middle East, and the Pacific.

Amy Borovoy. *The Too-Good Wife: Alcohol, Codependency, and the Politics of Nurturance in Postwar Japan*. Berkeley: University of California Press, 2005. This book explores the experiences of middle-class women in Tokyo who participated in a weekly support meeting for families of substance abusers. The women attempt to cope with their husbands' alcoholism while facing the dilemma that being a good wife may be part of the problem.

Deborah R. Connolly. *Homeless Mothers: Face to Face with Women and Poverty*. Minneapolis: University of Minnesota Press, 2000. Poor, White women on the margin of mainstream society in Portland, Oregon, describe how they attempt to be good mothers with no money, no home, and no help.

Charles N. Durran, James M. Freeman, and J.A. English-Lueck. *Busier Than Ever! Why American Families Can't Slow Down*. Stanford, CA: Stanford University Press, 2007. The authors followed the daily activities of 14 American families in California. Their findings show how people try to balance the demands of work and family in a cultural context in which "busyness," or always being busy, is an indication of success and the good life.

Helen Bradley Foster and Donald Clay Johnson, eds. *Wedding Dress across Cultures*. New York: Berg, 2003. Chapters examine the evolution and ritual functions of wedding attire in cultures such as those of urban Japan, Alaskan Indians, Swaziland, Morocco, Greece, and the Andes.

Jennifer Hirsch. *A Courtship after Marriage: Sexuality and Love in Mexican Transnational Marriages*. Berkeley: University of California Press, 2003. This study uses an innovative method of pairing 13 migrant women living in Atlanta, Georgia, with 13 nonmigrant counterparts in two rural towns in Mexico to learn about marriage and married life.

Suad Joseph, ed. *Intimate Selving in Arab Families: Gender, Self, and Identity*. Syracuse, NY: Syracuse University Press, 1999. Chapters discuss family life and relationships in Arab culture, with attention to connectivity, gender inequality, and the self. Case studies are from Lebanon and Egypt.

Laurel Kendall. *Getting Married in Korea: Of Gender, Morality, and Modernity*. Berkeley: University of California, 1996. This book examines preferences about desirable spouses, matchmaking, marriage ceremonies and their financing, and the effect of women's changing work roles on their marital aspirations.

Sulamith Heins Potter. *Family Life in a Northern Thai Village: A Structural Study in the Significance of Women*. Berkeley: University of California Press, 1977. This ethnography of matrifocal family life in rural Thailand focuses on work roles, rituals, and intrafamily relationships.

Kanchana Ruwanpura. *Matrilineal Communities, Patriarchal Realities: A Feminist Nirvana Uncovered*. Ann Arbor: University of Michigan Press, 2007. This book describes Muslim, Sinhala, and Tamil households headed by women in Sri Lanka.

Margaret Trawick. *Notes on Love in a Tamil Family*. Berkeley: University of California Press, 1992. This reflexive ethnography takes a close look at the daily dynamics of kinship in one Tamil (South Indian) family. Attention is given to sibling relationships, the role of older people, children's lives, and love and affection.

Toby Alice Volkman, ed. *Cultures of Transnational Adoption*. Durham, NC: Duke University Press, 2005. Chapters discuss Korean adoptees as a global family, transnational adoption in North America, shared parenthood among low-income people in Brazil, and representations of "waiting children."

Uyghurs (wee-gurs) are a Turkic ethnic population. Most live in China's Xinjiang Uyghur Autonomous Region (XUAR) and are Muslim. The Chinese state puts pressure on Uyghurs, particularly young women, to leave the XUAR to work in factories in Han regions of the south. The Uyghur migrants encounter language and other cultural barriers.

SOCIAL GROUPS AND SOCIAL STRATIFICATION

7

the BIG questions

◆ What are social groups and how do they vary cross-culturally?

◆ What is social stratification?

◆ What is civil society?

OUTLINE

Social Groups

Everyday Anthropology: Making Friends

Social Stratification

Eye on the Environment: Industrial Pollution and Activism in an African American Community in Georgia, the United States

Culturama: The Roma of Eastern Europe

Civil Society

147

In the early 1800s, when French political philosopher Alexis de Tocqueville visited the United States and characterized it as a "nation of joiners," he implied that people in some cultures are more likely to join groups than are people in other cultures. The questions of what motivates people to join groups, what holds people together in groups, and how groups deal with leadership and participation have intrigued scholars in many fields for centuries.

This chapter focuses on nonkin groups and microculture formation. Chapter 1 defined several factors related to microcultures: class, "race," ethnicity, indigeneity, gender, age, and institutions such as prisons and retirement homes. This chapter looks at how microcultures shape group identity and organization and the relationships among different groups in terms of hierarchy and power. It first examines a variety of social groups ranging from small scale to large scale and then considers inequalities among social groups. The last section looks at the concept of civil society and provides examples of it.

◆◆◆

Social Groups

A **social group** is a cluster of people beyond the domestic unit who are usually related on a basis other than kinship, although kinship relationships may exist between people in the group. Two basic categories exist: the **primary group**, consisting of people who interact with each other and know each other personally, and the **secondary group**, consisting of people who identify with each other on some common ground but who may never meet with one another or interact with each other personally.

Members of all social groups have a sense of rights and responsibilities in relation to the group. Membership in a primary group, because of the face-to-face interaction, involves more direct accountability about rights and responsibilities than does membership in a secondary group.

Modes of livelihood affect the formation of social groups, with the greatest variety of groups found in agricultural and industrial–informatics societies (see Figure 7.1).

---

social group a cluster of people beyond the domestic unit who are usually related on grounds other than kinship.

primary group a social group in which members meet on a face-to-face basis.

secondary group a group of people who identify with each other on some basis but may never meet with one another personally.

age set a group of people close in age who go through certain rituals, such as circumcision, at the same time.

One theory explaining this pattern is that mobile populations, such as foragers and pastoralists, are less likely to develop enduring social groups beyond kin relationships simply because they have less social density and less continuous interaction than more settled populations have. Although foragers and pastoralists do have less of a variety of social groups, they do not completely lack social groupings. A prominent form of social group among foragers and pastoralists is an **age set**, a group of people close in age who go through certain rituals, such as circumcision, at the same time.

Although it is generally true that settled populations have more social groups, as a way to organize society, some important exceptions exist. In accordance with this generalization, many informal and formal groups are active throughout Africa, Latin America, and Southeast Asia, but such groups are less prominent in South Asia, a region that includes Pakistan, India, Nepal, Bhutan, Bangladesh, and Sri Lanka. In Bangladesh (see Map 7.1), for example, a densely populated and agrarian country of South Asia, indigenous social groups are rare. The most prominent ties beyond the immediate household are kinship based (Miller and Khan 1986). In spite of the lack of indigenous social groups, Bangladesh has gained world renown since the later twentieth century for its success in forming local groups through an organization called the Grameen Bank, which offers *microcredit* (small loans) to poor people to help them start small businesses. Likewise, throughout the rest of South Asia, the modern era has seen the rise of many active social groups, including those dedicated to preserving traditional environmental knowledge, promoting women and children's health and survival, and advocating for lesbian and gay rights.

This section describes a variety of social groups, starting with the most face-to-face, primary groups of two or three people based on friendship. It then moves to larger and more formal groups, such as countercultural groups and activist groups.

FRIENDSHIP

Friendship refers to close social ties between at least two people in which the ties are informal, are voluntary, and involve personal, face-to-face interaction. Generally, friendship involves people who are nonkin, but in some cases kin are also friends. (Recall the Tory Islanders discussed in Chapter 6.) Friendship fits into the category of a primary social group. One question that cultural anthropologists ask is whether friendship is a cultural universal. Two factors make it difficult to answer this question. First, insufficient cross-cultural research exists to answer the question definitively. Second, defining friendship cross-culturally is problematic. It is likely, however, that something like "friendship" is a cultural universal but shaped in different degrees from culture to culture (see Everyday Anthropology).

Foraging	Horticulture	Pastoralism	Agriculture	Industrialism/Informatics
Characteristics				**Characteristics**
Informal and primary			Formal and secondary	
Egalitarian structure			Recognized leadership	
Ties based on balanced exchange		Ritual ties	Dues and fees	
Functions				**Functions**
Companionship		Special purposes		
		Work, war, lobbying government		
Types				**Types**
Friendship	Friendship		Friendship	
	Age-based work groups		Urban youth gangs	
	Gender-based work groups		Clubs, associations	
			Status Groups:	
			Class, "race," ethnicity, caste, age, gender	
			Institutional Groups:	
			Prisons, retirement homes	
			Quasi-Political Groups:	
			Human rights, environmental groups	

FIGURE 7.1 Modes of Livelihood and Social Groups

MAP 7.1 Bangladesh.
The People's Republic of Bangladesh is located on a deltaic floodplain with rich soil and risk of flooding. One of the world's most densely populated countries, Bangladesh has nearly 150 million people living in an area about the size of the state of Wisconsin. Bangladesh is the world's third-largest Muslim majority country.

SOCIAL CHARACTERISTICS OF FRIENDSHIP People choose their friends, and friends remain so on a voluntary basis. Even so, the criteria for who qualifies as a friend may be culturally structured. For instance, gender segregation may prevent cross-gender friendships and promote same-gender friendships, and racial segregation limits cross-"race" friendships. Another characteristic of friendship is that friends are supportive of each other, psychologically and sometimes materially. Support is mutual, shared back and forth in an expectable way (as in balanced exchange; see Chapter 3). Friendship generally occurs between social equals, although there are exceptions, such as friendships between older and younger people, between a supervisor and a staff worker, or between a teacher and a student.

Sharing stories is often a basis of friendship groups. According to a study that focused on interactions among men's friendship groups in rumshops in Guyana (gy-AH-nuh) (see Map 7.2), Indo-Guyanese men who have known each other since childhood spend time every day at the rumshop, eating, drinking, and regaling each other with stories (Sidnell 2000). Through shared storytelling about village history and other aspects of local knowledge, men display their equality with each other. The pattern of storytelling, referred to as "turn-at-talk," in which efforts are made to include everyone as a storyteller in turn, also serves to maintain equality and solidarity. These friendship groups are tightly knit, and the members can call on one another for economic, social, and political help.

everyday ANTHROPOLOGY

Making Friends

People's daily activities are often the basis of friendship ties. In Andalucia, southern Spain (see Map 2.4, p. 42), men and women pursue separate kinds of work and, relatedly, have different friendship patterns (Uhl 1991). Men's work takes place outside the house and neighborhood, either in the fields or in manufacturing jobs. Women devote most of their time to unpaid household work within the domestic domain. This dichotomy is somewhat fluid, however, as women's domestic roles sometimes take them to the market or the town hall.

For men, an important category of friend is an *amigo*, a friend with whom one casually interacts. This kind of friendship is acted out and maintained in bars where men drink together nightly. Bars are a man's world. Amigos share common experiences of school, sports and hobbies, and working together. In contrast, women refer to their friends using kin terms or as *vecina*, "neighbor," reflecting women's primary orientation to family and neighborhood.

Differences also emerge in the category of *amigos(as) del verdad*, or "true friends." True friends are those

A shepherd in Andalucia, southern Spain. In rural areas of Andalucia, as in much of the Mediterranean region, the division of labor is distinct and according to gender, with men working outside the home and women working inside or near the home. Friendship formation follows this pattern. Men form ties with men in cafes and bars after work, and women establish ties with other women in the neighborhood.

with whom one shares secrets without fear of betrayal. Men have more true friends than women do, a pattern that reflects their wider social networks.

◆ FOOD FOR THOUGHT

- What categories of friends do you have? Are friends in some categories "closer" or "truer" than others? What is the basis of close friendship?

In a low-income neighborhood in Rio de Janeiro, Brazil, men play dominoes and drink beer while others observe.

▶ *Discuss a comparable scene of female leisure activities in your microcultural experience.*

Participant observation and interviews with a sample of rural and urban, low-income Jamaicans reveals that cell phone use is frequent (Horst and Miller 2005). Jamaicans are keenly aware of their call lists and how often they have kept in touch with the many individuals on their lists. Cell phones allow for "linking up," or creating extensive networks that include close friends, possible future sexual partners, and members of one's church. Phone numbers of kin are also prominent on people's cell phone number lists. By linking up periodically with people on their lists, low-income Jamaicans maintain friendship and other ties with people on whom they can call when they need support. Cell phones allow a more extensive network of friends and other contacts than was previously possible.

FRIENDSHIP AMONG THE URBAN POOR Carol Stack's study of how friendship networks promote economic survival

MAP 7.2 Caribbean Countries of South America.
The ethnically and linguistically diverse countries of the Caribbean region of South America include Guyana, Suriname, and French Guiana. Guyana, or the Co-operative Republic of Guyana, is the only South American country whose official language is English. Other languages are Hindi, Wai Wai, and Arawak. Its population is 800,000. The Republiek Suriname, or Surinam, was formerly a colony of the Netherlands and is the smallest independent state in South America. Its population is 440,000. Dutch is the official language, but most Surinamese also speak Sranang Tongo, or Surinaams, a mixture of Dutch, English, Portuguese, French, and local languages. French Guiana is an overseas department of France and is thus part of the European Union. The smallest political unit in South America, its population is 200,000. Its official language is French, but several other languages are spoken, including indigenous Arawak and Carib.

among low-income, urban African Americans is a landmark contribution (1974). She conducted fieldwork in the late 1960s in "The Flats," the poorest section of a Black community in a large midwestern city. She found extensive networks of friends "supporting, reinforcing each other—devising schemes for self help, strategies for survival in a community of severe economic deprivation" (1974:28). Close friends are referred to by kin terms.

People in the Flats, especially women, maintain a set of friends through exchange: "swapping" goods (food, clothing) needed by someone at a particular time, sharing "child keeping," and giving or lending food stamps and money. Such exchanges are part of a clearly understood pattern—gifts and favors go back and forth over time. Friends thus bound together are obligated to each another and can call on each other in time of need. In opposition to theories that suggest the breakdown of social relationships among the very poor, this research documents how poor people strategize and cope through social ties.

CLUBS AND FRATERNITIES

Clubs and *fraternities* are social groups that define membership in terms of a sense of shared identity and objectives. They may comprise people of the same ethnic heritage (such as the Daughters of the American Revolution in the United States), occupation or business, religion, or gender. Although many clubs appear to exist primarily to serve functions of sociability and psychological support, deeper analysis often shows that these groups have economic and political roles as well.

Women's clubs in a lower class neighborhood in Paramaribo, Suriname (see Map 7.2), have multiple functions (Brana-Shute 1976). Here, as is common elsewhere in Latin America, clubs raise funds to sponsor special events and support individual celebrations, meet personal financial needs, and send cards and flowers for funerals. Members attend each other's birthday parties and death rites as a group. The clubs thus offer the women psychological support, entertainment, and financial help. A political aspect exists, too. Club members often belong to the same political party and attend political rallies and events together. The clubs therefore constitute political interest groups that can influence political outcomes. Politicians and party workers confirmed that real pressure is exerted on them by women individually and in groups.

College fraternities and sororities are highly selective groups that serve a variety of explicit functions, such as entertainment and social service. They also form bonds between members that may help in securing jobs after graduation. Few anthropologists have studied the "Greek system" on U.S. campuses. An exception is Peggy Sanday, who was inspired to study college fraternities after the gang rape of a woman student by several fraternity brothers at the campus where she teaches. Her book *Fraternity Gang Rape: Sex, Brotherhood, and Privilege on Campus* (1990) explores initiation rituals and how they are related to male bonding solidified by victimization and ridicule of women. Gang rape, or a "train," is a prevalent practice in some, not all, fraternities. Fraternity party invitations may hint at the possibility of a "train." Typically, the brothers seek out a "party girl"—a somewhat vulnerable young woman who may be especially needy of acceptance or especially high on alcohol or other substances (her drinks may have been "spiked"). They take her to one of the brothers' rooms, where she may or may not agree to have sex with one of the brothers, and she often passes out. Then a "train" of men have sex with her. Rarely prosecuted, the male participants reinforce their sense of privilege, power, and unity with one another through a group ritual involving abuse of a female outsider.

Cross-culturally, women do not tend to form *androphobic* ("man-hating" or otherwise anti-male) clubs, the logical parallel of *gynophobic* ("woman-hating" or otherwise anti-female) men's clubs. College sororities, for example, are not mirror images of college fraternities. Although some sororities' initiation rituals are psychologically brutal to the pledges,

(LEFT) Students gather outside a fraternity house near the University of San Francisco campus for a weekend party.

(RIGHT) Members of a fraternity at the University of Texas at Austin engage in public service by planting trees at an elementary school.

▶ *What knowledge do you have about the positive and negative social aspects of college fraternities and sororities? How could anthropological research provide a clearer picture?*

bonding among the members does not involve abusive behavior toward men.

COUNTERCULTURAL GROUPS

Several kinds of groups comprise people who, for one reason or another, are outside the "mainstream" of society and resist conforming to the dominant cultural pattern. The so-called hippies of the 1960s were one such group. One similarity among these groups, as with clubs and fraternities, is the importance of bonding through shared initiation and other rituals.

YOUTH GANGS The term **youth gang** refers to a group of young people, found mainly in urban areas, who are often considered a social problem by adults and law enforcement officials (Sanders 1994).

Youth gangs vary in terms of how formally they are organized. Like clubs and fraternities, gangs often have a recognized leader, formalized rituals of initiation for new members, and symbolic markers of identity, such as tattoos or special clothing. An example of an informal youth gang with no formal leadership hierarchy or initiation rituals is that of the "Masta Liu" in Honiara, the capital city of the Solomon Islands in the South Pacific (Jourdan 1995) (see Map 7.3). Unemployment is the primary unifying feature of the male youths who become Masta Liu. Most have migrated to the city from the countryside to escape what they consider an undesirable lifestyle there: working in the fields under control of their elders. Some Liu live with extended kin in the city; others organize Liu-only households. They spend their

time wandering around town, referred to locally as going *wakabaot*, in groups of up to 10:

> They stop at every shop on their way, eager to look at the merchandise but afraid to be kicked out by the security guards; they check out all the cinemas only to dream in front of the preview posters . . . not even having the $2 bill that will allow them to get in; they gaze for hours on end, and without moving, at the electronic equipment displayed in the Chinese shops, without saying a word: One can read in their gaze the silent dreams they create. (1995:210)

Street gangs are a more formal variety of youth gang. They generally have leaders and a hierarchy of membership roles and responsibilities. They are named, and their members mark their identity with tattoos or "colors." Much popular thinking associates street gangs with violence, but not all are involved in violence. An anthropologist who did research among nearly 40 street gangs in New York, Los Angeles, and Boston learned much about why individuals join gangs, providing insights that also contradict popular thinking (Jankowski 1991). One common perception is that young boys join gangs because they are from homes with no male authority figure with whom they identify. In the gangs studied, about half of the gang members were from intact nuclear households. Another common perception is that the gang replaces a missing feeling of family. This study showed that the same number of gang members reported having close family ties as those who did not.

Why, then, did young men join an urban gang? The research revealed that many gang members had a particular personality type called a *defiant individualist*. The defiant individualist type has five characteristics:

- Intense competitiveness
- Mistrust of others

---

youth gang a group of young people, found mainly in urban areas, who are often considered a social problem by adults and law enforcement officials.

- Self-reliance
- Social isolation
- A strong survival instinct

A structurist view suggests that poverty, especially urban poverty, leads to the development of this kind of personality, which is a reasonable response to the prevailing economic obstacles and uncertainty. To explain the global spread of urban youth gangs, structurists point to global economic changes in urban employment opportunities. In many countries, a declining urban industrial base has created persistent poverty in inner-city communities. At the same time, schooling and the popular media promote aspirations for a better life. Urban gang members, in this view, are the victims of large structural forces beyond their control that both inspire them to want

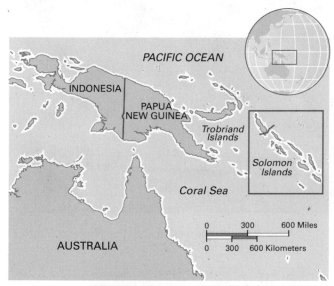

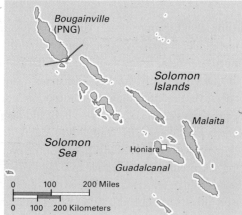

MAP 7.3   The Solomon Islands.
This country consists of nearly 1000 islands. Its capital, Honiara, is located on the island of Guadalcanal. The population is 540,000. Most of the people earn a living through small-scale farming and fishing. Commercial exploitation of local timber has led to severe deforestation. Over 70 languages are spoken, and an additional 4 have recently gone extinct. The majority of the people are Christian, mainly Anglican. The Solomons were the site of some of the bitterest fighting during World War II.

aspects of a successful lifestyle and prevent them from achieving the legal means to obtain their aspirations. Many of these youths want to be economically successful, but social conditions channel their interests and skills into illegal pursuits rather than into legal pathways to achievement.

BODY MODIFICATION GROUPS   One of the many countercultural movements in the United States includes people who have a sense of community strengthened through forms of body alteration. James Myers (1992) did research in California among people who feel that they are a special group because of their interest in permanent body modification, especially genital piercing, branding, and cutting. Fieldwork involved participant observation and interviews: Myers was involved in workshops organized for the San Francisco sadomasochist (SM) community; he attended the Fifth Annual Living in Leather Convention held in Portland, Oregon, in 1990; he spent time in tattoo and piercing studios; and he talked with students and others in his hometown who were involved in these forms of body modification. The study population included males and females, heterosexuals, gays, lesbians, bisexuals, and SMers. The single largest group was SM homosexuals and bisexuals. The study population was mainly White, and most had either attended or graduated from college.

Myers witnessed many modification sessions at workshops: Those seeking modification go up on stage and have their chosen procedure done by a well-known expert. Whatever the procedure, the volunteers exhibit little pain—usually just a sharp intake of breath at the moment the needle passes through or the brand touches skin. After that critical moment, the audience breathes an audible sigh of relief. The volunteer stands up and adjusts his or her clothing, and members of the audience applaud. This public event is a kind of initiation ritual that binds the expert, the volunteer, and the group together. Pain is an important part of many rites of passage. In this case, the audience witnesses and validates the experience and becomes joined to the initiate through witnessing.

The study revealed that a prominent motivation for seeking permanent body modification was a desire to identify with a specific group of people. As one participant said,

> It's not that we're sheep, getting pierced or cut just because everyone else is. I like to think it's because we're a very special group and we like doing something that sets us off from others. . . . Happiness is standing in line at a cafeteria and detecting that the straight-looking babe in front of you has her nipples pierced. I don't really care what her sexual orientation is, I can relate to her. (1992:292)

THINKING OUTSIDE THE BOX

Think of some examples in which socially excluded groups have contributed to changing styles of music, dress, and other forms of expressive culture of so-called mainstream groups.

(LEFT) A Tahitian chief wears tattoos that indicate his high status. (RIGHT) A woman with tattooed arms and pierced nose in the United States.

▶ *In your microcultural experience, what do tattoos mean to you when you see someone with them?*

COOPERATIVES

Cooperatives are a form of economic group in which surpluses are shared among the members and decision making follows the democratic principle of each individual member having one vote (Estrin 1996). Agricultural and credit cooperatives are the most common forms of cooperatives worldwide, followed by consumer cooperatives.

In Panama's eastern coastal region, indigenous Kuna (koo-nuh) women long have sewn beautiful *molas*, or cloth with appliquéd designs (see Map 7.4). Kuna make this cloth for their own use as clothing, but since the 1960s, molas have been important items for sale both on the world market and to tourists who come to Panama (Tice 1995). Revenue from selling molas to tourists as well as internationally is now an important part of

the household income of the Kuna. Some women continue to operate independently, buying their own cloth and thread and selling their molas either to an intermediary who exports them or in the local tourist market. But many women have joined cooperatives that offer them greater economic security. The cooperative buys cloth and thread in bulk and distributes it to the women. The women are paid almost the entire sale price for each mola, with only a small amount of the eventual sale prices being taken out for cooperative dues and administrative costs. Their earnings are steadier than what the fluctuating tourist season offers. Other benefits from being a member of the cooperative include its use as a consumer's cooperative (buying rice and sugar in bulk for members), a source of mutual strength and support, and a place for women to develop greater leadership skills and to take advantage of opportunities for political participation in the wider society.

SELF-HELP GROUPS

Recent years have seen a worldwide proliferation of *self-help groups,* or groups formed to achieve specific personal goals,

---

social stratification a set of hierarchical relationships among different groups as though they were arranged in layers, or "strata."

ascribed position a person's standing in society based on qualities that the person has gained through birth.

Kuna Indian woman selling molas, San Blas Islands, Panama.

▶ *Learn more about molas from the Web.*

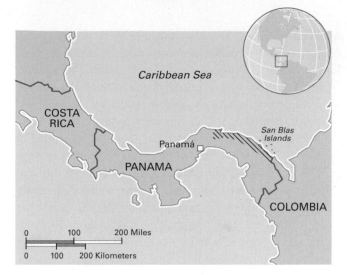

MAP 7.4 Kuna Region in Panama.
The Kuna are an indigenous people who live mainly in the eastern coastal region of Panama, including its offshore islands. Some live in cities, and a few live in villages in neighboring Colombia. The Kuna population is around 150,000. Farming, fishing, and tourism are important parts of the economy. Each community has its own political organization, and the Kuna as a whole are organized into the Kuna General Congress. Most speak Kuna, or Dulegaya ("People's Language"), and Spanish. They follow traditional religious practices, often with a mixture of Christian elements.

such as coping with illness or bereavement, or lifestyle changes such as trying to exercise more or lose weight. Self-help groups also increasingly are using the Internet to form virtual support communities. Anthropologists who study these groups focus on why members join, on rituals of solidarity, and on leadership and organization patterns.

An ethnography of Alcoholics Anonymous groups in Mexico City (see Map 4.3, p. 84) reports that most members are low-income, working-class males (Brandes 2002). They migrated to Mexico City from rural areas several decades earlier to find work and improve their standard of living. Their drinking problems are related both to their poverty and to the close links between alcohol consumption and male gender identity in Mexico: A "real man" consumes a lot of alcohol. Through a dynamic of shared stories and regular meetings, AA members in Mexico City achieve a high rate of sobriety.

The success of AA in Mexico is leading to a rapid proliferation of AA groups around the world. Membership globally is growing at about 10 percent a year, a remarkably high rate of growth for a self-help organization. At the end of the twentieth century, Latin America accounted for almost one-third of total AA membership worldwide. Thus, a model of a middle-class self-help organization that originated in the United States has been adopted and culturally localized by low-income men throughout Latin America.

◆◆◆

Social Stratification

Social stratification consists of hierarchical relationships among different groups, as though they were arranged in layers, or *strata*. Stratified groups may be unequal on a variety of measures, including material resources, power, human welfare, education, and symbolic attributes. People in groups in higher positions have privileges not experienced by those in lower echelon groups, and they are likely to be interested in maintaining their privileged positions. Social stratification appeared late in human history, most clearly with the emergence of agriculture. Now some form of social stratification is nearly universal.

Analysis of the categories—such as class, "race," gender, age, and indigeneity—within stratification systems reveals a crucial difference among them in the degree to which membership in a given category is an **ascribed position**, based on qualities of a person gained through birth, or an

THINKING OUTSIDE THE BOX

Do research on the current global distribution of Alcoholics Anonymous.

achieved position, based on qualities of a person gained through action. Ascribed positions may be based on one's "race," ethnicity, gender, age, or physical ability. These factors are generally out of the control of the individual, although some flexibility exists for gender (through surgery and hormonal treatments) and for certain kinds of physical conditions. Also, one can sometimes "pass" as a member of another "race" or ethnic group. Age is an interesting ascribed category because an individual goes through several different status levels associated with age. Achievement as a basis for group membership means that a person's membership in the group is based on some valued attainment. Ascribed systems are thus more "closed," and achievement-based systems more "open," in terms of mobility, either upward or downward, within the system. Some scholars of social status believe that modernization during the 20th century and increased social complexity led to a rise in achievement-based positions and a decline in ascription-based positions. The material that follows explores how social categories define group membership and relations of inequality among groups.

Societies place people into categories—student, husband, child, retired person, political leader, or member of Phi Beta Kappa—referred to as a person's **status**, or position or standing in society (Wolf 1996). Each status has an accompanying role, which is expected behavior for someone of a particular status, and a "script" for how to behave, look, and talk. Some statuses have more prestige attached to them than others. Within societies that have marked status positions, different status groups are marked by a particular lifestyle, including the goods they own, their leisure activities, and their linguistic styles. The maintenance of group position by the higher status categories is sometimes accomplished by exclusionary practices in relation to lower-status groups through a tendency toward group in-marriage and socializing only within the group. Groups, like individuals, have status, or standing, in society.

ACHIEVED STATUS: CLASS

Social class (defined in Chapter 1) refers to a person's or group's position in society and is defined primarily in economic terms. In many cultures, class is a key factor in determining a person's status, whereas in others, it is less important than, for example, birth into a certain family. Class and status, however, do not always match. A rich person may have become wealthy in disreputable ways and never gain high status. Both status and class groups are secondary groups,

---

achieved position   a person's standing in society based on qualities that the person has gained through action.

status   a person's position, or standing, in society.

mestizaje   literally, a racial mixture; in Central and South America, indigenous people who are cut off from their Indian roots, or literate and successful indigenous people who retain some traditional cultural practices.

because a person is unlikely to know every other member of the group, especially in large-scale societies.

In capitalist societies, the prevailing ideology is that the system allows for upward mobility and that every individual has the option of moving up. Some anthropologists refer to this ideology as *meritocratic individualism*, the belief that rewards go to those who deserve them (Durrenberger 2001). In contrast, a structurist perspective points to the power of economic class position in shaping a person's lifestyle and his or her ability to choose a different one. Obviously, a person who was born rich can, through individual agency, become poor, and a poor person can become rich. In spite of exceptions to the rule, a person born rich is more likely to lead a lifestyle typical of that class, just as a person born poor is more likely lead a lifestyle typical of that class.

The concept of class is central to the theories of Karl Marx. Situated within the context of Europe's Industrial Revolution and the growth of capitalism, Marx wrote that class differences, exploitation of the working class by the owners of capital, class consciousness among workers, and class conflict were forces of change that would eventually spell the downfall of capitalism.

ASCRIBED STATUS: "RACE," ETHNICITY, GENDER, AND CASTE

Four major ascribed systems of social stratification are based on divisions of people into unequally ranked groups on the basis of, respectively, "race," ethnicity (defined in Chapter 1), gender, and caste, the last a ranked group determined by birth and often linked to a particular occupation and to South Asian cultures. Like status and class groups, these four categories are secondary social groups, because no one can have a personal relationship with all other members of the entire group. Each system takes on local specificities, depending on the context. For example, "race" and ethnicity are interrelated and overlap with conceptions of culture in much of Latin America, although what they mean in terms of identity and status differs in different countries in the region (de la Cadena 2001). For some, the concept of **mestizaje** (mes-tee-SAH-hay), mestizo, literally means "racial" mixture. In Central and South America, it refers either to people who are cut off from their Indian roots or to literate and successful people who retain some indigenous cultural practices. One has to know the local system of categories and meanings attached to them to understand the dynamics of inequality that go with them.

Systems based on differences defined in terms of "race," ethnicity, gender, and caste share some important features with each other and with class-based systems. First, they relegate large numbers of people to particular levels of entitlement to livelihood, power, security, esteem, and freedom (Berreman 1979 [1975]:213). This simple fact should not be overlooked. Second, those with greater entitlements dominate those with lesser entitlements. Third, members of the dominant groups tend to seek to maintain their position, consciously or unconsciously. They do this through institutions that control ideology among the dominated and through institutions that physically suppress potential rebellion or subversion by the dominated (Harris 1971, quoted in Mencher 1974:469). Fourth, in spite of efforts to maintain systems of dominance, instances of subversion and rebellion do occur, indicating the potential for agency among the oppressed.

"RACE" Racial stratification is a relatively recent form of social inequality. It results from the unequal meeting of two formerly separate groups through colonization, slavery, and other large-group movements (Sanjek 1994). Europe's "age of discovery," beginning in the 1500s, ushered in a new era of global contact. In contrast, in relatively homogeneous cultures, ethnicity is a more important distinction than "race." In contemporary Nigeria, for example, the population is largely homogeneous and *ethnicity* is the more salient term (Jinadu 1994). A similar situation prevails in other African states as well as in the Middle East, Central Europe and Eurasia, and China.

A key feature of racial thinking is its insistence that behavioral differences among peoples are "natural," inborn, or biologically caused. Throughout the history of racial categorizations in the West, such features as head size, head shape, and brain size have been accepted as reasons for behavioral differences. Writing early in the twentieth century, Franz Boas contributed to de-linking supposed inborn, racial attributes from behavior (review Chapter 1). He showed that people with the same head size but from different cultures behaved differently and that people with various head sizes within the same cultures behaved similarly. For Boas and his followers, culture, not biology, is the key explanation for behavior. Thus, "race" is not a biological reality; there is no way to divide the human population into "races" based on certain biological features. Yet social race and racism exist. In other words, in many contexts the concept of "race" has a social reality in terms of people's entitlements, status, and treatment. In spite of some progress in reducing racism in the United States in the twentieth century, racial discrimination persists.

Racial classifications in the Caribbean and in Latin America involve complicated systems of status classification. The complexity results from the variety of contact over the centuries between peoples from Europe, Africa, Asia, and indigenous populations. Skin tone is one basis of racial classification, but it is mixed with other physical features and economic status as well. In Haiti, for example, racial categories take into account physical factors such as skin texture, depth of skin tone, hair color and appearance, and facial features (Trouillot 1994). Racial categories also include a person's income, social origin, level of formal education, personality or behavior, and kinship ties. Depending on how these variables are combined, a person occupies one category or another—and may even move between categories. Thus, a person with certain physical features who is poor will be considered to be a different "color" than a person with the same physical features who is well off.

An extreme example of racial stratification was the South African policy of apartheid, the legally sanctioned segregation of dominant Whites from non-Whites. White dominance in South Africa (see Map 7.5) began in the early 1800s with White migration and settlement. In the 1830s, slavery was abolished. At the same time, increasingly racist thinking developed among Whites (Johnson 1994:25). Racist images, including images of Africans as lazy and politically disorganized, served as part of the rationale for colonialist domination. In spite of years of African resistance to White domination, the Whites succeeded in maintaining and increasing their control for nearly two centuries. In South Africa, Blacks constitute 90 percent of the population, a numerical majority that was long dominated, through strict apartheid, by the White minority until 1994. During apartheid, every measure of the quality of life—infant mortality, longevity, education—showed great disparity between the Whites and the Africans. In addition to suffering from physical deprivation, Black South Africans experienced psychological suffering through constant personal insecurity caused by the threat and actuality of police raids and other forms of violence directed against them. Now, Black South Africans continue to face the scourge of continuing poverty and disentitlement as well as excess death and suffering from HIV/AIDS.

In contrast to the explicitly racist discrimination of South African apartheid, racism exists even where it is against the law to discriminate against people on the basis of race. In such contexts, structural violence as played out through racism is often denied by those in power, a fact that makes it especially difficult to fight. In the United States, racism plays out in many areas of life, including environmental pollution (see Eye on the Environment).

ETHNICITY Ethnicity is a sense of group membership based on a shared sense of identity that may be based on history, territory, language, or religion, or a combination of these (Comaroff 1987). Ethnicity can be a basis for claiming entitlements to resources (such as land, buildings, or artifacts) and for defending or regaining those resources.

States are interested in managing ethnicity to the extent that it does not threaten security. China has one of the most formalized systems for monitoring its many ethnic groups, and it has an official policy on ethnic minorities, meaning the non-Han groups (Wu 1990). The government lists 54 groups other than the Han majority, which constitutes about 94 percent of the total population. The other 6 percent of the population is made up of these 54 groups, about 67 million people. The non-Han minorities occupy about 60 percent of China's land mass and are located in border or "frontier" areas such as Tibet, Yunnan, Xinjiang, and Inner Mongolia. Basic criteria for

In 2003, the Treatment Action Campaign (TAC) began a program of civil disobedience to prompt the government of South Africa to sign and implement a National Prevention and Treatment Plan for HIV/AIDS. The TAC uses images of Hector Peterson, the first youth killed in the Soweto uprising against apartheid, and slogans such as "The Struggle Continues: Support HIV/AIDS Treatment Now."

▶ *Take a position, and be prepared to defend it, on whether or not a country's government should take responsibility for preventing and treating HIV/AIDS.*

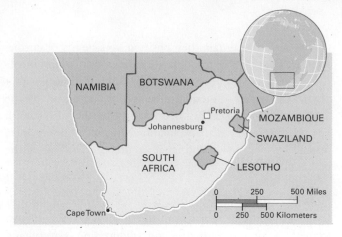

MAP 7.5 South Africa.
The Republic of South Africa experienced the highest level of colonial immigration of any African country. Its rich mineral wealth attracted interest from global powers through the Cold War era. Of its population of over 46 million, 80 percent are Black South Africans. The rest are of mixed ethnic backgrounds (referred to as "Coloureds"), Indian (from India), or White descendants of colonial immigrants. South Africa has 11 official languages, and it recognizes 8 nonofficial languages. Afrikaans and English are the major languages of the administration. Nonofficial languages include those of the San and other indigenous peoples.

defining an ethnic group include language, territory, economy, and "psychological disposition." The Chinese government establishes strict definitions of group membership and group characteristics; it even sets standards for ethnic costumes and dances. The Chinese treatment of the Tibetan people is especially severe and can be considered ethnocide, or annihilation of the culture of an ethnic group by a dominant group. In 1951, China forcibly incorporated Tibet, and the Chinese government undertook measures to bring about the social and economic transformation of what was formerly a decentralized, Buddhist feudal regime. This transformation has caused increasing ethnic conflict between Tibetans and Han Chinese, including demonstrations by Tibetans and crackdowns from the Chinese.

People of one ethnic group who move from one niche to another are at risk of exclusionary treatment by the local residents. Roma (often called Gypsies by outsiders, a term that Roma consider to be derogatory), are a **diaspora population**, a dispersed group living outside their original homeland. Roma are scattered throughout Europe and the United States (see Culturama). Their status within mainstream society is always marginal in terms of economic, political, and social measures.

diaspora population   a dispersed group of people living outside their original homeland.

patriarchy   the dominance of men in economic, political, social, and ideological domains.

matriarchy   the dominance of women in economic, political, social, and ideological domains.

Examples of marginality and stigma experienced by minority ethnic groups are plentiful. Incoming migrants are often at risk of discrimination, as is the case of Indo-Canadians, immigrants from India to Canada. Research undertaken with nearly 300 Indo-Canadians in Vancouver, British Columbia, revealed that half of the respondents reported experiencing some form of discrimination in the recent past (Nodwell and Guppy 1992). The percentage was higher among men (54 percent) than among women (45 percent). The higher percentage for men was consistent across the four categories of discrimination listed: verbal abuse, property damage, workplace discrimination, and physical harm. Overall, verbal abuse was the most frequent form of discrimination reported by both men and women. Indo-Canadians of the Sikh faith who were born in India say that they experience the highest levels of discrimination in Canada. Apparently, however, their actual experience of discrimination is not greater than that for other Indo-Canadians. The difference is that Sikhs who were born in India are more sensitive to discrimination than others. Sikhism, as taught and practiced in India, supports a strong sense of honor, which should be protected and, if wronged, avenged. The study discussed here helps explain differences in perception of discrimination among ethnic migrants. It does not, however, explain why such high levels of discriminatory treatment exist in a country committed to ethnic tolerance.

GENDER AND SEXISM Like other forms of social inequality, gender inequalities, based on perceived differences between people born male or female or somewhere in between,

A political leader of the Ashanti people, Ghana. British colonialists referred to such leaders with the English term "chief" although the English word "king" might have been more appropriate.

POLITICAL AND LEGAL SYSTEMS

8

the BIG questions

◆ What does political anthropology cover?

◆ What is the scope of legal anthropology?

◆ How are political and legal systems changing?

OUTLINE

Politics, Political Organization, and Leadership

Eye on the Environment: Water, Pollution, and International Politics

Social Order and Social Conflict

Critical Thinking: Yanomami: The "Fierce People"?

Change in Political and Legal Systems

Culturama: The Kurds of the Middle East

eye on the ENVIRONMENT

Industrial Pollution and Activism in an African American Community in Georgia, the United States

"But I know it's true" is an often-repeated phrase among African American residents of the Hyde Park area of Augusta, Georgia (Checker 2005, 2007). Following World War II, many rural African American families in Georgia bought land in Hyde Park, a swampy area, but nonetheless one that allowed them access to nearby jobs in factories or as domestic workers. The neighborhood was vibrant with shops and churches. It was, however, poorly serviced by the government and surrounded by several industrial enterprises, including Southern Wood Piedmont (SWP), a wood-preserving factory.

In the 1980s, several residents fell ill with uncommon and mysterious forms of cancer and skin diseases. SWP was found to be polluting the groundwater in the neighborhood with dioxins, chlorophenols, and other chemicals. The factory closed in 1988 and began efforts to remediate the contamination. A nearby low-income neighborhood that was predominantly White settled a class-action lawsuit against SWP and received compensation. The residents of Hyde Park were not told of the lawsuit or asked to join it, and they therefore received no compensation.

Hyde Park residents began to learn of other sources of industrial pollution, including polychlorinated biphenyls (PCBs). More cases emerged, especially among children, of rashes, lupus, respiratory and circulatory problems, and rare forms of cancer. People stopped letting their children play in the backyard, in order to avoid contact with contaminated ditch water and soil. They stopped growing vegetables in their home gardens. The values of their homes fell dramatically. In sum, they lost their health, their freedom to use their own property for play, and their economic security.

Over time, more studies showed high levels of chemicals and heavy metals in the groundwater and soil in Hyde Park. Georgia's Environmental Protection Division (EPD) continued to argue that levels were within normal ranges. Hyde Park residents, however, were convinced that the pollution was causing their health problems, as well as other problems. They organized in order to make their claims heard.

Environmental justice activism refers to social movements dedicated to (1) documenting the structural violence and inequality that place certain groups at risk of losing their entitlements to live in a safe and healthy environment and (2) helping such groups gain compensation or other forms of redress. Along these lines, Hyde Park residents and members of a nearby African American neighborhood formed the Hyde and Aragon Park Improvement Committee (HAPIC). HAPIC activists employ a unique blend of Black solidarity, church-based organizing principles, computers for research and communication, and partnerships with wider environmental groups, such as the Sierra Club, to make the committee's voice heard in the state political arena.

◆ **FOOD FOR THOUGHT**
● Do Internet research to learn about the current status of the Hyde Park residents' efforts to make their neighborhood livable and to gain compensation for damages to their health and household security.

vary from one culture to another. This book has already presented many examples of gender inequality, and more will appear in later chapters. The discussion that follows highlights some features of male dominance cross-culturally.

Patriarchy, or male dominance in economic, political, social, and ideological domains, is common but not universal. It also varies in severity and results. In its most severe forms, women and girls are completely under the power of men and can be killed by men, with no societal response. So-called *honor killings*, for example, of girls and women who defy rules of virginity or arranged marriage and are murdered by male kin, are examples of extreme patriarchy (Kurkiala 2003). Less violent, but also serious, is the effect of patriarchy on girls' education. In many countries, girls are not sent to school at all, or if they are, they attend for fewer years or attend schools of lower quality than their brothers.

The logical opposite of patriarchy is **matriarchy**, or female dominance in economic, political, social, and ideological domains. Matriarchy is so rare in contemporary cultures that anthropologists are not certain that it even exists—or has ever existed. Among the Iroquois at the time the European colonialists arrived, women controlled public finances, in the form of maize, and they determined whether or not war would be waged. They also chose the leaders, although the leaders were male. It is not clear whether the Iroquois were in fact matriarchal or might more accurately be considered gender egalitarian with a mixed and balanced gender system. A stronger case for a truly matriarchal society is found in the Minangkabau people of Malaysia and Indonesia (see Culturama, p. 132).

THINKING OUTSIDE THE BOX

With which ethnic or other kind of social group do you identify? What are the bases of this identification? Is your social group relatively high or low in terms of social status?

This chapter covers topics in political and legal anthropology, two subfields of cultural anthropology. *Political anthropology* addresses the area of human behavior and thought related to power—who has it and who does not, degrees of power, bases of power, abuses of power, relationships between political and religious power, political organization and government, social conflict and social control, and morality and law. *Legal anthropology* addresses issues of social order and conflict resolution cross-culturally.

♦♦♦

Politics, Political Organization, and Leadership

Compared with political scientists, cultural anthropologists take a broader view of *politics* that includes many kinds of behavior and thought beyond formal party politics, voting, and state governments. Cultural anthropologists offer examples of political systems and behavior that might not look "political" to people who have grown up in modern states. This section explores basic political concepts from an anthropological perspective.

This book uses the term *politics* to refer to the organized use of public power, not the more private micropolitics of family and domestic groups. **Power** is the ability to bring about results, often through the possession or use of forceful means. Closely related to power are authority and influence. **Authority** is the ability to take certain forms of action based on a person's achieved or ascribed status or moral reputation. Authority differs from power in that power is backed up by the potential use of force and power can be wielded by individuals without their having authority in the moral sense. **Influence** is the ability to achieve a desired end by exerting

---

power   the ability to take action in the face of resistance, through force if necessary.

authority   the ability to take action based on a person's achieved or ascribed status or moral reputation.

influence   the ability to achieve a desired end by exerting social or moral pressure on someone or some group.

political organization   groups within a culture that are responsible for public decision making and leadership, maintaining social cohesion and order, protecting group rights, and ensuring safety from external threats.

band   the form of political organization of foraging groups, with flexible membership and minimal leadership.

tribe   a form of political organization that comprises several bands or lineage groups, each with a similar language and lifestyle and occupying a distinct territory.

big-man system or **big-woman system**   a form of political organization midway between tribe and chiefdom and involving reliance on the leadership of key individuals who develop a political following through personal ties and redistributive feasts.

social or moral pressure on someone or some group. Unlike authority, influence may be exerted from a low-status, marginal position.

All three terms are relational. A person's power, authority, or influence exists in relation to other people. Power implies the greatest likelihood of a coercive and hierarchical relationship, and authority and influence offer the most scope for consensual, cooperative decision making. Power, authority, and influence are all related to politics, power being the strongest basis for action and decision making—and potentially the least moral.

Political anthropologists define **political organization** as the groups within a culture that are responsible for public decision making and leadership, maintaining social cohesion and order, protecting group rights, and ensuring safety from external threats.

Cultural anthropologists cluster the many forms of political organization that occur cross-culturally into four types that are loosely related to the modes of livelihood (see Figure 8.1).

BANDS

A **band**, the form of political organization associated with foraging groups, involves flexible membership and no formal leaders. Just as foraging has been the predominant mode of livelihood for almost all of human existence, the band is humanity's oldest form of political organization. A band comprises between 20 people and a few hundred people at most, all related through kinship. These units come together at certain times of the year, depending on their foraging patterns and ritual schedule.

Band membership is flexible: If a person has a serious disagreement with another person or a spouse, one option is to leave that band and join another. Leadership is informal, with no one person named as a permanent leader. Depending on events, such as organizing the group to relocate or to send people out to hunt, a particular person may be a leader for that event, someone whose advice and knowledge are especially respected.

All members of the group are social equals, and a band leader has no special status. He has a certain degree of authority or influence, perhaps as a respected hunter or storyteller, but he does not have power and cannot force others to accept his views. Social leveling mechanisms prevent anyone from accumulating much authority or influence. Political activity in bands involves mainly decision making about migration, food distribution, and the resolution of interpersonal conflicts. External conflict between groups is rare because territories of different bands are widely separated and the population density is low.

The band level of organization barely qualifies as a form of political organization, because groups are flexible, leadership is ephemeral, and there are no signs or emblems of political affiliation. Some anthropologists argue, therefore, that true politics did not exist in undisturbed band societies.

Foraging	Horticulture	Pastoralism	Agriculture	Industrialism/Informatics
Political Organization				**Political Organization**
Band	Tribe	Chiefdom	Confederacy	State
Leadership				**Leadership**
Band leader	Headman/Headwoman Big-man Big-woman	Chief Paramount chief		King/queen/president prime minister/emperor
Social Conflict				**Social Conflict**
Face-to-face Small-scale Rarely lethal	Armed conflict Revenge killing		War	International war Technological weapons Massively lethal Ethnic conflict Standing armies
Social Control				**Social Control**
Norms Social pressure Ostracism				Laws Formal judiciary Permanent police Imprisonment

Trends

Increased population density and residential centralization ⟶
More surpluses of resources and wealth ⟶
More social inequality/ranking ⟶
Less reliance on kinship relations as the basis of political structures ⟶
Increased internal and external social conflict ⟶
Increased power and responsibility of leaders ⟶
Increased burdens on the population to support political organization ⟶

FIGURE 8.1 Modes of Political Organization, Conflict, and Social Control

TRIBES

A **tribe** is a more formal type of political organization than the band. Typically associated with horticulture and pastoralism, tribal organization arose between 10,000 and 12,000 years ago with the emergence of these modes of livelihood. A tribe is a political group that comprises several bands or lineage groups, each with a similar language and lifestyle and each occupying a distinct territory. Tribal groups may be connected through a clan structure, in which most people claim descent from a common ancestor although they may be unable to trace the exact relationship. Kinship is the primary basis of membership. Tribal groupings contain from 100 to several thousand people. Tribes are found in the Middle East, South Asia, Southeast Asia, the Pacific, and Africa, as well as among Native Americans.

A tribal headman (most tribal leaders are male) is a more formal leader than a band leader. A headman must be hardworking and generous and must possess good personal skills. A headman is a political leader on a part-time basis only, yet this role is more demanding than that of a band leader. Depending on the mode of livelihood, a headman will be in charge of determining the times for moving herds, planting, and

harvesting and for setting the time for seasonal feasts and celebrations. Internal and external conflict resolution is also his responsibility. A headman relies mainly on authority and persuasion, rather than on power. These strategies are effective because tribal members are all kin and are loyal to each other.

BIG-MAN AND BIG-WOMAN LEADERSHIP In between tribal and chiefdom organizations is the **big-man system** or **big-woman system**, a form of political organization in which individuals build a political base and gain prestige, influence, and authority through a system of *redistribution* based on personal ties and grand feasts (review Chapter 3). Anthropological research in Melanesia, a large region in the South Pacific extending from New Guinea to Fiji, established the existence of big-man politics (Sahlins 1963). Similar

THINKING
OUTSIDE
THE BOX

Consider the concepts of power, authority, and influence as defined here in the context of campus politics or in some other context with which you are familiar.

The last queen of Hawai'i, Queen Lili'uokalani. Inheriting the throne from her brother, Queen Lili'uokalani reigned for only two years, from 1891 to 1893. She attempted to establish constitutional rights for Hawai'ians and Asians living in the islands. In 1893, she was deposed by a group of European and American businessmen who took political control of the islands. The status of Hawai'i is still contested today by local groups that seek autonomy from the United States.

▶ *What did you learn about Hawai'i in your high school history or government classes? Did you learn about Queen Lili'uokalani and her attempt to assert native rights?*

over people than leaders in bands, tribes, and chiefdoms have. Their leaders have more responsibilities as well:

- States engage in international relations in order to deal with other states about mutual concerns (see Eye on the Environment). The state may use force defensively to maintain its borders and offensively to extend its territory.
- States monopolize the use of force and the maintenance of law and order internally through laws, courts, and the police.
- States maintain standing armies and police (as opposed to part-time forces).
- States define citizenship and its rights and responsibilities. In complex societies, since early times, not all residents have been granted equal rights as citizens.

- States keep track of the number, age, gender, location, and wealth of their citizens through census systems that are regularly updated.
- States have the power to extract resources from citizens through taxation.
- States manipulate information. Information to protect the state and its leaders can be controlled both directly (through censorship, restricting access to certain information by the public, and promotion of favorable images via propaganda) and indirectly (through pressure on journalists, television networks, and other media to selectively present information or to present information in certain ways).

SYMBOLS OF STATE POWER Religious beliefs and symbols are often closely tied to the power of state leadership: The ruler may be considered to be a deity or part deity, or may be a high priest of the state religion, or perhaps be closely linked with the high priest, who serves as advisor. Architecture and urban planning remind the populace of the greatness of the state.

In democratic states, where leaders are elected by popular vote, and in socialist states, where political rhetoric emphasizes social equality, expense and elegance are muted by the adoption of more egalitarian ways of dress (even though in private, these leaders may live relatively opulent lives in terms of housing, food, and entertainment). The earlier practice of all Chinese leaders wearing a "Mao jacket," regardless of their rank, was a symbolic statement of their antihierarchical philosophy. A quick glance at a crowd of people, including the Prime Minister of Canada or Britain or the President of the United States, would not reveal who was the leader, because dress differences are avoided. Even members of British royalty wear "street clothes" on public occasions where regalia are not required.

Beyond clothing, other commodities associated with top leadership positions include the quality of housing, food, and modes of transportation. State leaders live in grand mansions and often have more than one residence. The King of Morocco, for example, has several official palaces around the country, and he travels regularly from one to another. President George W. Bush was considered "one of the people" because he liked to eat hamburgers. State leaders do not travel the way ordinary citizens do. For security reasons, their ground vehicles may have bulletproof windows, and a cavalcade of security vehicles protects the leader's vehicle. In many African countries, the most important new symbol of political power is an expensive imported car (Chalfin 2008).

GENDER AND LEADERSHIP IN STATES Most contemporary states are hierarchical and patriarchal, excluding members of lower classes and women from equal participation. Some states are less male dominated than others, but none is female dominated. One view of gender inequality in states suggests that increasing male dominance with the evolution of

Like air, water can move across state boundaries, carrying environmental pollution. Such movements can cause serious international political conflicts and lead to extended negotiations about reparations and planning to prevent future damages. One case is that of mining-related pollution of the Tisza (TEE-suh) River that flows from Romania to Hungary and beyond, within the Danube River basin.

In January 2000, a dam in Romania holding *tailings* (metal-processing by-products) from a gold mine breached and released water containing high levels of cyanide, copper, zinc, and other heavy metals into nearby streams (Harper 2005). Three days later, the *plume*, or water carrying the by-products, had reached Hungary's Tisza River. Within the month, it moved on to Serbia and Bulgaria and eventually reached the Black Sea.

In Hungary, the cyanide killed thousands of tons of fish and waterfowl and raised alarms about people's drinking water. Farmers in the affected region reported the death of cows, and they were unable to sell their farm produce due to negative public perceptions about polluted products. Although cyanide is lethal in the short run, it soon dissipates from the environment, as opposed to the heavy metals, which remain in the river's sediments and continue to affect riverine life for a long time.

In spite of the severity of the disaster, the Hungarian state was slow to file claims against the offending corporation or for compensation from Romania. Although postsocialist Hungarian political leaders took up the cause of environmental activism in their rhetoric, they did not follow through with action. This lack of action may be related to the heritage of

MAP 8.1 **The Danube and Tisza Rivers in Eastern Europe.**
The Danube River and its major tributary, the Tisza. Europe's largest remaining natural wetland is in the Danube delta. The core of the delta, which lies mainly in Romania but crosses into Ukraine, was declared a UNESCO World Natural Heritage Site in 1991.

state socialism, which did not take environmental problems seriously. Another explanatory factor is that a large number of Hungarians live in Romania, and Hungary's leaders may have wished to avoid an international confrontation that would put Hungarians in Romania at risk.

One positive development was that the European Union (EU) offered a wider political framework in which to address the issue of the Tisza River pollution. The Tisza disaster was the first environmental disaster in which the EU took a prominent role. In the end, Hungary decided to sue the mining company for damages in a civil lawsuit, rather than taking on an international lawsuit with its neighbor.

◆ FOOD FOR THOUGHT

- The exact reasons for the Hungarian government's inaction are not clear. How can one learn the true reasons behind politicians' actions or inactions?

Rescue workers remove dead fish from the Tisza River in the year 2000 following an accident at a gold mine in northwestern Romania that deposited cyanide and other toxic substances into the Tisza and that also flowed into the Danube River and the Black Sea. The accident caused environmental damage in a vast area involving several countries.

(LEFT) Afghanistan President Hamid Karzai wears a carefully assembled collection of regional political symbols. The striped cape is associated with northern tribes. The Persian-lamb hat is an Uzbek style popular in the capital city, Kabul. He also wears a tunic and loose trousers, which are associated with villagers, and sometimes adds a Western-style jacket. His clothing implies a statement of unity and diversity about his country. (CENTER) President Barack Obama typically wears a dark suit, white shirt and necktie for formal occasions. During a Hawai'i themed celebration at the White House, he sports a lei which signals his close links to the state where he was born and spent much of his youth. (RIGHT) President Ellen Sirleaf-Johnson of Liberia and U.S. Secretary of State Hillary Clinton make contrasting statements through their formal attire with Sirleaf-Johnson clearly signaling a connection to Africa and Clinton conveying a more neutral message in her trademark pantsuit.

the state is based on men's control of the technology of production and warfare (Harris 1993). Women in most cultures have limited access to these areas of power. In more peaceful states, such as Finland, Norway, Sweden, and Denmark, women's political roles are more prominent.

Strongly patriarchal contemporary states preserve male dominance through ideologies that restrict women's political power. In much of the Muslim Middle East, Central Asia, Pakistan, and northern India, the practice of purdah, female seclusion and segregation from the public world, limits women's public roles. In China, scientific beliefs that categorize women as less strong and dependable than men have long been used to rationalize the exclusion of women from politics (Dikötter 1998). Socialist states typically attempt to increase women's political roles, and the proportion of female members in legislative bodies is higher in socialist states than in capitalist democracies. But it is still not equal to that of men. Although women account for roughly half of the

world's population, they form only, on average, 16 percent of the world's parliamentary members (Lederer 2006). Regional differences range from an average of 40 percent female parliamentarians in the Nordic states to 8 percent in Arab states.

A few contemporary states have or recently had women as prime ministers or presidents. Powerful women heads of state in recent times include Indira Gandhi in India, Golda Meir in Israel, Margaret Thatcher in the United Kingdom, Benazir Bhutto in Pakistan, Michelle Bachelet in Chile, Angela Merkel in Germany, Ellen Johnson-Sirleaf in Liberia, and Tarja Halonen in Finland. Some female heads of state are related by kinship, as wife or daughter, to male heads of state. Indira Gandhi, for example, was the daughter of Jawaharlal Nehru, the popular first prime minister of independent India. It is unclear whether these women inherited the role or achieved it indirectly through their socialization, as a result of being born into political families.

◆◆◆

Social Order and Social Conflict

Informal cultural rules about proper behavior shape people's everyday life in countless ways, inducing most people, for example, to wait in line to get on a bus and to pay for a sandwich at the deli instead of stealing it. This section discusses social

---

social control   processes that, through both informal and formal mechanisms, maintain orderly social life.

norm   a generally agreed-upon standard for how people should behave, usually unwritten and learned unconsciously.

law   a binding rule created through enactment or custom that defines right and reasonable behavior and is enforceable by the threat of punishment.

order and peace, including informal arrangements and formal laws and systems of crime prevention and punishment. It begins with the cross-cultural study of social order and then moves to a discussion of conflict and violence.

In anthropology, **social control** is the process by which people maintain orderly life in groups. Social control systems include informal social controls that exist through socialization for proper behavior, education, and peer pressure. They may also include formal systems of codified rules about proper behavior and punishments for deviation. In the United States and Canada, the Amish (review Culturama in Chapter 4, p. 80) and Mennonites rely on informal social controls far more than do most microcultural groups. The Amish and Mennonites have no police force or legal system; the way social order is maintained is through religious teaching and group pressure. If a member veers from correct behavior, punishment such as ostracism ("shunning") may be applied.

NORMS AND LAWS

Cultural anthropologists distinguish two major instruments of social control: norms and laws. A **norm** is an accepted standard for how people should behave that is usually unwritten and learned unconsciously through socialization. All societies have norms. Norms include, for example, the expectation that children should follow their parents' advice, that people standing in line should be orderly, and that an individual should accept an offer of a handshake (in cultures where handshakes are the usual greeting) when meeting someone for the first time. Enforcement of norms is informal. For example, a violation may simply be considered rude and the violator would be avoided in the future. Sometimes, however, direct action may be taken, such as asking someone who disrupts a meeting to leave.

A **law** is a binding rule created through custom or official enactment that defines correct behavior and the punishment for misbehavior. Systems of law are more common and more elaborate in state-level societies, but many nonstate societies have formalized laws. Religion often provides legitimacy for law. Australian Aborigines believe that law came to humans during the *Dreamtime* (also called dreaming), a period in the mythological past when the ancestors created the world. The terms "law" and "religion" are synonymous in contemporary Islamic states. Secular Western states consider their laws to be religiously neutral, although, in fact, much Western law is based on Judeo-Christian beliefs.

SYSTEMS OF SOCIAL CONTROL

The material that follows considers forms of social control in small-scale societies as contrasted with large-scale societies. The former are characterized more by the use of norms. The latter, notably states, rely more on legal sanctions, although local-level groups, such as neighbors, practice social sanctions among themselves. A final topic considers the relationship between the law and social inequality.

SOCIAL CONTROL IN SMALL-SCALE SOCIETIES

Anthropologists distinguish between small-scale societies and large-scale societies in terms of conflict resolution, social order, and punishment of offenses.

Bands are small, close-knit groups, so disputes tend to be handled at the interpersonal level through discussion or one-on-one fights. Group members may act together to punish an offender through shaming and ridicule. Emphasis is on maintaining social order and restoring social equilibrium, not hurtfully punishing an offender. Ostracizing an offending member (forcing the person to leave the group) is a common means of punishment. Capital punishment (execution) is rare.

In some Australian Aboriginal societies, laws restrict access to religious rituals and paraphernalia to men who have gone through a ritual initiation. If an initiated man shared secrets with an uninitiated person, the elders would delegate one of their group to kill the offender. In such instances, the elders act like a court.

In small-scale, nonstate societies, punishment is often legitimized through belief in supernatural forces and their ability to affect people. Among the highland horticulturalists of the Indonesian island of Sumba (see Map 1.2, p. 14), one of the greatest offenses is to fail to keep a promise (Kuipers 1990). Breaking a promise will bring on "supernatural assault" by the ancestors of those who have been offended by the person's misbehavior. The punishment may come in the form of damage to crops, illness or death of a relative, destruction of the offender's house, or having one's clothing catch on fire. When such a disaster occurs, the only recourse is to sponsor a ritual that will appease the ancestors.

The overall goal in dealing with conflict in small-scale societies is to return the group to harmony. Village fission (breaking up) and ostracism are mechanisms for dealing with more serious conflict.

SOCIAL CONTROL IN STATES In densely populated societies with more social stratification and more wealth, increased social stress occurs in relation to the distribution of surplus, inheritance, and rights to land. In addition, an increased social scale means that not everyone knows everyone else. Face-to-face accountability exists only in localized groups. Three important factors in state systems of social control are as follows:

- Specialization of roles involved in social control
- Formal trials and courts
- Power-enforced forms of punishment, such as prisons and the death penalty

THINKING
OUTSIDE
THE BOX

What are some key symbols of state power in your home country?

Informal mechanisms of social control, however, exist alongside these formal systems at the local level.

SPECIALIZATION   The specialization of tasks related to law and order, such as those performed by police, judges, and lawyers, increases with the emergence of state organization. Full-time professionals such as judges and lawyers emerged with the state. These professionals are often members of powerful social groups, a fact that perpetuates elite biases in the justice process itself.

Policing is a form of social control that includes processes of surveillance and the threat of punishment related to maintaining social order (Reiner 1996). Police are the specific organization and personnel who discover, report, and investigate crimes. As a specialized group, police are associated with states.

Japan's low crime rate has attracted the attention of Western law-and-order specialists, who think that it may be the result of the police system there. They ask whether solutions to U.S. crime problems can be found in such Japanese policing practices as neighborhood police boxes, or small, local police offices, staffed by foot patrolmen and volunteer crime prevention groups organized on a neighborhood basis. Fieldwork among police detectives in the city of Sapporo reveals aspects of Japanese culture and policing that promote low crime rates (Miyazawa 1992). In Japan, the police operate under high expectations that no false arrests will be made and that all arrests should lead to confession. And, in fact, the rate of confession is high. The high rate of confession may be due to the fact that the police do an excellent job of targeting the guilty party, or it may result from the nearly complete control of interrogation by the police. The police are allowed to keep suspects isolated for long periods, a practice that wears down resistance. The suspect's statements are not recorded verbatim or taped; instead, the detectives write them down and the suspect is asked to sign them. Overall, policing culture in Japan gives more power to the police and less to the defendant than in the United States and has the potential to distort the process of justice.

TRIALS AND COURTS   In societies where spirits and ancestors define wrongdoing and punishment, a person's guilt is proved simply by the fact that misfortune has befallen him or her. If a person's crops were damaged by lightning, for instance,

---

policing   the exercise of social control through processes of surveillance and the threat of punishment related to maintaining social order.

trial by ordeal   a way of determining innocence or guilt in which the accused person is put to a test that may be painful, stressful, or fatal.

critical legal anthropology   an approach within the cross-cultural study of legal systems that examines the role of law and judicial processes in maintaining the dominance of powerful groups through discriminatory practices rather than protecting less powerful people.

then that person must have done something wrong. In other cases, guilt may be determined through **trial by ordeal**, a way of judging guilt or innocence in which the accused person is put through a test that is often painful. An accused person may be required to place his or her hand in boiling oil, for example, or to have a part of his or her body touched by a red-hot knife. Being burned is a sign of guilt, whereas not being burned means that the suspect is innocent.

The court system, with lawyers, judge, and jury, is used in many contemporary societies, although variation exists in how cases are presented and juries constituted. The goal of contemporary court trials is to ensure both justice and fairness. Analysis of courtroom dynamics and patterns of decision making in the United States and elsewhere, however, reveals serious problems in achieving these goals.

PRISONS AND THE DEATH PENALTY   Administering punishment involves doing something unpleasant to someone who has committed an offense. As noted earlier, the most extreme form of punishment in small-scale societies is ostracism and only rarely death. A common form of punishment in the case of theft or murder in pastoralist societies, especially Islamic cultures of the Middle East, is that the guilty party must pay compensation to members of the family that has been harmed.

The *prison*, as a place where people are forcibly detained as a form of punishment, has a long history but probably emerged only with the state. The dungeons of historic forts and castles are vivid evidence of the power of some people to detain and inflict suffering on others. In Europe, long-term detention of prisoners did not become common until the 1600s (Foucault 1977). The first prison in the United States was built in Philadelphia in the late 1700s (Sharff 1995).

The percentage of imprisoned people varies widely around the world. The United States imprisons more people than any other country in the world, followed by China (Pew Center 2008). In the United States, the prison population of 1.6 million has more than doubled since 1985 (Walmsley 2007). Prison populations have also doubled over that period in Brazil and Mexico.

It is important to look at the rate of imprisonment as well as sheer numbers. The national *incarceration rate* is calculated as the number of people in prison per 100,000 people in a country. Countries vary widely in their incarceration rate. The United States has the highest incarceration rate, 737 per 100,000 people, followed by Russia, 611; Turkmenistan, 489; Cuba, 487; Belarus, 426; South Africa, 335; Iran, 214; and Spain, 145 (Walmsley 2007).

It is also important to look inside national rates. In England and France, a disproportionate number of prisoners are Muslims (Moore 2008). Ethnic and gender differences in incarceration are marked in the United States. One in 15 black men is in prison, and 1 in 9 black men 20 to 34 years of age is in prison. One in 355 white women ages 35 to 39 years is in

This man, in a military prison in Chechnya, is accused by the Russian government of participating with Chechen rebel forces. Human rights activists have been concerned about the mistreatment of prisoners in Chechnya for several years.

▶ *What human rights do prisoners have in your country?*

prison, whereas 1 in 100 black women is behind bars. Among Hispanics, 1 in 36 adult Hispanic men is in prison. The state with the highest incarceration rate is Louisiana, and southern states in general have higher rates than northern states.

Inefficient justice systems may mean that many prisoners are in jail for many years awaiting trial; they have not been convicted of a crime, but they are imprisoned. In Haiti, 9 of every 10 prisoners are awaiting trial (Walmsley 2007).

SOCIAL INEQUALITY AND THE LAW Critical legal **anthropology** is an approach within the cross-cultural study of legal systems that examines the role of law and judicial processes in maintaining the dominance of powerful groups through discriminatory practices rather than protecting members of less powerful groups. Systematic discrimination against ethnic minorities, indigenous peoples, and women, among other categories, has been documented in judicial systems around the world, including those of long-standing democracies. This section presents an example from Australia.

At the invitation of Aboriginal leaders in Australia, Fay Gale and her colleagues conducted research comparing the treatment of Aboriginal youth and White youth in the judicial system (1990). The question posed by the Aboriginal leaders was "Why are our kids always in trouble?" Two directions can be pursued to find the answer. First, structural factors—such as Aboriginal displacement from their homeland, poverty, poor living conditions, and bleak future prospects—can be investigated. Second, the criminal justice system can be examined to see whether it treats Aboriginal and White youth equally. The researchers decided to direct their attention to the judicial system because little work had been done in that area by social scientists.

Findings show that Aboriginal youth are overrepresented at every level of the juvenile justice system, from apprehension (being caught by the police) through pretrial processes, to the ultimate stage of adjudication (the judge's decision) and disposition (the punishment): "A far greater proportion of Aboriginal than other young people follow the harshest route. . . . At each point in the system where discretion operates, young Aborigines are significantly more likely than other young persons to receive the most severe outcomes of those available to the decision-makers" (1990:3). At the time of apprehension (being caught by the police), the suspect can be either formally arrested or informally reported. A formal arrest is made to ensure that the offender will appear in court. Officers ask suspects for a home address and whether they have a job. Aboriginal youth are more likely than White youth to live in an extended family in a poor neighborhood, and they are more likely to be unemployed. Thus, they tend to be placed in the category "undependable," and they are formally arrested more than White youth for the same crime (see Figure 8.2). The next step determines whether the suspect will be tried in Children's Court or referred to Children's Aid Panels. The Children's Aid Panels in South Australia have gained acclaim worldwide for the opportunities they give to individuals to avoid becoming repeat offenders and take their proper place in society. But most Aboriginal youth offenders are denied access

	Aboriginal Youth (percent)	White Youth (percent)
Brought into system via arrest rather than police report	43.4	19.7
Referred to Children's Court rather than diverted to Children's Aid Panels	71.3	37.4
Proportion of court appearances resulting in detention	10.2	4.2

Note: Most of these youths are male; data are from 1979 to 1984.

Source: *Aboriginal Youth and The Criminal Justice System: The Injustice of Justice,* by Fay Gale, Rebecca Bailey-Harris, Joy Wundersitz, Copyright © Cambridge University Press 1990. Reprinted by permission of Cambridge University Press.

FIGURE 8.2 Comparison of Outcomes for Aboriginal and White Youth in the Australian Judicial System

CRITICAL thinking

Yanomami: The "Fierce People"?

The Yanomami are a horticultural people who live in dispersed villages of between 40 and 250 people in the Amazonian rainforest (Ross 1993). Since the 1960s, biological anthropologist Napoleon Chagnon has studied several Yanomami villages. He has written a widely read and frequently republished ethnography about the Yanomami, with early editions carrying the subtitle *The Fierce People* (1992 [1968]). He also helped produce classic ethnographic films about the Yanomami, including *The Feast* and *The Ax Fight*.

Chagnon's writings and films have promoted a view of the Yanomami as exceptionally violent and prone to lethal warfare. According to Chagnon, about one-third of adult Yanomami males die violently, about two-thirds of all adults lose at least one close relative through violence, and over 50 percent lose two or more close relatives (1992:205). He has reported that one village was raided 25 times during his first 15 months of fieldwork. Although village alliances are sometimes formed, they are fragile and allies may turn against each other unpredictably.

The Yanomami world, as depicted by Chagnon, is one of danger, threats, and counterthreats. Enemies, human and supernatural, are everywhere. Support from one's allies is uncertain. All of this uncertainty leads to what

Chagnon describes as the *waiteri* (a Yanomami word) *complex*, a set of behaviors and attitudes that includes a fierce political and personal stance for men and forms of individual and group communication that stress aggression and independence. Fierceness is a dominant theme in socialization, as boys learn how to fight with clubs, participate in chest-pounding duels with other boys, and use a spear. Adult males are aggressive and hostile toward adult females, and boys learn to be aggressive toward girls from an early age.

Chagnon provides a biological, Darwinian explanation for the fierceness shown by the Yanomami. He reports that the Yanomami explain that village raids and warfare are carried out so that men may obtain wives. Although the Yanomami prefer to marry within their village, a shortage of potential brides exists because of the Yanomami practice of female infanticide. Although the Yanomami prefer to marry endogamously, taking a wife from another group is preferable to remaining a bachelor. Men in other groups, however, are unwilling to give up their women—hence the necessity for raids. Other reasons for raids are suspicion of sorcery or theft of food.

Chagnon argues that within this system warfare contributes to

reproductive success because successful warriors are able to gain a wife or more than one wife (polygyny is allowed). Thus, successful warriors will have higher reproductive rates than unsuccessful warriors. Successful warriors, Chagnon suggests, have a genetic advantage for fierceness, which they pass on to their sons, leading to a higher growth rate of groups with violent males through genetic selection for fierceness. Male fierceness, in this view, is biologically adaptive.

Marvin Harris, taking the cultural materialist perspective, says that protein scarcity and population dynamics in the area are the underlying causes of warfare (1984). The Yanomami lack plentiful sources of meat, which is highly valued. Harris suggests that when game in an area becomes depleted, pressure rises to expand into the territory of neighboring groups, thus precipitating conflict. Such conflicts in turn result in high rates of adult male mortality. Combined with the effects of female infanticide, this meat-warfare complex keeps population growth rates down to a level that the environment can support.

A third view relies on historical data. Brian Ferguson (1990) argues that the high levels of violence among the Yanomami were caused by the intensified Western presence during the

---

to them and instead have to appear in court, where the vast majority of youthful offenders end up pleading guilty. The clear and disturbing finding from this study is that the mode of arrest tends to determine each subsequent stage in the system.

SOCIAL CONFLICT AND VIOLENCE

All systems of social control have to deal with the fact that conflict and violence may occur. This section considers the varieties of social conflict as studied by cultural anthropologists. Conflict can occur at any social level, from the private microlevel of the household to the public situation of international warfare.

---

war organized and purposeful group action directed against another group and involving lethal force.

ETHNIC CONFLICT Ethnic pluralism is a characteristic of most states in the world today. Ethnic conflict and grievances may result from an ethnic group's attempt to gain more autonomy or more equitable treatment. It may also be caused by a dominant group's actions to subordinate, oppress, or eliminate an ethnic group by *genocide* (killing large numbers of a distinct ethnic, racial, or religious group) or *ethnocide* (destroying the culture of a distinct group). In the past few decades, political violence has increasingly been enacted within states rather than between states. Political analysts and journalists often cite ethnicity, language, and religion as the causes of certain conflicts. It is true that ethnic identities give people an ideological commitment to a cause, but one must look beneath the labels to see whether deeper issues exist, such as claims to land, water, ports, and other material resources.

preceding 100 years. Furthermore, diseases introduced from outside, especially measles and malaria, severely depopulated the Yanomami and greatly increased their fears of sorcery (their explanation for disease). The attraction to Western goods such as steel axes and guns would also increase intergroup rivalry. Thus, Ferguson suggests that the "fierce people" are a creation of historical forces, especially contact with and pressure from outsiders.

Following Ferguson's position, but with a new angle, journalist Patrick Tierney points the finger of blame at Chagnon himself (2000). Tierney maintains that it was the presence of Chagnon, with his team of coresearchers and many boxes of trade goods, that triggered a series of lethal raids due to increased competition for those very goods. In addition, Tierney argues that Chagnon intentionally prompted the Yanomami to act fiercely in his films and to stage raids that created aggravated intergroup hostility beyond what had originally existed.

In 2001, the American Anthropological Association established a task force to examine five topics related to Tierney's allegations that Chagnon's and others' interactions with and representations of the Yanomami may have had a detrimental impact on them, contributing to "disorganization" among the Yanomami. The report of the El Dorado Task Force appears on the website www.aaanet.org of the

Napoleon Chagnon (center) in the field with two Yanomami men, 1995. Chagnon distributed goods such as steel axes and tobacco to the Yanomami to gain their cooperation in his research.

American Anthropological Association. The task force rejected all charges against Chagnon and instead emphasized the harmfulness of false accusations that might jeopardize future scientific research.

◆ **CRITICAL THINKING QUESTIONS**

- Which perspective presented here on Yanomami men's behavior appears most persuasive to you and why?
- What relevance does this case have to the theory that violence is a universal human trait?
- Do you think anthropological research could lead to increased violence among the study population?

Consider Central Asia (see Map 8.2), a vast region populated by many ethnic groups, none of which has a pristine indigenous claim to the land. Yet, in Central Asia, every dispute appears on the surface to have an ethnic basis: "Russians and Ukrainians versus Kazakhs over land rights and jobs in Kazakhstan, Uzbeks versus Tajiks over the status of Samarkhand and Bukhara, conflict between Kirghiz and Uzbeks in Kyrgyzstan, and riots between Caucasian Turks and Uzbeks in the Fergana Valley of Uzbekistan" (Clay 1990:48). Attributing the causes of all such problems to ethnic differences overlooks competition for resources that is based on regional, not ethnic, differences. Uzbekistan has most of the cities and irrigated farmland, whereas Kyrgyzstan and Tajikistan control most of the water and Turkmenistan has vast oil and gas riches.

WARFARE Several definitions of war exist (Reyna 1994), one of which is that it is an open and declared conflict between two political units. This definition, however, would rule out many war-like conflicts, including the American–Vietnam War because it was undeclared. Or war may be defined simply as organized aggression. This definition is too broad, because not all organized violence can be considered warfare. Perhaps the best definition is that **war** is organized conflict involving group action directed against another group and involving lethal force (Ferguson 1994, quoted in Reyna 1994:30).

Cultural variation exists in the frequency and seriousness of war. Intergroup conflicts among free-ranging foragers that would fit the definition of war do not exist in the ethnographic record. The informal, nonhierarchical political organization

MAP 8.2 Central Asian States.

The five states of Central Asia are Kazakhstan, Turkmenistan, Uzbekistan, Kyrgyzstan, and Tajikistan. Central Asia is a large, landlocked region that is historically linked with pastoralism and the famous Silk Road, a trade route connecting the Middle East with China. The region's terrain encompasses desert, plateaus, and mountains. Given its strategic location near several major world powers, it has often been a battleground of other states' interests. The predominant religion is Islam, and most Central Asians are Sunnis. Languages are of the Turkic language group. Central Asia has an indigenous form of rap-style music in which lyrical improvisers engage in battles, usually accompanied by a stringed instrument. These musical artists, or *akyns*, are now using their art to campaign for political candidates.

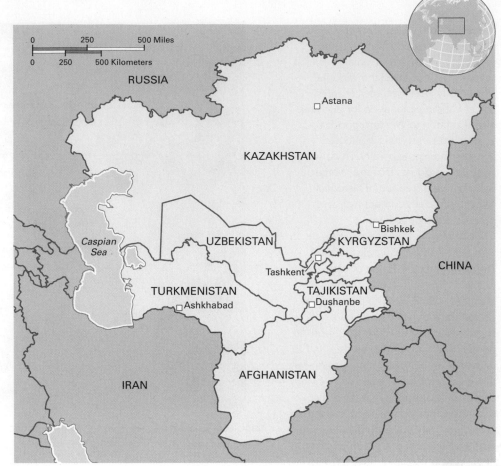

among bands is not conducive to waging armed conflict. Bands do not have specialized military forces or leaders.

Archaeological evidence indicates that warfare emerged during the Neolithic era with settled life. Plant and animal domestication required extensive land use and was accompanied by increased population density. The resulting economic and demographic pressures put more and larger groups in more direct and intense competition with each other.

No evidence of warlike behavior among bands exists, but it does among tribal groups. Tribal leadership patterns, including big-man systems, facilitate the mobilization of warrior groups for raids. Contemporary tribal groups everywhere, though, do not all have the same levels of warfare. At one extreme, with reported high levels of warfare, are the Yanomami of the Amazon (see Map 3.3, p. 57 and Critical Thinking).

In states, standing (permanent) armies and complex military hierarchies are supported by increased material resources through taxation and other forms of revenue generation. Greater state power allows for more powerful and effective military structures, which in turn increase the state's power. Thus, a mutually reinforcing relationship emerges between the military and the state. Although most states are highly militarized, not all are, nor are all states equally militarized. Costa Rica (see Map 11.1, p. 246) does not maintain an army.

Examining the causes of war between states has occupied scholars in many fields for centuries. Some experts have pointed to common, underlying causes, such as attempts to extend boundaries, secure more resources, ensure markets, support political and economic allies, and resist aggression from other states. Others point to humanitarian concerns that prompt participation in "just wars," to defend values such as freedom or to protect human rights that are defined as such by one country and are being violated in another.

Causes of war in Afghanistan have changed over time (Barfield 1994). Since the seventeenth century, warfare increasingly became a way in which kings justified their power in terms of the necessity to maintain independence from outside forces such as the British and Czarist Russia. The last Afghan king was murdered in a coup in 1978. When the Soviet Union invaded in 1979, no centralized ruling group existed to meet it. The Soviet Union deposed the ruling faction, set up one of its own, and then killed over 1 million people, caused 3 million to flee the country, and left millions of others to be displaced internally. Still, in spite of the lack of a central command, ethnic and sectarian differences, and being outmatched in equipment by Soviet forces, the Afghanis waged a war of resistance that eventually wore down the Soviets, who withdrew in 1989.

nation a group of people who share a language, culture, territorial base, political organization, and history.

A child soldier named Alfred walks to a UN disarmament camp in the Liberian city of Tubmanburg in 2004. Many countries have programs to help child soldiers adjust to life after war.

▶ *What might be the three most important challenges that child soldiers face in a postconflict situation?*

This case suggests that war was a more effective tool of domination in the premodern period, when it settled matters more definitively (Barfield 1994). In premodern times, fewer troops were needed to maintain dominance after a conquest, because continued internal revolts were less common and the main issue was defense against rivals from outside. Current events show clearly that attacking and taking over a country are only the first stages in a process much more complicated than the term *regime change* implies. Afghanistan is still attempting to recover and rebuild after four decades of war (Shahrani 2002). Cultural factors influencing the country's recovery include codes of honor that value political autonomy and require vengeance for harm received, the moral system of Islam, the drug economy, and the effects of intervention from outside powers involving foreign governments and corporations, including Unocal of California, Delta Oil of Saudi Arabia, and Bridas of Argentina. The difficulty of constructing a strong state with loyal citizens in the face of these conflicting internal and external factors is great.

◆◆◆
Change in Political and Legal Systems

In the early days of political and legal anthropology, researchers examined the varieties of political organization and social control in bands, tribes, chiefdoms, and states. Political and legal anthropologists are now more interested in political dynamics and change. This section provides three examples of change.

EMERGING NATIONS AND TRANSNATIONAL NATIONS

Many different definitions exist for a nation, and some of them overlap with definitions given for a state. One definition says that a **nation** is a group of people who share a language, culture, territorial base, political organization, and history (Clay 1990). In this sense, a nation is culturally homogeneous, and the United States would be considered not a nation, but rather a political unit composed of many nations. According to this definition, groups that lack a territorial base cannot be termed nations. A related term is the *nation–state*, which some say refers to a state that comprises only one nation, whereas others think that it refers to a state that comprises many nations. An example of the first view is the Iroquois nation (see Map 3.2, p. 57).

Depending on their resources and power, nations and other groups may constitute a political threat to state stability and control. Examples include the Kurds in the Middle East (see Culturama), the Maya of Mexico and Central America, Tamils in Sri Lanka, Tibetans in China, and Palestinians in the Middle East. In response to local political movements, states seek to create and maintain a sense of unified identity. Political scientist Benedict Anderson, in his book *Imagined Communities* (1991 [1983]), writes about the symbolic efforts that state builders employ to create a sense of belonging—an "imagined community"—among diverse peoples. Strategies include the imposition of one language as the national language; the construction of monuments and museums that emphasize unity; and the use of songs, dress, poetry, and other media messages to promote an image of a unified country. Some states, such as China, control religious expression in the interest of promoting loyalty to and identity with the state.

Globalization and increased international migration also prompt anthropologists to rethink the concept of the state (Trouillot 2001). The case of Puerto Rico (see Map 8.4) is particularly illuminating because of its continuing status as a quasi-colony of the United States (Duany 2000). Puerto Rico is neither fully a state of the United States nor an autonomous political unit with its own national identity. Furthermore, Puerto Rican people do not coexist in a bounded spatial territory. By the late 1990s, nearly as many Puerto Ricans lived in the United States mainland as on the island of Puerto Rico.

CULTURAMA

The Kurds of the Middle East

The Kurds are an ethnic group of between 20 and 30 million people, most of whom speak some dialect of the Kurdish language, which is related to Farsi, the language spoken in Iran, among other countries (Major 1996). The majority are Sunni Muslims. Kurdish kinship is strongly patrilineal, and Kurdish family and social relations are male dominated.

Their home region, called Kurdistan ("Place of the Kurds"), extends from Turkey into Iran, Iraq, and Syria. This area is grasslands, interspersed with mountains, with no coastline. Before World War I, many Kurds were full-time pastoralists, herding sheep and goats. Following the war and the creation of Iraq, Syria, and Kuwait, many Kurdish herders were unable to follow their traditional grazing because they crossed the new country borders. Herders no longer live in tents year-round, though some do for part of the year. Others are farmers. In towns and cities, Kurds own shops, are professionals, and are employed in many different occupations.

Reliable population data for the Kurds in the Middle East do not exist, and estimates vary widely. About half of all Kurds—between 10 and 15 million—live in Turkey, where they constitute 20 percent, or perhaps more, of the total population. Approximately 6 million live in Iran, 4 to 5 million in Iraq, and 1.5 million in Syria. Others live in Armenia, Germany, France, and the United States.

The Kurds have attempted to establish an independent state for decades, with no success and often facing harsh treatment from government forces. In Turkey, the state used to refer to them as "Mountain Turks" and in many ways still refuses to recognize them as a legitimate minority group. Use of the Kurdish language is restricted in Turkey. The Kurds have faced similar repression in Iraq, especially following their support of Iran in the 1980–1988 Iran–Iraq war. Saddam Hussein razed villages and used chemical weapons against the Kurds. After the Persian Gulf War, 2 million Kurds fled to Iran. Many others have emigrated to Europe and the United States. Iraqi Kurds gained political autonomy from Baghdad in 1991 following a successful uprising aided by Western forces.

Many Kurds feel united by the shared goal of statehood, but several strong internal political factions and a guerrilla movement in Turkey also exist among the Kurds. Kurds in Turkey seek the right to have Kurdish-language schooling and television and radio broadcasts, and they would like to have their folklore recognized as well. The Kurds are fond of music and dancing, and Kurdish villages are known for their distinct performance styles.

Thanks to Diane E. King, University of Kentucky, for reviewing this material.

MAP 8.3 Kurdish Region in the Middle East. Kurdistan includes parts of Iran, Iraq, Syria, Turkey, and Armenia. About half of all Kurds live in Turkey.

(LEFT) Herding goats and sheep is a major part of the economy throughout Kurdistan.

(CENTER) In Dohuk, Iraq, the Mazi Supermarket and Dream City are a combination shopping center and amusement park. The goods in the market come mainly from Dubai and Turkey.

Migration to Puerto Rico also occurs, creating cultural diversity there. Migrants include returning Puerto Ricans and others from the United States, such as Dominicans and Cubans.

These migration streams—outgoing and incoming—pose a dual complication to the sense of Puerto Rico as constituting a nation. First, half of the "nation" lives outside the home territory. Second, within the home territory, ethnic homogeneity does not exist because of the diversity of people who migrate there. The Puerto Ricans who are return migrants are different from the islanders because many have adopted English as their primary language. All of these processes foster the emergence of a transnational identity, which differs from a national identity centered in either the United States or Puerto Rico. (Chapter 12 provides additional material on transnationalism.)

DEMOCRATIZATION

Democratization is the process of transformation from an authoritarian regime to a democratic regime. This process includes several features: the end of torture, the liberation of political prisoners, the lifting of censorship, and the toleration of some opposition (Pasquino 1996). In some cases, what is achieved is more a relaxation of authoritarianism than a true transition to democracy, which would occur when the authoritarian regime is no longer in control. Political parties emerge, some presenting traditional interests and others oppositional.

The transition to democracy appears to be most difficult when the change is from highly authoritarian socialist regimes. This pattern is partly explained by the fact that democratization implies a transition from a planned economy to one based on market capitalism (Lempert 1996). The spotty record of democratization efforts also has to do with the fact that many principles of democracy do not fit in with local political traditions that are based solely on kinship and patronage.

THE UNITED NATIONS AND INTERNATIONAL PEACEKEEPING

What role might cultural anthropology play in international peacekeeping? Robert Carneiro (1994) has a pessimistic response. Carneiro says that during the long history of human political evolution from bands to states, warfare has been the major means by which political units enlarged their power and domain. Foreseeing no logical end to this process, he predicts that war will follow war until superstates become ever larger and one mega-state is the final result. He considers the United Nations powerless in dealing with the principal obstacle to world peace: state sovereignty interests. Carneiro indicts the United Nations for its lack of coercive power and its record of having resolved disputes through military intervention in only a few cases.

If war is inevitable, little hope exists that anthropological knowledge can be applied to peacemaking efforts. Nonetheless,

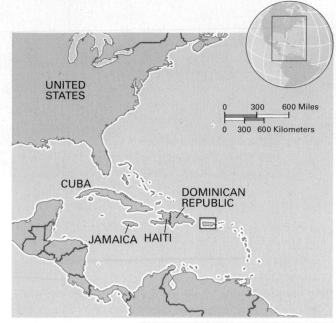

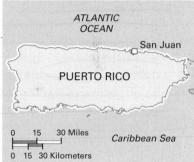

MAP 8.4   Puerto Rico.
The Commonwealth of Puerto Rico is a U.S. territory with commonwealth status. The indigenous population of the island, the Tainos, is extinct. Analysis of DNA of current inhabitants of Puerto Rico reveals a mixed ancestry, including the Taino, Spanish colonialists, and Africans who came to the island as slaves. The economy is based on agriculture, and sugarcane is the main crop. Tourism is also important, as are remittances. Official languages are Spanish and English. Roman Catholicism is the dominant religion, although Protestantism is increasing.

despite Carneiro's views, cultural anthropologists have shown that war is not a cultural universal and that some cultures solve disputes without resorting to war. The cultural anthropological perspective of critical cultural relativism (review this concept in Chapter 1) can provide useful background on issues of conflict and prompt a deeper dialogue between parties.

Two positive points emerge. The United Nations at least affords an arena for airing disputes. International peace organizations may thus play a role in world peace and order by providing a forum for analysis of the interrelationships among world problems and by exposing the causes and consequences of violence. Another positive direction is the role of NGOs and grassroots organizations in promoting local and global peacemaking through initiatives that bridge group interests.

the BIG questions REVISITED

◆ What does political anthropology cover?

Political anthropology is the study of power relationships in the public domain and how they vary and change cross-culturally. Political anthropologists study the concept of power itself and related concepts such as authority and influence. They have discovered differences and similarities between politics and political organization in small-scale and large-scale societies in leadership roles and responsibilities and in the distribution of power.

Foragers have a minimal form of political organization in the band. Band membership is flexible. If a band member has a serious disagreement with another person or spouse, one option is to leave that band and join another. Leadership in bands is informal. The tribe is a more formal type of political organization than the band. A tribe comprises several bands or lineage groups with a headman or headwoman as leader. Big-man and big-woman political systems are an expanded form of the tribe, and leaders have influence over people in several different villages. Chiefdoms may include several thousand people. Rank is inherited, and social divisions exist between members of the chiefly lineage and commoners.

The state is a centralized political unit encompassing many communities and possessing coercive power. States evolved in several locations with the emergence of intensive agriculture, increased surpluses, and increased population density. Most states are hierarchical and patriarchal.

◆ What is the scope of legal anthropology?

Legal anthropology encompasses the study of cultural variation in social order and social conflict. The more recent approach of critical legal anthropology points out how legal institutions often support and maintain social inequalities and injustice. Legal anthropologists also study the difference between norms and laws. Systems of social order and social control vary cross-culturally and over time.

Social control in small-scale societies seeks to restore order more than to punish offenders. The presence of a wide variety of legal specialists is more associated with the state than with small-scale societies, in which social shaming and shunning are common methods of punishment. In states, imprisonment and capital punishment may exist, reflecting the greater power of the state. Cross-cultural data on levels and forms of conflict and violence indicate that high levels of lethal violence are not universal and are more often associated with the state than with earlier forms of political organization. Social conflict ranges from face-to-face conflicts, such as those among neighbors or domestic partners, to larger group conflicts between ethnic groups and states. Solutions that would be effective at the interpersonal level often are not applicable to large-scale, impersonalized conflict.

Cultural anthropologists are turning their attention to studying global conflict and peace-keeping solutions. Key issues involve the role of cultural knowledge in dispute resolution and how international or local organizations can help achieve or maintain peace.

◆ How are political and legal systems changing?

The anthropological study of change in political and legal systems has documented several trends, many of which are related to the powerful influences of European colonialism and contemporary capitalist globalization. Postcolonial states struggle with internal ethnic divisions and pressures to democratize.

Ethnic politics has emerged within and across states as groups seek to compete for increased rights within the state or for separation from it. The Kurds are an example of an ethnic group fighting for political autonomy.

Cultural anthropologists are increasingly doing research on international topics, including the internal dynamics of international organizations such as the United Nations. Their work demonstrates the relevance of cultural anthropology in global peacekeeping and conflict resolution.

KEY CONCEPTS

authority, p. 168

band, p. 168

big-man or big-woman
    system, p. 169

chiefdom, p. 170

critical legal
    anthropology, p. 177

influence, p. 168

law, p. 175

moka, p. 170

nation, p. 181

norm, p. 175

policing, p. 176

political organization, p. 168

power, p. 168

social control, p. 175

state, p. 171

trial by ordeal, p. 176

tribe, p. 169

war, p. 179

SUGGESTED READINGS

Kimberley Coles. *Democratic Designs: International Intervention and Electoral Practices in Postwar Bosnia-Herzegovina.* Ann Arbor: University of Michigan Press, 2008. Coles provides an ethnographic analysis of the interaction between international humanitarian aid workers and the postwar political process by focusing on the electoral process.

Elizabeth F. Drexler. *Aceh, Indonesia: Securing the Insecure State.* Philadelphia: University of Pennsylvania Press, 2008. The author examines corruption, political violence, and the failure of international humanitarian interventions in the Indonesian province of Aceh.

Mona Etienne and Eleanor Leacock, eds. *Women and Colonization: Anthropological Perspectives.* New York: Praeger, 1980. This classic collection examines the impact of Western colonialism and missionary intervention on women of several indigenous groups of North America, South America, Africa, and the Pacific.

Magnus Fiskesjö. *The Thanksgiving Turkey Pardon, The Death of Teddy's Bear, and the Sovereign Exception of Guantánamo.* Chicago: Prickly Paradigm Press, 2003. This interpretation of the U.S. presidential ritual of "pardoning" a turkey every Thanksgiving sheds light on notions of the presidency and its power in the United States.

Thomas Gregor, ed. *A Natural History of Peace.* Nashville: University of Tennessee Press, 1996. This book contains essays on "what is peace?" reconciliation among nonhuman primates, the psychological bases of violent and nonviolent societies, case studies of Amazonia and American Indians, and international relations.

Susan F. Hirsch. *In the Moment of Greatest Calamity: Terrorism, Grief, and a Victim's Quest for Justice.* Princeton: Princeton University Press, 2006. The author's husband was killed in the 1998 bombing of the U.S. embassy in Kenya. In this book, Hirsch describes her experiences in Kenya in the aftermath of the bombing, her grief, and her witnessing of the bombing trials in Manhattan in 2001.

Beatriz Manz. *Paradise in Ashes: A Guatemalan Journey of Courage, Terror, and Hope.* Berkeley: University of California Press, 2004. Manz traces the lives and deaths of some Guatemalan Maya villagers who left their impoverished homeland in the mountains to build a new life in the lowlands. In their new location, they became victims of state-sponsored violence. Many were murdered, and others were forced to flee into the jungle. The survivors have returned to rebuild their homes and lives.

Bruce Miller. *The Problem of Justice: Tradition and Law in the Coast Salish World.* Lincoln: University of Nebraska Press, 2001. The author compares several legal systems operating in the Northwest Coast region from Washington state to British Columbia. The effects of colonialism differ from group to group. Some groups are strong and independent, whereas others are disintegrating.

Carolyn Nordstrom. *Shadows of War: Violence, Power, and International Profiteering in the Twenty-First Century.* Berkeley: University of California Press, 2004. Nordstrom did fieldwork in Sri Lanka and Mozambique to reveal the shadow economy that surrounds and supports war. She focuses on informal trading networks that involve goods ranging from guns to food and the people who profit from this economy.

Jennifer Schirmer. *The Guatemalan Military Project: A Violence Called Democracy.* Philadelphia: University of Pennsylvania Press, 1998. This book is an ethnography of the Guatemalan military, documenting its role in human rights violations through extensive interviews with military officers and trained torturers.

David Sneath. *The Headless State: Aristocratic Orders, Kinship Society, and Misrepresentations of Nomadic Inner Asia.* New York: Columbia University Press, 2008. The author describes how anthropologists since the nineteenth century have misrepresented Inner Asian nomadic political culture. His analysis continues through to the Soviet and post-Soviet periods and then offers a less essentialized interpretation.

9  **COMMUNICATION**

10 **RELIGION**

11 **EXPRESSIVE CULTURE**

ANTHROPOLOGY works

Brian Craik is a federal relations and environmental impact assessment anthropologist. "Working together" is his basic principle for achieving Native Peoples' rights in Canada. In his current position, Craik is the director of federal relations for the Grand Council of the Cree. The Cree, or Eeyou, number over 14,000. They live in the area of eastern James Bay and southern Hudson Bay in northern Québec, Canada.

Working for over 30 years as an applied anthropologist, Craik has combined his anthropological training with advocacy skills to assist the Cree in seeking social and environmental justice.

Craik is the first anthropologist in the world to become fluent in the Cree language (Preston 2006). After earning a doctorate in anthropology at McMaster University in the early 1970s, he began working as a consultant for various Cree communities.

In 1974, Craik joined Canada's Department of Indian Affairs and Northern Development. In that role, he helped to implement the James Bay and Northern Québec Agreement (JBNQA) that was signed in 1975. The JBNQA was a benchmark settlement related to land claims issues and compensation for damages. It awarded $225 million in compensation to the James Bay Cree and the Inuit of northern Québec, to be paid by Canada and Québec. The agreement defined Native rights to the land and laid out various protections to ensure the maintenance of those rights in the face of possible undesirable effects of commercial development. As part of this effort, Craik worked on the passage of the Cree/Naskapi (of Québec) Act, Canada's first Aboriginal local government act that helped protect the interests of Native Peoples.

In 1987, Craik left government work and returned to private consulting. In this role, he advised the James Bay Cree on relations with the federal government and on the environmental and social issues related to the Great Whale Project. Throughout the 1990s, Craik played a central role in reshaping several policy issues that affected the Cree, including leading the effort to halt the Great Whale River hydroelectric project.

The Cree have faced many threats to their culture and their environment since the arrival of the European colonizers. They formed the Grand Council of the Cree (sometimes the anglicized plural "Crees" is used) in response to the James Bay Hydroelectric Project (www.gcc.ca/gcc/fedrelations.php). Their political mobilization was inspired by the need to "stand in the way of development projects designed to serve others" (Craik 2004).

With Craik's assistance as a cultural broker, along with other factors, the Cree have developed political skills that enable them to resist external forces that seek to exploit their land and water to the benefit of outsiders and that will, if unchecked, continue to undermine, and indeed destroy, the Cree way of life. Cree now choose when to block a destructive project or when to work to change the terms of a project in order to reduce damage to their culture and gain financial benefits to promote Cree values and goals.

COMMUNICATION

9

the BIG questions

◆ How do humans communicate?

◆ How does communication relate to cultural diversity and inequality?

◆ How does language change?

OUTLINE

The Varieties of Human Communication

Lessons Applied: Anthropology and Public Understanding of the Language and Culture of People Who Are Deaf

Communication, Diversity, and Inequality

Language Change

Culturama: The Saami of Sápmi, or Lapland

Critical Thinking: Should Dying Languages Be Revived?

This chapter is about human communication and language, drawing on work in both linguistic anthropology and cultural anthropology. It looks at communication with a wide-angle lens to include topics from word choice to language extinction. The chapter first discusses how humans communicate and what distinguishes human communication from that of other animals. The second section offers examples of language, microcultures, and inequality. The third section discusses language change from its origins in the distant past to contemporary concerns about language loss.

◆◆◆
The Varieties of Human Communication

Humans can communicate with words, either spoken or signed, with gestures and other forms of body language such as clothing and hairstyle, and through methods such as telephone calls, postal mail, and e-mail.

LANGUAGE AND VERBAL COMMUNICATION

Most people are in almost constant communication—with other people, with supernaturals, or with pets. We communicate in face-to-face situations or indirectly through mail or e-mail. **Communication** is the process of sending and receiving messages. Among humans, it involves some form of **language**, a systematic set of symbols and signs with learned and shared meanings. Language may be spoken, hand-signed, written, or conveyed through body movements, body markings and modifications, hairstyle, dress, and accessories.

TWO FEATURES OF HUMAN LANGUAGE Over several centuries, scholars of language have proposed characteristics of human language that distinguish it from communication among other living beings. The following material describes the two most robust such characteristics.

First, human language has **productivity**, or the ability to create an infinite range of understandable expressions from a finite set of rules. This characteristic is a result of the rich variety of symbols and signs that humans use in their communication. In contrast, nonhuman primates have a more limited set of communicative resources. They rely on a **call system**, or a form of oral communication with a set repertoire of meaningful sounds generated in response to environmental factors. Nonhuman primates do not have the physiological capacity for speech that humans do. In captivity, however, some bonobos and chimpanzees have learned to communicate effectively with humans through sign language and by pointing to symbols on a chart. The world's most famous bonobo is, Kanzi, who lives at the Great Ape Trust in Des Moines, Iowa. He can understand much of what humans say to him, and he can respond by combining symbols on a printed board. He can also play simple video games, such as Ms. Pac-Man (http://www.greatapetrust.org).

Second, human language emphasizes the feature of **displacement**, the ability to refer to events and issues beyond the immediate present. The past and the future, in this view, are considered to be *displaced domains*. They include reference to people and events that may never exist at all, as in fantasy and fiction.

With respect to productivity and displacement in human language, the case of language among the Pirahã (pee-duh-hah) of Brazil raises many questions (Everett 2008) (see Map 9.1). Their language does not emphasize either productivity or displacement, though both exist to some

communication   the conveying of meaningful messages from one person or other living being to another.

language   a form of communication that is based on a systematic set of learned symbols and signs shared among a group and passed on from generation to generation.

productivity   a feature of human language whereby people are able to communicate a potentially infinite number of messages efficiently.

call system   a form of oral communication among nonhuman primates with a set repertoire of meaningful sounds generated in response to environmental factors.

displacement   a feature of human language whereby people are able to talk about events in the past and future.

phoneme   a sound that makes a difference for meaning in a spoken language.

Primatologist Sue Savage-Rumbaugh working with Kanzi, an adult male bonobo. Kanzi is involved in a long-term project about ape language. He has learned to use several symbols to communicate with researchers. Some chimpanzees, bonobos, orangutans, and gorillas are also able to communicate in American Sign Language and identify symbols on computer keyboards.

A Pirahã shelter. According to Daniel Everett, who has spent many years learning about their culture and language, the Pirahã do not lead a culturally deprived life. The Pirahã are content with their lifestyle, which includes leisure activities such as playing tag and other games. In spite of their wish to remain living as they are, their reservation is not secure from outside encroachment.

MAP 9.1 **Pirahã Reservation in Brazil.**
Linguistic anthropologist Daniel Everett helped to define the boundaries of the Pirahã reservation in the 1980s. With support from Cultural Survival and other sources, the demarcation was legally declared in 1994.

degree. The Pirahã are a group of about 350 foragers living on a reservation in the Amazonian rainforest near the Maici River. Their language contains only three pronouns, few words associated with time, no past-tense verbs, no color terms, and no numbers other than a word that translates into English roughly as "about one." The grammar is simple, with no subordinate clauses. Kinship terms are simple and few. The Pirahã have no myths or stories and no art other than necklaces and a few rudimentary stick figures. In spite of over 200 years of regular contact with Brazilians and neighboring Indians who speak a different language, the Pirahã remain monolingual.

Since 1977, linguist Daniel Everett has lived with the Pirahã and learned their language, so it is unlikely that he has overlooked major aspects of their language. He insists that their language is in no way "primitive" or inadequate. It has extremely complex verbs and rich and varied uses of stress and intonation, referred to in linguistics as *prosody*. The Pirahã especially enjoy verbal joking and teasing, both among themselves and with researchers.

FORMAL PROPERTIES OF VERBAL LANGUAGE Human language can be analyzed in terms of its formal properties: sounds, vocabulary, and syntax (sometimes called grammar), which are the formal building blocks of all languages. But languages differ widely in which sounds are important, what words are important in the vocabulary, and how people put words together to form meaningful sentences. Learning a new language usually involves learning different sets of sounds. The sounds that make a difference for meaning in a spoken language are called **phonemes**. The study of phonemes is called *phonetics*.

A native English-speaker learning to speak Hindi, the major language of North India, must learn to produce and recognize several new sounds. Four different "d" sounds exist. None is the same as an English "d," which is usually pronounced with the tongue placed on the ridge behind the upper front teeth (try it). One "d" in Hindi, which linguists refer to as a "dental" sound, is pronounced with the tongue pressed firmly behind the upper front teeth (try it) (see Figure 9.1). Next is a dental "d" that is also aspirated (pronounced "with air"); making this sound involves the tongue being in the same position as it is in making the dental "d," but now a puff of air is expelled (try it, and try the regular dental "d" again with no puff of air at all). Next is what is referred to as a "retroflex" sound, made by flipping the tongue back to the central dome of the roof of the mouth (try it, with no puff of air). Finally, there is the aspirated retroflex "d" with the tongue in the center of the roof of the mouth and a puff of air. Once you can do this, try the whole series again with a "t," because Hindi follows the same pattern with this letter as with the "d." Several other sounds in Hindi require careful use of aspiration and placement of the tongue for communicating the right word. A puff of air at the wrong time can produce a serious error, such as saying the word for "breast" when you want to say the word for "letter."

Every language has a vocabulary, or *lexicon*, which consists of all of the language's meaningful words. Speakers combine

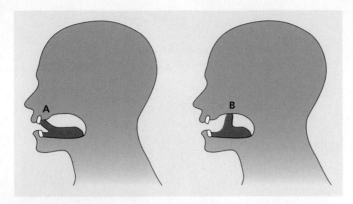

FIGURE 9.1 Dental and Retroflex Tongue Positions. When making a dental sound, the speaker places the tongue against the upper front teeth (position A in the diagram). When making a retroflex sound, the speaker places the tongue up against the roof of the mouth (position B in the diagram).

words into phrases and sentences to create meaning. *Semantics* refers to the study of the meaning of words, phrases, and sentences. Anthropologists add the concept of **ethnosemantics**, the study of the meaning of words, phrases, and sentences in particular cultural contexts. They find that languages classify the world in unpredictable ways, categorizing even such seemingly natural things as color and disease differently. (Recall the discussion of Subanun disease categories in Chapter 5.) Ethnosemantic research reveals much about how people define the world and their place in it, how they organize their social lives, and what is of value to them. *Focal vocabularies* are clusters of words that refer to important features of a particular culture. For example, many circumpolar languages have rich focal vocabularies related to snow (see Figure 9.2). In mountainous areas of Afghanistan, people use many terms for varieties of rocks.

Syntax, or grammar, consists of the patterns and rules by which words are organized to make sense in a sentence, or string. All languages have rules of syntax, although they vary in form. Even within the languages of contemporary Europe, syntactical variation exists. In German, for example, the verb often appears at the end of the sentence.

NONVERBAL LANGUAGE AND EMBODIED COMMUNICATION

Many forms of language and communication do not rely on verbal speech. Like verbal language, though, they are based on symbols and signs and have rules for their proper combination and meaning.

---

ethnosemantics the study of the meaning of words, phrases, and sentences in particular cultural contexts.

sign language a form of communication that uses mainly hand movements to convey messages.

SIGN LANGUAGE **Sign language** is a form of communication that uses mainly hand movements to convey messages. A sign language provides a fully competent communication system for its users, just as spoken language does (Baker 1999). Around the world, many varieties of sign language exist, including American Sign Language, British Sign Language, Japanese Sign Language, Russian Sign Language, and many varieties of indigenous Australian sign languages. Most sign languages are used by people who are hearing impaired as their main form of communication. But in many indigenous Australian communities, people who are able to communicate verbally often opt to use sign (Kendon 1988). They switch to sign language in situations in which verbal speech is forbidden or undesirable, for example, in some sacred contexts, for men during hunting, and for widows during mourning.

Although sign languages are complete and complex languages in their own right, they are often treated as second-class languages. A breakthrough in recognition of the validity and communicative competence of sign languages came in 1983 when the government of Sweden recognized Swedish Sign Language as a native language. Such recognition is especially important in contexts where a person's sense of identity, and even citizenship itself, is based on the ability to speak an officially accepted language. Anthropologists work with people who are deaf to help promote public understanding of the legitimacy of their language and to advocate for improved teaching of sign language (see Lessons Applied).

Gestures are movements, usually of the hands, that convey meanings. Some gestures may be universally meaningful, but most are culturally specific and often completely arbitrary. Some cultures have more highly developed gesture systems than others. Black urban youths in Pretoria and Johannesburg, South Africa, use a rich repertoire of gestures (Brookes 2004) (see Map 7.5, p. 158). Some of the gestures are widely

- Firm, even snow that falls in mild weather
- Thickly packed snow caused by intermittent freezing/thawing and high winds
- Hard-packed snow formed by strong wind
- Dry, large-grained, water-holding snow at the deepest layers, closest to the ground, found in late winter and spring
- Snow that forms a hard layer after rain
- Ice sheet on pastures formed by rain on open ground that freezes
- A layer of frozen snow between other snow layers that acts as an ice sheet

Source: Jernsletten 1997.

FIGURE 9.2 Kinds of "Snow" the Saami Recognize Related to Reindeer Herding

Ethnographic studies of the communication practices and wider culture of people who are deaf have great importance and practical application (Senghas and Monaghan 2002). This research demonstrates the limitations and inaccuracy of the *medical model* that construes deafness as a pathology or deficit and sees the goal as curing it. Instead, anthropologists propose the "cultural model," which views deafness simply as one possibility in the wide spectrum of cultural variation. In this view, a capital D is often used: Deaf culture.

Deafness in fact allows plenty of room for human agency. The strongest evidence of agency among people who are deaf is sign language itself, which exhibits adaptiveness, creativity, and change. This view helps to promote a nonvictim, nonpathological identity for people who are deaf and to reduce the social stigma often associated with deafness.

Anthropologists involved in Deaf culture studies are examining topics such as how people who are deaf become bilingual—for example, fluent in both English and Japanese sign languages. Their findings are being

In Uganda, James Mwadha, a deaf attendee at a meeting for Action on Disability and Development (ADD), signs to others in the group. ADD seeks to promote the rights of disabled people.

incorporated in improved ways of teaching sign language.

◆ **FOOD FOR THOUGHT**

- Choose five words and learn the signs for them in American Sign Language and in another culture's sign language. Are they the same or different, and how might one explain the similarity or difference?

---

used and recognized, but many vary by age, gender, and situation (see Figure 9.3). Men use more gestures than women do; the reason for this difference is not clear.

Greetings, an important part of communication in every known culture, often involve gestures (Duranti 1997b). They are typically among the first communicative routines that children learn, as do tourists and anyone trying to learn a foreign language. Greetings establish a social encounter. They usually involve both verbal and nonverbal language. Depending on the context and the social relationship, many variations exist for both the verbal and the nonverbal component. Contextual factors include the degree of formality or informality. Social factors include gender, ethnicity, class, and age.

SILENCE Silence is another form of nonverbal communication. Its use is often related to social status, but in unpredictable ways. In rural Siberia, an in-marrying daughter-in-law

has the lowest status in the household, and she rarely speaks (Humphrey 1978). In other contexts, silence is associated with power. For example, in U.S. courts lawyers speak more than anyone else and the judge speaks rarely but has more power than a lawyer, while the silent jury holds the most power (Lakoff 1990).

Silence is an important component of communication among many American Indian cultures. White outsiders, including social workers, have sometimes misinterpreted this

THINKING
OUTSIDE
THE BOX

Try to compose an English sentence with its main verb at the end.

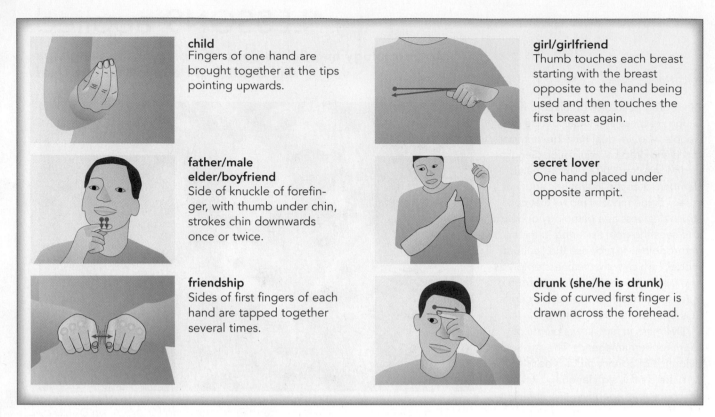

child
Fingers of one hand are brought together at the tips pointing upwards.

father/male elder/boyfriend
Side of knuckle of forefinger, with thumb under chin, strokes chin downwards once or twice.

friendship
Sides of first fingers of each hand are tapped together several times.

girl/girlfriend
Thumb touches each breast starting with the breast opposite to the hand being used and then touches the first breast again.

secret lover
One hand placed under opposite armpit.

drunk (she/he is drunk)
Side of curved first finger is drawn across the forehead.

FIGURE 9.3 Some South African Gestures Used by a Man

Source: From *A Repertoire of South African Quotable Gestures,* from *The Journal of Linguistic Anthropology,* Copyright © 2004 Blackwell Publishers Ltd. Reproduced with permission of Blackwell Publishers and the American Anthropological Association.

silence as a reflection of dignity or a lack of emotion or intelligence. How ethnocentric such judgments are is revealed by a study of silence among the Western Apache of Arizona (Basso 1972 [1970]) (see Map 9.2). The Western Apache use silence in four contexts:

- When meeting a stranger, especially at fairs, rodeos, or other public events. Speaking with a stranger immediately indicates interest in something such as money, work, or transportation, all possibly serving as reasons for exhibiting bad manners.

- In the early stages of courting. Sitting in silence and holding hands for several hours is appropriate. Speaking "too soon" would indicate sexual willingness or interest.

- When a parent and child meet after the child has been away at boarding school. They should be silent for about 15 minutes. It may be two or three days before sustained conversations are initiated.

- When "getting cussed out," especially at drinking parties.

An underlying similarity of all these contexts is the uncertainty, ambiguity, and unpredictability of the social relationships involved.

BODY LANGUAGE Human communication, in one way or another, often involves the body in sending and receiving messages. Beyond the mechanics of speaking, hearing, gesturing, and seeing, the body itself can function as a "text" that conveys messages. The full range of *body language* includes eye movements, posture, walking style, the way one stands and sits, cultural *inscriptions* on the body such as tattoos and hairstyles, and accessories such as dress, shoes, and jewelry. Body language follows patterns and rules just as verbal language does. As with verbal language, the rules and meanings are learned, often unconsciously. Without learning the rules and meanings, one will commit communication errors, which are sometimes funny and sometimes serious.

Different cultures emphasize different body language channels more than others. Some are more touch oriented than others, and some use facial expressions more. Eye contact is valued during Euro-American conversations, but in many Asian contexts direct eye contact is considered rude or perhaps a sexual invitation.

Clothing, hairstyles, and modification of or marks on the body convey messages about age, gender, sexual interest or availability, profession, wealth, and emotions. The color of one's clothing can send messages about a person's identity, class, gender, and more. In the United States, gender differentiation begins in the hospital nursery with the color coding of blue for boys and pink for girls. In parts of the Middle East, public dress is black for women and white for men.

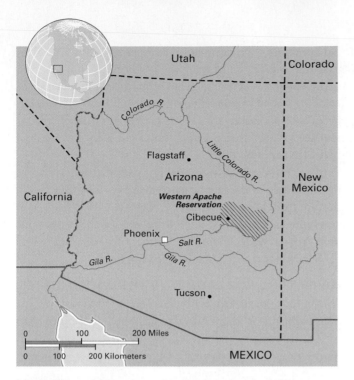

MAP 9.2 Western Apache Reservation in Arizona.
Before European colonialism, the Apache lived in a wide area extending from present-day Arizona to northwestern Texas. Originally foragers, they starting planting some food crops in the 1600s. After the arrival of the Spanish, the Apache gained horses from them and became skilled equestrian warriors. In the second half of the nineteenth century, the U.S. government was active in exterminating many Apache groups and forced those who survived to live on reservations in order to make way for White settlements.

Covering or not covering various parts of the body with clothing is another culturally coded matter. Consider the different meanings of head or face covering in Egypt and Kuwait (MacLeod 1992). Kuwaiti women's head covering distinguishes them as relatively wealthy, leisured, and honorable, as opposed to the immigrant women workers from Asia, who do not cover their heads. In contrast, the head covering in Egypt is done mainly by women from the lower and middle economic levels. For them, it is a way to accommodate conservative Islamic values while preserving their right to work outside the home. In Egypt, the head covering says, "I am a good Muslim and a good wife or daughter." In Kuwait, the headscarf says, "I am a wealthy Kuwaiti citizen." In many conservative Muslim contexts, it is important for a woman in public to cover more than her head by wearing a full-length loose garment. These rules, along with other patriarchal values, make it difficult for women in some Muslim contexts to participate in sports while in school and in public sporting events such as the international Olympics.

In Japan, the kimono provides an elaborate coding system signifying gender and life-cycle stage (Dalby 2001). The higher one's status, the shorter is the sleeve of one's kimono. Men's kimono sleeves come in one length: short. Unmarried

(TOP) Japanese businessmen meet each other, bow, and exchange business cards. Bowing is an important part of nonverbal communication in Japan. (BOTTOM) The *furisode* kimono is distinguished by its fine silk material, long sleeves, and elaborate colors and designs. A girl's 20th birthday gift is typically a furisode, marking her transition to young adulthood. Only unmarried women wear the furisode, so wearing one is a statement of marital availability. Fluttering the long, wide sleeves at a man is a way to express love for him.

▶ *What meanings do the styles and lengths of sleeves convey in your cultural world?*

A horse race at Ascot, England, attended by members of the elite.

▶ If you were going to the races at Ascot and wanted to be dressed properly, what should you wear?

women's sleeve length is nearly to the ground, whereas a married woman's sleeve is nearly as short as that of a man's.

COMMUNICATING WITH MEDIA AND INFORMATION TECHNOLOGY

Media anthropology is the cross-cultural study of communication through electronic media such as radio, television, film, recorded music, the Internet, and print media, including newspapers, magazines, and popular literature (Spitulnik 1993). Media anthropology is an important emerging area that links linguistic and cultural anthropology (Allen 1994). Media anthropologists study the media process and media content, the audience response, and the social effects of media presentations. **Critical media anthropology** asks to what degree access to media messages is liberating or controlling and whose interests the media serve. It is especially active in examining journalism, television, advertising, and new information technology, as the following examples illustrate.

THE POLITICS OF JOURNALISM Mark Pedelty studied war correspondents in El Salvador to learn about journalists and journalistic practices during war (1995) (see Map 12.4, p. 267). He found that the lives and identities of war correspondents are highly charged with violence and terror: "War correspondents have a unique relationship to terror . . .

that combines voyeurism and direct participation. . . . They need terror to . . . maintain their cultural identity as 'war correspondents'" (1995:2). The primary job of journalists, including war correspondents, is communication, but communication of a specific sort. They gather information that is time sensitive and often brutal. Their job is to provide brief stories for the public.

A critical media anthropology perspective reveals the important role of the news agency that pays their salary or, if they are freelancers or "stringers," that buys their story. War correspondents in El Salvador write a story about the same event differently, depending on whether they are sending it to a U.S. newspaper or a European newspaper.

ADVERTISING FOR LATINOS IN THE UNITED STATES
Within the U.S. advertising market, one of the most sought-after segments is the Latino population, also called "the

A satellite dish dominates the view of a village in Niger, West Africa. Throughout the world, the spread of electronic forms of communication have many and diverse social effects.

▶ Pretend you are a cultural anthropologist doing research on communication in this village. What do you want to study in order to assess the effects of satellite communication on the people and their culture?

---

critical media anthropology an approach within the cross-cultural study of media that examines how power interests shape people's access to media and influence the contents of its messages.

digital divide social inequality in access to new and emerging information technology, notably access to up-to-date computers, the Internet, and training related to their use.

Hispanic market" in the advertising industry (Dávila 2002). Interviews with staff of 16 Latino advertising agencies and content analysis of their advertisements reveal their approach of treating Latinos as a unified, culturally specific market. The dominant theme, or *trope*, is that of "the family" as being the most important feature of Latino culture, in contrast to the stereotype of the Anglo population as more individualistic. Recent milk-promotion advertisements for the Anglo population show a celebrity with a milk moustache. The Latino version shows a grandmother cooking a traditional milk-based dessert, and the caption reads, "Have you given your loved ones enough milk today?" (2002:270). In Spanish-language television and radio networks, a kind of "standard" Spanish is used, a generic form with no hint of regionalism or accent.

Latinos are, however, a highly heterogeneous population. By promoting a monolithic image of Latino culture, media messages may be contributing to identity change toward a more monolithic pattern. At the same time, they are certainly missing opportunities to tap into more specialized markets within the Latino population.

CROSSING THE DIGITAL DIVIDE IN RURAL HUNGARY

The term **digital divide** refers to social inequality in access to new and emerging information technology, especially access to up-to-date computers, the Internet, and training related to their use. Local attempts to overcome the digital divide between Hungary and countries in the European Union involve the development of the Hungarian Telecottage Association (HTA) (Wormald 2005) (see Map 9.3). The idea of the telecottage, which started in Sweden and Scotland, involves dedicating some space, such as an unused workshop or part of a house, for public use in which a computer with Internet access is provided.

The HTA, centered in Budapest, promotes village-based Internet access in order to improve the lives of rural people through enhanced communication. Most telecottages in Hungary are located in rural communities of fewer than 5000 people. The HTA website provides announcements about funding opportunities and relevant news. Although these innovations sound highly positive, interpersonal problems related to information hoarding by some managers and to who gets access first to information for posting on the website have emerged.

Like the Hungarian villagers, many marginalized people around the world, including indigenous people, women, and youth, realize the importance of having access to the Internet and to other information and communication technologies (ICTs). These technologies can help people preserve and learn their ancestral languages, record traditional agricultural and medical knowledge, and otherwise protect their culture and improve their lives (Lutz 2005, Turner 2002).

MAP 9.3   Hungary.
The Republic of Hungary has a population of around 10 million. The Roma population, variously estimated at between 450,000, and 600,000, has increased rapidly in recent years. Hungary's landscape is mainly plains with hills and low mountains to the north. One of the newest members of the European Union, Hungary has a growing economy. The main religion is Christianity, with Catholicism accounting for about half of the total; about 30 percent are atheists. Magyar, the Hungarian language, is one of the few European languages that does not belong to the Indo-European language family, but belongs instead to the Finno-Ugric family.

♦♦♦

Communication, Diversity, and Inequality

This section presents material about language, microcultures, and social inequality. It begins by presenting two models of the relationship between language and culture. Examples follow about class, gender and sexuality, "race" and ethnicity, and age.

LANGUAGE AND CULTURE: TWO THEORIES

During the twentieth century, two theoretical perspectives were influential in the study of the relationship between language and culture. They are presented here as two distinct

THINKING OUTSIDE THE BOX

Given Pedelty's findings, how "accurate" is the news as presented in mainstream media?

models, even though they actually overlap in real life and anthropologists tend to draw on both of them (Hill and Mannheim 1992).

The first was formulated by two early founding figures in linguistic anthropology, Edward Sapir and Benjamin Whorf. In the mid-twentieth century, they formulated an influential model called the **Sapir–Whorf hypothesis**, a perspective which says that people's language affects how they think. If a language has many words for variations of the English word "snow," for example, then someone who speaks that language can "think" about snow in more ways than someone can whose language has fewer "snow" terms. Among the Saami, whose traditional occupation was reindeer herding (see Culturama, p. 205), a rich set of terms exists for "snow" (review Figure 9.2, p. 192). If a language has no word for "snow," then someone who speaks that language cannot think of "snow." Thus, a language constitutes a *thought world,* and people who speak different languages inhabit different thought worlds. This catchy phrase became the basis for *linguistic determinism,* a theory stating that language determines consciousness of the world and behavior. Extreme linguistic determinism implies that the frames and definitions of a person's primary language are so strong that it is impossible to learn another language fully or, therefore, to understand another culture fully. Most anthropologists see value in the Sapir–Whorf hypothesis, but not in its extreme form.

A second approach to understanding the relationship between language and culture comes from scholars working in the area of **sociolinguistics**, a perspective that emphasizes how people's cultural and social context shapes their language and its meanings. Sociolinguists are, therefore, *cultural constructionists.*

Most anthropologists see some value in both perspectives since language, culture, context, and meaning are highly interactive: Language shapes culture and culture shapes language.

CRITICAL DISCOURSE ANALYSIS: GENDER AND "RACE"

Critical discourse analysis is an approach within linguistic anthropology that examines how power and social inequality are reflected in and reproduced through communication

---

Sapir–Whorf hypothesis   a perspective in linguistic anthropology which says that language determines thought.

sociolinguistics   a perspective in linguistic anthropology which says that culture, society, and a person's social position determine language.

critical discourse analysis   an approach within linguistic anthropology that examines how power and social inequality are reflected and reproduced in communication.

tag question   a question placed at the end of a sentence seeking affirmation.

(Blommaert and Bulcaen 2000). Critical discourse analysis reveals links between language and social inequality, power, and stigma. It also provides insights into agency and resistance through language. The material that follows presents examples of gender and racial power relations as played out through language.

GENDER IN EURO-AMERICAN CONVERSATIONS

Most languages contain gender differences in word choice, grammar, intonation, content, and style. Early studies of language and gender among white Euro-Americans revealed three general characteristics of female speech (Lakoff 1973):

- Politeness
- Rising intonation at the end of sentences
- Frequent use of **tag questions** (questions seeking affirmation and placed at the end of sentences, such as, "It's a nice day, *isn't it?*")

In English, male speech, in general, is less polite, maintains a flat and assertive tone in a sentence, and does not use tag questions. Related to politeness is the fact that, during cross-gender conversations, men tend to interrupt women more than women interrupt men.

Deborah Tannen's popular book *You Just Don't Understand* (1990) shows how differences in conversational styles between white Euro-American men and women lead to miscommunication. She says that "women speak and hear a language of connection and intimacy, whereas men speak and hear a language of status and independence" (1990:42). Although both men and women use *indirect response* (not really answering the question), their different motivations create different meanings embedded in their speech:

> **Michele:** What time is the concert?
> **Gary:** We have to be ready by seven-thirty. (1990:289)

Gary sees his role as one of protector in using an indirect response to Michele's question. He feels that he is simply "watching out for her" by getting to the real point of her question. Michele feels that Gary is withholding information by not answering her directly and is maintaining a power position. By contrast, a wife's indirect response to a question from her husband is prompted by her goal of being helpful in anticipating her husband's underlying interest:

> **Ned:** Are you just about finished?
> **Valerie:** Do you want to have supper now? (1990:289)

Cross-culturally, women's speech is not universally accommodating, subservient, and polite. In cultural contexts in which women's roles are prominent and valued, their language reflects and reinforces their position.

GENDER AND POLITENESS IN JAPANESE, AND THOSE NAUGHTY TEENAGE GIRLS   Gender registers in spoken Japanese reflect gender differences (Shibamoto 1987). Certain

	Male	Female
Box lunch	bentoo	obentoo
Money	kane	okane
Chopsticks	hasi	ohasi
Book	hon	ohon

Source: *Language, Gender, and Sex in Comparative Perspective*, by Susan U. Philips, Susan Steele, Chrisitne Tanz. Copyright © Cambridge University Press 1987. Reprinted with permission of Cambridge University Press.

FIGURE 9.4 Male-Unmarked and Female-Marked Nouns in Japanese

words and sentence structures convey femininity, humbleness, and politeness. One important contrast between male and female speech is the attachment, by female speakers, of the honorific prefix "o-" to nouns (see Figure 9.4). This addition gives women's speech a more refined and polite tone.

A contrasting pattern of gendered language comes from the *kogals*, young Japanese women between 14 and 22 years of age known for their female-centered coolness (Miller 2004). The kogals have distinctive language, clothing, hairstyles, makeup, attitude, and activities, all of which challenge prescriptive norms for young women. Their overall style is flashy and exuberant, combining global and local elements. Heavy users of cell phones, kogals use a complex and ever-changing set of *emoticons*, or "face characters" including icons for "wow," "ouch," "applause," and "I can't hear you." They have also invented a unique text message code for their cell phones that uses mixed scripts such as mathematical symbols and Cyrillic (Russian) letters.

The spoken language of the kogals is a rich and quickly changing mixture of slang, some classic but much newly created. They create new words through compounds and by adding the Japanese suffix "-ru," which turns a noun into a verb, such as *maku-ru* ("go to McDonald's"). They intentionally use strongly masculine language forms, openly talk about sex, and rework taboo sexual terms into new meanings. Reactions from mainstream society to kogals are mixed, ranging from horror to fascination. No matter what, they have cultural influence and are shaking up the gender order and language.

GAY LANGUAGE AND BELONGING IN INDONESIA

The national language of Indonesia is referred to as *bahasa Indonesia*. Many homosexual men in Indonesia speak *bahasa gay*, or "gay language" (Boellstorff 2004). Indonesia is the world's fourth-largest country in terms of population, with nearly 250 million citizens living on over 6,000 islands and speaking nearly 700 local languages. In spite of this cultural and linguistic diversity, bahasa gay is highly standardized.

Bahasa gay has a distinct vocabulary that plays humorously on mainstream language and provides a political commentary

A kogal in Tokyo's trendy Shibuyu district displays her cell phone that is covered with stickers. Her facial makeup and dress are characteristic of some, but not all, kogals. Various kogal makeup and dress styles, like their language, exist and keep changing.

on mainstream life. Some of the vocabulary changes involve sound-alikes; others add a suffix to a standard word. In terms of the state's strongly heterosexual image, Indonesian gays would seem to be a clearly excluded group. Nonetheless, bahasa gay is moving into mainstream linguistic culture, where it conveys agency and freedom from official control.

AFRICAN AMERICAN ENGLISH: PREJUDICE AND PRIDE

The topic of African American English (AAE), or African American Vernacular English (AAVE), is complicated by racism of the past and present (Jacobs-Huey 2006). Scholars debate whether AAE/AAVE is a language in its own right or a dialect (nonstandard version) of English. "Linguistic conservatives," who champion standard American Mainstream

THINKING
OUTSIDE
THE BOX

These broad generalizations about gender in Euro-American conversational styles do not apply to all situations. What are your microcultural rules?

English (AME), view AAE as an ungrammatical form of English that needs to be "corrected." In the current linguistic hierarchy in the United States, with AME at the top, speakers of AAE may be both proud of their language and feel stigmatized by those who judge AAE negatively and treat its speakers unfairly (Lanehart 1999).

African American English is a relatively new language, emerging out of slavery to develop a degree of standardization across the United States, along with many local variants. Some of its characteristic grammar results from its African roots. One of the most prominent is the use, or nonuse, of forms of the English verb "to be" (Lanehart 1999:217). In AAE, one says, "She married," which means "She is married" in AME. Viewed incorrectly by outsiders as "bad" English, "She married" follows a grammatical rule in AAE. That AME has its own grammar and usage rules is evident in the fact that when non-AME speakers attempt to speak it or imitate it, they often make mistakes (Jacobs-Huey 1997).

Ethnographic research on African American school-age children in a working-class neighborhood of southwest Philadelphia examined within-gender and cross-gender conversations, including *directives* (getting someone to do something), argument, he-said-she-said accusations, and storytelling (Goodwin 1990). All of these speech activities involve complex verbal strategies that are culturally embedded. In arguments, the children may bring in imaginary events as a "put-on," preceded by the cue term "psych," or use words of a song to create and maintain playfulness within an argument. Much of their arguments involve highly ritualized insults that work quickly to return an insult to the original giver. When a group of girls was practicing some dance steps and singing, a boy said, "You sound terrible." A girl responded, "We sound just like you look" (1990:183). The study revealed the importance of verbal play and art among the children. It also showed that girls often excel at verbal competitions in mixed gender settings.

Children who grow up speaking a version of AAE at home and with peer groups face a challenge in schools, where they are expected to perform in AME. Just like native Spanish speakers or any non–English-speaking new immigrants, African American children are implicitly expected to become bilingual in AAE and AME. More than vocabulary and grammar are involved. Teachers should understand that African American children may have culturally distinct styles of expression that should be recognized and valued. For example, in narrative style, African American children tend to use a spiral pattern, skipping around to different topics before addressing the theme, instead of adopting a linear style. Rather than being considered a deficiency, having AAE speakers in a classroom adds cultural diversity to those whose linguistic worlds are limited to AME.

Inspired by such findings, the Oakland School Board in California approved a resolution in 1996 to recognize *Ebonics*, or AAE, as the primary language, or vernacular, of African American students. The school developed a special teaching program, called the Bridge Program, in which AAE speakers were encouraged to learn Standard American English through a process of translation between AAE and SAE (Rickford 1997). After several months, students in the Bridge Program had progressed in their SAE reading ability much faster than African American students who were not in the program. Nevertheless, the program received so much negative publicity and raised such sensitive questions about the best way to enhance minority student learning that it was cancelled within the year.

The underlying issues of the so-called *Ebonics controversy* are still unresolved. One of the thorniest questions debated is whether AAE/AAVE/Ebonics is sufficiently distinct (either as a language separate from SAE or as a dialect) that U.S. schools should address it in their curriculum with special programs.

◆◆◆

Language Change

Languages, like the cultures of which they are a part, experience both continuity and change, and for similar reasons. Human creativity and contact lead to linguistic innovation and linguistic borrowing. War, imperialism, genocide, and other disasters may destroy languages. This section looks first at what is known about the origins of human language and provides a brief history of writing. Later parts discuss the influence of European colonialism on languages, nationalism and language, world languages, and contemporary language loss and revitalization.

THE ORIGINS AND HISTORY OF LANGUAGE

No one knows how verbal language began. Current evidence of other aspects of human cultural evolution suggests that verbal language began to develop between 100,000 and 50,000 years ago when early modern humans achieved both the physical and mental capacity for symbolic thinking and verbal communication. Facial expressions, gestures, and body postures were likely important features of early human communication, as they are among many nonhuman primate species today.

Early scholars of language were often misled by ethnocentric assumptions that the structure of European languages

---

historical linguistics the study of language change using formal methods that compare shifts over time and across space in aspects of language, such as phonetics, syntax, and semantics.

language family a group of languages descended from a parent language.

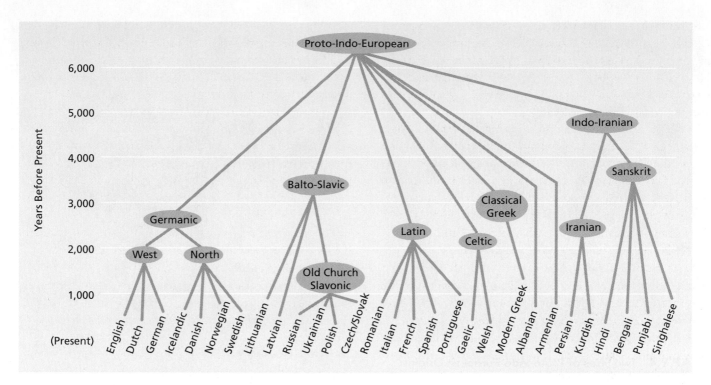

FIGURE 9.5 The Indo-European Language Family

was normative and that languages with different structures were less developed and deficient. For example, they considered the Chinese language primitive because it lacks the kinds of verbs that European languages have. As discussed at the beginning of this chapter, the Pirahã language appears simpler in many ways compared with English, as does the Pirahã culture, but both Pirahã and English have to be examined within their cultural contexts. Pirahã is a language that works for a rainforest foraging population. English works for a globalizing, technology-driven, consumerist culture. Languages of foraging cultures today can, with caution, provide insights about what foragers' language may have been like thousands of years ago. But they are not "frozen in time" examples of "Stone Age" language.

HISTORICAL LINGUISTICS

Historical linguistics is the study of language change through history. It relies on many specialized methods that compare shifts over time and across space in aspects of language such as phonetics, syntax, and meaning. It originated in the eighteenth century with a discovery made by Sir William Jones, a British colonial administrator working in India. During his spare time, he studied Sanskrit, a classical language of India. He noticed marked similarities among Sanskrit, Greek, and Latin in vocabulary and syntax. For example, the Sanskrit word for "father" is *pitr;* in Greek it is *patéras,* and in Latin it is *pater.* This was an astounding discovery for the time, given the prevailing European mentality that placed its cultural heritage firmly in the classical Graeco–Roman world

and depicted the "Orient" as completely separate from "Europe" (Bernal 1987).

Following Jones's discovery, other scholars began comparing lists of words and grammatical forms in different languages: for example, the French *père,* the German *Vater,* the Italian *padre,* the Old English *faeder,* the Old Norse *fadhir,* and the Swedish *far.* These lists allowed scholars to determine degrees of closeness and distance in the relationships among those languages. Later scholars contributed the concept of a **language family**, or groups of languages descended from a parent language (see Figure 9.5). Individual languages descended from the same language, such as French and Spanish (both descended from Latin), are referred to as *sister languages.*

Using comparative evidence from historical and contemporary Eurasian languages, historical linguists developed a hypothetical model of the original parent language, or *proto-language,* of most Eurasian languages. It is called *Proto-Indo-European (PIE).* Linguistic evidence suggests that PIE was located in Eurasia, either north or south of the Black Sea (see Map 9.4). From its area of origin, between 6000 and 8000 years ago, PIE spread into Europe, then into Central, South, and East Asia, where local versions developed over the centuries.

THINKING OUTSIDE THE BOX

Should AAE be suppressed in U.S. public schools in favor of promoting SAE? What are the pros and cons of a mono-language approach in education?

MAP 9.4 Two Sites of Proto-Indo-European Origins.
Two major theories about the location of PIE exist, with the site south of the Black Sea considered to be earlier.

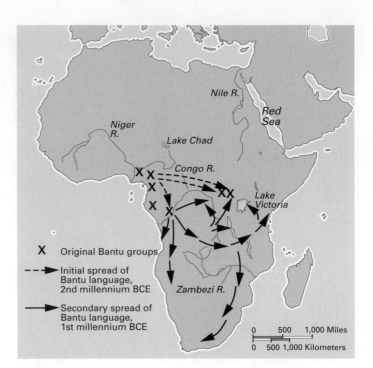

MAP 9.5 The Bantu Migrations in Africa.
Linguistic evidence for the migrations of Bantu-speaking people relies on similarities between languages in parts of eastern, central, and southern Africa and languages of the original Bantu homeland in West Africa. Over 600 African languages are derived from Proto-Bantu.

Similar linguistic methods reveal the existence of the original parent form of the Bantu language family, *Proto-Bantu* (Afolayan 2000). Scholars can trace the *Bantu expansion* in Africa starting around 5000 years ago (see Map 9.5). Today, some form of Bantu language is spoken by over 100 million people in Africa, not to mention the number of people in the African diaspora worldwide. Over 600 African languages are derived from Proto-Bantu. According to linguistic analysis, the homeland of Proto-Bantu is the present-day countries of Cameroon and Nigeria, West Africa. It is likely that Proto-Bantu spread through population migration as the farming population expanded and moved, over hundreds of years, into areas occupied by indigenous foragers. Bantu cultural imperialism may have wiped out some local languages, although it is impossible to document any such extinctions. Substantial linguistic evidence, however, suggests some interactions between the farmers and the foragers through which standard Bantu absorbed elements from local languages.

WRITING SYSTEMS

Evidence of the earliest written languages comes from Mesopotamia, Egypt, and China. The oldest writing system was in use in the fourth millennium BCE in Mesopotamia (Postgate et al. 1995). All early writing systems used **logographs**, signs that indicate a word, syllable, or sound. Over time, some logographs retained their original meaning; others were kept but given more abstract meaning, and nonlogographic symbols were added (see Figure 9.6).

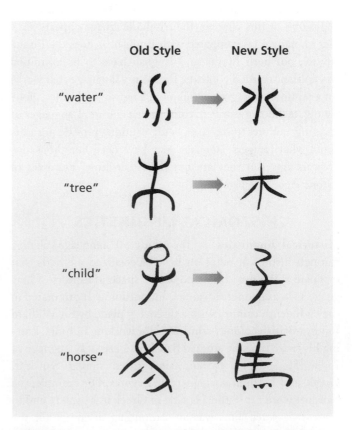

FIGURE 9.6 Logographic and Current Writing Styles in China

The emergence of writing is associated with the development of the state. Some scholars take writing as a key diagnostic feature that distinguishes the state from nonstate political forms because recordkeeping was such an essential task of the state. The Inca empire, centered in the Peruvian Andes, is a notable exception to this generalization. It used **khipu** (kee-poo), or cords of knotted strings of different colors, for keeping accounts and recording events. Scholars are not quite sure how khipu worked in the past because the Inca coding system is so complicated. Debates are ongoing as to whether khipu served as an actual language or more simply as an accounting system. Whatever is the answer, the world's largest empire in the fourteenth century relied on khipu.

Two interpretations of the function of early writing systems exist. The first says that early writing was mainly for ceremonial purposes. Evidence for this position consists of the prevalence of early writing on tombs, bone inscriptions, and temple carvings. The second says that early writing was mainly for secular use in government recordkeeping and trade. The archaeological record is biased toward durable substances, such as stone. Because ceremonial writing was intended to last, it was more likely to be inscribed on stone. Utilitarian writing, in contrast, was more likely to have been done on perishable materials because people would be less concerned with permanence. (Consider the way you treat shopping lists.) It is likely, however, that more utilitarian writing, as well as other forms of nonceremonial writing, also existed.

The scripts of much of South and Southeast Asia originated in the Aramaic system of the Middle East (Kuipers and McDermott 1996). The Aramaic system spread eastward to India, where it took on new forms, and then continued to move into much of Southeast Asia, including Indonesia and the Philippines, but excluding Vietnam. The functions of the scripts vary from context to context. Writing for recordkeeping and taxation exists but is subordinate to, and carries less status than, writing for communication with the spirits,

French colonialism added another cultural layer to Arabic influences in Morocco, resulting in many bilingual and trilingual shop signs.

▶ *Where have you seen multilingualism in public use? What languages were used and why?*

writing to record medical knowledge, and writing love poetry. Writing love poetry is exalted and esteemed, and is sometimes done in secret. Some love songs in the Philippine highlands have strict rules regulating such matters as how many syllables may be used per line. All adolescents want to learn the rules of writing love poetry and to be able to write it well.

COLONIALISM, NATIONALISM, AND GLOBALIZATION

European colonialism was a major force of language change. Not only did colonial powers declare their own language as the language of government, business, and education, but they often took direct steps to suppress indigenous languages and literatures. Widespread *bilingualism,* or competence in a language other than one's birth language, is one prominent effect of colonialism. Also, globalization is having substantial and complex effects on language.

EUROPEAN COLONIALISM AND CONTACT LANGUAGES
Beginning in the fifteenth century, European colonialism had dramatic effects on the people with whom it came into contact, as discussed elsewhere in this book. Language change is an important part of the story of colonialism and indigenous cultures. Depending on the type and duration of contact, it

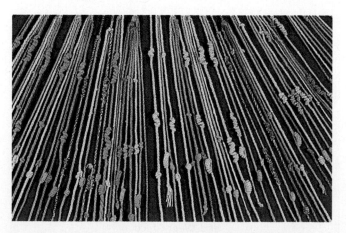

Khipu, or knotted strings, were the basis of state-level accounting in the Incan empire. The knots conveyed substantial information to those who could interpret their meaning.

---

logograph a symbol that conveys meaning through a form or picture resembling that to which it refers.

khipu cords of knotted strings used during the Inca empire for keeping accounts and recording events.

resulted in the development of new languages, the decline of others, and the extinction of many, along with the people who spoke them (Silverstein 1997). Two forms of new languages prompted by European colonialism are pidgins and creoles.

A **pidgin** is a language that blends elements of at least two parent languages and that emerges when two different cultures with different languages come in contact and must communicate (Baptista 2005). All speakers of pidgin have their own native language(s) but learn to speak pidgin as a second, rudimentary language. Pidgins are typically limited to specific functional domains, such as trade and basic social interactions. Many pidgins of the Western Hemisphere were the result of the Atlantic slave trade and plantation slavery. Owners needed to communicate with their slaves, and slaves from various parts of Africa needed to communicate with each other.

A pidgin often evolves into a **creole**, which is a language descended from a pidgin and which subsequently has its own native speakers, a richer vocabulary than a pidgin has, and a more developed grammar. Throughout the Western Hemisphere, many localized creoles have developed in areas such as Louisiana, Haiti, Ecuador, and Suriname. Though a living reminder of the heritage of slavery, Creole languages and associated literature and music are also evidence of resilience and creativity in the African diaspora.

Pidgins are common throughout the South Pacific. Tok Pisin, the pidgin language of Papua New Guinea, consists of a mixture of English, Samoan, Chinese, and Malayan. Tok Pisin (the indigenous pronunciation of "talk pidgin") is now a creole language and is recognized as one of the official languages of Papua New Guinea.

NATIONALISM AND LINGUISTIC ASSIMILATION

Nationalist policies of cultural assimilation of minorities have led to the suppression and loss of local dialects and the extinction of many indigenous and minority languages throughout the world. Direct policies of linguistic assimilation include the declaration of a standard language and rules about the language of instruction in public schools. Often, Christian missionaries worked to suppress indigenous languages as part of their attempts to "civilize" "pagan" peoples (see Culturama, p. 205). Indirect mechanisms include discrimination in hiring on the basis of language and social stigma.

---

pidgin   a contact language that blends elements of at least two languages and that emerges when people with different languages need to communicate.

creole   a language directly descended from a pidgin but possessing its own native speakers and involving linguistic expansion and elaboration.

global language   a language spoken widely throughout the world and in diverse cultural contexts, often replacing indigenous languages.

GLOBAL LANGUAGES   Ninety-six percent of the world's population speaks 4 percent of the world's languages (Crystal 2000). The eight most-spoken languages are Mandarin, Spanish, English, Bengali, Hindi, Portuguese, Russian, and Japanese, in that order. Languages that are gaining widespread currency are called **global languages**, or *world languages*. Global languages are spoken worldwide in diverse cultural contexts. As they spread to areas and cultures beyond their home area and culture, they take on new, localized identities. At the same time, the "mother language" picks up words and phrases from local languages (see Figure 9.7). Global languages may act as both a form of linguistic and economic opportunity and a form of cultural imperialism.

English is the most globalized language in history (Bhatt 2001, Crystal 2003). British English was first transplanted through colonial expansion to the present-day United States, Canada, Australia, New Zealand, South Asia, Africa, Hong Kong, and the Caribbean. English was the dominant language

Alcohol	Arabic, Middle East
Avocado	Nahuatl, Mexico/Central America
Banana	Mandingo, West Africa
Bogus	Hausa, West Africa
Candy	Arabic, Middle East
Caucus	Algonquin, Virginia/Delaware, North America
Chimpanzee	Bantu, West and Central Africa
Chocolate	Aztec Nahuatl, Mexico/Central America
Dungaree	Hindi, North India, South Asia
Gong	Malaysia, Southeast Asia
Hammock	Arawakan, South America
Hip/hep	Wolof, West Africa
Hurricane	Taino, Caribbean
Lime	Inca Quechua, South America
Moose	Algonquin, Virginia/Delaware, North America
Panda	Nepali, South Asia
Savannah	Taino, Caribbean
Shampoo	Hindi, North India, South Asia
Sugar	Sanskrit, South Asia
Tepee	Sioux, Dakotas, North America
Thug	Hindi, North India, South Asia
Tobacco	Arawak, South America
Tomato	Nahuatl, Mexico/Central America
Tundra	Saami, Lapland, Northern Europe
Tycoon	Japanese
Typhoon	Mandarin Chinese, East Asia
Zombie	Congo and Angola, Central and West Africa

FIGURE 9.7   Loan Words in North American English

CULTURAMA

The Saami of Sápmi, or Lapland

The Saami (SAH-mee) are indigenous people who live in the northernmost parts of Norway, Sweden, Finland, and western Russia (Gaski 1993). The area is called Sápmi, the land of the Saami, or Lapland. The total Saami population is around 100,000 people, with the majority in Norway (Magga and Skutnabb-Kangas 2001).

At the time of the earliest written records of 1000 years ago, all Saami hunted wild reindeer, among other land and sea species, and may have kept some tamed reindeer for transport (Paine 2004). Over time, herding domesticated reindeer developed and became the economic mainstay. In the past few hundred years, though, reindeer pastoralism has declined and is now a specialization of about 10 percent of the population. Settled Saami are farmers or work in trade, small-scale industry, handicrafts, services, and the professions.

Traditional Saami reindeer herding has been a family-based system. Men and women cared for the herd, and sons and daughters inherited the rights to the herd equally (Paine 2004). The value of social equality was strong, entailing both rights and privileges.

In their relationships with the modern state, the Saami have experienced discrimination, exclusion, loss of territorial rights, and cultural and linguistic repression. Environmental risks to Saami cultural survival include having been downwind of the prevailing winds after the 1986 Chernobyl disaster, having been near the earlier Soviet atomic testing grounds in Siberia, having had their ancestral territory and sacred spaces lost or damaged by hydroelectric dam construction, and having had grazing lands taken over for use as military training grounds (Anderson 2004).

State policies of cultural assimilation and forced Christianization in the twentieth century marginalized the Saami language and led to language loss (Magga and Skutnabb-Kangas 2001). Several Saami languages and dialects still exist, however, and spatially distant versions are mutually unintelligible (Gaski 1993:116).

Language is of central cultural value to the Saami, and efforts to maintain it have been under way since the 1960s. Besides the Saami language, a traditional song form, the *yoik*, is of particular importance (Anderson 2005). Yoik lyrics allow a subtle system of double meanings that can camouflage political content (Gaski 1997).

Thanks to Myrdene Anderson, Purdue University, for reviewing this material.

(LEFT) The well-known Saami singer–songwriter Marie Boine performs at the Easter Festival in Kautokeino, Sápmi, northern Norway.
(CENTER) A Saami herder with his reindeer in Kautokeino, the northernmost municipality in Norway and the first municipality to be given a Saami name.

MAP 9.6 The Saami of Sápmi, or Lapland. Sápmi spreads across Norway, Sweden, Finland, and Russia's Kola Peninsula.

CRITICAL thinking

Should Dying Languages Be Revived?

The Western media often carry articles about endangered biological species, such as certain frogs or birds, and the need to protect them from extinction. The reasons for concern about the loss of biological species are many. One major factor is simply that biological diversity is a good thing to have on the earth. Opponents of taking special measures to protect endangered species find support for their position in a Darwinian view that progress involves competition and the survival of those species which can make it. Economic progress might mean building a new shopping center or airport with a massive parking lot. If that means the extinction of a particular species of nonhuman primate, bird, flower, or worm, so be it, in the name of "progress."

Some parallels exist between the survival of endangered languages and that of endangered biological species (Maffi 2005). Supporters of language preservation and revitalization can point to the sheer fact of diversity on earth as a good thing, a sign of a culturally healthy planet with room for everyone's language. They will argue that a people's language is an intrinsic part of their culture. Without language, the culture, too, will die.

Others take the Darwinian view that languages, like species, live in a world of competition. Language survival means that the strong and fit carry on while the weak and unfit die out. They may point out that preserving linguistic heritage is useless because dying languages are part of a past that no longer exists. They resist spending public funds on language preservation and regard revitalization programs as wasteful.

◆ CRITICAL THINKING QUESTIONS

- Have you read or heard of an endangered biological species in the media recently? What was the species?
- Have you read or heard of an endangered language in the media lately? What was the language?
- Where do you stand on biological species preservation and on language preservation, and why?

---

in the colonies, used in government and commerce and taught in schools. Over time, regional and subregional varieties of English developed, often leading to a "New English" that a native speaker from England cannot understand at all. So many varieties of English now exist that scholars are beginning to talk of the *English language family*, which includes American English, "Spanglish," "Japlish," and "Tex-Mex."

ENDANGERED LANGUAGES AND LANGUAGE REVITALIZATION

The emergence of linguistic anthropology, as mentioned in Chapter 1, was prompted by the need to document disappearing indigenous languages in the United States. Today, anthropologists and other scholars, as well as descendant language communities themselves, are still concerned about the rapid loss of languages (Fishman 1991, Maffi 2005). The

task of documenting declining languages is urgent. It is often accompanied by applied work aimed at preserving and reviving endangered and dying languages (see Critical Thinking).

Scholars have proposed ways to assess degrees of language loss or decline (Walsh 2005). **Language shift**, or *language decay*, is a category of language decline describing what happens when speakers have a limited vocabulary in their native language and more often use a new language in which they may be semifluent or fluent (Hill 2001). An intermediary stage, **language endangerment**, is judged to exist when a language has fewer than 10,000 speakers. Near-extinction is a situation in which only a few elderly speakers are still living. **Language extinction**, or language death, occurs when the language has no competent speakers (Crystal 2000:11).

Keeping track of endangered and dying languages is difficult because no one is sure how many languages have existed in the recent past or even how many exist now (Crystal 2000). Estimates of the number of living languages today range between 5000 and 7000. Part of the explanation for the fuzzy numbers is the problem in separating languages from dialects. The largest number of languages of any world region is found on the island of New Guinea, which comprises the country of Papua New Guinea and the Indonesian territory of West Papua, and several neighboring small islands (Foley 2000). Over 1000 languages exist in this area, many from completely separate language families.

Language extinction is especially acute in the Australia–Pacific region, where 99.5 percent of the indigenous languages

---

language shift condition of a language in which speakers adopt a new language for most situations, begin to use their native language only in certain contexts, and may be only semifluent and have limited vocabulary in their native language.

language endangerment the condition of a language when it has fewer than 10,000 speakers.

language extinction the condition of a language in which speakers abandon it in favor of a new language to the extent that the native language loses functions and no longer has competent speakers.

Indigenous language dictionaries and usage guides are increasingly available on the Web and help indigenous peoples, such as these Australian boys, preserve their cultures.

▶ *Check out The Internet Guide to Australian Languages.*

have fewer than 100,000 speakers (Nettle and Romaine 2000:40). The situation of indigenous languages in the Americas, Siberia, Africa, and South and Southeast Asia is becoming increasingly serious. Over half of the world's languages have fewer than 10,000 speakers, and one-fourth have fewer than 1000 speakers.

Efforts to revive or maintain local languages face many challenges (Fishman 2001). Political opposition may come from governments that fear local identity movements. Governments are often averse to devoting financial resources to supporting minority language programs. Deciding which version of an endangered language to preserve may have political consequences at the local level (Nevins 2004). Notable achievements have been made, however, with perhaps one of the most robust examples of language maintenance occurring in French-speaking Québec.

Approaches to language maintenance and revitalization must respond to local circumstances and to factors such as how serious the degree of loss is, how many living speakers there are, what version of the language should be maintained or revived, and what resources for maintenance and revitalization programs are available. Major strategies include the following (Walsh 2005):

- Formal classroom instruction
- A master–apprentice system in which an elder teaches a nonspeaker in a one-on-one situation
- Web-based tools and services to support language learning

Each method has both promise and pitfalls. One thing is key: It takes living communities to activate and keep alive the knowledge of a language (Maffi 2003).

9

the BIG questions REVISITED

◆ How do humans communicate?

Human communication is the sending of meaningful messages through language. Language is a systematic set of symbols and signs with learned and shared meanings. It may be spoken, hand-signed, written, or conveyed through body movements, marking, or accessories.

Human language has two characteristics that distinguish it from communicative systems of other living beings: productivity, or the ability to create an infinite number of novel and understandable messages; and displacement, the ability to communicate about the past, the future, and imaginary things.

Language consists of basic sounds, vocabulary, and syntax. Cross-culturally, languages vary substantially in the details of all three features.

Humans use many forms of nonverbal language to communicate with each other. Sign language is a form of communication that uses mainly hand movements to communicate. Silence is a form of nonverbal communication with its own cultural values and meaning. Body language includes body movements and body placement in relation to other people, body modifications such as tattoos and piercing, dress, hairstyles, and odors.

Media anthropology sheds light on how culture shapes media messages and on the social dynamics that play out in media institutions. Critical media anthropology examines the power relations involved in the media.

◆ How does communication relate to cultural diversity and inequality?

The Sapir–Whorf hypothesis emphasizes how language shapes culture. A competing model, called sociolinguistics, emphasizes how one's culture and one's position in it shape language. Each position has merit, and many anthropologists draw on both models.

Critical discourse analysis studies how communication through language can serve the interests of the powerful, maintaining or even increasing social inequality. Although language can reinforce and expand social exclusion, it can also empower oppressed people, depending on the context. In mainstream North America, women's speech is generally more polite and accommodating than that of men. In Japan, gender codes emphasize politeness in women's speech, but some young Japanese women, the kogals, are creating a new linguistic style of resistance. Gay language in Indonesia is entering the mainstream as an expression of freedom from official control. African American English (AAE), in the view of many experts, has evolved into a standard language with local variants.

◆ How does language change?

The exact origins of human verbal language are not known. Historical linguistics and its discovery of language families provide insights about early human history and settlement patterns. The emergence of writing can be traced to around 6000 years ago, with the emergence of the state in Mesopotamia. Scripts have spread widely throughout the world, with the Aramaic system the basis of scripts in South and Southeast Asia. The functions of writing vary from context to context. In some situations official recordkeeping predominates, whereas in others writing is important for courtship.

The recent history of language change has been influenced by the colonialism of past centuries and by Western globalization in the current era. Nationalist policies of cultural integration often involve the repression of minority languages and the promotion of a standard language. Colonial contact created the context for the emergence of pidgin languages, many of which evolved into creoles. Western globalization supports the spread of English and the development of localized variants.

In the past 500 years, colonialism and globalization have resulted in the extinction of many indigenous and minority languages. Many others are in danger of dying. Applied linguistic anthropologists seek to preserve the world's linguistic diversity. They document languages and participate in designing programs for teaching dead and dying languages. A key element in language revitalization and survival is having communities use the language.

KEY CONCEPTS

call system, p. 190

communication, p. 190

creole, p. 204

critical discourse
analysis, p. 198

critical media anthropology,
p. 196

digital divide, p. 197

displacement, p. 190

ethnosemantics, p. 192

global language, p. 204

historical linguistics, p. 201

khipu, p. 203

language, p. 190

language endangerment,
p. 207

language extinction, p. 207

language family, p. 201

language shift, p. 206

logograph, p. 202

phoneme, p. 191

pidgin, p. 204

productivity, p. 190

Sapir–Whorf
hypothesis, p. 198

sign language, p. 192

sociolinguistics, p. 198

tag question, p. 198

SUGGESTED READINGS

Keith H. Basso, *Wisdom Sits in Places: Landscape and Language among the Western Apache.* Albuquerque: University of New Mexico Press, 1996. Fieldwork on the Fort Apache Indian Reservation, Arizona, reveals the importance of natural places in people's everyday life, thought, and language.

Thomas F. Carter, *The Quality of Home Runs: The Passion, Politics, and Language of Cuban Baseball.* Durham, NC: Duke University Press, 2009. This ethnography shows how men's talk about baseball in Cuba communicates masculinity, class, and national identity.

David Crystal, *English as a Global Language,* 2nd ed. New York: Cambridge University Press, 2003. This book discusses the history, current status, and future of English as a world language. It covers the role of English in international relations, the media, international travel, education, and "New Englishes."

Joshua A. Fishman, ed. *Can Threatened Languages Be Saved?* Buffalo: Multilingual Matters Ltd., 2001. Seventeen case studies examine language shift, language loss, and the attempts to reverse such changes.

Marjorie H. Goodwin. *He-Said-She-Said: Talk as Social Organization among Black Children.* Bloomington: Indiana University Press, 1990. A study of everyday talk among children of an urban African American community in the United States, this book shows how children construct social relationships among themselves through verbal interactions, including disputes, pretend play, and stories.

Niloofar Haeri, *Sacred Language, Ordinary People: Dilemmas of Culture and Politics in Egypt.* New York: Palgrave Macmillan, 2003. Classical Arabic is the official language of all Arab states and the language of the Qur'an, but no Arabs speak it as their mother tongue. This book uses research in Cairo to show how the state maintains its identity in people's everyday lives.

Lanita Jacobs-Huey. *From the Kitchen to the Parlor: Language and Becoming in African-American Women's Hair Care.* New York: Oxford University Press, 2006. Jacobs-Huey combines childhood experiences as the daughter of a cosmetologist with multisited fieldwork in the United States and England. She finds a complex world that is centered on hair and that relates to race, gender, religion, body esthetics, health, and verbal language.

William L. Leap. *Word's Out: Gay Men's English.* Minneapolis: University of Minnesota Press, 1996. Fieldwork among gay men in the Washington, DC, area produced this ethnography. It addresses gay men's speech as a cooperative mode of discourse, examines bathroom graffiti, and looks at discourse about HIV/AIDS.

Julie Lindquist. *A Place to Stand: Politics and Persuasion in a Working-Class Bar.* New York: Oxford University Press, 2002. The author did participant observation while working as a bartender in a White, working-class bar in the U.S. Midwest. The book is an ethnography of speaking in which the bar is a site of cultural performance related to White, working-class identity.

Karen Nakamura. *Deaf in Japan: Signing and the Politics of Identity.* Ithaca, NY: Cornell University Press, 2007. This book combines archival and ethnographic data to help understand ideas about modernity and Westernization.

Lisa Philips Valentine. *Making It Their Own: Ojibwe Communicative Practices.* Toronto: University of Toronto Press, 1995. This ethnography examines speech events in a small Ojibwe community in northern Ontario, Canada. It considers speech variations among speakers and examines code switching, multilingualism, and church music.

A San forager and ancient rock paintings in the Tsodilo hill region of northwestern Botswana. The hills have long been sacred to the San as the abode of the deceased and important spirits and deities. The area contains over 4,500 rock paintings. Tsodilo is a World Heritage Site that attracts many tourists and provides employment to San people as guides and sellers of crafts.

RELIGION

10

OUTLINE

Religion in Comparative Perspective

Eye on the Environment: Eagle Protection, National Parks, and the Preservation of Hopi Culture

World Religions and Local Variations

Everyday Anthropology: Tattoos and Sacred Power

Culturama: Hui Muslims of Xi'an, China

Directions of Religious Change

the BIG questions

◆ What is religion and what are the basic features of religions?

◆ How do world religions illustrate globalization and localization?

◆ What are some important aspects of religious change in contemporary times?

While studying the religious life of people of rural Greece, anthropologist Loring Danforth observed rituals in which participants walk across several yards of burning coals (1989). They do not get burned, they say, because their faith in a saint protects them. Back in the United States, Danforth met an American who regularly walks on fire as part of his New Age faith and who organizes training workshops for people who want to learn how to do it. Danforth himself walked on fire in a ceremony in rural Maine.

Not every anthropologist who studies religion undertakes such challenges, but they all share an interest in questions about humanity's understanding of the supernatural realm and relationships with it: Why do some religions have many gods and others just one? Why do some religions practice sacrifice? Why do some religions have more participation by women? How do religions respond to changing conditions in the political economy?

Religion has been a cornerstone topic in cultural anthropology since the beginnings of the discipline. The early focus, in the nineteenth century, was on religions of indigenous peoples living in places far from Europe. Now anthropologists also study the religions of state-level societies and the effects of globalization on religious change.

◆◆◆

Religion in Comparative Perspective

This section sets the stage for the chapter by discussing basic topics in the anthropology of religion, including how to define religion, theories about the origin of religion, and types of religious beliefs, rituals, and religious specialists.

WHAT IS RELIGION?

Since the earliest days of anthropology, scholars have proposed various definitions of religion. In the late 1800s, British anthropologist Sir Edward Tylor defined religion as the belief in spirits. A more comprehensive, current definition says that **religion** consists of beliefs and behavior related to supernatural beings and forces. This definition specifically avoids linking religion with belief in a supreme deity, because some religions have no concept of a supreme deity whereas others have multiple deities.

Religion is related to, but not the same as, a people's *worldview,* or way of understanding how the world came to

Christian fire walkers in northern Greece walking on hot coals. They reaffirm God's protection by not getting burned.
▶ *If you have a religious faith, are pain or other physical discomforts involved in any of the rituals?*

be, its design, and their place in it. Worldview is a broader concept and does not include the criterion of concern with a supernatural realm. An atheist has a worldview, but does not have a religion.

MAGIC VERSUS RELIGION Sir Edward Tylor wrote that magic, religion, and science are alike in that they are different ways in which people have tried to explain the physical world and events in it (1871). He considered science to be the superior, most rational of the three. Sir James Frazer, writing not long after Tylor, defined **magic** as people's attempt to compel supernatural forces and beings to act in certain ways (1978 [1890]). He contrasted magic with religion, which he said is the attempt to please supernatural forces or beings. Frazer differentiated two general principles of magic:

- *The law of similarity,* the basis of *imitative magic,* is founded on the assumption that if person or item X is like person or item Y, then actions done to person or item X will affect person or item Y. A familiar example is a voodoo doll. If someone sticks pins into a doll X that represents person Y, then person Y will experience pain or suffering.

- *The law of contagion,* the basis of *contagious magic,* says that persons or things once in contact with a person can still have an effect on that person. Common items for working contagious magic include a person's hair trimmings, nail clippings, teeth, saliva, blood, and fecal matter, as well as the placenta of a baby. In cultures where contagious magic is practiced, people are careful about disposing of their personal wastes so that no one else can get hold of them.

religion   beliefs and behavior related to supernatural beings and forces.

magic   the attempt to compel supernatural forces and beings to act in certain ways.

myth   a narrative with a plot that involves the supernaturals.

doctrine   direct and formalized statements about religious beliefs.

Tylor, Frazer, and other early anthropologists supported an evolutionary model (review Chapter 1), with magic preceding religion. They evaluated magic as being less spiritual and ethical than religion and therefore more "primitive." They assumed that, in time, magic would be completely replaced by the "higher" system of religion, which would eventually be replaced by science as the most rational way of thinking. They would be surprised to see the widespread presence of magical religions in the modern world, such as the so-called Wicca, or Neo-Pagan, religion that centers on respect for the Earth, nature, and the seasonal cycle. The pentacle is an important Wicca symbol (see Figure 10.1). As of 2007, the U.S. Department of Veterans Affairs added the pentacle to its list of approved religious symbols that can be placed on the headstones of the graves of deceased veterans and their family members.

Many people turn to magical behavior in situations of uncertainty. Magic, for example, is prominent in sports (Gmelch 1997 [1971]). Some baseball players in the United States repeat actions or use charms, including a special shirt or hat, to help them win. This practice is based on the assumption that if it worked before, it may work again. In baseball, pitching and hitting involve more uncertainty than fielding, and pitchers and hitters are more likely to use magic. Magical practices are also common in farming, fishing, the military, and love.

VARIETIES OF RELIGIOUS BELIEFS

Religions comprise beliefs and behavior. Scholars of religion generally address belief systems first because they appear to inform patterns of religious behavior. Religious beliefs are shared by a group, sometimes by millions of people, and are

Religion provides an important source of social cohesion and psychological support for many immigrant groups, whose places of worship attract both worshippers and cultural anthropologists interested in learning how religion fits into migrants' adaptation. This is a scene at a Lao Buddhist temple in Virginia.

▶ *Learn about Buddhism in North America from the Internet.*

FIGURE 10.1 A Pentacle. Sometimes called a pentagram, it is a five-pointed star surrounded by a circle. An important symbol in Neo-Pagan and Wiccan religions, the pentacle is also a magical tool used for summoning energies and commanding spirits.

passed on through the generations. Elders teach children through songs and narratives, artists paint the stories on rocks and walls, and sculptors create images in wood and stone that depict aspects of religious belief.

HOW BELIEFS ARE EXPRESSED Beliefs are expressed and transferred over the generations in two main forms:

- **Myth**, stories about supernatural forces or beings
- **Doctrine**, direct statements about religious beliefs

A myth is a narrative that has a plot with a beginning, middle, and end. The plot may involve recurrent motifs, the smallest units of narrative. Myths convey messages about supernatural forces or beings (or, simply, supernaturals) indirectly, through the story itself, rather than by using logic or formal argument. Greek and Roman myths, such as the stories of Zeus, Athena, Orpheus, and Persephone, are world famous. Some people would say that the Bible is a collection of myths; others would object to that categorization as suggesting that the stories are not "real" or "sacred." Myths have long been part of people's oral tradition, and many are still unwritten.

eye on the ENVIRONMENT

Eagle Protection, National Parks, and the Preservation of Hopi Culture

For many generations, young men of the Hopi tribe have searched each spring for golden eaglets in the cliffs of Arizona's Wupatki National Park and other parts of northeastern Arizona (Fenstemaker 2007). They bring the young eagles to the reservation and care for them until the summer, when, as mature birds, they are smothered in a ceremony that the Hopi believe frees the spirits of the birds, which convey messages to their ancestors who reside in the spiritual world. This ceremony is the most important Hopi ritual, but the tribe uses golden eagle feathers in all its rituals. For the Hopi, golden eagles are their link to the spiritual world, and their ritual use is essential to the continuity of Hopi culture.

In 1783, the U.S. Continental Congress adopted the bald eagle as the national symbol of the newly independent country. By 1940, numbers of bald eagles had dropped so low that the U.S. Congress passed the Bald Eagle Protection Act to preserve the species that had become established

as the symbol of American ideals of freedom. In 1962, Congress amended the act to include golden eagles, because the young of the two species are nearly indistinguishable.

In 1994, President Clinton promoted some official accommodation to Hopi beliefs about golden eagles. His administration established a repository for golden eagle feathers and other remains in Colorado. The demand is, however, higher than the supply.

The Hopi have a permit for an annual take of 40 golden eagles in northeastern Arizona, but they are excluded from Wupatki because of its status as a national park. The United States policy toward national parks follows the *Yellowstone model*, which aims to preserve the physical environment and species but excludes indigenous peoples and their cultures. This model has been applied widely throughout the world to the detriment of peoples who have long successfully lived in regions that are now off limits to them for hunting, fishing, and gathering.

In addition, many of these lands are sacred to them, but they are prevented from using them in traditional ways for the sake of "conservation" as defined by the government.

Anthropologists and others support environmental and species preservation, but not to the exclusion of heritage populations and cultures. They suggest that a case-by-case approach should be followed in considering exemptions to national laws. With regard to the golden eagles of Arizona, they point out that golden eagles are abundant and the Hopi requests for the spring take are small and present no threat to the survival of the species.

Environmentalists are concerned, however, that granting exemptions will establish dangerous precedents that will, over time, destroy pristine environments and precious species. Other environmentalists counter that more eagles are killed every year by airplanes or contact with electrical wires, or they die from eating prey that contains lead bullets.

Anthropologists ask why myths exist. Malinowski said that a myth is a *charter* for society in that it expresses core beliefs and teaches morality (1948). The French anthropologist Claude Lévi-Strauss, arguably the most famous mythologist, saw myths as functional in a philosophical and psychological way (1967). In his view, myths help people deal with the deep conceptual contradictions between, for example, life and death or good and evil, by providing stories in which these dualities find a solution in a mediating third factor. These mythological solutions are buried within a variety of surface details in the myth. For example, many myths of the Pueblo Indians of the U.S. Southwest juxtapose grass-eating animals (vegetarians) with predators (carnivores). The mediating third character is the raven, who is a carnivore but, unlike other creatures, does not have to kill to eat meat because it is a scavenger.

A cultural materialist perspective, also functionalist, says that myths store and transmit information related to making a living and managing economic crises (Sobel and Bettles 2000). Analysis of 28 myths of the Klamath and Modoc Indians (see Map 10.1) reveals that a consistent theme is uncertainty about the availability of food. Other prominent themes are

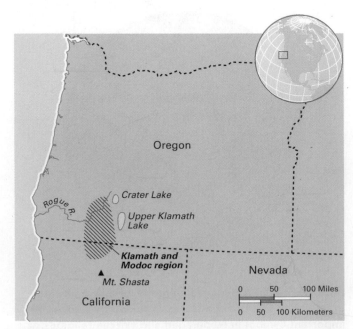

MAP 10.1 Klamath and Modoc Region in Oregon and California.

A Kachina doll. Among the Hopi, the word "Kachina" (kuh-CHEE-nuh) refers to a spirit or "life-bringer." Uncles carve Kachina dolls for their nieces to help them learn about the many spirits that exist in the Hopi religion. Kachina dolls, especially older ones, are highly sought after by non-Indians who collect Indian artifacts.

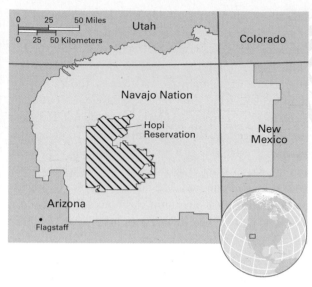

MAP 10.2 **Hopi Reservation in Arizona.**
The Hopi and Navajo tribes once shared the area known as Big Mountain. U.S. Acts of Congress in 1974 and 1996 divided the area into two reservations, leaving the Hopi completely surrounded by the much larger Navajo reservation. About 7000 people live on the Hopi Reservation.

In contrast to the Yellowstone model, anthropologists advocate for a *parks and people approach*, which builds on community-based conservation that does not exclude heritage populations from continuing to enjoy the economic and religious benefits of their territory while also sharing with the wider population.

◆ **FOOD FOR THOUGHT**

- Consider how you would feel if you were told that you could no longer practice the most important annual ritual in your religion but that other people could have a touristic experience at the place where you would normally practice the ritual. For secular students, consider a secular ritual; for example, watching the Super Bowl.

how to cope with hunger, food storage, resource diversification, resource conservation, spatial mobility, reciprocity, and supernatural forces. Thus, myths are repositories of knowledge related to economic survival and environmental conservation.

Doctrine, the other major form in which beliefs are expressed, explicitly defines the supernaturals, the world and how it came to be, and people's roles in relation to the supernaturals and to other humans. Doctrine is written and formal. It is close to law because it links incorrect beliefs and behaviors with punishments. Doctrine is associated with institutionalized, large-scale religions rather than small-scale "folk" religions.

Doctrine, however, can and does change (Bowen 1998). Over the centuries, various popes have pronounced new doctrine for the Catholic Church. A papal declaration of 1854, made with the intent of reinvigorating European Catholicism, bestowed authenticity on the concept of the Immaculate Conception, an idea with substantial popular support.

Muslim doctrine is expressed in the Qur'an, the basic holy text of the Islamic faith, which consists of revelations made to the prophet Muhammad in the seventh century and of collections of Muhammad's statements and deeds. In Kuala Lumpur, Malaysia (see Map 6.3, p. 132), a small group of highly educated women called the Sisters in Islam regularly debate with members of the local *ulama*, religious authorities who are responsible for interpreting Islamic doctrine, especially concerning families, education, and commercial affairs (Ong 1995). Debates concern such issues as polygamy, divorce, women's work roles, and women's clothing.

BELIEFS ABOUT SUPERNATURAL FORCES AND BEINGS Supernaturals range from impersonal forces to those who look just like humans. Supernaturals can be supreme and all-powerful creators or smaller-scale, annoying spirits that take up residence in people through possession.

The term **animatism** refers to a belief system in which the supernatural is conceived of as an impersonal power. An important example is *mana*, a concept widespread throughout the South Pacific region, including Melanesia, Polynesia, and Micronesia. Mana is a force outside nature that works

---

animatism a belief system in which the supernatural is conceived of as an impersonal power.

automatically; it is neither spirit nor deity. It manifests itself in objects and people and is associated with personal status and power, because some people accumulate more of it than others.

Some supernaturals are *zoomorphic*, deities in the shape, or partial shape, of animals. No satisfactory theory has appeared to explain why some religions develop zoomorphic deities and for what purposes, and why others do not. Religions of classical Greece and Rome and ancient and contemporary Hinduism are especially rich in zoomorphic supernaturals. *Anthropomorphic* supernaturals, deities in the form of humans, are common but not universal. The human tendency to perceive of supernaturals in their own form was noted 2500 years ago by the Greek philosopher Xenophanes, who lived sometime between 570 and 470 BCE. He said,

> But if horses or oxen, or lions had hands and could draw with their hands and accomplish such works as men, horses would draw the figures of their gods as similar to horses and the oxen as similar to oxen, and they would make the bodies of the sort which each of them had. (Lesher 2001:25)

The question, though, of why some religions have anthropomorphic deities and others do not remains unanswered.

Anthropomorphic supernaturals, like humans, can be moved by praise, flattery, and gifts. They have emotions. They get annoyed if neglected. They can be loving and caring, or they can be distant and nonresponsive. Most anthropomorphic supernaturals are adults, though some are children. Supernaturals tend to have similar marital and sexual relationships as the humans who worship them do. Divine marriages are heterosexual, and in some societies male gods have multiple wives. Although many supernaturals have children, grandchildren are not prominent. In *pantheons* (collectivities of deities), a division of labor reflects specializations in human society. There may be deities of forests, rivers, the sky, wind and rain, agriculture, childbirth, disease, warfare, and marital happiness. The supernaturals have political roles and hierarchies. High gods, such as Jupiter and Juno of classical Roman religion, are all-powerful, with a range of less powerful deities and spirits below them.

In some cultures, deceased ancestors can be supernaturals. Many African, Asian, and American Indian religions have a cult of the ancestors in which the living must do certain things to please the dead ancestors and may also ask for their help in time of need (see Eye on the Environment, p. 214). In contemporary Japan, ancestor worship is the principal religious activity of many families. Three national holidays recognize the importance of ancestors: the annual summer visit of the dead to their homes and the visits by the living to graves during the two equinoxes.

BELIEFS ABOUT SACRED SPACE Beliefs about sacred space probably exist in all religions, but such beliefs are more prominent in some religions than others. Sacred spaces, such as rock formations or rapids in a river, may or may not be permanently marked (Bradley 2000). Among the Saami (see

Uluru, Kata Tjuta National Park, Australia. Located roughly in the center of Australia in the Northern Territory and 280 miles south of Alice Springs, Uluru is an Aboriginal sacred site and a World Heritage Site. Tourists often want to make the arduous climb to the top, although the Anangu people who are the custodians urge people to consider other ways to enjoy the region.

Culturama in Chapter 9, p. 205), traditional religious beliefs were closely tied to sacred natural sites (Mulk 1994). The sites, often unmarked, included rock formations resembling humans, animals, or birds. The Saami sacrificed fish and other animals at these sites until strong pressures from Christian missionaries forced them to repress their practices and beliefs. Many Saami today know where the sacred sites are, but they will not reveal them to outsiders.

Another important form of sacred space that has no permanent mark occurs in a domestic ritual conducted by Muslim women throughout the world. The ritual is called the *khatam quran* (khuh-tum kuh-rahn), the "sealing" or reading of the holy book of the Qur'an (Werbner 1988). Among Pakistani migrants living in the city of Manchester, northern England (see Map 10.3), this ritual involves a gathering of women who read the Qur'an and then share a ritual meal. The reason for gathering is to give thanks or seek divine blessing. During the ritual, the otherwise nonsacred space of the house becomes sacred. A "portable" ritual such as this one is especially helpful in the adaptation of migrants to their new contexts, because it can be conducted without a formally consecrated ritual space. All that is required is a place, a supportive group of kin and friends, and the Qur'an.

Religions of the Aboriginal people of Australia are closely tied to sacred space. During a mythological past called the Dreamtime, the ancestors walked the earth and marked out the territory belonging to a particular group. People's knowledge of where the ancestors roamed is secret. In several cases that have recently been brought to the courts, Aboriginal peoples have claimed title to land that is being sought by commercial developers. Some anthropologists have provided expert testimony

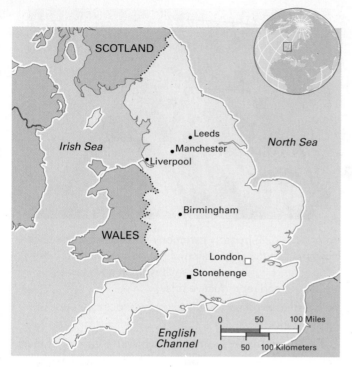

MAP 10.3 England.

England is the largest in area and the most populous of the constituent countries of the United Kingdom. Its population of 50 million accounts for 84 percent of the total. DNA analysis reveals that a majority of the English are of Germanic descent, as is their language. The terrain is mainly rolling hills, with some mountains in the north and east. London is by far the largest city, with Manchester and Birmingham competing for second place. English is the dominant language, with its diverse regional accents. Many other languages brought into the country by immigrant communities are spoken as first languages, including several South Asian languages, Polish, Greek, and Cantonese. An estimated 250,000 people speak British Sign Language. Although the Church of England is the state religion, everyone in England has the right to religious freedom.

documenting the validity of the Aboriginal claims to their sacred space. In one such case, secret Aboriginal knowledge about a sacred place and its associated beliefs was gender specific: The place belonged to women, and its location could not be told to men (Bell 1998). The anthropologist who was hired to support the women's claims was a woman, so the women could tell her about the sacred places, but she could not convey that knowledge in court to the male judge, a situation that demanded considerable ingenuity on the part of the anthropological consultant.

RITUAL PRACTICES

A **ritual** is patterned, repetitive behavior focused on the supernatural realm. Such *sacred rituals* are the enactment of beliefs expressed in myth and doctrine, for example, the Christian ritual of communion. Sacred rituals are distinct from *secular rituals*, such as a sorority or fraternity initiation, which has no connection to the supernatural realm. Some ritual events combine sacred and secular elements. The U.S. holiday of Thanksgiving originated as a Christian sacred meal with the primary purpose of giving thanks to God for the survival of the pilgrims (Siskind 1992). Its original Christian meaning is not maintained by everyone who celebrates the holiday today. Secular features of the holiday, such as watching football, may be of greater importance than the ritual aspect of thanking God for plentiful food.

Anthropologists categorize sacred rituals in many ways. One division is based on their timing. Regularly performed rituals are called *periodic rituals*. Many periodic rituals are performed annually to mark a seasonal milestone such as planting or harvesting or to commemorate some important event. For example, Buddha's Day, an important periodic ritual in Buddhism, commemorates the birth, enlightenment, and death of the Buddha (all on one day). On this day, Buddhists gather at monasteries, hear sermons about the Buddha, and perform rituals such as pouring water over images of the Buddha. Calendrical events, such as the shortest day of the year, the longest day, the new moon, and the full moon, often shape ritual cycles. *Nonperiodic rituals*, in contrast, occur irregularly, at unpredictable times, in response to unscheduled events, such as a drought or flood, or to mark events in a person's life, such as illness, infertility, birth, marriage, or death. The following material presents highlights of various types of ritual.

LIFE-CYCLE RITUALS A **life-cycle ritual**, or rite of passage, marks a change in status from one life stage to another of an individual or group. Victor Turner's (1969) fieldwork among the Ndembu (en-dem-boo), horticulturalists of northwestern Zambia, provides insights into the phases of life-cycle rituals. Turner found that, among the Ndembu and cross-culturally, life-cycle rituals have three phases: separation, transition, and reintegration.

- In the first phase, the initiate (the person undergoing the ritual) is separated physically, socially, or symbolically from normal life. Special dress may mark the separation. In many cultures of the Amazon and in East and West Africa, adolescents are secluded for several years in separate huts or areas away from the village.

- The transition, or *liminal*, phase, is when the person is no longer in the previous status but is not yet a member of the next stage. *Liminality* often involves the learning of specialized skills that will equip the person for the new status.

- Reintegration, the last stage, occurs when the initiate emerges and is welcomed by the community as an individual occupying the new status.

ritual patterned behavior that has to do with the supernatural realm.

life-cycle ritual a ritual that marks a change in status from one life stage to another; also called *rite of passage*.

Differences in the cross-cultural distribution of puberty rituals for boys and girls reflect the economic value and status of males and females (review Chapter 4). Most societies have some form of puberty ceremony for boys, but puberty ceremonies for girls are less common. In societies where female labor is important and valued, girls have elaborate, and sometimes painful, puberty rites (Brown 1978). Where their labor is not important, menarche is unmarked and there is no puberty ceremony. Puberty rites function to socialize future members of the labor force, among other things. For example, among the Bemba of northern Zambia, during her initiation a girl learns to distinguish 40 kinds of mushrooms and to know which are edible and which are poisonous.

PILGRIMAGE Pilgrimage is round-trip travel to a sacred place or places for purposes of religious devotion or ritual. Prominent pilgrimage places are Varanasi (var-uh-nuh-see) in India (formerly called Banaras or Benares) for Hindus; Mecca in Saudi Arabia for Muslims; Bodh Gaya in India for Buddhists; Jerusalem in Israel for Jews, Christians, and Muslims; and Lourdes in France for Christians. Pilgrimage often involves hardship, with the implication that the more suffering that is involved, the more merit the pilgrim accumulates. Compared with a weekly trip to church or synagogue, pilgrimage removes a person further from everyday life, is more demanding, and therefore is potentially more transformative.

Victor Turner applied the three sequences of life-cycle rituals to pilgrimage: The pilgrim first separates from everyday life, then enters the liminal stage during the actual pilgrimage, and finally returns to be reintegrated into society in a transformed state (1969). A person who has gone on a pilgrimage often gains enhanced public status as well as spiritual benefits.

RITUALS OF INVERSION In a **ritual of inversion**, normal social roles and relations are temporarily inverted. A functionalist perspective says that these rituals allow for social pressure to be released. They also provide a reminder about the propriety of normal, everyday roles and practices to which people must return once the ritual is over.

---

pilgrimage   round-trip travel to a sacred place or places for purposes of religious devotion or ritual.

ritual of inversion   a ritual in which normal social roles and order are temporarily reversed.

sacrifice   a ritual in which something is offered to the supernaturals.

priest/priestess   a male or female full-time religious specialist whose position is based mainly on abilities gained through formal training.

world religion   a term coined in the nineteenth century to refer to a religion that is based on written sources, has many followers, is regionally widespread, and is concerned with salvation.

An Apache girl's puberty ceremony. Cross-cultural research indicates that the celebration of girls' puberty is more likely to occur in cultures in which adult women have valued productive and reproductive roles.

▶ *How does this theory apply to your microcultural experience?*

Carnival (or *carnaval* in Portuguese) is a ritual of inversion with roots in the northern Mediterranean region. It is celebrated widely throughout southern Europe and the Western Hemisphere. Carnival is a period of riotous celebration before the Christian fast of Lent. It begins at different times in different places, but always ends on Mardi Gras (or Shrove Tuesday), the day before the fasting period of Lent begins. The word *carnival*, from Latin, means "flesh farewell," referring to the fact that believers give up eating meat during Lent.

In Bosa, a town in Sardegna (Sardinia), Italy (see Map 12.6, p. 273), carnival involves social-role reversal and the relaxing of usual social norms. Discotheques extend their hours, mothers allow their daughters to stay out late, and men and women flirt with each other in public in ways that are forbidden during the rest of the year (Counihan 1985). Carnival in Bosa has three major phases. The first is impromptu street theater and masquerades that take place over several weeks, usually on Sundays. The skits are social critiques of current events and local happenings. In the masquerades, men dress up as exaggerated women:

> Young boys thrust their padded breasts forward with their hands while brassily hiking up their skirts to reveal their thighs. . . . A youth stuffs his shirt front with melons and holds them proudly out. . . . The high school gym teacher dresses as a nun and lifts up his habit to reveal suggestive red underwear. Two men wearing nothing but bikinis, wigs, and high heels feign a stripper's dance on a table top. (1985:15)

The second phase occurs on the morning of Mardi Gras, when hundreds of Bosans, mostly men, dress in black, like widows, and flood the streets. They accost passersby, shaking in their faces dolls and other objects that are maimed in some way or bloodied. They shriek at the top of their lungs as if mourning, and they say, "Give us milk, milk for our babies. . . . They are dying, they are neglected, their mothers have been gallivanting since St. Anthony's Day and have abandoned their poor children" (1985:16).

The third phase, called Giolzi, takes place during the evening. Men and women dress in white, wearing sheets for cloaks and pillowcases for hoods. They blacken their faces. Rushing into the street, they hold hands and chant the word "*Giolzi*." They storm at people, pretending to search their bodies for Giolzi and then say, "Got it!" It is not clear what Giolzi is, but whatever it is, it represents something that makes everyone happy.

How does a cultural anthropologist interpret these events? Carnival allows people for a short time to act out roles that are normally denied them. It is also a time when everyone has fun. In this way, rituals of inversion may function as a mechanism for maintaining social order. After a few days of revelry, everyone returns to his or her original place for another year.

SACRIFICE Many rituals involve **sacrifice**, or the offering of something for transfer to the supernaturals. Sacrifice has a long history throughout the world and is probably one of the oldest forms of ritual. It may involve killing and offering animals; making human offerings (of whole people, parts of a person's body, or bloodletting); or offering vegetables, fruits, grains, flowers, or other products. One interpretation of flowers as sacrificial offerings is that they, like vegetables and fruits, are symbolic replacements for former animal sacrifices (Goody 1993).

Spanish documents from the sixteenth century describe the Aztec practice of public sacrifice of humans and other animals to please the gods. The details are gory and involve marching thousands of human victims up to the top of a temple and then cutting out their hearts so that the blood spurts forth. Debate exists among anthropologists as to how many victims were actually sacrificed and why. Cultural materialist Marvin Harris has argued that the numbers were large, up to 100,000 at particular sites, and that the remains of the victims were butchered and eaten by commoners (1977). He maintains that the Aztec state, through such rituals, demonstrated its power and provided protein to the masses. In opposition to Harris, symbolic anthropologist Peggy Sanday takes an emic perspective and says that the sacrifices were necessary to please the gods and had nothing to do with maintaining the worldly power of leaders or feeding the masses (1986).

RELIGIOUS SPECIALISTS

Not all rituals require the presence of a *religious specialist*, or someone with extensive, formal training, but all require some level of knowledge on the part of the performer(s) about how to do them correctly. Even the daily, household veneration of an ancestor requires some knowledge gained through informal learning. At the other extreme, many rituals cannot be done without a highly trained specialist.

SHAMANS AND PRIESTS General features of the categories of shaman and priest illustrate key differences between these two types of specialists. (Many other specialists fit somewhere in between.) A *shaman* or *shamanka* (defined in Chapter 5) is a religious specialist who has a direct relationship with the supernaturals, often by being "called." A potential shaman may be recognized by special signs, such as the ability to go into a trance. Anyone who demonstrates shamanic abilities can become a shaman; in other words, this is an openly available role. Shamans are more often associated with nonstate societies, yet faith healers and evangelists of the United States could fit into this category. (Review the discussion in Chapter 5 of shamanic specialists as healers.)

In states, the more complex occupational specialization in religion means that there is a wider variety of types of specialists, especially what anthropologists refer to as *priests* (not the same as the specific modern role of the Catholic priest), and promotes the development of religious hierarchies and power structures. The terms **priest** and **priestess** refer to a category of full-time religious specialists whose position is based mainly on abilities gained through formal training. A priest may receive a divine call, but more often the role is hereditary, passed on through priestly lineages. In terms of ritual performance, shamans are more involved with nonperiodic rituals. Priests perform a wider range of rituals, including periodic state rituals. In contrast to shamans, who rarely have secular power, priests and priestly lineages often do.

OTHER SPECIALISTS Many other specialized religious roles exist cross-culturally. *Diviners* are specialists who are able to discover the will and wishes of the supernaturals through techniques such as reading animal entrails. Palm readers and tarot card readers fit into the category of diviners.

Prophets are specialists who convey divine revelations usually gained through visions or dreams. They often possess charisma, an especially attractive and powerful personality, and may be able to perform miracles. Prophets have founded new religions, some long-lasting and others short-lived.

Witches use psychic powers and affect people through emotion and thought. Mainstream society often condemns witchcraft as negative. Some scholars of ancient and contemporary witchcraft differentiate between positive forms that involve healing and negative forms that seek to harm people.

◆◆◆

World Religions and Local Variations

The term **world religion** was coined in the nineteenth century to refer to religions that were based on written sources, with many followers that crossed country borders and that had a concern with salvation (the belief that human beings require deliverance from an imperfect world). At that time, the term referred only to Christianity, Islam, and Buddhism. It was later expanded to include Judaism, Hinduism, Confucianism, Taoism, and Shintoism. Because of the global importance of the African diaspora that began with the European colonial slave trade, a sixth category of world religions is included here that describes key elements shared among the diversity of traditional African belief systems even though they are oral, not text-based, traditions.

For many centuries, the world religions have traveled outside their original borders through intentional attempts to expand and gain converts or through the migration of believers to new locales. European colonialism was a major force that led to the expansion of Christianity through the missionary work of Protestant sects. The increased rate of population migration since the twentieth century (Chapter 12) and the expansion of television and the Internet give even greater impetus to religious movement and change. Each world religion comprises many local variants, raising a "predicament" for centrally organized religions in terms of how to maintain a balance between standardization based on core beliefs and the local variations (Hefner 1998).

The material that follows first discusses the five traditional world religions in terms of their history, distribution, and basic teachings. The world religions are presented in order by historical age, based on the dates of written texts. For each world religion, an example of a local variation is presented. When a world religion moves into a new cultural region, it encounters local religious traditions. In many cases, the incoming religion and local religions coexist as separate traditions, either as complements or competitors, in what is called **religious pluralism**. In **religious syncretism**, elements of two or more religions blend together. Religious syncretism is most likely to occur when aspects of two religions form a

close match with each other. For example, if a local myth involves a hero who has something to do with snakes, there may be a syncretistic link with the Catholic belief in St. Patrick, who is believed to have driven snakes out of Ireland.

Many situations of nonfit also exist. For example, Christian missionaries have had difficulty translating the Bible into some indigenous languages because of a lack of matching words or concepts and because of differing kinship and social structures. Some Amazonian groups, such as the Pirahã (review Chapter 9), have no word that corresponds to the Christian concept of "heaven" (Everett 1995, personal communication). In other cases, matrilineal peoples have found it difficult to understand the significance of the Christian construct of "god the father."

An early nineteenth-century painting of the Virgin of Guadalupe by Isidro Escamilla, a Mexican artist. The Virgin of Guadalupe, or Our Lady of Guadalupe, is Mexico's most popular image. Her depiction involves syncretism with the indigenous Aztec goddess Tonantzin, part of a conscious strategy of Christian clergy to convert the Indians. Today, the Virgin of Guadalupe conveys messages of sacrifice and nurturance as well as strength and hope. She appeals to Mexican mothers, nationalists, and feminists alike.

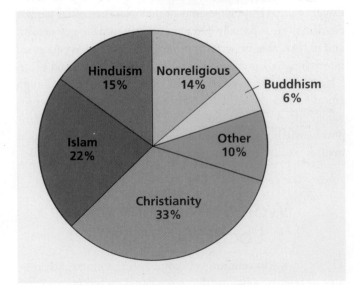

FIGURE 10.2 Population Distribution of Major World Religions. Judaism, due to its relatively small numbers, is classified in "Other."

The two world religions that emphasize *proselytizing,* or seeking converts, are Christianity and Islam. Their encounters with local religions have sometimes been violent, involving the physical destruction of sacred places and objects (Corbey 2003). Common methods include burning, overturning, dismantling, or cutting up sacred objects, dumping them into rivers, and hiding them in caves. European Christian missionaries in the 1800s often confiscated sacred goods and shipped them to Europe for sale to private owners or museums. Both Christian and Islamic conversion efforts frequently involved the construction of their own places of worship on top of the original sacred site. Conflict between these two religions is, unfortunately, not a matter of the past only.

HINDUISM

Over 900 million people in the world are Hindus. (*Note:* Population statistics for the world religions are rough averages derived from several Internet sources.) About 97 percent of all Hindus live in India, where Hinduism accounts for 80 percent of the population. The rest live throughout the world in countries such as Bangladesh, Myanmar, Pakistan, Sri Lanka, the United States, Canada, the United Kingdom, Malaysia, Fiji, Trinidad, Guyana, and Hong Kong.

A Hindu is born a Hindu, and Hinduism does not actively seek converts. The core texts of Hinduism are the four Vedas, which were composed in Sanskrit in northern India between 1200 and 900 BCE. Many other scholarly texts, epics and stories, and oral traditions enrich the Hindu tradition. The two most widely known stories are the *Mahabharata* (muh-huh-bhar-uh-tuh), the story of a war between two patrilineages in which Krishna plays an important role, and the *Ramayana* (ruh-my-uh-nuh), the story of King Rama and his devoted wife, Sita. Throughout India, many local stories also exist, some containing elements from pre-Vedic times.

Hinduism offers a rich polytheism and, at the same time, a philosophical tradition that reduces the multiplicity of deities into oneness. Deities range from a simple stone placed at the foot of a tree to elegantly carved and painted icons of gods such as Shiva and Vishnu and the goddesses Durga and Saraswati. Everyday worship of a deity involves lighting a lamp in front of the god, chanting hymns and mantras (sacred phrases), and taking *darshan* (dar-shun), which means seeing the deity, usually in the form of an icon (Eck 1985). These acts bring blessings to the worshipper. Local variations of worship often involve deities and rituals unknown elsewhere. For example, fire walking is an important part of goddess worship in southern and eastern India (Freeman 1981) and among some Hindu groups living outside India, notably in Fiji (Brown 1984).

Caste differences in beliefs and practices are also marked, even within the same village. Lower caste deities prefer offerings of meat sacrifices and alcohol, whereas upper caste deities prefer flowers, rice, and fruit.

A NAYAR FERTILITY RITUAL The matrilineal Nayars (nye-ers) of Kerala, South India (see Map 13.2, p. 282), perform a nonperiodic ritual as a remedy for the curse of the serpent deities who cause infertility in women (Neff 1994). This ritual illustrates the unity of Hinduism in several ritual elements: the use of a camphor flame and incense, the importance of serpent deities, and the offering of flowers to the deity. Locally specific elements are related to the matrilineal cultural context of Kerala.

The all-night ritual includes, first, women painting a sacred design of intertwined serpents on the floor. Several hours of worshipping the deity follow, with the camphor flame, incense, and flowers. Music comes from drumming, playing the cymbals, and singing. The presence of the deity is fully achieved when one of the women goes into a trance. Through her, matrilineal family members may speak to the deity and be blessed.

Among the Nayars, a woman's mother, mother's brothers, and brothers are responsible for ensuring that her desires for motherhood are fulfilled. They share her interest in continuing the matrilineage. What the women say during the trance is important. They typically draw attention to family disharmonies or neglect of the deities. This message diverts blame from the infertile woman for whom the ritual is being held. It reminds family and lineage members of their responsibilities to each other.

HINDU WOMEN AND KARMA IN NORTHERN ENGLAND One of Hinduism's basic concepts is *karma,* translated as "destiny" or "fate." A person's karma is determined at birth on the basis of his or her previous life and how it was conducted. The karma concept has prompted many outsiders to judge Hindus as fatalistic, lacking a sense of agency. But anthropological research on how people actually think about karma in their everyday lives reveals much individual variation, from fatalism to a strong sense of being in charge of one's destiny. One study looked at women's perceptions of karma among Hindus living in the city of Leeds, northern England (Knott 1996) (see Map 10.3, p. 217). Some of the women are fatalistic in their attitudes and behavior. One woman who had a strongly fatalistic view of karma said,

> When a baby's born . . . we have a ritual on the sixth day. That's when you name the baby, you know. And on that day, we believe the goddess comes and writes your future . . . we leave a blank white paper and a pen and we just leave it [overnight]. . . . So I believe that my future—whatever happens—is what she has written for me. That tells me [that] I have to do what I can do, and if I have a mishap in between I have to accept that. (1996:24)

---

religious pluralism   the condition in which one or more religions coexist either as complementary to each other or as competing systems.

religious syncretism   the blending of features of two or more religions.

Celebration of Holi, a spring festival popular among Hindus worldwide. In this scene in New Delhi, a young woman sprays colored water on a young man as part of the joyous event. The deeper meaning of Holi is tied to a myth about a demon.

▶ Is the arrival of spring ritually marked in your culture?

Another woman said that her sufferings were caused by the irresponsibility of her father and the "bad husband" to whom she had been married. She challenged her karma and left her husband: "I could not accept the karma of being with Nirmal [her husband]. If I had done so, what would have become of my children?" (1996:25). Because Hindu women's karma dictates being married and having children, leaving one's husband is a major act of resistance.

Options for women seeking support when questioning or changing their karmic roles can be religious, such as praying more and fasting, or secular, such as seeking the advice of a psychological counselor or social worker. Some Hindu women in England have become counselors, working in support of other women's independence and self-confidence. They illustrate how human agency can work against traditional religious rules.

BUDDHISM

Buddhism originated in a founding figure, Siddhartha Gautama (ca. 566–486 BCE), revered as the Buddha, or Awakened One (Eckel 1995:135). It began in northern India, where the Buddha grew up. From there, it spread throughout the subcontinent, into inner Asia and China, to Sri Lanka, and on to Southeast Asia. In the past 200 years, Buddhism has spread to Europe and North America. Buddhism's popularity declined in India, and Buddhists now constitute less than 1 percent of India's population. Its global spread is matched by a great diversity of doctrine and practice, to the extent that it is difficult to point to a single essential feature other than the importance of Gautama Buddha. No one text is accepted as authoritative for all forms of Buddhism. Many Buddhists worship the Buddha as a deity, but others do not. Instead, they honor his teachings and

follow the pathway he suggested for reaching *nirvana* (nurvah-nuh), or release from worldly life. The total number of Buddhists worldwide is around 400 million.

Buddhism arose as a protest against Hinduism, especially caste inequality, but it retained and revised several Hindu concepts, such as karma. In Buddhism, everyone has the potential for achieving nirvana (enlightenment and the overcoming of human suffering in this life), the ultimate goal of the religion. Good deeds are one way to achieve a better rebirth with each incarnation, until finally, release from *samsara* (the cycle of birth, reincarnation, death, and so on) is achieved. Compassion toward others, including animals, is a key virtue. Branches of Buddhism have different texts that they consider their canon. The major division is between the Theravada Buddhism practiced in Southeast Asia and the Mahayana Buddhism of Tibet, China, Taiwan, Korea, and Japan. Buddhism is associated with a strong tradition of monasticism through which monks and nuns renounce the everyday world and spend their lives meditating and doing good works. Buddhists have many and varied annual festivals and rituals. Some events bring pilgrims from around the world to Sarnath, near Varanasi, North India, where the Buddha gave his first teaching, and to Gaya, where he gained enlightenment.

LOCAL SPIRITS AND BUDDHISM IN SOUTHEAST ASIA Wherever Buddhism exists outside India, it is never the exclusive religion of the devotees, because it arrived to find established local religions already in place (Spiro 1967). In Myanmar (formerly Burma), Buddhism and indigenous traditions coexist without one being dominant. Indigenous beliefs remain strong because they offer a way of dealing with everyday problems. Buddhist beliefs about karma in

Buddhism gained an established footing in Japan in the eighth century. The city of Nara was an important early center of Buddhism. An emperor sponsored the casting of this huge bronze statue of the Buddha.

▶ Is there a Buddhist temple where you live? If so, have you visited it? If not, find out where the nearest one is and visit it if possible.

Myanmar are similar to those in Hinduism: A person's karma is the result of previous births and determines his or her present condition. If something bad happens, the person can do little but suffer through it.

In contrast, indigenous supernaturalism says that the bad things happen because of the actions of capricious spirits called *nats*. Ritual actions, however, can combat the influence of nats. Thus, people can deal with nats but not with karma. The continuity of belief in nats is an example of human agency and creativity. Burmese people kept what was important to them from their traditional beliefs and adopted aspects of the new religion.

Buddhism became an important cultural force and the basis for social integration in Myanmar. A typical village may have one or more Buddhist monasteries and several resident monks. All boys are ordained as temporary members of the monastic order. Almost every villager observes Buddhist holy days. Nonetheless, although Buddhism is held to be the supreme truth, the spirits retain control when it comes to dealing with everyday problems such as a toothache or a monetary loss. In Myanmar, the two traditions exist in a pluralistic situation as two separate options.

Other studies of religion in Southeast Asia provide examples in which there is more thorough blending, or syncretism, of local religions with Buddhism (see Everyday Anthropology).

JUDAISM

The first Judaic religious system was defined around 500 BCE, following the destruction of the Temple in Jerusalem by the Babylonians in 586 BCE (Neusner 1995). The early writings, called the Pentateuch (pen-ta-took), established the theme of exile and return as a paradigm for Judaism that endures today. The Pentateuch is also called the Five Books of Moses, or the Torah. Followers of Judaism share in the belief in the Torah as the revelation of God's truth through Israel, a term for the "holy people." The Torah explains the relationship between the supernatural and human realms and guides people in how to carry out the worldview through appropriate actions. A key feature of all forms of Judaism is the identification of what is wrong with the present and how to escape, overcome, or survive that situation. Jewish life is symbolically interpreted as a tension between exile and return, given its foundational myth in the exile of the Jews from Israel and their period of slavery in Egypt.

Judaism is monotheistic, teaching that God is one, unique, and all powerful. Humans have a moral duty to follow Jewish law, to protect and preserve life and health, and to follow certain duties, such as observing the Sabbath. The high regard for human life is reflected in the general opposition to abortion within Jewish law and in opposition to the death penalty. Words, both spoken and written, are important in Judaism. There is an emphasis on truth telling in life and on the use of established literary formulas at precise times during worship. These formulas are encoded in a *sidur* (sih-door), or prayer book. Dietary patterns distinguish Judaism from other religions; for example, rules of kosher eating forbid the mixing of milk or milk products with meat.

Contemporary varieties of Judaism range from conservative Hasidism to Reform Judaism, which emerged in the early 1800s. One difference between these two perspectives concerns the question of who is Jewish. Jewish law traditionally defined a Jewish person as someone born of a Jewish mother. In contrast, reform Judaism recognizes as Jewish the offspring of a Jewish father and a non-Jewish mother. Currently, the Jewish population numbers about 15 million worldwide, with about half living in North America, a quarter in Israel, and 20 percent in Europe and Russia. Smaller populations are scattered across the globe.

WHO'S WHO AT THE KOTEL The most sacred place to all Jews is the Kotel (ko-TELL), or Western Wall in Jerusalem (see Map 10.5, p. 226). Since the 1967 war, which brought Jerusalem under Israeli rule, the Kotel has been the most important religious shrine and pilgrimage site of Israel. The Kotel is located at one edge of the Temple Mount (also called Haram Sharif), an area sacred to Jews, Muslims, and Christians. According to Jewish scriptures, God asked Abraham to sacrifice his son Isaac on this hill. Later, King Solomon built the First Temple here in the middle of the tenth century BCE. It was destroyed by Nebuchadnezzsar (neh-boo-kud-NEZZ-er) in 587 BCE, when the Jews were led into captivity in Babylon. Around 500 BCE, King Herod built the Second Temple on the same site. The Kotel is a remnant of the Second Temple. Jews of all varieties, as well as non-Jews, come to the Kotel in vast numbers from around the world. The Kotel plaza is open to everyone, pilgrims and tourists alike. The wall is made of massive rectangular stones weighing between 2 and 8 tons each. At its base is a synagogue area partitioned into men's and women's sections.

This single site brings together a variety of Jewish worshippers and secular visitors. The great diversity among the visitors is evident in the various styles of dress and gesture:

> The Hasid . . . with a fur shtreimel on his head may enter the synagogue area alongside a man in shorts who utilizes a cardboard skullcap available for "secular" visitors. American youngsters in jeans may ponder Israeli soldiers of their own age, dressed in uniform, and wonder what their lot might have been if they [had been] born in another country. Women from Yemen, wearing embroidered trousers under their dresses, edge close to the Wall as do women accoutred in contemporary styles whose religiosity may have been filtered through a modern education. . . . (Storper-Perez and Goldberg 1994:321)

In spite of plaques that state the prohibition against begging, beggars offer to "sell a blessing" to visitors. They may remind visitors that it was the poor who built the wall in the first place. Another category of people is young Jewish men who, in search of prospective "born again" Jews, "hang around"

everyday ANTHROPOLOGY

Tattoos and Sacred Power

Fieldwork with Shan people in northern Thailand reveals the importance of tattooing, a tradition shared with much of Southeast Asia (Tannenbaum 1987). Shan tattooing blends aspects of Buddhism with local spirit beliefs and even elements of Hinduism as practiced by some groups in neighboring Myanmar.

Among the Shan, three types of tattoos exist:

- Tattoos that act on other people, causing them to like or fear the bearer, and that cause the spirits to be kind

- Tattoos that act on the bearer, increasing the bearer's skill

- Tattoos that create a barrier around the person that prevents animals from biting, knives from cutting, and bullets from entering the body

Tattoos are done in two colors—red, and blue-black. The first two types tend to be done in red; the third type tends to be done in blue black. Different designs are associated with each type. For example, the two-tailed lizard is a common tattoo in the first type.

The first type of tattoo is popular among many people, because it brings health to the bearer. It is the main type among women, used to prevent, as well as cure, an illness. A person who falls ill may get a tattoo incorporating a letter of the Shan alphabet in the design, either on the calf, around a body joint, around the mouth, or on the top of the tongue. Some of the most powerful designs in this category are placed on the back or over the heart.

The most powerful tattoo in this category, called the Five Buddha tattoo, is not allowed for women. Men who get this tattoo have to follow five Buddhist precepts at all times: Refrain from killing, stealing, improper sexual behavior, lying, and intoxication. The tattoo is red, but it also includes exfoliated skin from a Buddhist monk. That makes it different from all other tattoos and makes its bearer like a monk. Whereas most tattoos in the first category cause other people to look favorably on the bearer, the Five Buddha tattoo inspires fear and awe.

Tattoos in the second category are related to words. Some increase people's memory and help them on exams. Others strengthen a person's speaking ability. The most powerful tattoos in this group give a person such great verbal skills that he or she can intimidate others. They increase courage as well. One tattoo in the category is the Saraswati tattoo, which depicts, among other things, the head of Saraswati, the Hindu goddess of knowledge, on the bearer's right shoulder. To call on Saraswati for help, the person brushes his or her lips on the tattoo.

The third category of tattoos, those which provide a protective barrier, has one subset that prevents bites from insects, snakes, dogs, cats, tigers, and so on. If the person has the tattoo and gets bitten nonetheless, the tattoo helps reduce the pain. A general antibite tattoo depicts a cat and is on the lower arm. More powerful tattoos in this third category protect people from weapons. They seal off the body. A person should be careful not to get too many of these tattoos, however, because they seal the body off completely and therefore prevent good fortune from entering it. Someone with many of these tattoos is likely to be poor or unlucky.

---

looking for a "hit" (in their words). Most of the hits are young Americans, who are urged to take their Jewishness more seriously and, if male, to be sure to marry a Jewish woman. Other regulars are Hebrew-speaking men who are available to organize a prayer service. One of the most frequent forms of religious expression at the Kotel is the insertion of written prayers into the crevices of the wall.

The social heterogeneity of the Jewish people is thus transcended in a single space, creating some sense of what Victor Turner (1969) called *communitas*, a sense of collective unity that bridges individual differences.

PASSOVER IN KERALA The Jews of the Kochi (ko-chee) area of Kerala, South India, have lived there for about 1000 years (Katz and Goldberg 1989) (see Map 13.2, p. 282). The Maharaja of Kochi had respect for the Jewish people, who were mainly merchants. He relied on them for external trade and contacts. In recognition of this relationship, he allowed a synagogue, which is still standing, to be built next to his palace. Syncretism is apparent in Kochi Jewish lifestyle, social structure, and rituals. Basic aspects of Judaism are retained, along with many aspects of Hindu practices.

Three aspects of syncretism with Hinduism are apparent in Passover, one of the most important annual rituals of the Jewish faith. First, the Western/European Passover celebration is typically joyous and a time of feasting. In contrast, the Kochi version has adopted a tone of austerity and is called "the fasting feast." Second, Kochi Passover allows no role for children, whereas, at a traditional Western/European ritual meal, or *seder* (say-der), children usually ask four questions as a starting point of the narrative. The adult Kochi Jews chant the questions in unison. (In Hinduism, children do not have solo roles in rituals.) Third, a Kochi seder stresses purity even more than standard Jewish requirements do. Standard rules about maintaining the purity of kosher wine usually mean that no gentile (non-Jew) should touch it. But Kochi Jews expand the rule to

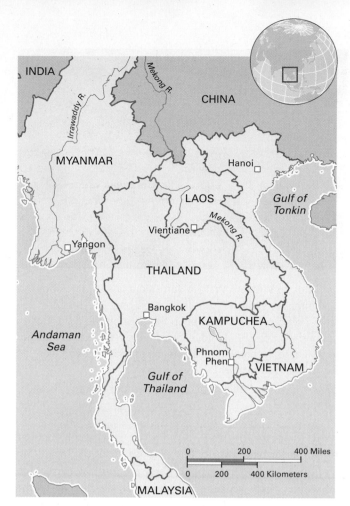

MAP 10.4 Mainland Southeast Asia.
Mainland Southeast Asia comprises Myanmar, Thailand, Laos, Vietnam, Kampuchea, and Malaysia. Although each country has a distinct history, the region shares a tropical monsoon climate, emphasis on wet-rice agriculture, and ethnic contrasts between highlanders and lowlanders. Many national and ethnic languages exist. Languages in the Mon-Khmer language family have the most speakers. Theravada Buddhism, Islam, and Christianity are the major religions. Growth in industry and informatics has created an economic upsurge in many parts of the region.

The Shan people do not question why or how their tattoos work. They simply believe that they do. In the case of the Saraswati tattoo, they blend what anthropologists classify as magic with religious beliefs from Buddhism and Hinduism. Sacred power is the key that links all these beliefs together into a coherent system for the Shan.

◆ **FOOD FOR THOUGHT**

- What do people in your microculture do to get people to like them, to succeed on exams, and to protect the body from harmful intrusions?

say that if the shelf or table on which the wine sits is touched by a gentile, the wine is impure. This extra level of "contagion" is influenced by Hindu concepts of pollution.

CHRISTIANITY

Christianity has many ties with Judaism, from which it sprang. One of the strongest ties is the biblical teaching of a coming savior, or *messiah* (anointed one). Christianity began in the eastern Mediterranean in the second quarter of the first century (Cunningham 1995). Most of the early believers were Jews who took up the belief in Jesus Christ as the messiah who came to earth in fulfillment of prophesies contained in the Hebrew scriptures.

Today, Christianity is the largest of the world religions, with about 2 billion adherents, roughly one-third of the world's population. It is the majority religion of Australia, New Zealand, the Philippines, Papua New Guinea, most countries of Europe and of North and South America, and about a dozen

southern African countries. Christianity is a minority religion throughout Asia, but Asian Christians constitute 16 percent of the world's Christians and are thus a significant population.

Christians accept the Bible (Old and New Testaments) as containing the basic teachings of their faith, believe that a supreme God sent His son to earth as a sacrifice for the welfare of humanity, and look to Jesus as the model to follow for moral guidance. The three largest branches of Christianity are Roman Catholic, Protestant, and Eastern Orthodox. Within each of these branches, various denominations exist. The greatest growth in Christianity is occurring in sub-Saharan Africa, India, Indonesia, and Eastern Europe.

PROTESTANTISM AMONG WHITE APPALACHIANS
Studies of Protestantism in Appalachia describe local traditions that outsiders who are accustomed to standard, urban versions may view as "deviant." For example, some churches in rural West Virginia and North Carolina, called Old Regulars, practice

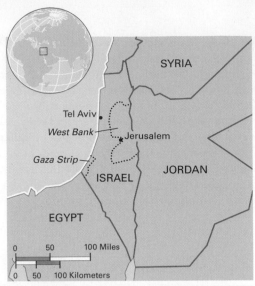

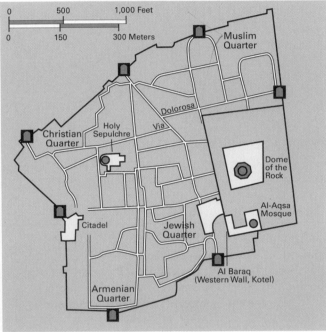

MAP 10.5   Sacred Sites in the Old City of Jerusalem, Israel.
Jerusalem is the holiest city of Judaism, the third holiest city of Islam, and holy to Christians. The section called the Old City is surrounded by walls that have been built, razed, relocated, and rebuilt over several hundred years. The Old City contains four quarters—Armenian, Christian, Jewish, and Muslim—and many sacred sites, such as the Kotel and the Via Dolorosa.

three obligatory rituals: footwashing, communion (a ritual commemorating the Last Supper that Jesus had with his disciples), and baptism (Dorgan 1989). The footwashing ceremony occurs once a year in conjunction with communion, usually as an extension of the Sunday service. An elder is called to the front of the church, and he preaches for 10 to 20 minutes. A round of handshaking and embracing follows. Two deaconesses then come forward to "prepare the table" by uncovering the sacramental elements placed there earlier under a white tablecloth. The elements are unleavened bread,

The Kotel, or Western Wall, in Jerusalem is a sacred place of pilgrimage, especially for Jews. Men pray in a section marked off on the left, women in the area on the right. Both men and women should cover their heads, and when leaving the wall area, women should take care to keep their faces toward it and avoid turning their backs to it.

▶ *Think of some behavioral rules at another sacred place you know.*

serving plates for the bread, cups for the wine, and a decanter or quart jar or two of wine. The deacons break the bread into pieces and the moderator pours the wine into the cups. Men and women form separate groups as the deacons serve the bread and wine. The deacons serve each other, and then it is time for the footwashing.

The moderator begins by quoting from the New Testament (John 13:4): "He riseth from supper, and laid aside his garments; and he took a towel and girded himself." The moderator takes a towel and basin from the communion table, puts water in it, and selects a senior elder and removes his shoes and socks. The moderator washes his feet slowly and attentively. Other members come forward and take towels and basins and take turns washing others' feet and having their feet washed. Soon "the church is filled with crying, shouting, and praising as these highly poignant exchanges unleash a flood of emotions" (Dorgan 1989:106). A functional interpretation of the ritual of footwashing is that it helps maintain social cohesion.

Another feature of worship in some small Protestant churches in Appalachia, especially remote areas of rural West Virginia, involves the handling of poisonous snakes. This practice finds legitimation in the New Testament (Daugherty 1997 [1976]). According to a passage in Mark (16:15–18), "In my name shall they cast out devils; they shall speak with new tongues; they shall take up serpents; and if they drink any deadly thing, it shall not hurt them; they shall lay hands on the sick, and they shall recover." Members of "Holiness-type" churches believe that the handling of poisonous snakes is the supreme act of devotion to God. Biblical literalists, these people choose serpent handling as their way of celebrating life, death, and resurrection and of proving that only Jesus has the power to deliver them from death. Most serpent handlers have been bitten many times, but few have died.

One interpretation says that the risks of handling poisonous snakes mirror the risks of the environment. In Appalachia, unemployment rates are high and many people are economically poor. The structurist view (review Chapter 1) points to the fact that serpent handling increased when local people lost their land rights to big mining and forestry companies (Tidball and Toumey 2003:4). As their lives became more economically insecure, they turned to a way of increasing their sense of stability through a dramatic religious ritual. Outsiders might ask whether such dangerous ritual practices indicate that the people are psychologically disturbed. Psychological tests indicate that members of Holiness churches are more emotionally healthy, on average, than members of mainline Protestant churches.

THE LAST SUPPER IN FIJI Among Christians in Fiji (see Map 5.6, p. 117), the image of the Last Supper is a dominant motif (Toren 1988). This scene, depicted on tapestry hangings, adorns most churches and many houses. People say, "Christ is the head of this household, he eats with us and overhears us" (1988:697). The image's popularity is the result of its fit with Fijian notions of communal eating and kava drinking. Seating rules at such events place the people of highest status, such as the chief and others close to him, at the "above" side of the room, away from the entrance. Others sit at the "lower" end, facing the highly ranked people. Intermediate positions are located on either side of the person of honor, in ranked order.

Leonardo Da Vinci's fifteenth-century painting of the Last Supper places Jesus Christ in the position of a Fijian chief, with the disciples in an ordered arrangement around him. The disciples and the viewers "face" the chief and eat and drink together, as is appropriate in Fijian society. The positioning parallels the orderly placement of Fijian people around the kava as encountered "virtually every day in the village" (1988:706). This kind of cultural fit is a clear example of religious syncretism.

ISLAM

Islam is based on the teachings of the prophet Muhammad (570–632 CE) and is thus the youngest of the world religions (Martin 1995:498–513). The Arabic word *Islam* means "submission" to the will of the one god, Allah, through which peace will be achieved. Followers of Islam, known as Muslims, believe that Muhammad was God's final prophet. Islam has several denominations with essentially similar beliefs but also distinct theological and legal approaches. The two major schools of thought are Sunni and Shi'a. About 85 percent of the total Muslim population worldwide is Sunni, and about 15 percent is Shi'a. Sufism is a more mystical variant of Islam, with much smaller numbers of adherents. Many other subgroups exist.

Every year, millions of Muslim pilgrims do the Hajj to Mecca, in Saudi Arabia. The Hajj is one of the Five Pillars of Sunni Islam and is also important in Shi'a Islam. A person who has done the Hajj is referred to as a *hajji*, a term of honor.

The Five Pillars of Islam are profession of faith in Allah, daily prayer, fasting, contributing alms for the poor, and the *Hajj* (pilgrimage to Mecca). The five pillars are central to Sunni Islam but less so to other branches of Islam, such as the Shi'as and the Sufis.

The total number of Muslims worldwide is about 1.4 billion, making it the second-largest religion. Muslim-majority nations are located in northern Africa; the Middle East, including Afghanistan, Pakistan, and Bangladesh in South Asia; and several nations in Central Asia and Southeast Asia. Most of the world's Muslims (60 percent) live in South Asia or Southeast Asia. Muslims live as minorities in many other countries, including China, where they seek to maintain their religious practices (see Culturama, p. 228). Although Islam originally flourished among pastoralists, only 2 percent of its adherents are now in that category.

A common and inaccurate stereotype of Islam prevalent among many non-Muslims is that it is the same no matter

THINKING
OUTSIDE
THE BOX

Visit the Vatican website and explore the Vatican's position on the "Da Vinci code" phenomenon.

locations, they have been influenced by foreign religions, notably Islam and various types of Christianity. The out-migration of African peoples has brought African religions to new locations, where they have been localized in their new contexts and also revitalized (Clarke 2004).

Many religious syncretisms in North and South America combine African traditions with aspects of Christianity, indigenous Indian religions, and other traditions. Widely popular in Brazil are Afro-Brazilian religions such as *umbanda*, *santería*, and *condomblé* that appeal to people of all social classes, urban and rural, especially for providing social support and alleviation of stress (refer to photo on p. 107) (Burdick 2004).

RAS TAFARI Also called Rastafarianism, Ras Tafari is an Afro-Caribbean religion with its original roots in Jamaica. It is not known how many Rastafarians there are, because they refuse to be counted (Smith 1995:23). Ras Tafari is a protest religion that shares only a few of the features of the African religions just mentioned. It traces its history to several preachers of the early twentieth century who taught that Ras ("Prince") Tafari, then the Ethiopian emperor Haile Selassie, was the "Lion of Judah" who would lead Blacks to the African promised land.

Rastafarianism does not have an organized set of doctrines or written texts. Shared beliefs of the many diffuse groups in the Caribbean, the United States, and Europe include the belief that Ethiopia is heaven on earth, that Haile Selassie is a living god, and that all Blacks will be able to return to the homeland through his help. Since the death of Haile Selassie in 1975, more emphasis has been placed on pan-African unity and Black power, and less on Ethiopia.

Rastafarianism is particularly strong in Jamaica, where it is associated with reggae music, dreadlocks, and *ganja*

Bob Marley, legendary reggae artist and Rastafarian, performing at the Roxy Theater in Hollywood, California, in 1979. Marley died in 1981 at the age of 36, but he is still the most revered reggae musician. He launched the global spread of Jamaican music. Reggae is a genre of Jamaican music associated with Rastafarianism. Its songs address poverty, social injustice, love, and sexuality.

(marijuana) smoking. Variations within the Rastafarian movement in Jamaica range from the belief that one must fight oppression to the position that living a peaceful life brings victory against evil.

◆◆◆
Directions of Religious Change

All religions have mythologies and doctrines that provide for continuity in their beliefs and practices. Yet no religion is frozen and unchanging. Cultural anthropologists have traced the resurgence of religions that seemed to be headed toward extinction through colonial forces, and they have documented the emergence of new religions. Likewise, they are observing the contemporary struggle of once-suppressed religions in socialist states to find a new position in the postsocialist world. Religious *icons* (images, pictures, or other forms of representation), once a prominent feature in Russian Orthodox churches, had been removed and placed in museums. The churches want them back.

Indigenous people's beliefs about the sacredness of their land are an important part of their attempts to protect their territory from encroachment and development by outside commercial interests. The world of religious change offers these examples, and far more, as windows into wider cultural change.

REVITALIZATION MOVEMENTS

Revitalization movements are religious movements that seek to bring about positive change through reestablishing a religion that has been threatened by outside forces or through adopting new practices and beliefs. These movements often arise in the context of rapid cultural change and appear to represent a way for people to try to make sense of their changing world and their place in it. One such movement that emerged as a response of Native Americans to the invasion of their land by Europeans and Euro-Americans was the Ghost Dance movement (Kehoe 1989). In the early 1870s, a shaman named Wodziwob of the Paiute (pie-yoot) tribe in California declared that the world would soon be destroyed and then renewed: Native Americans, plants, and animals would come back to life. He instructed people to perform a circle dance, known as the Ghost Dance, at night.

The movement spread to other tribes in California, Oregon, and Idaho but ended when the prophet died and his prophecy was unfulfilled. A similar movement emerged in 1890, led by another Paiute prophet, Wovoka, who had a vision during a total eclipse. His message was the same: destruction, renewal, and the need to perform circle dances in anticipation of the impending event. The dance spread widely and had various effects. Among the Pawnee, it provided the basis for a cultural revival of old ceremonies that had fallen into disuse. The Sioux altered Wovoka's message and adopted a more overtly hostile stance toward the government and White people. Newspapers began to carry stories about the "messiah craze," referring to Wovoka. Ultimately, the government took action against the Sioux, killing Chief Sitting Bull and Chief Big Foot and about 300 Sioux at Wounded Knee. In the 1970s, the Ghost Dance was revived again by the American Indian Movement, an activist organization that seeks to advance Native American rights.

Cargo cults are a type of revitalization movement that emerged throughout Melanesia in response to Western influences. Most prominent in the first half of the nineteenth century, cargo cult behavior emphasized the acquisition of Western trade goods, or *cargo* in local terms. Typically, a prophetic leader emerged with a vision of how the cargo will arrive. In one instance, the leader predicted that a ship would come, bringing not only cargo but also the people's dead ancestors. Followers set up tables for the expected guests, complete with flower arrangements.

Later, after World War II and the islanders' experiences of aircraft arrivals bringing cargo, the mode of anticipated arrival changed to planes. Once again, people would wait expectantly for the arrival of the plane. Cargo cults emerged as a response to the disruptive effects of new goods being suddenly introduced into indigenous settings. The outsiders imposed a new form of exchange system that emphasized the importance of Western goods and suppressed the importance of indigenous valuables such as shells and pigs. This transformation undermined traditional patterns of gaining status through the exchange of indigenous goods. Cargo cult leaders sought help, in the only way they knew, in obtaining Western goods so that they could acquire social status in the new system.

CONTESTED SACRED SITES

Religious conflict often becomes focused on sacred sites. One place of recurrent conflict is Jerusalem, where many religions and sects within religions compete for control of sacred terrain. Three major religions claim that they have primary rights: Islam, Judaism, and Christianity. Among the Christians, several different sects vie for control of the Church of the Holy Sepulchre (see Map 10.5, p. 226). In India, frequent conflicts over sacred sites occur between Hindus and Muslims. Hindus claim that Muslim mosques have been built on sites sacred to Hindus. On some occasions, the Hindus have destroyed the mosques. Many conflicts that involve secular issues surrounding sacred sites also exist worldwide. In the United States, White racists have burned African American churches. In Israel, some Jewish leaders object to archaeological research because they believe that the ancient Jewish burial places should remain undisturbed.

A similar situation exists among indigenous populations in the Western Hemisphere. Their sacred sites and burial grounds have often been destroyed for the sake of urban growth, petroleum and mineral extraction, and recreational sports. Resistance to such destruction is growing, with indigenous people finding creative ways to protect, restore, and manage their heritage.

John Frum Movement supporters stand guard around one of the cult's flagpoles at Sulphur Bay village, on Tanna Island, Vanuatu, in the region of Melanesia.

▶ *Does this scene remind you of anything from your culture?*

RELIGIOUS FREEDOM AS A HUMAN RIGHT

According to a United Nations Declaration, freedom from religious persecution is a universal human right. Yet violations of this right by countries and by competing religions are common. Sometimes people who are persecuted on religious grounds can seek and obtain sanctuary in other places or nations. Thousands of Tibetan Buddhist refugees, including their leader, the Dalai Lama, fled Tibet after it was taken over by the Chinese. Several Tibetan communities have been established in exile in India, the United States, and Canada, where the Tibetan people attempt to keep their religion, language, and heritage alive.

Religions are often the focal point of conflict and dissension and sometimes a source of conflict resolution. As an integral part of the heritage of humanity, religions are best understood within a cross-cultural and contextualized perspective. Such an understanding is essential for building a more peaceful future.

---

revitalization movement a socioreligious movement, usually organized by a prophetic leader, that seeks to construct a more satisfying situation by reviving all or parts of a religion that has been threatened by outside forces or by adopting new practices and beliefs.

cargo cult a form of revitalization movement that emerged in Melanesia in response to Western and Japanese influences.

the BIG questions REVISITED

◆ **What is religion and what are the basic features of religions?**

Early cultural anthropologists defined religion in contrast to magic and suggested that religion was a more evolved form of thinking about the supernatural realm. They collected information on religions of non-Western cultures and constructed theories about the origin and functions of religion. Since then, ethnographers have described many religious systems and documented a rich variety of beliefs, forms of ritual behavior, and types of religious specialists. Beliefs are expressed in either myth or doctrine and often are concerned with defining the roles and characteristics of supernatural beings and how humans should relate to them.

Religious beliefs are enacted in rituals that are periodic or nonperiodic. Some common rituals worldwide are life-cycle rites, pilgrimage, rituals of inversion, and sacrifice. Rituals are transformative for the participants.

Many rituals require the involvement of a trained religious specialist, such as a shaman/shamanka or priest/priestess. Compared with the situation in states, religious specialist roles in nonstate contexts are fewer, less than full time, and less formalized, and they carry less secular power. In states, religious specialists are often organized into hierarchies, and many specialists gain substantial secular power.

◆ **How do world religions illustrate globalization and localization?**

The five so-called world religions are based on texts and generally agreed-on teachings and beliefs shared by many people around the world. In order of historic age, these religions are Hinduism, Buddhism, Judaism, Christianity, and Islam. Christianity has the largest number of adherents, with Islam second and Hinduism third. Due to accelerated global population migration in the past few centuries, many formerly local religions now have a worldwide membership. Because of Western colonialism and slavery, African religions are prominent in the Western Hemisphere, with a variety of syncretistic religions attracting many adherents.

As members of the world religions have moved around the globe, religious beliefs and practices have become contextualized into localized variants. When a new religion moves into a culture, it may be blended with local systems (syncretism), may coexist with indigenous religions in a pluralistic fashion, or may take over and obliterate the original beliefs.

◆ **What are some important aspects of religious change in contemporary times?**

Religious movements of the past two centuries have often been prompted by colonialism and other forms of social contact. In some instances, indigenous religious leaders and cults have arisen in an attempt to resist unwanted outside forces of change. In other cases, they evolve as ways of incorporating selected outside elements. Revitalization movements, such as the Ghost Dance movement in the United States Plains region, look to the past and attempt to recover lost and suppressed religious beliefs and practices.

Issues of contemporary importance include the increasing amount of conflict surrounding sacred sites, hostilities related to the effects of secular power interests on religious institutions and spaces, and religious freedom as a human right.

KEY CONCEPTS

animatism, p. 215

cargo cult, p. 231

doctrine, p. 213

life-cycle ritual, p. 217

magic, p. 212

myth, p. 213

pilgrimage, p. 218

priest/priestess,
  p. 219

religion, p. 212

religious pluralism, p. 220

religious syncretism,
  p. 220

revitalization movement,
  p. 230

ritual, p. 217

ritual of inversion,
  p. 218

sacrifice, p. 219

world religion, p. 219

SUGGESTED READINGS

Paulo Apolito. *The Internet and the Madonna: Religious Visionary Experience on the Web*. Antony Shugaar, trans. Chicago: University of Chicago Press, 2003. This book traces the Christian cult of Mary as it has developed and grown through the medium of the World Wide Web.

Janet Bennion. *Desert Patriarchy: Mormon and Mennonite Communities in the Chihuahua Valley*. Tucson: University of Arizona Press, 2004. The ethnographer, raised in a Mormon family, reports on her fieldwork among Mormons in a desert region in Mexico.

Karen McCarthy Brown. *Mama Lola: A Vodou Priestess in Brooklyn*. Berkeley: University of California Press, 1991. This life story of Mama Lola, a voodoo practitioner, is set within an ethnographic study of a Haitian community in New York City.

Sondra L. Hausner. *Wandering with Sadhus: Ascetics in the Hindu Himalayas*. Bloomington: Indiana University Press, 2008. This ethnographic study explores the interactions of Hindu ascetics in northern India with ordinary households and considers how these believers are part of the public community in spite of their commitment to solitary religious practices.

Klara Bonsack Kelley and Harris Francis. *Navajo Sacred Places*. Bloomington: Indiana University Press, 1994. The authors report on the results of a research project undertaken to learn about Navajo cultural resources, especially sacred sites, and the stories associated with them in order to help protect these places.

Melvin Konner. *Unsettled: An Anthropology of the Jews*. New York: Penguin Compass, 2003. A biological anthropologist is the author of this cultural history of the Jewish people and their religion. It extends from the origins of Judaism among pastoralists in the Middle East through enslavement in the Roman Empire, to the Holocaust and the creation of Israel.

J. David Lewis-Williams and D. G. Pearce. *San Spirituality: Roots, Expression, and Social Consequences*. New York: AltaMira Press, 2004. This book examines the interplay of cosmology, myth, ritual, and art among the San people of southern Africa.

Charlene Makley. *The Violence of Liberation: Gender and Tibetan Buddhist Revival in Post-Mao China*. Berkeley: University of California Press, 2007. Makley combines archival research with fieldwork in a Buddhist monastery in Tibet. She describes the incorporation of the region of Labrang into China.

Fatima Mernissi. *Beyond the Veil: Male–Female Dynamics in Modern Muslim Society*. Bloomington: Indiana University Press, revised edition, 1987. The author considers how Islam perceives female sexuality and regulates it on behalf of the social order.

Todd Sanders. *Beyond Bodies: Rainmaking and Sense Making in Tanzania*. Toronto: University of Toronto Press, 2008. This study of rainmaking rituals among the Inhanzu of central Tanzania reveals ideas about gender roles and relations.

Maureen Trudelle Schwarz. *Blood and Voice: Navajo Women Ceremonial Practitioners*. Tucson: University of Arizona Press, 2003. Contemporary Navajo women are increasingly taking on the ritual role of ceremonial Singer, formerly the domain of men. This book describes how women gain sacred knowledge and explains how they overcome the tradition that only men can be Singers.

Stephen Selka. *Religion and the Politics of Ethnic Identity in Bahia, Brazil*. Gainesville: University Press of Florida, 2008. This study shows how Catholicism, evangelical Protestantism, and the traditional Brazilian religion of Candomblé shape the discourse of race and identity in northeastern Brazil.

Katharine L. Wiegele. *Investing in Miracles: El Shaddai and the Transformation of Popular Catholicism in the Philippines*. Honolulu: University of Hawai'i Press, 2005. This book examines the widespread popularity in the Philippines of Brother Mike, a charismatic businessman who became a preacher. He appears at huge outdoor rallies and uses mass media to spread his message of economic prosperity within a Catholic framework.

Zhou Shaming. *Funeral Rituals in Eastern Shandong, China: An Anthropological Study*. Lewiston, NY: Edwin Mellen Press, 2009. This work is the first detailed Western study of contemporary funeral rituals in villages in north China and reveals a shift in the meaning and content of the funeral rituals which are related to changing generational values and the new emphasis on the interests of the living in favor of those of the dead.

Brazilian country music singer Inaia performs at the opening ceremony of the Barretos Rodeo in Berretos in the Brazilian state of São Paulo.

EXPRESSIVE CULTURE

11

the BIG questions

◆ How is culture expressed through art?

◆ What do play and leisure activities reveal about culture?

◆ How is expressive culture changing in contemporary times?

OUTLINE

Art and Culture

Critical Thinking: Probing the Categories of Art

Play, Leisure, and Culture

Change in Expressive Culture

Culturama: The Gullah of South Carolina

Lessons Applied: A Strategy on Cultural Heritage for the World Bank

This chapter considers a vast area of human behavior and thought called **expressive culture**, or behavior and beliefs related to art, leisure, and play. (Definitions of these terms are provided later.) It begins with a discussion of theoretical perspectives on cross-cultural art and how anthropologists study art and expressive culture. The second section considers the topics of play and leisure cross-culturally. The last section provides examples of change in expressive culture.

◆◆◆

Art and Culture

Compared with the definition of art and how to study the subject as presented in art history classes you may have taken, the approach of cultural anthropologists is rather different. Their findings, here as in other cultural domains, stretch and subvert Western concepts and categories and prompt us to look at art within its context. Thus, anthropologists consider many kinds of products, practices, and processes to be art. They also study the artist and the artist's place in society. In addition, they ask questions about how art, and expressive culture more generally, is related to microcultural variation, inequality, and power. They question how cross-cultural art is to be selected and put on display in museums.

WHAT IS ART?

Are ancient rock carvings art? Is subway graffiti art? An embroidered robe? A painting of a can of Campbell's soup? Philosophers, art critics, anthropologists, and art lovers have all struggled with the question *What is art?* The issue of how to define art involves more than mere word games. The way art is defined affects the manner in which a person values and treats artistic creations and those who create art (see Critical Thinking).

Anthropologists propose broad definitions of art to take into account emic definitions cross-culturally. One definition says that **art** is the application of imagination, skill, and style to matter, movement, and sound that goes beyond the purely practical (Nanda 1994:383). Such imagination, skill, and style can be applied to many substances and activities, and the product can be considered art—for example, a beautifully presented meal, a well-told story, or a perfectly formed basket. In this sense, art is a human universal, and no culture can be said to lack artistic activity completely. The Pirahã of the Brazilian Amazon, however, appear to have very little visual art, but they do have verbal art (review Chapter 9).

In addition to studying the art product itself, anthropologists pay attention to the process of making art, variations in art and its preferred forms cross-culturally, and the way culture constructs and changes artistic traditions. They also consider various categories of art. Within the general category of art, subcategories exist, sometimes denoting eras, such as Paleolithic or modern art. Other subcategories are based on the medium of expression, such as graphic or plastic arts (painting, drawing, sculpture, weaving, basketry, and architecture); decorative arts (interior design, landscaping, gardens, costume design, and body adornment such as hairstyles, tattooing, and painting); performance arts (music, dance, and theater); and verbal arts (poetry, writing, rhetoric, and telling stories and jokes). A long-standing distinction in the Western view exists between *fine art* and *folk art*. This distinction is based on a Western-centric judgment that defines fine art as rare, expensive art produced by artists usually trained in the Western classical tradition. This is the kind of art that is included in college courses called "Fine Arts." The implication is that all other art is less than fine and is more appropriately called folk art, ethnic art, primitive art, or crafts. Characteristics of Western fine art are as follows: The product is created by a formally schooled artist, it is made for sale on the market, it is clearly associated with a particular artist, its uniqueness is valued, and it is not primarily utilitarian but is rather "art for art's sake." In contrast, all the rest of the world's art that is non-Western and nonclassical is supposedly characterized by the opposite features:

- It is created by an artist who has not received formal training.

- It is not produced for the market.

- The artist is anonymous and does not sign or individually claim the product.

- It is made primarily for everyday use, such as food procurement, processing, or storage; in ritual; or in war.

A closer examination of these two categories is in order. All cultures have art, and all cultures have a sense of what makes something art versus non-art. The term *esthetics* refers to socially accepted notions of quality (Thompson 1971). Before anthropologists proved otherwise, Western art experts believed that esthetics either did not exist or was poorly developed in non-Western cultures. We now know that esthetic principles, or established criteria for artistic quality, exist everywhere, whether or not they are written down and formalized. **Ethno-esthetics** refers to culturally specific definitions of what art is.

The standards for wood carving in West Africa illustrate the importance of considering cross-cultural variation in the criteria for art (Thompson 1971). Among the

---

expressive culture   behaviors and beliefs related to art, leisure, and play.

art   the application of imagination, skill, and style to matter, movement, and sound that goes beyond what is purely practical.

ethno-esthetics   culturally specific definitions of what art is.

Probably every reader of this book, at one time or another, has looked at an object in an art museum or in an art book or magazine and exclaimed, "But that's not art!" As a critical thinking research project on "What is art?" visit two museums, either in person or on the Internet. One of these should be a museum of either fine art or modern art. The other should be a museum of natural history. In the former, examine at least five items on display. In the latter, examine several items on display that have to do with human cultures (that is, skip the bugs and rocks).

Take notes on all the items that you are examining. Then answer the following questions.

◆ **CRITICAL THINKING QUESTIONS**

• What is the object?

• What contextual explanation does the museum provide about the object?
• Was the object intended as a work of art or as something else?
• In your opinion, is it art or not, and why or why not?
• Compare your notes on the objects in the two types of museums. What do your notes tell you about categories of art?

Yorùbà (YOR-uh-buh) of Nigeria, esthetic guidelines for wood carving include these:

• Figures should be depicted midway between complete abstraction and complete realism so that they resemble "somebody," but no one in particular. Portraiture in the Western sense is considered dangerous.

• Humans should be depicted at their optimal physical peak, not in infancy or old age.

• Line and form should have clarity.

• The sculpture should have the quality of luminosity achieved through a polished surface and the play of incisions and shadows.

• The piece should exhibit symmetry.

Some anthropological studies have documented intra-cultural differences in esthetic standards, as well as cross-cultural variation. For example, an anthropologist showed computer-generated graphics to the Shipibo (shih-PEE-bo) Indians of the Peruvian Amazon and learned that the men liked the abstract designs whereas the women thought they were ugly (Roe, cited in Anderson and Field 1993). If you are wondering why this difference would exist, consider the interpretation of the anthropologist: Shipibo men are the shamans and take hallucinogenic drugs that may give them familiarity with more "psychedelic"/abstract images.

STUDYING ART IN SOCIETY

The anthropological study of art seeks to understand not only the products of art but also who makes it and why, the role of art in society, and its wider social meanings. Franz Boas was the first anthropologist to emphasize the importance of studying the artist in society. Functionalism (review Chapter 1) was the most important theory informing anthropological research on art in the first half of the twentieth century.

Yorùbà wood carving follows esthetic principles that require clarity of line and form, a polished surface that creates a play of light and shadows, symmetry, and the depiction of human figures that are neither completely abstract nor completely realistic.

▶ *Have you seen African sculptures that follow these principles? Visit an African art museum on the Web for further exploration.*

Anthropologists wrote about how paintings, dance, theater, and songs serve to socialize children into the culture, provide a sense of social identity and group boundaries, and promote healing. Art may legitimize political leaders and enhance efforts in war through body painting, adornment, and magical decorations on shields and weapons. Art may also serve as a form of social control, as in African masks worn by dancers who represent deities visiting humans to remind them of the moral order. Art, like language, can be a catalyst for political resistance or a rallying point for ethnic solidarity in the face of oppression.

The anthropology of art relies on a range of methods in data gathering and analysis. The basic method is participant observation, supplemented by collecting and analyzing oral or written material such as video and tape recordings. Thus, strong ties often exist between cultural and linguistic anthropologists in the study of art.

Many anthropologists have become apprentices in an artistic tradition. For John Chernoff, learning to play African drums was an important part of building rapport during his fieldwork in Ghana and an essential aspect of his ability to gain an understanding of the importance of music in Ghanaian society (1979). His book, *African Rhythm and African Sensibility*, takes into account the position and role of the ethnographer and how it shapes what the ethnographer learns. Reading the book's introduction will convince you that fieldwork in cultural anthropology is far more than simply gathering the data you think you need for the project you have in mind, especially if your project concerns processes of creativity and expression.

Chernoff argues that only by relinquishing a scientific approach can a researcher learn about creativity and how it is related to society. As one of his drumming teachers said, "The heart sees before the eyes." Chernoff had to do more than practice participant observation. His heart had to participate, too. During his early months in the field, Chernoff often found himself wondering why he was there. To write a book? To tell people back in the United States about Ghana? No doubt, many of the Ghanaians he met wondered the same thing, especially given that his early efforts at drumming were pretty bad, although he did not realize it because he always drank copious amounts of gin before playing. Eventually, he became the student of a master drummer and went through a formal initiation ceremony. For the ceremony, he had to kill two chickens himself and eat parts of them in a form that most North Americans will never see in a grocery store. Still he was not playing well enough. He went through another ritual to make his wrist "smart" so that it would turn faster, like a cat chasing a mouse. For that ritual, he had to go into the bush, 10 miles outside town, and collect ingredients. The ritual worked. Having a cat's hand was a good thing, but anthropologically it was more important to Chernoff that he had begun to gain an understanding of drumming in its social and ritual contexts.

Chernoff learned about Ghanaian family life and how it is connected to individual performers and to rituals that have to do with music. He also grew to see where his performance fell short and what he needed to do to improve. He gained great respect for the artists who taught him and admiration for their striving for respect. Chernoff's personality was an important ingredient of the learning process. He comments, "I assumed that I did not know what to do in most situations. I accepted what people told me about myself and what I should be doing. . . . I waited to see what people would make of me. . . . By staying cool I learned the meaning of character" (1979:170).

Expressive culture in Sumba, Indonesia. (TOP) A woman weaves ikat (IH-kut) cloth on a bamboo loom. Ikat is a style of weaving that uses a tie-dye process on either the warp or weft before the threads are woven. The process will create a design in the final product. Double ikat is when both warp and weft threads are tie-dyed before weaving. The motif on this piece of ikat is the Tree of Life flanked by roosters. (BOTTOM) Linguistic anthropologist Joel Kuipers interviews a ritual speaker who is adept at verbal arts performance.

▶ *What is a form of verbal art in your culture?*

FOCUS ON THE ARTIST   In the early twentieth century, Franz Boas urged his students to go beyond the study of the products of art and study the artists. One goal of the anthropologist, he said, is to study art from the artist's perspective. Ruth Bunzel's (1972 [1929]) research with Native American potters in the U.S. Southwest is a classic example of this focus. While undergoing training as an apprentice potter, she asked individual potters about their choices for pot designs. One Zuni (zoo-nee) potter commented, "I always know the whole design before I start to paint" (1972:49). A Laguna potter said, " I learned this design from my mother. I learned most of my designs from my mother" (1972:52). Bunzel discovered the importance of both individual agency and following tradition.

The social status of artists is another aspect of the focus on the artist. Artists may be revered and wealthy as individuals or as a group, or they may be stigmatized and economically marginal. In ancient Mexico, goldworkers were highly respected. In American Indian groups of the Pacific Northwest coast, male carvers and painters had to be initiated into a secret society, and they had higher status than other men. Often a gender division exists. Among the Navajo of Arizona, women weave and men do silversmithing. In the Caribbean, women of African descent are noted for their carvings of calabashes (large gourds). In the contemporary United States, most famous and successful graphic artists are men, although the profession includes many women. Depending on the genre, race/ethnicity/indigeneity is another factor shaping success as an artist.

As with other occupations, the performing arts are more specialized in state-level societies. Generally, among free-ranging foragers, little specialization exists. Artistic activity is open to all, and artistic products are shared equally by all. Some people may be especially appreciated as singers, storytellers, or carvers. With increasing social complexity and a market for art, specialized training is required to produce certain kinds of art, and the products are sought after by those who can afford them. Class differences in artistic styles and preferences emerge along with the increasingly complex division of labor.

MICROCULTURES, ART, AND POWER   Art forms and styles, like language, are often associated with microcultural groups' identity and sense of pride. For example, the Berbers of highland Morocco are associated with woolen carpets, Maya Indians with woven and embroidered blouses, and the Inuit of Alaska with stone carvings of figurines. Cultural anthropologists provide many examples of linkages between various microcultural dimensions and power issues. In some instances, more powerful groups appropriate the art forms of less powerful groups. In others, forms of art are said to be expressive of resistance.

An example of how gender relations play out in expressive culture comes from a study of male strip dancing in Florida (Margolis and Arnold 1993). Advertisements in the media tell women that seeing a male strip dancer is "their chance," "their night out." Going to a male strip show is marketed as a time of reversal of traditional gender roles in which men are dominant and women submissive. Are gender roles actually reversed in a male stripper bar? The short answer is no. Women customers are treated like juveniles. As they stand in line waiting for the show to open, the manager instructs them on how to tip. They are symbolically dominated by the dancers, who take on various roles such as lion tamers. The *dive-bomb* is further evidence of women's subordinate position. The dive-bomb is a form of tipping the dancer in which the woman customer gets on her hands and knees and tucks a bill held between her teeth into the dancer's g-string. The interpretation of all this behavior is that, rather than reversing the gender hierarchy, it reinforces it.

Not all forms of popular art and performance are mechanisms of social control and maintenance of hierarchies. In the United States, for example, hip-hop and urban Black youths' verbal arts and rap music can be seen as a form of protest through performance (Smitherman 1997). Their lyrics report on their experience of economic oppression, the danger of drugs, and men's disrespect for women. The global spread of hip-hop and related music is another example of social resistance through song and performance.

PERFORMANCE ARTS

The performance arts include music, dance, theater, rhetoric (speechmaking), and narrative (storytelling). One important area has developed its own name: **ethnomusicology**, the cross-cultural study of music. Ethnomusicologists study a

Kanye West performs on the main stage at the 2006 Coachella Valley Music and Arts Festival in Indio, California.

▶ *Do your parents or grandparents know who Kanye West is?*

ethnomusicology   the cross-cultural study of music.

range of topics, including the form of the music itself, the social position of musicians, how music interacts with other domains of culture such as religion or healing, and change in musical traditions. This section provides examples about music and gender in Malaysia, music and globalization in Brazil, and theater and society in India.

MUSIC AND GENDER AMONG THE TEMIAR OF MALAYSIA An important topic for ethnomusicologists is gender differences in access to performance roles in music. (For ideas about research on this topic, see Figure 11.1) A cultural materialist perspective would predict that in cultures where gender roles are quite egalitarian, access to and meanings in music will also be egalitarian for males and females. This is the case among the Temiar (tem-ee-yar), foragers of the highlands of peninsular Malaysia (see Map 6.3, p. 132). Their musical traditions emphasize balance and complementarity between males and females (Roseman 1987).

Among the Temiar, kinship and marriage rules are flexible and open. Marriages are based on the mutual desires of the partners. Descent is bilineal (review Chapter 6), and marital residence follows no particular rule after a period of bride service. Marriages often end in separation, and serial monogamy is common. Men, however, do have a slight edge over women in political and ritual spheres. They are typically the village leaders, and they are the spirit mediums who sing the songs that energize the spirits.

> If you were doing an ethnographic study of gender roles in musical performance, the following questions would be useful in starting the inquiry. But they would not exhaust the topic. Can you think of questions that should be added to the list?
>
> 1. Are men and women equally encouraged to use certain instruments and repertoires?
> 2. Is musical training available to all?
> 3. Do male and female repertoires overlap? If so, how, when, and for what reasons?
> 4. Are the performances of men and women public, private, or both? Are women and men allowed to perform together? In what circumstances?
> 5. Do members of the culture give equal value to the performances of men and women? On what criteria are these evaluations based, and are they the same for men and women performers?
>
> Source: From "Power and Gender in the Musical Experiences of Women," pp. 224–225 by Carol E Robertson in *Women and Music in Cross-Cultural Perspective*, ed. by Ellen Koskoff. Copyright © 1987. Reprinted by permission of the Greenwood Publishing Group, Inc. Westport, CT.

FIGURE 11.1 Five Ethnographic Questions about Gender and Music

Although the spirits enter the community through male singers, the male spirit-medium role is not of greater importance or status than a woman's performance role in singing choruses. The singing of the male spirit medium and the female chorus is blurred through overlap between phrases and repetition. The performance is one of general community participation, with integrated male and female roles, as in Temiar society in general.

COUNTRY MUSIC AND GLOBALIZATION IN BRAZIL Linguistic anthropologist Alexander Dent studies the growing popularity of *música sertaneja* (MOO-see-kah ser-tah-NAY-shah), Brazilian country music (2005). Música sertaneja draws heavily on U.S. country music, but it is significantly localized within Brazilian contexts. Brazilian performers creatively use North American country music songs, such as "Achy Breaky Heart," to convey messages about gender relationships, intimacy, the family, the past, and the importance of the countryside that make sense in the Brazilian context. In their performances and recordings, they use an American genre to critique American-driven processes such as extreme capitalism and globalization and to critique the Brazilian adoption of such Western ways.

A prominent feature of Brazilian country music is performance by a *dupla* (doo-plah), or two "brothers," who may or may not be biological brothers. They emphasize their similarity by cutting their hair the same way and wearing similar clothes. Musically, they blend their voices, with neither voice dominating the other. When performing, they sing part of a song with their arms over each other's shoulders and gaze at each other affectionately. The *dupla* and their music emphasize kinship and caring as important aspects of Brazilian tradition that should be preserved.

THEATER AND MYTH IN SOUTH INDIA Theater is a type of enactment that seeks to entertain through movement and through words related to dance, music, parades, competitive games and sports, and verbal art (Beeman 1993). Cross-culturally, strong connections exist among myth, ritual, and performance.

One theatrical tradition that offers a blend of mythology, acting, and music is the Kathakali (kuh-tuh-kal-lee) ritual dance-drama of southern India (Zarrilli 1990). Stylized hand gestures, elaborate makeup, and costumes contribute to the attraction of these performances, which dramatize India's great Hindu epics, especially the *Mahabharata* (review Chapter 10) and the *Ramayana*. Costumes and makeup transform the actor into one of several well-known characters from Indian mythology. The audience easily recognizes the basic character types at their first entrance by the performers' costumes and makeup. Six types of makeup exist to depict characters ranging from the most refined to the most vulgar. Kings and heroes have green facial makeup, reflecting their refinement and moral uprightness. Vulgar characters are associated with

Many forms of theater combine the use of facial makeup, masks, and costumes to transform an actor into someone (or something) else. This Kathakali dancer is applying makeup before a performance in Kerala, South India.

black facial makeup and occasionally black beards. With their black faces dotted with red and white, they are the most frightening of the Kathakali characters.

ARCHITECTURE AND DECORATIVE ARTS

Like all art forms, architecture is interwoven with other aspects of culture. Architecture may reflect and protect social rank and class differences, as well as gender, age, and ethnic differences (Guidoni 1987). Decorative arts—including interior decoration of homes and buildings, and external design features such as gardens—likewise reflect people's social position and "taste." Local cultures have long defined preferred standards in these areas of expression, but global influences from the West and elsewhere, such as Japan and other non-Western cultures, have been adopted and adapted by other traditions.

ARCHITECTURE AND INTERIOR DESIGN Foragers, being highly mobile, build dwellings as needed and then abandon them. (Refer to the photo on p. 53 of Ju/'hoansi shelter.) Having few personal possessions and no surplus goods, they need no permanent storage structures. The construction of dwellings does not require the efforts of groups larger than

the family unit. Foragers' dwellings are an image of the family and not of the wider society. The dwellings' positioning in relation to each other reflects the relations among families.

More elaborate shelters and greater social cohesiveness in planning occur as foraging is combined with horticulture, as in the semipermanent settlements of the Amazon rainforest. People live in the settlement part of the year but break into smaller groups that spread out into a larger area for foraging. Important decisions concern how the site will fare with respect to the weather, the availability of drinking water, and defensibility. The central plaza must be elevated for drainage and drainage channels dug around the hearths. The overall plan is circular. In some groups, separate shelters are built for extended family groups; in others, they are joined into a continuous circle with connected roofs. In some cases, the headman has a separate and larger shelter.

Pastoralists have designed ingenious portable structures, such as the North American teepee and the Mongolian *ger*, or yert. The teepee is a conical tent made with a framework of four wooden poles tied at the top with thongs, to which are joined other poles to complete the cone. This frame is then covered with buffalo hide. A ger is also a circular, portable dwelling, but its roof is flatter. The covering is made of cloth. This lightweight structure is easy to set up, take down, and transport, and it is adaptable to all weather conditions. Encampments are often arranged around the teepees or gers in several concentric circles. Social status was the structuring principle, and the council of chiefs and the head chief were located in the center.

With the development of the state, urban areas grew and showed the effects of centralized planning and power, for example, in grid-style planning of streets rather than haphazard placement. The symbolic demonstration of the power, grandeur, and identity of states was and is expressed architecturally through the construction of impressive urban monuments: temples, administrative buildings, memorials, and museums.

Interior decoration of domestic dwellings also became more elaborate. In settled agricultural communities and urban centers, where permanent housing is the norm, decoration is more likely to be found in homes. Wall paintings, sculptures, and other features distinguish the homes of wealthier individuals. Research on interior decoration in contemporary Japan involved studying the contents of home-decorating magazines and doing participant observation within homes (Rosenberger 1992). Findings reveal how people incorporate and localize selected aspects of Western decorating styles.

---

theater   a form of enactment, related to other forms such as dance, music, parades, competitive games and sports, and verbal art, that seeks to entertain through acting, movement, and sound.

(LEFT) The Duomo in Florence, Italy. The Duomo, or Cathedral of Santa Maria del Fiore, was begun in 1296. Its massive dome, designed by architect and sculptor Filippo Brunelleschi, was not completed until 1436. The goal was to surpass all other edifices in height and beauty. The Duomo still physically dominates the city of Florence and also attracts many tourists from around the world. (RIGHT) Burj Dubai, or Dubai Tower, in Dubai, United Arab Emirates, is currently the tallest building the world. Its immense height signals the importance of Dubai in the modern world and, more generally, the success and prosperity of the Middle East.

Home-decorating magazines target middle- and upper-class Japanese housewives who seek to express their status through new consumption styles. A trend is the abandonment of three features of traditional Japanese design: *tatami, shoji,* and *fusuma.* Tatami are 2-inch-thick mats that are about 3 feet wide and 6 feet long. A room's size is measured in terms of the number of tatami it holds. Shoji are the sliding screen doors of tatami rooms; one door is covered with glass and the other with translucent rice paper often printed with a design of leaves or waves. Fusuma are sliding wall panels made of thick paper; they are removable so that rooms can be enlarged for gatherings. The tatami room usually contains a low table in the center, with pillows for seating on the floor. A special alcove may contain a flower arrangement, ancestors' pictures,

heterotopia   a new situation formed from elements drawn from multiple and diverse contexts.

and a Buddhist altar. Futons are stored in closets around the edges and brought out at night for sleeping.

In distancing themselves from the old style, "modern" Japanese housewives make several changes. The kitchen has a central rather than marginal location and is merged with a space called the DK (dining-kitchen) or LDK (living-dining-kitchen), with wood, tile, or carpeting on the floor. Western products such as carpeting and curtains (instead of the fusuma, the tatami, and shoji) are used to cover surfaces and to separate rooms. The LDK has a couch, a dining set, a VCR, a stereo, and an array of small items on display, such as Western-style teapots, cuckoo clocks, and knickknacks.

These design choices accompany deeper social changes that involve new aspirations about marriage and family relationships. Home-decorating magazines promote the idea that the modern style brings with it happier children who earn better grades and closer husband–wife ties. Tensions exist, however, between these ideals and the realities of middle- and upper-class life in Japan. Women feel compelled to work either part time or full time to be able to contribute income for satisfying their new consumer needs in spite of societal pressure against careers and for devoting more time to domestic pursuits to provide the kind of life portrayed in the magazines. Children are in the conflicting position of being indulged as new consumer targets, while the traditional value of self-discipline still holds. Husbands are in the conflicting position of needing to be more attentive to wife and home, whereas the corporate world calls them for a "7–11" working day. Last, the Western image of the happy nuclear family contains no plan for the aged. Only the wealthiest Japanese families manage to satisfy both individualistic desires and filial duties because they can afford a large house in which they dedicate a separate floor for the husband's parents, complete with tatami mats. Less wealthy people have a more difficult time dealing with conflicting values about the care of aged parents.

GARDENS AND FLOWERS Gardens for use, especially for food production, are differentiated from gardens for decorative purposes. The concept of the decorative garden is not a cultural universal. Circumpolar peoples cannot construct gardens in the snow, and highly mobile pastoralists have no gardens because they are on the move. The decorative garden is a product of state-level societies, especially in the Middle East, Europe, and Asia (Goody 1993). Within these contexts, variation exists in what are considered to be the appropriate contents and designs for gardens. A Japanese garden may contain no blooming flowers, focusing instead on the shape and placement of trees, shrubs, stones, and bodies of water.

Elite Muslim culture, with its core in the Middle East, has long been associated with formal decorative gardens. A garden, enclosed with four walls, is symbolically equivalent to the concept of paradise. The Islamic garden pattern involves a square design with a symmetrical layout, fountains, waterways, and straight pathways, all enclosed within walls. Islamic gardens often surrounded the tombs of prominent people. India's Taj Mahal, built by a Muslim emperor, follows this pattern, with one modification: The tomb is placed at one edge of the garden rather than in the center. The result is a dramatic stretch of fountains and flowers leading from the main gate to the monument.

The contents of a personal garden, like a dinner menu with all its special ingredients or a collection of souvenirs from around the world with all their memories and meanings, make a statement about its owner's identity and status. For example, in Europe during the height of colonialism, imperial gardens contained specimens from remote corners of the globe, collected through scientific expeditions. Such gardens were created through the collection and placement of plants from many parts of the world and are thus examples of what the French cultural theorist Michel Foucault refers to as a **heterotopia**, or a place formed from elements drawn from multiple and diverse contexts (Foucault 1970). Heterotopias can be constructed in architecture, cuisine, dress, and more. In the case of the colonial European gardens, the heterotopic message conveyed the owner's worldliness and intellectual status.

Cut flowers are now important economic products. They provide income for gardeners throughout the world, and they are also exchange items. In France, women receive flowers from men more than any other kind of gift (Goody 1993:316). In much of the world, special occasions require gifts of flowers: In the West, as well as in East Asia, funerals are times for displays of flowers. Ritual offerings to the deities in Hinduism are often flowers such as marigolds woven into a chain or necklace.

Flowers are prominent motifs in Western and Asian secular and sacred art, but less so in African art (Goody 1993). Some possible reasons for this variation include ecological and economic factors. Eurasia's more temperate environment possesses a greater variety of blooming plants than Africa's does. Also, sheer economic necessity in developing countries of Africa limits the amount of space that can be used for decorative purposes. In wealthy African kingdoms, prominent luxury goods include fabrics, gold ornaments, and wooden carvings rather than flowers. This pattern of production is changing with globalization, and many African countries now grow flowers for export to the world market.

◆◆◆

Play, Leisure, and Culture

This section turns to the area of expressive culture related to what people do for "fun." It is impossible to draw a clear line between the concepts of *play* or *leisure* and art or performance, however, because they often overlap. For example, a person could paint watercolors in her leisure time, yet simultaneously be creating a work of art. In most cases, though, play and leisure can be distinguished from other activities (Huizinga, as summarized in Hutter 1996). In the case of play,

- it is an unnecessary activity.
- it serves no direct utilitarian purpose for the participants.
- it is limited in terms of time.
- it has rules.
- it may contain chance and tension.

THINKING
OUTSIDE
THE BOX

Think of some occasions in your cultural world in which cut flowers are important. What role do they play?

Leisure activities often overlap with play, but many leisure activities, such as reading or lying on a beach, would not be considered play because they lack rules, chance, and tension. Within the broad category of play and leisure activities, several subcategories exist, including varieties of games, hobbies, and recreational travel. Although play and leisure, as well as their subcategories, may be pursued from a nonutilitarian perspective, they are often situated in a wider context of commercial and political interests. Major international competitions are a good example of such complexities. China's hosting of the 2008 summer Olympics was an opportunity for China to demonstrate its status as a world leader.

Cultural anthropologists study play and leisure within their cultural contexts as part of social systems. They ask, for example, why some leisure activities involve teams rather than individuals; what the social roles and statuses of people involved in particular activities are; what the goals of the games are and how those goals are achieved; how much danger or violence is involved; how certain activities are related to group identity; and how such activities link or separate different groups within or between societies or countries.

GAMES AND SPORTS AS A CULTURAL MICROCOSM

Games and sports, like religious rituals and festivals, can be interpreted as reflections of social relationships and cultural ideals. In Clifford Geertz's terms, they are both *models of a culture,* depicting basic ideals, and *models for a culture,* socializing people into certain values and ideals (1996). American football can be seen as a model for corporate culture in its clear hierarchy with leadership vested in one person (the quarterback) and its goal of territorial expansion by taking over areas from the competition.

A comparison of baseball as played in the United States and in Japan reveals core values about social relationships in each country (Whiting 1979). The differences emerge clearly when U.S. players are hired by Japanese teams. The U.S. players bring with them an intense sense of individualism, which promotes the value of "doing your own thing." This pattern conflicts with a primary value that influences the playing style in Japan: **wa**, meaning discipline and self-sacrifice for the good of the group. In Japanese baseball, players must seek to achieve and maintain team harmony. Japanese baseball players have a negative view of extremely individualistic, egotistical plays and strategies.

---

wa   Japanese word meaning discipline and self-sacrifice for the good of the group.

blood sport   competition that explicitly seeks to bring about a flow of blood from, or even the death of, human–human contestants, human–animal contestants, or animal–animal contestants.

SPORTS AND SPIRITUALITY: MALE WRESTLING IN INDIA   In many contexts, sports are closely tied to religion and spirituality. Asian martial arts, for example, require forms of concentration much like meditation, leading to spiritual self-control. Male wrestling in India, a popular form of entertainment at rural fairs and other public events, involves a strong link with spiritual development and asceticism (Alter 1992).

In some ways, these wrestlers are just like other members of Indian society. They go to work, and they marry and have families, but their dedication to wrestling involves important differences. A wrestler's daily routine is one of self-discipline. Every act—defecation, bathing, comportment, devotion—is integrated into a daily regimen of discipline. Wrestlers come to the *akhara* (AKH-uh-ruh), equivalent to a gymnasium, early in the morning for practice under the supervision of a guru or other senior akhara member. They practice moves with different partners for two to three hours. In the early evening, they return for more exercise. In all, a strong young wrestler will do around 2000 push-ups and 1000 deep-knee bends a day in sets of 50 to 100.

The wrestler's diet is strictly defined. Most wrestlers are mainly vegetarian. Although they avoid alcohol and tobacco, they do consume *bhang,* a beverage made of blended milk, spices, almonds, and concentrated marijuana. In addition to regular meals, wrestlers consume large quantities of milk, ghee (clarified butter), and almonds. These substances are sources of strength because, according to traditional dietary principles, they help to build up the body's semen.

Several aspects of the wrestler's life are similar to those of a Hindu *sannyasi* (sun-YAH-see) or holy man, who renounces life in the normal world. The aspiring sannyasi studies under a guru and learns to follow a strict routine of discipline and meditation called yoga, and he adheres to a restricted diet to achieve control of the body and its life force. Both wrestler and sannyasi roles focus on discipline to achieve a controlled

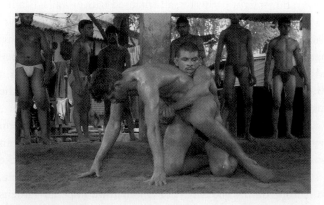

Wrestlers in a village in northern India. They follow a rigorous regimen of dietary restrictions and exercise in order to keep their bodies and minds under control.

▶ *Think of another sport that emphasizes dietary restrictions.*

self. Therefore, in India, wrestling does not involve the "dumb jock" stereotype that it sometimes does in North America. Rather, wrestlers have respect because their sport requires perfected physical, spiritual, and moral health.

PLAY, PLEASURE, AND PAIN Many leisure activities combine pleasure and pain. Serious injuries can result from mountain climbing, horseback riding, or playing touch football in the backyard. A more intentionally dangerous category of sports is **blood sports**, competitions that explicitly seek to bring about a flow of blood or even death. Blood sports may involve human contestants, humans contesting against animal competitors, or animals or birds fighting other animals or birds (Donlon 1990). In the United States and Europe, professional boxing is an example of a popular blood sport that few, if any, anthropologists have studied so far. Cultural anthropologists have looked at the use of animals in blood sports such as cockfights and bullfights. These sports are variously interpreted as providing sadistic pleasure, as offering vicarious self-validation (usually of males) through the triumph of their representative pit bulls or fighting cocks, and as the triumph of culture over nature in the symbolism of bullfighting.

Even the seemingly pleasurable leisure experience of a Turkish bath can involve discomfort and pain. One phase involves scrubbing the skin vigorously several times with a rough natural sponge, a pumice stone, or a piece of cork wood wrapped in cloth (Staats 1994). The scrubbing removes layers of dead skin and opens the pores so that the skin will be beautiful. In Turkey, an option for men is a massage that can be quite violent, involving deep probes of leg muscles, cracking of the back, and being walked on by the often weighty masseur. In Ukraine, being struck repeatedly on one's bare skin with birch branches is the final stage of the bath. Violent scrubbing, scraping, and beating of the skin, along with radical temperature changes in the water, are combined with valued social interaction at the bathhouse.

LEISURE TRAVEL

Anthropologists who study leisure travel, or tourism, often comment that their research is dismissed as trivial and based on "hanging out" at beautiful beaches or at five-star hotels. Research on tourism, however, is just as challenging as the anthropological study of any other topic.

Tourism is one of the major economic forces in the world, and it has dramatic effects on people and places in tourist destination areas. A large percentage of worldwide tourism involves individuals from Europe, North America, and Japan traveling to less industrialized countries. Ethnic tourism, cultural tourism, and ecotourism are attracting increasing numbers of travelers. They are often marketed as providing a view of "authentic" cultures. Images of indigenous people figure prominently in travel brochures and advertisements (Bruner 2005).

Many international tourists seek "cultural tourism" so that they can participate in what is presented to them as a "traditional" cultural context. Safari tour groups in Africa, as in this visit to Maasailand, combine sightings of exotic wildlife and contact with Maasai people.

▶ *Go to the Web to learn about cultural tourism opportunities among the Maasai.*

Tourist promotional literature often presents a "myth" of other peoples and places and offers travel as a form of escape to a mythical land of wonder. Research on Western travel literature shows that, from the time of the earliest explorers to the present, it has been full of *primitivist* images about indigenous peoples who are portrayed as having static or "stone age" traditions, largely unchanged by the forces of Western colonialism, nationalism, economic development, and even tourism. Tourists often seek to find the culture that the tourist industry defines rather than gaining a genuine, more complicated, and perhaps less photogenic view of it. For the tourist, obtaining these desired cultural images through mass tourism involves packaging the "primitive" with the "modern" because most tourists want comfort and convenience along with their "authentic" experience. Thus, advertisements minimize the foreignness of the host country, noting, for example, that English is spoken and that the destination is remote, yet accessible, while simultaneously promoting primitivist and racist imagery.

The strains among accuracy in presenting a cultural experience, sensationalism, and social stigma emerge clearly in

THINKING OUTSIDE THE BOX

In your cultural world, what are some examples of leisure activities that combine pleasure and pain? As a research project, conduct some informal interviews with participants to learn why they are attracted to such activities.

High-end tourism in Costa Rica.

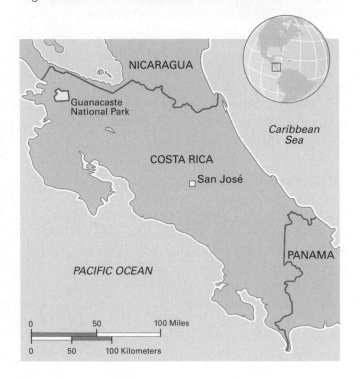

MAP 11.1 Costa Rica.
The Republic of Costa Rica was the first country in the world to constitutionally abolish its army, and it has largely escaped the violence that its neighbors have endured. Agriculture is the basis of the economy, with tourism—especially ecotourism—playing an increasing role. Most of the 4 million inhabitants of Costa Rica are descended from Spanish colonialists. Less than 3 percent are Afro-Costa Ricans, and less than 2 percent, or around 50,000, are indigenous people. Seventy-five percent of the people are Roman Catholic and 14 percent Protestant. The official language is Spanish.

research on tourism in the coal-mining region of Appalachia in Virginia (LaLone 2003). Mary LaLone pinpoints some of the challenges that arise in representing Appalachian culture with accuracy and dignity while at the same time responding to marketing demands of tourists. For example, in portraying people's everyday lives, accuracy says that it is right to show people wearing shoes and using indoor plumbing, whereas tourists may expect and want to see displays of "hillbilly life" that emphasize poverty, shoelessness, outhouses, feuding, and "moonshining" (producing and consuming illicit alcohol). LaLone suggests that cultural anthropologists can help find a way toward the interpretation and presentation of a region's heritage that provides a more complex view so that hosts retain their dignity, accuracy is maintained, and tourists learn more than they expected.

The anthropology of tourism has focused on the impact of global and local tourism on indigenous peoples and places. Such studies are important in exposing the degree to which tourism helps or harms local people and local ecosystems. For example, the formation of Amboseli National Park in Kenya prevented Maasai herders from accessing traditional water resources (Drake 1991). The project staff promised benefits (such as shares of the revenues from the park) to the Maasai if they stayed off the reserve, but most of the benefits never materialized. In contrast, in Costa Rica local people were included in the early planning stages of the Guanacaste National Park (see Map 11.1), and now they play a greater role in the park management system and share in some of the benefits.

Local people with long-standing rights to land, water, and other resources often attempt to exercise agency and take an active role in transforming the effects of tourism to their advantage, designing and managing tourist projects (Natcher, Davis, and Hickey 2005; Miller 2009). The Gullah people of South Carolina are one such example (see Culturama). The last section of this chapter provides others.

◆◆◆

Change in Expressive Culture

Nowhere are forms and patterns of expressive culture frozen in time. Much change is influenced by Western culture through globalization, but influence does not occur in only one direction. African musical styles have transformed the U.S. musical scene since the days of slavery. Japan has exerted a strong influence on upper-class garden styles in the United States. Cultures in which tradition and conformity have been valued in pottery making, dress, or theater find themselves having to make choices about whether to innovate and, if so, how. Many contemporary artists (including musicians and playwrights) from Latin America to China are fusing ancient and "traditional" motifs and styles with more contemporary themes and messages.

Changes occur through the use of new materials and technology and through the incorporation of new ideas, tastes, and meanings. These changes often accompany other aspects of social change, such as colonialism, global tourism, or political transitions.

The Gullah of South Carolina

The Gullah (goo-luh) culture in South Carolina stretches along the coast, going inland about 30 miles (National Park Service 2005). The Gullah are descended from African slaves originating in West and Central Africa. In the early eighteenth century, Charleston, South Carolina, was the location of the largest trans-Atlantic slave market on the coast of British North America.

The enslaved people brought with them many forms of knowledge and practice. Rice was a central part of their African heritage and identity. They knew how to plant it in swamps, harvest it, and prepare it. Gullah ancestors in colonial South Carolina were influential in developing tidal irrigation methods of rice growing, using irrigation and management of the tides to increase yields compared with yields from rainfall-dependent plantings.

Experts at net fishing, the Gullah made handwoven nets that are masterpieces of folk art. Their textile arts include a form of quilting, or sewing strips of cloth together into a larger piece. Gullah women combined their African quilting styles with those of Europeans to form new styles and patterns. Many quilts tell a story in their several panels.

Gullah cuisine combines African elements such as rice, yams, peas, okra, hot peppers, peanuts, watermelon, and sesame seeds with European ingredients and with American Indian foods such as corn, squash, tomatoes, and berries (National Park Service 2005). Popular dishes are stews of seafood and vegetables served over rice. Rice is the cornerstone of the meal, and the family rice pot is a treasured possession passed down over the generations.

Gullah culture in South Carolina has become a major tourist attraction, including music, crafts, and cuisine. If there is a single item that tourists identify with the Gullah, it is sweetgrass baskets. Basketmaking, once common among all Gullah people in South Carolina, is now a specialized activity. In South Carolina, it is thriving in the Charleston area largely through a combination of tourist demand and the creativity of local artists. Both men and women "sew" the baskets. They sell them in shops in Charleston's historic center and along Highway 17.

As the success of the basketmakers has grown and the popularity of the baskets increased, so too, has the need for sweetgrass. Sweetgrass baskets thus are a focal point of conflict between Gullah cultural producers and local economic developers who are destroying the land on which the sweetgrass grows. Because tourism low-country South Carolina is increasingly dependent on cultural tourism some planners are trying to find ways to devote land to growing sweetgrass.

The story of the Gullah of South Carolina begins with their rich African cultural heritage, through their suffering as slaves, to racism and social exclusion, and to their current situation in which their expressive culture is a key factor in the state economy.

(LEFT) The hands of Charleston artist Mary Jackson are shown making a sweetgrass basket. (CENTER) Drummers at the Gullah Festival in Beaufort (BO-fert). The Festival celebrates the culture and accomplishments of the Gullah people.

MAP 11.2 The Gullah Region of South Carolina. The heartland of Gullah culture is in the low-country

COLONIALISM AND SYNCRETISM

Western colonialism had dramatic effects on the expressive culture of indigenous peoples. In some instances, colonial disapproval of particular art forms and activities resulted in their extinction. For example, when colonialists banned head-hunting in various cultures, the change also meant that body decoration, weapon decoration, and other related expressive activities were abandoned. This section provides an example of how colonial repression of indigenous forms succeeded, but only temporarily.

In the Trobriand Islands of Papua New Guinea (see Map 2.1, p. 33), British administrators and missionaries sought to eradicate the frequent tribal warfare as part of a pacification process. One strategy was to replace it with intertribal competitive sports (Leach 1975). In 1903, a British missionary introduced the British game of cricket in the Trobriands as a way of promoting a new morality, separate from the warring traditions. As played in England, cricket involves particular rules of play and a proper look of pure white uniforms. In the early stages of the adoption of cricket in the Trobriands, the game followed the British pattern closely. As time passed and the game spread into more parts of the islands, it developed localized and syncretized versions.

Throughout the Trobriands, the islanders merged cricket into indigenous political competition between big-men (Foster 2006). Big-men leaders urged their followers to increase production in anticipation of a cricket match because matches were followed by a redistributive feast. (Review the discussion of moka in Chapter 8.) The British missionaries discouraged traditional magic in favor of Christian beliefs, but the Trobriand Islanders brought war-related magic into cricket. For example, they used spells against opposing teams, and they decorated bats like war weapons. Weather magic was important, too. If things were not going well, a ritual specialist might use a spell to bring rain and force cancellation of the game.

Over time, the Trobrianders stopped wearing the crisp white uniforms and instead painted their bodies and adorned themselves with feathers and shells. The teams announced their entry into the host village with songs and dances, praising their team in contrast to the opposition. Syncretism is notable in team songs and dances, which draw on Western elements. An example is the famous entry song of the "P-K" team. (P-K is the name of a Western chewing gum.) The P-K team chose its name because the stickiness of gum is like the ability of their bat to hit the ball. Other teams incorporated sounds and motions of airplanes, objects that they first saw during World War II. The songs and dances were explicitly sexual and enjoyed by all, in spite of Christian missionary attempts to suppress the "immoral" aspects of Trobriand culture, which included sexual metaphors about large yams in songs and thrusting hip movements in dances, among other things.

The Trobrianders also changed some of the rules of play. The home team should always win, but not by too many runs. In this way, guests show respect to the hosts. Winning is not the major goal. The feast after the match is the climax, in which hosts demonstrate their generosity to their guests, establishing the requirement for the next match and feast.

TOURISM'S COMPLEX EFFECTS

Global tourism has had varied effects on indigenous arts. Often, tourist demand for ethnic arts and souvenirs has led to the mass production of sculpture, woven goods, or jewelry of a lesser quality than was created before the demand. Tourists' interests in seeing an abbreviated form of traditionally long

In the Trobriand Islands, British missionaries tried in the late nineteenth century to substitute their game of cricket for intertribal rivalries and warfare. It did not take long, however, for the Trobriand people to transform British rules and style to Trobriand ways.

▶ *If you wanted to watch a cricket match, what would be the closest place for you to go?*

MAP 11.3 Turkey.

Turkey straddles two continents, with most of its territory being in Asia. Its largest city, Istanbul, is located in the European part. The capital city, Ankara, is located in the Asian part, called Anatolia. Turkey's culture is a blend between East and West. Its population is over 70 million. Under the leadership of Mustafa Kamal Atatürk, a constitutional, representative political system was established in 1923, following the breakup of the Ottoman Empire after World War I. Turkish is the only official language of the country. It is also widely spoken in countries that were once part of the Ottoman Empire, including Albania, Bosnia-Herzegovina, the Republic of Macedonia, Greece, Romania, and Serbia. Over 2 million Turkish-speaking immigrants live in Germany. Islam is the overwhelmingly predominant religion of Turkey, with 99 percent of the people Muslim. Of these, 75 percent are Sunni, 20 percent Shia, and 5 percent Sufi. According to the constitution, Turkey is a secular state, so there is no official state religion. The most popular sport is football (soccer). The most serious internal security issue is the Kurdish quest for greater cultural autonomy and rights.

dance or theater performances has led to the presentation of "cuts" rather than an entire piece. As a result, some scholars say that tourism leads to the decline in quality and authenticity of indigenous arts.

Tourist support for indigenous arts, however, is often the sole force maintaining them because local people in a particular culture may themselves be more interested in foreign music, art, or sports. Vietnamese water puppetry is an ancient performance mode, dating back at least to the Ly Dynasty of 1121 (Contreras 1995). Traditionally, water puppet shows took place in the spring during a lull in the farm work, or at special festival times. The stage for this performance art is either a small natural pond or an artificial water tank with a backdrop that hides the puppeteers from the audience. The

A belly dancer performing in Istanbul, Turkey. Belly dancing may have originated in Egypt. In Turkey, it is influenced by Egyptian styles and also by Roma traditions, because many prominent contemporary Turkish belly dancers are Roma. Turkish belly dancing is distinguished by its highly energetic and athletic style and the adept use of *zils*, or finger cymbals.

puppeteers operate carved and painted wooden figures with bamboo poles, wires, and strings, making them appear to glide over the water on their own. Since the 1980s, water puppetry has grown in popularity among Vietnamese people and international tourists (Foley 2001). It has spread from its core area in the Red River Delta in the northern part of the country to being nationwide and from being a seasonal performance to being year-round.

A more complicated situation exists in the growth of belly dancing as an essential touristic performance in Istanbul, Turkey (Potuoğlu-Cook 2006). International and Turkish tourists associate belly dancing with the Ottoman past, and it is increasingly available in various venues, including classical concerts, restaurants, and nightclubs in Istanbul and other major cities (see Map 11.3). In spite of Muslim values about female modesty, commercial interests are promoting this performance mode. Even middle-class housewives are taking belly dancing lessons, a sign that a formerly stigmatized and lower class activity is gentrifying. The rising popularity of belly dancing is evidence of Turkey's growing cosmopolitanism.

One positive result of global tourism is the growing international and local support for the preservation of **material cultural heritage**, which includes sites, monuments and buildings, and movable objects considered of outstanding world value in terms of history, art, and science (Cernea 2001). UNESCO proposed the basic definition of material cultural heritage in 1972. Since then, several hundred locations worldwide have been placed on its World Heritage List

---

material cultural heritage   the sites, monuments, buildings, and movable objects considered to have outstanding value to humanity.

LESSONS applied

A Strategy on Cultural Heritage for the World Bank

With headquarters in Washington, DC, and offices throughout the world, the World Bank is an international organization funded by member nations that works to promote and finance economic development in poor countries. Even though most of its permanent professional staff are economists, the Bank has begun to pay more attention to noneconomic factors that affect development projects.

A major move in that direction occurred in 1972 when the Bank hired its first anthropologist, Michael Cernea (CHAIR-nyuh). For three decades, Cernea has drawn attention to the cultural dimensions of development, especially in terms of the importance of local participation in development projects and people-centered approaches to project-forced resettlement (when, for example, large dams are being planned). His most recent campaign is to convince top officials at the World Bank that the Bank should become involved in supporting cultural heritage projects as potential pathways to development.

The World Bank already has in place a "do no harm" rule when it approves projects such as roads, dams, and mines. Cernea agrees that a "do no harm" rule is basic to preventing the outright destruction of cultural heritage, but he points out that it is a passive rule and does nothing to provide resources to preserve sites. Cernea wants the Bank to move beyond its "do no harm" rule. He's written a strategy that is active, not passive. It has two objectives:

- The World Bank should support cultural heritage projects that help to reduce local poverty by creating employment and generating capital from tourism.

- Projects should emphasize the educational value of preserving cultural heritage to local people and international visitors on the grounds that cultural understanding promotes goodwill and good relations at all levels—local, state, and international.

Cernea offers two suggestions for better management of cultural heritage projects: selectivity in site selection on the basis of the impact of the project on reducing poverty; and building partnerships for project planning and implementation among local, national, and international institutions.

◆ FOOD FOR THOUGHT

- On the Internet, find the UNESCO World Heritage Site that is nearest to where you live. What does the site contain, and what can you learn about its potential role in generating income for the local people?

---

and receive some financial support for preservation. Many other invaluable sites are lost, and will be lost in the future, through destructive engineering projects, urbanization, war, looting, private collecting, and climate change.

Applied anthropologists are involved in promoting improved stewardship of material cultural heritage. Some are motivated by a desire to preserve the record of humanity for future generations or for science. Others see that material cultural heritage, especially in poorer countries, can promote improvements in human welfare, and they endorse forging a link between material cultural heritage and sustainable development (see Lessons Applied).

In 2003, UNESCO ratified a new policy aimed at protecting **intangible cultural heritage,** or **living heritage** manifested in oral traditions, languages, performing arts, rituals and festive events, knowledge and practices about nature and the universe, and craftmaking. Support for this policy is based on the understanding that intangible culture provides people with a sense of identity and continuity, promotes respect for cultural diversity and human creativity, is compatible with the promotion of human rights, and supports sustainable development. Through this initiative, member countries of the United Nations are to make lists of valuable forms of intangible culture and take steps to preserve them. This policy has stimulated discussion and debate among cultural anthropologists, who see culture as more than a list of traits—highly contextualized, always changing, and not amenable to being managed or preserved through policy mandates (Handler 2003).

Cultural anthropologists point to the fact that the preservation of expressive culture sometimes occurs as a form of resistance to outside development forces. One example of this phenomenon is the resurgence of the hula, a traditional Hawai'ian dance (Stillman 1996). Beginning in the early 1970s, the *Hawai'ian Renaissance* grew out of political protest, mainly against American colonialism. Hawai'ian youth began speaking out against encroaching development that was displacing indigenous people from their land and destroying their natural resources. They launched a concerted effort to revive the Hawai'ian language, the hula, and canoe paddling, among other things. Since then, hula schools have proliferated, and hula competitions among the islands are widely attended by local people and international tourists.

---

intangible cultural heritage   UNESCO's view of culture as manifested in oral traditions, languages, performing arts, rituals and festive events, knowledge and practices about nature and the universe, and craftmaking.

Classical dancers perform in Thailand. The intricate hand motions, with their impact augmented by metal finger extenders, have meanings that accompany the narrative being acted out. International tourism is a major support for such performance arts in Thailand.

▶ Learn about UNESCO's recent declaration about intangible cultural heritage, and speculate on what it may mean for the preservation of particular cultural forms.

The 1990s saw the inauguration of the International Hula Festival in Honolulu, which attracts competitors from around the world. Although the hula competitions have helped ensure the survival of this ancient art form, some Hawai'ians voice concerns. First, they feel that allowing non-Hawai'ians to compete is compromising the quality of the dancing. Second, the format of the competition violates traditional rules of style and presentation, which require more time than is allowed, so important dances have to be cut. Third, for Hawai'ians, hula has close ties to religious beliefs and stories about the deities (Silva 2004). Performing hula in a mainly secular format is offensive to the gods and violates the true Hawai'ian way.

Another approach to preserving cultural heritage that is not top-down is "people-first" cultural heritage projects (Miller 2009). These are projects designed by the people whose culture is to be preserved—designed for their benefit and managed by them. A growing number of examples worldwide demonstrate the value of *people-first cultural heritage preservation* as having strong positive, measurable effects. One major area of impact is on the very survival of a culture through territorial entitlements, community security, poverty reduction, improved mental health, and the education of youth in traditional knowledge. Other important domains where people-first cultural heritage preservation has demonstrable positive effects include minority rights, conflict prevention and resolution, and environmental conservation and sustainability.

An example of people-first heritage preservation with implications for territorial entitlements and cultural survival is the Waanyi Women's History Project in Northern Queensland,

Australia (Smith, Morgan, and van der Meer 2003). This is a case of a community-driven project devoted to archiving cultural heritage and to establishing local community management. The "community" is a group of Waanyi (waan-yee) women who value their family history as heritage. The traditional way of maintaining this heritage has been to pass it on verbally from mother to daughter. The women wanted to have a written record of their history and documentation of sites and places of significance to them. They hired an anthropologist consultant to collect and record their narratives. An interesting feature of the case, which contrasts with traditional academic research, is that the knowledge generated cannot be published. The role of the researcher is limited to supporting the aspirations of the Waanyi women.

The project generated new sources of cash income for some Waanyi women through their employment in the National Park as "cultural rangers" responsible for the conservation of women's sites. It thus helped reduce material deprivation and entitlement insecurity. This project offers a clear case of a locally initiated and locally controlled heritage project with financial benefits going to the women and not to outsiders.

THINKING OUTSIDE THE BOX

Use UNESCO's interactive map of World Heritage Sites at http://whc.unesco.org/en/254 (Google Earth is required, but is available for free) to explore at least three sites. Follow up by looking at photographs of each site at http://ourplaceworldheritage.com.

11

the BIG questions REVISITED

◆ How is culture expressed through art?

Cultural anthropologists choose a broad definition of art that takes into account cross-cultural variations. From the anthropological perspective, all cultures have some form of art and a concept of what is good art.

Ethnographers document the ways in which art is related to many aspects of culture: economics, politics, human development and psychology, healing, social control, and entertainment. Art may serve to reinforce social patterns, and it may also be a vehicle of protest and resistance.

Anthropologists who study art examine it within its cultural context. To do this, anthropologists often become apprentices, learning how to make pots or play drums and, in that way, gaining both artistic skills and valuable insights into the culture of art, artists, the meanings of art, the role of the artist in society, and how art changes. A current trend is to examine how art and other forms of expressive culture are related to power issues and social inequality.

Various categories of art exist cross-culturally, and different cultures emphasize different forms. These categories include performance arts, architecture and decorative arts, graphic arts, and more.

◆ What do play and leisure activities reveal about culture?

Anthropological studies of play and leisure examine these activities within their cultural contexts. Cultural anthropologists view games as cultural microcosms, both reflecting and reinforcing dominant social values. Sports and leisure activities, although engaged in for nonutilitarian purposes, are often tied to economic and political interests. In some contexts, sports are related to religion and spirituality.

Tourism is a rapidly growing part of the world economy with vast implications for culture. Anthropologists who study tourism examine both its impact on local cultures and questions of authenticity in the touristic experience. Tourism

companies often market "other" cultures to appeal to consumers, a phenomenon that perpetuates stereotypes and denigrates the "host" culture. Some cultural anthropologists work with the tourism industry and local people to find better ways of representing culture that are more accurate, less stigmatizing to the host culture, and more informative for tourists. Local groups are actively seeking ways to share in the benefits of large-scale tourism and conservation projects and to contribute to cultural and environmental sustainability.

◆ How is expressive culture changing in contemporary times?

Major forces of change in expressive culture include Western colonialism, contemporary tourism, and globalization in general. As with other kinds of cultural change through contact, expressive culture may reject, adopt, or adapt new elements. Cultural resistance and syncretism are increasingly frequent, as exemplified in the Trobriand Islanders' co-optation and re-creation of cricket as a performative event leading up to a traditional feast.

In some cases, outside forces have led to the extinction of local forms of expressive culture. In others, outside forces have promoted continuity or the recovery of practices that had been lost. The rising popularity of belly dancing among the middle and upper classes of Istanbul is partly inspired by the demand for its performance by international tourists. Resistance to colonialism and neocolonialism has often inspired cultural revitalization, as in the Hawai'ian Renaissance and community-designed projects in Australia.

UNESCO's policies about the preservation of material cultural heritage and intangible cultural heritage are increasing worldwide attention to, and protection of, many sites and cultural practices. At the same time, increased tourist interest sometimes has detrimental effects on the sustainability of a site and the vitality of a cultural practice. In contrast to international policies, many local indigenous groups are taking cultural rights into their own hands and trying to preserve and protect their heritage for themselves and their descendants, rather than for tourists.

KEY CONCEPTS

art, p. 236

blood sports, p. 245

ethno-esthetics, p. 236

ethnomusicology, p. 239

expressive culture, p. 236

heterotopia, p. 243

intangible cultural heritage, p. 250

material cultural heritage, p. 249

theater, p. 240

wa, p. 244

SUGGESTED READINGS

Eduardo Archetti. *Masculinities: Football, Polo, and the Tango in Argentina*. New York: Berg, 1999. An Argentinean anthropologist examines expressive culture in Buenos Aires and how it is related to elite tastes, gender, and international competitiveness.

Edna G. Bay, ed. *Asen, Ancestors, and Vodun: Tracing Change in African Art*. Champaign-Urbana: University of Illinois Press, 2008. Focusing on southern Benin, this book documents the rise and decline of the sculptural production of *asen,* metal art objects created to honor the spirits of ancestors and vodun deities.

Jennifer Loureide Biddle. *Breasts, Bodies, Canvas: Central Desert Art as Experience*. Seattle: University of Washington Press, 2008. This study of artists in Australia's Central Desert draws on fieldwork among the Walpiri people.

Kevin K. Birth. *Bacchanalian Sentiments: Musical Experiences and Political Counterpoints in Trinidad*. Durham, NC: Duke University Press, 2008. The author explores links among several Trinidadian musical styles and political consciousness on the island.

Tara Browner. *Heartbeat of the People: Music and Dance of the Northern Pow-Wow*. Urbana: University of Illinois Press, 2002. An ethnomusicologist of Choctaw heritage uses archival research on the pow-wow and participant observation to show how elements of the pow-wow in North America have changed.

Shirley F. Campbell. *The Art of Kula*. New York: Berg, 2002. The author focuses on designs painted on kula canoes and finds that kula art and its associated male ideology linked to the sea competes with female ideology and symbolism linked to the earth.

Michael M. Cernea. *Cultural Heritage and Development: A Framework for Action in the Middle East and North Africa*. Washington, DC: The World Bank, 2001. Following an overview of cultural heritage projects and possibilities in the Middle East and North Africa, Cernea presents a strategy to reduce poverty with high-impact cultural heritage projects.

Michael Chibnik. *Carving Tradition: The Making and Marketing of Oaxacan Wood Carvings*. Austin: University of Texas Press, 2003. Chibnik examines the production of, and international trade in, Oaxacan wood carvings. Wood carving is not an indigenous art form in Oaxaca but was developed to appeal to tourists.

Debra L. Klein. *Yorùbá Bàt` Goes Global: Artists, Culture Brokers, and Fans*. Chicago: University of Chicago Press, 2007. The author describes the musical traditions of southwestern Nigeria, which are declining at home while being embraced internationally.

Alaina Lemon. *Between Two Fires: Gypsy Performance and Romani Memory from Pushkin to Post-Socialism*. Durham, NC: Duke University Press, 2000. This book examines how theater in Moscow both liberates Roma in Russia and reinforces their status as stigmatized outsiders.

Beverly B. Mack. *Muslim Women Sing: Hausa Popular Song*. CD included. Bloomington: Indiana University Press, 2004. This ethnography provides an intimate portrait of the life and art of Hausa women singers in northern Nigeria. It shows how Hausa women exercise agency and creativity through music and dance.

Roger Magazine. *Golden and Blue Like My Heart: Masculinity, Youth, and Power among Soccer Fans in Mexico City*. Tucson: University of Arizona Press, 2007. This book is an ethnography of fan clubs devoted to the Pumas, one of the most popular soccer teams in Mexico City.

Fiona Magowan. *Melodies in Mourning: Music and Emotion in Northern Australia*. Albuquerque, NM: School of American Research Press, 2007. Through the study of music and ritual life, this book focuses on women's experiences and child socialization among the Yolngu, an Aboriginal people of Arnhem Land in Australia's Northern Territory.

Jay R. Mandle and Joan D. Mandle. *Caribbean Hoops: The Development of West Indian Basketball*. Amsterdam: Gordon and Breach Publishers, 1994. This book describes and analyzes the emergence of (mainly men's) basketball as a popular sport in several Caribbean nations and explores regional differences in how the sport is played and viewed within the Caribbean.

Louise Meintjes. *Sound of Africa! Making Music Zulu in a South African Studio*. Durham, NC: Duke University Press, 2003. A South African anthropologist reveals the connections among music, culture, and state building. Focused on one studio in Johannesburg, this ethnography describes the roles of artists, sound engineers, emcees, and producers.

Laura Miller. *Beauty Up: Selling and Consuming Body Aesthetics in Japan*. Berkeley: University of California Press, 2006. The author, a linguistic anthropologist, examines the diversity of Japanese personal beauty practices of both males and females. She links eyelid surgery, body hair removal, and beauty products to a wider context of body esthetics.

12  PEOPLE ON THE MOVE

13  PEOPLE DEFINING DEVELOPMENT

PART V

CONTEMPORARY CULTURAL CHANGE

ANTHROPOLOGY works

Mamphela Ramphele's life story moves from her birth in 1947 in rural South Africa to her growing up in a context of racial apartheid and gender discrimination, to her adulthood and achievement as a political activist, medical doctor, anthropologist, teacher, university administrator, mother, and now one of the four managing directors of the World Bank.

As a child, Ramphele saw the injustices of apartheid inflicted on her family when the government retaliated against her relatives who worked for social equality. This experience spurred her on to political activism while she was still pursuing her education. Speaking about her school years, Ramphele says that although she knew she was intelligent, she had a difficult time overcoming the sense of inferiority that apartheid instilled in Black people.

In the early 1970s, Ramphele completed her medical studies at the University of Natal in South Africa. At the same time, she became an activist working for social justice. She founded the South Africa's Black Consciousness movement to abolish segregation and repression at a time when the White government was engaged in some of the most brutal activities against Black South Africans in its history.

As a consequence of her activism, she was censured under the Terrorism Act. Exiled for six years to Northern Transvaal, Ramphele worked there with the rural poor, setting up community health programs.

In the 1980s, after her release, she became a research fellow with the South African Development Research Unit at the University of Cape Town and earned a doctorate in anthropology. Her dissertation, *A Bed Called Home: Life in the Migrant Labour Hostels of Cape Town*, was later published as a book. In 1996, Ramphele was elected vice-chancellor of the University of Cape Town, the first Black and the first woman in the position.

Since 2000, Ramphele has been working with the World Bank, of which she is the first South African to hold a position as managing director. She oversees human development activities in the areas of education; health, nutrition, and population; and social protection. She also monitors and guides the World Bank's relationships with client governments in strengthening socioeconomic support programs. She has worked to reduce child mortality, eradicate polio, and reduce the prevalence of HIV/AIDS, TB, and malaria.

In 2001, the South African Women for Women organization honored Ramphele with a Woman of Distinction Award that recognizes her "energetic leadership, her commitment to excellence, and her continuing dedication to transforming the lives of those around her."

The Marsh Arab people suffered under the rule of Saddam Hussein from government projects that drained their marshes and political repression. Many who fled the country as refugees are now returning and plans are under way for restoring some of the marshes.

PEOPLE ON THE MOVE

12

the BIG questions

◆ What are the major categories of migration?

◆ What are examples of the new immigrants in the United States and Canada?

◆ How do anthropologists contribute to migration policies and programs?

OUTLINE

Categories of Migration

Critical Thinking: Haitian Cane Cutters in the Dominican Republic: A Case of Structure or Human Agency?

Culturama: The Maya of Guatemala

The New Immigrants to the United States and Canada

Migration Politics, Policies, and Programs in a Globalizing World

Lessons Applied: Studying African Pastoralists' Movements for Risk Assessment and Service Delivery

The current generation of North American youth will move more times during their lives than previous generations did. College graduates are likely to change jobs an average of eight times during their careers, and these changes are likely to require relocation.

Environmental, economic, familial, and political factors are causing population movements worldwide at seemingly all-time high levels. Research in anthropology shows, however, that frequent moves during a person's life and mass movements have occurred throughout human evolution. Foragers, horticulturalists, and pastoralists relocate frequently as a normal part of their lives.

Migration is the movement of a person or people from one place to another. Its causes are linked to major aspects of life, such as providing for one's food or for marriage. It often has profound effects on a person's economic and social status, for better or worse, as well as on health, language, religious identity, and education.

Thus, migration is of great interest to many academics and many professions. Historians, economists, political scientists, sociologists, and scholars of religion, literature, art, and music have studied migration. The professions of law, medicine, education, business, architecture, urban planning, public administration, and social work have specialties that focus on the process of migration and the period of adaptation following a move. Experts working in these areas share with anthropologists an interest in such issues as the kinds of people who migrate, causes of migration, processes of migration, health and psychosocial adaptations to new locations, and implications for planning and policy.

Cultural anthropologists do research on many issues related to migration. They study how migration is related to economic and reproductive systems, health and human development over the life cycle, marriage and household formation, politics and social order, and religion and expressive culture. Because migration affects all areas of human life, the topic pulls together the material in preceding chapters of this book.

Chinese Canadians also live mainly in urban areas such as Vancouver and Toronto. In Vancouver, they constitute about 16 percent of the population. Vancouver's Chinatown is a vibrant tourist site and a place where Chinese Canadians reaffirm their cultural heritage, as in the celebration, shown here, of Chinese New Year.

▶ *When does Chinese New Year take place, and how is the date determined?*

Three tendencies characterize research on migration in cultural anthropology:

- Fieldwork experience in more than one location in order to understand the places of origin and destination.

- The combination of macro- and microperspectives. Studying migration challenges the traditional fieldwork focus on one village or neighborhood, creating the need to take into account national and global economic, political, and social forces.

- Involvement in applied work. Many opportunities exist for anthropologists to contribute their knowledge and insights toward improving government policies and programs related to migration. Anthropologists assist efforts to address the situation of people forced to move by war, environmental destruction, and massive building projects such as dams.

This chapter first presents information on the most important categories of migrants and the opportunities and challenges they face. The second section provides descriptions of several examples of immigrants to the United States and Canada. The last section considers urgent issues related to migration, such as human rights and risk assessment and prevention programs.

---

migration   movement from one place to another.

internal migration   movement within country boundaries.

international migration   movement across country boundaries.

transnational migration   regular movement of a person between two or more countries resulting in a new cultural identity.

push–pull theory   an explanation for rural-to-urban migration that emphasizes people's incentives to move because of a lack of opportunity in rural areas (the "push") compared with urban areas (the "pull").

◆◆◆
Categories of Migration

Migration and its effects on people come in many forms. Both vary in terms of the distance involved, the purpose of the move, whether the move was forced or a matter of choice, and the migrant's status in the new destination. Microcultures play an important role in migration and its consequences for the migrant, as the rest of this chapter will document.

CATEGORIES BASED ON SPATIAL BOUNDARIES

This section reviews the basic features of three categories of population movement defined in terms of the spatial boundaries crossed:

- **Internal migration**, movement within country boundaries
- **International migration**, movement across country boundaries
- **Transnational migration**, movement in which a person regularly moves back and forth between two or more countries and forms a new cultural identity transcending a single geopolitical unit

INTERNAL MIGRATION   Rural-to-urban migration was the dominant form of internal population movements in most countries during the twentieth century. A major reason that people migrate to urban areas is the availability of work. According to the **push–pull theory** of labor migration, rural areas are unable to support population growth and rising expectations about the quality of life (*the push factor*). Cities (*the pull factor*), in contrast, attract people, especially youths, for employment and lifestyle reasons. According to this theory, rural people weigh the costs and benefits of rural versus urban life and then decide to go or stay. The theory is related to the approach in anthropology that emphasizes human agency, or choice (review Chapter 1). Many instances of urban migration, however, are shaped by structural forces that are beyond the control of the individual, such as war or poverty.

INTERNATIONAL MIGRATION   International migration has grown in volume and significance since 1945 and especially since the mid-1980s. Around 100 million people, or nearly 2 percent of the world's population, including legal and undocumented immigrants, live outside of their home countries. Migrants who move for work-related reasons constitute most of the people in this category. The driving forces behind the trend are economic and political changes that affect labor demands and human welfare (see Critical Thinking).

The major destination countries of early international immigration were the United States, Canada, Australia, New Zealand, and Argentina. The immigration policies that these countries applied in the early twentieth century are labeled "White immigration" because they explicitly limited non-White immigration (Ongley 1995). In the 1960s, Canada made its immigration policies less racially discriminatory and more focused on skills and experience. The "White Australia" policy formally ended in 1973. In both the Canadian and Australian cases, a combination of changing labor needs and interest in improving those countries' international image prompted the reforms.

During the 1980s and 1990s, the United States, Canada, and Australia experienced large-scale immigration from new sources, especially from Asia, and—to the United States—from Latin America and the Caribbean. These trends continue in the twenty-first century.

The earlier classic areas of outmigration—northern, western, and southern Europe—are now, instead, receiving many immigrants, including refugees from Africa and the Middle East. International migration flows in the Middle East are complex, with some countries, such as Turkey, experiencing substantial movements both in and out. Millions of Turkish people immigrated to Germany in the later decades of the twentieth century. Turkey, in turn, has received many Iraqi and Iranian Kurdish refugees (review Culturama, Chapter 8, p. 182). Over 2 million Palestinian refugees and their descendants live in Jordan and Lebanon. Israel has attracted Jewish immigrants from Europe, northern Africa, the United States, and Russia.

TRANSNATIONAL MIGRATION   Transnational migration is increasing along with other aspects of globalization. It is important to recall, however, that rising rates of transnational migration are related to the creation of state boundaries in recent centuries. Pastoralists with extensive seasonal herding routes were "transnational" migrants long before state boundaries cut across their pathways.

Much contemporary transnational migration is motivated by economic factors. The spread of the global corporate economy is the basis for the growth of one category of transnational migrants nicknamed "astronauts": businesspeople (mainly men) who spend most of their time flying among different cities as investment bankers or corporate executives. At the lower end of the income scale are transnational migrant laborers, who spend substantial amounts of time working in different places and whose movements depend on the demand for their labor.

An important feature of transnational migration is how it affects a migrant's identity, sense of citizenship, and entitlements. Constant movement weakens the sense of having one home and promotes instead a sense of belonging to a community of similar transnational migrants whose lives "in between" take on a new cultural reality.

As a response to the increased rate of transnational migration and the growth of overseas diaspora populations

CRITICAL thinking

Haitian Cane Cutters in the Dominican Republic: A Case of Structure or Human Agency?

The circulation of male labor from villages in Haiti (see Map 13.3, p. 284) to work on sugar estates in the neighboring Dominican Republic is the oldest and perhaps largest continuing population movement within the Caribbean region (Martínez 1996). Beginning in the early twentieth century, Dominican sugarcane growers began to recruit Haitian workers, called **braceros** (bruh-SARE-ohs) in Spanish— agricultural laborers permitted entry to a country to work for a limited time. Between 1852 and 1986, an agreement between the two countries' governments regulated and organized the labor recruitment. Since then, recruitment has become a private matter, with men crossing the border on their own or with recruiters working in Haiti without official approval.

Many studies and reports have addressed this system of labor migration. Two competing perspectives exist:

- View 1, the structurist position: The bracero system is neo-slavery and a clear violation of human rights.
- View 2, the human agency position: Braceros are not slaves because they migrate voluntarily.

View 1

Supporters of this position point to interviews with Haitian braceros in the Dominican Republic that indicate, they say, a consistent pattern of labor rights abuses. Haitian recruiters approach poor men, and boys as young as 7 years old, and promise them easy, well-paid employment in the Dominican Republic. Those who agree to go are taken to the frontier on foot and then either transported directly to a sugar estate in the Dominican Republic or turned over to Dominican soldiers for a fee for each recruit and then passed on to the sugar estate. Once there, the workers are given only one option for survival: cutting sugarcane, for which even the most experienced workers can earn only about US$2 a day. Working and living conditions on the estates are bad. The cane cutters are coerced into working even if they are ill, and working hours start before dawn and extend into the night. Many estate owners prevent Haitian laborers from leaving by having armed guards patrol the estate grounds at night. Many of the workers say that they cannot save enough from their meager wages to return home.

View 2

According to this view, reports of coercion are greatly exaggerated and miss the point that most Haitian labor migrants cross the border of their own

Hakka women of rural southern China are touristically defined by their "lampshade" hats. This Hakka woman migrated to Hong Kong for work and wears a traditional Hakka woman's hat as she pursues an urban lifestyle.

(review the definition in Chapter 7), many "sending" countries (countries that are the source of emigrants) are redefining themselves as *transnational countries*. A transnational country is a country with a substantial proportion of its population living outside the country's boundaries (Glick Schiller and Fouron 1999). Examples are Haiti, Colombia, Mexico, Brazil, the Dominican Republic, Portugal, Greece, and the Philippines. These countries grant continuing citizenship to emigrants and their descendants in order to foster a sense of belonging and willingness to continue to send **remittances**, or transfers of money or goods from a migrant to his or her family back home. Remittances are an increasingly large, though difficult to quantify, proportion of the global economy and often a large part of a country's economy. For example, at least 60 percent of the gross domestic product of the small Pacific island country of Tonga comes from remittances from members of the Tongan diaspora (Lee 2003:32) (see Map 12.1). India is the country that receives the largest total amount of money through remittances.

CATEGORIES BASED ON REASON FOR MOVING

Migrants are also categorized on the basis of their reason for relocating. The spatial categories just discussed overlap with

A Haitian migrant laborer. It is a matter of debate how much choice such a laborer has regarding whether he will migrate to the neighboring Dominican Republic for short-term work cutting cane, given the fact that he cannot find paid work in Haiti.

volition. On the basis of his fieldwork in Haiti, cultural anthropologist Samuel Martínez comments that "Recruitment by force in Haiti seems virtually unheard of. On the contrary, if this is a system of slavery, it may be the first in history to turn away potential recruits" (1996:20). Some recruits have even paid bribes to recruiters in order to be hired. Most people, even young people, are aware of the terrible working conditions in the Dominican Republic, so they are making an informed choice when they decide to migrate. Repeat migration is common and is further evidence of free choice. The major means of maintaining labor discipline and productivity on the sugar estates is not force but wage incentives, especially piecework. The life histories of braceros show that many of them move from one estate to another, thus discrediting the view that the estates are "concentration camps."

Martínez does, however, raise the issue of how free the "choice" to migrate to the Dominican Republic really is, given the extreme poverty in which many Haitians live. In Haiti, few work opportunities exist, and the prevailing wage for rural workers is US$1 a day. Thus, the poor are not truly free to choose to work in their home country: Labor migration to the Dominican Republic becomes a necessity.

In this view, what looks like a free choice to participate in the bracero system is actually "illusory" or structured choice. It is based on the unavailability of the option to work for a decent wage in Haiti and on the forced, or structured, choice to work in the Dominican Republic.

◆ **CRITICAL THINKING QUESTIONS**

- What are the comparative strengths of View 1 and View 2?
- What does each perspective support in terms of policy recommendations?
- How does the concept of structured choice change those policy recommendations?

---

the categories based on reason. An international migrant, for example, may also be a person who moved for employment reasons. Migrants experience different kinds of spatial change and, at the same time, have various reasons for moving.

LABOR MIGRANTS Many thousands of people migrate each year to work for a specific length of time. They do not intend to establish permanent residence and are often explicitly barred from doing so. This form of migration, when legally contracted, is called *wage labor migration*. The period of work may be brief, or it may last several years.

Asian women are the fastest-growing category among the world's more than 35 million migrant workers (www.ilo.org). Over 1.5 million Asian women are working abroad. Most are in domestic service jobs, and some work as nurses and teachers. Major sending countries are Indonesia, the Philippines, Sri Lanka, and Thailand. Main receiving countries are Saudi Arabia and Kuwait, and, to a lesser degree, Hong Kong, Japan, Taiwan, Singapore, Malaysia, and Brunei. Such women are usually alone and are not allowed to marry or have children in the countries where they are temporary workers. International migrant workers are sometimes illegally recruited and have no legal protection against poor or unjust working conditions.

Circular migration is a regular pattern of population movement between two or more places. It may occur within or between countries. Internal circular migrants include, for example, female domestic workers throughout Latin America and the Caribbean. These women have their permanent residences in rural areas, but they work for long periods for better-off people in the cities. They may leave their children in the care of grandparents in the country, sending remittances for the children's support.

DISPLACED PERSONS **Displaced persons** are people who are evicted from their homes, communities, or countries and forced to move elsewhere (Guggenheim and Cernea 1993). Colonialism, slavery, war, persecution, natural disasters, and large-scale mining and dam building are major causes of population displacement.

---

bracero an agricultural laborer who is permitted entry to a country to work for a limited time.

remittance the transfer of money or goods by a migrant to his or her family in the country of origin.

circular migration repeated movement between two or more places, either within or between countries.

displaced person someone who is forced to leave his or her home and community or country.

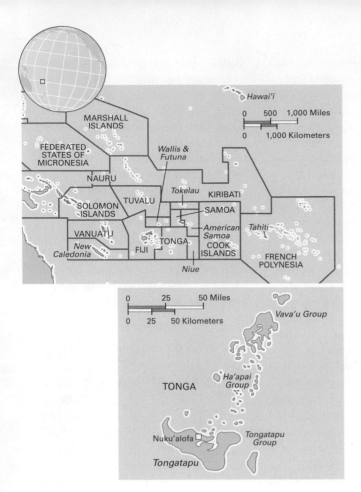

MAP 12.1 Tonga.

The Kingdom of Tonga is an archipelago of 169 islands, nick-named by Captain Cook as the Friendly Islands on the basis of his reception there. A constitutional monarchy, Tonga has great reverence for its king, stemming from a tradition of the sacred paramount chief. The current king, who has reigned since 1965, is Taufa'ahau Tupou IV. Before him, Queen Salote Tupou II reigned from 1918 to 1965. The population is around 113,000, with two-thirds living on the main island, Tongatapu. Rural Tongans are small-scale farmers. Most Tongans are ethnically Polynesian, and Christianity is by far the dominant religion. Languages are Tongan and English. Many Tongans have emigrated, and remittances are a major part of the economy.

Refugees are internationally displaced persons. Many refugees are forced to relocate because they are victims or potential victims of persecution on the basis of their race, religion, nationality, ethnicity, gender, or political views (Camino

---

refugee someone who is forced to leave his or her home, community, or country.

internally displaced person (IDP) someone who is forced to leave his or her home and community but who remains in the same country.

development-induced displacement the forced migration of a population due to development projects, such as the construction of a dam.

and Krulfeld 1994). Refugees constitute a large and growing category of displaced persons. An accurate count of all refugees globally is unavailable, but it is about 16 million people, meaning that about 1 of every 500 people is a refugee (UNHCR 2008). Around one-fourth of the world's refugees are Palestinians.

Women and children, who form the bulk of refugees, are vulnerable to abuse in refugee camps, including rape and trading sex for food (Martin 2005). Some case studies, however, shed a more positive light on the refugee experience (Burton 2004). Many refugee women from El Salvador, for example, learned to read and write in the camps and found positive role models in the humanitarian aid workers and their vision of social equality.

Internally displaced persons (IDPs) are people who are forced to leave their homes and communities but who remain within their country. They are the fastest-growing category of displaced people, with an estimated number of total IDPs worldwide of 51 million people (UNHCR 2008). Africa is the continent with the most IDPs. Within Africa, Sudan (see Map 13.6, p. 291) has the highest number, estimated at 2.7 million people. Iraq has an estimated 2.8 million IDPs, making it the country with the largest number of IDPs.

Many IDPs, like refugees, live for extended periods in camps under miserable conditions and with no access to basic

An Iraqi girl carries her sister at a camp for internally displaced persons (IDPs) near Falluja in 2004. Iraq has the largest number of IDPs of any country in the world. Some IDPs live in the same city but in a different neighborhood because they fear their former neighbors.

As construction of the massive Three Gorges Dam project proceeds in China, residents of a village that will be flooded by the dam collect their belongings from their homes as the bulldozers arrive.

▶ *Do research so that you can present a five-minute briefing on the social and environmental implications of the Three Gorges Dam to the people in the "affected" areas.*

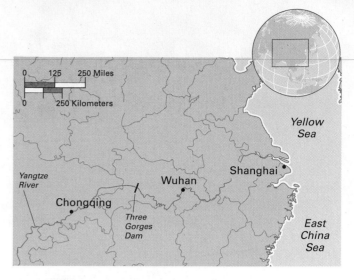

MAP 12.2 **Site of Three Gorges Dam in China.**
The Three Gorges Dam, the world's biggest dam, is one of several projects that are transforming China's environment. The dam will create a vast reservoir upstream to Chongqing. Engineers believe that the dam will solve the problem of annual flooding of the Yangtze River, the world's third-largest river, and generate immense amounts of power. Environmentalists point to the downsides, which include the decline of many important fish species, destabilizing slopes, and eroding islands in the Yangtze River delta. Cultural anthropologists are concerned about the forced migration of over 1 million people from 13 major cities and 140 villages, and the loss of rural farming livelihoods as land is flooded. Archaeologists decry the loss of unknown numbers of prehistoric and historic sites now buried under water. Others mourn the loss of one of the most beautiful places in the world, with its "gumdrop" mountains and breathtaking vistas that have inspired artists for centuries.

supports such as health care and schools. Because IDPs do not cross country boundaries, they do not come under the purview of the United Nations or any other international body. These institutions have limited authority over problems within countries. Several people have taken up the cause of IDPs and worked to raise international awareness of the immensity of the problem. Such efforts have led to the formal definition of IDPs and to legal recognition of their status.

Political violence is a major cause of people becoming IDPs. But other factors come into play as well, including natural disasters and large-scale development projects (discussed in Chapter 13). Dam construction, mining, and other projects have displaced millions in the past several decades. Dam construction alone is estimated to have displaced around 80 million people since 1950 (Worldwatch Institute 2003). Forced migration due to development projects is called **development-induced displacement**. Depending on a country's policy, people displaced by development may or may not be compensated financially for the loss of their homes and homeland. Even with monetary compensation, it is rarely possible to replace the life one had and the local knowledge that made life livable.

Mega-dam projects, or dam construction projects that involve costs in the billions of dollars and affect massive areas of land and huge numbers of people, are now attracting the attention of concerned people worldwide who support local resistance to massive population displacement. One of the most notorious cases is India's construction of a series of high dams in its Narmada River Valley, which cuts across the middle of the country from the west coast. This massive project involves relocating hundreds of thousands of people. The relocation is against the residents' wishes, and government compensation to the "oustees" for the loss of their homes, land, and livelihood is inadequate. Thousands of people in the Narmada Valley have organized protests over the many years of construction, and international environmental organizations have lent support. Celebrated Indian novelist Arundhati Roy joined the cause by learning everything she could about the 20 years of government planning for the Narmada dam projects, interviewing people who have been relocated, and writing a passionate statement called *The Cost of Living* (1999) in opposition to the project. In her book, a man who was displaced and living in a barren resettlement area tells how he used to pick 48 kinds of fruit in the forest. In the resettlement area, he and his family have to purchase all their food, and they cannot afford to eat any fruit at all (1999:54–55).

Governments promote mega-dam projects as important to the general welfare of the country. The uncalculated costs, however, are high for the local people who are displaced (see Map 12.2). The benefits are skewed toward corporate profits, energy for industrial plants, and energy and water for urban consumers who can pay.

CULTURAMA

The Maya of Guatemala

The term *Maya* refers to a diverse range of indigenous people who share elements of a common culture and speak varieties of the Mayan language. (*Note:* The adjective includes a final *n* only when referring to the language.) Most Maya people live in Mexico and Guatemala, with smaller populations in Belize and the western parts of Honduras and El Salvador. Their total population in Mexico and Central America is about 6 million.

In Guatemala, the Maya live mainly in the western highlands. The Spanish treated the Maya as subservient, exploited their labor, and took their land. Descendants of a formerly rich and powerful civilization, most Maya now live in poverty and lack basic human rights.

The Maya in Guatemala suffered years of genocide during the country's 36-year civil war, when about 200,000 Maya "disappeared" and were brutally murdered by government military forces (Manz 2004). Many more were forcibly displaced from their homeland, and today around 250,000 Maya live as IDPs (Fitigu 2005). Thousands left the country as refugees, fleeing to Mexico and the United States.

Beatriz Manz tells a chilling story of one group of K'iche' Maya and their struggle to survive during the war (2004). Manz began her fieldwork in 1973 among the Maya living in the rural areas near the highland town of Santa Cruz del Quiché in the province of El Quiché. The Maya farmed small plots, growing maize and other food items, but found it increasingly difficult to grow enough food for their families. An American Catholic priest came to them with an idea for a new settlement, over the mountains to the east, in Santa María Tzeá.

Several Maya from the highlands decided to establish a new village. They divided land into equal-size plots so that everyone had enough to support their families. Over time, more settlers came from the highland village. They cleared land for houses, farms, workshops, and a school.

In the late 1970s, their lives were increasingly under surveillance by the Guatemalan military, who suspected the village of harboring insurgents. In the early 1980s, the military began taking village men away. These men were never seen alive again. In 1982, a brutal attack left the village in flames and survivors fleeing into the jungle. Some went to Mexico, where they lived in exile for years, and others migrated as refugees to the United States. The peace accords of 1996 officially ended the bloodshed. Many of the villagers returned and began to rebuild.

Thanks to Beatriz Manz, University of California at Berkeley, for reviewing this material.

(LEFT) Maya women pray in a church 55 miles southeast of Guatemala City in 2003. The coffins contain the remains of the victims of a 1982 massacre inside the church. (CENTER) Maya women are active in market trade.

MAP 12.3 Guatemala. Within the Republic of Guatemala, the Maya constitute about 40 percent of the country's population of 14.6 million.

The manner in which displaced persons are relocated affects how well they will adjust to their new lives. Displaced persons in general have little choice about when and where they move, and refugees typically have the least choice of all. The Maya people of Guatemala suffered horribly during years of state violence and genocide. Many became refugees, relocating to Mexico and the United States. Others fit into the category of internally displaced persons (see Culturama).

Cultural anthropologists have done substantial research on refugee populations, especially those affected by war and other forms of violence and terror (Camino and Krulfeld 1994, Hirschon 1989, Manz 2004). They have discovered some key factors that ease or increase relocation stresses. One critical factor is the extent to which the new location resembles or differs from the home place in features such as climate, language, and food (Muecke 1987). Generally, the more different the places of origin and destination are, the greater are the adaptational demands and stress. Other key factors are the refugee's ability to get a job commensurate with his or her training and experience, the presence of family members, and whether people in the new location are welcoming or hostile to the refugees.

INSTITUTIONAL MIGRANTS **Institutional migrants** are people who move into a social institution, either voluntarily or involuntarily. They include monks and nuns, the elderly, prisoners, and boarding school or college students. This section considers examples of students and soldiers within the category of institutional migrants.

Student adjustment is similar to many other forms of migration, especially in terms of risks for mental stress. International students face serious challenges of spatial and cultural relocation. They are at greater risk of adjustment stress than are local students. Many international students report mental health problems, depending on age, marital status, and other factors. Spouses who accompany international students also suffer the strains of dislocation.

Soldiers are often sent on long-distance assignments for lengthy periods. Their destination may have detrimental physical and mental health effects on them, in addition to the fact that they may face combat. During the British and French colonial expansion, thousands of soldiers were assigned to tropical countries (Curtin 1989). Colonial soldiers faced new diseases in their destination areas. Their death rates from disease were twice as high as those of soldiers who stayed home, with two exceptions—in Tahiti and Hawai'i—where soldiers experienced better health than soldiers at home.

Anthropologists have published little about the effects of military migration on people in the military and on local people. One matter is clear, however: Military people on assignment need more in-depth training about how to communicate with local people and about the importance of respecting local people's cultures. A pocket-size handbook on Iraqi etiquette used by some U.S. troops in Iraq provides limited guidelines (Lorch 2003). It says, for example, that one should avoid arguments and should not take more than three cups of coffee or tea if one is a guest. Also, one should not use the "thumbs up" gesture because its meaning is obscene, and one should not sit with one's feet on a desk because that is rude. Such basics are helpful, but they do little to provide more in-depth cultural awareness that can make all the difference in conflict and postconflict situations.

During wartime, soldiers are trained primarily to seek out and destroy the enemy, not to engage in cross-cultural communication. As mentioned in Chapter 8, winning a war in contemporary times often hinges on what the conquerors do after the outright conflict is over, and that often means keeping troops stationed on foreign soil for a long time. Such extended assignments take a heavy toll on military personnel's mental health and appear to be linked to high rates of suicide, interpersonal violence, stress-based acts of violence against people in the occupied country, and readjustment problems after returning home.

◆◆◆

The New Immigrants to the United States and Canada

The term **new immigrant** refers to a person who moved internationally since the 1960s. The category of new immigrants worldwide includes rapidly increasing proportions of refugees, most of whom are destitute and desperate for asylum. Three trends characterize the new international migration in the twenty-first century:

- *Globalization*: More countries are involved in international migration, leading to increased cultural diversity in both sending and receiving countries.

- *Acceleration*: Growth in numbers of migrants has occurred worldwide.

- *Feminization*: Women are a growing percentage of international migrants to and from all regions and in all types of migration; some types exhibit a majority of women.

In the United States, the category of new immigrants refers to people who arrived after the 1965 amendments to the Immigration and Naturalization Act. This change made it possible for far more people from developing countries to enter, especially if they were professionals or trained in some desired skill. Later, the *family reunification* provision allowed permanent residents and naturalized citizens to bring in close family members. Most of the new immigrants in the United States are

---

institutional migrant   someone who moves into a social institution (such as a school or prison) either voluntarily or involuntarily.

new immigrant   an international migrant who has moved since the 1960s.

(LEFT) Latino immigrants studying English in a program in Virginia. (RIGHT) A Dominican Day parade in New York City.
▶ *Learn about an ethnic festival or event that is being held in the near future. Attend it and observe what signs and symbols of ethnicity are displayed, who attends, and what major messages about identity are conveyed.*

from Asia, Latin America, and the Caribbean, although increasing numbers are from Eastern Europe, especially Russia.

The United States offers two kinds of visas for foreigners: immigrant visas (also called residence visas) and nonimmigrant visas for tourists and students (Pessar 1995:6). An immigration visa is usually valid indefinitely and allows its holder to be employed and to apply for citizenship. A nonimmigrant visa is issued for a limited period and usually bars its holder from paid employment. Some immigrants are granted visas because of their special skills in relation to labor market needs, but most are admitted under the family unification provision.

THE NEW IMMIGRANTS FROM LATIN AMERICA AND THE CARIBBEAN

Since the 1960s, substantial movements of the *Latino* population (people who share roots in former Spanish colonies in the Western Hemisphere) have occurred, mainly to the United States. Latinos are about 10 percent of the U.S. population, excluding the population of Puerto Rico.

In the United States as a whole, and in some cities, such as Los Angeles, Miami, San Antonio, and New York, Latinos are the largest minority group. Within the category of Latino new immigrants, the three largest subgroups are Mexicans, Puerto Ricans, and Cubans. Large numbers also come from the Dominican Republic, Colombia, Ecuador, El Salvador, Nicaragua, and Peru.

Mexico is by far the major source of foreign-born immigrants to the United States (www.migrationinformation.org). Nearly 12 million foreign-born Mexicans live in the United States, a number that doubled from 1995 to 2006. Most live in

---

chain migration   a form of population movement in which a first wave of migrants comes and then attracts relatives and friends to join them in the destination.

the traditional destination states of California, Texas, and Illinois, but increasing numbers are settling in other states, such as Georgia, North Carolina, Nebraska, and Ohio. Mexico is also the major source of unauthorized immigration into the United States. Due to the large number of out-migrants, many rural areas in Mexico are left with mainly elderly people and their grandchildren until the Christmas holidays, when migrant workers return to join their families for a week or two.

CHAIN MIGRATION OF DOMINICANS   The Dominican Republic has ranked among the top 10 source countries of immigrants to the United States since the 1960s (Pessar 1995) (see Map 13.3, p. 284), and Dominicans are one of the fastest-growing immigrant groups in the United States. They live in clusters in a few states, with their highest concentration in New York State.

Patricia Pessar conducted fieldwork in the Dominican Republic and with Dominican immigrants living in New York City. She studied aspects of the departure process, such as getting a visa, arrival, and adaptation. Like many anthropologists who study immigrants, she became involved in helping some of her participants: "Along the way I also endeavored to repay people's help by brokering for them with institutions such as the Immigration and Naturalization Service, social service agencies, schools, and hospitals" (1995:xv).

For Dominican immigrants, as for many other immigrant groups, the *cadena*, or chain, links one immigrant to another. **Chain migration** is a form of population movement in which a first wave of migrants comes and then attracts relatives and friends to join them in the destination place. Most Dominicans who are legal immigrants have sponsored other family members. Thus, many Dominicans have entered the United States through the family unification provision. The policy, however, defines a family as a nuclear unit (review Chapter 6) and excludes important members of Dominican extended families, such as cousins and ritual kin (*compadres*). To overcome this barrier, some Dominicans use a technique called the *business marriage*. In a business marriage, an individual seeking to migrate pays a legal immigrant or citizen a fee, perhaps $2,000, to contract a "marriage" with that person. The migrant then acquires a visa through the family unification provision. A business marriage does not involve cohabitation or sexual relations; it is meant to be broken.

In New York City, most Dominicans work in manufacturing industries, including the garment industry. They are more concentrated in these industries than is any other ethnic group. Recent declines in manufacturing jobs in New York City, and the redefining of better positions into less desirable ones, have therefore disproportionately affected Dominicans. Retail and wholesale trade is another sector that employs large numbers of Dominicans and that has declined since the late 1960s. Other Dominicans have established their own retail businesses, or *bodegas*. Many bodegas are located in unsafe areas, and some owners have been assaulted or killed. Declining economic opportunities for Dominicans are aggravated by the arrival of even newer immigrants, especially from Mexico and Central America, who are willing to accept even lower wages than Dominicans do and worse working conditions.

Although many middle-class and upper-class Dominican migrants secured fairly solid employment in the United States on their arrival, they have declined economically since then. Dominicans have the highest poverty rate in New York City, 37 percent, compared with a city average of 17 percent. Wages are higher for men than women. Poverty is concentrated among women-headed households with young children, and women are more likely than men to be on public assistance.

Still, Dominican women in the United States are more often regularly employed than they would be in the Dominican Republic. This pattern upsets a patriarchal norm in which the nuclear family depends on male earnings and female domestic responsibilities. A woman's earning power means that husband–wife decision making is more egalitarian. A working Dominican woman is likely to obtain more assistance from the man in doing household chores. All of these changes help explain why more Dominican men are eager to return to the Dominican Republic than women are. As one man said, "Your country is a country for women; mine is for men" (Pessar 1995:81). Although most Dominicans left their homeland in search of a better life, many hope to return to the Dominican Republic. A common saying is that in the United States, "there is work but there is no life."

SALVADORANS: ESCAPING WAR TO STRUGGLE WITH POVERTY
Salvadorans are the fourth largest Latino population in the United States, numbering around 1,200,000 in 2006 (www.migrationinformation.org). The civil war in El Salvador, which began in 1979 and continued for over a decade, was the major stimulus for Salvadoran emigration (Mahler

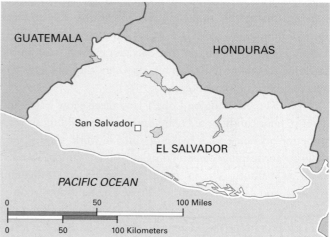

MAP 12.4 El Salvador.
In recent times, the Republic of El Salvador has tended to emphasize one or two major export crops, with coffee being dominant. Coffee growing requires high-altitude land, and coffee production has displaced many of the indigenous people. The country's total population is nearly 7 million. About 90 percent are mestizo, 9 percent of European descent (mostly Spanish), and 1 percent indigenous. The dominant language is Spanish, although some indigenous people speak Nahuat, a dialect of Nahuatl. Eighty-three percent of the people are Roman Catholic, and Protestants are 15 percent and growing in number.

1995) (see Map 12.4). By 1984, one-fourth of the country's population consisted of either refugees or IDPs (Burton 2004). Most of the refugees came to the United States. About half of all Salvadorans in the United States live in California, especially Los Angeles (Baker-Christales 2004), with another large cluster in the Washington, DC, area. Many also settled

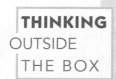

THINKING OUTSIDE THE BOX

Find a detailed map that shows the geography of the United States, Mexico, and Central America, including El Salvador. Trace a possible overland migration route to the United States, and find the three rivers that Salvadoran refugees had to cross.

around New York City, including some 60,000 who moved to suburban areas of Long Island.

Middle-class and upper-class Salvadorans obtained tourist or even immigration visas relatively easily. The poor, however, were less successful, and many entered the United States illegally as a *mojado* (mo-HAH-do), derogatory slang meaning a "wetback." Like Mexican illegal immigrants, Salavadorans use the term *mojado* to describe their journey. The Salvadorans, though, had to cross three rivers instead of one. These three crossings are a prominent theme of their escape stories, which are full of physical and psychological hardship, including hunger, arrests, and women being beaten and raped along the way. Once they arrive, things are still not easy, especially in the search for work and housing. Lack of education and marketable skills limit the job search. For undocumented immigrants, getting a decent job is even harder. These factors make it more likely that Salvadorans will work in the informal sector (review Chapter 3), where they are easy targets for economic exploitation.

Salvadorans living on Long Island receive low wages and labor in poor conditions. Their jobs involve providing services to better-off households. Men do outside work, such as gardening, landscaping, construction, and pool cleaning. Women work as nannies, live-in maids, housecleaners, restaurant workers, and caregivers for the elderly. The Salvadorans often hold down more than one job—for example, working at a McDonald's in the morning and cleaning houses in the afternoon. Men's pride prevents them from taking lowly ("female") jobs such as washing dishes. Women are more flexible and hence are more likely than men to find work. For the poorest of Salvadoran refugees, even exploitative jobs may be an economic improvement compared with conditions back home, where they could not support their families at all.

The Salvadorans were attracted to Long Island by its thriving informal economy, a sector where checking for visas was less likely to occur. Unfortunately, the cost of living on Long Island is higher than in many other places. The combination of low wages and high costs of living has kept most Salvadorans in the category of the working poor, with few prospects for improvement. They attempt to cope with high housing costs by crowding many people into units meant for small families. Compared with El Salvador, where most people, except for the urban poor, owned their own homes, only a few Salvadorans on Long Island own homes. Residential space and costs are shared among extended kin and nonkin who pay rent. This situation causes intrahousehold tension and stress. In spite of all these difficulties, most Salvadorans evaluate their experience in the United States positively.

THE NEW IMMIGRANTS FROM ASIA

Research on how international migrants change their behavior in the new destination have addressed, among other things, the question of whether different consumption patterns emerge and, if so, how, why, and what effects such changes have on other aspects of their culture.

CHANGING PATTERNS OF CONSUMPTION AMONG HONG KONG CHINESE A Canadian study examined consumption patterns among four groups: Anglo-Canadians, Hong Kong immigrants who had arrived within the previous seven years, long-time Hong Kong immigrants, and Hong Kong residents (Lee and Tse 1994). Since 1987, Hong Kong has been the single largest source of migrants to Canada. The new immigrant settlement pattern in Canada is one of urban clustering. The Hong Kong Chinese have developed their own shopping centers, television and radio stations, newspapers, and country clubs. Because of generally high incomes, Hong Kong immigrants have greatly boosted Canadian buying power.

For most of the poor Hong Kong migrants, however, the move brought a lowered economic situation, reflected in consumption patterns. New immigrants may have to reduce spending on entertainment and expensive items. Primary needs of the new immigrants in the 1990s included items that only about half of all households owned: TVs, a car, a house, a VCR, carpets, and a microwave oven. Items in the second-needs category were a dining room set, a barbecue, a deep freezer, and a dehumidifier. Long-time immigrants owned more secondary products.

At the same time, businesses in Canada have responded to Hong Kong immigrant tastes by providing Hong Kong–style restaurants, Chinese branch banks, and China-oriented travel agencies. Supermarkets offer specialized Asian sections. Thus, traditional patterns and ties are maintained to some extent. Two characteristics of Hong Kong immigrants distinguish them from other groups discussed in this section: their relatively secure economic status and their high level of education. Still, in Canada, they often have a difficult time finding suitable employment. Some have named Canada "Kan Lan Tai," meaning a difficult place to prosper, a fact that leads many to become "astronauts," or transnational migrants.

THREE PATTERNS OF ADAPTATION AMONG THE VIETNAMESE Over 125 million refugees left Vietnam during and after the wartime 1970s. Most relocated to the United States, but many others went to Canada, Australia, France, Germany, and Britain (Gold 1992). Vietnamese immigrants in the United States constitute the nation's third-largest Asian American minority group. Three distinct subgroups are the 1975-era elite, the "boat people," and the ethnic Chinese. Although they interact frequently, they have retained distinct patterns of adaptation.

The first group, the 1975-era elite, avoided many of the traumatic elements of flight. They were U.S. employees and members of the South Vietnamese government and military. They left before having to live under the communists, and they spent little time in refugee camps. Most came with intact families and received generous financial assistance from the

United States. Using their education and English language skills, most found good jobs quickly and adjusted rapidly.

The boat people began to enter the United States after the outbreak of the Vietnam–China conflict of 1978. Mainly of rural origin, they had lived for three years or more under communism. Their exit, either by overcrowded and leaky boats or on foot through Cambodia, was dangerous and difficult. Over 50 percent died on the way. Those who survived faced many months in refugee camps in Thailand, Malaysia, the Philippines, or Hong Kong before being admitted to the United States. Because many more men than women escaped as boat people, these refugees are less likely to have arrived with intact families. They were less well educated than the earlier wave, with half lacking competence in English. They faced the depressed U.S. economy of the 1980s. By the time of their arrival, the U.S. government had severely reduced refugee cash assistance and had canceled other benefits. These refugees had a much more difficult time adjusting to life in the United States than the 1975-era elite did.

The ethnic Chinese, a distinct and socially marginalized class of entrepreneurs in Vietnam, arrived in the United States mainly as boat people. Following the 1987 outbreak of hostilities between Vietnam and China, the ethnic Chinese were allowed to leave Vietnam. Some, using contacts in the overseas Chinese community, were able to reestablish their roles as entrepreneurs. Most have had a difficult time in the United States because they lacked a Western-style education. They were also sometimes subject to discrimination from other Vietnamese in the United States.

The general picture of first-generation Vietnamese adjustment in the United States shows high rates of unemployment, welfare dependency, and poverty. Interviews with Vietnamese refugees in southern California reveal generational change and fading traditions among youths. Vietnamese teenagers in southern California, for example, have adopted the lifestyle of low-income U.S. teenagers. Their Euro-American friends are more important to them than their Vietnamese heritage is. Given social variations and regional differences in adaptation throughout the United States, however, generalizations about Vietnamese Americans must be made with extreme caution.

HINDUS OF NEW YORK CITY MAINTAIN THEIR CULTURE With the 1965 change in legislation in the United States, a first wave of South Asian immigrants dominated by male professionals from India arrived (Bhardwaj and Rao 1990). Members of this first wave settled primarily in eastern and western cities. Subsequent immigrants from India, who were less well educated and less wealthy, tend to be concentrated in New York and New Jersey. New York City has the largest population of South Asian Indians in the United States, with about one-eighth of the total number of South Asians in the nation (Mogelonsky 1995).

Hindu worshippers at the Geeta Temple in Elmhurst, Queens, pass their hands over a camphor lamp flame as a blessing. Queens, one of the five boroughs of New York City, is one of the most ethnically diverse communities in the world.

Members of the highly educated first wave are concentrated in professional fields such as medicine, engineering, and management (Helweg and Helweg 1990). One of the major immigrant groups in Silicon Valley, California, is South Asian Indians. Members of the less educated, later wave find work in family-run businesses or service industries. Indians dominate some trades, such as convenience stores. They have penetrated the ownership of budget hotels and motels and operate nearly half of the total number of establishments in this niche. More than 40 percent of New York City's licensed cab drivers are Indians, Pakistanis, or Bangladeshis (Mogelonsky 1995).

The South Asian Indian population in the United States is one of the better-off immigrant groups and is considered an immigrant success story. South Asian Indians place high value on their children's education and urge them to pursue higher education in fields such as medicine and engineering. They tend to have few children and invest heavily in their schooling and social advancement.

A continuing concern of many members of the first wave is the maintenance of Hindu cultural values in the face of patterns prevalent in mainstream U.S. culture, such as dating, premarital sex, drinking, and drugs (Lessinger 1995). The Hindu population supports the construction of Hindu temples that offer Sunday school classes for young people and cultural events as a way of passing on the Hindu heritage to the next generation. South Asian Hindus attempt to appeal to their youths by accommodating to their lifestyles and preferences in terms of things such as the kind of food served after rituals. Vegetarian pizza is now a common temple menu item for the young people.

Another challenge for Hinduism in the United States and Canada is to establish temples that offer ritual diversity that speaks to Hindus of many varieties. In New York City, the growth of one temple shows how its ritual flexibility helped it to expand. The Ganesha (guh-NAY-shuh) Temple was founded in 1997 under leadership from Hindus from southern

LESSONS applied

Studying African Pastoralists' Movements for Risk Assessment and Service Delivery

Pastoralists are often vulnerable to malnutrition as a consequence of climate changes, fluctuations in food supply, and war and political upheaval. Because of their spatial mobility, they are difficult to reach with relief aid during a crisis. Cultural anthropologists are devising ways to gather and manage basic information about pastoralists' movements and nutritional needs in order to improve service delivery (Watkins and Fleisher 2002). The data required for such proactive planning include the following:

- Information on the number of migrants and the size of their herds in a particular location at a particular time. Such data can inform planners about the level of services required for public health programs,

educational programs, and veterinary services. This information can be used to assess the demand on particular grazing areas and water sources and is therefore important in predicting possible future crises.

- Information on patterns of migratory movements. This information can enable planners to move services to where the people are, rather than expecting people to move to the services. Some nongovernmental organizations, for example, are providing mobile banking services and mobile veterinary services. Information about pastoralist movements can be used as an early warning to prevent social conflicts that might result if several groups arrived in the same place at the same time.

And conflict resolution mechanisms can be put in place more effectively if conflict does occur.

The data collection involves interviews with pastoralists, often with one or two key participants, whom the anthropologists select for their specialized knowledge. Interviews cover topics such as the migratory paths followed (both typical and atypical), population levels, the sizes of herds, and the nutritional and water requirements of people and animals. Given the complex social systems of pastoralists, the data gathering must also include information on group leadership, decision-making practices, and concepts about land and water rights.

The anthropologists organize this information into a computerized

---

India. Temple rituals at first were the same as those conducted in southern Indian temples. Over the years, though, in order to widen its reach, the temple expanded its rituals to include those which would appeal to Hindus from other regions of India. The congregation has grown, and the physical structure has expanded to provide for this growth. The daily and yearly cycle has become more elaborate and more varied than what one would find at a typical Hindu temple in southern India. The Ganesha temple in New York City is an important pilgrimage destination for Hindus from throughout India.

THE NEW IMMIGRANTS FROM THE FORMER SOVIET UNION

The breakup of the Soviet Union into 15 separate countries spurred the movement of over 9 million people throughout Eastern Europe and Central Asia. Many, of Slavic descent, lived in Central Asia during the existence of the Soviet Union and seek to return to their homelands. Another large category includes people who were forcibly relocated to Siberia or Central Asia. Since 1988, refugees from the former Soviet Union have been one of the largest refugee nationalities to enter the United States (Gold 1995).

SOVIET JEWS FLEE PERSECUTION Many of the refugees from the former Soviet Union are Soviet Jews. Although most Soviet Jews live in Israel, since the mid-1960s over 300,000 have settled in the United States, especially in California (Gold 1995). Several features characterize the experience of

Soviet Jewish refugees in the United States. First, their origins in the Soviet Union accustomed them to the fact that the government controlled most aspects of life and provided many public services, including jobs, housing, day care, and health care. In their new locations, they had to find ways of meeting these needs in a market economy. Second, Soviet

In January 2004, more than 50,000 Russian immigrants to Israel returned to Russia. Motivations for the move back include the difficult living conditions for many Russian immigrants in Israel, violence, and the improving economic situation in Russia. Nonetheless, people from Russia continue to migrate to Israel, and they now number over 1 million people, about 13 percent of the population.

▶ Learn how many people left Russia after the breakup of the Soviet Union in 1989 and where they went.

database, linking the ethnographic data with other data collected and managed through what is called a geographic information system (GIS), which includes data on the environment and climate information from satellites. The anthropologists then construct various scenarios and assess the relative risks that they pose to the people's health. Impending crises can be foreseen, and warnings can be issued to governments and international aid agencies.

In 2006, after three years of drought, women of eastern Kenya search out increasingly scarce pasture for their declining herd of goats. As they walk through a dust storm, clouds and a rainbow in the distance are signs that rain is coming. Heavy rains did come in the next few days, but the pastoralists in the region, like these women, had lost most of their animals during the drought and were dependent on food aid and other forms of humanitarian assistance for survival. Global climate change is linked to increasingly severe swings in climatic conditions in this region.

◆ FOOD FOR THOUGHT

- The tracking system described here remains outside the control of the pastoralists themselves. How might it be managed so that they can participate more meaningfully and gain greater autonomy?

Jews, as "White Europeans," become members of the "racial" majority group. Their high level of education places them in the elite of new immigrant groups. Third, they have access to established and prosperous communities of American Jews, which provides them with sponsors when they arrive. Most other new immigrant groups do not have these advantages.

Soviet Jewish immigrants, however, face several challenges. Many have a difficult time finding a job commensurate with their education and previous work in the Soviet Union. Throughout the United States, many Soviet Jewish immigrants remain unemployed or work at menial jobs far beneath their qualifications. This pattern is especially true for women. They were employed professionals in the Soviet Union but can find no work in the United States other than housecleaning or babysitting. Another major challenge involves marriage options. Cultural norms promote intraethnic marriage, but the number in the U.S. marriage pool is small.

◆◆◆

Migration Politics, Policies, and Programs in a Globalizing World

The major questions related to migration politics, policies, and programs concern state and international policies of inclusion and exclusion of particular categories of people. The human rights of various categories of migrants vary dramatically.

Migrants of all sorts, including long-standing migratory groups such as pastoralists and horticulturalists, seek ways of protecting their lifestyles, maintaining their health, and creating security for the future.

PROTECTING MIGRANTS' HEALTH

Health risks to migrants are many and varied, depending on the wide variety of migrant types and destinations. One group of migrants of special concern consists of those whose livelihoods depend on long-standing economic systems requiring spatial mobility, such as foragers, horticulturalists, and pastoralists. The frequency of drought and food shortages in the Sahel region of Africa (see Map 12.5) in recent decades is prompting research by cultural anthropologists to learn how to prevent such situations through better monitoring and an enhanced provision of services (see Lessons Applied).

INCLUSION AND EXCLUSION

National policies that set quotas on the quantity and types of immigrants who are welcome and that determine how they are treated are dictated largely by political and economic interests. Even in cases of seemingly humanitarian quotas, governments undertake a cost–benefit analysis of how much will be gained and how much will be lost. Governments show their political support or disapproval of other governments through their immigration policies. One of the most obvious economic factors affecting policy is labor flow. Cheap, including illegal, immigrant labor is used around the world to maintain profits for

MAP 12.5 Sahel Region.

The word *sahel* comes from the Arabic for "shore" or "border," referring in this case to the area between the Sahara desert and the more fertile regions to the south. Primarily savanna, the region has been the home to many rich kingdoms that controlled Saharan trade routes. Most people make their living from pastoralism and semisedentary cattle raising. The region recently experienced several major droughts, leading to the widespread death of herd animals, widespread human starvation and malnutrition, and forced population displacement.

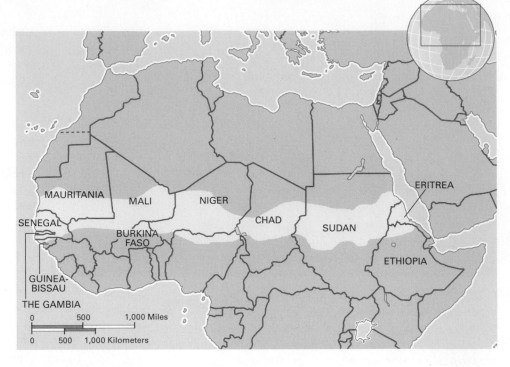

MAURITANIA
MALI
NIGER
SENEGAL
CHAD
SUDAN
ERITREA
BURKINA FASO
ETHIOPIA
GUINEA-BISSAU
THE GAMBIA

| 0 | 500 | 1,000 Miles |
| 0 | 500 | 1,000 Kilometers |

Memorials to illegal border crossers on the Mexico side of a fence along the U.S.–Mexico border. U.S.-built barriers along the border with Mexico have existed for decades. Recent increases in illegal crossings and a closed-border policy prompted President George W. Bush to push for the Secure Fence Act of 2007, which authorized the construction of 700 additional miles of fencing. Human rights supporters say that the fences simply push immigrants to attempt to cross into the United States in more desolate and dangerous areas, adding to the mortality rate of illegal immigrants.

▶ *The World Trade Organization supports the free trade of goods between countries. Where does it stand, if at all, on the free movement of labor between countries?*

businesses and services for the better off. Flows of such labor undermine labor unions and the status of established workers.

State immigration policies are played out in local communities. In some instances, local resentments are associated with a so-called **lifeboat mentality**, a view that seeks to limit enlarging a particular group because of perceived constraints on resources. This perspective may be part of the explanation for many recent outbreaks of hostility throughout the world in which host populations, instead of being gracious and sharing what they have, seek to drive out the immigrants to protect their own entitlements.

Labor immigrants are not always the subject of resentment, as a study of Palermo, Italy, shows (Cole 1996). The number of immigrants has grown substantially in southern Italy since the early 1980s. The city of Palermo, on the island of Sicilia, or Sicily (see Map 12.6), has a total population of 1 million people, of which nearly 30,000 are immigrants from Africa, Asia, and elsewhere. Does working-class racism exist among the working class in Palermo? Two conditions seem to predict that it would: large numbers of foreign immigrants and a high rate of unemployment. So far, however, instead of expressing racist condemnation of the immigrants, working-class residents of Palermo accept the immigrants as fellow poor people. One critical factor may be the lack of competition for jobs because Palermitans and immigrants occupy different economic niches. African immigrant men work in less desirable jobs in bars and restaurants, as building cleaners, or as street vendors. African and Asian women work as domestic servants in the better-off neighborhoods. Sicilians do refer to immigrants by certain racial or ethnic names, but these seem to be used interchangeably and imprecisely. For example, a common term for all immigrants, Asian or African, is *turchi*,

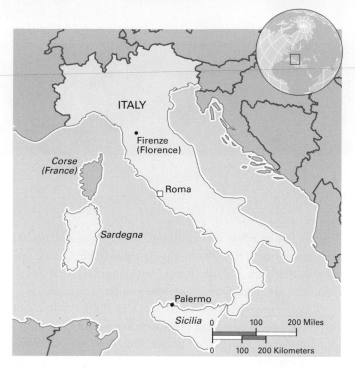

MAP 12.6 Italy.

Officially the Italian Republic, the country includes the mainland and two large islands. Italy has the seventh highest GDP in the world. The country's population of nearly 60 million makes it one of the most densely populated countries in Europe. Roman Catholicism is the dominant religion. Recent waves of immigration, especially from northern Africa, have increased the number of Muslims to perhaps 1 million. The official language is standard Italian, descended from the Tuscan dialect of Firenze (Florence), but many cherished dialects of Italian continue to be spoken throughout the country. Italy has the largest number of UNESCO World Heritage Sites of any country.

which means "Turks," but it can also be applied teasingly to a Sicilian. In a questionnaire given to schoolchildren, the great majority agreed with the statement that "a person's race is not important." Although the tolerance among Palermo's working class may be only temporary and may change to resentment if economic conditions change or the numbers of immigrants increase, it nonetheless suggests that working-class racism against immigrants is not inevitable.

Recent politically conservative trends in the United States have succeeded in reversing earlier, more progressive immigration policies. Police raids in areas thought to have many undocumented migrants have brought mass expulsions. This lifeboat mentality of exclusiveness is held mainly by the dominant White majority and others who have achieved the "American dream" and resent competition from outsiders.

MIGRATION AND HUMAN RIGHTS

Several questions arise about migration and human rights. One of the most basic is whether migration is forced or voluntary (review Critical Thinking, this chapter). Forced migration itself may be considered a violation of a person's human rights. Another issue is whether members of a displaced group have a guaranteed **right of return**, or a refugee's entitlement to return to and live in his or her homeland. The right of return has been considered a basic human right in the West since the time of the signing of the Magna Carta. It is included in UN General Assembly Resolution 194, passed in 1948, and was elevated by the United Nations to an "inalienable right" in 1974.

The right of return is a pressing issue for the hundreds of thousands of Palestinians who fled or were driven from their homes during the 1948 war. They went mainly to Jordan, the West Bank/East Jerusalem, Gaza, Lebanon, Syria, and other Arab states. Jordan and Syria have granted Palestinian refugees rights equal to those of their citizens. In Lebanon, where estimates of the number of Palestinian refugees range between 200,000 and 600,000, the government refuses them such rights (Salam 1994). Israel favors the lower number because it makes the problem seem less severe. The Palestinians favor the higher number to highlight the seriousness of their plight. The Lebanese government also favors the higher number to emphasize its burden in hosting so many refugees. Palestinians know that they are not welcome in Lebanon, but they cannot return to Israel because Israel denies them the right of return. Israel responds to the Palestinians' claims by saying that its acceptance of Jewish immigrants from Arab countries constitutes an equal exchange.

The right of return can be considered, just as validly, within states, even though most have no policy close to that of the United Nations. A stark instance of internal displacement and loss of rights to return home comes from the 2005 hurricanes in New Orleans and the coastal counties of Mississippi and Louisiana. The "racial" lines of displacement are nowhere clearer than in the statistics for the city of New Orleans (Lyman 2006). Before Hurricane Katrina, the population of New Orleans was 54 percent White, 36 percent Black, and 6 percent Latino. In 2006, the population was 68 percent White and 21 percent Black, with no change in the Latino percentage. The causes of the differential displacement of the Black population are one problem. The fact that many Black people still have little chance of returning to their homes—*differential resettlement*—and rebuilding their lives is another.

---

lifeboat mentality   a view that seeks to limit enlarging a particular group because of perceived constraints on resources.

right of return   the United Nations' guaranteed right of a refugee to return to his or her home country to live.

the BIG questions REVISITED

◆ What are the major categories of migration?

Migrants are classified as internal, international, or transnational. Another category is based on the migrants' reason for moving. On this dimension, migrants are classified as labor migrants, institutional migrants, or displaced persons. People's adjustment to their new situations depends on the degree of voluntarism involved in the move, the degree of cultural and environmental difference between the place of origin and the destination, and how closely expectations about the new location are met, especially in terms of making a living and establishing social ties.

Displaced persons are one of the fastest-growing categories of migrants. Refugees fleeing from political persecution or warfare face serious adjustment challenges because they often leave their home countries with few material resources and frequently have experienced much psychological suffering. The number of internally displaced persons is growing even faster than the number of refugees. Mega-dams and other large-scale development projects result in thousands of people becoming IDPs, and these individuals do not fall under the purview of international organizations such as the United Nations. Still, their situation is attracting the attention of a global consortium of governments and nongovernmental organizations.

◆ What are examples of the new immigrants in the United States and Canada?

Worldwide, the "new immigrants" are contributing to growing transnational connections and to the formation of increasingly multicultural populations within states. In the United States, the new immigrants from Latin America, especially Mexico, are the largest and fastest-growing category. In the United States, members of most refugee immigrant groups tend to have jobs at the lower end of the economic scale. Jewish refugees from the Soviet Union experience a major gap in what their employment was like in Russia versus their limited options in the United States. Immigrants from East and South Asia, who are more likely than others to have immigrated to the United States voluntarily, have achieved greater levels of economic success than most other new immigrant groups.

Immigrant groups throughout the world may face discrimination in their new destinations, although the degree to which it occurs among those already residing in those locales varies with the level of perceived competition for resources. Immigrants from India in Canada experience discriminatory practices that differ on the basis of their gender.

◆ How do anthropologists contribute to migration policies and programs?

Anthropologists have studied national and international migration policies and practices in terms of social inclusion and exclusion. Fieldwork in particular contexts reveals a range of patterns between local residents and immigrants. Working-class resentment among local people against immigrants is not universal and varies with the overall amount and type of employment available.

Anthropologists examine possible infringements of the human rights of migrants, especially as regards the degree of voluntarism in their move and the conditions they face in the destination area. Another human rights issue related to migration is the right of return. The United Nations proclaimed the right of return for internationally displaced populations. Most countries, however, have no such policy. Internally displaced persons, including the evacuees from the 2005 hurricanes in the United States, have no guarantee that they can return to their home area.

Cultural anthropologists find many roles in applied work related to migration. Gathering data on migratory movements of traditionally mobile people, such as pastoralists, can help make humanitarian aid programs more timely and effective.

KEY CONCEPTS

bracero, p. 260

chain migration, p. 266

circular migration, p. 261

development-induced
  displacement, p. 263

displaced person, p. 261

institutional migrant, p. 265

internal migration, p. 259

internally displaced person
  (IDP), p. 262

international migration,
  p. 259

lifeboat mentality, p. 272

migration, p. 258

new immigrant, p. 265

push–pull theory, p. 259

refugee, p. 262

remittance, p. 260

right of return, p. 273

transnational
  migration, p. 259

SUGGESTED READINGS

Rogaia Mustafa Abusharaf. *Wanderings: Sudanese Migrants and Exiles in North America.* Ithaca, NY: Cornell University Press, 2002. Abusharaf provides historical background on the first wave of Sudanese migration to the United States and Canada, information on various Sudanese groups that have migrated, and an interpretation of Sudanese identity in North America.

Beth Baker-Cristales. *Salvadoran Migration to Southern California: Redefining El Hermano Lejano.* Gainesville: University of Florida Press, 2004. This book provides a history of Salvadoran migration to the United States and a detailed description of the lives of Salvadoran migrants in Los Angeles.

Jeffrey H. Cohen. *The Culture of Migration in Southern Mexico.* Austin: University of Texas Press, 2004. Migration is a way of life for many individuals and entire families in the Mexican state of Oaxaca. Some migrants go to other parts of Mexico and others to the United States. Cohen discusses outmigration in 12 communities and its effects on the people who remain.

Sheba Mariam George. *When Women Come First: Gender and Class in Transnational Migration.* Berkeley: University of California Press, 2005. This book traces the experiences of women nurses from Kerala, India, who migrate to work in the United States, the effects on their marriages, and how husbands adapt through active involvement in religion.

Farha Ghannam. *Remaking the Modern: Space, Relocation, and the Politics of Identity in a Global Cairo.* Berkeley: University of California Press, 2002. As part of a plan to modernize Cairo, the government relocated low-income residents from valuable real estate in downtown Cairo to public housing outside the city. Ghannam explores how the displaced people deal with the loss of social networks and the stigma of living in public housing.

Julianne Hammer. *Palestinians Born in Exile: Diaspora and the Search for a Homeland.* Austin: University of Texas Press, 2004. In the decade following the 1993 Oslo Peace Accords, 100,000 diasporic Palestinians moved to the West Bank and Gaza. This ethnography documents the experiences of young adults and their adjustment to the move.

Josiah McC. Heyman. *Finding a Moral Heart for U.S. Immigration Policy: An Anthropological Perspective.* Washington, DC: American Ethnological Society, Monograph Series, Number 7, 1998. This critique finds that current U.S. immigration policy is basically anti-immigrationist. The author suggests steps toward a more inclusive policy.

Helen Morton Lee. *Tongans Overseas: Between Two Shores.* Honolulu: University of Hawai'i Press, 2003. This book about Tongan migrants in Melbourne uses participant observation and analysis of messages on a Tongan Internet forum called Kava Bowl.

Ann Aurelia López. *The Farmworkers' Journey.* Berkeley: University of California Press, 2007. Interviews conducted over a 10-year period document the lives of farm workers who migrate from west-central Mexico to central California.

Martin F. Manalansan, IV. *Global Divas: Filipino Gay Men in the Diaspora.* Durham, NC: Duke University Press, 2004. This book is based on the life narratives of 50 Filipino gay men in New York City and participant observation in homes, bars, hospitals, restaurants, and the Gay Pride Parade.

Ann V. Millard and Jorge Chapa, with others. *Apple Pie and Enchiladas: Latino Newcomers in the Rural Midwest.* Austin: University of Texas Press, 2004. Many Latinos migrate to the rural Midwest in the United States to work in food-processing plants and small factories. The authors explore relations between the local Anglos and the immigrants.

Karen Richman. *Migration and Vodou.* Gainesville: University of Florida Press, 2005. This book and its accompanying CD reveal the innovative ways that Haitian migrants in South Florida maintain their religious traditions and familial connections.

Archana B. Verma. *The Making of Little Punjab in Canada: Patterns of Immigration.* Thousand Oaks, CA: Sage Publications, 2002. Verma describes the historical connections between Hindu migrants from a village in India's northern state of Punjab to Vancouver Island, British Columbia.

A traditional custodian of the Ngarrindjeri people in South Australia holds a box containing four skulls of Australian Aborigines at a ceremony at Manchester University, England, 2003. The skulls were returned to a sacred keeping place after having been in England for 100 years.

PEOPLE DEFINING DEVELOPMENT

13

the BIG questions

◆ What is development and what are the approaches to achieving it?

◆ How has development affected indigenous people and women, and how are they redefining development?

◆ What are urgent issues in development?

OUTLINE

Defining Development and Approaches to It

Lessons Applied: The Saami, Snowmobiles, and the Need for Social Impact Analysis

Culturama: The Peyizan yo of Haiti

Development, Indigenous People, and Women

Eye on the Environment: Oil, Environmental Degradation, and Human Rights in the Nigerian Delta

Urgent Issues in Development

We have had many visitors to Walpole Island since the French "discovered us" in the seventeenth century in our territory, Bkejwanong. In many cases, these visitors failed to recognize who we were and to appreciate our traditions. They tried to place us in their European framework of knowledge, denying that we possessed our indigenous knowledge. They attempted to steal our lands, water, and knowledge. We resisted. They left and never came back. We continued to share our knowledge with the next visitors to our place. ... It was a long-term strategy that has lasted more than three hundred years. (Dr. Dean Jacobs, Executive Director of Walpole Island First Nation, from his foreword in VanWynsberghe 2002:ix)

These are the words of a leader of the Walpole Island First Nation, located in southern Ontario, Canada (see Map 13.1). They, along with many other indigenous groups worldwide, have taken strong action in recent decades to protect their culture and natural environment. The Walpole Island First Nation organized itself and successfully fought to control industrial waste that was polluting its water and land. In the process, the people have regained their pride and cultural integrity.

The subfield of development anthropology looks at how culture and "development" interact to improve people's lives and reduce poverty. Thus, it has a strong applied component, as well as a critical component that asks hard questions about the causes of poverty. This chapter's first section considers concepts related to change and development and various approaches to development. The second section focuses on development in relation to indigenous peoples and women. The third section looks at urgent issues in development and what cultural anthropology can contribute to them.

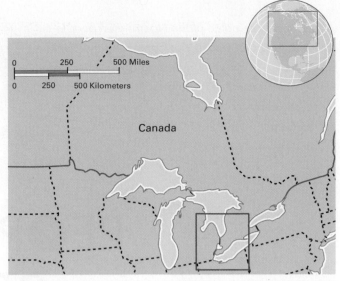

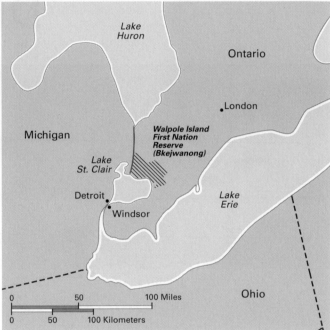

MAP 13.1 Walpole Island Reservation in Southern Ontario, Canada.

◆◆◆

Defining Development and Approaches to It

This chapter focuses on the topic of contemporary cultural change as shaped by **development**, or directed change aimed at improving human welfare. A major focus of development

efforts is preventing or reducing poverty. Poverty is extremely difficult to define, but one workable definition says that **poverty** is the lack of tangible and intangible assets that contribute to life and the quality of life. Some approaches to reducing poverty focus on *basic needs* such as access to decent food, water, housing, and clothing, factors without which a person may die or certainly fail to thrive. More expanded definitions include access to things such as education and personal security (freedom from fear). Development experts in Paris, Rome, and Washington, DC, spend much time discussing how to measure poverty rates, how to assess whether poverty is increasing or decreasing and why, and what kinds of policies and programs are best to reduce poverty. More locally, real people in real places experience poverty and attempt to deal with it.

---

development   change directed toward improving human welfare.

poverty   the lack of tangible and intangible assets that contribute to life and the quality of life.

invention   the discovery of something new.

diffusion   the spread of culture through contact.

acculturation   a form of cultural change in which a minority culture becomes more like the dominant culture.

assimilation   a form of cultural change in which a culture is thoroughly acculturated, or decultured, and is no longer distinguishable as having a separate identity.

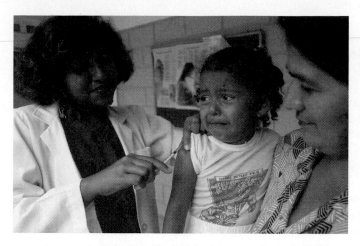
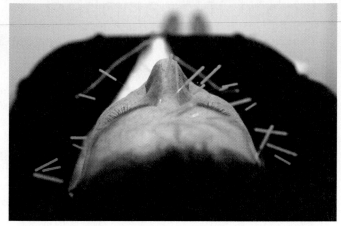

(LEFT) A doctor administering polio vaccine in Ecuador. In 1985, the Pan American Health Organization (PAHO) established a plan for eradicating the polio virus from the Americas by 1990. (RIGHT) A patient rests with acupuncture needles on her face during a "face lift" treatment (to remove wrinkles and make the individual look younger) in New York City. This acupuncture procedure, based in traditional Chinese medicine, follows the theory that the face is where the essence of yin and the energy of yang meet. The procedure seeks to adjust imbalances in yin and yang through the insertion of needles at particular places in the face.

▶ *Do research to find out whether traditional Chinese acupuncture had a specialization in "face lifting." If not, can you learn when, where, and why this specialization emerged?*

TWO PROCESSES OF CULTURAL CHANGE

Two basic processes underlie all cultural change. The first is **invention**, the discovery of something new. The second is **diffusion**, the spread of culture through contact.

INVENTION Most inventions evolve gradually through experimentation and the accumulation of knowledge, but some appear suddenly. Examples of technological inventions that have created cultural change include the printing press, gunpowder, the polio vaccine, and satellite communication. Conceptual innovations, such as Jeffersonian democracy, are also inventions. Many inventions bring about positive cultural change, but not all inventions have positive social outcomes. Inventions inspired by a socially positive goal may have mixed or unintended negative consequences.

DIFFUSION Diffusion is logically related to invention because new discoveries are likely to spread. Diffusion can occur in several ways. First, in mutual borrowing, two societies that are roughly equal in power exchange aspects of their culture. Second, diffusion sometimes involves a transfer from a dominant culture to a less powerful culture. This process may occur through force or, more subtly, through education or marketing processes that promote the adoption of new practices and beliefs. Third, a more powerful culture may appropriate aspects of a less powerful culture, through *cultural imperialism*. Last, a less powerful and even oppressed cultural group often provides sources of cultural change in a dominant culture.

Changes in a minority culture that make it more like the dominant culture are referred to as **acculturation**. In extreme cases, a culture becomes so thoroughly acculturated that it is **assimilated**, or *decultured*—that is, it is no longer distinguishable as having a separate identity. In the most extreme cases, the impact on the minority culture is that it becomes extinct. These processes parallel degrees of language change resulting from contact with dominating cultures and languages. Such changes have occurred among many indigenous people as the result of globalization and the introduction of new technology (see Lessons Applied). Other responses to acculturative influences include the partial acceptance of something new with localization and syncretism, as in the case of the game of cricket in the Trobriand Islands (Chapter 11), or rejection and resistance.

THEORIES AND MODELS OF DEVELOPMENT

This subsection reviews theories and models of development and the various kinds of institutions involved in development. It then examines development projects and how anthropologists work with, or sometimes against, those projects.

No single view of development or how to achieve it exists. Debates about these issues are heated and involve experts from many disciplines, governments, and local people worldwide.

THINKING OUTSIDE THE BOX

Choose two inventions made in your lifetime, and assess how they affect your everyday activities, social interactions, and ways of thinking.

LESSONS applied

The Saami, Snowmobiles, and the Need for Social Impact Analysis

How might the adoption of a new belief or practice benefit or harm a particular culture and its various members? Although often difficult to answer, this question must always be asked. A classic study of the snowmobile disaster among a Saami group in Finland offers a careful response to the question in a context of rapid technological diffusion (Pelto 1973). In the 1950s, the Saami of Finland (review Culturama, Chapter 9, p. 205) had an economy based on reindeer herding, which provided most of their diet.

Besides supplying meat, reindeer had other important economic and social functions. They were used as draft animals, especially for hauling wood for fuel. Their hides were made into clothing and their sinews used for sewing. Reindeer were key items of exchange, in both external trade and internal gift-giving. Parents gave a child a reindeer to mark the appearance of the child's first tooth. When a couple became engaged, they exchanged a reindeer with each other to mark the commitment.

By the 1960s, all this had changed because of the introduction of the snowmobile. Previously, people herded the reindeer herds on skis. The use of snowmobiles for herd management had several unintended and interrelated consequences, all of which were detrimental to the herding way of life.

First, the herds were no longer kept domesticated for part of the year, a practice during which they became tame. Instead, they were allowed to roam freely all year and thus became wilder. Second, snowmobiles allowed herders to cover larger amounts of territory at roundup time and to do more than one roundup. As the number of snowmobiles increased, herd sizes declined dramatically. The reasons for the decline included the stress inflicted on the reindeer by the extra distance traveled during roundups, the multiple roundups instead of a single one, and the fear aroused by the noisy snowmobiles. Furthermore, roundups were held at a time when the females were near the end of their pregnancies, a factor that induced reproductive stress.

Negative economic changes occurred, including a new dependence on the outside through the cash economy. Cash is needed in order to purchase a snowmobile, buy gasoline, and pay for parts and repairs. This delocalization of the economy created social inequality, which had not existed before. Other economic and related repercussions ensued as well:

- The cash cost of effective participation in herding exceeded the resources of some families, which then had to drop out of participation in herding.

- The snowmobile pushed many Saami into debt.

- Dependence on cash and indebtedness forced many Saami to migrate to cities for work.

Snowmobiles also changed Saami gender relations by increasing the prominence of young men in herding (Larsson 2005). Before the snowmobiles, reindeer herding was a family operation. Although men did more of the long-distance herding, women also worked closely with the herd. After snowmobiles were adopted, parents began steering their sons toward herding and their daughters toward education and professional careers. Two rationales for such gender tracking are that driving a snowmobile is difficult because the vehicle is heavy and that the driver may get stuck somewhere. The use of snowmobiles also changed the age pattern of reindeer herding in favor of youth over age; thus, older herders were squeezed out.

Pertti Pelto, the anthropologist who first documented this case, calls these transformations a disaster for Saami culture (1973). He offers a recommendation for the future: Communities confronting the adoption of new technology should have a chance to weigh evidence on the pros and cons and make an informed judgment. Pelto's work is one of the early warnings from anthropology about the need for a **social impact assessment**—a study that attempts to predict the potential social costs and benefits of particular innovations before change is undertaken.

◆ FOOD FOR THOUGHT

- If you were a Saami herder, what would you have done if you had been able to consider a social impact assessment of the effects of snowmobiles on your culture?

A Saami herder riding a skidoo in northern Norway leads his herd.

Five theories or models of development are presented here. They differ in terms of the following characteristics:

- The definition of development
- The goal of development
- Measures of development
- Attention to environmental and financial sustainability

MODERNIZATION **Modernization** is a form of change marked by economic growth through industrialization and market expansion, political consolidation through the state, technological innovation, literacy, and options for social mobility. It originated in Western Europe in the beginning of the seventeenth century with the emerging emphasis on secular rationality and scientific thinking as the pathways to progress (Norgaard 1994). Given the insights of rationality and science, modernization is thought to spread inevitably throughout the world and lead to improvement in people's lives everywhere. The major goals of modernization are material progress and individual betterment.

Supporters and critics of modernization are found in both rich and poor countries. Supporters claim that the benefits of modernization (improved transportation, electricity, biomedical health care, and telecommunications) are worth the costs to the environment and society.

Others take a critical view and regard modernization as problematic because of its focus on ever-increasing consumption levels and heavy use of nonrenewable resources. Many cultural anthropologists are critical of Westernization and modernization because their research shows how modernization often brings environmental ruin, increases social inequality, destroys indigenous cultures, and reduces global cultural and biological diversity. In spite of strong cautionary critiques from anthropologists, environmentalists, and others about the detrimental effects of modernization, most countries worldwide have not slowed their attempts to achieve it. Some governments and citizen groups, however, are promoting lifestyles that rely less on nonrenewable resources and include a concern for protecting the environment.

GROWTH-ORIENTED DEVELOPMENT Development as "induced" change, brought about through applying modernization theory in so-called developing countries, emerged after World War II. At that time, the United States began to expand its role as a world leader, and aid for development was part of its international policy agenda. International development, as defined by major Western development institutions, is similar to modernization in terms of its goals. The process emphasizes economic growth as the most crucial element. According to growth-oriented development theory, investments in economic growth will lead to improved human welfare through the *trickle-down effect:* the gradual increase in wealth among the less well off as it filters down from the more well off.

Schoolgirls in Bhutan. The government of Bhutan rejects the Western concept of the gross domestic product (GDP) as the best measure of a country's success and instead uses a measure called gross domestic happiness (GDH).

▶ *Go to the Internet to learn more about Bhutan and the government's aspirations for its people.*

Promoting economic growth in developing countries includes two strategies:

- Increasing economic productivity and trade through modernized agriculture and manufacturing and through participation in world markets.
- Reducing government expenditures on public services such as schools and health in order to reduce debt and reallocate resources to increase productivity. This strategy, called *structural adjustment,* has been promoted by the World Bank since the 1980s.

One measure for assessing the achievement of development through this model is the rate of growth of the economy, especially the *gross domestic product,* or *GDP.*

social impact assessment   a study conducted to predict the potential social costs and benefits of particular innovations before change is undertaken.

modernization   a model of change based on belief in the inevitable advance of science and Western secularism and processes, including industrial growth, consolidation of the state, bureaucratization, a market economy, technological innovation, literacy, and options for social mobility.

DISTRIBUTIONAL DEVELOPMENT *Distributional development* contrasts with growth-oriented development in its emphasis on social equity in benefits, especially in terms of increased income, literacy, and health. It rejects the trickle-down process as ineffective in reaching poor people. Its position is based on evidence that growth-oriented strategies, applied without concern for distribution, actually increase social inequality. In this view, the growth model ensures that "the rich get richer and the poor get poorer."

The distributional approach opposes structural adjustment policies because they further undermine the welfare of the poor by removing the few entitlements they had in the form of services. Advocates of the distributional model see the need for benevolent governments to ensure equitable access to crucial resources in order to enhance the ability of the poor to provide for their own needs (Gardner and Lewis 1996).

Although conservative, "neoliberal" economists argue that redistribution is neither realistic nor feasible, supporters of the distributive approach point to cases in the model that have worked. As an example, anthropological research in a village in central Kerala (KARE-uh-luh), a state in southern India (see Map 13.2), assessed whether redistribution was an effective development strategy (Franke 1993). The findings showed the answer to be affirmative. Even though Kerala's per capita income is the lowest of any state in India, it has the highest social indicators in the country in health and literacy.

Government attention to distribution in Kerala came about through democratic channels, including demonstrations and pressure on the government by popular movements and labor unions. These groups forced the state to reallocate land ownership, thereby alleviating social inequality somewhat. In other instances, people pressured government leaders to improve village conditions by providing school lunches for poor children, increasing school attendance by dalit children (review Chapter 7), and investing in school facilities. Through public action, Nadur village became a better place to live for many people.

HUMAN DEVELOPMENT Another alternative to the growth-first model is called *human development*, the strategy that emphasizes investing in human welfare. The United Nations adopted the phrase "human development" to emphasize the need for improvements in human welfare in terms of health, education, and personal security and safety. In this model, investments in improving human welfare will lead to economic development. The reverse is not invariably true: The level of economic growth of a country (or region within a country) is not necessarily correlated with its level of human development, as is clear from the case of Kerala. Thus, in this view, economic growth is neither an end in itself nor even a necessary component of development as measured by human welfare. Economic resources, combined with distributive policies, are a strong basis for attaining high levels of human development.

SUSTAINABLE DEVELOPMENT *Sustainable development* refers to forms of improvement that do not destroy nonrenewable resources and are financially supportable over time. Advocates of sustainable development argue that the economic growth of wealthy countries has been, and still is, costly in terms of the natural environment and people whose lives depend on fragile ecosystems. They say that such growth cannot be sustained at even its present level, not to mention projected demands as more countries become industrialized.

INSTITUTIONAL APPROACHES TO DEVELOPMENT

Cultural anthropologists are increasingly aware of the importance of examining the institutions, organizations, and specialists involved in development policy making, programs, and projects. With this knowledge, cultural anthropologists have a better chance of shaping development policies and programs. Institutional research includes studying the management systems of both large-scale institutions such as the World Bank and small-scale organizations in diverse settings.

MAP 13.2 Kerala, South India.
With a population of 30 million, Kerala has living standards, literacy rates, and health indicators that are high compared with the rest of India. Kerala comprises 14 districts and three historical regions: Travancore in the south, Kochi in the central part, and Malabar in the north. Long a socialist democracy, Kerala now allows the free market and foreign direct investment to play larger roles. A major tourist destination because of its tropical ecology and cultural features such as dramatic martial arts and theater, Kerala also hosts a growing Ayurvedic health tourism industry along its coast.

Topics include behavior within the institutions, social interactions with the "client population," and institutional discourse. This section describes first some large development institutions and then some smaller organizations.

LARGE-SCALE DEVELOPMENT INSTITUTIONS Two major types of large-scale development institutions exist. First are the *multilateral institutions*—those which include several countries as "donor" members. Second are the *bilateral institutions*—those which involve only two countries: a "donor" and a "recipient."

The largest multilaterals are the United Nations and the World Bank. Each is a vast and complex social system. The United Nations, established in 1945, includes over 160 member states. Each country contributes money according to its ability, and each has one vote in the General Assembly. Several UN agencies exist, fulfilling a range of functions, such as the United Nations Development Programme (UNDP), Food and Agriculture Organization (FAO), World Health Organization (WHO), United Nations Children's Fund (UNICEF), United Nations Educational, Scientific, and Cultural Organization (UNESCO), and United Nations High Commissioner for Refugees (UNHCR).

The World Bank is supported by contributions from over 150 member countries. Founded in 1944, the Bank is dedicated to promoting the concept of economic growth worldwide. Its main strategy is to promote international investment through loans. The World Bank is guided by a board of governors made up of the finance ministers of member countries. The World Bank system assigns each country a number of votes based on the size of its financial commitment. The economic superpowers, therefore, dominate.

The World Bank system includes the International Bank for Reconstruction and Development (IBRD) and the International Development Association (IDA). Both are administered at the World Bank headquarters in Washington, DC. They lend for similar types of projects and often in the same country, but their loan conditions differ. The IBRD provides loans to poor countries that are generally regarded as "bad risks" on the world commercial market. Thus, the IBRD is a source of interest-bearing loans to countries that otherwise would not be able to borrow. The IBRD has recorded a profit every year of its existence. Most of its loans support large infrastructure projects such as roads and dams. The IDA is the "soft-loan" side of the World Bank. It provides interest-free loans (although there is a 0.75 percent annual service charge) and a flexible repayment schedule averaging between 35 and 40 years (Rich 1994). These concessional loans are granted to the poorest countries.

Prominent bilateral institutions include the Japan International Cooperation Agency (JICA), the United States Agency for International Development (USAID), the Canadian International Development Agency (CIDA), Britain's

The USAID has funded many development projects worldwide, such as this "improved road" in rural Bangladesh. Proceeds from the toll gate will help pay for maintenance of the road. The rickshaws are parked while their drivers pay their toll. The large white vehicle belongs to USAID and was being used by American researchers.

▶ *What kinds of user fees have you paid in the past few months? Did you think that the fees were fair?*

Department for International Development (DfID), the Swedish Agency for International Development (SIDA), and the Danish Organization for International Development (DANIDA). These agencies vary in terms of the total size of their aid programs, the types of programs they support, and the proportion of aid disbursed as loans that have to be repaid with interest as opposed to aid disbursed as grants that do not require repayment. The USAID tends to give more loans than grants, compared with other bilaterals.

Loans and grants also differ in terms of whether they are *tied* or *untied*. Tied loans and grants require that a certain percentage of project expenditures go for goods, expertise, and services originating in the donor country. For example, a tied loan to a certain country for road construction would require allocating a designated percentage of the funds to donor country construction companies, to airfare for donor country road experts, and to in-country expenses, such as hotels, food, and local transportation, for donor country experts. When loans or grants are untied, the recipient country may decide

THINKING
OUTSIDE
THE BOX

Visit the website of one multilateral development organization and one bilateral organization to learn about their goals, programs, and internship opportunities. For current information on territorial rights of indigenous peoples, consult the websites of Cultural Survival (www.cs.org) and Survival International (www.survival-international.org).

CULTURAMA

The Peyizan yo of Haiti

Haiti and the Dominican Republic share the island of Hispaniola. Following the island's discovery by Columbus in 1492, Spanish colonialists exterminated the island's indigenous Arawak Indians. In 1697, the French took control of what is now Haiti and instituted an exceptionally cruel system of African plantation slavery. In the late 1700s, the half million slaves revolted. In what is the only successful slave revolution in history, they ousted the French and established the first Black republic in the Western Hemisphere.

Haiti's population of over 8 million people occupies a territory somewhat smaller than the state of Maryland in the United States (www.unfpa.org). The land is rugged, hilly, or mountainous. Over 90 percent of the forests have been cleared. Haiti is the poorest country in the Western Hemisphere. Extreme inequality exists between the urban elite, who live in the capital city of Port-au-Prince, and everyone else.

The people in the countryside are the *peyizan yo* (the plural form of *peyizan*), a Creole term for small farmers who produce for their own use and for the market (Smith 2001). Many also participate in small-scale marketing. Most peyizan yo in Haiti own their land. They grow vegetables, fruits (especially mangoes), sugarcane, rice, and corn.

Accurate health statistics are not available, but even rough estimates show that Haiti has the highest prevalence of HIV/AIDS of any country in the region. Medical anthropologist Paul Farmer emphasizes the role of colonialism in the past and global structural inequalities now in causing these high rates (1992).

Colonial plantation owners grew fabulously rich from this island. It produced more wealth for France than all of France's other colonies combined and more than the 13 colonies in North America produced for Britain. Why is Haiti so poor now? Colonialism launched environmental degradation by clearing forests. After the revolution, the new citizens carried with them the traumatic history of slavery. Now, neocolonialism and globalization are leaving new scars. For decades, the United States has played, and still plays, a powerful role in supporting conservative political regimes.

In contrast to these structural explanations, some people point to problems with the Haitian people: They cannot work together, and they lack a vision of the future. Opposed to these views are the findings of Jennie Smith's ethnographic research in southwestern Haiti, which shed light on the life of the peyizan yo and offer perspectives on their development (2001). She found many active social organizations with functions such as labor sharing, to help each member get his or her field planted on time, and cost sharing, to help pay for health care or funerals. Also, the peyizan yo had clear opinions about their vision for the future, including hopes for relative economic equality, political leaders with a sense of social service, *respe* (respect), and access of citizens to basic social services.

Thanks to Jennie Smith-Pariola, Berry College, for reviewing this material.

  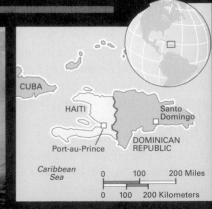

(LEFT) A woman repays her loan at a small-scale savings and loan business in rural Haiti. Many of the credit union members use their loans to set up small businesses. (CENTER) Food riots erupted in Port-au-Prince in 2008, and a soldier in the UN peacekeeping forces was shot dead. The Haitian Senate dismissed the standing prime minister.

MAP 13.3 Haiti. The Republic of Haiti occupies one-third of the Caribbean island of Hispaniola.

freely how to use the funds. The USAID offers more tied than untied aid, whereas countries such as Sweden, the Netherlands, and Norway tend to give untied aid.

Another difference among the bilaterals is the proportion of their total aid that goes to the poorest countries. The United Kingdom's DfID sends more than 80 percent of its aid to the poorest countries, whereas most of U.S. foreign aid dollars go to Egypt and Israel. Emphasis on certain types of aid also varies from one bilateral institution to another. Cuba has long played a unique role in bilateral aid, concentrating on aid for training health-care providers and for promoting preventive health care (Feinsilver 1993). Its development assistance goes to socialist countries, including many in Africa and, in Latin America, Venezuela, and Bolivia.

GRASSROOTS APPROACHES Many countries have experimented with *grassroots approaches* to development, or locally initiated small-scale projects. This alternative to the top-down development pursued by the large-scale agencies described in the previous section is more likely to be culturally appropriate, supported through local participation, and successful.

The term **social capital** refers to the intangible resources that exist through social ties, trust, and cooperation. Many local grassroots organizations around the world use social capital to provide basic social needs (see Culturama).

Religious organizations sponsor a wide variety of grassroots development projects. In the Philippines, the Basic Ecclesiastical Community (BEC) movement is based on Christian teachings and follows the model of Jesus as a supporter of the poor and oppressed (Nadeau 2002) (see Map 5.1, p. 103). BECs seek to follow the general principles of liberation theology, which blends Christian principles of compassion and social justice, political consciousness raising among the oppressed, and communal activism. In the rural areas, several BECs have successfully built trust among group members and leaders and developed people's awareness of the excesses of global capitalism and the dangers of private greed and accumulation. Part of their success is due to the fact that members were able to pursue new economic strategies outside the constraints of capitalism and that require little capital input, such as organic farming.

A BEC in Cebu City, on the Island of Cebu (suh-BOO), the Philippines, however, was unsuccessful. It faced the challenge of organizing people who make a living scavenging in a nearby city dump. Both adults and children scavenge for materials that are then sorted and sold for recycling, such as plastic. They work for 14 hours a day, seven days a week. It is an organized operation, with district officials monitoring the dump. Customary arrangements among the scavengers regulate their work areas. Scavenging requires no formal education and few tools—just a basket and a steel hook, and a kerosene lantern for nighttime work. Scavengers

Scavenging for a livelihood in an urban dump in the Philippines.
▶ *What kind of an entitlement is this?*

earn more than other nonskilled laborers in the city. In the BEC meetings, the scavengers found little on which to build solidarity. Instead, they bickered with each other and complained about each other to the leaders. The sheer poverty of the people was so great that communal values could not compete against their daily economic struggle. In cases of extreme poverty with limited or no options for alternative forms of income generation, government programs may be required to complement faith-based, grassroots initiatives.

THE DEVELOPMENT PROJECT

Development institutions, whether they are large multilaterals or local nongovernmental organizations (NGOs), implement their goals through the **development project**, a set of activities designed to put development policies into action. For example, suppose a government sets a policy of increased

---

social capital   the intangible resources existing in social ties, trust, and cooperation.

development project   a set of activities designed to put development policies into action.

Project identification	Selecting a project to fit a particular purpose
Project design	Preparing the details of the project
Project appraisal	Assessing the project's budgetary aspects
Project implementation	Putting the project in place
Project evaluation	Assessing whether the project goals were fulfilled

FIGURE 13.1 The Development Project Cycle

agricultural production by a certain percent within a designated period. A development project to achieve the policy goal might be the construction of irrigation canals that would supply water to a targeted number of farmers.

THE DEVELOPMENT PROJECT CYCLE Although details vary among organizations, all development projects have a **project cycle**, or the full process of a project from initial planning to completion (Cernea 1985). The project cycle includes five basic steps from beginning to end (see Figure 13.1).

Since the 1970s, applied anthropologists have been involved in development projects. Early on, they were hired primarily to do project evaluations, to determine whether the project had achieved its goals. Their research shows that projects were often dismal failures (Cochrane 1979). Three major reasons for these failures are as follows:

- The project did not fit the cultural and environmental context.

- The project benefits did not reach the target group, such as the poor or women; instead, project benefits went to elites or some other less needy group.

- The intended beneficiaries were worse off after the project than before it.

project cycle the steps of a development project from initial planning to completion: project identification, project design, project appraisal, project implementation, and project evaluation.

cultural fit a characteristic of informed and effective project design in which planners take local culture into account; opposite of "one-size-fits-all" project design.

traditional development anthropology an approach to international development in which the anthropologist accepts the role of helping to make development work better by providing cultural information to planners.

critical development anthropology an approach to international development in which the anthropologist takes on a critical-thinking role and asks why and to whose benefit particular development policies and programs are pursued.

One factor underlying these three problems is poor project design. The projects were designed by bureaucrats, usually Western economists, who lived in cities far from the project site with no firsthand experience of the lives of the target population. These experts applied a universal formula ("one size fits all") to all situations (Cochrane 2009). The cultural anthropologists who evaluated the projects, in contrast, knew the local people and context and were therefore shocked by the degree of nonfit between the projects and the people.

Applied anthropologists gained a reputation in development circles as troublemakers—people to be avoided by those who favored a move-ahead approach to getting projects funded and implemented. Applied anthropologists are still considered a nuisance by many development policy makers and planners, but sometimes, at least, a necessary nuisance. On a more positive note, through persistent efforts they have made progress in gaining a role earlier in the project cycle, at the stages of project identification and design.

CULTURAL FIT A review of many development projects over the past few decades reveals the importance of **cultural fit**, or taking the local culture into account in project design (Kottak 1985). A glaring case of nonfit between a project and its target population is a project intended to improve nutrition and health in some South Pacific islands by promoting increased milk consumption (Cochrane 1974). The project involved the transfer of large quantities of powdered milk from the United States to an island community. The local people, however, were lactose intolerant (unable to digest raw milk), and they all soon had diarrhea. They stopped drinking the milk and used the powder to whitewash their houses. Beyond wasting resources, inappropriately designed projects result in the exclusion of the intended beneficiaries. Two examples are when a person's signature is required but the people do not know how to write and when photo identification cards are requested from Muslim women, whose faces may not be shown in public.

Applied anthropologists can provide insights into how to achieve cultural fit in order to enhance the success of a project. Anthropologist Gerald Murray played a positive role in redesigning a costly and unsuccessful reforestation project supported by USAID in Haiti (1987). Since the colonial era in Haiti (see Map 13.3, p. 284), deforestation has been dramatic, with an estimated 50 million trees cut annually. Some of the deforestation is driven by the market demand for wood for construction and for charcoal in the capital city of Port-au-Prince. Another reason is that the peyizan yo, or small farmers, need cleared land for growing crops and grazing their goats. The ecological consequences of so much clearing, however, are extensive erosion of the soil and declining fertility of the land.

In the 1980s, USAID sent millions of tree seedlings to Haiti and the Haitian government urged rural people to plant them. The peyizan yo, however, refused to plant the seedlings on their land and instead fed them to their goats. Murray, who had done his doctoral dissertation on rural Haitian land tenure practices, was called on by USAID to diagnose the problem and suggest an alternative approach. He advised that the kind of seedling promoted be changed from that of fruit trees, in which the peyizan yo saw little benefit because they are not to be cut, to that of fast-growing trees, such as eucalyptus, which could be cut as early as four years after planting and sold in Port-au-Prince. The peyizan yo quickly accepted this plan because it would yield profits in the foreseeable future. The cultural nonfit was that USAID wanted trees to stay in place for many years, but the peyizan yo viewed trees as things that were meant to be cut in the short term.

THE ANTHROPOLOGICAL CRITIQUE OF DEVELOPMENT PROJECTS

The early decades of development anthropology were dominated by what I call **traditional development anthropology**. In traditional development anthropology, the anthropologist takes on a role of helping to make development policies and programs work better. It is the "add an anthropologist and stir" approach to development. Like good applied anthropology in any domain, traditional developmental anthropology does work. For example, an anthropologist familiar with a local culture can provide information about what kinds of consumer goods would be desired by the people or what might persuade people to relocate with less resistance. The anthropologist may act as a cultural broker, someone who uses knowledge of both the *donor culture* and the *recipient culture* to devise a workable plan.

Concern exists among many anthropologists about development projects that have negative effects on local people and their environments. For example, a comparison of the welfare of local inhabitants of the middle Senegal River valley (see Map 13.4) before and after the construction of a large dam shows that people's level of food insecurity increased after the dam was built (Horowitz and Salem-Murdock 1993). Before the dam, periodic flooding of the plain provided for a dense population supporting itself with agriculture, fishing, forestry, and herding. After the dam was constructed, water was released less often. The people downstream lacked sufficient water for their crops, and fishing was no longer a dependable source of food. At other times, dam managers released a large flood of water, damaging farmers' crops. Many downstream residents have had to leave the area because of the effects of the dam; they are victims of development-induced displacement (review Chapter 12). Downstream people now have high rates of schistosomiasis, a severely debilitating disease caused by parasites, because the disease spreads quickly in the slow-moving water below the dam.

Other "dam stories" document the negative effects of dam construction on local people, including the destruction of

MAP 13.4 Senegal.
The Republic of Senegal is mainly rolling sandy plains of the western Sahel. Senegal's economy has been struggling. Social inequality is extreme, and urban unemployment is high. The population of Senegal is over 11 million, of which 70 percent live in rural areas. Of the many ethnic groups, the Wolof are the largest. Islam is the major religion, practiced by 94 percent of the population, with Christians making up 4 percent. Sufi brotherhoods are the organizing principle of Islam in Senegal.

their economy, social organization, sacred space, sense of home, and environment (Loker 2004). Such mega-projects force thousands, even millions, of people in the affected area to cope with the changes in one way or another. Many leave; others stay and try to replace what they have lost by clearing new land and rebuilding. Most end up in situations far worse than the one in which they lived originally.

The growing awareness of the detrimental effects of many supposedly positive development projects has led to the emergence of what I call **critical development anthropology**. In this approach, the anthropologist takes on a critical-thinking role. The question is not What can I do to make this project successful? Instead, the anthropologist asks, Is this a good project from the perspective of the local people and their environment? If the answer is yes, then an applied anthropologist can take a supportive role. If the answer is no, then the anthropologist can intervene with relevant information, taking on the role of either a whistle-blower to stop the project or an advocate promoting ideas about how to change the project in order to mitigate harm. In the case of the Senegal River dam project, applied anthropologists worked in collaboration with engineers and local people to devise an alternative management plan for the water flow in which regular and controlled amounts of water were released. In many other cases, the process has less of a positive outcome, with planners ignoring the anthropologist's advice (Loker 2000).

Development, Indigenous People, and Women

This section considers two categories of people who are increasingly taking an active role in redefining development in their own terms: indigenous people and women. Although they are overlapping categories, the section presents material about them separately for purposes of illustration.

INDIGENOUS PEOPLE AND DEVELOPMENT

Indigenous peoples have been victimized by many aspects of growth-oriented development, as they were by colonialism before it. But now many indigenous groups are redefining development and taking it into their own hands.

As noted in Chapter 1, indigenous people are usually a numerical minority in the states that control their territory. The United Nations distinguishes between indigenous peoples and other minority groups such as African Americans, the Roma, and the Tamils of Sri Lanka. It is more useful to view all "minority" groups as forming a continuum, from purely indigenous groups to minority/ethnic groups that are not geographically original to a place but that share many problems with indigenous peoples as a result of displacement and living within a more powerful majority culture (Maybury-Lewis 1997b).

Indigenous peoples differ from most minorities in that they tend to occupy remote areas and, often, areas rich in natural

In the southern part of Madagascar, there is pressure to grow more rice, which means irrigating more land. The expansion of intensive rice cultivation will bring the death of many baobab trees and threaten the habitats of wild animal species, including lemurs.

▶ *Assume that you have just been appointed as Madagascar's minister of people, nature, and development. What do you want your research staff to brief you about during your first month of service?*

resources. Remoteness has, to some extent, protected them from outsiders. Now, however, governments, international business, conservationists, and tourists increasingly recognize that the lands of these people contain valuable natural resources, such as gas in the circumpolar region, gold in Papua New Guinea and the Amazon, sapphires in Madagascar, hydroelectric potential in large rivers throughout the world, and cultural attractions.

Accurate statistics on indigenous populations do not exist. Several reasons account for this lack of information (Kennedy and Perz 2000). First, no one agrees about whom to count as indigenous. Second, some governments do not bother to conduct a census of indigenous people, or if they do, they may undercount indigenous people in order to downplay recognition of their existence. Third, it is often physically difficult, if not impossible, to carry out census operations in indigenous areas. The indigenous people of North Sentinel Island in India's Andaman Islands remain uncounted because Indian officials cannot land on the island without being shot at with arrows (Singh 1994).

Rough estimates of the total population of indigenous people worldwide range between 300 million and 350 million people, or about 5 percent of the world's population (Hughes 2003). The greatest numbers are in Asia, including Central Asia, South Asia, East Asia, and Southeast Asia. Canada's First Nation population is under 2 million. The Indian population in the United States numbers around 1 million.

INDIGENOUS PEOPLE AS VICTIMS OF COLONIALISM AND DEVELOPMENT Like colonialism, contemporary global and state political and economic interests often involve the takeover and control of indigenous people's territory. Over the past several hundred years, many indigenous groups and their cultures have been exterminated as a result of contact with outsiders. Death and population decline have resulted from contagious diseases, slavery, warfare, and other forms of violence. With colonialism, indigenous people experienced wholesale attacks as outsiders sought to take over their land by force, prevented them from practicing their traditional lifestyles, and integrated them into the colonial state as marginalized subjects. The loss of economic, political, and expressive autonomy have had devastating physical and psychological effects on indigenous peoples. Reductions in the biodiversity of their natural environments are directly linked to impoverishment, despair, and overall cultural decline (Maffi 2005, Arambiza and Painter 2006). These processes are common worldwide, creating unforeseen new risks for indigenous people's welfare.

In Southeast Asia, states use policies of "planned resettlement" that displace indigenous people, or "hill tribes," in the name of progress (Evrard and Goudineau 2004). Development programs for the hill tribes in Thailand, for example, reveal the links among international interests, state goals, and the well-being of the tribes (Kesmanee 1994). The hill tribes include groups such as the Karen, Hmong, Mian, Lahu, Lisu, and Akha. They total about half a million people. International pressures are applied to have the hill tribes replace the cultivation of opium with other cash crops. International aid agencies therefore sponsor alternative agricultural projects and tourism. The Thai government, however, is more concerned with political stability and security in the area, given its strategic location, and therefore promotes development projects such as roads and markets to establish links between the highlands and the lowlands. Either way, the hill tribes are the target of outsiders' interests; thus, they face a challenge to the promotion of their own agendas.

Efforts to find viable substitute crops for opium have been unsuccessful, especially among the Hmong, who are most dependent on opium as a cash crop. Alternative crops require the heavy use of fertilizers and pesticides, which are costly to the farmers and greatly increase environmental pollution; moreover, such crops are less lucrative for the farmers. Logging companies have gained access to the hills and have done far more damage to the forests than the highlanders' horticultural practices have. Increased penetration of the hill areas by lowlanders and international tourists have promoted rising HIV/AIDS rates, illegal trafficking of girls and boys for sex, and opium addiction among the highlanders.

The Thai government, like the government of neighboring Laos, has attempted to relocate highland horticulturalists to the plains through various resettlement schemes. Highlanders who opt for relocation find the lowland plots to be unproductive because of poor soil quality. Relocated highlanders find that their quality of life and economic status decline in the lowlands. Yet another new risk for the resettlers in Thailand and Laos is that they are now heavy consumers of methamphetamines, an addictive, euphoria-inducing compound with serious negative side effects, such as rapid weight loss, tooth decay, diarrhea, nausea, and agitation (Lyttleton 2004). Overall, 50 years of so-called development have been disastrous for Southeast Asia's hill peoples.

INDIGENOUS PEOPLE AND TERRITORIAL ENTITLEMENTS

Throughout their history of contact with the outside world, indigenous peoples have actively sought to resist the deleterious effects of "civilization." Since the 1980s, more effective and highly organized forms of protest have become prominent. Indigenous groups now hire lawyers and other experts as consultants in order to reclaim and defend their territorial rights, gain self-determination, and secure protection from outside risks. Many indigenous people have themselves become trained as lawyers, researchers, and advocates. Conflicts range from lawsuits to attempts at secession (Stidsen 2006).

This section provides an overview on the status of indigenous people's territorial rights claims. Within each large world region, country-by-country variation exists in legal codes and in the adherence to any such codes that may exist.

LATIN AMERICA Few Latin American countries provide legal protection against encroachment on the land of indigenous groups. Nicaragua, Peru, Colombia, Ecuador, Bolivia, and Brazil have taken the lead in enacting policies that legitimize indigenous rights to land and in demarcating and titling indigenous territories (Stocks 2005). A wide gap often exists, however, between policy and actual protection. Despite these efforts, increasing numbers of Indians throughout the entire region of Latin America have been forced off their land in the past few decades through poverty, violence, and environmental degradation due to encroachment by logging companies, mining operations, ranch developers, and others. In response, many migrate to cities and seek wage labor. Those who remain face extreme poverty, malnutrition, and personal and group insecurity.

A surge of political activism by indigenous people has occurred since the 1990s, sometimes involving physical resistance. Violence continues to erupt between indigenous groups and state-supported power structures, especially in the southern Mexican state of Chiapas (see Map 4.3, p. 84). In 2005, participants at the First Symposium on Isolated Indigenous Peoples of the Amazon created a group called the International Alliance for the Protection of Isolated Indigenous Peoples. The group seeks to make the relevant state governments aware of the current endangered situation of many indigenous people. These people demand their right to isolation, if that is their choice, and to protection from unwelcome outside contact and encroachment. In 2008, the International Alliance of Forest Peoples formed to push for indigenous people's participation in global climate change talks and to devise a plan whereby wealthy countries would compensate developing countries for conserving tropical forests (Barrionuevo 2008).

CANADA In Canada, the law distinguishes between two different types of Native Peoples and their land claims (Plant 1994). *Specific claims* concern problems arising from previous agreements or treaties, and *comprehensive claims* are those made by Native Peoples who have not been displaced and have made no treaties or agreements. Most of the former claims have led to monetary compensation. In the latter category, interest in oil and mineral exploration has prompted governments to negotiate with indigenous people in an effort to have the latter's native claims either relinquished or redefined. In some provinces, especially British Columbia, claims affect most of the province. The Nunavut land claim was settled, granting about 25,000 Inuit access to a vast tract of land, including subsurface rights (Jensen 2004) (see Map 13.5).

ASIA In Asia, most countries have been reluctant to recognize the territorial rights of indigenous people (Plant 1994). In Bangladesh, the Chittagong Hill Tracts in the southeast is being massively encroached upon by settlers from the crowded plains region (see Map 7.1, p. 149). Encroachers from the lowlands now occupy the most fertile land, and the

see Anthropology Works, p. 187). In southern Africa, several San groups joined together to claim a share in the profits from commercial marketing of hoodia as a diet pill (review Culturama, Chapter 1, p. 21). Indigenous groups are taking advantage of new technology and media to build and maintain links with each other over large areas.

Although it is tempting to see hope in the newly emerging forms of resistance, self-determination, and organization among indigenous peoples, such hope cannot be generalized to all indigenous groups. Many are making progress in asserting their claims, and their economic status is improving, but many others are suffering extreme political and economic repression and possible extinction.

WOMEN AND DEVELOPMENT

The category of women contrasts with that of indigenous peoples because women, as a group, do not have a recognized territory associated with them. But the effects of colonialism, and now development, on women are similar to their effects on indigenous people: Women have often lost economic entitlements and political power in their communities. Matrilineal kinship, for example, which keeps property in the female line (review Chapter 6), is in decline throughout the world. Westernization and modernization are frequently the cause of this change. Another factor that has had a pervasive negative effect on women's status is the **male bias in development**, or the design and implementation of development projects with men as beneficiaries and without regard to their impact on women's roles and status.

THE MALE BIAS IN DEVELOPMENT In the 1970s, researchers began to notice and write about the fact that development projects were male biased (Boserup 1970, Tinker 1976). Many projects completely bypassed women as beneficiaries, targeting men for such initiatives as growing cash crops and learning about new technology. This male bias in development contributed to increased gender inequality by giving men greater access to new sources of income and by depriving women of their traditional economic roles. The development experts' image of a farmer, for example, was male, not female.

Women's projects were typically focused on the domestic domain—for example, infant feeding practices, child care, and family planning. This emphasis led to the *domestication of women* worldwide, meaning that their lives became more focused on the domestic domain and more removed from the public domain (Rogers 1979). For example, agricultural projects bypassed female horticulturalists, who were taught to spend more time in the house bathing their babies, and political leadership projects focused on men and left women out even in contexts where women traditionally had public political roles.

The male bias in development also contributed to the failure of some projects. In the West African country of Burkina Faso (see Map 12.5, p. 272), a reforestation project included men as the sole participants, whose tasks would include planting and caring for the trees. Cultural patterns there, however, dictate that men do not water plants; women do. The men planted the seedlings and left them. Excluding women from the project ensured its failure. The exclusion of women from development continues to be a problem, in spite of many years of attempting to keep women's issues on the development agenda.

The inclusion of women's knowledge, concerns, and voices in research has brought new and important issues to the fore, redefining development to fits women's needs (see Figure 13.2). One such issue is gender-based violence. This issue has gained attention even among large multilateral organizations, whose experts now realize that women cannot participate in a credit program, for example, if they fear that their husbands will beat them for leaving the house. The United Nations Commission on the Status of Women drafted a declaration in opposition of violence against women that was adopted by the General Assembly in 1993 (Heise, Pitanguy, and Germain 1994). Article 1 of the declaration states that violence against women includes "any act of gender-based violence that results in, or is likely to result in, physical, sexual or psychological harm or suffering to women, including threats of such acts, coercion or arbitrary deprivations of liberty, whether occurring in public or private life"

Prebirth	Sex-selective abortion, battering during pregnancy, coerced pregnancy
Infancy	Infanticide, emotional and physical abuse, deprivation of food and medical care
Girlhood	Child marriage, genital mutilation, sexual abuse by family members and strangers, rape, deprivation of food and medical care, child prostitution
Adolescence	Dating and courtship violence, forced prostitution, rape, sexual abuse in the workplace, sexual harassment
Adulthood	Rape and partner abuse, partner homicide, sexual abuse in the workplace, sexual harassment
Old Age	Abuse and neglect of widows, elder abuse

Source: Adapted from Heise, Pitanguy, and Germain 1994:5.

FIGURE 13.2 Violence against Girls and Women throughout the Life Cycle

male bias in development the design and implementation of development projects with men as beneficiaries and without regard to the impact of the projects on women's roles and status.

Grameen Bank, a development project in Bangladesh that provides small loans to poor people, is one of the most successful examples of improving human welfare through microcredit, or small loans. Professor Mohammed Yunnus (center) founded Grameen Bank and continues to be a source of charismatic leadership for it.

▶ *How does the success of Grameen Bank cause you to question your previous image of Bangladesh?*

(Economic and Social Council 1992). This definition cites women as the focus of concern but also includes girls.

WOMEN'S ORGANIZATIONS FOR CHANGE In many countries, women have improved their status and welfare through forming organizations, which are sometimes part of their traditional culture and sometimes a response to outside inspiration. These organizations range from mothers' clubs that help provide for communal child care to credit organizations that give women opportunities to start their own businesses. Some are local and small scale; others are global, such as Women's World Banking, an international organization that started in India and Bangladesh and grew out of credit programs for poor working women.

An informal system of social networks emerged to help support poor Maya women vendors in San Cristóbal, Chiapas, Mexico (Sullivan 1992) (see Map 4.3, p. 84). Many of the vendors who work in the city square have fled from the highlands because of long-term political conflict there. They manufacture and sell goods to tourists, earning an important portion of household income. In the city, they find social support in an expanded network that helps compensate for the loss of support from the extensive godparenthood system (review Chapter 6) of the highlands. The vendors' new networks include relatives, neighbors, church members, and other vendors, regardless of their religious, political, economic, or social background.

The networks first developed in response to a series of rapes and robberies that began in 1987. Because the offenders were persons of power and influence, the women did not dare to press charges. Mostly single mothers and widows, they adopted a strategy of self-protection. First, they began to gather during the slow period each afternoon. Second, they always travel in groups. Third, they carry sharpened corset bones and prongs: "If a man insults one of them, the group surrounds him and jabs him in the groin" (Sullivan 1992:39–40). Fourth, if a woman is robbed, the other women surround her, comfort her, and help contribute something toward compensating her for her loss. The mid-afternoon gatherings developed into support groups that provide financial assistance, child care, medical advice, and training in job skills. The groups have publicly demonstrated against city

In the town of San Cristóbal de las Casas, the capital city of Chiapas state in Mexico, a Maya vendor sells her goods. The city is located near the Tzotzil Maya communities of Chamula and Zinacantán.

eye on the ENVIRONMENT

Oil, Environmental Degradation, and Human Rights in the Nigerian Delta

During the British colonial era, Nigeria provided wealth for the Crown through the export of palm oil (Osha 2006). In the postcolonial era of globalization, a different kind of oil dominates the country's economy: petroleum. Starting in the 1950s, with the discovery of vast petroleum reserves in Nigeria's Delta region, several European and American companies have explored for, drilled, and exported crude oil to the extent that Nigeria occupies an important position in the world economy. But the local people have gained few economic benefits from the oil industry and instead have reaped major losses in their agricultural and fishing livelihoods due to environmental pollution. The people of the delta are poorer now than in the 1960s. In addition to economic loss, they have lost personal security. Many have become victims of the violence that has increased in the region since the 1990s through state and corporate repression of a local resistance movement. Many others have become IDPs (review Chapter 12), leaving the delta region to escape the pervasive violence.

One of the most detrimentally affected groups is the Ogoni people who live in the southeastern portion of the delta. Ogoni author and Nobel prizewinner Ken Saro-Wiwa founded the Movement for Survival of the

A farmer walks through an oil-soaked field. About 500,000 Ogoni people live in Ogoniland, a deltaic region in southern Nigeria. The fertility of the Niger delta has supported farming and fishing populations at high density for many years. Since Shell discovered oil there in 1958, 100 oil wells were constructed in Ogoniland and countless oil spills have occurred.

Ogoni People (MOSOP) in 1992 to protest Shell's actions in Ogoniland and the Nigerian government's

militarized repression in the region. In 1995, he and eight other Ogoni activists were arrested and tried under

officials' attempts to prevent them from continuing their vending. Through their collective efforts, they have succeeded in bringing greater security into their lives.

A last example of women's empowerment and personal risk reduction through organized efforts comes from Kazakhstan, Central Asia (see Map 8.2, p. 180). In response to the widespread domestic violence of husbands against wives, an NGO called the Society of Muslim Women (SMW) defines domestic violence as a problem that the Islamic faith should address at the grassroots level (Snajdr 2005). The organization declines to work with the police and civic activists, who provide secular responses that involve criminalization of the offense, arrest of offenders, and other public procedures.

Instead, SMW views domestic violence as a private matter that should be dealt with by using Islamic and Kazakh values. Its three approaches are counseling and shelter for abused women and couples' mediation. SMW's guiding principle is to find a way, if possible, to rebuild the family, something that may sound conservative, and even dangerous, in a situation where wife abuse is reported to occur in four out of five marriages. Yet, without funding or professional training, SMW members have provided support for countless women. They help the women overcome isolation by offering shelter, which conforms to the Kazakh custom of hospitality and the Muslim virtue of patience. SMW support gives the spouses time to think about their relationship and shifts blame from the

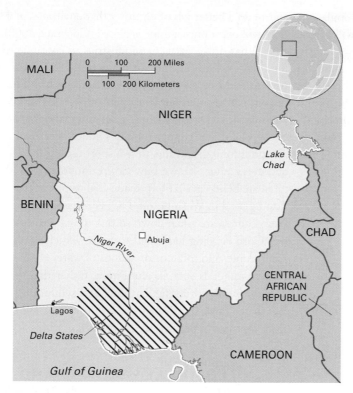

MAP 13.7 Nigeria and the Niger Delta.
Nigeria is the most populous country in Africa, with over 140 million people. It has more than 250 ethnic groups, with the largest being the Fulani, Hausa, Yorúbà, and Igbo. Nigerians speak over 500 languages; English is the official language. Nigeria is Africa's biggest petroleum producer, with an average of 2 million barrels a day extracted in the Niger Delta. The delta makes up 7.5 percent of Nigeria's landmass, but its population of 31 million accounts for 22 percent of the population. The Niger Delta's petroleum industry supports a high economic growth rate for the country, making it one of the fastest growing economies in the world. Yet little of this wealth filters back to the local people of the delta, who bear the brunt of the environmental and cultural damage caused by the petroleum industry. Oil spills are a frequent problem. Traditional economic pursuits, such as fishing, have been negatively affected. One of the world's richest wetlands and richest areas of cultural diversity, with over 40 ethnic groups, is endangered by large-scale petroleum mining that benefits people in the capital city and in other countries.

suspicious circumstances and then executed by hanging.

In a 1992 speech to the United Nations Working Group on Indigenous Populations, Saro-Wiwa eloquently points to the connections among resource extraction, the environment, and Ogoni human and cultural rights:

> Environmental degradation has been a lethal weapon in the war against the indigenous Ogoni people. ... Oil exploration has turned Ogoni into a wasteland: lands, streams, and creeks are totally and continually polluted; the atmosphere has been poisoned, charged as it is with hydrocarbon vapors, methane, carbon monoxide, carbon dioxide, and soot emitted by gas which has been flared 24 hours a day for 33 years in close proximity to human habitation . . . . All one sees and feels around is death. (quoted in Sachs 1996:13–16)

Many social scientists agree with Saro-Wiwa that such forms of development violate human and cultural rights because they undermine a people's way of life and threaten its continued existence (Johnston 1994).

◆ **FOOD FOR THOUGHT**

• Use the Internet to explore the concept of corporate social responsibility, and be prepared to discuss its relationship to the Ogoni situation.

victims by invoking Islamic values of familial commitment and gender equality. Nationalist rhetoric shifts blame for men's alcoholism from the individual to the Russian occupation. Thus, SMW works within the bounds of Kazakh culture and uses that culture for positive outcomes within those bounds.

◆◆◆

Urgent Issues in Development

This chapter opened with a quotation about the people of Walpole Island Reservation in Canada and their ongoing attempt to recover from the damage that colonialism and neocolonialism have wreaked on their culture and natural environment. In spite of much progress of local people and women in redefining development to improve their lives, rather than the lives of external groups such as international businesses and neocolonial states, the bulk of "development" money still goes for mega-projects that do more for people who already have resources than for the poor.

As discussed earlier in the chapter, development projects are the main mechanism through which development institutions implement their goals. These projects are typically designed by outsiders, often with little local knowledge, and they follow a universal, one-size-fits-all pattern. They range from mega-projects such as massive dams to small projects, with the former being much more damaging to local people than the latter. The so-called beneficiaries or target population are often not consulted at all about projects that will affect their community. Critics of such externally imposed and often damaging initiatives refer to them as **development aggression**, the imposition of development projects and policies without the free, prior, and informed consent of the affected people (Tauli-Corpuz 2005). Such development violates the human rights of local people, including their right to pursue a livelihood in their homeland and to prevent environmental destruction of their territory. It also contributes nothing to prevent or alleviate poverty.

LIFE PROJECTS AND HUMAN RIGHTS

Moving beyond critique, indigenous people, women, and others who are victimized by development aggression are redefining what should be done to improve their lives or protect them from further decline. They propose the concept of the life project rather than the development project. A **life project** is local people's vision of the direction they want to take in life, informed by their knowledge, history, and context, and how to achieve that vision.

Life projects can be considered a human right and thus in accord with the UN's Declaration of Human Rights that was ratified in 1948. Development that leads to environmental degradation, including loss of biological diversity, air and water pollution, deforestation, and soil erosion, is a human rights abuse. Many examples exist worldwide of how rich natural resources are improperly exploited to the gain of a few and the detriment of many, turning a blessing into what is now considered a curse (see Eye on the Environment).

The major extractive industries of mining, oil, and gas are driven by the profit motive to the extent that they are disinclined to take local people's interests and environmental concerns seriously. An **extractive industry** is a business that explores for, removes, processes, and sells minerals, oil, and gas that are found on or beneath the earth's surface and are nonrenewable. The many tragic cases of local violence around the world where local people seek to prevent or remove an extractive industry project from their land, however, have been a wake-up call to some companies. Rio Tinto, one of the largest mining companies in the world, seeks to use cultural anthropology expertise to find ways to treat "affected peoples" more fairly

and to do a better job of ensuring that environmental "mitigation" will occur once a mine is closed (Cochrane 2008).

What drives extractive industries to continue to explore for gold, drill for oil, and cut down trees? What drives countries to build mega-dams and mega-highways? The demand lies with all of us, in our consumerist lifestyle that requires diamonds for engagement rings, gold and platinum for computers and gold and copper for cell phones, electrical power for air conditioning, and fuel to transport us, our food and water, and everything else we buy. Entire mountains in West Virginia are being leveled to provide coal to power the air conditioning used in Washington, DC. Forests in Brazil and Papua New Guinea are taken down so that we can read the newspaper. Corn is being harvested to move vehicles rather than to feed people, and millions of gallons of water are being used to process minerals such as aluminum, rather than being available for human drinking, bathing, and swimming, or for fish and water fowl. It will take a lot to turn this pattern around from destructive projects to life projects.

CULTURAL HERITAGE AND DEVELOPMENT: LINKING THE PAST AND PRESENT TO THE FUTURE

Chapter 11 discussed the potential of cultural heritage, both tangible and nontangible, in creating employment opportunities for local people through cultural tourism. This section goes more deeply into the complicated connections between cultural heritage and improving people's welfare from a life project perspective.

The connection of cultural heritage tourism to development is a double-edged sword, with both benefits and costs (Bauer 2006). Promoting cultural heritage through tourism requires an expansion of supportive infrastructure such as roads and hotels and electricity, the provision of food and other supplies for tourists, and labor to provide services for tourists. Thus, at the same time that it generates revenue, such tourism can preserve and protect cultural heritage, but the presence of the tourism industry and the tourists themselves may damage and even destroy it. Such famous World Heritage Sites as Angkor Wat in Cambodia and Machu Picchu in Peru are physically suffering the strains of huge numbers of tourists. Venice, the world's most touristed city, is also a World Heritage Site. Given its particular attraction as a city of canals, it is at particular risk of overload and environmental degradation from the ever-increasing number of tourist boats in the canals, not to mention the massive amount of solid and liquid trash that tourists leave behind (David and Marvin 2004). Although promotional literature advertising Venice to tourists shows a romantic scene of a couple in a gondola or sitting alone in the Piazza San Marco, the reality is that the couple would be surrounded by crowds of tourists and heckled by ambitious local entrepreneurs.

---

development aggression   the imposition of development projects and policies without the free, prior, and informed consent of the affected people.

life project   local people's definition of the direction they want to take in life, informed by their knowledge, history, and context.

extractive industry   a business that explores for, removes, processes, and sells minerals, oil, and gas that are found on or beneath the earth's surface and are nonrenewable.

World Heritage Sites both benefit and suffer from the designation because of the many tourists drawn to them. Angkor Wat, which means "The Temple City," was designated as a World Heritage Site in 1983. It was built in the twelfth century as a Hindu temple, but later additions to it were Buddhist. Current tourist numbers are putting the site in danger due to trash, pedestrian traffic, and hotel development in the vicinity. In 1983, fewer than 8,000 tourists visited the site. Projections for 2010 are 3 million.

▶ *Plan a trip to Angkor Wat, and learn whether "green" options exist and whether the site offers ways to reduce damage from tourists.*

A growing area related to cultural heritage preservation is intellectual property rights law, or cultural property rights law. Lawyers worldwide are increasingly involved in providing legal definitions and protections of rights to various forms of cultural knowledge and behavior. The legalization of culture is another double-edged sword: On one hand, laws may help people, such as the San of southern Africa, to gain a share of the profits from the hoodia plant. On the other hand, the legalization of culture can transform much of everyday life into a legal battle requiring expensive legal specialists. For thousands of years, the San had full and unquestioned entitlement to hoodia and its benefits. They did not need to hire international lawyers.

Everything from website addresses that may use tribal names to the designation of what is or is not champagne can now become grounds for litigation. And money, you can be sure, is involved from the start to the finish, as is the more difficult to quantify sense of identity of people who define themselves in relation to a place, a product, or a taste.

CULTURAL ANTHROPOLOGY AND THE FUTURE

Over the next several years, culture as defined, understood, and argued about—will be a major factor in international, regional, and local development and change. Determining how cultural anthropologists can contribute more effectively to a better future for humanity is a challenge for a field with its intellectual roots in studying *what is* rather than *what might be*. But just as local people everywhere are redefining development and reclaiming their culture, so are they also helping to redefine the theory, practice, and application of cultural anthropology. Although we live in a time of war, it is also a time of hope, in which insights and strength often come from those with the least in terms of material wealth but with cultural wealth beyond measure.

Haitian dancers perform on Discover Miami Day at Miami's Little Haiti Caribbean Marketplace. Haitian culture in Miami is an increasingly popular tourist attraction in North America.

13

the BIG questions REVISITED

◆ What is development and what are the approaches to achieving it?

Several theories or models of development exist, including modernization, growth-oriented development, distributional development, human development, and sustainable development. They differ in terms of how they define development and how to achieve it.

Institutional approaches to development, whether pursued by large-scale or grassroots organizations, tend to rely on the development project as a vehicle of local change. Cultural anthropologists have been hired as consultants on development projects, typically at the end of the project cycle to provide evaluations. Anthropologists have pushed for involvement earlier in the project so that their cultural knowledge can be used in project planning to avoid common errors. A one-size-fits-all project design often results in failed projects because of a lack of cultural fit.

In traditional development anthropology, anthropological knowledge contributes to a development project by adding insights that will make the project work. In critical development anthropology, anthropological knowledge may suggest that the most socially beneficial path is either to stop the project or to redesign it.

◆ How has development affected indigenous people and women, and how are they redefining development?

Indigenous people and women have been affected by international development in various ways, often negatively. They are taking an increasingly active role in redefining development to better suit their vision of the future.

Colonialism, neocolonialism, and globalization have eroded the entitlements and standard of living of indigenous peoples and women worldwide. Often, such losses are tied to environmental degradation and violence. Indigenous peoples throughout the world suffer because they lack a secure claim to their ancestral territories. They seek social recognition of territorial claims from state governments and protection from encroachment. Some governments are responding to their claims; others are not. Establishing organizations has been a major source of strength for promoting indigenous people's rights.

Western development planning and projects have long suffered from a male bias in project design. Excluding women from projects serves to domesticate women and often results in failed projects. Women are stating their needs and visions for the future, thus redefining development in ways that are helpful to them. They have added the issue of violence against women and girls to the policy agendas of development institutions worldwide, including the large multilateral organizations.

◆ What are urgent issues in development?

Three urgent issues, as informed by cultural anthropology and the views and voices of people themselves, are the redefinition of development projects as life projects, or people-centered projects; the relationship between human rights and development; and the role of cultural heritage in development. Indigenous people, women, and others adversely affected by certain forms of development are promoting these new kinds of development in order to enhance their prospects for the future.

The concept of the life project is a human right and a right to live in one's cultural world without encroachment, threat, or discrimination. Cultural anthropologists contribute insights from different cultures about perceptions of basic human and cultural rights, and this knowledge, linked to advocacy, may be able to help prevent human/cultural rights abuses in the future.

People's cultural heritage can be a path toward improved welfare, but it is a double-edged sword. Promoting cultural tourism can protect culture but also lead to damage and destruction. An emerging area is the legalization of cultural heritage through intellectual property rights law, another double-edged sword.

Culture is a central issue of our time, and local people are working with cultural anthropologists to address the challenges of an increasingly globalized and insecure, but exciting, world.

KEY CONCEPTS

acculturation, p. 279

assimilation, p. 279

critical development
  anthropology, p. 287

cultural fit, p. 286

development, p. 278

development aggression, p. 296

development project, p. 285

diffusion, p. 279

extractive industry, p. 296

invention, p. 279

life project, p. 296

male bias in development, p. 292

modernization, p. 281

poverty, p. 278

project cycle, p. 286

social capital, p. 285

social impact assessment, p. 280

traditional development
  anthropology, p. 287

SUGGESTED READINGS

Mario Blaser, Harvey A. Feit, and Glenn McRae, eds. *In the Way of Development: Indigenous Peoples, Life Projects and Globalization.* New York: Zed Books, 2004. The authors are indigenous leaders, social activists, and anthropologists. Topics include the environment, women's status, social justice, participation, and dealing with mega-development projects.

Glynn Cochrane. *Festival Elephants and the Myth of Global Poverty.* Boston: Pearson, 2009. Over 40 years of experience in international development inform this memoir and critique. Cochrane argues that no single form of global poverty exists but that poverty is local and must be addressed with local solutions.

Ann Frechette. *Tibetans in Nepal: The Dynamics of International Assistance among a Community in Exile.* New York: Berghahn Books, 2002. This book explores how a long history of international assistance to refugees has affected individual and community identity and values. Focusing on Tibetans in Nepal, Frechette shows how aid complicates exiled Tibetans' attempts to define and maintain a sense of community.

Dorothy L. Hodgson. *Once Intrepid Warriors: Gender, Ethnicity, and the Cultural Politics of Maasai Development.* Bloomington: Indiana University Press, 2004. This ethnography shows how Maasai identity and gender connect with development and globalization to shape Maasai life today.

Gideon M. Kressel. *Let Shepherding Endure: Applied Anthropology and the Preservation of a Cultural Tradition in Israel and the Middle East.* Albany: SUNY Press, 2003. This book presents a case study of the Bedu of the Negev, southern Israel. It discusses how globalization is encroaching on herders to their great detriment. The author lays out an applied anthropology program for reconstituting and promoting pastoralism.

William Loker. *Changing Places: Environment, Development, and Social Change in Rural Honduras.* Durham, NC: Carolina Academic Press, 2004. Loker uses qualitative and quantitative data to assess the social and environmental effects of a large dam in the El Cajón region of Honduras.

Mark Moberg. *Citrus, Strategy, and Class: The Politics of Development in Southern Belize.* Iowa City: University of Iowa Press, 1992. Moberg compares the involvement of two villages in Belize in the global citrus market. He describes the formation of a rural class and the increasing dependency of rural Belize on the global market.

David Mosse. *Cultivating Development: An Ethnography of Aid Policy and Practice.* Ann Arbor, MI: Pluto Press, 2005. Mosse uses his experience as a development worker in India to analyze and critique how the structure of aid shapes the actions of development workers. The subject matter is policy making and projects viewed from a critical ethnographic perspective.

Richard J. Perry. *From Time Immemorial: Indigenous Peoples and State Systems.* Austin: University of Texas Press, 1996. Perry provides a comparative review of the history and status of indigenous peoples of Mexico, the United States, Canada, and Australia. Topics covered are state policies, state violence, resistance of the indigenous people, and efforts at self-determination.

Joanne Rappaport. *Intercultural Utopias: Public Intellectuals, Cultural Experimentation, and Ethnography.* Durham, NC: Duke University Press, 2005. The author draws on collaborative research with indigenous activists in Colombia. She documents the country's complex indigenous political movement, with a focus on the southwestern Cauca region and its long history of indigenous mobilization and ethnic pluralism.

John Sherry. *Land, Wind and Hard Words: A Story of Navajo Activism.* Albuquerque: University of New Mexico Press, 2002. This book presents the story of the community-based activists of a Navajo environmental organization called Diné CARE, which seeks to protect Navajo forests from logging.

Jennie M. Smith. *When the Hands Are Many: Community Organization and Social Change in Rural Haiti.* Ithaca, NY: Cornell University Press, 2001. Fieldwork in southwest Haiti reveals how poor rural people use social organizing and expressive culture to unite in resistance to the larger forces that impoverish them.

John van Willigen. *Anthropology in Action: A Source Book on Anthropological Practice.* Boulder, CO: Westview Press, 1991. This book first provides brief overviews of ethics, publications, and professional organizations in applied anthropology. Case studies follow, arranged alphabetically by topic, from "Agriculture" to "Women in Development."

PHOTO CREDITS

GLOSSARY

acculturation   a form of cultural change in which a minority culture becomes more like the dominant culture.

achieved position   a person's standing in society based on qualities that the person has gained through action.

adolescence   a culturally defined period of maturation from the time of puberty until adulthood that occurs in some, but not all, cultures.

agency   the ability of humans to make choices and exercise free will even within dominating structures.

age set   a group of people close in age who go through certain rituals, such as circumcision, at the same time.

agriculture   a mode of livelihood that involves growing crops with the use of plowing, irrigation, and fertilizer.

amazon   a person who is biologically female but takes on a male gender role.

animatism   a belief system in which the supernatural is conceived of as an impersonal power.

animism   the belief in souls or "doubles."

anthropology   the study of humanity, including its prehistoric origins and contemporary human diversity.

applied anthropology   the use of anthropological knowledge to prevent or solve problems or to shape and achieve policy goals.

applied medical anthropology   the application of anthropological knowledge to furthering the goals of health care providers.

archaeology   the study of past human cultures through their material remains.

art   the application of imagination, skill, and style to matter, movement, and sound that goes beyond what is purely practical.

ascribed position   a person's standing in society based on qualities that the person has gained through birth.

assimilation   a form of culture change in which a culture is thoroughly acculturated, or decultured, and is no longer distinguishable as having a separate identity.

authority   the ability to take action based on a person's achieved or ascribed status or moral reputation.

balanced exchange   a system of transfers in which the goal is either immediate or eventual equality in value.

band   the form of political organization of foraging groups, with flexible membership and minimal leadership.

berdache   a blurred gender category, usually referring to a person who is biologically male but who takes on a female gender role.

big-man system or big-woman system   a form of political organization midway between tribe and chiefdom and involving leadership by individuals who maintain a political following through personal ties and redistributive feasts.

bilineal descent   tracing descent through both parents.

biological anthropology   the study of humans as biological organisms, including evolution and contemporary variation.

biological determinism   a theory that explains human behavior and ideas as shaped mainly by biological features such as genes and hormones.

blood sport   competition that explicitly seeks to bring about a flow of blood from, or even death of, human–human contestants, human–animal contestants, or animal–animal contestants.

bracero   an agricultural laborer who is permitted entry to a country to work for a limited time.

brideprice   a form of marriage exchange involving the transfer of cash and goods from the groom's family to the bride's family.

bride-service   a form of marriage exchange in which the groom works for his father-in-law for a certain length of time before returning home with the bride.

call system   a form of oral communication among nonhuman primates with a set repertoire of meaningful sounds generated in response to environmental factors.

cargo cult   a form of revitalization movement that emerged in Melanesia in response to Western and Japanese influences.

caste system   a form of social stratification linked with Hinduism and based on a person's birth into a particular group.

chain migration   a population movement in which a first wave of migrants comes and then attracts relatives and friends to join them in the destination.

chiefdom   a form of political organization in which permanently allied tribes and villages have one recognized leader who holds an "office."

circular migration   a regular pattern of population movement between two or more places, either within or between countries.

civil society   the collection of interest groups that function outside the government to organize economic and other aspects of life.

class   a way of categorizing people on the basis of their economic positions in society, usually measured in terms of income or wealth.

collaborative research   an approach to learning about culture that involves anthropologists working with members of the study population as partners and participants rather than as "subjects."

communication   the conveying of meaningful messages from one person or other living being to another.

community healing   healing that emphasizes the social context as a key component and that is likely to be carried out within the public domain.

consumerism   a mode of consumption in which people's demands are many and infinite and the means of satisfying them are insufficient and become depleted in the effort to satisfy the demands.

couvade   customs applying to the behavior of fathers during and shortly after the birth of their children.

creole   a language directly descended from a pidgin but possessing its own native speakers and involving linguistic expansion and elaboration.

critical development anthropology   an approach to international development in which the anthropologist takes on a critical-thinking role and asks why and to whose benefit particular development policies and programs are pursued.

critical discourse analysis   an approach within linguistic anthropology that examines how power and social inequality are reflected and reproduced in communication.

critical legal anthropology   an approach within the cross-cultural study of legal systems that examines the role of law and judicial processes in maintaining the dominance of powerful groups through discriminatory practices rather than protecting less powerful people.

critical media anthropology an approach within the cross-cultural study of media that examines how power interests shape people's access to media and influence the contents of its messages.

critical medical anthropology an approach within medical anthropology involving the analysis of how economic and political structures shape people's health status, their access to health care, and the prevailing medical systems that exist in relation to them.

cross-cousin offspring of either one's father's sister or one's mother's brother.

cultural anthropology the study of living peoples and their cultures, including variation and change.

cultural broker a person who is familiar with the practices and beliefs of two cultures and who can promote cross-cultural understanding to prevent or mediate conflicts.

cultural constructionism a theory that explains human behavior and ideas as shaped mainly by learning.

cultural fit a characteristic of informed and effective project design in which planners take local culture into account; opposite of "one-size-fits-all" project design.

cultural materialism a theorya theory that takes material features of life, such as the environment, natural resources, and mode of livelihood, as the bases for explaining social organization and ideology.

cultural relativism the perspective that each culture must be understood in terms of the values and ideas of that culture and should not be judged by the standards of another culture.

culture people's learned and shared behaviors and beliefs.

culture shock persistent feelings of uneasiness, loneliness, and anxiety that often occur when a person has shifted from one culture to a different one.

culture-specific syndrome a collection of signs and symptoms that is restricted to a particular culture or a limited number of cultures.

dalit the preferred name for the socially defined lowest groups in the Indian caste system; the name means "oppressed" or "ground down."

deductive approach (to research) a research method that involves posing a research question or hypothesis, gathering data related to the question, and then assessing the findings in relation to the original hypothesis.

demographic transition the change from the agricultural pattern of high fertility and high mortality to the industrial pattern of low fertility and low mortality.

descent the tracing of kinship relationships through parentage.

development change directed toward improving human welfare.

development aggression the imposition of development projects and policies without the free, prior, and informed consent of the affected people.

development-induced displacement (DID) the forced migration of a population due to development projects, such as the construction of a dam.

development project a set of activities designed to put development policies into action.

diaspora population dispersed group of people living outside their original homeland.

diffusion the spread of culture through contact.

digital divide social inequality in access to new and emerging information technology, notably access to up-to-date computers, the Internet, and training related to their use.

disease in the disease–illness dichotomy, a biological health problem that is objective and universal.

disease of development a health problem caused or increased by economic development activities that have detrimental effects on the environment and people's relationship with it.

displaced person someone who is forced to leave his or her home and community or country.

displacement a feature of human language whereby people are able to talk about events in the past and future.

doctrine direct and formalized statements about religious beliefs.

dowry a form of marriage exchange involving the transfer of cash and goods from the bride's family to the newly married couple and, sometimes, to the groom's family.

ecological/epidemiological approach an approach within medical anthropology that considers how aspects of the natural environment and social environment interact to cause illness.

emic insiders' perceptions and categories and their explanations for why they do what they do.

endogamy marriage within a particular group or locality.

ethnicity a shared sense of identity among a group based on a heritage, language, or culture.

ethnocentrism judging another culture by the standards of one's own culture rather than by the standards of that particular culture.

ethno-esthetics culturally specific definitions of what art is.

ethno-etiology a culturally specific causal explanation for health problems and suffering.

ethnography a firsthand, detailed description of a living culture, based on personal observation.

ethnomedicine the study of cross-cultural health systems.

ethnomusicology the cross-cultural study of music.

ethnosemantics the study of the meaning of words, phrases, and sentences in particular cultural contexts.

etic an analytical framework used by outside analysts in studying culture.

exogamy marriage outside a particular group or locality.

expected reciprocity an exchange of approximately equally valued goods or services, usually between people roughly equal in social status.

expressive culture behaviors and beliefs related to art, leisure, and play.

extended household a coresidential group that comprises more than one parent–child unit.

extensive strategy a form of livelihood involving the temporary use of large areas of land and a high degree of spatial mobility.

extractive industry a business that explores for, removes, processes, and sells minerals, oil, and gas that are found on or beneath the earth's surface and are nonrenewable.

family a group of people who consider themselves related through a form of kinship, such as descent, marriage, or sharing.

family farming a form of agriculture in which farmers produce mainly to support themselves and also produce goods for sale in the market system.

female genital cutting (FGC) a range of practices that result in partial or total removal of the clitoris and labia.

fertility the rate of births in a population or the rate of population increase in general.

fieldwork research in the field, which is anyplace where people and culture are found.

foraging obtaining food available in nature through gathering, fishing, hunting, or scavenging.

functionalism the theory that a culture is similar to a biological organism, in which parts work to support the operation and maintenance of the whole.

gender culturally constructed and learned behaviors and ideas attributed to males, females, or blended genders.

gender pluralism the existence within a culture of multiple categories of femininity, masculinity, and blurred genders that are tolerated and legitimate.

genealogy a record of a person's relatives constructed beginning with the earliest ancestors.

generalized reciprocity a form of exchange that involves the least conscious interest in material gain or thought of what might be received in return and when a return might occur.

globalization increased and intensified international ties related to the spread of Western, especially U.S., capitalism that affects all world cultures.

global language a language spoken widely throughout the world and in diverse cultural contexts often replacing indigenous languages.

heterotopia a new situation formed from elements drawn from multiple and diverse contexts.

hijra in India, a blurred gender role in which a person, usually biologically male, takes on female dress and behavior.

historical linguistics the study of language change using formal methods that compare shifts over time and across space in aspects of language such as phonetics, syntax, and semantics.

historical trauma the intergenerational transfer of the detrimental effects of colonialism from parents to children.

holism the perspective in anthropology that cultures are complex systems that cannot be fully understood without paying attention to their different components, including economic and reproductive systems, social organization, and ideology.

horticulture a mode of livelihood based on growing domesticated crops in gardens with the use of simple hand tools.

household either one person living alone or a group of people who may or may not be related by kinship and who share living space.

humoral healing healing that emphasizes balance among natural elements within the body.

illness in the disease–illness dichotomy, culturally shaped perceptions and experiences of a health problem.

incest taboo a strongly held prohibition against marrying or having sex with particular kin.

indigenous knowledge local understanding of the environment, climate, plants, and animals.

indigenous peoples groups of people who have a long-standing connection with their home territories that predates colonial or outside societies prevailing in that territories.

inductive approach (to research) a research approach that avoids hypothesis formation in advance of the research and instead takes its lead from the culture being studied.

industrial agriculture a form of agriculture that is capital intensive, substituting machinery and purchased inputs for human and animal labor.

industrial collectivized agriculture a form of industrialized agriculture that involves state control of land, technology, and goods produced.

industrialism/informatics a mode of livelihood in which goods are produced through mass employment in business and commercial operations and through the creation and movement of information via electronic media.

infanticide the killing of an infant or child.

influence the ability to achieve a desired end by exerting social or moral pressure on someone or some group.

informed consent an aspect of fieldwork ethics requiring that the researcher inform the research participants of the intent, scope, and possible effects of the proposed study and seek their consent to be in the study.

institutional migrant someone who moves into a social institution (such as a school or prison) either voluntarily or involuntarily.

intangible cultural heritage UNESCO's view of culture as manifested in oral traditions, languages, performing arts, rituals and festive events, knowledge and practices about nature and the universe, and craftmaking.

intensive strategy a form of livelihood that involves continuous use of the same land and resources.

internal migration the movement of a population within country boundaries.

internally displaced person (IDP) someone who is forced to leave his or her home and community but who remains in the same country.

interpretive anthropology a theory which says that cultures are best understood by studying what people think about, their ideas, and the meanings that are important to them.

interview a research technique that involves gathering verbal data through questions or guided conversation between the interviewer and at least one other person.

invention the discovery of something new.

isogamy marriage between status equals.

khipu cords of knotted strings used during the Inca empire for keeping accounts and recording events.

kinship system the predominant form of kin relationships in a culture and the kinds of behavior involved.

kula a trading network, linking many of the Trobriand Islands, in which men have long-standing partnerships for the exchange of everyday goods, such as food, and highly valued necklaces and armlets.

language a form of communication that is based on a systematic set of learned symbols and signs shared among a group and passed on from generation to generation.

language endangerment the condition of a language when it has fewer than 10,000 speakers.

language extinction the condition of a language in which speakers abandon it in favor of a new language to the extent that the native language loses functions and no longer has competent speakers.

language family a group of languages descended from a parent language.

language shift the condition of a language in which speakers adopt a new language for most situations, begin to use their native language only in certain contexts, and may be only semi-fluent and have limited vocabulary in their native language.

law a binding rule created through enactment or custom that defines right and reasonable behavior and is enforceable by the threat of punishment.

lifeboat mentality a view that seeks to limit enlarging a particular group because of perceived constraints on resources.

life-cycle ritual a ritual that marks a change in status from one life stage to another; also called *rite of passage*.

life project local people's definition of the direction they want to take in life, informed by their knowledge, history, and context.

linguistic anthropology the study of human communication, including its origins, history, and contemporary variation and change.

localization the transformation of global culture by local cultures into something new.

logograph a symbol that conveys meaning through a form or picture resembling that to which it refers.

magic the attempt to compel supernatural forces and beings to act in certain ways.

male bias in development the design and implementation of development projects with men as beneficiaries and without regard to the impact of the projects on women's roles and status.

market exchange a form of unbalanced exchange that involves the buying and selling of commodities under competitive conditions in which the forces of supply and demand determine value.

marriage a union, usually between two people, who are likely to be, but are not necessarily, coresident, sexually involved with each other, and procreative.

material cultural heritage the sites, monuments, buildings, and movable objects considered to have outstanding value to humanity.

matrescence motherhood, or the cultural process of becoming a mother.

matriarchy the dominance of women in economic, political, social, and ideological domains.

matrilineal descent a kinship system that highlights the importance of women by tracing descent through the female line, favoring marital residence with or near the bride's family, and providing for property to be inherited through the female line.

medicalization the labeling of a particular issue or problem as medical and requiring medical treatment when, in fact, that issue or problem is economic or political.

medical pluralism the existence of more than one health system in a culture; also, a government policy to promote the integration of local healing systems into biomedical practice.

menarche the onset of menstruation.

menopause the cessation of menstruation.

mestizaje literally, a racial mixture; in Central and South America, indigenous people who are cut off from their Indian roots, or literate and successful indigenous people who retain some traditional cultural practices.

microculture a distinct pattern of learned and shared behavior and thinking found within larger cultures.

migration the movement of a person or people from one place to another.

minimalism a mode of consumption that emphasizes simplicity, is characterized by few and finite consumer demands, and involves an adequate and sustainable means of achieving the demands.

mode of consumption the dominant pattern, in a culture, of using things up or spending resources in order to satisfy demands.

mode of exchange the dominant pattern, in a culture, of transferring goods, services, and other items between and among people and groups.

mode of livelihood the dominant pattern, in a culture, of making a living.

mode of reproduction the predominant pattern, in a culture, of population change through the combined effect of fertility (birth rate) and mortality (death rate).

modernization a model of change based on belief in the inevitable advance of science and Western secularism and processes, including industrial growth, consolidation of the state, bureaucratization, a market economy, technological innovation, literacy, and options for social mobility.

moka a strategy for developing political leadership in highland Papua New Guinea that involves exchanging gifts and favors with individuals and sponsoring large feasts where further gift giving occurs.

monogamy marriage between two people.

multisited research fieldwork conducted in more than one location in order to understand the behaviors and ideas of dispersed members of a culture or the relationships among different levels, such as state policy and local culture.

myth a narrative with a plot that involves the supernaturals.

nation a group of people who share a language, culture, territorial base, political organization, and history.

new immigrant an international migrant who has moved since the 1960s.

norm a generally agreed-upon standard for how people should behave, usually unwritten and learned unconsciously.

nuclear household a domestic unit containing one adult couple (married or partners), with or without children.

parallel cousin offspring of either one's father's brother or one's mother's sister.

participant observation basic fieldwork method in cultural anthropology that involves living in a culture for a long time while gathering data.

pastoralism a mode of livelihood based on keeping domesticated animals and using their products, such as meat and milk, for most of the diet.

patrescence fatherhood, or the cultural process of becoming a father.

patriarchy the dominance of men in economic, political, social, and ideological domains.

patrilineal descent a kinship system that highlights the importance of men in tracing descent, determining marital residence with or near the groom's family, and providing for inheritance of property through the male line.

personality an individual's patterned and characteristic way of behaving, thinking, and feeling.

phoneme a sound that makes a difference for meaning in a spoken language.

phytotherapy healing through the use of plants.

pidgin a contact language that blends elements of at least two languages and that emerges when people with different languages need to communicate.

pilgrimage round-trip travel to a sacred place or places for purposes of religious devotion or ritual.

placebo effect a positive result from a healing method due to a symbolic or otherwise nonmaterial factor.

policing the exercise of social control through processes of surveillance and the threat of punishment related to maintaining social order.

political organization the groups within a culture that are responsible for public decision making and leadership, maintaining social cohesion and order, protecting group rights, and ensuring safety from external threats.

polyandry marriage of one wife with more than one husband.

polygamy marriage involving multiple spouses.

polygyny marriage of one husband with more than one wife.

potlatch a feast held by Pacific Northwest Indian cultures in which guests are invited to eat and to receive gifts from the hosts.

poverty the lack of tangible and intangible assets that contribute to life and the quality of life.

power the ability to take action in the face of resistance, through force if necessary.

priest/priestess a male/female full-time religious specialist whose position is based mainly on abilities gained through formal training.

primary group a social group in which members meet on a face-to-face basis.

productivity a feature of human language whereby people are able to communicate a potentially infinite number of messages efficiently.

project cycle the steps of a development project from initial planning to completion: project identification, project design, project appraisal, project implementation, and project evaluation.

pronatalism an attitude or policy that encourages childbearing.

puberty a time in the human life cycle that occurs universally and involves a set of biological markers and sexual maturation.

pure gift something given with no expectation or thought of a return.

push–pull theory an explanation for rural-to-urban migration that emphasizes people's incentives to move because of a lack of opportunity in rural areas (the "push") compared with urban areas (the "pull").

qualitative data non-numeric information.

quantitative data numeric information.

questionnaire a formal research instrument containing a pre-set series of questions that the anthropologist asks in a face-to-face setting, by mail, or by e-mail.

"race" a classification of people into groups on the basis of supposedly homogeneous biological traits such as skin color or hair characteristics.

rainforest an environment found at mid-latitudes, of tall, broad-leaf evergreen trees, with annual rainfall of 400 centimeters (or 60 inches) and no dry season.

rapport a trusting relationship between the researcher and the study population.

redistribution a form of exchange that involves one person collecting goods or money from many members of a group that, at a later time and at a public event, "returns" the pooled goods to everyone who contributed.

refugee someone who is forced to leave his or her home, community, or country.

religion beliefs and behavior related to supernatural beings and forces.

religious pluralism a situation in which one or more religions coexist either as complementary to each other or as competing systems.

religious syncretism the blending of features of two or more religions.

remittance the transfer of money or goods by a migrant to his or her family in the country of origin.

revitalization movement a religious movement, usually organized by a prophetic leader, that seeks to construct a more satisfying situation by reviving all or parts of a religion that has been threatened by outside forces or by adopting new practices and beliefs.

right of return the United Nations' guaranteed right of a refugee to return to his or her home country to live.

ritual a patterned behavior that has to do with the supernatural realm.

ritual of inversion a ritual in which normal social roles and order are temporarily reversed.

sacrifice a ritual in which something is offered to the supernaturals.

Sapir–Whorf hypothesis a perspective in linguistic anthropology which says that culture, society, and a person's social position determine language.

secondary group people who identify with each other on some basis but may never meet with one another personally.

shaman/shamanka a male/female healer who gains his or her status through a direct relationship with the supernaturals, often by being "called."

sign language a form of communication that uses mainly hand movements to convey messages.

social capital the intangible resources existing in social ties, trust, and cooperation.

social control processes that, through both informal and formal mechanisms, maintain orderly social life.

social group a cluster of people beyond the domestic unit who are usually related on grounds other than kinship.

social impact assessment a study conducted to predict the potential social costs and benefits of particular innovations before change is undertaken.

social stratification hierarchical relationships among different groups as though they were arranged in layers, or "strata."

sociocultural fit a characteristic of informed and effective project design in which planners take local culture into account; opposite of one-size-fits-all project design.

sociolinguistics a perspective in linguistic anthropology which says that culture, society, and a person's social position determine language.

somatization the process through which the body absorbs social stress and manifests symptoms of suffering.

state a form of political organization in which a centralized political unit encompasses many communities and has a bureaucratic structure and in which its leaders possess coercive power.

status a person's position, or standing, in society.

structural suffering human health problems caused by such economic and political situations as war, famine, terrorism, forced migration, and poverty.

structurism a theoretical position concerning human behavior and ideas that says large forces such as the economy, social and political organizations, and the media shape what people do and think.

susto fright/shock disease, a culture-specific illness found in Spain and Portugal and among Latino people wherever they live; symptoms include back pain, fatigue, weakness, and lack of appetite.

symbol an object, word, or action with culturally defined meaning that stands for something else; most symbols are arbitrary.

synchronic a "one-time" view of a culture that devotes little or no attention to its past.

tag question a question placed at the end of a sentence seeking affirmation.

theater a form of enactment, related to other forms such as dance, music, parades, competitive games and sports, and verbal art, that seeks to entertain through acting, movement, and sound.

toponymy the naming of places.

trade the formalized exchange of one thing for another according to set standards of value.

traditional development anthropology an approach to international development in which the anthropologist accepts the role of helping to make development work better by providing cultural information to planners.

transnational migration a form of population movement in which a person regularly moves between two or more countries and forms a new cultural identity transcending a single geopolitical unit.

trial by ordeal a way of determining innocence or guilt in which the accused person is put to a test that may be painful, stressful, or fatal.

tribe a form of political organization that comprises several bands or lineage groups, each with a similar language and lifestyle and occupying a distinct territory.

unbalanced exchange a system of transfers in which one party seeks to make a profit.

unilineal descent tracing descent through only one parent.

use rights a system of property relations in which a person or group has socially recognized priority in access to particular resources, such as gathering, hunting, and fishing areas and water holes.

wa Japanese word meaning discipline and self-sacrifice for the good of the group.

war organized and purposeful group action directed against another group and involving lethal force.

Western biomedicine (WBM) a healing approach based on modern Western science that emphasizes technology for diagnosing and treating health problems related to the human body.

world religion a term coined in the nineteenth century to refer to a religion that is based on written sources, has many followers, is regionally widespread, and is concerned with salvation.

youth gang a group of young people, found mainly in urban areas, who are often considered a social problem by adults and law enforcement officials.

REFERENCES

Abu-Lughod, Lila. 1993. *Writing Women's Worlds: Bedouin Stories.* Berkeley: University of California Press.

Adams, Abigail E. 2002. Dyke to Dyke: Ritual Reproduction at a U.S. Men's Military College. In *The Best of Anthropology Today* (pp. 34–42). Jonathan Benthall, ed. New York: Routledge.

Adams, Vincanne. 1988. Modes of Production and Medicine: An Examination of the Theory in Light of Sherpa Traditional Medicine. *Social Science and Medicine* 27:505–513.

Afolayan, E. 2000. Bantu Expansion and Its Consequences. In *African History before 1885* (pp. 113–136). T. Falola, ed. Durham, NC: Carolina Academic Press.

Agar, Michael and Heather Schacht Reisinger. 2003. Going for the Global: The Case of Ecstasy. *Human Organization* 62(1):1–11.

Ahmadu, Fuambai. 2000. Rites and Wrongs: An Insider/Outside Reflects on Power and Excision. In *Female "Circumcision" in Africa: Culture, Controversy, and Change* (pp. 283–312). Bettina Shell-Duncan and Ylva Hernlund, eds. Boulder, CO: Lynne Reiner Publishers.

Albro, Robert and Joanne Bauer. 2005. Introduction. Human Rights Dialogue: An International Forum for Debating Human Rights. Special issue on Cultural Rights: What They Are, Why They Matter, How They Can Be Realized. *Carnegie Journal* 2(12):2–3.

Allen, Catherine J. 2002. *The Hold Life Has: Coca and Cultural Identity in an Andean Community.* Washington, DC: Smithsonian Institution Press.

Allen, Susan. 1994. What Is Media Anthropology? A Personal View and a Suggested Structure. In *Media Anthropology: Informing Global Citizens* (pp. 15–32). Susan L. Allen, ed. Westport, CT: Bergin & Garvey.

Alter, Joseph S. 1992. The Sannyasi and the Indian Wrestler: Anatomy of a Relationship. *American Ethnologist* 19(2):317–336.

Amster, Matthew H. 2000. It Takes a Village to Dismantle a Longhouse. *Thresholds* 20:65–71.

Ancrenaz, Marc, Olivier Gimenez, Laurentius Ambu, Karine Ancrenaz, Patrick Andau, Benoît Goossens, John Payne, Arzi Sawang, Augustine Tuuga, and Isabelle Lackmann-Ancrenaz. 2005. Aerial Surveys Give New Estimates for Orangutans in Sabah, Malaysia. *PloS Biology* 3(1):e3. www.plosbiology.org.

Anderson, Benedict. 1991 [1983]. *Imagined Communities: Reflections on the Origin and Spread of Nationalism.* New York: Verso.

Anderson, Myrdene. 2004. Reflections on the Saami at Loose Ends. In *Cultural Shaping of Violence: Victimization, Escalation, Response* (pp. 285–291). Myrdene Anderson, ed. West Lafayette, IN: Purdue University Press.

———. 2005. The Saami Yoik: Translating Hum, Chant and/or Song. In *Song and Significance: Virtues and Vices of Vocal Translation* (pp. 213–233). Dinda Gorlée, ed. Amsterdam: Rodopi.

Anderson, Richard L. and Karen L. Field. 1993. Chapter Introduction. In *Art in Small-Scale Societies: Contemporary Readings* (p. 247). Richard L. Anderson and Karen L. Fields, eds. Englewood Cliffs, NJ: Prentice-Hall.

Applbaum, Kalman D. 1995. Marriage with the Proper Stranger: Arranged Marriage in Metropolitan Japan. *Ethnology* 34(1): 37–51.

Arambiza, Evelio and Michael Painter. 2006. Biodiversity Conservation and the Quality of Life of Indigenous People in the Bolivian Chaco. *Human Organization* 65:20–34.

Ariès, Philippe. 1962. *Centuries of Childhood: A Social History of Family Life.* Trans. Robert Baldick. New York: Vintage Books.

Baker, Colin. 1999. Sign Language and the Deaf Community. In *Handbook of Language and Ethnic Identity* (pp. 122–139). Joshua A. Fishman, ed. New York: Oxford University Press.

Baker-Christales, Beth. 2004. *Salvadoran Migration to Southern California: Redefining El Hermano Lejano.* Gainesville: University of Florida Press.

Baptista, Marlyse. 2005. New Directions in Pidgin and Creole Studies. *Annual Review of Anthropology* 34:34–42.

Barfield, Thomas J. 1994. Prospects for Plural Societies in Central Asia. *Cultural Survival Quarterly* 18(2&3):48–51.

———. 2001. Pastoral Nomads or Nomadic Pastoralists. In *The Dictionary of Anthropology* (pp. 348–350). Thomas Barfield, ed. Malden, MA: Blackwell Publishers.

Barkey, Nanette, Benjamin C. Campbell, and Paul W. Leslie. 2001. A Comparison of Health Complaints of Settled and Nomadic Turkana Men. *Medical Anthropology Quarterly* 15:391–408.

Barnard, Alan and Anthony Good. 1984. *Research Practices in the Study of Kinship.* New York: Academic Press.

Barrionuevo, Alexei. Amazon's "Forest People" Seek a Role in Striking Global Climate Agreements. *New York Times.* April 5:6.

Bartlett, Peggy F. 1989. Industrial Agriculture. In *Economic Anthropology* (pp. 253–292). Stuart Plattner, ed. Stanford, CA: Stanford University Press.

Barth, Frederik. 1993. *Balinese Worlds.* Chicago: University of Chicago Press.

Basch, Linda, Nina Glick Schiller, and Christina Szanton Blanc. 1994. *Nations Unbound: Transnational Projects, Postcolonial Predicaments, and Deterritorialized Nation–States.* Langhorne, PA: Gordon and Breach Science Publishers.

Basso, Keith. H. 1972 [1970]. "To Give Up on Words": Silence in Apache Culture. In *Language and Social Context* (pp. 67–86). Pier Paolo Giglioni, ed. Baltimore: Penguin Books.

Bauer, Alexander A. 2006. Heritage Preservation in Law and Policy: Handling the Double-Edged Sword of Development. Paper presented at the International Conference on Cultural Heritage and Development, Bibliothèca Alexandrina, Alexandria, Egypt, January.

Beals, Alan R. 1980. *Gopalpur: A South Indian Village. Fieldwork Edition.* New York: Holt, Rinehart and Winston.

Beeman, William O. 1993. The Anthropology of Theater and Spectacle. *Annual Review of Anthropology* 22:363–393.

Belikov, Vladimir. 1994. Language Death in Siberia. *UNESCO Courier* 1994(2):32–36.

Bell, Diane. 1998. *Ngarrindjeri Wurruwarrin: A World That Is, Was, and Will Be.* North Melbourne, Australia: Spinifex.

Bernal, Martin. 1987. *Black Athena: The Afroasiatic Roots of Classical Civilization.* New Brunswick, NJ: Rutgers University Press.

Berreman, Gerald D. 1979 [1975]. Race, Caste, and Other Invidious Distinctions in Social Stratification. In *Caste and Other Inequities:*

Essays on Inequality (pp. 178–222). Gerald D. Berreman, ed. New Delhi: Manohar.

Bestor, Theodore C. 2004. *Tsukiji: The Fish Market at the Center of the World.* Berkeley: University of California Press.

Beyene, Yewoubdar. 1989. *From Menarche to Menopause: Reproductive Lives of Peasant Women in Two Cultures.* Albany: State University of New York Press.

Bhardwaj, Surinder M. and N. Madhusudana Rao. 1990. Asian Indians in the United States: A Geographic Appraisal. In *South Asians Overseas: Migration and Ethnicity* (pp. 197–218). Colin Clarke, Ceri Peach, and Steven Vertovec, eds. New York: Cambridge University Press.

Bhatt, Rakesh M. 2001. World Englishes. *Annual Review of Anthropology* 30:527–550.

Bilharz, Joy. 1995. First among Equals? The Changing Status of Seneca Women. In *Women and Power in Native North America* (pp. 101–112). Laura F. Klein and Lillian A. Ackerman, eds. Norman: University of Oklahoma Press.

Billig, Michael S. 1992. The Marriage Squeeze and the Rise of Groomprice in India's Kerala State. *Journal of Comparative Family Studies* 23:197–216.

Blackwood, Evelyn. 1995. Senior Women, Model Mothers, and Dutiful Wives: Managing Gender Contradictions in a Minangkabau Village. In *Bewitching Women, Pious Men: Gender and Body Politics in Southeast Asia* (pp. 124–158). Aihwa Ong and Michael Peletz, eds. Berkeley: University of California Press.

Bledsoe, Caroline H. 1983. Stealing Food as a Problem in Demography and Nutrition. Paper presented at the annual meeting of the American Anthropological Association.

Blommaert, Jan and Chris Bulcaen. 2000. Critical Discourse Analysis. *Annual Review of Anthropology* 29:447–466.

Blood, Robert O. 1967. *Love Match and Arranged Marriage.* New York: Free Press.

Bodenhorn, Barbara. 2000. "He Used to Be My Relative." Exploring the Bases of Relatedness among the Inupiat of Northern Alaska. In *Cultures of Relatedness: New Approaches to the Study of Kinship* (pp. 128–148). Janet Carsten, ed. New York: Cambridge University Press.

Bodley, John H. 1990. *Victims of Progress,* 3rd ed. Mountain View, CA: Mayfield Publishing.

Boellstorff, Tom. 2004. Gay Language and Indonesia: Registering Belonging. *Journal of Linguistic Anthropology* 14:248–268.

Boserup, Ester. 1970. *Woman's Role in Economic Development.* New York: St. Martin's Press.

Bourdieu, Pierre. 1984. *Distinction: A Social Critique of the Judgement of Taste.* Trans. Richard Nice. Cambridge, MA: Harvard University Press.

Bourgois, Philippe I. 1995. *In Search of Respect: Selling Crack in El Barrio.* New York: Cambridge University Press.

Bowen, John R. 1992. On Scriptural Essentialism and Ritual Variation: Muslim Sacrifice in Sumatra. *American Ethnologist* 19(4):656–671.

———. 1998. *Religions in Practice: An Approach to the Anthropology of Religion.* Boston: Allyn and Bacon.

Bradley, Richard. 2000. *An Archaeology of Natural Places.* New York: Routledge.

Brana-Shute, Rosemary. 1976. Women, Clubs, and Politics: The Case of a Lower-Class Neighborhood in Paramaribo, Suriname. *Urban Anthropology* 5(2):157–185.

Brandes, Stanley H. 1985. *Forty: The Age and the Symbol.* Knoxville: University of Tennessee Press.

———. 2002. *Staying Sober in Mexico City.* Austin: University of Texas Press.

Brave Heart, Mary Yellow Horse. 2004. The Historical Trauma Response among Natives and Its Relationship to Substance Abuse. In *Healing and Mental Health for Native Americans: Speaking in Red* (pp. 7–18). Ethan Nebelkopf and Mary Phillips, eds. Walnut Creek, CA: AltaMira Press.

Brink, Judy H. 1991. The Effect of Emigration of Husbands on the Status of Their Wives: An Egyptian Case. *International Journal of Middle East Studies* 23:201–211.

Brookes, Heather. 2004. A Repertoire of South African Quotable Gestures. *Journal of Linguistic Anthropology* 14:186–224.

Brooks, Alison S. and Patricia Draper. 1998 [1991]. Anthropological Perspectives on Aging. In *Anthropology Explored: The Best of AnthroNotes* (pp. 286–297). Ruth Osterweis Selig and Marilyn R. London, eds. Washington, DC: Smithsonian Press.

Broude, Gwen J. 1988. Rethinking the Couvade: Cross-Cultural Evidence. *American Anthropologist* 90(4):902–911.

Brown, Carolyn Henning. 1984. Tourism and Ethnic Competition in a Ritual Form: The Firewalkers of Fiji. *Oceania* 54:223–244.

Brown, Judith K. 1970. A Note on the Division of Labor by Sex. *American Anthropologist* 72(5):1073–1078.

———. 1975. Iroquois Women: An Ethnohistoric Note. In *Toward an Anthropology of Women* (pp. 235–251). Rayna R. Reiter, ed. New York: Monthly Review Press.

———. 1978. The Recruitment of a Female Labor Force. *Anthropos* 73(1/2):41–48.

———. 1999. Introduction: Definitions, Assumptions, Themes, and Issues. In *To Have and To Hit: Cultural Perspectives on Wife Beating,* 2nd ed. (pp. 3–26). Dorothy Ayers Counts, Judith K. Brown, and Jacquelyn C. Campbell, eds. Urbana: University of Illinois Press.

Browner, Carole H. 1986. The Politics of Reproduction in a Mexican Village. *Signs: Journal of Women in Culture and Society* 11(4):710–724.

Browner, Carole H. and Nancy Ann Press. 1995. The Normalization of Prenatal Diagnostic Screening. In *Conceiving the New World Order: The Global Politics of Reproduction* (pp. 307–322). Faye D. Ginsberg and Rayna Rapp, eds. Berkeley: University of California Press.

———. 1996. The Production of Authoritative Knowledge in American Prenatal Care. *Medical Anthropology Quarterly* 10(2):141–156.

Bruner, Edward M. 2005. *Culture on Tour: Ethnographies of Travel.* Chicago: University of Chicago Press.

Bunzel, Ruth. 1972 [1929]. *The Pueblo Potter: A Study of Creative Imagination in Primitive Art.* New York: Dover Publications.

Burdick, John. 2004. *Legacies of Liberation: The Progressive Catholic Church in Brazil at the Turn of a New Century.* Burlington, VT: Ashgate Publishers.

Burton, Barbara. 2004. The Transmigration of Rights: Women, Movement and the Grassroots in Latin American and Caribbean Communities. *Development and Change* 35:773–798.

Call, Vaughn, Susan Sprecher, and Pepper Schwartz. 1995. The Incidence and Frequency of Marital Sex in a National Sample. *Journal of Marriage and the Family* 57:639–652.

Camino, Linda A. and Ruth M. Krulfeld, eds. 1994. *Reconstructing Lives, Recapturing Meaning: Refugee Identity, Gender and Culture Change.* Basel: Gordon and Breach Publishers.

Caplan, Pat. 2000. "Eating British Beef with Confidence": A Consideration of Consumers' Responses to BSE in Britain. In *Risk Revisited* (pp. 184–203). Pat Caplan, ed. Sterling, VA: Pluto Press.

Carneiro, Robert L. 1994. War and Peace: Alternating Realities in Human History. In *Studying War: Anthropological Perspectives* (pp. 3–27). S. P. Reyna and R. E. Downs, eds. Langhorne, PA: Gordon and Breach Science Publishers.

Carstairs, G. Morris. 1967. *The Twice Born.* Bloomington: Indiana University Press.

Carsten, Janet. 1995. Children in Between: Fostering and the Process of Kinship on Pulau Langkawi, Malaysia. *Man* (n.s.) 26:425–443.

Carsten, Janet, ed. 2000. *Cultures of Relatedness: New Approaches to the Study of Kinship.* New York: Cambridge University Press.

Carter, William E., José V. Morales, and Mauricio P. Mamani. 1981. Medicinal Uses of Coca in Bolivia. In *Health in the Andes* (pp. 119–149). Joseph W. Bastien and John M. Donahue, eds. Washington, DC: American Anthropological Association.

Cassell, Joan. 1991. *Expected Miracles: Surgeons at Work.* Philadelphia: Temple University Press.

Cátedra, María. 1992. *This World, Other Worlds: Sickness, Suicide, Death, and the Afterlife among the Vaqueiros de Alzada of Spain.* Chicago: University of Chicago Press.

Cernea, Michael M. 1985. Sociological Knowledge for Development Projects. In *Putting People First: Sociological Variables and Rural Development* (pp. 3–22). Michael M. Cernea, ed. New York: Oxford University Press.

———. 2001. *Cultural Heritage and Development: A Framework for Action in the Middle East and North Africa.* Washington, DC: The World Bank.

Chagnon, Napoleon. 1968. *Yanomamö, The Fierce People.* New York: Holt, Rinehart and Winston.

———. 1992. *Yanomamö,* 4th ed. New York: Harcourt Brace Jovanovich.

Chalfin, Brenda. 2004. *Shea Butter Republic: State Power, Global Markets, and the Making of an Indigenous Commodity.* New York: Routledge.

———. 2008. Cars, the Customs Service, and Sumptuary Rule in Neoliberal Ghana. *Comparative Studies in Society and History* 50:424–453.

Chavez, Leo R. 1992. *Shadowed Lives: Undocumented Immigrants in American Society.* New York: Harcourt Brace Jovanovich.

Checker, Melissa. 2005. Polluted Promises: *Environmental Racism and the Search for Justice in a Southern Town.* New York: New York University Press.

———. 2007. "But I Know It's True": Environmental Risk Assessment, Justice, and Anthropology. *Human Organization* 66:112–124.

Cherlin. Andrew J. 1996. *Public and Private Families: An Introduction.* New York: McGraw-Hill.

Cherlin, Andrew J. and Frank F. Furstenberg, Jr. 1992 [1983]. The American Family in the Year 2000. In *One World, Many Cultures* (pp. 2–9). Stuart Hirschberg, ed. New York: Macmillan Publishing.

Chernoff, John Miller. 1979. *African Rhythm and African Sensibility: Aesthetics and African Musical Idioms.* Chicago: University of Chicago Press.

Childs, Larry and Celina Chelala. 1994. Drought, Rebellion and Social Change in Northern Mali: The Challenges Facing Tamacheq Herders. *Cultural Survival Quarterly* 18(4):16–19.

Chin, Elizabeth. 2001. *Purchasing Power: Black Kids and American Consumer Culture.* Minneapolis: University of Minnesota Press.

Chiñas, Beverly Newbold. 1992. *The Isthmus Zapotecs: A Matrifocal Culture of Mexico.* New York: Harcourt Brace Jovanovich.

Chowdhury, A. N. 1996. The Definition and Classification of Koro. *Culture, Medicine and Psychiatry* 20(1):41–65.

Clarke, Maxine Kumari. 2004. *Mapping Yorùbá Networks: Power and Agency in the Making of Transnational Communities.* Durham, NC: Duke University Press.

Clay, Jason W. 1990. What's a Nation: Latest Thinking. *Mother Jones* 15(7):28–30.

Cochrane, D. Glynn. 1974. Barbara Miller's class lecture notes in Applied Anthropology, Syracuse University.

———. 1979. *The Cultural Appraisal of Development Projects.* New York: Praeger Publishers.

———. 2009. Festival of Elephants and the Myth of Global Poverty. Boston: Pearson.

Cohen, Mark Nathan. 1989. *Health and the Rise of Civilization.* New Haven, CT: Yale University Press.

Cohen, Roberta. 2002. Nowhere to Run, No Place to Hide. *Bulletin of the Atomic Scientists,* November/December:36–45.

Cohn, Bernard S. 1971. *India: The Social Anthropology of a Civilization.* New York: Prentice-Hall.

Cole, Douglas. 1991. *Chifly Feasts: The Enduring Kwakiutl Potlatch.* Aldona Jonatis, ed. Seattle: University of Washington Press/ New York: American Museum of Natural History.

Cole, Jeffrey. 1996. Working-Class Reactions to the New Immigration in Palermo (Italy). *Critique of Anthropology* 16(2):199–220.

Colley, Sarah. 2002. *Uncovering Australia: Archaeology, Indigenous People and the Public.* Washington, DC: Smithsonian Institution Press.

Comaroff, John L. 1987. Of Totemism and Ethnicity: Consciousness, Practice and Signs of Inequality. *Ethnos* 52(3–4):301–323.

Contreras, Gloria. 1995. Teaching about Vietnamese Culture: Water Puppetry as the Soul of the Rice Fields. *The Social Studies* 86(1):25–28.

Coon Come, Matthew. 2004. Survival in the Context of Mega-Resource Development: Experiences of the James Bay Crees and the First Nations of Canada. In *In the Way of Development: Indigenous Peoples, Life Projects, and Globalization* (pp. 153–165). Mario Blaser, Harvey A. Feit, and Glenn McRae, eds. New York: Zed Books in Association with the International Development Research Centre.

Corbey, Raymond. 2003. Destroying the Graven Image: Religious Iconoclasm on the Christian Frontier. *Anthropology Today* 19:10–14.

Cornia, Giovanni Andrea. 1994. Poverty, Food Consumption, and Nutrition During the Transition to the Market Economy in Eastern Europe. *American Economic Review* 84(2):297–302.

Counihan, Carole M. 1985. Transvestism and Gender in a Sardinian Carnival. *Anthropology* 9(1&2):11–24.

Coward, E. Walter, Jr. 1976. Indigenous Organisation, Bureaucracy and Development: The Case of Irrigation. *The Journal of Development Studies* 13(1):92–105.

———. 1979. Principles of Social Organization in an Indigenous Irrigation System. *Human Organization* 38(1):28–36.

Craik, Brian. 2004. The Importance of Working Together: Exclusions, Conflicts and Participation in James Bay, Quebec. In *In the Way of Development: Indigenous Peoples, Life Projects, and Globalization* (pp. 166–186). Mario Blaser, Harvey A. Feit, and Glenn McRae, eds. Zed Books in Association with the International Development Research Centre.

Crowe, D. 1996. *A History of the Gypsies of Eastern Europe and Russia.* New York: St. Martin's Press.

Crystal, David. 2000. *Language Death.* New York: Cambridge University Press.

———. 2003. *English as a Global Language,* 2nd ed. New York: Cambridge University Press.

Cunningham, Lawrence S. 1995. Christianity. In *The HarperCollins Dictionary of Religion* (pp. 240–253). Jonathan Z. Smith, ed. New York: HarperCollins.

Curtin, Philip D. 1989. *Death by Migration: Europe's Encounter with the Tropical World in the Nineteenth Century.* New York: Cambridge University Press.

Dalby, Liza Crihfield. 1998. *Geisha,* 2nd ed. New York: Vintage Books.

———. 2001. *Kimono: Fashioning Culture.* Seattle: University of Washington Press.

Daly, Martin and Margo Wilson. 1984. A Sociobiological Analysis of Human Infanticide. In *Infanticide: Comparative and Evolutionary Perspectives* (pp. 487–582). Glen Hausfater and Sarah Blaffer Hrdy, eds. New York: Aldine.

Danforth, Loring M. 1989. *Firewalking and Religious Healing: The Anestenaria of Greece and the American Firewalking Movement.* Princeton, NJ: Princeton University Press.

Dannhaeuser, Norbert. 1989. Marketing in Developing Urban Areas. In *Economic Anthropology* (pp. 222–252). Stuart Plattner, ed. Stanford, CA: Stanford University Press.

Daugherty, Mary Lee. 1997 [1976]. Serpent-Handling as Sacrament. In *Magic, Witchcraft, and Religion* (pp. 347–352). Arthur C. Lehmann and James E. Myers, eds. Mountain View, CA: Mayfield Publishing.

Dávila, Arlene. 2002. Culture in the Ad World: Producing the Latin Look. In *Media Worlds: Anthropology on New Terrain* (pp. 264–280). Faye D. Ginsburg, Lila Abu-Lughod, and Brian Larkin, eds. Berkeley: University of California Press.

David, Robert C. and Garry R. Marvin. 2004. *Venice, the Tourist Maze: A Cultural Critique of the World's Most Touristed City.* Berkeley: University of California Press.

Davis, Susan Schaefer and Douglas A. Davis. 1987. *Adolescence in a Moroccan Town: Making Social Sense.* New Brunswick: Rutgers University Press.

Davis-Floyd, Robbie E. 1987. Obstetric Training as a Rite of Passage. *Medical Anthropology Quarterly* 1:288–318.

———. 1992. *Birth as an American Rite of Passage.* Berkeley: University of California Press.

de la Cadena, Marisol. 2001. Reconstructing Race: Racism, Culture and Mestizaje in Latin America. *NACLA Report on the Americas* 34:16–23.

de la Pradelle, Michelle. Amy Jacobs, trans. 2006. *Market Day in Provence.* Chicago: University of Chicago Press.

Deitrick, Lynn. 2002. Commentary: Cultural Brokerage in the Newborn Nursery. *Practicing Anthropology* 24:53–54.

Dent, Alexander Sebastian. 2005. Cross-Culture "Countries": Covers, Conjuncture, and the Whiff of Nashville in *Música Sertaneja* (Brazilian Commercial Country Music). *Popular Music and Society* 28:207–227.

Devereaux, George. 1976. *A Typological Study of Abortion in Primitive Societies: A Typological, Distributional, and Dynamic Analysis of the Prevention of Birth in 400 Preindustrial Societies.* New York: International Universities Press.

Diamond, Jared. 1994 [1987]. The Worst Mistake in the History of the Human Race. In *Applying Cultural Anthropology: A Reader* (pp. 105–108). Aaron Podolefsky and Peter J. Brown, eds. Mountain View, CA: Mayfield Publishing.

Dickemann, Mildred. 1975. Demographic Consequences of Infanticide in Man. *Annual Review of Ecology and Systematics* 6:107–137.

DiFerdinando, George. 1999. Emerging Infectious Diseases: Biology and Behavior in the Inner City. In *Urbanism, Health, and Human Biology in Industrialised Countries* (pp. 87–110). Lawrence M. Schell and Stanley J. Ulijaszek, eds. New York: Cambridge University Press.

digim'Rina, Linus S. 2005. Food Security through Traditions: Replanting Trees and Wise Practices." *People and Culture in Oceania* 20:13–36.

digim'Rina, Linus S. 2006. Personal communication.

Dikötter, Frank. 1998. Hairy Barbarians, Furry Primates and Wild Men: Medical Science and Cultural Representations of Hair in China. In *Hair: Its Power and Meaning in Asian Cultures* (pp. 51–74). Alf Hiltebeitel and Barbara D. Miller, eds. Albany: State University of New York Press.

Divale, William T. 1974. Migration, External Warfare, and Matrilocal Residence. *Behavior Science Research* 9:75–133.

Divale, William T. and Marvin Harris. 1976. Population, Warfare and the Male Supremacist Complex. *American Anthropologist* 78:521–538.

Doi, Yaruko and Masami Minowa. 2003. Gender Differences in Excessive Daytime Sleepiness among Japanese Workers. *Social Science and Medicine* 56:883–894.

Donlon, Jon. 1990. Fighting Cocks, Feathered Warriors, and Little Heroes. *Play & Culture* 3:273–285.

Dorgan, Howard. 1989. *The Old Regular Baptists of Central Appalachia: Brothers and Sisters in Hope.* Knoxville: University of Tennessee Press.

Drake, Susan P. 1991. Local Participation in Ecotourism Projects. In *Nature Tourism: Managing for the Environment* (pp. 132–155). Tensie Whelan, ed. Washington, DC: Island Press.

Dreifus, Claudia. 2000. Saving the Orangutan, Preserving Paradise. *New York Times,* March 21:D3.

Drucker, Charles. 1988. Dam the Chico: Hydropower Development and Tribal Resistance. In *Tribal Peoples and Development Issues: A Global Overview* (pp. 151–165). John H. Bodley, ed. Mountain View, CA: Mayfield Publishing.

Duany, Jorge. 2000. Nation on the Move: The Construction of Cultural Identities in Puerto Rico and the Diaspora. *American Ethnologist* 27:5–30.

Duranti, Alessandro. 1994. *From Grammar to Politics: Linguistic Anthropology in a Western Samoan Village.* Berkeley: University of California Press.

———. 1997a. *Linguistic Anthropology.* New York: Cambridge University Press.

———. 1997b. Universal and Culture-Specific Properties of Greetings. *Journal of Linguistic Anthropology* 7:63–97.

Durkheim, Emile. 1965 [1915]. *The Elementary Forms of the Religious Life.* New York: Free Press.

Durrenberger, E. Paul. 2001. Explorations of Class and Class Consciousness in the U.S. *Journal of Anthropological Research* 57:41–60.

Eck, Diana L. 1985. *Darsán: Seeing the Divine Image in India,* 2nd ed. Chambersburg, PA: Anima Books.

Eckel, Malcolm David. 1995. Buddhism. In *The HarperCollins Dictionary of Religion* (pp. 135–150). Jonathan Z. Smith, ed. New York: HarperCollins.

Economic and Social Council. 1992. *Report of the Working Group on Violence against Women.* Vienna: United Nations. E/CN.6/WG.2/1992/L.3.

Eisler, Kim Isaac. 2001. *Revenge of the Pequots: How a Small Native American Tribe Created the World's Most Profitable Casino.* New York: Simon and Schuster.

Ember, Carol R. 1983. The Relative Decline in Women's Contribution to Agriculture with Intensification. *American Anthropologist* 85(2):285–304.

Englund, Harri. 1998. Death, Trauma and Ritual: Mozambican Refugees in Malawi. *Social Science and Medicine* 46(9):1165–1174.

Ennis-McMillan, Michael C. 2001. Suffering from Water: Social Origins of Bodily Distress in a Mexican Community. *Medical Anthropology Quarterly* 15(3):368–390.

Erickson, Barbra E. 2007. Toxin or Medicine?Explanatory Models of Radon in Montana Health Mines. *Medical Anthropology Quarterly* 21:1–21.

Ervin, Alexander M., Antonet T. Kaye, Giselle M. Marcotte, and Randy D. Belon. 1991. *Community Needs, Saskatoon—The 1990's: The Saskatoon Needs Assessment Project.* Saskatoon, Canada: University of Saskatchewan, Department of Anthropology.

Escobar, Arturo. 2002. Gender, Place, and Networks: A Political Ecology of Cyberculture. In *Development: A Cultural Studies Reader* (pp. 239–256). Susan Schech and Jane Haggis, eds. Malden, MA: Blackwell Publishers.

Esman, Milton. 1996. Ethnic Politics. In *The Social Science Encyclopedia* (pp. 259–260). Adam Kuper and Jessica Kuper, eds. New York: Routledge.

Estrin, Saul. 1996. Co-operatives. In *The Social Science Encyclopedia* (pp. 138–139). Adam Kuper and Jessica Kuper, eds. New York: Routledge.

Etienne, Mona and Eleanor Leacock, eds. 1980. *Women and Colonization: Anthropological Perspectives.* New York: Praeger.

Evans-Pritchard, E. E. 1951. *Kinship and Marriage among the Nuer.* Oxford: Clarendon.

Everett, Daniel L. 1995. Personal communication.

———. 2005. Cultural Constraints on Grammar and Cognition in Pirahã: Another Look at Design Features in Human Language. *Current Anthropology* 46:621–634, 641–646.

———. 2008. *Don't Sleep, There Are Snakes: Life and Language in the Amazonian Jungle.* New York: Knopf Publishing Group.

Evrard, Olivier and Yves Goudineau. 2004. Planned Resettlement, Unexpected Migrations and Cultural Trauma in Laos. *Development and Change* 35:937–962.

Fabian, Johannes. 1995. Ethnographic Misunderstanding and the Perils of Context. *American Anthropologist* 97(1):41–50.

Fabrega, Horacio, Jr. and Barbara D. Miller. 1995. Adolescent Psychiatry as a Product of Contemporary Anglo-American Society. *Social Science and Medicine* 40(7):881–894.

Fadiman, Anne. 1997. *The Spirit Catches You and You Fall Down: A Hmong Child, Her American Doctors, and the Collision of Two Cultures.* New York: Farrar, Straus and Giroux.

Faiola, Anthony. 2005. Sick of Their Husbands in Graying Japan: Stress Disorder Diagnosed in Many Women after Spouses Retire. *Washington Post,* October 10: A1, A16.

Farmer, Paul. 1992. *AIDS and Accusation: Haiti and the Geography of Blame.* Berkeley: University of California Press.

———. 2005. *Pathologies of Power: Health, Human Rights, and the New War on the Poor.* Berkeley: University of California Press.

Fasulo, Linda. 2003. *An Insider's Guide to the UN.* New Haven, CT: Yale University Press.

Feinsilver, Julie M. 1993. *Healing the Masses: Cuban Health Politics at Home and Abroad.* Berkeley: University of California Press.

Fenstemaker, Sarah. 2007. Conservation Clash and the Case for Exemptions: How Eagle Protection Conflicts with Hopi Cultural Preservation. *International Journal of Cultural Property* 14:315–328.

Ferguson, R. Brian. 1990. Blood of the Leviathan: Western Contact and Amazonian Warfare. *American Ethnologist* 17(1):237–257.

Ferguson, James. 1994. *The Anti-Politics Machine: "Development," Depoliticization, and Bureaucratic Power in Lesotho.* Minneapolis: University of Minnesota Press.

Fields, Jason and Lynne M. Casper. 2000. *America's Families and Living Arrangements: Population Characteristics.* Washington, DC:

United States Census Bureau. Current Population Reports P20-537.

Fisher, James. 1990. *Sherpas: Reflections on Change in Himalayan Nepal.* Berkeley: University of California Press.

Fishman, Joshua A. 1991. *Reversing Language Shift: Theoretical and Empirical Foundations of Assistance to Threatened Languages.* Clevedon, UK: Multilingual Matters Ltd.

Fishman, Joshua A., ed. 2001. *Can Threatened Languages Be Saved? Reversing Language Shift, Revisited: A 21st Century Perspective.* Buffalo, NY: Multilingual Matters Ltd.

Fitigu, Yodit. 2005. Forgotten People: Internally Displaced Persons in Guatemala. www.refugeesinternational.org/content/article/detail/6344.

Foley, Kathy. 2001. The Metonymy of Art: Vietnamese Water Puppetry as Representation of Modern Vietnam. *The Drama Review* 45(4):129–141.

Foley, William A. 2000. The Languages of New Guinea. *Annual Review of Anthropology* 29:357–404.

Foster, Helen Bradley and Donald Clay Johnson, eds. 2003. *Wedding Dress across Cultures.* New York: Berg.

Foster, Robert J. 2002. *Materializing the Nation: Commodities, Consumption, and Media in Papua New Guinea.* Bloomington: Indiana University Press.

———. 2006. From Trobriand Cricket to Rugby Nation: The Mission of Sport in Papua New Guinea. *The International Journal of the History of Sport* 23(5):739–758.

Foucault, Michel. 1970. *The Order of Things: An Archaeology of the Human Sciences.* New York: Random House.

———. 1977. *Discipline and Punish: The Birth of the Prison.* New York: Pantheon Books.

Fox, Robin. 1995 [1978]. *The Tory Islanders: A People of the Celtic Fringe.* Notre Dame: University of Notre Dame Press.

Frake, Charles O. 1961. The Diagnosis of Disease among the Subanun of Mindanao. *American Anthropologist* 63:113–132.

Franke, Richard W. 1993. *Life is a Little Better: Redistribution as a Development Strategy in Nadur Village, Kerala.* Boulder, CO: Westview Press.

Frankel, Francine R. 1971. *India's Green Revolution: Economic Gains and Political Costs.* Princeton, NJ: Princeton University Press.

Fratkin, Elliot. 1998. *Ariaal Pastoralists of Kenya: Surviving Drought and Development in Africa's Arid Lands.* Boston: Allyn and Bacon.

Frazer, Sir James. 1978 [1890]. *The Golden Bough: A Study in Magic and Religion.* New York: Macmillan.

Freeman, Derek. 1983. *Margaret Mead and Samoa: The Making and Unmaking of an Anthropological Myth.* Cambridge, MA: Harvard University Press.

Freeman, James A. 1981. A Firewalking Ceremony that Failed. In *Social and Cultural Context of Medicine in India* (pp. 308–336). Giri Raj Gupta, ed. New Delhi: Vikas Publishing.

———. 1989. *Hearts of Sorrow: Vietnamese-American Lives.* Stanford, CA: Stanford University Press.

Frieze, Irene, Jacquelynne E. Parsons, Paula B. Johnson, Diane N. Ruble, Gail L. Zellman, Esther Sales, Jeanne Marecek, Gwendolyn Lewis, Joan Hertzberg, and Deborah Lee. 1978. *Women and Sex Roles: A Social Psychological Perspective.* New York: W. W. Norton.

Furst, Peter T. 1989. The Water of Life: Symbolism and Natural History on the Northwest Coast. *Dialectical Anthropology* 14:95–115.

Gable, Eric. 1995. The Decolonization of Consciousness: Local Skeptics and the "Will to Be Modern" in a West African Village. *American Ethnologist* 22(2):242–257.

Galdikas, Biruté. 1995. *Reflections of Eden: My Years with the Orang-utans of Borneo*. Boston: Little, Brown.

Gale, Faye, Rebecca Bailey-Harris, and Joy Wundersitz. 1990. *Aboriginal Youth and the Criminal Justice System: The Injustice of Justice?* New York: Cambridge University Press.

Gardner, Katy and David Lewis. 1996. *Anthropology, Development and the Post-Modern Challenge*. Sterling, VA: Pluto Press.

Garland, David. 1996. Social Control. In *The Social Science Encyclopedia* (pp. 780–783). Adam Kuper and Jessica Kuper, eds. Routledge: New York.

Gaski, Harald. 1993. The Sami People: The "White Indians" of Scandinavia. *American Indian Culture and Research Journal* 17:115–128.

———. 1997. Introduction: Sami Culture in a New Era. In *Sami Culture in a New Era: The Norwegian Sami Experience* (pp. 9–28). Harald Gaski, ed. Seattle: University of Washington Press.

Geertz, Clifford. 1966. Religion as a Cultural System. In *Anthropological Approaches to the Study of Religion* (pp. 1–46). Michael Banton, ed. London: Tavistock.

Gegiow vs. Uhl. 1915. No. 340. Supreme Court of the United States.

Gillette, Maris Boyd. 2000. *Between Mecca and Beijing: Modernization and Consumption among Urban Chinese Families*. Stanford: Stanford University Press.

Ginsberg, Faye D. and Rayna Rapp. 1991. The Politics of Reproduction. *Annual Review of Anthropology* 20:311–343.

Glick Schiller, Nina and Georges E. Fouron. 1999. Terrains of Blood and Nation: Haitian Transnational Social Fields. *Ethnic and Racial Studies* 22:340–365.

Gmelch, George. 1997 [1971]. Baseball Magic. In *Magic, Witchcraft, and Religion* (pp. 276–282). Arthur C. Lehmann and James E. Myers, eds. Mountain View, CA: Mayfield Publishing.

Gold, Stevan J. 1992. *Refugee Communities: A Comparative Field Study*. Newbury Park: Sage Publications.

———. 1995. *From the Workers' State to the Golden State: Jews from the Former Soviet Union in California*. Boston: Allyn and Bacon.

Goldstein-Gidoni, Ofra. 2003. Producers of "Japan" in Israel: Cultural Appropriation in a Non-Colonial Context. *Ethnos* 68(3): 365–390.

Goodwin, Marjorie H. 1990. *He-Said-She-Said: Talk as Social Organization among Black Children*. Bloomington: Indiana University Press.

Goody, Jack. 1976. *Production and Reproduction: A Comparative Study of the Domestic Domain*. New York: Cambridge University Press.

———. 1993. *The Culture of Flowers*. New York: Cambridge University Press.

Goossens, Benoît, Lounès Chikhi, Marc Ancrenaz, Isabelle Lackman-Ancrenaz, Patrick Andau, and Michael W. Bruford. 2006. Genetic Signature of Anthropogenic Population Collapse in Orangutans. *PloS Biology* 4(2):e25. www.plosbiology.org.

Greenhalgh, Susan. 2003. Science, Modernity, and the Making of China's One-Child Policy. *Population and Development Review* 29:163–196.

———. 2008. *Just One Child: Science and Policy in Deng's China*. Berkeley: University of California Press.

Gregg, Jessica L. 2003. *Virtually Virgins: Sexual Strategies and Cervical Cancer in Recife, Brazil*. Stanford: Stanford University Press.

Gremillion, Helen. 1992. Psychiatry as Social Ordering: Anorexia Nervosa, a Paradigm. *Social Science and Medicine* 35(1):57–71.

Grinker, Roy Richard. 1994. *Houses in the Rainforest: Ethnicity and Inequality among Farmers and Foragers in Central Africa*. Berkeley: University of California Press.

Gross, Daniel R. 1984. Time Allocation: A Tool for the Study of Cultural Behavior. *Annual Review of Anthropology* 13:519–558.

Gruenbaum, Ellen. 2001. *The Female Circumcision Controversy: An Anthropological Perspective*. Philadelphia: University of Pennsylvania Press.

Guggenheim, Scott E. and Michael M. Cernea. 1993. Anthropological Approaches to Involuntary Resettlement: Policy, Practice, and Theory. In *Anthropological Approaches to Resettlement: Policy, Practice, and Theory* (pp. 1–12). Michael M. Cernea and Scott E. Guggenheim, eds. Boulder, CO: Westview Press.

Guidoni, Enrico. 1987. *Primitive Architecture*. Trans. Robert Erich Wolf. New York: Rizzoli.

Günes-Ayata, Ayse. 1995. Women's Participation in Politics in Turkey. In *Women in Modern Turkish Society: A Reader* (pp. 235–249). Sirin Tekeli, ed. London: Zed Books.

Hackenberg, Robert A., B. H. Hackenberg, H. F. Magalit, and El Cabral. 1983. Migration, Modernization and Hypertension: Blood Pressure Levels in Four Philippine Communities. *Medical Anthropology* 7(1):45–71.

Hacker, Andrew. 1992. *Two Nations: Black and White, Separate, Hostile, Unequal*. New York: Ballantine Books.

Haddix McCay, Kimber. 2001. Leaving Your Wife and Your Brothers: When Polyandrous Marriages Fall Apart. *Evolution and Human Behavior* 22:47–60.

Hamabata, Matthews Masayuki. 1990. *Crested Kimono: Power and Love in the Japanese Business Family*. Ithaca, NY: Cornell University Press.

Hammond, Peter B. 1966. *Yatenga: Technology in the Culture of a West African Kingdom*. New York: Free Press.

Hancock, Graham. 1989. *Lords of Poverty: The Power, Prestige, and Corruption of the International Aid Business*. New York: Atlantic Monthly Press.

Handler, Richard. 2003. Cultural Property and Cultural Theory. *Journal of Social Archaeology* 3:353–365.

Harner, Michael. 1977. The Ecological Basis of Aztec Sacrifice. *American Ethnologist* 4:117–135.

Harper, Krista. 2005. "Wild Capitalism" and "Ecocolonialism": A Tale of Two Rivers. *American Ethnologist* 107:221–233.

Harris, Marvin. 1974. *Cows, Pigs, Wars and Witches: The Riddles of Culture*. New York: Random House.

———. 1975. *Culture, People, Nature: An Introduction to General Anthropology*, 2nd ed. New York: Thomas Y. Crowell.

———. 1977. *Cannibals and Kings: The Origins of Culture*. New York: Random House.

———. 1984. Animal Capture and Yanomamo Warfare: Retrospect and New Evidence. *Journal of Anthropological Research* 40(10):183–201.

———. 1989. *Our Kind: The Evolution of Human Life and Culture*. New York: Harper & Row Publishers.

———. 1992. Distinguished Lecture: Anthropology and the Theoretical and Paradigmatic Significance of the Collapse of Soviet and East European Communism. *American Anthropologist* 94:295–305.

———. 1993. The Evolution of Human Gender Hierarchies. In *Sex and Gender Hierarchies* (pp. 57–80). Barbara D. Miller, ed. New York: Cambridge University Press.

Hawn, Carleen. 2002. Please Feedback the Animals. *Forbes* 170(9):168–169.

Hefner, Robert W. 1998. Multiple Modernities: Christianity, Islam, and Hinduism in a Globalizing Age. *Annual Review of Anthropology* 27:83–104.

Heise, Lori L., Jacqueline Pitanguy, and Adrienne Germain. 1994. Violence against Women: The Hidden Health Burden. *World Bank Discussion Papers No. 255*. Washington, DC: The World Bank.

Helweg, Arthur W. and Usha M. Helweg. 1990. *An Immigrant Success Story: East Indians in America.* Philadelphia: University of Pennsylvania Press.

Henshaw, Anne. 2006. Pausing along the Journey: Learning Landscapes, Environmental Change, and Toponymy amongst the Sikusilarmiut. Arctic Anthropology 43:52–66.

Herdt, Gilbert. 1987. *The Sambia: Ritual and Gender in New Guinea.* New York: Holt, Rinehart and Winston.

Hewlett, Barry S. 1991. *Intimate Fathers: The Nature and Context of Aka Pygmy Paternal Care.* Ann Arbor: University of Michigan Press.

Hill, Jane H. 2001. Dimensions of Attrition in Language Death. In *On Biocultural Diversity: Linking Language, Knowledge, and the Environment* (pp. 175–189). Luisa Maffi, ed. Washington, DC: Smithsonian Institution Press.

Hill, Jane H. and Bruce Mannheim. 1992. Language and World View. *Annual Review of Anthropology* 21:381–406.

Hiltebeitel, Alf. 1988. *The Cult of Draupadi: Mythologies from Gingee to Kuruksetra.* Chicago: University of Chicago Press.

Hirschon, Renee. 1989. *Heirs of the Catastrophe: The Social Life of Asia Minor Refugees in Piraeus.* New York: Oxford University Press.

Hodge, Robert W. and Naohiro Ogawa. 1991. *Fertility Change in Contemporary Japan.* Chicago: University of Chicago Press.

Hoffman, Danny. 2003. Frontline Anthropology: Research in a Time of War. *Anthropology Today* 19:9–12.

Hoffman, Danny and Stephen Lubkemann. 2005. Warscape Ethnography in West Africa and the Anthropology of "Events." *Anthropological Quarterly* 78:315–327.

Holland, Dorothy C. and Margaret A. Eisenhart. 1990. *Educated in Romance: Women, Achievement, and College Culture.* Chicago: University of Chicago Press.

Hopkins, Nicholas S. and Sohair R. Mehanna. 2000. Social Action against Everyday Pollution in Egypt. *Human Organization* 59:245–254.

Hornbein, George and Marie Hornbein. 1992. *Salamanders: A Night at the Phi Delt House.* Video. College Park: Documentary Resource Center.

Horowitz, Irving L. 1967. *The Rise and Fall of Project Camelot: Studies in the Relationship between Social Science and Practical Politics.* Boston: MIT Press.

Horowitz, Michael M. and Muneera Salem-Murdock. 1993. Development-Induced Food Insecurity in the Middle Senegal Valley. *GeoJournal* 30(2):179–184.

Horst, Heather and Daniel Miller. 2005. From Kinship to Link-up: Cell Phones and Social Networking in Jamaica. *Current Anthropology* 46:755–764, 773–778.

Howell, Nancy. 1979. *Demography of the Dobe !Kung.* New York: Academic Press.

———. 1990. *Surviving Fieldwork: A Report of the Advisory Panel on Health and Safety in Fieldwork.* Washington, DC: American Anthropological Association.

Huang, Shu-Min. 1993. A Cross-Cultural Experience: A Chinese Anthropologist in the United States. In *Distance Mirrors: America as a Foreign Culture* (pp. 39–45). Philip R. DeVita and James D. Armstrong, eds. Belmont, CA: Wadsworth.

Hughes, Charles C. and John M. Hunter. 1970. Disease and "Development" in Africa. *Social Science and Medicine* 3:443–493.

Hughes, Lotte. 2003. *The No-Nonsense Guide to Indigenous Peoples.* London: Verso.

Humphrey, Caroline. 1978. Women, Taboo and the Suppression of Attention. In *Defining Females: The Nature of Women in Society* (pp. 89–108). Shirley Ardener, ed. New York: John Wiley and Sons.

Hunte, Pamela A. 1985. Indigenous Methods of Fertility Regulation in Afghanistan. In *Women's Medicine: A Cross-Cultural Study of Indigenous Fertility Regulation* (pp. 44–75). Lucile F. Newman, ed. New Brunswick, NJ: Rutgers University Press.

Hutter, Michael. 1996. The Value of Play. In *The Value of Culture: On the Relationship between Economics and the Arts* (pp. 122–137). Arjo Klamer, ed. Amsterdam: Amsterdam University Press.

Ingham, John M. 1996. *Psychological Anthropology Reconsidered.* New York: Cambridge University Press.

Inhorn, Marcia C. 2003. Global Infertility and the Globalization of New Reproductive Technologies: Illustrations from Egypt. *Social Science and Medicine* 56:1837–1851.

———. 2004. Middle Eastern Masculinities in the Age of New Reproductive Technologies: Male Infertility and Stigma in Egypt and Lebanon. *Medical Anthropology Quarterly* 18(2):162–182.

International Alliance for the Protection of Isolated Indigenous Peoples. 2005. *Belém Declaration on Isolated Indigenous Peoples.* Adopted at the First International Symposium on Isolated Indigenous Peoples of the Amazon, Belém, Brazil, November.

IUCN/SSC Conservation Breeding Specialist Group. 2004. *Orangutan: Population and Habitat Viability Assessment: Final Report.* Apple Valley, MN: IUCN/SSC Conservation Breeding Specialist Group. www.cbsg.org.

Jacobs-Huey, Lanita. 1997. Is There an Authentic African American Speech Community: Carla Revisited. *University of Pennsylvania Working Papers in Linguistics* 4(1):331–370.

———. 2002. The Natives Are Gazing and Talking Back: Reviewing the Problematics of Positionality, Voice, and Accountability among "Native" Anthropologists. *American Anthropologist* 104:791–804.

———. 2006. *From the Kitchen to the Parlor: Language and Becoming in African American Women's Hair Care.* New York: Oxford University Press.

Janes, Craig R. 1990. *Migration, Social Change, and Health: A Samoan Community in Urban California.* Stanford, CA: Stanford University Press.

———. 1995. The Transformations of Tibetan Medicine. *Medical Anthropology Quarterly* 9(1):6–39.

Jankowski, Martín Sánchez. 1991. *Islands in the Street: Gangs and American Urban Society.* Berkeley: University of California Press.

Jenkins, Gwynne. 2003. Burning Bridges: Policy, Practice, and the Destruction of Midwifery in Rural Costa Rica. *Social Science and Medicine* 56:1893–1909.

Jenkins, Gwynne L. and Marcia C. Inhorn. 2003. Reproduction Gone Awry: Medical Anthropology Perspectives. *Social Science and Medicine* 56:1831–1836.

Jensen, Marianne Wiben, ed. Elaine Bolton, trans. 2004. Land Rights: A Key Issue. *Indigenous Affairs* 4.

Jernsletten, Nils. 1997. Sami Traditional Terminology: Professional Terms Concerning Salmon, Reindeer and Snow. In *Sami Culture in a New Era: The Norwegian Sami Experience* (pp. 86–106). Harald Gaski, ed. Seattle: University of Washington Press.

Jet. 1995. Baseball Team Members Who Used KKK Symbol Will Receive Multi-Cultural Training. *Jet* 88(18):39–40, September 11.

Jinadu, L. Adele. 1994. The Dialectics of Theory and Research on Race and Ethnicity in Nigeria. In *"Race," Ethnicity and Nation: International Perspectives on Social Conflict* (pp. 163–178). Peter Ratcliffe, ed. London: University College of London Press.

Johnson, Walter R. 1994. *Dismantling Apartheid: A South African Town in Transition.* Ithaca, NY: Cornell University Press.

Johnson-Hanks, Jennifer. 2002. On the Limits of Life Stages in Ethnography: Toward a Theory of Vital Conjectures. *American Anthropologist* 104:865–880.

Johnston, Barbara Rose. 1994. Environmental Degradation and Human Rights Abuse. In *Who Pays the Price? The Sociocultural Context of Environmental Crisis* (pp. 7–16). Barbara Rose Johnston, ed. Washington, DC: Island Press.

Jonaitis, Aldona. 1995. *A Wealth of Thought: Franz Boas on Native American Art.* Seattle: University of Washington Press.

Joralemon, Donald. 1982. New World Depopulation and the Case of Disease. *Journal of Anthropological Research* 38:108–127.

Jordan, Brigitte. 1983. *Birth in Four Cultures*, 3rd ed. Montreal: Eden Press.

Joseph, Suad. 1994. Brother/Sister Relationships: Connectivity, Love, and Power in the Reproduction of Patriarchy in Lebanon. *American Ethnologist* 21:50–73.

Jourdan, Christine. 1995. Masta Liu. In *Youth Cultures: A Cross-Cultural Perspective* (pp. 202–222). Vered Amit-Talai and Helena Wulff, eds. New York: Routledge.

Judd, Ellen. 2002. *The Chinese Women's Movement: Between State and Market.* Stanford, CA: Stanford University Press.

Kaberry, Phyllis. 1952. *Women of the Grassfields: A Study of the Economic Position of Women in Bamenda, British Cameroons.* London: Her Majesty's Stationery Office.

Kapchan, Deborah A. 1994. Moroccan Female Performers Defining the Social Body. *Journal of American Folklore* 107(423):82–105.

Karan, P. P. and Cotton Mather. 1985. Tourism and Environment in the Mount Everest Region. *Geographical Review* 75(1):93–95.

Kassam, Aneesa. 2002. Ethnodevelopment in the Oromia Regional State of Ethiopia. In *Participating in Development: Approaches to Indigenous Knowledge* (pp. 65–81). Paul Sillitoe, Alan Bicker, and Johan Pottier, eds. ASA Monographs No. 39. New York: Routledge.

Katz, Nathan and Ellen S. Goldberg. 1989. Asceticism and Caste in the Passover Observances of the Cochin Jews. *Journal of the American Academy of Religion* 57(1):53–81.

Katz, Richard. 1982. *Boiling Energy: Community Healing among the Kalahari Kung.* Cambridge, MA: Harvard University Press.

Katz, Richard, Megan Biesele, and Verna St. Denis. 1997. *Healing Makes Our Hearts Happy: Spirituality and Cultural Transformation among the Kalahari Jul'hoansi.* Rochester, VT: Inner Traditions.

Kaul, Adam. 2004. The Anthropologist as Barman and Tour-guide: Reflections on Fieldwork in a Touristed Destination. *Durham Anthropology Journal* 12:22–36.

Kawanishi, Y. 2004. Japanese Youth: The Other Half of the Crisis? *Asian Affairs* 35:22–32.

Kehoe, Alice Beck. 1989. *The Ghost Dance: History and Revitalization.* Philadelphia: Holt.

Kendon, A. 1988. Parallels and Divergences between Warlpiri Sign Language and Spoken Warlpiri: Analyses of Spoken and Signed Discourse. *Oceania* 58:239–254.

Kennedy, David P. and Stephen G. Perz. 2000. Who Are Brazil's Indígenas? Contributions of Census Data Analysis to Anthropological Demography of Indigenous Populations. *Human Organization* 59:311–324.

Kerns, Virginia. 1999. Preventing Violence against Women: A Central American Case. In *To Have and To Hit: Cultural Perspectives on Wife Beating,* 2nd ed. (pp. 153–168). Dorothy Ayers Counts, Judith K. Brown, and Jacquelyn C. Campbell, eds. Urbana: University of Illinois Press.

Keskitalo, Jan Henry. 1997. Sami Post-Secondary Education: Ideals and Realities. In *Sami Culture in a New Era: The Norwegian Sami Experience* (pp. 155–171). Harald Gaski, ed. Seattle: University of Washington Press.

Kesmanee, Chupinit. 1994. Dubious Development Concepts in the Thai Highlands: The Chao Khao in Transition. *Law & Society Review* 28:673–683.

Kirsch, Stuart. 2002. Anthropology and Advocacy: A Case Study of the Campaign against the Ok Tedi Mine. *Critique of Anthropology* 22:175–200.

Kleinman, Arthur. 1995. *Writing at the Margin: Discourse between Anthropology and Medicine.* Berkeley: University of California Press.

Klima, Alan. 2002. *The Funeral Casino: Meditation, Massacre, and Exchange with the Dead in Thailand.* Princeton: Princeton University Press.

Knott, Kim. 1996. Hindu Women, Destiny and Stridharma. *Religion* 26:15–35.

Kolenda, Pauline M. 1978. *Caste in Contemporary India: Beyond Organic Solidarity.* Prospect Heights, IL: Waveland Press.

Kondo, Dorinne. 1997. *About Face: Performing "Race" in Fashion and Theater.* New York: Routledge.

Konner, Melvin. 1989. Homosexuality: Who and Why? *New York Times Magazine.* April 2:60–61.

Kottak, Conrad Phillip. 1985. When People Don't Come First: Some Sociological Lessons from Completed Projects. In *Putting People First: Sociological Variables and Rural Development* (pp. 325–356). Michael M. Cernea, ed. New York: Oxford University Press.

———. 1992. *Assault on Paradise: Social Change in a Brazilian Village.* New York: McGraw-Hill.

Kovats-Bernat, J. Christopher. 2002. Negotiating Dangerous Fields: Pragmatic Strategies for Fieldwork amid Violence and Terror. *American Anthropologist* 104:1–15.

Kramer, Jennifer. 2005. Personal communication.

Krantzler, Nora J. 1987. Traditional Medicine as "Medical Neglect": Dilemmas in the Case Management of a Samoan Teenager with Diabetes. In *Child Survival: Cultural Perspectives on the Treatment and Maltreatment of Children* (pp. 325–337). Nancy Scheper-Hughes, ed. Boston: D. Reidel.

Kraybill, Donald B. and Steven M. Nolt. 2004. *Amish Enterprise: From Plows to Profits,* 2nd ed. Baltimore: Johns Hopkins University Press.

Kroeber, A. L. and Clyde Kluckhohn. 1952. *Culture: A Critical Review of Concepts and Definitions.* New York: Vintage Books.

Kuipers, Joel C. 1990. *Power in Performance: The Creation of Textual Authority in Weyéwa Ritual Speech.* Philadelphia: University of Pennsylvania Press.

———. 1991. Matters of Taste in Weyéwa. In *The Varieties of Sensory Experience: A Sourcebook in the Anthropology of the Senses* (pp. 111–127). David Howes, ed. Toronto: University of Toronto Press.

———. 2004. Ethnography of Language in the Age of Video: "Voices" in Context of Religious and Clinical Authority. In *Discourse and Technology: Multimodal Discourse Analysis* (pp. 167–183). Philip LeVine and Ron Scollon, eds. Washington, DC: Georgetown University Press.

Kuipers, Joel C. and Ray McDermott. 1996. Insular Southeast Asian Scripts. In *The World's Writing Systems* (pp. 474–484). Peter T. Daniels and William Bright, eds. New York: Oxford University Press.

Kumar, Krishna. 1996. Civil Society. In *The Social Science Encyclopedia* (pp. 88–90). Adam Kuper and Jessica Kuper, eds. New York: Routledge.

Kurin, Richard. 1980. Doctor, Lawyer, Indian Chief. *Natural History* 89(11):6–24.

Kurkiala, Mikael. 2003. Interpreting Honor Killings: The Story of Fadime Sahindal (1975–2002) in the Swedish Press. *Anthropology Today* 19:6–7.

Kuwayama, Takami. 2004. *Native Anthropology: The Japanese Challenge to Western Academic Hegemony*. Melbourne, Australia: Trans Pacific Press.

Kwiatkowski, Lynn M. 1998. *Struggling with Development: The Politics of Hunger and Gender in the Philippines*. Boulder, CO: Westview Press.

Labov, William. 1966. *The Social Stratification of English in New York City*. Washington, DC: Center for Applied Linguistics.

Lacey, Marc. 2002. Where 9/11 News Is Late, But Aid Is Swift. *New York Times*, June 3:A1, A7.

Ladányi, János. 1993. Patterns of Residential Segregation and the Gypsy Minority in Budapest. *International Journal of Urban and Regional Research* 17(1):30–41.

Laderman, Carol. 1988. A Welcoming Soil: Islamic Humoralism on the Malay Peninsula. In *Paths to Asian Medical Knowledge* (pp. 272–288). Charles Leslie and Allan Young, eds. Berkeley: University of California Press.

LaFleur, William. 1992. *Liquid Life: Abortion and Buddhism in Japan*. Princeton, NJ: Princeton University Press.

Lakoff, Robin. 1973. Language and Woman's Place. *Language in Society* 2:45–79.

———. 1990. *Talking Power: The Politics of Language in Our Lives*. New York: Basic Books.

LaLone, Mary B. 2003. Walking the Line between Alternative Interpretations in Heritage Education and Tourism: A Demonstration of the Complexities with an Appalachian Coal Mining Example. In *Signifying Serpents and Mardi Gras Runners: Representing Identity in Selected Souths* (pp. 72–92). Southern Anthropological Proceedings, No. 36. Celeste Ray and Luke Eric Lassiter, eds. Athens: University of Georgia Press.

Lamphere, Louise. 1992. Introduction: The Shaping of Diversity. In *Structuring Diversity: Ethnographic Perspectives on the New Immigration* (pp. 1–34). Louise Lamphere, ed. Chicago: University of Chicago Press.

Lane, Sandra D., Robert H. Keefe, Robert A. Rubenstein, Brooke A. Levandowski, Michael Freedman, Alan Rosenthal, Donald A. Cibula, and Maria Czerwinski. 2004. Marriage Promotion and Missing Men: African American Women in a Demographic Double Bind. *Medical Anthropology Quarterly* 18:405–428.

Lanehart, Sonja L. 1999. African American Vernacular English. In *Handbook of Language and Ethnic Identity* (pp. 211–225). Joshua A. Fishman, ed. New York: Oxford University Press.

Larsen, Ulla and Marida Hollos. 2003. Women's Empowerment and Fertility Decline among the Pare of Kilimanjaro Region, Northern Tanzania. *Social Science and Medicine* 57:1099–1115.

Larsen, Ulla and Sharon Yan. 2000. Does Female Circumcision Affect Infertility and Fertility? A Study of the Central African Republic, Côte d'Ivoire, and Tanzania. *Demography* 37:313–321.

Larsson, Sara. 2005. Legislating Gender Equality: In Saami Land, Women Are Encouraged to Become Lawyers—But Many Would Rather Be Reindeer Herders. *Cultural Survival Quarterly* 28(4):28–29.

Lassiter, Luke Eric, Hurley Goodall, Elizabeth Campbell, and Michelle Natasya Johnson. 2004. *The Other Side of Middletown: Exploring Muncie's African American Community*. Walnut Creek, CA: AltaMira Press.

Leach, Jerry W. 1975. *Trobriand Cricket: An Ingenious Response to Colonialism*. Video.

Lederer, Edith. 2006. Record Number of Women in Politics. *Guardian Weekly*, March 10–15:9.

Lee, Gary R. and Mindy Kezis. 1979. Family Structure and the Status of the Elderly. *Journal of Comparative Family Studies* 10:429–443.

Lee, Helen Morton. 2003. *Tongans Overseas: Between Two Shores*. Honolulu: University of Hawai'i Press.

Lee, Richard B. 1969. Eating Christmas in the Kalahari. *Natural History*, December 14–22, 60–63.

Lee, Richard Borshay. 1979. *The !Kung San: Men, Women, and Work in a Foraging Society*. New York: Cambridge University Press.

Lee, Wai-Na and David K. Tse. 1994. Becoming Canadian: Understanding How Hong Kong Immigrants Change Their Consumption. *Pacific Affairs* 67(1):70–95.

Lempert, David. 1996. *Daily Life in a Crumbling Empire*. 2 volumes. New York: Columbia University Press.

Lepowsky, Maria. 1990. Big Men, Big Women, and Cultural Autonomy. *Ethnology* 29(10):35–50.

———. 1993. *Fruit of the Motherland: Gender in an Egalitarian Society*. New York: Columbia University Press.

Lesher, James H., trans. 2001. *Xenophanes of Colophon: Fragments*. Toronto: University of Toronto Press.

Lessinger, Johanna. 1995. *From the Ganges to the Hudson: Indian Immigrants in New York City*. Boston: Allyn and Bacon.

Levine, Robert, Suguru Sato, Tsukasa Hashimoto, and Jyoti Verma. 1995. Love and Marriage in Eleven Cultures. *Journal of Cross-Cultural Psychology* 26:554–571.

Levinson, David. 1989. *Family Violence in Cross-Cultural Perspective*. Newbury Park, CA: Sage Publications.

Lévi-Strauss, Claude. 1967. *Structural Anthropology*. New York: Anchor Books.

———. 1968. *Tristes Tropiques: An Anthropological Study of Primitive Societies in Brazil*. New York: Atheneum.

———. 1969 [1949]. *The Elementary Structures of Kinship*. Boston: Beacon Press.

Levy, Jerrold E., Eric B. Henderson, and Tracy J. Andrews. 1989. The Effects of Regional Variation and Temporal Change in Matrilineal Elements of Navajo Social Organization. *Journal of Anthropological Research* 45(4):351–377.

Lew, Irvina. 1994. Bathing as Science: Ancient Sea Cures Gain Support from New Research. *Condé Nast Traveler* 29(12):86–90.

Lewis, Oscar. 1966. The Culture of Poverty. *Scientific American* 215:19–25.

Leynaud, Emile. 1961. Fraternités d'âge et sociétés de culture dans la Haute-Vallée du Niger. *Cahiers d'Etudes Africaines* 6:41–68.

Lightfoot, David. 2006. *How New Languages Emerge*. New York: Cambridge University Press.

Lincoln, Kenneth. 1993. *Indi'n Humor: Bicultural Play in Native America*. New York: Oxford University Press.

Lindenbaum, Shirley. 1979. *Kuru Sorcery: Disease and Danger in the New Guinea Highlands*. Mountain View, CA: Mayfield Publishing.

Lipka, Jerry, Maureen P. Hogan, Joan Parker Webster, Evelyn Yanez, Barbara Adams, Stacy Clark, and Doreen Lacy. 2005. Math in a Cultural Context: Two Case Studies of a Successful Culturally Based Math Project. *Anthropology and Education Quarterly* 36(4):367–385.

Lock, Margaret. 1993. *Encounters with Aging: Mythologies of Menopause in Japan and North America*. Berkeley: University of California Press.

Loker, William. 2000. Sowing Discord, Planting Doubts: Rhetoric and Reality in an Environment and Development Project in Honduras. *Human Organization* 59:300–310.

———. 2003. Dam Impacts in a Time of Globalization: Using Multiple Methods to Document Social and Environmental Change in Rural Honduras. *Current Anthropology* 44(supplement): S112–S121.

——. 2004. *Changing Places: Environment, Development, and Social Change in Rural Honduras*. Durham, NC: Carolina Academic Press.

Long, Susan Orpett. 2005. *Final Days: Japanese Culture and Choice at the End of Life*. Honolulu: University of Hawai'i Press.

Lorch, Donatella. 2003. Do Read This for War. *Newsweek* 141(11):13.

Low, Setha M. 1995. Indigenous Architecture and the Spanish American Plaza in Mesoamerica and the Caribbean. *American Anthropologist* 97(4):748–762.

Lubkemann, Stephen C. 2002. Refugees. In *World at Risk: A Global Issues Sourcebook* (pp. 522–544). Washington, DC: CQ Press.

——. 2005. Migratory Coping in Wartime Mozambique: An Anthropology of Violence and Displacement in "Fragmented Wars." *Journal of Peace Research* 42:493–508.

Lutz, Ellen L. 2005. The Many Meanings of Technology: A Message from our Executive Editor. *Cultural Survival Quarterly* 29(2):5.

Lyman, Rick. 2006. Reports Reveal Hurricanes' Impact on Human Landscape. *New York Times*, May 6, p. A16.

Lyttleton, Chris. 2004. Relative Pleasures: Drugs, Development and Modern Dependencies in Asia's Golden Triangle. *Development and Change* 35:909–935.

MacLeod, Arlene Elowe. 1992. Hegemonic Relations and Gender Resistance: The New Veiling as Accommodating Protest in Cairo. *Signs: The Journal of Women in Culture and Society* 17(3):533–557.

Macnair, Peter. 1995. From Kwakiutl to Kwakwa̲ ka'wakw. In *Native Peoples: The Canadian Experience*, 2nd ed. (pp. 586–605). R. Bruce Morrison and C. Roderick Wilson, eds. Toronto: McClelland & Stewart.

Maffi, Luisa. 2003. The "Business" of Language Endangerment: Saving Language or Helping People Keep Them Alive? In *Language in the Twenty-First Century: Selected Papers of the Millennial Conference of the Center for Research and Documentation on World Language Problems* (pp. 67–86). H. Tonkin and T. Reagan, eds. Amsterdam: John Benjamins.

——. 2005. Linguistic, Cultural, and Biological Diversity. *Annual Review of Anthropology* 34:599–617.

Magga, Ole Henrik and Tove Skutnabb-Kangas. 2001. The Saami Languages: The Present and the Future. *Cultural Survival Quarterly* 25(2):26–31.

Mahler, Sarah J. 1995. *Salvadorans in Suburbia: Symbiosis and Conflict*. Boston: Allyn and Bacon.

Major, Marc R. 1996. No Friends but the Mountains: A Simulation on Kurdistan. *Social Education* 60(3):C1–C8.

Malinowski, Bronislaw. 1929. *The Sexual Life of Savages*. New York: Harcourt, Brace & World.

——. 1948. *Magic, Science and Religion, and Other Essays*. Boston: Beacon Press.

——. 1961 [1922]. *Argonauts of the Western Pacific*. New York: E. P. Dutton & Co.

Mamdani, Mahmoud. 1972. *The Myth of Population Control: Family, Caste, and Class in an Indian Village*. New York: Monthly Review Press.

——. 2002. Good Muslim, Bad Muslim: A Political Perspective on Culture and Terrorism. *American Anthropologist* 104:766–775.

Manz, Beatriz. 2004. *Paradise in Ashes: A Guatemalan Journey of Courage, Terror, and Hope*. Berkeley: University of California Press.

Marcus, George. 1995. Ethnography in/of the World System: The Emergence of Multi-Sited Ethnography. *Annual Review of Anthropology* 24:95–117.

Margolis, Maxine. 1994. *Little Brazil: An Ethnography of Brazilian Immigrants in New York City*. Princeton, NJ: Princeton University Press.

Margolis, Maxine L. and Marigene Arnold. 1993. Turning the Tables? Male Strippers and the Gender Hierarchy in America. In *Sex and Gender Hierarchies* (pp. 334–350). Barbara D. Miller, ed. New York: Cambridge University Press.

Martin, Richard C. 1995. Islam. In *The HarperCollins Dictionary of Religion* (pp. 498–513). Jonathan Z. Smith, ed. New York: HarperCollins.

Martin, Sarah. 2005. *Must Boys Be Boys? Ending Sexual Exploitation and Abuse in UN Peacekeeping Missions*. Washington, DC: Refugees International.

Martínez, Samuel. 1996. Indifference with Indignation: Anthropology, Human Rights, and the Haitian Bracero. *American Anthropologist* 98(1):17–25.

Masquelier, Adeline. 2005. The Scorpion's Sting: Youth, Marriage and the Struggle for Social Maturity in Niger. *Journal of the Royal Anthropological Institute* 11:59–83.

Maybury-Lewis, David. 1997a. Museums and Indigenous Cultures. *Cultural Survival Quarterly* 21(1):3.

——. 1997b. *Indigenous Peoples, Ethnic Groups, and the State*. Boston: Allyn and Bacon.

McCallum, Cecilia. 2005. Explaining Caesarean Section in Salvador da Bahia, Brazil. *Sociology of Health and Illness* 27(2):215–242.

McCallum, Cecilia and Ana Paula dos Reis. 2005. Childbirth as Ritual in Brazil: Young Mothers' Experiences. *Ethnos* 70(3):335–360.

McCully, Patrick. 2003. Big Dams, Big Trouble. *New Internationalist* 354:14–15.

McDade, T. W., V. Reyes-Garcia, P. Blackinton, S. Tanner, T. Huanca, and W. R. Leonard. 2007. Ethnobotanical Knowledge is Associated with Indices of Child Health in the Bolivian Amazon. *Proceedings of the National Academy of Sciences* 104: 6134–6139.

McElroy, Ann and Patricia K. Townsend. 1996. *Medical Anthropology in Ecological Perspective*, 3rd ed. Boulder, CO: Westview Press.

McMahon, April M. S. 1994. *Understanding Language Change*. New York: Cambridge University Press.

Mead, Margaret. 1961 [1928]. *Coming of Age in Samoa: A Psychological Study of Primitive Youth for Western Civilization*. New York: Dell Publishing.

——. 1986. Field Work in the Pacific Islands, 1925–1967. In *Women in the Field: Anthropological Experiences* (pp. 293–331). Peggy Golde, ed. Berkeley: University of California Press.

Meador, Elizabeth. 2005. The Making of Marginality: Schooling for Mexican Immigrants in the Rural Southwest. *Anthropology and Education Quarterly* 36(2):149–164.

Meigs, Anna S. 1984. *Food, Sex, and Pollution: A New Guinea Religion*. New Brunswick, NJ: Rutgers University Press.

Mencher, Joan P. 1974. The Caste System Upside Down, or The Not-So-Mysterious East. *Current Anthropology* 15(4):469–493.

Mernissi, Fatima. 1987. *Beyond the Veil: Male–Female Dynamics in Modern Muslim Society*. Revised edition. Bloomington: Indiana University Press.

Merry, Sally Engle. 2006. *Human Rights and Gender Violence: Translating International Law into Local Justice*. Chicago: University of Chicago Press.

Messer, Ellen. 1993. Anthropology and Human Rights. *Annual Review of Anthropology* 22:221–249.

Michaelson, Evelyn Jacobson and Walter Goldschmidt. 1971. Female Roles and Male Dominance among Peasants. *Southwestern Journal of Anthropology* 27:330–352.

Michaud, Catherine M., W. Scott Gordon, and Michael R. Reich. 2005. *The Global Burden of Disease Due to Schistosomiasis.* Cambridge, MA: Harvard School of Public Health, Harvard Center for Population and Development Studies, Schistosomiasis Research Program Working Paper Series. Volume 14, Number 1.

Miller, Barbara D. 1987. Social Patterns of Food Expenditure Among Low-Income Jamaicans. In *Papers and Recommendations of the Workshop on Food and Nutrition Security in Jamaica in the 1980s and Beyond.* Kenneth A. Leslie and Lloyd B. Rankine, eds. Kingston, Jamaica: The Caribbean Food and Nutrition Institute.

———. 1993. Surveying the Anthropology of Sex and Gender Hierarchies. In *Sex and Gender Hierarchies* (pp. 3–31). Barbara D. Miller, ed. New York: Cambridge University Press.

———. 2005. Putting People First to Strengthen Cultural Heritage Advocacy: Rationale, Results, and an Advocacy Tool. Paper presented at the Workshop on Preserving the World's Heritage, Cumberland, SC, October.

———. 2009. Heritage Management Inside Out and Upside Down: Questioning Top-Down and Outside Approaches. *Heritage Management* 2:5-9.

Miller, Barbara D. and Showkat Hayat Khan. 1986. Incorporating Voluntarism into Rural Development in Bangladesh. *Third World Planning Review* 8(2):139–152.

Miller, Bruce G. 1994. Contemporary Native Women: Role Flexibility and Politics. *Anthropologica* 36:57–72.

Miller, Daniel, ed. 2001. *Car Cultures.* New York: Berg.

Miller, Laura. 2004. Those Naughty Teenage Girls: Japanese Kogals, Slang, and Media Assessments. *Journal of Linguistic Anthropology* 14:225–247.

Milton, Katherine. 1992. Civilization and Its Discontents. *Natural History* 3(92):37–92.

Miner, Horace. 1965 [1956]. Body Ritual among the Nacirema. In *Reader in Comparative Religion: An Anthropological Approach* (pp. 414–418). William A. Lessa and Evon Z. Vogt, eds. New York: Harper & Row.

Mines, Mattison. 1994. *Public Faces, Private Voices: Community and Individuality in South India.* Berkeley: University of California Press.

Mintz, Sidney. 1985. *Sweetness and Power: The Place of Sugar in Modern History.* New York: Viking.

Miyazawa, Setsuo. 1992. *Policing in Japan: A Study on Making Crime.* Frank G. Bennett, Jr. with John O. Haley, trans. Albany: State University of New York Press.

Modell, Judith S. 1994. *Kinship with Strangers: Adoption and Interpretations of Kinship in American Culture.* Berkeley: University of California Press.

Moerman, Daniel. 2002. *Meaning, Medicine and the "Placebo" Effect.* New York: Cambridge University Press.

Mogelonsky, Marcia. 1995. Asian-Indian Americans. *American Demographics* 17(8):32–39.

Montesquieu, Charles. 1949 [1748]. *The Spirit of the Laws.* Trans. T. Nugent. New York: Hafner.

Moore, Molly. 2008. In France, Prisons Filled with Muslims. *Washington Post* April 29:A1, A4.

Morgan, Lewis Henry. 1851. *The League of the [Ho-de-nesau, or] Iroquois.* New York: Russell Sage.

Morris, Brian. 1998. *The Power of Animals: An Ethnography.* New York: Berg.

Morris, Rosalind. 1994. Three Sexes and Four Sexualities: Redressing the Discourses on Gender and Sexuality in Contemporary Thailand. *Positions* 2:15–43.

Muecke, Marjorie A. 1987. Resettled Refugees: Reconstruction of Identity of Lao in Seattle. *Urban Anthropology* 16(3–4): 273–289.

Mulk, Inga-Maria. 1994. Sacrificial Places and Their Meaning in Saami Society. In *Sacred Sites, Sacred Places* (pp. 121–131). David L. Carmichael, Jane Hubert, Brian Reeves, and Audhild Schanche, eds. New York: Routledge.

Mullings, Leith. 2005. Towards an Anti-Racist Anthropology: Interrogating Racism. *Annual Review of Anthropology* 34:667–693.

Murdock, George Peter. 1965 [1949]. *Social Structure.* New York: Free Press.

Murray, Gerald F. 1987. The Domestication of Wood in Haiti: A Case Study of Applied Evolution. In *Anthropological Praxis: Translating Knowledge into Action* (pp. 233–240). Robert M. Wulff and Shirley J. Fiske, eds. Boulder, CO: Westview Press.

Myerhoff, Barbara. 1978. *Number Our Days.* New York: Simon and Schuster.

Myers, James. 1992. Nonmainstream Body Modification: Genital Piercing, Branding, Burning, and Cutting. *Journal of Contemporary Ethnography* 21(3):267–306.

Myers, Norman. 2000. Sustainable Consumption. *Science* 287 (March 31):2419.

Myrskylä, Mikko, Hans-Peter Kohler, and Francesco C. Billari. 2009. Advances in Development Reverse Fertility Trends. Nature 460(6):741–743.

Nadeau, Kathleen M. 2002. *Liberation Theology in the Philippines: Faith in a Revolution.* Westport: Praeger.

Nader, Laura. 1972. Up the Anthropologist—Perspectives Gained from Studying Up. In *Reinventing Anthropology* (pp. 284–311). Dell Hymes, ed. New York: Vintage Books.

Nag, Moni. 1972. Sex, Culture and Human Fertility: India and the United States. *Current Anthropology* 13:231–238.

———. 1983. Modernization Affects Fertility. *Populi* 10:56–77.

Nag, Moni, Benjamin N. F. White, and R. Creighton Peet. 1978. An Anthropological Approach to the Study of the Economic Value of Children in Java and Nepal. *Current Anthropology* 19(2):293–301.

Nanda, Serena. 1990. *Neither Man nor Woman: The Hijras of India.* Belmont, CA: Wadsworth.

———. 1994. *Cultural Anthropology.* Wadsworth, CA: Wadsworth.

Natcher, David C., Susan Davis, and Clifford G. Hickey. 2005. Co-Management: Managing Relationships, Not Resources. *Human Organization* 64:240–250.

National Park Service. 2005. *Low Country Gullah Culture: Special Resource Study and Final Environmental Impact Statement.* Atlanta: NPS Southeast Regional Office. www.nps.gov.

Neff, Deborah L. 1994. The Social Construction of Infertility: The Case of the Matrilineal Nayars in South India. *Social Science and Medicine* 39(4):475–485.

Nettle, Daniel and Suzanne Romaine. 2000. *Vanishing Voices: The Extinction of the World's Languages.* New York: Oxford University Press.

Neusner, Jacob. 1995. Judaism. In *The HarperCollins Dictionary of Religion* (pp. 598–607). Jonathan Z. Smith, ed. New York: HarperCollins.

Nevins, M. Eleanor. 2004. Learning to Listen: Confronting Two Meanings of Language Loss in the Contemporary White Mountain Apache Speech Community. *Journal of Linguistic Anthropology* 14:269–288.

Newman, Lucile. 1972. *Birth Control: An Anthropological View.* Module No. 27. Reading, MA: Addison-Wesley.

Newman, Lucile, ed. 1985. *Women's Medicine: A Cross-Cultural Study of Indigenous Fertility Regulation.* New Brunswick: Rutgers University Pres.

Ngokwey, Ndolamb. 1988. Pluralistic Etiological Systems in Their Social Context: A Brazilian Case Study. *Social Science and Medicine* 26:793–802.

Nichter, Mark. 1992. Of Ticks, Kings, Spirits and the Promise of Vaccines. In *Paths to Asian Medical Knowledge* (pp. 224–253). Charles Leslie and Allan Young, eds. Berkeley: University of California Press.

———. 1996. Vaccinations in the Third World: A Consideration of Community Demand. In *Anthropology and International Health: Asian Case Studies* (pp. 329–365). Mark Nichter and Mimi Nichter, eds. Amsterdam: Gordon and Breach Publishers.

Nodwell, Evelyn and Neil Guppy. 1992. The Effects of Publicly Displayed Ethnicity on Interpersonal Discrimination: Indo-Canadians in Vancouver. *The Canadian Review of Sociology and Anthropology* 29(1):87–99.

Nordstrom, Carolyn. 1997. *A Different Kind of War Story*. Philadelphia: University of Pennsylvania Press.

Norgaard, Richard B. 1994. *Development Betrayed: The End of Progress and the Coevolutionary Revisioning of the Future*. New York: Routledge.

Obeyesekere, Gananath. 1981. *Medusa's Hair: An Essay on Personal Symbols and Religious Experience*. Chicago: University of Chicago Press.

Ohnuki-Tierney, Emiko. 1980. Shamans and Imu: Among Two Ainu Groups. In *The Culture-Bound Syndromes* (pp. 91–110). Ronald C. Simons and Charles C. Hughes, eds. Dordrecht: D. Reidel Publishing.

Oinas, Felix J. 1993. Couvade in Estonia. *Slavic & East European Journal* 37(3):339–345.

Ong, Aihwa. 1995. State versus Islam: Malay Families, Women's Bodies, and the Body Politic in Malaysia. In *Bewitching Women, Pious Men: Gender and Body Politics in Southeast Asia* (pp. 159–194). Aihwa Ong and Michael G. Peletz, eds. Berkeley: University of California Press.

Ongley, Patrick. 1995. Post–1945 International Migration: New Zealand, Australia and Canada Compared. *International Migration Review* 29(3):765–793.

Ortner, Sherry. 1999. *Life and Death on Mt. Everest: Sherpas and Himalayan Mountaineering*. Princeton, NJ: Princeton University Press.

Osha, Sanya. 2006. Birth of the Ogoni Protest Movement. *Journal of Asian and African Studies* 41:13–38.

Paine, Robert. 2004. Saami Reindeer Pastoralism: Quo Vadis? *Ethnos* 69:23–42.

Paley, Julia. 2002. Toward an Anthropology of Democracy. *Annual Review of Anthropology* 31:469–496.

Parker, Richard G. 1991. *Bodies, Pleasures, and Passions: Sexual Culture in Contemporary Brazil*. Boston: Beacon Press.

Parrillo, Vincent N. 1997. *Strangers to These Shores: Race and Ethnic Relations in the United States*. Boston: Allyn and Bacon.

Parry, Jonathan P. 1996. Caste. In *The Social Science Encyclopedia* (pp. 76–77). Adam Kuper and Jessica Kuper, eds. New York: Routledge.

Pasquino, Gianfranco. 1996. Democratization. In *The Social Science Encyclopedia* (pp. 173–174). Adam Kuper and Jessica Kuper, eds. New York: Routledge.

Patterson, Thomas C. 2001. *A Social History of Anthropology in the United States*. New York: Berg.

Paxson, Heather. 2003. With or Against Nature: IVF, Gender and Reproductive Agency in Athens, Greece. *Social Science and Medicine* 56:1853–1866.

Peacock, James L. and Dorothy C. Holland. 1993. The Narrated Self: Life Stories in Process. *Ethos* 21(4):367–383.

Pedelty, Mark. 1995. *War Stories: The Culture of Foreign Correspondents*. New York: Routledge.

Peletz, Michael. 2006. Transgenderism and Gender Pluralism in Southeast Asia since Early Modern Times. *Current Anthropology* 47(2):309–325, 333–340.

Pelto, Pertti. 1973. *The Snowmobile Revolution: Technology and Social Change in the Arctic*. Menlo Park, CA: Cummings.

People's Daily. 2003. Xi'an Protects Oldest Residential Area. April 9.

Perry, Richard J. 1996. *From Time Immemorial: Indigenous Peoples and State Systems*. Austin: University of Texas Press.

Pessar, Patricia R. 1995. *A Visa for a Dream: Dominicans in the United States*. Boston: Allyn and Bacon.

Petryna, Adriana, Andrew Lakoff, and Arthur Kleinman, eds. 2007. *Global Pharmaceuticals: Ethics, Markets, Practices*. Durham, NC: Duke University Press.

Pew Center. 2008. One in 100: Behind Bars in America. www.pewcenteronthestates.org.

Pieterse, Jan Nederveen. 2004. *Globalization and Culture*. Global Mélange. New York: Rowman and Littlefield.

Plant, Roger. 1994. *Land Rights and Minorities*. London: Minority Rights Group.

———. 1998. *Issues in Indigenous Poverty*. Washington, DC: Interamerican Development Bank. No. IND-105.

Plattner, Stuart. 1989. Markets and Marketplaces. In *Economic Anthropology* (pp. 171–208). Stuart Plattner, ed. Stanford, CA: Stanford University Press.

Population Reference Bureau. 2005. *2005 World Population Data Sheet*. Washington, DC: Population Reference Bureau.

Posey, Darrell Addison. 1990. Intellectual Property Rights: What Is the Position of Ethnobiology? *Journal of Ethnobiology* 10:93–98.

Postgate, Nicholas, Tao Wang, and Toby Wilkinson. 1995. The Evidence for Early Writing: Utilitarian or Ceremonial? *Antiquity* 69:459–480.

Potter, Jack M. 1976. *Thai Peasant Social Structure*. Chicago: University of Chicago Press.

Potter, Sulamith Heins. 1977. *Family Life in a Northern Thai Village: A Study in the Structural Significance of Women*. Berkeley: University of California Press.

Pratt, Jeff. 2007. Food Values: The Local and the Authentic. *Critique of Anthropology* 27:285–300.

Price, David H. 1995. Water Theft in Egypt's Fayoum Oasis: Emics, Etics, and the Illegal. In *Science, Materialism, and the Study of Culture* (pp. 96–110). Martin F. Murphy and Maxine L. Margolis, eds. Gainesville: University of Florida Press.

———. 2003. Personal communication, response to "Six Questions Survey," author's files, Washington, DC.

Psychology Today. 1995. Child Support. 28:16.

Purdum, Elizabeth D. and J. Anthony Paredes. 1989. *Facing the Death Penalty: Essays on Cruel and Unusual Punishment*. Philadelphia: Temple University Press.

Potuoğlu-Cook, Öykü. 2006. Beyond the Glitter: Belly Dance and Neoliberal Gentrification in Istanbul. *Cultural Anthropology* 21:633–660.

Radcliffe-Brown, A. R. 1964 [1922]. *The Andaman Islanders*. Cambridge, UK: Cambridge University Press.

Raheja, Gloria Goodwin. 1988. *The Poison in the Gift: Ritual, Presentation, and the Dominant Caste in a North Indian Village*. Chicago: University of Chicago Press.

Ramesh, A., C. R. Srikumari, and S. Sukumar. 1989. Parallel Cousin Marriages in Madras, Tamil Nadu: New Trends in Dravidian Kinship. *Social Biology* 36(3/4):248–254.

Ramphele, Mamphela. 1996. Political Widowhood in South Africa: The Embodiment of Ambiguity. *Daedalus* 125(1):99–17.

Raphael, Dana. 1975. Matrescence: Becoming a Mother: A "New/Old" *Rite de Passage*. In *Being Female: Reproduction, Power, and Change* (pp. 65–72). Dana Raphael, ed. The Hague: Mouton Publishers.

Rathje, William and Cullen Murphy. 1992. *Rubbish! The Archaeology of Garbage*. New York: Harper & Row.

Rehbun, L. A. 1994. Swallowing Frogs: Anger and Illness in Northeast Brazil. *Medical Anthropology Quarterly* 8:360–382.

Reid, Russell M. 1992. Cultural and Medical Perspectives on Geophagia. *Medical Anthropology* 13:337–351.

Reiner, R. 1996. Police. In *The Social Science Encyclopedia* (pp. 619–621). Adam Kuper and Jessica Kuper, eds. New York: Routledge.

Reyna, Stephen P. 1994. A Mode of Domination Approach to Organized Violence. In *Studying War: Anthropological Perspectives* (pp. 29–65). S. P. Reyna and R. E. Downs, eds. Langhorne, PA: Gordon and Breach Science Publishers.

Rhodes, Lorna A. 2001. Toward an Anthropology of Prisons. *Annual Review of Anthropology* 30:65–83.

Rich, Bruce. 1994. *Mortgaging the Earth: The World Bank, Environmental Impoverishment, and the Crisis of Development*. Boston: Beacon Press.

Rickford, John. 1997. Unequal Partnership: Sociolinguistics and the African American Speech Community. *Language in Society* 26:161–198.

Robson, Colin. 1993. *Real World Research: A Resource for Social Scientists and Practitioner–Researchers*. Cambridge, MA: Blackwell Publishers.

Rogers, Barbara. 1979. *The Domestication of Women: Discrimination in Developing Societies*. New York: St. Martin's Press.

Roscoe, Will. 1991. *The Zuni Man–Woman*. Albuquerque: University of New Mexico Press.

Roseman, Marina. 1987. Inversion and Conjuncture: Male and Female Performance among the Temiar of Peninsular Malaysia. In *Women and Music in Cross-Cultural Perspective* (pp. 131–149). Ellen Koskoff, ed. New York: Greenwood Press.

Rosenberger, Nancy. 1992. Images of the West: Home Style in Japanese Magazines. In *Re-made in Japan: Everyday Life and Consumer Taste in a Changing Society* (pp. 106–125). James J. Tobin, ed. New Haven, CT: Yale University Press.

Rosenblatt, Paul C., Patricia R. Walsh, and Douglas A. Jackson. 1976. *Grief and Mourning in Cross-Cultural Perspective*. New Haven, CT: HRAF Press.

Ross, Marc Howard. 1993. *The Culture of Conflict: Interpretations and Interests in Comparative Perspective*. New Haven, CT: Yale University Press.

Roy, Arundhati. 1999. *The Cost of Living*. New York: Modern Library.

Rubel, Arthur J., Carl W. O'Nell, and Rolando Collado-Ardon. 1984. *Susto: A Folk Illness*. Berkeley: University of California Press.

Rylko-Bauer, Barbara, Merrill Singer, and John van Willigen. 2006. Reclaiming Applied Anthropology: Its Past, Present, and Future. *American Anthropologist* 108:178–190.

Sachs, Aaron. 1996. Dying for Oil. *WorldWatch*, June:10–21.

Sahlins, Marshall. 1963. Poor Man, Rich Man, Big Man, Chief. *Comparative Studies in Society and History* 5:285–303.

Saitoti, Tepilit Ole. 1986. *The Worlds of a Maasai Warrior*. New York: Random House.

Salam, Nawaf A. 1994. Between Repatriation and Resettlement: Palestinian Refugees in Lebanon. *Journal of Palestine Studies* 24:18–27.

Salamandra, Christa. 2004. *A New Old Damascus: Authenticity and Distinction in Urban Syria*. Bloomington: Indiana University Press.

Salih, M. A. Mohamed. 1999. Land Alienation and Genocide in the Nuba Mountains, Sudan. *Cultural Survival Quarterly* 22(4): 36–38.

Sanday, Peggy Reeves. 1973. Toward a Theory of the Status of Women. *American Anthropologist* 75:1682–1700.

———. 1986. *Divine Hunger: Cannibalism as a Cultural System*. New York: Cambridge University Press.

———. 1990. *Fraternity Gang Rape: Sex, Brotherhood, and Privilege on Campus*. New York: New York University Press.

———. 2002. *Women at the Center: Life in a Modern Matriarchy*. Ithaca, NY: Cornell University Press.

Sanders, Douglas E. 1999. Indigenous Peoples: Issues of Definition. *International Journal of Cultural Property* 8:4–13.

Sanders, William B. 1994. *Gangbangs and Drive-Bys: Grounded Culture and Juvenile Gang Violence*. New York: Aldine de Gruyter.

Sanjek, Roger. 1990. A Vocabulary for Fieldnotes. In *Fieldnotes: The Making of Anthropology* (pp. 92–138). Roger Sanjek, ed. Ithaca, NY: Cornell University Press.

———. 1994. The Enduring Inequalities of Race. In *Race* (pp. 1–17). Steven Gregory and Roger Sanjek, eds. New Brunswick, NJ: Rutgers University Press.

———. 2000. Keeping Ethnography Alive in an Urbanizing World. *Human Organization* 53:280–288.

Sargent, Carolyn F. 2005. Counselling Contraception for Malian Migrants in Paris: Global, State and Personal Politics. *Human Organization* 64:147–156.

Saugestad, Sidsel. 2001. *The Inconvenient Indigenous: Remote Area Development in Botswana, Donor Assistance, and the First People of the Kalahari*. Uppsala, Sweden: The Nordic Afrika Institute.

Sault, Nicole L. 1985. Baptismal Sponsorship as a Source of Power for Zapotec Women of Oaxaca, Mexico. *Journal of Latin American Lore* 11(2):225–243.

———. 1994. How the Body Shapes Parenthood: "Surrogate" Mothers in the United States and Godmothers in Mexico. In *Many Mirrors: Body Image and Social Relations* (pp. 292–318). Nicole Sault, ed. Brunswick, NJ: Rutgers University Press.

Savishinsky, Joel S. 1974. *The Trail of the Hare: Life and Stress in an Arctic Community*. New York: Gordon and Breach.

Savishinsky, Joel S. 1991. *The Ends of Time: Life and Work in a Nursing Home*. New York: Bergin & Garvey.

Schaft, Kai and David L. Brown. 2000. Social Capital and Grassroots Development: The Case of Roma Self-Governance in Hungary. *Social Problems* 47(2):201–219.

Scheffel, David Z. 2004. Slovak Roma on the Threshold of Europe. *Anthropology Today* 20(1):6–12.

Scheper-Hughes, Nancy. 1992. *Death without Weeping: The Violence of Everyday Life in Brazil*. Berkeley: University of California Press.

Schlegel, Alice. 1995. A Cross-Cultural Approach to Adolescence. *Ethos* 23(1):15–32.

Schlegel, Alice and Herbert Barry, III. 1991. *Adolescence: An Anthropological Inquiry*. New York: Free Press.

Schneider, David M. 1968. *American Kinship: A Cultural Account*. Englewood Cliffs, NJ: Prentice-Hall.

Scott, James C. 1998. *Seeing Like a State: How Certain Schemes to Improve the Human Condition Have Failed*. New Haven, CT: Yale University Press.

Scrimshaw, Susan. 1984. Infanticide in Human Populations: Societal and Individual Concerns. In *Infanticide: Comparative and*

Evolutionary Perspectives (pp. 463–486). Glenn Hausfater and Sarah Blaffer Hrdy, eds. New York: Aldine.

Scudder, Thayer. 1973. The Human Ecology of Big Dam Projects: River Basin Development and Resettlement. *Annual Review of Anthropology* 2:45–55.

Senghas, Richard J. and Leila Monaghan. 2002. Signs of Their Times: Deaf Communities and the Culture of Language. *Annual Review of Anthropology* 31:69–97.

Shachtman, Tom. 2006. *Rumspringa: To Be or Not to Be Amish.* New York: North Point Press.

Shahrani, Nazif M. 2002. War, Factionalism, and the State in Afghanistan. *American Anthropologist* 104:715–722.

Shanklin, Eugenia. 2000. Representations of Race and Racism in American Anthropology. *Current Anthropology* 41(1):99–103.

Shapiro, Thomas M. 2004. *The Hidden Cost of Being African American.* New York: Oxford University Press.

Sharff, Jagna Wojcicka. 1995. "We Are All Chickens for the Colonel": A Cultural Materialist View of Prisons. In *Science, Materialism, and the Study of Culture* (pp. 132–158). Martin F. Murphy and Maxine L. Margolis, eds. Gainesville: University of Florida Press.

Sheriff, Robin E. 2000. Exposing Silence as Cultural Censorship: A Brazilian Case. *American Anthropologist* 102:114–132.

Shibamoto, Janet. 1987. The Womanly Woman: Manipulation of Stereotypical and Nonstereotypical Features of Japanese Female Speech. In *Language, Gender, and Sex in Comparative Perspective* (pp. 26–49). Susan U. Philips, Susan Steel, and Christine Tanz, eds. New York: Cambridge University Press.

Shore, Bradd. 1998. Status Reversal: The Coming of Age in Samoa. In *Welcome to Middle Age! (And Other Cultural Fictions)* (pp. 101–138). Richard A. Shweder, ed. Chicago: University of Chicago Press.

Short, James F. 1996. Gangs. In *The Social Science Encyclopedia* (pp. 325–326). Adam Kuper and Jessica Kuper, eds. New York: Routledge.

Shostak, Marjorie. 1981. *Nisa: The Life and Times of a !Kung Woman.* Cambridge, MA: Harvard University Press.

Shweder, Richard A. 1998. Preface. In *Welcome to Middle Age! (And Other Cultural Fictions)* (pp. vii–viii). Chicago: University of Chicago Press.

———. 2003. *Why Do Men Barbecue? Recipes for Cultural Psychology.* Cambridge, MA: Harvard University Press.

Sidnell, Jack. 2000. *Primus inter pares:* Storytelling and Male Peer Groups in an Indo-Guyanese Rumshop. *American Ethnologist* 27:72–99.

Silva, Noenoe K. 2004. *Aloha Betrayed: Native Hawaiian Resistance to American Colonialism.* Durham, NC: Duke University Press.

Silver, Ira. 1993. Marketing Authenticity in Third World Countries. *Annals of Tourism Research* 20:302–318.

Silverstein, Michael. 1997. Encountering Language and Languages of Encounter in North American Ethnohistory. *Journal of Linguistic Anthropology* 6:126–144.

Singh, K. S. 1994. *The Scheduled Tribes. Anthropological Survey of India, People of India, National Series Volume III.* Delhi: Oxford University Press.

Siskind, Janet. 1992. The Invention of Thanksgiving: A Ritual of American Nationality. *Critique of Anthropology* 12(2):167–191.

Skocpol, Theda. 1979. *States and Social Revolutions: A Comparative Analysis of France, Russia, and China.* New York: Cambridge University Press.

Smith, Jennie M. 2001. *When the Hands Are Many: Community Organization and Change in Rural Haiti.* Ithaca, NY: Cornell University Press.

Smith, Jonathan Z., ed. 1995. *The HarperCollins Dictionary of Religion.* New York: HarperCollins.

Smith, Laurajane, Anna Morgan, and Anita van der Meer. 2003. Community-driven Research in Cultural Heritage Management: The Waanyi Women's History Project. *International Journal of Heritage Studies* 9(1):65–80.

Smitherman, Geneva. 1997. "The Chain Remain the Same": Communicative Practices in the Hip Hop Nation. *Black Studies* 28(1):3–25.

Snajdr, Edward. 2005. Gender, Power, and the Performance of Justice: Muslim Women's Responses to Domestic Violence in Kazakhstan. *American Ethnologist* 32:294–311.

Sobel, Elizabeth and Gordon Bettles. 2000. Winter Hunger, Winter Myths: Subsistence Risk and Mythology among the Klamath and Modoc. *Journal of Anthropological Archaeology* 19:276–316.

Sperber, Dan. 1985. *On Anthropological Knowledge: Three Essays.* New York: Cambridge University Press.

Spilde Contreras, Kate. 2006. Indian Gaming in California Brings Jobs and Income to Areas that Need It Most. Indian Gaming. www.indiangaming.com/regulatory/view/?id=35.

Spiro, Melford. 1967. *Burmese Supernaturalism: A Study in the Explanation and Reduction of Suffering.* Englewood Cliffs, NJ: Prentice-Hall.

———. 1990. On the Strange and the Familiar in Recent Anthropological Thought. In *Cultural Psychology: Essays on Comparative Human Development* (pp. 47–61). James W. Stigler, Richard A. Shweder, and Gilbert Herdt, eds. Chicago: University of Chicago Press.

Spitulnik, Deborah. 1993. Anthropology and Mass Media. *Annual Review of Anthropology* 22:293–315.

Srinivas, M. N. 1959. The Dominant Caste in Rampura. *American Anthropologist* 1:1–16.

Staats, Valerie. 1994. Ritual, Strategy or Convention: Social Meaning in Traditional Women's Baths in Morocco. *Frontiers: A Journal of Women's Studies* 14(3):1–18.

Stack, Carol. 1974. *All Our Kin: Strategies for Survival in a Black Community.* New York: Harper & Row.

Stephen, Lynn. 1995. Women's Rights Are Human Rights: The Merging of Feminine and Feminist Interests among El Salvador's Mothers of the Disappeared (CO-MADRES). *American Ethnologist* 22(4):807–827.

Stidsen, Sille, comp. and ed. Elaine Bolton, trans. 2006. *The Indigenous World 2006.* Rutger, NJ: Transaction Books.

Stillman, Amy Ku'uleialoha. 1996. Hawaiian Hula Competitions: Event, Repertoire, Perfor-mance and Tradition. *Journal of American Folklore* 109(434):357–380.

Stivens, Maila, Cecelia Ng, and Jomo K. S., with Jahara Bee. 1994. *Malay Peasant Women and the Land.* Atlantic Highlands, NJ: Zed Books.

Stocks, Anthony. 2005. Too Much for Too Few: Problems of Indigenous Land Rights in Latin America. *Annual Review of Anthropology* 34:85–104.

Stoler, Ann Laura. 1985. *Capitalism and Confrontation in Sumatra's Plantation Belt, 1870–1979.* New Haven, CT: Yale University Press.

Storper-Perez, Danielle and Harvey E. Goldberg. 1994. The Kotel: Toward an Ethnographic Portrait. *Religion* 24:309–332.

Strathern, Andrew. 1971. *The Rope of Moka: Big-Men and Ceremonial Exchange in Mount Hagen, New Guinea.* London: Cambridge University Press.

Stringer, Martin D. 1999. Rethinking Animism: Thoughts from the Infancy of Our Discipline. *Journal of the Royal Anthropological Institute* 5:541–556.

Stronza, Amanda. 2001. Anthropology of Tourism: Forging New Ground for Ecotourism and Other Alternatives. *Annual Review of Anthropology* 30:261–283.

Sullivan, Kathleen. 1992. Protagonists of Change: Indigenous Street Vendors in San Cristobal, Mexico, Are Adapting Tradition and Customs to Fit New Life Styles. *Cultural Survival Quarterly* 16:38–40.

Suttles, Wayne. 1991. The Traditional Kwakiutl Potlatch. In *Chiefly Feasts: The Enduring Kwakiutl Potlatch* (pp. 71–134). Aldona Jonaitis, ed. Washington, DC: American Museum of Natural History.

Tannen, Deborah. 1990. *You Just Don't Understand: Women and Men in Conversation.* New York: Morrow.

Tannenbaum, Nicola B. 1987. Tattoos: Invulnerability and Power in Shan Cosmology. *American Ethnologist* 14:693–711.

Tauli-Corpuz, Victoria. 2005. Indigenous Peoples and the Millennium Development Goals. Paper submitted to the Fourth Session of the UN Permanent Forum on Indigenous Issues, New York City, May 16–27. www.tebtebba.org.

Taussig, Michael. 1978. Nutrition, Development, and Foreign Aid: A Case Study of U.S.-Directed Health Care in a Colombian Plantation Zone. *International Journal of Health Services* 8:101–121.

———. 2004. *My Cocaine Museum.* Chicago: University of Chicago Press.

Thomas, Frédéric, François Renaud, Eric Benefice, Thierry de Meeüs, and Jean-François Guégan. 2001. International Variability of Ages at Menarche and Menopause: Patterns and Main Determinants. *Human Biology* 73(2):271–290.

Thompson, Nile R. and C. Dale Sloat. 2004. The Use of Oral Literature to Provide Community Health Education on the Southern Northwest Coast. *American Indian Culture and Research Journal* 28(3):1–28.

Thompson, Robert Farris. 1971. Aesthetics in Traditional Africa. In *Art and Aesthetics in Primitive Societies* (pp. 374–381). Carol F. Jopling, ed. New York: E. P. Dutton.

Tice, Karin E. 1995. *Kuna Crafts, Gender, and the Global Economy.* Austin: University of Texas Press.

Tidball, Keith G. and Christopher P. Toumey. 2003. Signifying Serpents: Hermeneutic Change in Appalachian Pentecostal Serpent Handling. In *Signifying Serpents and Mardi Gras Runners: Representing Identity in Selected Souths* (pp. 1–18). Southern Anthropological Society Proceedings, No. 36. Celeste Ray and Luke Eric Lassiter, eds. Athens: University of Georgia Press.

Tierney, Patrick. 2000. *Darkness in El Dorado: How Scientists and Journalists Devastated the Amazon.* New York: W. W. Norton.

Tiffany, Walter W. 1979. New Directions in Political Anthropology: The Use of Corporate Models for the Analysis of Political Organizations. In *Political Anthropology: The State of the Art* (pp. 63–75). S. Lee Seaton and Henri J. M. Claessen, eds. New York: Mouton.

Tinker, Irene. 1976. The Adverse Impact of Development on Women. In *Women and World Development* (pp. 22–34). Irene Tinker and Michele Bo Bramsen, eds. Washington, DC: Overseas Development Council.

Tooker, Elisabeth. 1992. Lewis H. Morgan and His Contemporaries. *American Anthropologist* 94(2):357–375.

Toren, Christina. 1988. Making the Present, Revealing the Past: The Mutability and Continuity of Tradition as Process. *Man* (n.s.) 23:696–717.

Trelease, Murray L. 1975. Dying among Alaskan Indians: A Matter of Choice. In *Death: The Final Stage of Growth* (pp. 33–37).

Elisabeth Kübler-Ross, ed. Englewood Cliffs, NJ: Prentice-Hall.

Trotter, Robert T. II. 1987. A Case of Lead Poisoning from Folk Remedies in Mexican American Communities. In *Anthropological Praxis: Translating Knowledge into Action* (pp. 146–159). Robert M. Wulff and Shirley J. Fiske, eds. Boulder, CO: Westview Press.

Trouillot, Michel-Rolph. 1994. *Haiti: State against Nation: The Origins and Legacy of Duvalierism.* New York: Monthly Review Press.

———. 2001. The Anthropology of the State in the Age of Globalization. *Current Anthropology* 42:125–133, 135–138.

Turner, Terrence. 2002. Representation, Politics, and Cultural Imagination in Indigenous Video: General Points and Kayapo Examples. In *Media Worlds: Anthropology on New Terrain* (pp. 75–89). Faye D. Ginsburg and Lila Abu-Lughod, eds. Berkeley: University of California Press.

Turner, Victor W. 1969. *The Ritual Process: Structure and Anti-Structure.* Chicago: Aldine.

Tylor, Edward Burnett. 1871. *Primitive Culture: Researches into the Development of Mythology, Philosophy, Religion, Art, and Custom.* 2 volumes. London: J. Murray.

Uhl, Sarah. 1991. Forbidden Friends: Cultural Veils of Female Friendship in Andalusia. *American Ethnologist* 18(1):90–105.

UNFPA. Accessed June 15, 2006. www.unfpa.org.

UNHCR. 2008. 2007 Global Trends: Refugees, Asylum-seekers, Returnees, Internally Displaced Persons, and Stateless Persons. New York: The United Nations, United Nations High Commission for Refugees.

United Nations Development Programme. 1995. *Human Development Report 1994.* New York: Oxford University Press.

United Nations Environment Programme. 2002. *Impact of Global Warming on Mountain Areas Confirmed by UNEP-Backed Mountaineers.* News Release.

Uphoff, Norman T. and Milton J. Esman. 1984. *Local Organizations: Intermediaries in Rural Development.* Ithaca, NY: Cornell University Press.

van der Geest, Sjaak, Susan Reynolds Whyte, and Anita Hardon. 1996. The Anthropology of Pharmaceuticals: A Biographical Approach. *Annual Review of Anthropology* 25:153–178.

Van Gennep, Arnold. 1960 [1908]. *The Rites of Passage.* Chicago: University of Chicago Press.

Van Wynsberghe, Robert M. 2002. *AlterNatives: Community, Identity, and Environmental Justice on Walpole Island.* Boston: Allyn and Bacon.

Vellinga, Marcel. 2004. *Constituting Unity and Difference: Vernacular Architecture in a Minangkabau Village.* Leiden: KITLV Press.

Walmsley, Roy. 2007. Prison Planet. *Foreign Policy* May/June: 30–31.

Walsh, Michael. 2005. Will Indigenous Languages Survive? *Annual Review of Anthropology* 34:293–315.

Ward, Martha C. 1989. Once Upon a Time. In *Nest in the Wind: Adventures in Anthropology on a Tropical Island* (pp. 1–22). Martha C. Ward, ed. Prospect Heights, IL: Waveland Press.

Warren, Carol A. B. 1988. *Gender Issues in Field Research. Qualitative Research Methods, Volume 9.* Newbury Park, CA: Sage Publications.

Warren, Seth. 2001. Oil and Human Rights in Sudan. *Cultural Survival Quarterly* 25(3):20.

Watkins, Ben and Michael L. Fleisher. 2002. Tracking Pastoralist Migration: Lessons from the Ethiopian Somali National Regional State. *Human Organization* 61:328–338.

Watson, James, L., ed. 1997. *Golden Arches East: McDonald's in East Asia.* Stanford, CA: Stanford University Press.

Watson, Rubie S. 1986. The Named and the Nameless: Gender and Person in Chinese Society. *American Ethnologist* 13(4): 619–631.

Weatherford, J. 1981. *Tribes on the Hill.* New York: Random House.

Weber, Linda R., Andrew Miracle, and Tom Skehan. 1994. Interviewing Early Adolescents: Some Methodological Considerations. *Human Organization* 53(1):42–47.

Websdale, Neil. 1995. An Ethnographic Assessment of the Policing of Domestic Violence in Rural Eastern Kentucky. *Social Justice* 22(1):102–122.

Webster, Gloria Cranmer. 1991. The Contemporary Potlatch. In *Chiefly Feasts: The Enduring Kwakiutl Potlatch* (pp. 227–250). Aldona Jonaitis, ed. Washington, DC: American Museum of Natural History.

Weiner, Annette B. 1976. *Women of Value, Men of Renown: New Perspectives in Trobriand Exchange.* Austin: University of Texas Press.

———. 1988. *The Trobrianders of Papua New Guinea.* New York: Holt, Rinehart and Winston.

Werbner, Pnina. 1988. "Sealing the Koran": Offering and Sacrifice among Pakistani Labour Migrants. *Cultural Dynamics* 1:77–97.

Whitehead, Tony Larry. 1986. Breakdown, Resolution, and Coherence: The Fieldwork Experience of a Big, Brown, Pretty-talking Man in a West Indian Community. In *Self, Sex, and Gender in Cross-Cultural Fieldwork* (pp. 213–239). Tony Larry Whitehead and Mary Ellen Conway, eds. Chicago: University of Illinois Press.

Whiting, Beatrice B. and John W. M. Whiting. 1975. *Children of Six Cultures: A Psycho-Cultural Analysis.* Cambridge, MA: Harvard University Press.

Whiting, Robert, 1979. You've Gotta Have "Wa." *Sports Illustrated,* September 24:60–71.

Whyte, Martin King. 1993. Wedding Behavior and Family Strategies in Chengdu. In *Chinese Families in the Post-Mao Era* (pp. 189–216). Deborah Davis and Stevan Harrell, eds. Berkeley: University of California Press.

Wikan, Unni. 1977. Man Becomes Woman: Transsexualism in Oman as a Key to Gender Roles. *Man* 12(2):304–319.

———. 2000. Citizenship on Trial: Nadia's Case. *Daedalus* 129:55–76.

Williams, Brett. 1984. Why Migrant Women Feed Their Husbands Tamales: Foodways as a Basis for a Revisionist View of Tejano Family Life. In *Ethnic and Regional Foodways in the United States: The Performance of Group Identity* (pp. 113–126). Linda Keller Brown and Kay Mussell, eds. Knoxville: University of Tennessee Press.

Williams, Brett. 1994. Babies and Banks: The "Reproductive Underclass" and the Raced, Gendered Masking of Debt. In *Race* (pp. 348–365). Steven Gregory and Roger Sanjek, eds. Ithaca, NY: Cornell University Press.

Williams, Walter. 1992. *The Spirit and the Flesh: Sexual Diversity in American Indian Cultures,* 2nd ed. Boston: Beacon Press.

Williamson, Nancy. 1976. *Sons or Daughters: A Cross-Cultural Study of Parental Preferences.* Beverly Hills, CA: Sage Publications.

Wolf, Charlotte. 1996. Status. In *The Social Science Encyclopedia* (pp. 842–843). Adam Kuper and Jessica Kuper, eds. New York: Routledge.

Wolf, Margery. 1968. *The House of Lim: A Study of a Chinese Farm Family.* New York: Appleton-Century-Crofts.

World Bank. 2003. *Roma Poverty Remains Key Hurdle to Shared Prosperity in Central and Eastern Europe.* Washington, DC: The World Bank. www.worldbank.org/roma.

Worldwatch Institute. 2003. *Vital Signs 2003: The Trends That Are Shaping Our Future.* Washington, DC: Worldwatch Institute/ W.W. Norton.

Wormald, Tom. 2005. Visions of the Future: Technology and the Imagination in Hungarian Civil Society. *Anthropology Matters* 7(1):1–10. http://www.anthropologymatters.com.

Wu, David Y. H. 1990. Chinese Minority Policy and the Meaning of Minority Culture: The Example of Bai in Yunnan, China. *Human Organization* 49(1):1–13.

www.greatapetrust.org/bonobo/meet/kanzi.php.

www.migrationinformation.org.

www.ilo.org

www.npr.org.

Xizhe, Peng. 1991. *Demographic Transition in China: Fertility Trends since the 1980s.* New York: Oxford University Press.

Zaidi, S. Akbar. 1988. Poverty and Disease: Need for Structural Change. *Social Science and Medicine* 27:119–127.

Zarrilli, Phillip B. 1990. Kathakali. In *Indian Theatre: Traditions of Performance* (pp. 315–357). Farley P. Richmond, Darius L. Swann, and Phillip B. Zarrilli, eds. Honolulu: University of Hawaii Press.

Zureik, Elia. 1994. Palestinian Refugees and Peace. *Journal of Palestine Studies* 24(1):5–17.

Sources for "Anthropology in the Real World"

Part I: Susan Squires

American Breakfast & the Mother-in-Law: How an Anthropologist Created Go-Gurt. National Association for the Practice of Anthropology. (2003–2004). www.practicinganthropology.org/ learn/index.cfm?print=1storyid=4.

Boss, Shira J. (2 January 2001). Anthropologists on the Job. *The Christian Science Moni*tor. http://csmonitor.com/cgi-bin/ durableRedirect.pl?/durable/2001/01/02/fp9sl-csm.shtml.

Squires, Susan. Ph.D., Research Director, Tactics LLC. (2004). Southwestern Anthropological Association. www2.sjsu.edu/ depts/anthropology/swaa/pages/PgSquares.html.

Walsh, Sharon. (23 May 2001). Corporate Anthropology: Dirt-Free Research. CNN.com/CAREER. www.cnn.com/2001/ CAREER/dayonthejob/05/23/corp.anthropologist.idg/.

Part II: Lara Tabac

Lara Tabac. (29 September 2003). Slate. http://slate.msn.com/id/ 2088748/entry/2088987/.

Part III: Fredy Peccerelli

AAAS Human Rights Action Network. American Association for the Advancement of Science. (21 March 2002). http://shr.aaas.org/ news/050204_peccerelli.html.

Black, Richard. Guatemala Rights Scientist Honoured. BBC. (15 February 2004). http://news.bbc.co.uk/go/pr/fr/-/2/hi/ science/nature/3489743.stm.

Digging for Truth in Guatemala. American Association for the Advancement of Science Public Release. (14 February 2004). www.eurekalert.org/pub_releases/2004-02/aaft-dft020504.php.

Elton, Catherine. (27 March 2002). Despite Threats, Guatemalan Scientists Dig for the Truth. *The Christian Science Monitor.* www.csmonitor.com/2002/0327/pO8s01-woam.html.

Peccerelli, Fredy. (2004). Executive Director of the Guatemalan Forensic Anthropology Foundation Speaks at AAAS. American Association for the Advancement of Science. http://shr.aaas.org/news/050204_peccerelli.html.

Part IV: Brian Craik

Craik, Brian. (n.d.). The Importance of Working Together: Exclusions, Conflicts and Participation in James Bay, Quebec. IDRC Books Online. www.idrc.ca/en/ev-64530-201-1-DO_TOPIC.html.

Grand Council of the Crees website. (7 August 2006). www.gcc.ca/gcc/fedrelations.php.

Preston, Richard J. (12 May 2006). Reflections on Becoming an Applied Anthropologist. The 2006 Weaver-Tremblay Lecture, presented at the Canadian Anthropology Section/Société Canadien Anthropologie, Concordia University, Montreal. www.socsci.mcmaster.ca/anthro/emplibrary/prestonawardreflection.

Part V: Mamphela Ramphele

Across Boundaries. (21 April 1997). Online NewsHour: Zair: End of an Era. 1999, MacNeil-Lehrer Productions. www.pbs.org/newshur/bb/africa/april97/ramph_4-21.html.

New Vice-Chancellor Appointed. (10 December 1996). University of Capetown Department of Development and Public Affairs. web.uct.ac.za/depts/dpa/news/ramphele.html.

Ramphele, Mamphela. Dr. Mamphela Ramphele's Biography. www.sahistory.org.za/pages/people/ramphele-m.html.

INDEX

Words and page numbers in boldface type indicate key concepts; italicized page numbers indicate photos, figures, and maps.

Abortion
  in Afghanistan, 84–85
  indigenous methods of, 84
  poverty as motivator of, 85
  and religion, 85
Absolute cultural relativism, *22*
Abu-Lughod, Lila, 43
Acculturation, 278–279
Achieved position, 156
Achieved status, 156
Adams, Abigail, 91
Adams, Vincanne, *116*
Adolescence, 90. *See also* Adolescent females; Adolescent males; Initiation
  as distinct from puberty, 90
  gender identity and, 90–94
  life cycle rituals and, 217
  and sexual preference, 92
  stress and, 23
Adolescent females
  female genital cutting (FGC) as initiation rite, 90–*92*
  first menstruation, 82
  gender and politeness among Japanese, 198–199
  kogals of Japan, *199*
  puberty ritual among Bemba of Zambia, 218
  as a recent life-cycle stage in Morocco, 90
Adolescent males
  circumcision, 91,*93*, 148
  fraternities in the U.S., 151–152
  initiation rites among the Sambia of Papua New Guinea, 90
  puberty ritual, 218
  youth gangs in the U.S., *149*, 152–153
Adoption and fostering, 130–131, *133*
Adulthood. *See* Middle age; Parenthood; Senior years
Afghanistan
  focal vocabulary in mountainous regions, 192
  and Islam, 181
  President Hamid Karzai and unifying message of his clothing, *174*
  regime change in, 181
  warfare in, 180–181

Africa. *See also* specific countries, regions, and peoples
  arranged marriages in, 136
  Bantu migration, *202*
  circumcision (male), 91
  daughter preference south of the Sahara, 84
  female genital cutting and, 90–*92*
  horticulture and, 56–57
  internally displaced persons in, *262*, *294*
  matrilineal descent and, 129, 139
  pastoralism in, 58, *272*
  patrilineal descent and, 129
  religions in, *133*, 216
  Sahel region of, 91, 271–*272*, 287, 290
  territorial rights of indigenous people, 291–292
  woman-woman marriage in, 134
African Americans
  African American English (AAE) or African American English Vernacular (AAEV), 199–200
  ebonics and, 200
  displacement following Hurricane Katrina, 273
  hairstyles of women, 31
  industrial pollution and activism among community in Augusta, Georgia, *159*
  and inequality of consumption, 66
  and Stack's fieldwork of social networks among women of "The Flats," 151
  women and marriage, 135–136
African Rhythm and African Sensibility (Chernoff), 238
Age. *See also* Adolescence; Adulthood; Birth; Middle age
  as basis of task allocation among foragers, 55
  and effect on fieldwork, 37
  as microculture, *19*–20
  U.S. Congress ("The Hill") as gerontocracy, 22
Age set, 148
Agency, 12, 13
  braceros and, *260–261*
  female genital cutting, *92–93*
  karma and, 221–222
  push-pull theory of migration and, 259
  structurism *vs.*, 24

Aggression, *178*–180. *See also* Social conflict; Violence
Agriculture
  beginnings in Neolithic period, 58
  corporate farm, 60
  family farming, *58*
  hypotheses explaining male dominance in, *59*
  industrial agriculture and its social effects, *60*
  as intensive strategy, 58
  migrant labor, *61*
  as mode of reproduction, 78
  Old Order Amish of the U.S. and Canada, 79, *80*
  progressivist view of, *62*
  property relations, 60
  revisionist view of, *61*
  social inequality as cost of, *62*, *63*
  as unsustainable system, 61
  wet rice agriculture, 60
Ahmadu, Fuambai, *92*
Aka of the Central African Republic and the Democratic Republic of Congo
  gender equality among, *95*
  fathers as caretakers, *95*
  map and description, *95*
Alcoholic beverages and social drinking, 15
Alcoholics Anonymous as self-help social group in Mexico City, 155
Algonquin confederacy, 171
Allah, 227
Allen, Catherine, 32
Altar, in Togo, *229*
Alternative food movements and exchange, 73
Amazon (person), 94
Amazon region. *See also* specific countries, regions, and peoples
  botanical knowledge in, *109*
  changing patterns of consumption, 71
  development in, 288–289
  hybridization in, 19
  sleeping habits in, 16
Amboseli Park (Kenya), 246
American Anthropological Association (AAA)
  ethics code of, 44
  and Yanomami research controversy, *179*
American Association for the Advancement of Science, *123*

American Indians. *See also specific peoples*
   anthropological study of, 30
   Bunzel's study of potters, 239
   dance performance of, *23*
   effect of casinos on, *69*
   ethnomedical knowledge of, 103
   map of precolonial distribution of tribes
      in U.S., *112*
   map of reservations in U.S., *113*
American War (Vietnam War), 44
Amish people of the United States and
      Canada, *80*
   informal social control among, 175
Andalucia (Spain), 150
Andaman Islanders of India
   bones of dead relatives, *30*
   as foragers, 55
Anderson, Benedict, 181
Anemia in northeastern Brazil, *86*
Animatism, 215
Anthropology, 6. *See also* Applied
      anthropology; Archaeology; Biological
      anthropology; Cultural anthropology;
      Linguistic anthropology
   careers in, *3, 123*
   definition and description of, 6
   fields of, *6–9*
Antinatalism, 83–84
Anti-racist anthropology, 13
Applied anthropology, *6*, 9
   relevance of cultural integration to, 18
Applied medical anthropology, 118
Archaeology, *6*, 7
   and written language, 203
   of everyday life, 8
   specialties in, 7–8
Architecture and decorative arts, 241–243
Argentina, 79, *163*, 259
Argonauts of the Western Pacific
      (Malinowski), *32*
Armchair anthropology, 30
Art. *See also* Architecture and decorative arts
   as catalyst for political resistance, 237
   definition of, *236*
   esthetics, 236
   fine art versus folk art, 236
   as human universal, 236
   microcultural variation of, 236
   as social control, 237
Aryan supremacists, 22
Ascot, England, *196*
Ascribed status, 154–156
Ashanti people of Ghana, political
      leader, *166*
Asia. *See also specific countries, regions, and peoples*
Assimilation, 278–279
Australia. See Australian Aborigines
Australian Aborigines
   Dream Time, 175, 216
   language preservation of, *207*
   laws, 175
   Miriam people, 291

native title activism of, 291
Ngarrindjeri nation and return of skulls
      to, *276*
religions of, 216–217
social inequality and the law, *177–178*
Uluru as sacred space, *216*
women's culture, 217
youth in justice system, *177–178*
Authority, 168
Ax Fight, The (film, Chagnon), *178*
Aztecs of Mexico, human sacrifice and
      cannibalism among, 219

Bachelet, Michele, 174
Baffin Island, Northeast Canada
   map and description, *41*
Bailey, Robert, *28*
Balanced exchange, 66–67
Band, 168–*169*
Bangladesh
   Chittagong Hill Tracts in, 289
   and Grameen Bank, *293*
   and kinship-based social groups, 148
   map and description, *149*
   smallpox and its eradication, *119*
   and USAID-funded development
      projects, *283*
Bantu expansion
   and language, 202, *204*
   map of migrations of, *202*
BCE (Before the Common Era), 10
Bed Called Home (Ramphele), *255*
Bedu people of Egypt and Yemen, 43
   and female genital cutting, 91
   as patrilineal, *129*
Beliefs
   animatism, 215
   anthropomorphic deities, 216
   patheons, 216
   about sacred space, 216
   zoomorphic deities, 216
Belize, 139, *264*
Benedict, Ruth, *12*
Berdache, 93–94
Bestor, Ted, 68
Bhutan
   gross domestic happiness (GDH) in lieu
      of GDP, *281*
Bhutto, Benazir, 174
Big-man or **big-woman system, 168**
Biological anthropology, 6–7
   subfields of, 7
Biological determinism, 23
   versus cultural constructionism, 24
Biological evolution, 11
Birth
   and bonding, 87
   and conflict regarding honey ritual and
      newborn, 87
   effect of context of, 87
Birth control methods, 82–83
Bledsoe, Caroline, 70

Blood sport, 244–245
Boas, Franz, *12*
   on art, 237, 239
   on potlatching, *72*
   on "race," 157
   research methods, 39, 40
Bolivia
   Tsimané of Amazon region and botanical
      knowledge of women, *109*
Botswana
   map, *21*
   and San, *21, 210*
Bourdieu, Pierre, 65
Bourgois, Philippe, 45
Bracero, 260–261
Brazil
   anemia in, 86
   carnaval as ritual of inversion, 218
   country music (*música sertaneja*) and
      globalization, *235, 240*
   foragers of Amazon and nutritional
      effects of Western contact on, 71
   friendship in Rio de Janeiro, *150*
   HIV-positive girl, *102*
   infanticide in Bom Jesus, *86*
   structural suffering of urban poor of
      northeastern Brazil, 106
   as transnational country, 260
   Umbanda religion of, *107*
Breastfeeding, *78*, 84, 95, 130
Brideprice, 136
Brideservice, 136
Bridewealth, 136
Buddhism, 222–223
   concept of nirvana, 222
   Dalai Lama fleeing Tibet, 231
   in Japan, *222*
   Lao Buddhist temple in Virginia, *213*
   Mahayan Buddhism, 222
   in Myanmar, 222–223
   population distribution of, *116, 213, 220,*
      222–223
   Theravada Buddhism, 222
Bunzel, Ruth, 239
Burkina Faso
   failed reforestation project in, 292
Bush, George W., 141, 172, *272*
"Bushmen," *22*. *See also* San

Cambodia
   Angkor Wat as World Heritage Site,
      296, *297*
Canada
   Chinese Canadians, *258*
   Grand Council of the Cree, *187*, 291
   and immigrants from Hong Kong, 268
   Inuit of Baffin Island, *41*
   marginality of Indo-Canadians and
      Sikhs, 158
   and Native People's land claims, 289
   new immigrants from the Caribbean,
      Latin America, and Asia, 265–270

Walpole Island First Nation, map and description, *278*, 295
Canadian International Development Agency (CIDA), 283
Cannibalism
and *kuru* among Fore of Papua New Guinea, 65
Capital punishment, 175
Capitalism
and inequality, 66
Caribbean region. *See specific countries, regions, and peoples*
Carneiro, Robert, 183
Carnival (carnaval) as ritual of inversion, *218*
Caste system, 156, *161*–162
and Hinduism, 161
Cátedra, María, 42
Catholicism, 85–86, *103, 109, 183, 197,* 215, *273*
Center for California Native Nations (CCNN), *69*
Central America. *See specific countries, regions, and peoples*
Central Asia. *See also specific countries, regions, and peoples*
ethnic groups in, 179
map and description of states, *180*
Cernea, Michael, 250
Chagnon, Napoleon, 178–179
Chain migration, 266
of Dominicans, 266–267
Chechnya prisons, *177*
Chernoff, John, 238
Chiefdom, 170–171
Child-rearing
Margaret Mead's study of, 13
Chin, Elizabeth, 66
China
and 2008 Olympics as demonstration of world leader status, 244
acupuncture as "face lift" in New York City, *280*
and ethnic domination of Han Chinese over Tibetans, 20
ethnic groups in, 157–158
Hakka migration, *262*
and hookworm infection among female rice paddy farmers, *110*
Hui Muslim minority of Xi'an, *228*
as increasingly consumerist, 64
and logographic origins of current writing styles, *202*–203
map and description of effect of Three Gorges Dam, *263*
map of Xi'an, Shaanxi province, *228*
women's movement in, 162
Christianity, 225–227. *See also* Catholicism
and Appalachian practices, 225–227
and the Bible, 225
branches of, 225

population distribution of, *103, 109, 183, 197, 220,* 225–227
as proselytizing religion, 221
and syncretism in Fiji, 227
Circular migration, 261
Civil society, 162–163
CO-MADRES of El Salvador, 163
"Mothers of the Disappeared," Argentina, *163*
new social movements, 163
women's movement in China, 162
Clash of civilizations model, *19*
Class, 18–19
and its effect on fieldwork, 36
and Karl Marx, 156
as microculture, *19*
Clinton, Hillary, *174*
Clothing
and adaptation to cold, 54, *55*
of contemporary political leaders, 172, 174
as embodied language, 151, 190, 194–195, 199
exchange and, 73, 151
fieldwork and, 34, 38
and gender roles, 20, 93–94, 139, 215
for life-cycle rituals, 153
kimonos, *195*–196
and social organization, 63
wedding, *82,* 141–142
Coca, 108
Code of Ethics of the American Anthropological Association, 44
Collaborative research, 44–*45*
Colombia
and immigration to the U.S., 266
Colonialism, 63, 111, 139, 141, 184, *195,* 243, 246
language change, 200, *203, 204*
tourism and, 245
CO-MADRES, 163
Coming of Age in Samoa (Mead), 90
Communication, 190–196. *See also* Language
American Sign Language, *190*
changes in, 200, 203
and colonialism's effect on, 203–204
definition of, 190
and displacement, *190*
and emergence of writing, *202*–203
and globalization, 203–204
Indo-European language family, *201*
khipu of Inca in Peruvian Andes, *203*
linguistic determinism, 198
origins of, 200–201
phoneme, *190*
pidgin, *204*
and productivity of, *190*
Proto-Indo-European (PIE) origins, 201, *202*
Sapir-Whorf hypothesis, *198*
sociolinguistics, *198*

versus call system of nonhuman primates, *190*
Communitas, 224
Community healing, 106
Consumerism, 62
and globalization, 63
and narcissism, 89
and unbalanced exchange, 66
Consumption
depersonalized consumption, 64
as game of distinction, 64
and laws of supply and demand, 63
microcultures of, 65–66
modes of, 62–66
personalized consumption, 64
two meanings of, 62–63
Contemporary human biological variation, 7. *See also* Race
Contreras, Kate Spilde, *69*
Cooperatives, 154
The Cost of Living (Roy), 263
Costa Rica
overview and map, *246*
Guanacaste National Park (and map), *246*
and medicalization of birth, 108
Countercultural groups, 152–154
body modification groups, 153–*154*
street gangs, 152–153
youth gangs, 152
Couvade, 94
Craft cooperatives in Panama, *155*
Craik, Brian, *187*
Creole, *204*
Creolization, 19
Critical cultural relativism, 22–23
Critical development anthropology, 286–**287**
Critical discourse analysis, 198
gay language in Indonesia, 199
gender in Euro-American conversation, 198
gendered language in Japan, 198–199
Critical legal anthropology, 176
Critical medical anthropology, *112*–113
Cross-cousin, *134, 135*
Cuba, 285
Cultural anthropology, 9
careers in, 3, 24–25
characteristics of, 13–14, 23
debates in, 23
definition of, 6–7, 13–14
economic anthropology, 52
goals of, 22
history of, 10, 30, 45
Cultural broker, 87, 287
Cultural change, 278
diffusion, *278*–279
invention, *278*–279
Cultural constructionism, 24
versus biological determinism, 23–24

Cultural diversity, 23
Cultural evolution, 11
Cultural heritage, 296–297
   and development, 296–297
   preservation of, 297
   and tourism, 296–297
Cultural imperialism, 23, 279
Cultural interaction, 18
   four models of, *19*
Cultural materialism, 12, 13, 14
   and etic approach, 38
   interpretation of Aztec human
      sacrifice, 219
   interpretation of Hindu taboo on killing
      cows and eating beef, 24
   three-level model of, 24
   versus interpretive anthropology, 24
Cultural relativism, 12, 22
   and female genital cutting, 91
Cultural resource management (CRM), 9
Cultural sensitivity, 87
Cultural Survival organization, 23, 70
Culture, 6–7
   as opposed to nature, 14–15
   change of, 18, 31
Culture shock, 36, 37
Culture-specific syndrome, 104
   anorexia nervosa, 105
   bulimia, 105
   and spread of through
      globalization, 105
   and *sufriendo del agua,* 106
   susto, 105

Dalby, Liza, *37*
Dalit, 161
Dam construction
   effect on environment, *173*
   effect on people, *170*
   and development-induced displacement
      (DID), *263,* 287
   health effects of, 115, 120
   mega-dam project in India's Narmada
      River Valley, 263
   opposition to, 291
   prompting migration, 258
Danforth, Loring, 212
Dani people of Irian Jaya, New Guinea, *6*
Danish Organization for International
     Development (DANIDA), 283
Darfur, 290
Darwin, Charles, 11
Data analysis, 43
Death
   and blood sports, *244–245*
   death penalty as form of social control,
      175–176
   and grief, 97
   infanticide, 86
   maternal death, 85
   modes of livelihood and reproduction,
      78–79

   and mortuary ritual in Trobriand
      Islands, *32*
   religious perspectives on, 222, 226–227
   and social inequality, 113
   Western denial of, 96
Deductive approach (to research)**, 36,**
   37–38
   and etic approach, *38*
Deitrick, Lynn, *87*
Democratic Republic of Congo. *See* the
     Ituri people
Democratization, 183
Demographic transition, 79
Dent, Alexander, 240
Department for International Development
     (DfID), UK, 283, 285
Descent, 128–130
   bilineal, *128–129*
   and change in due to colonialism and
      globalization, 139–140
   matrilineal, *128,* 129
   patrilineal, *128,* 129
   unilineal, *128,* 129
Descriptive linguistics, 9
Development, 278–299. *See also* Dam
     construction
   anthropology, 278–297
   grassroots approaches to, 285
   five theories or models of, 281–283
   Grameen Bank and, 148, *293*
   indigenous people and, 288–292
   institutions, 282–283, 285
   women and, 293–295
Development aggression, 296
Development project, 285–286
   and cultural fit, 286
   donor culture, 287
   project cycle of, *286*
   recipient culture, 287
   and role of applied anthropologists, 286
Dialect, 33, 182, 199, 200, 204, *205,* 206,
     267, 273
Diaspora population, 158, 202, 204, 220,
     229, 259, 260
Difference, 19
Differential resettlement, 273
Diffusion, 278–279, *280*
Digital divide, 196
   in rural Hungary, 197
Discourse, 9
   and power relations, 9
Disease, 102
   as biological, 103
Disease-illness dichotomy, 103
Disease of development, 115
Displaced person, 261–262
   development-induced displacement,
     262, 287
   refugees, 262
Displacement (as characteristic of
     language), **190**
Distributional development, 282

DNA, 7
Doctrine, 212–213
   and Catholicism, 215
   in Qur'an, 215
Dogs
   importance to Hare Indians of Canada's
     Northwest Territories, *54*
Dominican Republic
   and business marriage, 267
   and chain migration from, *266*
   Haitian *braceros* and, *260–261*
   new immigrants to the U.S. from,
     266–267
   as transnational country, 260
Douglas, Mary, *12*
Dowry, 136
Dreamtime, 175, 216
Dress. *See* Clothing
Drugs, illegal
   use in U.S., 71
Duomo in Florence, Italy, *242*
Dying languages, 206–207

Eagle protection, Hopi religion and, *214–215*
East Asia. *See specific countries, regions, and
     peoples*
Eastern Europe. *See specific countries, regions,
     and peoples*
Ecological/epidemiological approach (in
     medical anthropology)**, 110**–112
   and etic perspective, 111
   to understanding hookworm infections in
     China, 111
Economic systems, 52
Ecotourism, 245
Ecuador
   family farming in the highlands of, *59*
   and immigration to the U.S., 266
   polio vaccination, *280*
El Salvador
   and new immigrants to the U.S,
     266–268
   and journalistic practices during Civil
     War, 196
   map and description of, *267*
   and refugee women of, *262*
   as working poor in Long Island, NY, 268
Emic approach, 38
   and diversity of labeling health
     problems, 102
Enculturation, 86
Endangered language, *206–207*
Endogamy, 134, 135
England
   and Hindu women's beliefs in Leeds,
     221–222
   map and description of, 217
English language
   as global language, *204*
   language family, 206
Environment
   cultural materialism and, 12, *178*

cultural rights, *187*, 251, 278
development projects, 281, 282, *285*, 288, *294–295*
effect on language, 190
and health, 105–106
pollution of the Danube River basin, *173*
protection of endangered eagles versus cultural rights, 214
role of racism, 157, *159*
threats to Saami, *205*
Eskimo kinship terms, *128*
Ethics, 34, 44, 81
Ethiopia
and food, *15*
Etic, 38
Ethnicity, 156
as ascribed status, 157–158
effect on fieldwork, 36
and "ethnic cleansing," 20
as microculture, *19*
in contrast to "race," 20
Ethnocentrism, 22, 23
Ethnoesthetics, 236, 237
Ethno-etiology, 104, 105–106
Ethnography, 44
Ethnomedicine, 102, 103
Ethnomusicology, 239–240
Ethnosemantics, 192
Europe. *See specific countries, regions, and peoples*
European colonialism. *See* Colonialism
Everett, Daniel, 191
Exogamy, 134, 135
Expected reciprocity, 66
Exploitation, 67, 70, *153,* 156, 161, 268
Expressive culture, 236–252. *See also* Art; Play and leisure
and change through globalization, 246, 248
as form of resistance, 250–251
and syncretism in, 248
Extended household, 136, 137, 138, 142
Extensive strategy, 52, 53, 56, 58
Extractive industry, 296

Facial expressions as form of communication, 194
Family, 127–131
Family reunification, 265
Farmer, Paul, *284*
The Feast, (film, Chagnon), *178*
Female genital cutting (FGC), **90, 91,** *92–93*
and health risks of, *92*
Feminist anthropology, 13, 31
Feminization, new immigration and, 265
Ferguson, Brian, *178–179*
Fertility, 78, *79*
below-replacement level, 79
and birth control, 82–83
culture's effect on, 81
decision-making at family, state, and global levels, 83–84

and family planning in Egypt, *83*
and frequency of sexual intercourse, 82
and in vitro fertilization (IVF), 85–86
replacement–level, 79
and social stigma related to male infertility in Cairo and Beirut, 86
Fieldwork, 30
ethics of, 44
process of, 31
risks of, 45
safety issues, 44
Fierce People, The (Chagnon), *178*
First People of the Kalahari (FPK), *21*
Fishing, 15, 33, 41, 42, 52, 54, 55, 56, 153, 155, 213, *214, 247,* 287, 294
Focal vocabulary, 192
Food
breakfast, 3
cassava, as grown by horticulturalists in Niger, *56*
and children's nutrition, 3
prestige foods, 56
"Folk medicine." *See* Ethnomedicine
Foraging, 52. *See also* Fishing, Hunting, Gathering
in the Andaman Islands, 55
and artistic activity, 239
and band as form of political organization, 168, *169*
circumpolar foraging, 53–54
diet, *53*
division of labor in, 54–55
as egalitarian, 63
as extensive strategy, 53
gender division of labor, *53*
knowledge of natural environment of foragers, 53
and minimalist consumption, 63
as mode of livelihood, 52
as original affluent society, 56
shelters of foragers, *53*–54, 241
social groups, *149*
as sustainable, 55
temperate-climate foraging, 53–54
tools used by foragers, 53
use rights among foragers, 55
Fore people of Papua New Guinea and *kuru,* 65
map and description, 65
Forensic anthropology, 9
Former Soviet Union. *See specific countries, regions, and peoples*
Foucault, Michel, 176, 243
Fox, Robin, 126
Fraternity Gang Rape: Sex, Brotherhood, and Privilege on Campus (Sanday), 151
Frazer, Sir James, 11–*12,* 212–213
French Enlightenment, 11
French structuralism, *12*–13

Friendship, 148–151
Functionalism, 12
Galdikas, Biruté, *10–11*
Gale, Fay, 177
Gandhi, Indira, 174
Gandhi, Mahatma, 161
Gang rape, 151–152
"Garbage Project," 8
Gardens, 243
Islamic gardens as representation of paradise, 243
Japanese influence on U.S. gardens, 246
Garifuna people of Belize
infrequent incidents of spousal abuse, 139
Gathering, 15, 19, 52–55, *109, 214*
Gay and lesbian anthropology, 13
Geertz, Clifford, *12,* 14, 244
Gender, 20
as ascribed status, 158–159
cross-culturally, 88
as culturally constructed, 88
effect on fieldwork, 36–37
in infancy, 88
innate differences, 88
matriarchy, *159,* 160
patriarchy, *159,* 160
reversal of in male strip dancing, 239
segregation and inequality according to, 37, 158–159
violence based on, *292*
Gender identity, 86, 90
Gender pluralism, 92–94
in Thailand, 94
Genealogy, 127–128
Generalized reciprocity, 66
Geographic information system (GIS), *271*
Gestures as form of communication, 190
Ghana. *See also* Hausa people
Chernoff's study of drumming, 238
fostering in Accra, 131
map and description, *133*
Gillette, Maris Boyd, 228
Global language, 204
Global warming, *116*
Globalization, 18
effects of, 19–20, 102
infectious diseases, 114
and rethinking concept of state, 181
and spread of non-Western healing, 114
Godparenthood, 130
Great Ape Trust, 190
Greece
Christian fire walkers, *212*
as transnational country, 260
Grinker, Roy Richard, 70
Groomprice, 136
Groomservice, 136
Gross domestic product (GDP), *281*
Growth-oriented development, 281
and trickle-down effect, 281

Guatemala
    Guatemalan Forensic Anthropology
        Foundation (FAFG), *123*
    map of, *264*
    Maya people of, *8, 264*
    political violence in, *123, 264*
Gullah people of South Carolina, 246–247
    crafts and tourism of, 246
    overview and map, *247*
Gusii of Kenya, 57
    children in *Six Cultures Study*, 89
Guyana
    friendship among Indo-Guyanese
        men, 149

Hairstyles, 190, 194, 199, 208, 236
Haiti
    braceros migrating to work in the
        Dominican Republic, *260–261*
    culture and dancers in Miami, *297*
    map, *284*
    Peyizan yo people and their development,
        284, 286–287
    racial categories and inequality, 156
    as transnational country, 260
Hajj, 227
Halonen, Tarja, 174
Hamabata, Matthews
    gift giving in Japan and, 35
Han people of China, 20
Hare Indians of Canada, *54*
    map and description, *55*
Harris, Marvin, *12, 14, 178*
    cultural materialist interpretation of Aztec
        human sacrifice, 219
Hawai'i
    hula, 250–251
    Queen Lili'uokalani, *172*
Hawthorne effect, 38
Head-hunting, 18, 248
Headman, *169*, 241
Healing, 102, 106–110
    community healing, 106
    healers, 107–*108*
    humoral healing, 106–107
    and minerals, 109–110
    phytotherapy, *108–110*
Health, 102
    effect of environment on, 111
    effect of globalization on, 102
    effect of urbanization on, 111
    and three theoretical approaches to,
        110–114
Hecht, Tobias, *36*
Herdt, Gilbert, *12*, 90
Herodotus, 10
Heterotopia, 242–243
Hierarchy, 19. *See also* Social stratification
Hijra, 94
Hindi language
    dental and retroflex sounds of, 191–*192*
Hinduism, 221–222

abstinence and, 83
caste system and, 221
celebration of Holi, *222*
concept of *karma*, 221
and cultural values of immigrants to New
    York City, *269*
Nayar fertility ritual, 221
polytheism of, 221
Vedas, 221
Historical archaeology, 7
Historical linguistics, 9, *200*, 201
Historical trauma, 110, 111
HIV/AIDS
    and female genital cutting, *92*
    and globalization, 114–*115*
    and increase among Hill Tribes of
        Southeast Asia, 289
    and sexuality, 81
Hmong of Thailand, 289
    and opium cultivation, 289
Holism, 12, 18, 31
Holocaust, 22
Homosexuality, 94
Homo sapiens, 7
Hong Kong
    and naming system in Ha Tsuen village,
        130–131
Hoodia cactus, 21
Honor killing , 159
Hopi of the U.S.
    golden eagle in spiritual beliefs,
        214–215
    map of reservation, *215*
    as matrilineal, 129
    significance of Kachina doll, *215*
Horticulture, 56
    and children, 57
    division of labor in, 56
    fallowing as critical to, 57
    regions where practiced, 56
    settlements of, 241
    social groups within system, *149*
    stages of, *56*
    tools used, 56
    and tribe as system of political
        organization, *169*
    use rights, 57
Household, 137–139
    domestic violence, *139*
    extended, 137
    multigenerational, 143
    nuclear, 137
    sibling relationships within, 138
    spouse-partner relationships
        within, 138
    widows and widowers, 139
Howell, Nancy, 45
Huasa people of Ghana
    and dowry, *137*
Human development strategy, *255,*
    258, 282
Human Rights, 273–274, *294, 296*

of Haitian *braceros* working in the
    Dominican Republic, *260–261*
Humoral healing system, 106–107, 117
Hungary
    digital divide, *196*, 197
    map and description of, 197
Hunting, 15, *21, 41, 52, 54*–56, 89, *109,*
    140, 192, *214*
Hurricane Katrina, 273
Hurston, Zora Neale, *12*
Hussein, Saddam, *182, 256*
Hybridization, 19
Hypergyny, 135
Hypogyny, 135

Identity
    and ethnicity, 20
Ikat cloth, *238*
Illness, 102
    as cultural, 103
Imagined Communities (Anderson), *181*
Incest taboo, 134
Inclusion and exclusion of migrants,
    271–273
India
    caste system, *161*–162
    Dharavi slum *50*
    diseases of development, 115
    eating behavior in, 15
    elimination practices, 17
    family planning, 85
    fieldwork in, 34, 37, 45
    gender division of labor in family farming,
        59, 60
    healing, 107–*108*
    hijras, *94*
    importance of sons, 79, 94, *108*
    Kerala, map and description of
        development there, *282*
    kinship, 127, 135
    sexual practices in, 83
    and Six Cultures Study, *88, 89*
    taboo against eating cattle, 244–245
    and vaccination programs, *119*
    white sari as symbol, *18*
Indigenous knowledge, 40, *41*
Indigenous people, 288
    as victims of colonialism and
        development, 288–289
    and territorial entitlements, 289–292
Indo-European language family, *197,*
    201–202
Indonesia
    "gay language" in, *199*
    expressive culture in, *238*
    map, *10, 14*
    and social control among highlanders of
        Sumba, 175
Inductive approach (to research), **38**
    and emic approach, *38*
Industrialism/informatics
    definition of, 61

formal sector in, 61
informal sector in, 61
social groups within system, *149*
social inequality in, 63
underground economy in, 61
Inequality. *See* Social inequality
Infancy. *See* Birth
Infanticide, 86
    in Bom Jesus, northeastern Brazil, *86*
    direct form of, 86
    indirect form of, 86
Influence, 168
Informed consent, 34, 296
Infrastructure
    as in cultural materialist explanation of
        culture, 24
Initiation
    and adolescence, 90–91, *92–93*, 94, 151, 218
    of Australian Aborigines, 175
    cross-cultural groups and, 152–153
    of healers, *108*
    Indian caste system and, 161
    religion and, 229
    rituals of, 217
Institutions
    as microculture, *19, 22*
Institutional migrant, 265
Intangible cultural heritage, 250
Intensive strategy, 58
Internal migration, *258–259*
    push-pull theory of labor rural-to-urban
        internal migration, 259
Internally displaced person, 262–263, 267
International migration, *258–259*
    and effect on household relationships, 143
    growth since 1945, 259
International peacekeeping, 183
Internet, 196–197, *207*, 220
Interpretive anthropology, 12, 13, 14
    and emic approach, 38
    interpretation of Aztec human
        sacrifice, 219
    interpretation of Hindu taboo on killing
        cows and eating beef, 24
    and qualitative data, 43
    versus cultural materialism, 24
Interpretivist approach to health systems, 112
Interview, 38
Inuit 12, *41*
    attitudes toward death, 96
    behavior as basis of determining
        kinship, 126
    map and description of Nunavut
        Province, *290*
    and Nunavut land claim, 289
Iraq
    conflict in, 23, 32
    Marsh Arab people, *256*
    IDPs, *260*, 262
    Kurds, *182*
    migrants to Turkey, 259
    U.S. troops and Iraqi etiquette, 265

Ireland
    map and description, *126*
    Troy Islanders of, 126
Iroquois of North America
    as confederated chiefdom, 171
        kinship terminology, *128*
    map and description, *57*
    as matriarchy, *159*
    as matrilineal, 129
    as nation, 181
    and the role of women in horticultural
        society, *57*
Islam, 227, 229
    comparison of celebration of Eid-ul-Adha
        in highland Sumatra and Morocco, 229
    Five Pillars of, 227
    Khatam quran ritual, 216
    Population distribution of, *180, 220,*
        227–229, 249, 291, 298
    as proselytizing religion, 221
    and Sufism, 227
    Sunni and Shi'a schools of, 227
    Wahhabist, 229
Isogamy, 135
Israel
    children's birthday parties and class
        distinction, 65
    and displacement of Palestinians, 273
    immigration to, 259, *270*
    map of, *226*
    and migration of Jewish refugees for
        former Soviet Union, *270*
Italy
    acceptance of labor immigrants in
        Palermo, 272–273
    map and description of, *273*
    and Venice as overtourited, 296
Ituri people of the Democratic Republic of
    Congo, *28*

Jacobs-Huey, Lanita, *31*
    and study of African American women's
        hairstyles, 31
Jamaica
    friendship and cell phone use, 150
    low-income neighborhoods, *19*
    quantitative data analysis in study
        of, *43*
    Tony Whitehead's fieldwork in, 36
Japan
    ancestor worship in, 216
    baseball and *wa*, 244
    below-replacement level fertility and
        aging population, *81*
    bowing as nonverbal communication, *195*
    and Buddhism, *222*
    excessive daytime sleepiness (EDS), 17
    and kimono, *195*
    and low crime rate due to policing
        culture, 176
Japan International Cooperation Agency
    (JICA), 283

Jesus Christ
    and Last Supper motif in Fiji, 227
    as Messiah in Christianity, 225
Johnson-Sirleaf, Ellen, *174*
Jones, Sir William, 201
Jordan, Brigitte, 87
Judaism, 223–225
    as monotheistic, 223
    and Pentateuch, 223
    population distribution of, *220*
    sacredness of Kotel in Jerusalem,
        223–224, *226*
    and syncretism in Kerala, India, 224–225
Judd, Ellen, 162
Ju/'hoansi people of Southern Africa, 21, 39
    and bilineal descent among, 129
    breastfeeding and, 78
    as foragers, *53–54*
    health status of, 56
    as minimalists, 63
    and open community healing of, *106*
    reproduction among, 78
    use rights among, 55

Kalahari people. *See* San peoples.
Kayapo people of Brazil, *170*
Kazakhstan
    and the Society of Muslim Women
        (SMW), 294
Khaldun, Ibn, 10
Kelabit people of Borneo, *142*
    changing household structure of, 142
Kentucky
    map and description of, *140*
    wife abuse in rural areas, *140*
Kenya
    effect of drought on pastoralists of, *271*
Khipu, *203*
Kimono
    furisode, *195*
Kinship, 126–137
    through adoption and fostering,
        130–131, 133
    "blood" as basis of, 126
    through descent, 128
    diagrams, *127*
    and geneaologies, 127
    and household structure, *127*
    and position of ego, 127
    and relationship to modes of
        livelihood, *127*
    terminology, 128
    through marriage, 128, 133–137
    through ritual, 130
    through sharing, 128, 130–131
Klamath and Modoc Indians of Oregon and
    California
    map of region, *214*
    myths of, 214–215
Kogal, 199
Konner, Melvin, 92
Kuipers, Joel, *238*

Kula, *32*
Kuna of Panama
 craft cooperatives of, *155*
 and shaman assisting childbirth, 112
Kurds of Middle East, *182*
 map of region, *182*
Kurin, Richard
 false role assignment of, 35
Kuwait, veiling in, 195
Kwakwaka'wakw of Canada
 map, *72*
 and potlatch, 62, *72–73*

Labor migration, 261
LaLone, Mary, 246
Language, 190
Language endangerment, 206
Language extinction, 206
Language family, *197*, 200, *201*, 202, 206, *225*
Language revitalization, 206
Language shift/language decay, 206
Laos, *225*, 289–290
Lassiter, Luke Eric, 44, *45*
Last Supper, in Fiji, 227
Latin America. *See specific countries, regions, peoples*
Latinos
 and advertising aimed toward, 196–197
 and lead poisoning among Mexican American children, 118
 and substantial immigration since the 1960s to the U.S. of, *266–268*
 and *susto,* 104–105
Law of contagion, in magic, 212
Law of similarity, in magic, 212
Leacock, Eleanor, *12*
Leakey, Lewis, *11*
Lebanon
 sibling relationships within households in Beirut, 138–139
Lee, Richard, *21*, 45
Legal anthropology
 Critical legal anthropology, 176
Leisure, 243–244. *See also* Travel
Leó Francisco de, *8*
Lesbian, 13, 94, 148, 153
Lese and Efe of Democratic Republic of Congo
 map and description of region, *70*
 relationships of unequal exchange among, *70*
Leveling mechanisms, 63–64
Lévi-Strauss, Claude, *12–13*
 and critical cultural relativism, *22–23*
 French structuralism, 13
 and myth, 214
Liberia
 child solider in, *181*
Life project, 296
Lifeboat mentality, *272–273*
Life-cycle ritual, 217, 218
Lindenbaum, Shirley, 65

Linguistic anthropology, 6, 190–207. *See also* Communication, Language)
 definition of, 6–7
 subfields of, 9
Linguistic determinism, 198
Loans to poor countries, 283–*284,* 293
Localization, 18
 as model of cultural interaction, *19*
Logograph, *202*
Lost semen complex, 83
Lubkemann, Stephen, *8*

Maasai of Kenya and Tanzania, 90–*91*
 adoption among, 131
 circumcision ceremony, 91
 effect of cultural tourism on, *245*–246
 extended adolescence among males, 90
 map and description, *91*
Mabo, Eddie Koiko, *291*
Madagascar
 and environmental problems, *288*
Magic, 212
 contagious magic, 212
 imitative magic, 212
 laws of contagion and similarity in, 212
 use in sports, 213
Mahabharata, 221
Malaysia
 and humoral healing system of Orang Asli, 107
 map and orangutan range, *10*
 and music of Temiar, 240
 and sharing-based kinship, 130
 Sisters in Islam, Kuala Lumpur, 215
Male bias in development, 292–293
Malinowski, Bronislaw, 11–*12, 32*
 as "father" of participant observation, 30
 and first anthropological study of sexuality, 81
 and myth as charter for society, 214
 and study of kula as mode of exchange, 66
Mana, 215
Manioc, *56, 57,* 95
Manz, Beatriz, 264
Marcus, George, *12*
Marital residence, *127, 128,* 129, *130, 140,* 240
Marriage, 134
 age at first marriage, 141
 arranged marriages, 136
 crisis among African American women, 141
 difficulty defining cross-culturally, 133–134
 gay marriage, *133*
 marriage gifts and exchange, *136*
 matrilocality, 129
 monogamy, 137
 neolocality, 129
 parallel-cousin marriage, *134*
 patrilocality, 129

polyandry, 137
polygamy, 137
 role of romantic love in, 135
 sexual activity and marital satisfaction, 138
 woman-woman marriage among Nuer of southern Sudan, 134
Marsh Arabs of Iraq, *256*
Martínez, Samuel, *261*
Marxist theory, 13
 and class, 19
Material cultural heritage, 249
 global tourism's support of, 249–250
Matrescence, 94
Matriarchy, 158, 159
Matrilineal descent, 127–129, *132,* 137, 139, 141, 220–221, 292
Matrilocality, 129
Mawri of Niger
 and marriage crisis among men, 141
Maya people, *4–5, 8*
 birth context of, 87
 and blouses as artistic production of, 239
 and godparenthood, 133
 map, *264*
 as migrant agricultural laborers in California, 61
 political violence in Guatemala against, *123, 264,* 265
 and women vendors, *293*
McDonaldization model of cultural interaction, *19*
Mead, Margaret, *12–13*
 on gender roles, 13
 studies of adolescence, 90
 theory of child rearing and personality, 13
Meaning effect, 112
Media, 12–13, 60–61, 66, 71, 112, 153, 172, 181, 196–197, 239, 292
Media anthropology, 196–197
 critical media anthropology, *196*
 digital divide, *196*–197
Medical anthropology, 49, 102
 applied medical anthropology, 118
 critical medical anthropology, 112–113
 information and communication technologies (ICTs), 197
 theoretical approaches to, 102
 and vaccination programs in developing countries, *119*
Medical pluralism, 115, 117
Medicalization, 112–114
Medicine, Beatrice, *12*
Meir, Golda, 174
Melanesia
 and big-man redistributive political organization of, 169
Men
 division of labor, 15, *53–61*
 drinking, 15

exchange, 67, 70
homosexuality among, 199
language, 198
Malinowski's focus on, *32*
sleep patterns, 17
Menarche, 82
Mende people of Sierra Leone
and food stealing by children, 70
Menopause, 82, 96
Merkel, Angela, 174
Mernissi, Fatima, 90
Merry, Sally Engle, *12*
Mestizaje, 156
Mexico
and immigration to the U.S., 266
map and description, *84*
and Maya people, *4–5*
and structural suffering of women in
Valley of Mexico, 106
as transnational country, 260
and unauthorized immigration from,
266, *272*
Microculture, 14, 19
and effect on fieldwork and rapport, 36
formation of, 148
Middle age, 96
Middle East. *See also specific countries,*
regions, and peoples
Aramaic writing system in, 203
ethnicity in, 157
gardens and, 243
gendered public dress in, 194
Kurds of, *182*
marriage preferences in, 134, 136
migration and, 259
pastoralism in, 58
patriarchy in, 174
patrilineal descent in, 129
punishment in, 176
tribes in, 169
Midwifery, *78*, 108
Migration, 258–274
definition of, 258
health risks of, 271
and questions about human rights, 273
research approaches, 258
and role of microcultures, 259
Milton, Katherine, 71
Minangkabau people of Indonesia
bride, 124
and decline of matrilineal kinship due to
Dutch colonialism, Islam, and
as matriarchy, 159
Minimalism, 62
and balanced exchange, 66
among foragers, horticulturalists, and
pastoralists, 63
Mode of consumption, 52, 62, *63. See also*
Minimalism; Consumerism
Mode of exchange, 52, *63. See also* Balanced
exchange; Unbalanced exchange
and effects of globalization on, 71–73

Mode of production, 52, *63. See also*
Foraging; Horticulture; Pastoralism;
Agriculture
Mode of reproduction, 78–81
stratified reproduction, 81
Modell, Judith, 131
Modernization, 141, 156
and economic and symbolic significance
of water buffalo, *132*
as form of change, *281, 292*
map and description, *132*
as matrilineal group, 129, *132*
of mortality, 86
as theory of development, 281
Moka, 67
Mongolia
Ger (yert) of pastoralists, 241
Monogamy, 137
Montesquieu, Charles, 11
Morgan, Lewis Henry, 11–*12*
and study of Iroquois, 30
Morocco
adolescence among females, 90
and Berber carpets as art form, 239
map and description, *82*
and wedding customs blending Berber
and Western traditions, 142
Movement for the Survival of the Ogoni
People (MOSOP), Nigeria, 294
Muhammad, 227. *See also* Islam
Mullings, Leith, *12*
Multisited research, 30–31
Mumbai (Bombay), India, *50*
Murray, Gerald, 286
Myanmar
coexistence of Buddhism and indigenous
beliefs, 222–223
and *nats*, 223
Myers, James, 153
Myth, 212–215
from cultural materialist perspective, 214
from functionalist perspective, 214

Nacirema, 9–10
Nader, Laura, *12*
and studying up, 36
Namibia
map, 21
and San, *21*
Nation, *180–181*
Nation-state, 181
Native Americans. *See* American Indians
Natural selection, 11 *See* Darwin, Charles
Navajo of the American Southwest, *100*
and adolescence, 90
gendered division of artistic
creation, 239
and matrilineal descent, 141
as pastoralists, 58
Neolocality, 129
Nepal
map and description, *116*

and selective medical pluralism of Sherpa,
116, 117
New immigrant, 265–273
New international migration
acceleration of, 265
and family reunification in the U.S.,
265–266
feminization of, 265
globalization of, 265
the New World
and spread of infection disease during
European colonization of, 111
New World archaeology, 7–8
New York City Department of Health and
Mental Hygiene (DOHMH), *49*
Nicaragua
and immigration to the U.S., 266
Niger, West Africa
Tuareg pastoralists, *189,* 290
Nigeria
and displacement of Ogoni people due to
oil, *294–295*
map and description of, *295*
Nisa: The Life and Times of a !Kung Woman
(Shostak), 39
Nongovernmental organization
(NGO), 285
Nonkin group, 148
Nonverbal language
body language, 194
clothing, 194–195
cultural inscriptions, 194
Deaf culture, *193*
gestures in South Africa, 192–*194*
greetings, 193
sign language, *192*
silence, 193–194
Swedish Sign Language, 192
Norm, 169, *174*
and laws, 175–176
North America. *See specific countries, regions,*
peoples
Norway
Experience of Moroccan immigrants
in, 143
Nuclear household, 137
Nuer of southern Sudan
and woman-woman marriage, 134
Nutrition, 7, 71, 79, 109, 111, 113,
270, 286

Obama, President Barack
and clothing, *174*
Obeyeskekere, Gananath, 39
Ogoni people of southern Nigeria, *294–295*
Old World archaeology, 7–8
Oman, Gulf State of
and xanith, 93
One-Child-per-Couple Policy, China, 85
Orangutans, 6
conservation of, *10–11*
logging threatening, *10*

Orangutans *(Cont.)*
  Orangutan Foundation International
    (OFI), *11*
Oromo people of Ethiopia, 291
  Hundee NGO and participatory
    approach to development, 291

Paleoanthropology, 7
Panama
  Kuna women's cooperative, 154–*155*
  map and description, *155*
Papua New Guinea (PNG)
  and cultural integration of intertribal
    warfare, 18
  and gender segregation, 20
  and *kuru* epidemic in highlands, 65
  map, *17, 33*
  and *moka*, 170
  and Tok Pisin, 204
  and the Trobriand Islanders of, *33*
Parallel-cousin, 128, *134*
Parenthood, 90, 98
Participant observation, 30, 38
Pastoralism, 58
  animal species raised in this system, 58
  division of labor in, 58
  settlements of, 241
  social groups within system, *149*
  study of movement and nutritional needs
    of, *270–271*
  as sustainable system, 58
  and tribe as system of political
    organization, *169*
Patresence, 94
Patriarchy, 159, 160
Patrilineal descent, 128–129
Patrilocality, 129
Peacock, Nadine, *28*
Peccerelli, Fredy, *123*
Pedelty, Mark, 196
Pelto, Pertti, *280*
"People-first" cultural heritage, 251
  Waanyi Women's History Project
    in Northern Queensland,
    Australia, 251
Pequot Indians of Connecticut
  and Foxwoods Resort and Casino, 69
Performance art, 239–241
  ethnomusicology, *239–240*
  and gender, *240*
  and Kathakali theater in South India,
    240–241
  theater, *241*
Personality, 86
  and its formation through
    enculturation, 86
Peru
  and Machu Picchu as World Heritage
    Site, 296
  and immigration to the U.S., 266
Pessar, Patricia, 266
Phonemes, 191

Philippines
  Basic Ecclesiastical Community's (BEC)
    approach to development, 285
  map and description, *103*
  Subanun people's categories of *nuka*,
    103, 192
  as transnational country, 260
Physical anthropology, 6–7. *See also*
  Biological anthropology
Phytotherapy, 108–*110*
Pidgin, 204
Pirahã foragers of Brazil
  language among, 190–*191*, 201, 220
  map and description of reservation, *191*
  stratified reproduction and inequality
    among, 81
  verbal art of, 236
Placebo effect, 112
Play and leisure, 243–244
  characteristics of, 243
  games and sports as models of and models
    for a culture, 244
  male wrestling in India, *244*–245
Policing, 176
Political anthropology, 168–183
Political organization, 168–174
  definition of, 168
  state, *170*, 171–172, 174. *See also* States
  tribe, *168*, 169
Politics, 168
Polyandry, 137
Polygamy, 137
Polygyny, 136
Polytheism, 221
Polo, Marco, 10
Portugal
  and *susto*, 104–105
  as transnational country, 260
Postmodernism, 13
Potlatch, *62*
  as social safety net, 62
Poverty, *278*
  and basic needs, 278
Power, 168
Practical anthropology, 7
Prehistoric archaeology, 7
Prehistory, 52, 84, 98
Priest/priestess, 161–162, 172, 218–219, 232
Primary group, 148
Productivity (of human language), **190**
Project Camelot, 44
Project cycle, 286
Pronatalism, 78–79, 84
  among Mennonites, Hutterites, and
    Amish, 79
  in North India, 79
Primatology, 7
Puberty, 90, 98
  ceremonies, *218*
Public anthropology, 13
Pueblo Indians of U.S. Southwest
  and animal myths, 214

Puerto Rico
  and immigration to the U.S., 266
  map and description, *183*
  and transnational identity, 181, 183
Purdah, 174
Pure gift, 67
Push-pull theory of labor migration, *258*

Qualitative data, 38, 43
Quantitative data, 38, 43
Qur'an, 215–216, *228*
Queer anthropology. *See* Gay and lesbian
  anthropology
Questionnaire, 38

Race, 20
  and ascribed status, 156–157
  and its effect on fieldwork, 36
  and status classifications in Caribbean
    and Latin America, 157
  and structural violence and environmental
    pollution, 157, *159*
Rainforest, *10*
Ramphele, Mamphela, *255*
Rape, 163, 262, 268, 292–293
  fraternity gang rape, 163
Rapport, 34
  help of gatekeepers in, 34
Ras Tafari of Jamaica, *230*
  and *ganja* (marijuana), 230
Ramayana, 240
Redistribution, *66*, 67
Refugee, 262. *See also* Displaced persons
Religion, 212–231
  African religions, 229–230
  beliefs, 213. *See also* Beliefs
  definition of, *212*
  doctrine, *212*–213. *See also*
    Doctrine
  myth, *212*–213. *See also* Myth
  and ritual, 217. *See also* Ritual
  and social cohesion, *213*
  symbols, 213
  versus magic, *212*. *See also* Magic
  Wicca, *213*
Religious change, 230–231
Religious conflict, 231
Religious pluralism, 220, 221
Religious specialists
  diviners, 219
  priest/priestess, *218*
  prophets, 219
  shaman/shamanka, *106*–108, 219
  witches, 219
Religious syncretism, 220–221
  and Mexico's Virgin of Guadalupe
    as example, *220*
Remittance, 260–261
Replacement-level fertility, 79
Research methods, 30
  archival and historical sources, 40
  collaborative research, 44

and data collection, 37
ethics of, 34
field notes, 42
informed consent, 34
institutional review boards (IRBs), 34
interview, 38–39
life history, 39
multidisciplinary projects, *40*
multisited research, 30–31
pilot study, 39
restudy, 32
textual materials, 40
time allocation study, 40
Reverse culture shock, 37
Revitalization movement, 230, 231
and cargo cult in Melanesia, *231*
and Ghost Dance movement, 230–231
Right of return, *273*
Rio Tinto, 296
Ritual, 217–219
initiation of Bembe girls in
Zambia, 218
life-cycle rituals, 217
liminality phase of, *217*
nonperiodic rituals, 217
periodic rituals, 217
pilgrimage, 218
ritual of inversion, *218*
sacred rituals, 217
sacrifice, *218*–219
secular rituals, 217
Turner's three phases of, 217
Ritual of inversion, 218–219
Roma
as diaspora population, *158*
map of Roma population in Eastern
Europe, *160*
marginality of, *160*
as minority ethnic group, 20
Rosaldo, Michelle Zimbalist, *12*, 45
Roy, Arundhati, 263

Saami of northern Scandinavia
focal vocabulary related to kinds of
"snow," *192*
and impact of snowmobile, *280*
language, *205*
map and description, *205*
as pastoralists, 58, *205*
and sacred space, 216
Sacrifice, 218–219, 221
and religions of Middle East, 223, 225,
229, 232
Sahel region of Africa
and displacement of Tuareg
pastoralists, 290
frequency of drought and food shortage
in, 271
map and description of, *272*
Salamanders, ethnographic film, 15
Salamandra, Christa
study of popular culture in Syria by, 35

Sambia people of highland Papua
New Guinea
and institutionalized homosexuality
during male adolescence, 90
Samoa and American Samoa
map and description, *117*
and miscommunication in diabetes case in
Hawaii, 117–118
San of Southern Africa, *21*
and commercial marketing of hoodia,
292, 297
and legislation to protect in South
Africa, 290
as minority ethnic group, 20
Sanday, Peggy, 151
emic perspective of Aztec human
sacrifice, 219
Sapir, Edward, 198
Sapir-Whorf hypothesis, 198, 208
Sardegna (Sardinia), Italy
ritual of inversion in Bosa, 218–219
Saro-Wiwa, Ken, *294–295*
Savage-Rumbaugh, Sue, *190*
Savishinsky, Joel, *54*
Scheper-Hughes, Nancy, *12*, 86, 88, 114
Schistosomiasis, 287
Secondary group, 148
Semantics, 192
Senegal
map and description, *287*
Senior years, 98
Sexuality
cultural dynamics of in India, 83
heterosexuality, 93
homosexuality, 93
importance of bride's virginity in northern
Morocco, 82
intercourse, 81–82
sexually transmitted diseases (STDs), 81
Shaman/Shamanka, *101,* 106, **107,** 108,
112, 117, 219, 230, 232, 237
Shipibo people of the Peruvian Amazon
cultural and gender differences in
esthetics, 237
Shostak, Marjorie, 39
Siberia
silence of daughter-in-law, 193
Sign language, 192
Singapore
traditional medicines of, *110*
The Six Cultures Study, 57, 60, *88*–89
Sleep
cross-culturally, 15–16
Smith, Jennie, *284*
Social capital, 285
Social conflict, 179–181
ethnocide, 178
genocide, 178
war, *178*
Social control, 175–178
law, 175
norm, 175

policing, *176*
and prisons, 176
in states, 175
trial by ordeal, *176*
Social groups, 148–152
clubs, 151
cooperatives, 154
countercultural groups, 152–153. *See also*
Countercultural groups
fraternities, 151–*152*
primary and secondary, *148*
self-help groups, 154–155
sororities, 151
Social impact assessment, 280, 281
Social inequality and poverty
and morbity, 113
and mortality, 113
Social order, 174–177
Social stratification, 154, 155–162
Society of Muslim Women (SMW), 294
Sociolinguistics, 9
Solomon Islands in South Pacific, 152
map and description, *153*
"Masta Liu" young gang, 152
Somatization, 104
Son preference in South and East Asia, 83
South Africa
and Apartheid, 157
Mamphela Ramphele's life and
work, *255*
map, *21*
traditional healers and HIV/AIDS, *102*
South America. *See also specific countries,*
regions, and peoples
co-sleeping in Amazon region, 16
use of coca in Andean region as
phytotherapy, 108–109
South Baffin Island Place Name Project, *41*
Southeast Asia. *See also specific countries,*
regions, and peoples
map and description of, *225*
Spain, *64*
Asturias, *42*
friendship in Andalucia, *150*
map and description, *42*
and *susto,* 104–105
Squires, Susan, 3
Sri Lanka
Hindu religious devotees in, 39, *40*
Stack, Carol, 150–151
States, 170, 171
gender and leadership in, 172–173
and patriarchy, 174
symbols of power in, 172
Status, 156
Stoler, Ann, 40
Structural linguistics. *See also* Descriptive
linguistics
Structural suffering, 104–106
Structure
as in cultural materialist explanation of
culture, 24

Structurism, 12–13
  versus agency, 24
Sudan
  and IDPs, 262
  map and description, *291*
  and violence, 290
Superstructure
  as in cultural materialist explanation of
    culture, 24
Suriname
  women's groups in lower-class Paramaribo
    neighborhood, 151
Sustainable development, 282–283
Susto, 104–105
  and social marginality, 105
Swedish Agency for International
    Development (SIDA), 283
Symbolic anthropology, 13
Symbol, 17–18
Syncretism. *See also* Hybridization
Syria
  hyssop, *108*
  map and description, *35*

Tabac, Laura, *49*
Taboos
  food, 95
Tag question, 198
Tamils of Sri Lanka
  as minority ethnic group, 20
Tannen, Deborah, 198
Tanzania
  HIV/AIDS in children, *115*
Tarahumara people of northern Mexico, *76*
Tejanos
  and social significance of tamales, *16*
Thailand
  development and the Hill tribes, 289–290
  and gender, 20
  importance of tattoos among Shan,
    224–225
  tourism's support of dance
    performance, *251*
Tibet
  and polyandrous marriage, *138*
Tierney, Patrick, *179*
Tocqueville, Alexis de, 148
Togo, West Africa
  religion in, *229*
Tonga
  map and description, *262*
  and remittances, 260
Toponymy, 40, *41*
Torah, 223. *See also* Judaism
Torres Strait Islands of Australia, 291
Tory Islands of Ireland
  friendship among, 148
  and kinship terms, 126
Traditional development anthropology,
    286, 287
  Critical development anthropology,
    286, 287

Transnational countries, 260
Transnational immigration, *258,* 259–260
  and "astronauts," 259
  increase with globalization, 259
Travel and tourism, 245–250
  ecotourism, 245
  effect on arts, 248–249
  impact on indigenous peoples and
    places, 245
Tribe, 168–170
Trobriand Islands, *33. See also* Papua New
    Guinea
  and adolescence, 90
  Kilivila, language of, *33*
  kinship of, *33*
  Kiriwina Islands, also known as, *33*
  kula, 67
  localization of cricket, *248,* 279
  Malinowski's study of, 30, *32*
  map, *33*
  Weiner's restudy of, *32*
Trotter, Robert, 118
Tsukiji, Tokyo
  Ted Bestor's study of the fish market, *68*
Tuareg of Africa's Sahel region, 290
Turkana men of northwest Kenya
  and health of settled versus pastoralist
    men, 111
Turkey
  belly dancing in Istanbul, *249*
  map and description, *249*
  outmigration of Turkish people in the
    twentieth century, 259
Turner, Victor
  and *communitas,* 224
  fieldwork among Ndembu of
    Zambia, 217
  three phases of ritual, 217
Tylor, Sir Edward, 11–*12,* 14, 212–213

Unbalanced exchange, 66, 67
  casinos, *69*
  gambling, 68
  market exchange, 67–68
  marketplace, 68
  slavery, 70
  theft, 70
  trade, 68
Underwater archaeology, 8
Unilineal descent, 128, 129
Use rights, 55. *See also* Foraging
United Arab Emirates
  Burj Dubai (Dubai Tower) as symbol, *242*
United Nations
  Commission on the Status of
    Women, 292
  as multilateral development
    institution, 283
  role in peacekeeping, 183
  UN Children's Fund (UNICEF), 283
  UN Declaration of Human Rights, 297
  UN Development Program (UNDP), 283

UN Educational, Scientific, and Cultural
    Organization (UNESCO), 8,
    249–250, 283
UN Food and Agriculture Organization
    (FAO), 283
UN High Commissioner for Refugees
    (UNHCR), 283
UN Working Group on Indigenous
    Populations, *295*
UN World Health Organization
    (WHO), 283
United States
  birth context in, 87
  as consumerist country, 64
  ecstasy use and exchange networks, 71
  high incarceration rate, 176
  immigration policies of, 273
  migration of Jewish refugees from former
    Soviet Union, 270
  new immigrants from the Caribbean,
    Latin America, and Asia, 265–270
  and racism, 65
  in *Six Cultures Study,* 89
  and tuberculosis, 111
United States Agency for International
    Development (USAID), *283*
  and reforestation project in Haiti,
    286–297
  and tied aid, 285
U.S. National Parks
  Parks and people approach to
    preservation, *215*
  Yellowstone model of preservation of
    physical environment, *214*
Use rights, 55
Uyghurs, *146*

Verandah anthropology, 30
Verbal language, 191–192
  ethnosemantics, 192
  focal vocabularies, 192
  lexicon, 191–192
  phonemes, 191
  properties of, 191
  semantics, 192
  syntax, 192
Vietnam
  and adaptation patterns of immigrants
    from, 268–269
  homeless children in Ho Chi
    Minh City, *64*
  Vietnam War, 44, 179
Violence
  domestic violence, 139–*140,* 144
  against females throughout the life
    cycle, *292*
  and IDPs, 263
  versus Roma of Eastern Europe, *160*
  state violence against Maya in Guatemala,
    123, 265
  street violence among urban poor, 113, 152
  structural violence and racism, 157, *159*

in Sudan and Darfur, 290
and warfare, 179
Virgin of Guadalupe, *220*
Virginia Military Institute (VMI) initiation
rites, *91–92*
Voodoo, 212

Wa, **244**
War zone anthropology, 45
Weyéwa people of Indonesia
map, *14*
and their categories of food flavor, 15
Weiner, Annette, *32*
West, Kanye, *239*
Western Apache of Arizona
and girls' puberty ceremony, *218*
map and description, *195*
and silence, 194
Western biomedicine (WBM), **102**
classification and description of
afflictions, 104
*The International Classification of Diseases
(ICD)*, 104
training in, 114
Whitehead, Tony
study of Haversham, Jamaica, 36
Whorf, Benjamin, 198
Women
Aboriginal, 217, 251
and abortion, 85
African American, 31, 141, 151
and alcohol consumption, 15
and art, 239
Chinese women's movement, 162–163
CO-MADRES of El Salvador, 163
culture-specific syndromes affecting,
104, 106
and development, 288, 292–293, 296

and division of labor, *53–59*
domestic roles of, 15, 17, 70, 89
of Dominican descent, 267
dress of, 195–196
Egyptian Bedu, 43
Hindu, 221–222
in India, *18*, 135, 142, 162
and Islam, 141, 143, 215–216, *228*, 229
and Judaism, *226*
Ju/'hoansi, 78, *106*
and marriage, 133, 135–137, 141
middle age, 96
and migration, *261–262*, 265, 268, 272
and music, *240*
in politics, 170–171, 174
in prisons, 177
as refugees, 262, 269, 271
religious participation of, 212
and reproduction, 79, 85, 95
and sexuality, 82
in Spain, *150*
and speech, 198–199
violence toward, *139–140*, 143, 151, *292*
Women of Value, Men of Renown
(Weiner), *32*
Women's World Banking, 293
Working Group of Indigenous Minorities in
Southern Africa (WIMSA), *21*
World Bank, *11*
and consideration of cultural dimensions
of development, *250*
International Bank for Reconstruction
and Development (IBRD), 283
International Development Association
(IDA), 283
as multilateral development
institution, 283

and South African Mamphela
Ramphele, *255*
and structural adjustment as development
strategy, 281
World Health Organization, 119
World Heritage Site, *297*
World religion(s), *218*, 219–231. *See also*
Buddhism; Christianity; Hinduism;
Islam; Judaism
population distribution of major world
religions, *220*
and proselytizing, 221
Writing Women's Worlds (Abu-Lughod), 43

Xanith, 93
Xi'an, China
Hui Muslims of, *228*
map, *228*

Yanomami of Brazil and Venezuela, *89*
and Iroquois kinship naming
system, 128
map and description, *57*
purported "fierceness" of, *178–179*
and the role of women in horticultural
society, *57*
Yorúbà people of Nigeria
and wood carving, 236–237
You Just Don't Understand (Tannen,
1990), 198
Youth gang, *149*, **152**–153
Yugoslavia
and "ethnic cleansing," 20
Yunnus, Professor Mohammed, *293*

Zapotec Indians of Oaxaca, Mexico
as family farmers, *59*
Zoomorphic supernaturals, 216